The Adam Smith Review
Volume 6

Adam Smith's contribution to economics is well-recognized but in recent years scholars have been exploring anew the multidisciplinary nature of his works. *The Adam Smith Review* is a refereed annual review that provides a unique forum for interdisciplinary debate on all aspects of Adam Smith's works, his place in history, and the significance of his writings to the modern world. It is aimed at facilitating debate between scholars working across the humanities and social sciences, thus emulating the reach of the Enlightenment world which Smith helped to shape.

The sixth volume of the series contains contributions from specialists across a range of disciplines, including Vivienne Brown, Maria A. Carrasco, Douglas J. Den Uyl, Jon Elster, Niall Ferguson, Samuel Fleischacker, Christel Fricke, Lisa Hill, Duncan Kelly, Karl Ove Moene, John O'Neill, Maria Pia Paganelli, Alessandro Roncaglia, Carola Freiin von Villiez, and Jonathan B. Wight.

Topics examined include:

- Smith and the conditions of a moral society
- the fate of Anglo-American capitalism
- Smith and Shaftesbury.

Fonna Forman-Barzilai is Associate Professor of Political Theory at the University of California–San Diego, USA. She is Editor of *The Adam Smith Review* on behalf of the International Adam Smith Society.

The Adam Smith Review
Published in association with the International Adam Smith Society
Edited by Fonna Forman-Barzilai
Department of Political Science, University of California–San Diego

Book reviews
Edited by Craig Smith
Department of Moral Philosophy, University of St Andrews

Editorial assistant
Christian R. Donath
Department of Political Science, University of California–San Diego

The Adam Smith Review is a multidisciplinary annual review sponsored by the International Adam Smith Society. It aims to provide a unique forum for vigorous debate and the highest standards of scholarship on all aspects of Adam Smith's works, his place in history, and the significance of his writings for the modern world. *The Adam Smith Review* aims to facilitate interchange between scholars working within different disciplinary and theoretical perspectives, and to this end it is open to all areas of research relating to Adam Smith. The Review also hopes to broaden the field of English-language debate on Smith by occasionally including translations of scholarly works at present available only in languages other than English.

The Adam Smith Review is intended as a resource for Adam Smith scholarship in the widest sense. The Editor welcomes comments and suggestions, including proposals for symposia or themed sections in the Review. Future issues are open to comments and debate relating to previously published papers.

The website of *The Adam Smith Review* is: www.adamsmithreview.org/

For details of membership of the International Adam Smith Society and reduced rates for purchasing the Review, please contact the Membership Secretary, Remey Debes, (rdebes@memphis.edu).

Books available in this series

The Adam Smith Review (Volume 1)
Edited by Vivienne Brown
Published in 2004. Please note*: available paperback*

The Adam Smith Review (Volume 2)
Edited by Vivienne Brown
Published in 2006. Please note*: available in paperback*

The Adam Smith Review (Volume 3)
Edited by Vivienne Brown
Published in 2007

The Adam Smith Review (Volume 4)
Edited by Vivienne Brown
Published in 2008

The Philosophy of Adam Smith
The Adam Smith Review, Volume 5: Essays Commemorating the 250th Anniversary of the *Theory of Moral Sentiments*
Edited by Vivienne Brown and Samuel Fleischacker
Published in 2010

The Adam Smith Review (Volume 6)
Edited by Fonna Forman-Barzilai
Published in 2011

The Adam Smith Review

Volume 6

Edited by
Fonna Forman-Barzilai

LONDON AND NEW YORK

IASS

First published 2011
by Routledge
2 Park Square, Milton Park, Abingdon, Oxon, OX14 4RN

Simultaneously published in the USA and Canada
by Routledge
711 Third Avenue, New York, NY 10017

Routledge is an imprint of the Taylor & Francis Group, an informa business

British Library Cataloguing in Publication Data
A catalogue record for this book is available from the British Library

Library of Congress Cataloging in Publication Data
A catalogue record has been requested for this book

ISSN: 1743-5285
ISBN: 978-0-415-66722-7 (hbk)
ISBN: 978-0-203-81723-0 (ebk)

Typeset in Times New Roman by
Exeter Premedia Services Private Ltd., Chennai, India

Printed and bound in Great Britain by
CPI Antony Rowe, Chippenham, Wiltshire

From the editor

As I assume editorial responsibilities for *The Adam Smith Review*, I would like to thank Founding Editor Vivienne Brown for her vision in establishing the journal, and for so masterfully editing it over these past years. We are all in her debt. In the spirit of publishing the very best peer-reviewed work on Adam Smith across the humanities and social sciences, we press forward!

My thanks to the Editorial Board and to Craig Smith, the new Book Reviews Editor, for their support during the transition of editorial operations, and to Christian Donath, my Editorial Assistant, for his hard work as we prepared the current volume for publication. Thanks also to the University of California–San Diego for material support.

It is my great pleasure to welcome the following new members to the Editorial Board, many of whom contributed substantially to the preparation of this volume:

Christopher J. Berry (University of Glasgow, UK)
Vivienne Brown (Open University, UK)
Laurence W. Dickey (University of Wisconsin, USA)
Istvan Hont (King's College, Cambridge, UK)
Iain McLean (Nuffield College, Oxford, UK)
Martha C. Nussbaum (University of Chicago, USA)
Amartya Sen (Harvard University, USA and Cambridge University, UK)
Shannon C. Stimson (University of California–Berkeley, USA)

Fonna Forman-Barzilai
Editor

Contents

Notes on contributors

Tony Aspromourgos is Professor of Economics at the University of Sydney. He has published extensively on the history of economics, particularly with reference to the seventeenth and eighteenth centuries, and is a member of the Editorial Board of the *European Journal of the History of Economic Thought*. He is the author of *On the Origins of Classical Economics* (1996) and *The Science of Wealth* (2009).

Magali Bessone is an assistant professor of philosophy at the University of Rennes 1 (France). She currently works on modern and contemporary theories of justice and democracy, with a special focus on races and racism, and international criminal justice. She has published a translation of W. E. B. Du Bois' *The Souls of Black Folk* (2004), a book on the origins of the American Republic, *T. Jefferson et A. Hamilton* (2007) and recently co-edited *Peines de guerre. La justice pénale internationale et l'ex-Yougoslavie*, with Isabelle Delpla (2010).

Michaël Biziou is Professor of Philosophy at the University of Nice–Sophia Antipolis (France). He works both on eighteenth-century British philosophy and on contemporary theories of liberalism. He has translated Smith's *Theory of Moral Sentiments* into French (Paris: PUF, 1999), and is currently translating Hume's *Treatise of Human Nature* (Paris: Vrin, to be published). He has published three books: *Le concept de système dans la tradition anglo-écossaise des sentiments moraux. De la métaphysique à l'économie politique (Shaftesbury, Hutcheson, Hume et Smith)* (Lille: ANRT, 2000), *Adam Smith et l'origine du libéralisme* (Paris: PUF, 2003) and *Shaftesbury. Le sens moral* (Paris: PUF, 2005). He has also edited 'Adam Smith et la Théorie des sentiments moraux', special issue of *Revue philosophique de la France et de l'étranger* (Paris: PUF, 2000, no. 4), and *Adam Smith philosophe. De la morale à l'économie, ou philosophie du libéralisme*, co-edited with Magali Bessone (Rennes: Presses Universitaires de Rennes, 2009).

Vivienne Brown is Professor Emerita of Philosophy and Intellectual History in the Economics Department, The Open University, UK. She is the author of *Adam Smith's Discourse: Canonicity, Commerce and Conscience*, and the founding editor of *The Adam Smith Review* (vols 1–5). She is currently working on an interdisciplinary project on agency, action and rights, and a collection of essays on Adam Smith.

Maria A. Carrasco is Professor of Philosophy at the Pontificia Universidad Católica de Chile; Santiago, Chile. She is the author of several articles on Adam Smith, both in English and Spanish. Her papers on this topic include 'Adam Smith's Reconstruction of Practical Reason', *The Review of Metaphysics* (2004); 'Adam Smith: Liberalismo y Razón Práctica', *Revista Pensamiento*, España (2006); 'Adam Smith on Morality, Justice, and the Political Constitution of Liberty', *Journal of Scottish Philosophy* (2008); 'Hutcheson y Smith: Hacia un Sentimentalismo "Sofisticado"', *Revista de Filosofía de la Universidad de Chile* (2009); 'Adam Smith y el Relativismo', *Anuario Filosófico*, Spain (2009); 'Adam Smith's "Sympathetic Impartiality" and Universality', *Revista de Instituciones, Ideas y Mercados* (*RIIM*), Argentina (2010); 'Adam Smith: Self-command, Practical Reason and Deontological Insights', *British Journal for the History of Philosophy* (forthcoming); 'Hutcheson, Smith and Utilitarianism', *The Review of Metaphysics* (2011). She is also co-editor of the monographic issue on Adam Smith of the Spanish journal *Empresa y Humanismo* (2009); and author of the book *Consecuencialismo. Por qué no* (Eunsa, Spain, 1999).

Michael Clark is currently a visiting assistant professor at the University of Baltimore while he is completing his Ph.D. at George Mason University. He earned his undergraduate degree from Hillsdale College in 2004. In 2009 he was selected as a Merrick School of Business top ten teacher at the University of Baltimore. His Ph.D. dissertation is being completed under Daniel Klein. His dissertation explores Adam Smith's insights on strategic writing and how they potentially apply to Smith's own works. Michael's academic interests include political economy and liberty, Smithian economics, Austrian economics, and public choice economics.

Sergio Volodia Cremaschi is Associate Professor of Moral Philosophy at the Amedeo Avogadro University (Vercelli). Besides papers on Adam Smith, Malthus, and Ricardo, he has authored a book on applied ethics, *Normativity Within the Bounds of Plural Reasons* (Uppsala, 2007); a trilogy on the history of ethics, *L'etica del Novecento* (Rome, 2005); *L'etica moderna* (Rome, 2007); *L'etica occidentale da Pitagora ai francescani* (Rome, forthcoming); a monograph on Adam Smith, *Il sistema della ricchezza* (Milan, 1984); and another on Spinoza, *L'automa spirituale* (Milan, 1979).

Douglas J. Den Uyl was born in Monroe, Michigan and attended Kalamazoo College (B.A. in Political Science and Philosophy), the University of Chicago (M.A. Political Science) and Marquette University (Ph.D. Philosophy). He is interested in the history of ideas and has published essays or books on Spinoza, Smith, Shaftesbury, Mandeville and others. His interests also include moral and political theory. His most recent publication is the co-authorship of the 2006 book *Norms of Liberty*. He co-founded the American Association for the Philosophic Study of Society, The North American Spinoza Society, and The International Adam Smith Society. He taught Philosophy and was Department Chair and Full Professor at Bellarmine College (now Bellarmine University) before coming to Liberty Fund where he is now Vice President of Educational Programs.

Jon Elster is Robert K. Merton Professor of Social Science at Columbia University and Professor, Chaire de Rationalité et Sciences Sociales, at the Collège de France. His recent publications include *L'irrationalité* (2010), *Alexis de Tocqueville: The First Social Scientist* (2009) and *Le désintéressement* (2009).

Niall Ferguson is Laurence A. Tisch Professor of History at Harvard University and William Ziegler Professor at Harvard Business School. He is the author of several works of financial history, notably *The World's Banker: The History of the House of Rothschild* (1998); *The Cash Nexus: Money and Power in the Modern World, 1700–2000* (2001); *The Ascent of Money: A Financial History of the World* (2008); and *High Financier: The Lives and Time of Siegmund Warburg* (2010). He is a Senior Research Fellow of Jesus College, Oxford, a contributing editor of the *Financial Times* and serves on the board of the Centre for Policy Studies.

Samuel Fleischacker is a Professor of Philosophy at the University of Illinois–Chicago. His publications include *A Third Concept of Liberty: Judgment and Freedom in Kant and Adam Smith* (Princeton, 1999) and *On Adam Smith's Wealth of Nations: A Philosophical Companion* (Princeton, 2003). He was President of the International Adam Smith Society from 2006 to 2010.

Carola Freiin von Villiez is Professor of Legal and Social Philosophy at the University of Duisburg-Essen in Germany and currently also Academic Director of the Ethics Programme at the University of Oslo in Norway. Her main research interests are in Legal Philosophy (a.o. normative sources of international law), Political Philosophy (a.o. theory of institutions), Ethics (foundational and applied) and History of Philosophy (Kant, Smith, Rawls). Her publications include *Grenzen der Rechtfertigung? Internationale Gerechtigkeit durch transnationale Legitimation* (Borders of Justice? International Justice through Transnational Legitimation), Paderborn 2005, Mentis).

Christel Fricke is Professor of Philosophy in the Department of Philosophy, Classics, History of Art and Ideas at the University of Oslo, Norway. From 2007 to 2010, she was Director of the Centre for the Study of Mind in Nature, Oslo, of which she is still a member. She has published extensively on aesthetics and the history of modern philosophy (with a particular focus on Immanuel Kant and Adam Smith). She co-edited (with Hans-Peter Schütt) a volume with papers on *Adam Smith as a Moral Philosopher* (published in German, Berlin 2005, de Gruyter), and is at present editing *The Ethics of Forgiveness* (Routledge, 2011).

Paul Gunn is a Ph.D. student in the Department of Politics at Queen Mary College, University of London. His thesis, entitled 'The Epistemic Deficiencies of Deliberative Democracy: An Austrian View', explores the merits of modern liberal and democratic arguments in the context of the so-called politics of difference. He is interested in the ability of classical liberal and Austrian economic approaches to solve social problems, and his doctoral research seeks to use these viewpoints as lenses to examine the efficacy of modern political theories.

Ryan Patrick Hanley is Associate Professor of Political Science at Marquette University. His research in the history of political philosophy focuses on the Scottish Enlightenment. He is the author of *Adam Smith and the Character of Virtue* (Cambridge University Press, 2009), and co-editor, with Darrin M. McMahon, of *The Enlightenment: Critical Concepts in History*, 5 vols (Routledge, 2010). In addition, Professor Hanley is the editor of the Penguin Classics edition of Adam Smith's *Theory of Moral Sentiments* (Penguin, 2010), and current President of the International Adam Smith Society.

Lisa Hill is Professor of Politics in the School of History and Politics, University of Adelaide. Her research interests are in political theory, intellectual history and issues in electoral law. She has written a monograph on the social and political thought of Adam Ferguson (entitled *The Passionate Society*) and has published numerous articles on Adam Smith in such journals as *Review of Politics*, *History of Political Thought*, *History of the Human Sciences*, and *European Journal of the History of Economic Thought*.

Ragnvald Kalleberg is a Professor of Sociology in the Department of Sociology and Human Geography at the University of Oslo. His research interests include: universities as knowledge organizations, the history of sociology, academics as intellectuals, and research ethics. Some of his recent publications include 'A Reconstruction of the Ethos of Science' (*Journal of Classical Sociology*, 2007), 'Can Normative Disputes Be Settled Rationally?' (in M. Cherkaoui and P. Hamilton, eds (2009) *Raymond Boudon: A Life in Sociology* (Oxford, Bardwell Press); and 'The Ethos of Science and the Ethos of Democracy', in Craig Calhoun, ed. (2010) *Robert K. Merton: Sociology of Science and Sociology as Science* (New York, Columbia University Press).

Duncan Kelly is University Senior Lecturer in Political Theory, in the Department of Politics and International Studies, University of

Cambridge, and a Fellow of Jesus College, Cambridge. He is the author of *The State of the Political: Conceptions of Politics and the State in the Thought of Max Weber, Carl Schmitt and Franz Neumann* (Oxford University Press/The British Academy, 2003), and *The Propriety of Liberty: Persons, Passions and Judgement in Modern Political Thought* (Princeton University Press, 2010). He is also Editor of the volume *Lineages of Empire* (Oxford University Press/The British Academy, 2009).

Gavin Kennedy is Professor Emeritus at Heriot-Watt University, UK, and author of The Economist *Essential Negotiator* (2004), *Adam Smith's Lost Legacy* (2005) and *Adam Smith: A Moral Philosopher and His Political Economy* (2008).

Catherine Labio is Associate Professor of English at the University of Colorado at Boulder. She is the author of *Origins and the Enlightenment: Aesthetic Epistemology from Descartes to Kant* (2004) and is working on a book on literature and economics since the eighteenth century.

Raino Malnes is Professor of Political Science at the University of Oslo, Adjunct Professor at the Norwegian Defence College, and Research Coordinator at the Center for Study of Mind in Nature (CSMN). His publications include *Valuing the Environment* (Manchester University Press, 1995), *Meningen med samfunnsvitenskap* (The Point of Social Science; Gyldendal Akademisk, 2008) and *Politisk tenkning* (Political Thought; co-author Knut Midgaard, Universitetsforlaget, 2009).

Stephen McKenna is Associate Professor and Chair of Media Studies at the Catholic University of America. In addition to his work on Adam Smith, he has published on the rhetoric of advertising and American presidential rhetoric. He is the co-editor of *The World's Greatest Speeches* (Dover, 1999).

Karl Ove Moene is Professor of Economics at the Department of Economics, University of Oslo, and the director of the Center of Excellence ESOP (Equality Social Organization and Performance), funded by the Norwegian Research Council and the University of Oslo. His most recent publications include articles on governance, polarization between the rich and the poor, and social democracy as a development strategy.

John O'Neill is Hallsworth Professor of Political Economy at Manchester University. He has written widely on philosophy and political economy, political theory, environmental policy, ethics, and the philosophy of science. His books include *Markets, Deliberation and Environment* (Routledge, 2007), *The Market: Ethics, Knowledge and Politics* (Routledge, 1998) and *Ecology, Policy and Politics: Human Well-Being and the Natural World* (Routledge, 1993). He is also co-author with Alan Holland and Andrew Light of *Environmental Values* (Routledge, 2008). He is co-editor with Tim Hayward of *Justice, Property and the Environment: Social and*

Legal Perspectives (Ashgate, 1997), and with Ian Bateman and Kerry Turner of *Environmental Ethics and Philosophy* (Edward Elgar, 2001).

James R. Otteson is joint Professor of Philosophy and Economics at Yeshiva University in New York, and the Charles G. Koch Senior Fellow at the Fund for American Studies in Washington, DC. He is author of *Adam Smith's Marketplace of Life* (Cambridge, 2002) and *Actual Ethics* (Cambridge, 2006), the latter of which won the Templeton Enterprise Award in 2007. His latest book is *Adam Smith* (Continuum, 2011).

Maria Pia Paganelli is an Assistant Professor of Economics at Trinity University and an affiliated faculty at New York University. She received her Ph.D. from George Mason University. She has written numerous articles, published in leading journals of the field, on Adam Smith, David Hume and eighteenth-century money theory and won the European Society for the History of Economic Thought 2009 best article of the year prize.

Sandra Peart is Dean of the Jepson School and Professor of Leadership Studies at the University of Richmond, Virginia. She obtained her doctorate in economics from the University of Toronto. She serves on the editorial board of the *Journal of the History of Economic Thought* and is a past president of the History of Economics Society where she began and directed the Young Scholars program. For the past eleven years she has co-directed, with David Levy, the annual Summer Institute for the History of Economic Thought. Peart has written on ethics and economics, rationality, utilitarianism, race and eugenics, the transition to 'modern' economics, central planning, and the political economy of leadership. Her most recent book, edited with David Levy, was published by the University of Michigan Press in 2008: *The Street Porter and the Philosopher: Conversations on Analytical Egalitarianism*. With David Levy, she is now writing a book on the role of experts and expertise in society.

Hugh Rockoff is a Professor at Rutgers, the State University of New Jersey, and a Research Associate of the National Bureau of Economic Research. His research focuses on the monetary and banking history of the United States, and on wartime economic controls. He is also the author, with Gary Walton, of a textbook: *History of the American Economy*.

Alessandro Roncaglia is Professor of Economics at La Sapienza University of Rome, Italy, and member of the Accademia Nazionale dei Lincei. He is editor of *Moneta e Credito* and *PSL Quarterly Review* (earlier, *BNL Quarterly Review*), and member of the editorial board of the *Journal of Post Keynesian Economics*. His publications include The *Wealth of Ideas* (Cambridge University Press, 2005), and *Piero Sraffa* (Palgrave Macmillan, 2009).

Robert Urquhart teaches economics at the University of Denver. He has written on a number of figures in early political economic thought, including Steuart, Hume, Tucker, and Locke, as well as Smith. He has also written a book on the concept of incommensurable choice.

Jonathan B. Wight is Professor of Economics at the University of Richmond, Virginia. Recent work includes 'Adam Smith on Instincts, Ethics, and Informal Learning: Proximate Mechanisms in Multilevel Selection', *Review of Social Economy* 67, 1 (2009). He is also the author of *Teaching the Ethical Foundations of Economics* (with J. Morton, 2007) and the academic novel, *Saving Adam Smith* (2002).

Jeffrey T. Young is the A. Barton Hepburn Professor of Economics at St. Lawrence University. His research interests include the economics and moral philosophy of Adam Smith and David Hume. He is also interested in Malthusian population theory, and its role in modern economic and environmental thought. In addition to journal articles his publications include *Economics as a Moral Science: The Political Economy of Adam Smith* (1997) and, as editor, *The Elgar Companion to Adam Smith* (2009).

Symposium

Adam Smith and the conditions of a moral society

Introduction

Adam Smith and the conditions of a moral society

Christel Fricke

An international Adam Smith conference celebrating the 250th anniversary of *The Theory of Moral Sentiments* was held in Oslo, Norway, on August 27–29, 2009. It was jointly hosted and funded by three Oslo-based research institutions: the Centre for the Study of Mind in Nature (CSMN/Christel Fricke and Raino Malnes), the Centre for the Study of Equality, Social Organization, and Performance (ESOP/Kalle Moene) and the Seminar on Theory of Science (Ragnvald Kalleberg).

We are here publishing some of the contributions to the conference. All have been peer reviewed and revised for publication in the *Adam Smith Review*.

Adam Smith wrote the TMS before academic disciplines were distinguished as they are today. He deals with a number of topics which are now seen as falling into the area of competence of different academic disciplines, including not only moral philosophy but also sociology, political science, psychology, history, pedagogy, law and economics (the latter in so far as what Smith has to say in the TMS about, for example, the driving forces of human motivation and interaction, as well as about both national and international justice, provides an important background for properly understanding his theory of national economics in the WN). And this list of disciplines may not even be complete.

Whereas philosophy takes its own history to be among its main areas of research, nothing similar is the case for any of these other disciplines. However, reading the TMS today is more than a matter of purely historical interest. For Smith, morality is on the one hand an achievement of human civilization and on the other a result of individual learning. Both of these aspects of the phenomenon of morality are of great interest in present debates. Questions concerning individual humans' emotional dispositions and moral capacities, the role of socialization and moral learning, the impact of culture on moral development, the driving forces and dynamics of human interaction, the process of civilization and the evolution of human morality are high up on the agenda of scholars interested in human nature and, in particular, the nature of morality and its evolution. In his TMS, Smith explores the social, economical and political conditions of a moral society

The Adam Smith Review, 6: 3–8 © The International Adam Smith Society
ISSN 1743-5285, ISBN 0–415–66722–7

and its historical development as part of the process of civilization, laying out a blueprint for the moral foundations of modernity. Based on observations of human behaviour, he argues that human beings are by nature disposed to take an interest in other people's well being, even if their own utility is not affected by it. Whereas Smith speaks of human 'sympathy', this disposition is now labelled as 'altruism'. Smith rejects the originally Hobbesian claim that humans are intrinsically selfish, interested in nothing but their own well being and utility. The view of human nature as exclusively selfish survives today in the notion of the 'homo oeconomicus'. Smith's rejection of this anthropological claim has, in the meantime, been strengthened by experimental research in motivational psychology and behavioural economics. Today, his TMS can provide ample inspiration for further research in philosophy and the behavioural sciences. It is for this reason that the organizers of the Oslo conference have joined forces and invited philosophers, economists, political scientists and sociologists to comment on Adam Smith's moral theory from their respective points of view.

The papers published here address the controversy over the questions whether or not the TMS does contain a normative moral theory and, in so far as it does, which view of morality Smith defended. Furthermore, contributors discuss various aspects of Smith's account of the nature and dynamics of the reactive attitudes of gratitude and resentment. These attitudes are shaping human interaction not only inside circles of families and friends but also among members of a commercial society who meet on the marketplace. The papers published here reveal the TMS as a source of philosophical, sociological, political and economic thought which can help us to further develop our modern understanding of human nature and the conditions of a moral society.

Maria Alejandra Carrasco takes a close look at Smith's genetic explanation of the emergence of moral conscience with a particular focus on the transition from developmental psychology to moral philosophy proper. In her account of the way in which Adam Smith builds a 'bridge' from the amoral (psychological) to the moral sphere she distinguishes four kinds of sympathy: (1) sympathy as a transfusion of sentiments which one can find in very young children and even in higher developed animals; (2) identification sympathy as depending on practical imagination which opens up to circumstance and as including a capacity to evaluate an agent's passions and actions; (3) mutual sympathy between an agent and a spectator, where the agent becomes the 'spectator of the spectator'; and (4) moral sympathy, as due to the appearance of the impartial spectator within. Carrasco sees the move from (3) to (4) as representing the transition from the psychological to the moral realm, a reflexive turn that produces second-order or rational desires. The moral ideal – as far as it is at all achievable by humans – is incorporated by the 'wise and virtuous'. Carrasco reads Smith's account of reflection-based impartial sympathy as anticipating Richard Hare's account of an impartial judgment (as approved of by anybody in the same circumstances) and Kurt Baier's account of such a judgment (as based on a reversibility test).

Carola Freiin von Villiez accommodates both the descriptive and the prescriptive elements of the TMS as essential parts of one normative moral theory. She argues that, according to Smith, communal moral standards are natural side-effects of the interactions between individuals. These interactions are to be understood in terms of a process of moral progress. Von Villiez distinguishes between three main steps in this process, according to the degree of impartiality of the sympathetic feelings of the respective spectator and the corresponding degree of justification of his judgment: at first, the spectator relies on 'empathy' as the criterion for *natural justification*, afterwards on 'social consensus' as the criterion for *conventional justification,* and finally on 'universality' as the criterion for *moral justification.* Only judgments based on universally valid norms, on 'moral norms proper' are moral in the strict sense of the term. The step from the second to the third level is marked by the acquisition of conscience. Persons with conscience do not depend on actual social consensus for their moral judgment; rather, they rely on the internalized spectator and his capacity to distinguish praiseworthiness from actual praise. According to von Villiez, the distinction between praise and praiseworthiness is ultimately conductive to ideally impartial norms, that is, to moral norms proper.

Christel Fricke suggests a third reading of the TMS as a normative moral theory. According to her, the core of this theory is Smith's account of the rules of justice – rather than his theory of conscience, as many scholars assume, including both Carrasco and von Villiez. The rules of justice are not constituted by the spectatorial process between a person concerned and her impartial spectator. This is because an (implicit) endorsement of these rules is a condition for the person concerned and her spectator for engaging in a spectatorial process in the first place and for the possibility of their agreeing on shared moral standards. Shared moral standards arising from a spectatorial process have both factual and justified authority. The rules of justice, however, have absolute authority. Human beings are naturally motivated to act in accordance with the rules of justice; but the process of socialization within a particular culture gives rise to prejudices about who is (and who is not) among those whose feelings and interests have to be respected. Smith's moral account of the socialization of a child (and his account of civilization at large) is therefore ambivalent: On the one hand, socialization is indispensable for a child's moral education. But on the other hand, any process of socialization takes place under contingent conditions and gives rise to prejudices about who is to be respected as an equal. The rules of justice prescribe respect for all people as equals, independently of their cultural identity, and that their interests be taken into account. Universal respect is a requirement of impartiality.

Samuel Fleischacker takes Smith's claim according to which self-deceit is 'the source of half the disorders of human life' literally and explores from this starting point Smith's notion of the self and the dangers of self-deceit. Sources of self-deceit are to be found in the passions, and a person can limit the impact of the passions on his judgment and volition by relying on rules of action. For Smith, the self is essentially a social self but not, as for Hume, a social construction which is not identical over time. The self is essentially divided between a spectator and an agent. For this reason, self-consciousness as well as self-deceit are for Smith phenomena governed by norms of agency and by moral norms in particular. Finally, Fleischacker relates Smith's account of self-deceit to the phenomenon of akrasia.

Duncan Kelly explores Smith's theory of propriety in the framework of his account of 'persuasive agency', claiming that 'the propriety of agency is a measure of how persuasive its claims to our sympathy might be, particularly when seen from the vantage point of the impartial spectator'. Kelly employs the character of Cordelia from Shakespeare's *King Lear* as an example of the challenges of impartial propriety. Cordelia's expression of her love for her father is proper in the eyes of the spectators: Persuasive as her communicative action is, Cordelia gains the spectators' sympathy. But her audience on stage, and her father in particular, fails to recognize the real propriety of her speech – as it is not in accordance with the formal propriety as defined by the etiquette at the court. The case of Cordelia illustrates the possible discrepancy between standards of propriety as arbitrarily defined by a particular group and those impartial standards of propriety to which we appeal in our natural desire for approbation. Action should be governed by propriety, but it should aim at persuading those whose sympathy is with impartial propriety.

The papers mentioned so far draw on Smith's theory of human interaction and its emotional drives as sources of morality without paying much attention to the substantive changes which Smith witnessed in the society of his time. It is these changes that Lisa Hill addresses in her paper: changes from a pre-commercial to a commercial society. Hill draws on sociological theory in order to examine Smith's understanding of the social physics of life in the commercial age. According to her, Smith was fascinated by the social changes he witnessed in his own time, changes brought about by material progress as well as social and economic expansion: He saw strangers meeting in the marketplace, in need of a legal framework that could provide mutual trust where such trust had not been previously established by extensive former personal acquaintance. Accordingly, Smith describes the affective, social and moral psychology of a world that was moving from homogeneity and the exigencies of security to differentiation and the demands of commerce. While being aware of the dissolution of the primordial ties of blood and territory, Smith explained how commercial society could still be adequately regulated and held together – by contract, the cool virtues, the division of labour, a minimal and properly managed state and a regular system of justice and police. Whereas Hill diagnoses a certain ambivalence in Smith's attitude to commercial society, she argues that he saw the ideal of a liberal commercial society to be more 'pacific, orderly and predictable than its stadial predecessors ... partly because its regulating mechanisms are generated *outside* intensely emotional and exclusivistic social units like the family, the village, the *umma* or the feudal estate'.

John O'Neill shares Hill's interest in the interaction of members of a commercial society as explored by Smith. He takes his starting point from recent debates about the politics of recognition: Is recognition a cultural matter that can be studied without taking economic inequalities into account, or is it intrinsically shaped by economic inequalities? Whereas the debate has extensively explored the Hegelian theory of recognition, including Hegel's discussion of Rousseauean views, O'Neill explores the particular position of Adam Smith and the way Smith responds to the egalitarian challenges raised by Rousseau (and others). According to O'Neill, Smith provides a theory of recognition which understands the economy as a sphere of recognition and the distribution of goods within the economy as closely related to problems of recognition. Smith's attitude to the commercial society is to some extent ambivalent: He is aware of the social invisibility of the poor as an example of misrecognition in commercial society, that is, of the divorce of recognition from its proper object. But, according to O'Neill, Smith is defending commercial society nevertheless, describing it as a social order in which independent agents mutually recognize each other as such.

In his contribution, Jon Elster focuses on the topic of strong reciprocity as explored by Seneca and Adam Smith. Strong reciprocity can be either negative (resentment) or positive (gratitude). On behalf of the phenomenon of strong reciprocity, Elster distinguishes between two questions: There is on the one hand the normative question about the right response to an action (the right degree of resentment or gratitude) and on the other the positive question about the motivational impact these feelings actually have. Elster explores both Seneca's and Smith's answers to these questions, compares them to each other and then looks at their views from the point of view of contemporary experimental research in behavioural economics. He draws attention to two phenomena in particular: Experimental findings confirm that people are naturally disposed to excessive retaliation of suffered harm. But if a third person punishes the offender rather than the victim himself, the punishment is more moderate. Furthermore, Smith is anticipating that a victim would gain more pleasure from punishing his offender himself than from seeing him punished by a third person. This claim has not yet been tested in experiments. Both phenomena provide interesting aspects to be taken into account when addressing the normative question about the right degree of gratitude, resentment and punishment as a response to an act of benevolence or offence.

Vivienne Brown argues that the TMS provides resources for showing why it might be rational for players to cooperate in a one-shot Prisoners' Dilemma game. She develops a new mode of practical reasoning for interdependent players which shows that it might be individually rational, not self-sacrificial, to cooperate in such a game. She argues that the respective mode of reasoning, which shows that 'instrumental cooperation' can be the outcome of individual maximization given the nature of players' interdependence, is in tune with Smith's account of intersubjectivity in the TMS. According to this account, individual agents internalize their awareness of interdependence: Smith develops an intersubjective conception of the 'self' which allows new insights for understanding social dilemmas.

Karl Ove Moene reminds us of the historical fact that Smith's WN has been instrumentalized by conservative liberalist economists: In Smith's name, they campaigned against any political interference in the market. Smith's reputation as a liberalist capitalist who ignored the needs of the people at the poor end of society has made him a welcome target of left-wing anti-market-mechanism ideology. Moene sets off to free Smith from his ideological captivity. He argues that Smith was defending a policy of economics and society that is best captured by comparing it to the so-called Scandinavian model: The Scandinavian model is distinguished by comprehensive labour market organizations, a large welfare state and a system of routine consultation among government and representatives of interest organizations. The typical policies are wage compression, lowering high wages and raising low wages; the provision of basic goods for all citizens as a right of citizenship; and a government commitment to full employment. In his re-reading of the WN, Moene argues that these aspects of the Scandinavian model of social democratic development owe more to Adam Smith than to Karl Marx.

From psychology to moral normativity

Maria A. Carrasco

Adam Smith 'constructs' the moral world, says Samuel Fleischacker, from some amoral, innate tendencies of human nature.[1] Along the same line of interpretation D. D. Raphael affirms that Smith gives a psychological genetic explanation of the emergence of moral conscience;[2] which originating from our most basic and innate drives, advances to a reasonable account of human moral nature. Psychology – which here, for the sake of clarity, will only refer to 'our innate desire for pleasure' – is in this theory like the infrastructure that supports the gradually formed 'superstructure' of morality – or the desire for good in itself and for its own sake.[3] Our psychological constitution both sustains and is the condition that enables morality. However, the moral dimension in Smith's *Theory of Moral Sentiments* (TMS) is independent of psychology. Many important interpreters affirm that morality is a mere internalization of social norms, which would ultimately be justified in psychology.[4] On the contrary, I will argue that morality is a new and distinct dimension, which emerges from a different source and has a different kind of normative authority. They are distinct spheres that, despite their genetic connection, can be distinguished in Smith's ethics.

My proposal is that Adam Smith builds this 'bridge' from the amoral to the moral through the development of his notion of sympathy – 'the backbone of Smith's theory', as Carola von Villiez calls it.[5] Reconstructing the TMS around this concept – which along with the impartial spectator are the two 'pillars' of this ethics – will show how Smith is able to give an account of the human moral dimension starting from the empirical *factum* of our innate drive to sympathize.[6] Nonetheless, this will not mean that psychology is the cause of morality as if it were an epiphenomenon or could be reduced to it. Human moral conscience develops gradually, in the same way as self-consciousness or the capacity for abstract reasoning do. At some stage of the normal process of maturation we 'acquire', so to speak, moral conscience,[7] and become – as Smith characterizes us – morally accountable beings (Corr. p. 52, TMS III.1.4).

The difference and independence of the psychological and the moral dimensions is manifest in Smith's brief but unequivocal description of that small group of men who – I will contend – embody his underlying normative ideal: the 'wise and virtuous'. These men, who represent the apex of virtue in

The Adam Smith Review, 6: 9–29 © The International Adam Smith Society
ISSN 1743-5285, ISBN 0-415-66722-7

Smith's theory, also suffer from conflicts of motivation, revealing that there are two distinct motives (psychological and moral) competing in their breasts. In spite of their continuous efforts to identify themselves with the 'impartial spectator within' and to cultivate the resolution of mind and delicacy of sentiments required for virtue (cf. TMS VII.iii.3.10), their innate psychological tendencies or passive feelings will always coexist with their habitual *moral* feelings.

In order to make my point, I will start by presenting the (reconstructed) evolution of Smith's concept of sympathy. In the first section, I will explain psychological sympathy in order to, in the second section, show why and how what I call 'moral sympathy' reveals a new and different dimension in human beings. In the third section, I will describe what I take to be Smith's normative ideal, embodied in the 'wise and virtuous'. And I will finish suggesting that the structure of moral judgments in the TMS is intrinsically connected to Smith's normative theory, and that his innovative concept of sympathy changes the metaethical qualification of his system: his self-described sentimentalist morality (cf. TMS VII.iii.3.16) becomes an ethics closer to a kind of modern practical reason theory.[8]

From amoral to moral sympathy: the psychological dimension

Roughly speaking, it is possible to identify four kinds of sympathy in Smith's TMS, which are qualitatively different and increasingly complex, although they are not mutually exclusive.[9] Two of them might be called 'one-way sympathies', and the other two, 'two-way or mutual sympathies'. These 'mutual sympathies' are Smith's specific creations, and those that change the axis of his theory from a mere sentimentalism to an ethics closer to practical reason. Nevertheless, each of these concepts is the foundation or the ground upon which the following one rests.

One-way sympathies[10]

The first two kinds, or one-way sympathies, are quickly described in the first chapter of the book. One is the most basic meaning, the contagion or transfusion of sentiments – as Smith characterizes it – between an agent and a spectator (TMS I.i.1.6). This 'mechanical' sympathy lacks one of the central features of Smith's final notion: the identification through practical imagination between the actors. However, it already gives us some important information about this concept: morality is a social phenomenon; it emerges from the interaction between human beings.

Mechanical sympathy is simply to laugh when somebody else is laughing or to yawn when another yawns. Even animals are subject to this 'infection of feelings', such as when dogs start howling upon hearing other dog's howls. The most primitive manifestation of it, or some kind of proto-empathy, might be motor mimicry.[11] As Robert Gordon reports, infants and animals may also replicate emotions, i.e. have some sort of very basic sympathetic responses which travel by way of a purely non-cognitive channel.[12] Smith does not ignore this rudimentary understanding of the concept of sympathy, probably because its observation was the starting point of all the theories that give a prominent role to this notion, and also because it was not completely absent among his contemporaries. Hutcheson, for instance, describes it as an internal sense through which, '*previous to any reasoning or meditation*, we rejoice in the prosperity of others, and sorrow with them in their misfortunes'.[13] But Smith does qualify it as a very imperfect sympathy (TMS I.i.1.9); and he not only broadens its meaning to 'a fellow-feeling with *any* passion whatever' (TMS I.i.1.5. My emphasis) but he also shows that there are some cases, like resentment (TMS I.i.1.8), where this kind of sympathy cannot explain the spectator's affective reactions. This case, indeed, makes him reformulate the definition of sympathy. But his new definition retains the social element, innateness and psychological strength that the first notion manifests.

The second one-way sympathy, introduced as early as in the second paragraph of the TMS, already includes a feature that will afterwards be the core of Smith's concept of sympathy: practical imagination. This new concept, which I will call 'identification-sympathy', is not just a transfusion but, as it were, an 'entering' of the spectator into the agent's breast and what he thinks the other is feeling. In Smith's own words: 'The emotions of the by-stander always correspond to those with what, by bringing the case home to himself he imagines should be the sentiments of the sufferer' (TMS I.i.1.4). Some of his examples are the torments we feel while seeing our brother on the rack (cf. TMS I.i.1.2) or the restlessness at the sight of the ulcers exposed by beggars (cf. TMS I.i.1.3).

Therefore, in identification-sympathy, the spectator must be 'open to context;' he does not merely replicate the agent's feelings but, through an imaginary change of positions, he now focuses on the circumstances that produce those feelings.[14] Haakonssen, comparing this notion with Hume's, says that Smith 'simply … broaden[s] the causal factors in the creation of the sympathetic reaction of the spectator *to include* the situation in which the original passion and its expression occurred'.[15] However, regardless of the truth of this claim, this twist cannot be seen as a *simple* one, since it implies the most profound consequences for Smith's technical understanding of sympathy and his whole moral theory. First, it introduces reason into this innate psychological tendency; and second, it sets the foundation for the judgments of propriety of the agent's passions/actions.

Regarding the latter, Smith says: 'We blush for the impudence or rudeness of another though he himself appears to have no sense of the impropriety of his own behaviour; because we cannot help feeling with what confusion we ourselves should be covered, have we behaved in so absurd a manner' (TMS I.i.1.10). This situation does not express contagion but a clear judgment of the other's conduct. How can Smith justify this judgment? Evaluation implies comparison, and within the framework of identification-sympathy, that will be made between the agent and what *I* imagine would be *my feelings* in that situation. '[I]t is only this "tension" between persons that gives rise to all evaluations of persons, of which the act of sympathy is the necessary first step'.[16]

Despite Smith not actually describing this mental process, he gives enough hints to reconstruct it. In order to be evaluative, 'sympathy' has to become a twofold process. First of all, I (the spectator) must completely identify with the agent: 'I not only change circumstances with you, but I change persons and characters' (TMS VII.iii.1.4);[17] and then, in the second step, I only change positions or circumstances with the agent, keeping my self-identification (i.e. I do not change 'persons and characters').[18] Finally, I compare the agent's (attributed) feelings with those I imagine I would feel in that situation, and only if they coincide will I judge them as proper to what 'the situation deserves' (TMS I.i.2.6). This is what I will call 'subjective propriety'.[19]

Phenomenologically, this evaluation through identification-sympathy can be explained as the superimposing of two maps. We all live our lives within an egocentric map, self-identified and with our particular circumstances. When we have to identify with another, 'to enter into his breast' or to imaginarily become the other person, we must re-center that map or, as Gordon puts it, to make 'an imaginary shift in the reference of indexicals'.[20] This is the job that actors usually do: they bracket out their self-identification to get completely absorbed in the role they are playing (personality, circumstances, etc.).[21]

This first movement of complete identification, this 'simulation', as Gordon calls it, 'is a procedure we consciously use in everyday moral thinking'.[22] However, complete identification has no standard with which it could be compared, and thus no possibility of evaluation.[23] That is why there is a second step, which is a similar process except that we keep our self-identification. Propriety assessments then, require a second re-centering of our egocentric map, but only with regard to the relevant circumstances of the situation (if I were performing Hamlet, I would imagine how *I*, Maria, would act in *his* circumstances).[24] I finally compare these maps, superimposing the partially adjusted map of the spectator (Maria in Hamlet's circumstances) on top of the reconstructed imaginary map of the agent (Hamlet), and according to their correspondence I approve or disapprove of him.[25]

The other consequence that this 'broadening the casual factors' of sympathy produced in Smith's innovative notion was the introduction of reason. Resentment is the best example: Before sympathizing with the agent's resentment, the spectator 'analyzes' the situation to define how appropriate those feelings are. Here Smith patently introduces intentionality and practical imagination in this innate psychological tendency, which in this case cannot be shared with irrational animals. Indeed, before 'barking' at the supposed aggressor of his master, as a dog automatically does, the human spectator evaluates if the victim's resentment is proportionate to the harm received (cf. TMS II.i.4.3). And only if the spectator thinks that the victim's feelings are proper, does he sympathize with him. Clearly this case involves some 'measure of understanding – at times sophisticated understanding;'[26] not theoretical but some sort of comprehension of the situation of the other.

There are two particularly interesting examples of identification-sympathy in the TMS, which refer to extraordinary situations and thus better reveal other relevant features of the formal structure of Smith's concept of sympathy. The first is 'illusive sympathy', as when we identify with a dead person who obviously cannot feel the sentiments we imagine he would feel if he were conscious of his circumstances (cf. TMS I.i.1.13 and II.i.2.5). This situation shows that for Smith the key to 'propriety' is not the agent's actual feelings but those 'we imagine they should be'. The second is 'conditional sympathy' (TMS I.i.3.4), where Smith shows how this imaginary identification may also work the other way round: sometimes we are not able to correspond to the agent's feelings, but since we know from experience that they are proportionate to their situation, we approve of them.

All these cases manifest the fundamental qualitative difference between this second one-way sympathy and mere contagion. Identification-sympathy involves an act of practical imagination; it requires the assistance of reason. We ought to be able to identify 'kinds of situations', to abstract their essential features in order to categorize them. Only through this cognitive process can we later recognize concrete situations with all their contingent circumstances, and know what the appropriate feelings for them are. To know 'from experience' means that we have already categorized situations, and hence we are able to recognize their exemplars and to judge accordingly, without needing to return to our actual affective reactions.

Consequently, in this still very basic level of sympathy, there are already some essential elements of the increasingly complex concept Smith is putting forward. First of all, interpersonality: sympathy requires two actors, an agent and a spectator. Second, openness to context. Identification with the other's feelings is an understanding, through practical imagination, of the situation the other is experiencing. And finally, evaluation and judgment of propriety. Identification-sympathy implies the comparison between the agent's actual or virtual feelings with those that would be the spectator's feelings in the same circumstances. From this comparison arises the judgment of subjective propriety according to what the spectator's thinks the situation deserves. All these characteristics, quickly exposed in the first pages of the TMS, already change Smith's concept of sympathy from his predecessor's mere 'power of perception' (TMS III.4.5)[27] into a 'principle of approving of propriety' of the sentiments of the other.

Mutual sympathy

The first great leap Smith makes with his novel notion of sympathy, which will signify the decisive qualitative difference with his contemporaries' 'spectatorial ethics', is the introduction of mutual sympathy.[28] Smith does not seem to give to this new feature the meta-ethical importance it has for the definition of his theory, which will eventually set it apart from classic sentimentalism. Without any preamble, in the second chapter of the book he brings in his original notion of the 'pleasure of mutual sympathy'. 'Nothing pleases us more – he says – than to observe in other men a fellow-feeling with all the emotions of our own breast; nor are we ever so much shocked as by the appearance of the contrary' (TMS I.i.2.1); and further: 'As the person who is principally interested in any event is pleased with our sympathy, and hurt by the want of it, so we, too, seem to be pleased when we are able to sympathize with him, and to be hurt when we are unable to do so' (TMS I.i.2.6). This seemingly innocent empirical observation transforms at least in two different ways the spectatorial ethics. First, it makes it a 'mutual spectatorship': the agent, until now uninvolved with the judgment, becomes an active participant in the sympathy process. He turns out to be a 'spectator of the spectator', and as he vividly desires the pleasure of mutual sympathy, he strives to identify himself with the spectator, he looks at himself through the other's eyes and brings his feelings up to the point which the spectator would approve of them. Second, the spectator, who has so far been evaluating 'from the outside', shall also enter into the situation to get the pleasure of mutual sympathy, moderating his feelings in order to match them with the agent's.[29] Henceforth, under this new concept, sympathy becomes performative. There is observation, but an observation that also and necessarily implies action: both the spectator and the agent have to modify their feelings if they want the pleasure of mutual sympathy. And their efforts will give rise, correspondingly, to the virtues of humanity and those of self-command.[30]

Unsurprisingly, Smith's highly original notion was not well understood by his contemporaries. After the first edition of the TMS he was criticized by his friend David Hume, who said that sympathizing with painful feelings could never give pleasure and ironically commented that, if that was the case, 'A hospital would be a more entertaining place than a ball'.[31] Naturally, for him, sympathy just meant one-way sympathy. Therefore, Smith had to explain his innovative concept in a footnote added in the TMS's second edition saying what was only implicit in the first:

> It has been objected to me that as I found the sentiment of approbation, which is always agreeable, upon sympathy, it is inconsistent with my system to admit any disagreeable sympathy. I answer, that in the sentiment of approbation there are two things to be taken notice of; first, the sympathetic passion of the spectator; and, secondly, the emotion which arises from his observing the perfect coincidence between this sympathetic passion in himself, and the original passion in the person principally concerned. This last emotion, in which the sentiment of approbation properly consists, is always agreeable and delightful.
>
> (TMS I.iii.1.9)

Smith, in this passage, distinguishes between the three steps I have already described for subjective propriety judgments: complete identification, partial identification and comparison. However, once he includes the common desire for mutual sympathy, the 'superimposed maps' no longer remain static. If the spectator finds no coincidence between his and the agent's feelings, he will strive, through the virtues of humanity, to better identify himself with the agent, to better *understand* his situation and get as close as possible to his affective responses. The agent, in turn, who is now a spectator too, will struggle to moderate his passions/actions while applying the virtues of self-command. And the point of propriety will correspond to where they are able to coincide: it will be a 'consensual propriety'. Henceforth, following the *factum* of our innate psychological tendency of the pleasure of mutual sympathy, the formal structure of the judgments of propriety in Smith's TMS is completely transformed.[32] In this third stage, there is no longer an external judge imposing his standards from a third person viewpoint, but propriety is set by internal consensus.

Furthermore, when mutual sympathy becomes more widespread,[33] it also has deep social consequences. Being relational, the spectator's private feelings will no longer be the measure of propriety, but it will require the contrast, attunement and eventual concordance of both the agent's and the average spectators' feelings. Propriety then becomes culture-relative and is embodied in social norms, which will be the new standard for judgments. The agents, seeking the pleasure of mutual sympathy, will have to adjust their sentiments to what they think their culture believes each particular situation deserves. And the spectators will try to correspond to what, in von Villiez's terms, would be the 'communal observer'.

This consensual propriety is indeed normative, but its authority is completely factual, it proceeds from our desire of mutual sympathy or to feel approved of by our peers.[34] And this psychological sympathy, meaning the concordance of sentiments between two real, affectively connected and socially embedded people, is necessarily relativistic. However, if in the TMS morality is not reducible to psychology, Smith cannot stop here.[35] Psychological sympathy might suffice for the harmony within society (cf. TMS I. i.4.7); but regarding morality, where more than a social bond is aimed for, psychological sympathy is not enough.

Mutual moral sympathy

Smith's Copernican revolution, which finally shifts his psychological sympathy into moral sympathy and our raw sentiments into moral sentiments, is mainly developed in the Part III of the book. The point of inflection is the appearance of the impartial spectator within, who by 'moralizing' our self-centered passions through impartiality, changes – as far as human weakness allows – a conventional and relativistic ethics into one closer to practical reason.

Identification-sympathy is a surprisingly appropriate vehicle for this ethics, which connects the universality of reason (given, in this case, through impartiality) with the particularities of each different situation. Practical reason, that is nothing but reason guiding action, has to be 'open to context': to our ever-changing world, full of contingencies that cannot be captured in universal theoretical laws, but where real actions take place.[36] Henceforth, an ethics of practical reason will always be 'situation-relative', because circumstances are always changing and judgments have to be made each time anew.[37] Identification-sympathy then, is a perfect vehicle for identifying, as practical reason's judgments require, the relevant circumstances that in each particular occasion need to be considered.

Therefore, based on the infrastructure of mutual psychological sympathy, Smith shows how at some point of our development moral conscience naturally and necessarily appears. A very young child – he says, has no self-command,

> but, whatever are its emotions, whether fear, or grief, or anger, it endeavours always, by the violence of its outcries, to alarm, as much as it can, the attention of its nurse, or of its parents. While it remains under the custody of such partial protectors, its anger is the first and, perhaps, the only passion which it is taught to moderate.
>
> (TMS III.3.22)

Nevertheless, when that child starts going to school, he faces for the first time people who are not disposed to accept his innate self-centered desires. At this point he realizes that without restraining the expression of his passions he will never get their approval and the most desired pleasure of mutual sympathy. The indifferent eyes of our peers are the efficient cause that forces us to look at ourselves from the outside, from their unconcerned standpoint, where we discover that we are nothing 'but one in a multitude of equals' (cf. TMS III.3.4). These indifferent spectators are like the mirrors or looking-glasses Smith alludes to – following Hume's metaphor about a hypothetical solitary human creature – in which we see ourselves as we really are (cf. TMS III.1.4). That is precisely why, just like the solitary man, when we 'enter into society' our 'desires and aversions … will now often become the causes of new desires and new aversions' (TMS III.1.3). Indeed, our raw uneducated passions will give rise, for the first time, to *moral sentiments.*

Therefore our psychological desire for mutual sympathy is the first motivation for moral conduct, or as Griswold says, 'the midwife of virtues'.[38] Our peers' indifferent eyes prompt us to look at ourselves ex-centrically, to distance ourselves from our first-order desires inducing us to that reflexive turn that will produce second-order or rational desires, finally bringing the 'impartial spectator' to existence. *He* is the one that will inform those second-order passions – our same passions although mediated by internalized patterns of deliberation – continuously reminding us that, as we are all equals, we can never make an exception of ourselves if we wish to gain other people's sympathy.

However, in this Third Part of the TMS Smith emphasizes that we desire not only praise (or 'other people's sympathy') but also praiseworthiness (cf. TMS III.2.1); that these desires, in spite of their resemblance and connection are different and independent of one another (cf. TMS III.2.32); that none of them may be derived from the other (cf. TMS III.2.2), and that '[i]n every well-formed mind [the desire of praiseworthiness] seems to be the strongest of the two' (TMS III.2.7). Indeed, for Smith, 'The secret of education is to direct vanity to proper objects' (TMS VI.iii.46); i.e. the mere desire of *praise* to that of *praiseworthiness.* Hence the reflexive turn we are psychologically forced to make and through which we see ourselves as we really are – one in a multitude of equals, 'in no respect better than any other in it' (TMS III.3.5) – also opens to us a new dimension, unveiling a different motive for actions (praiseworthiness instead of praise) with its own and different justification (equality instead of pleasure).[39]

Moreover, this moral dimension is not an external imposed reality for us.[40] Mutual respect as beings of equal worth is already implicit in our most primitive concerns, as our 'immediate and instinctive approbation of the most sacred and necessarily law of retaliation' (TMS II.i.2.5).[41] But most importantly, after realizing we are all equals, when somebody hurts us we resent the fact that the person who inflicted the injury looks at us as if we are inferior; 'we resent disrespect of our dignity, our status as persons who *may not* be treated in certain ways'.[42] And because of sympathy, when another is hurt we resent the harm done to them in exactly the same was as if the injury was inflicted on us. In other words, identification-sympathy implies what Darwall has described as 'reciprocal recognition of one another as having equal dignity'.[43]

Consequently, our self-distancing reveals to us a *moral value* (equal dignity) which becomes a different standard to guide and measure our actions. We are able to perceive it because morality is natural for us (Smith, probably responding Hume, affirms that we detest vices *for their own sake*: 'why should it not; if we hate and detest them because they are the natural and proper object of hatred and detestation' – TMS II.ii.3.8; and that we also love virtue 'for its own sake, and without any further view' – TMS VII.iii.2.7). Furthermore, this moral value is also universally binding, independent of our interests or desires, since it gives reasons to every 'equal' to respect it.[44]

In sum, psychological sympathy becomes moral sympathy when its motivation (or 'the sentiment or affection of the heart … upon which all virtue or vice depends' – TMS II.i introd.2) changes: when we start to intend praiseworthiness or virtue in our passions/actions instead of the pleasure of actual praise.[45] This happens when our first-order passions start to be informed, mediated or modeled by the 'impartial spectator within' (or 'reason, principle, conscience' – TMS III.3.5); when they become second-order passions or, properly speaking, *moral* sentiments.[46]

Henceforth, returning to the superimposed maps example, in mutual moral sympathy the spectator's map is not his own egocentric or culture-centric map, but the supposed impartial spectator's. *Before* judging, *before* sympathizing or entering into the agent's breast, the actual spectator brackets out his natural self-centeredness, his consciously known cultural prejudices, his interests, biases and emotional ties;[47] in order to become, as much as possible, a 'man in general', an 'abstract man', 'the representative of mankind' (TMS III.2.31). After this self-removal, he 'draws a new map' founded on the impartial spectator's feelings, and thus with some fixed and stable references that should be the same for every moral being.[48] This is the 'map' that we will compare with the agent's. Hence in moral judgments we project ourselves into the other person as an *impartial* spectator,[49] ponder their feelings from that *impartial* standpoint and judge of their propriety according to what that particular situation in its particular context *impartially* deserves. The agent, who may now be the same spectator judging himself, will struggle to align his passions with this new standard; and far from the psychological 'how would *I* feel if *I* were in your circumstances', when making moral judgments we renounce to our self-identification to ask: 'How would *anybody* feel if they were really you (with all your particular characteristics) in your circumstances?' This *anybody* is the 'impartial spectator within'. Sympathetic-impartiality then will be the means of attaining propriety, which might now be called 'moral (not just consensual) propriety', since it is no longer the coincidence of the actual spectator's partial feelings but the coincidence with the moral feelings of the impartial spectator.[50]

In conclusion, the inciting incident of our moral life is that moment when our first-order desires start to be mediated by the impartial spectator. First-order desires will never disappear from our nature though, and will often struggle with the newly acquired habit of self-command. This is why Smith suggests that the entrance into 'the great school of self-command' is the entrance into the moral domain and that it coincides with the emergence of the impartial spectator in our breast (cf. TMS II.3.22). Moreover, if first-order and second-order desires may coexist and even oppose each other, they must belong to different dimensions in human beings, each of them with their own particularities. This may be illustrated by a very simple example. When, after listening to a friend's account about treating unjustly another, the other friend says 'I really understand where you are coming from, but I cannot justify your action', she is implicitly showing that psychological sympathy and moral sympathy belong to different spheres (and that they are not exclusive). The 'I' who *understands* is my actual being; it is 'I' evaluating from my particular position in the world. The 'I' who does not *justify* though, is also myself, but not self-identified. This time, I am evaluating from a standpoint we can all share, and from which I can rationally argue why that particular action is morally wrong. Otherwise, my *understanding* would be enough to justify actions.[51]

Therefore, if 'moral beings are accountable beings', (TMS III.1.4) as Smith says, psychological sympathy and consensual propriety are not enough for that accounting. We need *rational* reasons, and not only subjective feelings, to validate our judgments or to give them – as von Villiez asserts – truly 'intersubjective authority'. And only moral or impartiality mediated sympathy can open that *locus* where we may all coincide; this is to say, our common moral world.

Smith's normative ideal

Despite saying that his theory is about facts and not values (cf. TMS II. i.5.10), if we accept that Smith recognizes an independent moral dimension in human beings we acknowledge that he believes in moral good and evil.[52] He does not clearly distinguish these dimensions until describing the emergence of moral conscience, but from the beginning of the book he suggests his normative ideal. He says:

> *Two* different roads are presented to us, equally leading to the attainment of this so much desired object [to be respected and to be respectable]; the one, by the study of wisdom and the practice of virtue; the other, by the acquisition of wealth and greatness. *Two* different characters are presented to our emulation; the one, of proud ambition and ostentatious avidity; the other, of humble modesty and equitable justice. *Two* different models, *two* different pictures, are held out to us, according to which we may fashion our own character and behaviour.
>
> (TMS I.iii.3.2. My emphasis)

We all want praise, to feel approved of, to feel sympathy. But despite wisdom and virtue being the only human features that strictly deserve praise, as Smith emphatically declares (cf. TMS I.iii.3.1–3), few people take that path. The road is open to everybody;[53] but it is harder, slower, narrower and not always as visible as wealth and honor, which is the 'second road' we may choose to attain others' sympathy. Virtue or true praiseworthiness may even require the sacrifice of worldly praise, keeping only the consolation of the 'impartial spectator's approval' or that 'second tribunal' which we can appeal to judge of our conduct (cf. TMS III.2.32).

The wise and virtuous

Smith dedicates relatively few pages to describe the 'wise and virtuous character' in his work. But these passages reveal at least that he acknowledges their existence, or the possibility of their existence, and what he considers the consummation of morality: 'the best head joined to the best heart' (TMS VI. i.15). Indeed, Smith distinguishes from the beginning between 'virtue' – or 'excellence, something uncommonly great and beautiful, which rises far above what is vulgar and ordinary' (TMS I.i.5.6) – and mere propriety, understood as decency, the common degree of virtue most people reach and aspire to.[54] There are scarce references to the 'wise and virtuous' in the book, but they are an important clue to understanding his notion of morality and the underlying normative ideal of the 'common moral world' he attempts to explain as emerging from our psychological tendencies.

The 'wise and virtuous' in Smith's theory are the best students in the 'school of self-command', perhaps the only ones who have really taken on board its meaning. They are the ones who are permanently exercising that habit in order to identify themselves, as much as possible, with the 'impartial spectator within' and his moral evaluations. Unlike the majority of people, content with minimal propriety of just following general rules,[55] the wise and virtuous understand that, in our ever-changing practical world, every situation is different, and the indeterminable circumstances that have to be taken into account ask for renewed moral judgments to capture the most subtle differences and attain perfect propriety. This is exactly the reason why self-command is a *habit*, a disposition that has to be developed and improved, although 'the longest life is very seldom sufficient to bring to complete perfection' (TMS III.3.22). A wise and virtuous man then, is continuously sharpening the 'eye of [his] mind' (TMS III.3.2) because, unsatisfied with social norms, he would rather follow the 'ideal of perfection' that he has been gradually forming

> from his observations upon the character and conduct both of himself and of other people. It is the slow, gradual, and progressive work of the great demigod within the breast … [The virtuous man] has studied this idea more than other people, he comprehends it more distinctly, he has formed a much more correct image of it, and is much more deeply enamoured of its exquisite and divine beauty. He endeavours as well as he can, to assimilate his own character to this archetype of perfection.
> (TMS VI.3.25)[56]

There are some authors who identify this 'archetype' with a 'perfect communal observer' or perfectly internalized social norms; however, this poses some problems. In the first place, if it were this perfect *superego*, the love of praiseworthiness would derive from love of praise, as Smith emphatically denies. But it would also be difficult to justify why Smith qualifies what the majority of people do – to follow the road of wealth and honor (cf. TMS I.iii.3) – as a *corruption* of moral sentiments; or why he says that 'when custom and fashion coincide with *the natural principles* of right and wrong, they heighten the delicacy of our sentiments' (TMS V.2.2. My emphasis), or that 'the man who associates chiefly with the profligate and the dissolute … must soon *lose*, at least, all his *original abhorrence* of profligacy and dissolution of manners' (TMS VI.ii.1.17. My emphasis). If social or communal norms set the moral standards, there would be nothing *to lose*.

On the contrary, although the wise and virtuous can never be completely sure about their moral choices, they can, and indeed do, go against what is socially accepted and approved of (cf. TMS I.iii.2.8). Griswold explains: 'Although the impartial spectator is rooted in common life … it may (as metaphor allows) grow above the soil of common life, thus supplying a vantage point that is appropriately critical and sympathetic'.[57] Moreover, when Smith criticizes Plato and Aristotle for not condemning infanticide, he suggests that wise men ought to reflect and sometimes question social norms. He explicitly says that the opinion of these philosophers, given their superior wisdom, '*ought* to have been more just and accurate' (TMS V.2.15. My emphasis). In other words, Smith really believes that some people might think beyond established customs. Observation, comparison (with other cultures, for instance), study, reflection and the disposition to question their own cultural beliefs, are completely natural causes for improving moral knowledge without recurring to any metaphysical assumption. Indeed, although it is usually highlighted that 'well-informed spectators' form more precise judgments (TMS III.2.32); it is rarely noticed, but *very important*, that Smith also talks about 'well-formed' minds (TMS III.2.7), which means that he considers that conscience may always be more delicate, more sensitive and thus more just.

Henceforth, the wise and virtuous in the TMS are those who best exemplify that moment of rationality introduced into our sentiments by the reflexive turn that engenders the impartial spectator and actualizes our moral practical reasoning. These people are those who deliberately strive to reach the best identification with the others in order to 'enter' into their passions with the best impartial perspective – as truly *moral* judgments require – to judge with the most perfect *moral* propriety accomplished through the most perfect *moral* sympathy.

In sum, his brief but substantial description of the 'virtuous' shows that, although both founded on and being sustained by our natural drive for sympathy, morality and psychology are different and independent dimensions in human nature. This is made even more evident by the fact that a virtuous man also suffers conflicts of motivation: '[In the] paroxysms of distress' – says Smith –

> [h]is own natural feeling … presses hard upon him, and he cannot, without a very great effort, fix his attention upon that of the impartial spectator. … His natural, his untaught and undisciplined feelings, are continually calling it off to the other. He does not, in this case, perfectly identify himself with the ideal man within the breast. … The different views of both characters exist in his mind separate and distinct from one another, and each directing him to a behaviour different from that to which the other directs him.
>
> (TMS III.iii.28)[58]

If there are two different principles competing in the breast, there must also be two different dimensions: 'The jurisdictions of those two tribunals are founded upon principles which, though in some respects resembling and akin, are, however, in reality different and distinct' (TMS III.2.32). The love of praise and the love of praiseworthiness are both natural for us, but they come from different sources.[59] Moral conscience, although awakened and many times perfected by social interaction, cannot be reduced to psychology.

Sentimentalism and practical reason

As a final point, I will suggest that the formal structure of moral judgments in Smith's theory manifests, at least partially, both the ideal of virtue and the meta-ethical justification of this theory. Smith identifies himself as a sentimentalist moral philosopher claiming that 'If virtue … necessarily pleases for its own sake, and if vice as certainly displeases the mind, it cannot be reason, but immediate sense and feeling, which, in this manner, reconciles us to the one and alienates us from the other' (TMS VII.iii.2.7). This is true regarding his ethics. But the point is that those feelings, according to the TMS, are not our first-order uneducated passions but the feelings of the impartial spectator, i.e. passions that have been moralized by impartiality: passions *already* informed by reason. Therefore moral desires, which set the goals and standards for moral actions, are mediated by those internalized patterns of deliberation that have given rise to moral sentiments. Propriety is neither set nor recognized by the pleasure of psychological mutual sympathy but by mutual moral sympathy: the coincidence in virtue.[60]

In Part III of the TMS where he describes the impartial spectator, Smith also illustrates how moral deliberation operates (cf. TMS II.2.31).[61] Through sympathy, the impartial spectator is open to context and may identify the relevant circumstances that have to be taken into account on each particular occasion. Hence moral perception is the perception of the impartial spectator, whose affective reactions already include 'a blending of deliberation, understanding and insight'.[62] The spectator projects himself into the agent as an *impartial* spectator, with a specific principle of decision that allows his moral sentiments to immediately perceive and be pleased by virtue.

Moral sympathy and the impartial spectator are like the two sides of a coin. Moral judgments, although situation-relative, are also intrinsically connected to the universality of reason. In the figure of the impartial spectator and his sympathetic-impartial judgments contingencies are assumed, selected according to their relevance and ordered by a universal principle:[63] the voice of that 'man in the breast' who continuously reminds us of our equal dignity. Hence in this theory, the impartial spectator is the one that bridges the gap between particularity and universality and works as the vehicle of practical reason.

Furthermore, in Part VII of the TMS Smith describes 'virtue' as 'the proper government and direction of all our affections. … according to the objects that they pursue, and the degree of vehemence with which they pursue them'.[64] A few paragraphs later he says that virtue, for Aristotle, is 'the habit of mediocrity according to right reason', and he immediately adds: 'It is unnecessary to observe that this account of virtue corresponds *pretty exactly* with what has been said above concerning the propriety and impropriety of conduct' (TMS VII.ii.1.12. My emphasis). In other words, virtuous actions in the TMS are concrete forms of behavior which manifest certain habitual patterns of rational deliberation or principles of decision. And if Aristotle's notion of virtue is *pretty exactly* the same as Smith's, then 'right reason' or the principle of decision for the latter is represented by the prescriptions of the impartial spectator. This figure is the one that articulates, in what I have been calling sympathetic-impartiality, complete unnatural detachment with spontaneous absolute engagement. In other words, the interplay of universality and particularity that characterizes practical reason.

A special feature of this account of virtue is its meta-ethical validation. In general, contemporary ethical systems consider impartiality as a necessary condition for moral rational justification. There are two well-known 'tests of impartiality'.[65] One is Richard Hare's which says that a judgment is an impartial judgment if and only if it would be approved of by anybody in the same circumstances. The second is Kurt Baier's reversibility test: one acts impartially if and only if one would act in the same way in the case that the roles were exchanged. The judgment of the impartial spectator and the sympathetic imaginary exchange of positions are, respectively, the expression of both these criteria. The supposed impartial spectator is the 'third (internalized) stance' that validates Smith's moral propriety and which is lacking in Aristotle's more or less vague notion of '*right* reason'. In Tugenhdat's words: 'It might have required Smith's unique and brilliant idea of connecting the principle of impartiality with that of affective concord – an idea whose significance has been forgotten – to make the virtues again accessible to the modern consciousness'.[66] Consequently both Smith's ideal of virtue and the metaethical justification of his theory may be already alluded to in the formal structure of moral judgments; and the 'descriptive' and the 'normative' analysis, in the TMS, would then be indiscernible.[67]

In brief, through a genetic explanation Smith advances from a human's innate psychological constitution, which includes our tendency for mutual sympathy and therefore judgments of (more or less relativistic) propriety, to an account of how moral judgments are made. By the introduction of the impartial spectator he is able to move from psychological to moral sympathy, from propriety to moral propriety, from an order of mere affective satisfaction to an order of moral values where sympathetic-impartiality is the justification of virtue. Perfect sympathetic-impartiality may never be attained because of the weakness of our nature and the disinterest of the majority of people. However, the factual existence of immorality, uncertainty and biases, do not invalidate Smith's account of a human's moral dimension which is – let's say – 'uncovered' by our reflexive judgments and executed via 'mutual moral sympathy'.

Acknowledgments

I am greatly indebted to Stephen Darwall and most particularly to Christel Fricke for their very helpful comments on this paper. This research has been funded by Fondecyt Project 1100494, Conicyt, Chile.

Notes

1 Cf. Fleischacker (1996: 404).
2 Raphael (2007: 7).
3 In other words, 'psychologically' something will be considered 'good' as long as it is desired. Conventional norms, for instance, will belong to this sphere when, even if they oppose an individual's actual desires, they are followed in order to gain approval of the community. In contrast, declaring something as 'morally good' needs a different, person-neutral and independent standard to justify it.
4 See, for instance, T. D. Campbell (1971), Otteson (2002) or Forman-Barzilai (2006).
5 von Villiez (2006: 117).
6 Cf. Tugendhat (2004: 88): 'the book proceeds from the fact of sympathy, whose normative implications are shown only gradually'.
7 Moral conscience in this theory is embodied by the figure of the 'impartial spectator within'. When people's actions are disapproved of by their peers – says Smith – they may still appeal 'to the tribunal of their own *consciences*, to that of the supposed *impartial and well-informed spectator*, to that of the man within the breast, the great judge and arbiter of their conduct' (TMS III.2.32. My emphasis). Cf. Haakonssen (1981: 57): 'When men in this way develop and internalize a morality which aspires to certain independence, we can talk of the operation of their conscience, of the impartial spectator in them'.
8 I develop this interpretation in Carrasco (2004).
9 Many commentators distinguish 'kinds of sympathies' in the TMS, depending on the specific aspect they focus on (see, for instance, Forman-Barzilai's two 'stages' of sympathy [2005] or von Villiez's three 'degrees' corresponding to three dimensions of moral judgments [2006]). My distinction is founded, simultaneously, on the relationship between agent and spectator and that between psychological and moral spheres.
10 As Stephen Darwall clarifies, the term 'sympathy' in Smith, as well as in Hume, is used to describe the distinctive forms of what now we call 'empathy', 'which [in general] involves something like a sharing of the other's mental state, frequently, as from her standpoint' (Darwall 1998: 263). See also Montes (2004: 48).
11 Cf. Sherman (1990: 104).
12 Gordon (1995: 728). A very important difference between von Villiez's typology of sympathies and mine is that she correlates them to degrees of moral judgments. Indeed, regarding the 'contagion sympathy' she says: 'These emotive reactions already contain an implicit judgment of the situation observed' (von Villiez 2006: 118). On the contrary, I think that this sympathy does not include any kind of judgment; let alone *moral* judgments.
13 Hutcheson (2007: 33). My emphasis. On the same page he affirms that this happens 'by a sort of contagion or infection'.
14 This is what Darwall (1998: 270) has called 'projective empathy', where 'the attention is focused not on the other, but on her situation as we imagine she sees it, or as we think she should see it'.
15 Haakonssen (1981: 46).
16 Haakonssen (1981: 48–49).
17 Cf. Montes (2004: 48), who describes this imaginary change of positions not only as 'to be in the other's shoes' but also 'to know where those shoes are standing'.

18 The complete identification corresponds to what Fontaine (1997: 263) calls 'empathetic identification', and this second step would be his 'partial empathetic identification'.

19 'Every faculty in one man is the measure by which he judges of the like faculty in another. I judge of your sight by my sight, of your ear by my ear, of your reason by my reason … ' (TMS I.i.3.10).

20 Gordon (1995: 734).

21 It must be noticed that acting is a 'know-how', a profession that is improved by experience (repetition and habituation). It is important to highlight that it is a know-*how*; i.e. it is practical knowledge; and that it can be improved with practice. Both these characteristics are two fundamental features of Smith's notion of sympathy (cf. TMS III.3.2) and essential to any ethics of practical reason.

22 Gordon (1995: 740).

23 Sugden (2002: 74).

24 From the first person standpoint – says Darwall (1998: 268) – feelings present themselves 'as warranted by features of the situation to which they apparently respond'. When I am performing Hamlet, I do not question his passions and actions. However – Darwall continues – this doesn't mean that we have to *believe* the emotion warranted. Being Maria, I do not have to approve of his conduct.

25 In Gordon's words, decision procedure implies imagining being in X's situation, once with the adjustments required to imagine being X in that situation, and then again without these adjustments. Only if your response is the same in each case, do you approve of X's conduct (1995: 741). Gordon criticizes Smith for not having distinguished these two moments in judgment making; however, in the footnote added to the second edition of the TMS (further quoted), he seems to explain them quite clearly.

26 Griswold (1999: 87).

27 Cf. Hutcheson (2007: 33).

28 Cf. Haakonssen (1981) highlights 'mutuality' as a crucial feature in Smith's moral theory (52), saying that 'mutual sympathy unintendedly creates common moral standards' (55). As I will also show, it changes the way propriety is set and transforms it from the previous 'subjective propriety' to what I will call 'consensual propriety'.

29 This changing of moral standpoint is highlighted by Darwall (2006: 46), who extensively explains its consequences and identifies Smith as the first modern philosopher to introduce it.

30 'In order to produce this concord, as nature teaches the spectator to assume the circumstances of the person principally concerned, so she teaches this last in some measure to assume those of the spectator' (TMS I.i.4.8). Mutual sympathy explains why in the TMS Smith had to supplement 'the great law of Christianity' with 'the great precept of Nature' in order to reach perfect virtue (cf. TMS I.i.5.1 and I.i.5.5).

31 Corr. 36, July 1759; p. 43.

32 Von Villiez makes an outstanding depiction of these mental processes through her concept of 'reciprocal role-reversal', which 'indicates the overriding significance of comprehensive information for proper moral judgments in the TMS' (2006: 117).

33 'Mutual sympathy' may well be between individual agents, like a mother and her child setting the point of propriety of the latter's cry, which – because of their emotional ties – will probably be different from the point of propriety reached by a neighbor and the same child's cry (Smith exemplifies these dissimilarities of propriety in TMS III.3.39–40 and V.2.10: 'We expect more indulgence from a friend than from a stranger'). However, we may also think in 'mutual social sympathy', which will establish the standards of behavior for a given community. This 'social' sympathy is the one described by von Villiez as the 'second degree of sympathy'.

34 The coincidence with the communal observer remains in the psychological realm, since what is aimed for is 'to be approved of' by our culture and not 'to be the proper object of approval'. There is not an independent justification for our actions; they are motivated and justified by the same innate psychological desire for sympathy.

35 Many authors think he does. One of the problems this raises is the impossibility of cross-cultural moral judgments. I discuss this point in Carrasco (2009).

36 The psychological genetic explanation of the moral dimension in Smith is an essential element for interpreting him as a practical reason's ethicist. It is precisely because morality is a 'superstructure' sustained on our innate psychological tendency to sympathize that Smith's notion of impartiality is not an abstract, unemotional, impersonal and rigid impartiality (cf. Griswold 1999: 141); but rather what I call here 'sympathetic-impartiality'.

37 Being 'situation-relative' is far from being relativistic or conventionalist. Practical reason's moral judgments are guided by a rationally justifiable principle ('impartiality') which, as Haakonssen (1996: 152) says, 'is thus similar to universality in requiring that individuals in relevantly similar circumstances must be judged similarly, if the judgment and the will are to be considered moral'. Moral sympathy is not the attunement of sentiments of actual spectators but the attunement with a particular standard, which will ultimately be the moral justification for actions.

38 Griswold (1999: 122). Notice that a 'midwife' helps to deliver a baby; but thereafter she is no longer necessary.

39 This difference may be compared to Charles Taylor's insightful distinction between kinds of second-order desires: the 'weak' and the 'strong or qualitative' desires, which 'involve [judgments] of right or wrong, better or worse, higher or lower, which are not rendered valid by our own desires, inclinations or choices, but rather stand independent of these and offer standards by which they can be judged' (1989: 4).

40 Ingraining morality in psychological sympathy warrants, in Smith's ethics, that '[n]ormativity is built into the emotions in question, it is not a foreign element that has to be added from outside', Griswold (2000: 166).

41 Regarding this 'law' Smith says that 'Nature, antecedent to all reflections upon the utility of punishment … stamped [it] upon the human heart, in the strongest and most indelible characters' (TMS II.i.2.5); and he even compares its innateness and strength to 'hunger, thirst, the passions that unite the two sexes' (TMS II.i.5.10).

42 Cf. Darwall (2005). Although Smith does not talk about dignity but only about 'equal respect', if he describes 'injustice' as treating an equal as an inferior, it is plausible to infer that we owe respect to each other because we recognize in others the same value we identify in ourselves, i.e. dignity.

43 Darwall (2004: 129).

44 It might always be discussed who belongs to this group of 'equals'. In Smith though, it is quite clear that our (moral) 'equals' are – at least – those towards whom we can have moral feelings: they must be able to both produce pleasure/pain in others on purpose, and to repent (cf. in TMS II.iii.1.6). Henceforth, he is talking about all rational beings, regardless of their particular culture or their communal observer's opinions. These people *ought* to be respected (and to respect us) as beings of equal dignity.

45 Naturally, I am not saying that virtuous actions are not pleasant (on the contrary, self-approbation or a 'clear conscience' is a requisite for happiness – cf. TMS I.iii.1.7), but the difference is the object directly intended by the action: virtue or pleasure. Generally, though not necessarily, pleasure is a secondary effect of virtue.

46 Cf. Griswold (2000: 67). 'Emotions become moral … only when, first of all, they meet the relevant criterion as specified by the impartial spectator'.

47 Cf. Griswold (1999: 136): 'the impartial spectator lacks only those emotions (such as envy or excessive self-love) that interfere with good judgment'.
48 This does not imply that the content of virtues is the same everywhere, but, as Tugendhat (2004: 98) says, 'The important progress made by Smith consists … in grounding [the virtues] in a universalistic moral principle'.
49 Darwall (1999: 142), and also Darwall (2004: 131): '[I]mpartiality disciplines the *way* in which we enter into the agent's or patient's point of view; it does not provide its own external perspective'.
50 Griswold, (1999: 139). The 'supposed impartial spectator's map' is not an external pattern of morality which may be located altogether outside the ethical community. It is our own map although illuminated by an impartial light, i.e. considering ourselves as 'one in a multitude of equals'.
51 And Smith's concept of sympathy will necessarily found a relativistic ethics.
52 To recognize them does not mean that we, 'so weak and imperfect … creature[s]' (TMS II.i.5.10) are able to know with absolute certainty what are morally good/evil characters/actions/passions. However, this factual restriction does not make any difference to Smith's underlying normative and meta-ethical claims.
53 Cf. Otteson (2002: 61) and Hanley (2009: 196).
54 Cf. Hanley (2009: 43).
55 Moral norms, which summarize indefinite 'impartial spectator's judgments', are an essential element in the TMS. First, they prevent self-deceit. Sometimes the psychological strength of our passions makes us believe that we are being impartial when it is not true. Second, they also guide the conduct of that majority of people who primarily care about behaving in a socially approved manner.
56 This quotation touches on the role of teleology in the TMS. There are several interpretations of it (cf. Hanley 2009: 183ff.). My own thesis, developed in Carrasco (2004: 108–12) is more Aristotelian than Hanley's slightly Stoical view. In Charles Taylor's terms the 'archetype of perfection' would be something like the horizon that illuminates a wise man's choices, the 'kind of man he wants to be', and the reference he uses to make his strong qualitative discriminations.
57 Griswold (2000: 165).
58 In this long quotation Smith also suggests the existence of two different orders of sympathies; the psychological one, which might be the mere correspondence of sentiments between the agent and any compassionate bystander, and the moral one, which is the correspondence in virtue.
59 The problem with this last argument is that some interpreters point to a textual evolution between the TMS's editions, which would mean that Smith, throughout his life, changed his views about this topic (cf. TMS Introduction, p. 16). However, the independence of dimensions was already suggested by the Scottish author in 1759, when explaining to his editor why the 'impartial spectator' was not a mere internalization of cultural conventions (cf. Corr. pp. 48–57).
60 As it has been said, pleasure is not absent from virtue. Indeed Smith highlights that only the vain are satisfied without self-approbation; that virtuous men's friendships are the happiest of all, that they recover sooner from tragedies, etc.
61 Otteson says that the impartial spectator is a metaphor for explaining how people in practice make moral judgments; but that for those few who turn the focus of their deliberations to the nature of moral judgments, the impartial spectator becomes a device consciously employed to render accurate assessments (2002: 46–47).
62 Griswold (1999: 88).
63 For this reason the rules of justice, which embody the principle of impartiality and safeguard our mutual respect for our equal dignity, may have precise and exact norms; while all the other virtues, being context-relative, cannot have any fixed content (cf. TMS VI.ii.1.22).

64 TMS VII.ii.introd.1. This is the general definition of the systems of 'propriety' which, in Part VII, is identified with 'virtue' (cf. Hanley 2009: 43).

65 Cf. *The Encyclopedia of Ethics*, Becker and Becker (eds), corresponding to the voice 'Impartiality' by Bernard Wert (Becker and Becker 1992: 599–600). These tests are taken, respectively, from Hare, R. M., *Freedom and Reason* (Oxford University Press, 1963); and Baier, K., *The Moral Point of View* (Cornell University Press, 1958). See also Wert, B., *Morality: Its Nature and Justification* (Oxford University Press, 1998), where the author analyzes the concept of 'impartiality' and might give an answer to Fleischacker's (2005) claim that Smith's notion of impartiality is not enough to set him apart from ethical relativism.

66 Tugendhat (2004: 102).

67 Many important interpreters contend that the TMS exposes a descriptive-scientific analysis rather than a normative and prescriptive one (cf. Campbell, Raphael, etc.); but there is an equally important group who highlights its moral character (cf. Hanley's recent (2009) book *Adam Smith and the Character of Virtue*).

Bibliography

Becker, Lawrence and Becker, Charlotte (eds) (1992) *The Encyclopedia of Ethics*, Harlem, NY: Garland.

Campbell, T. D. (1971) *Adam Smith's Science of Morals*, London: Allen & Unwin.

Carrasco, Maria A. (2004) 'Adam Smith's Reconstruction of Practical Reason', *The Review of Metaphysics* 58: 81–116.

——(2009) 'Adam Smith y el Relativismo', *Anuario Filosófico* XLII(1): 179–204.

Darwall, Stephen (1998) 'Empathy, Sympathy, Care', *Philosophical Studies*, 89: 261–82.

——(1999) 'Sympathetic Liberalism: Recent Work on Adam Smith', *Philosophy and Public Affairs*, 28(2): 137–64.

——(2004) 'Equal Dignity in Adam Smith', *The Adam Smith Review* vol. 1: 129–34.

——(2005) 'Smith über die Gleichheit der Würde und den Standpunkt der 2. Person', in Fricke, Christel and Schütt, Hans-Peter (eds) *Adam Smith als Moralphilosoph*, Berlin: Walter de Gruyter, 178–89.

——(2006) *The Second Person Standpoint*, Cambridge, MA: Harvard University Press.

Fleischacker, Samuel (1996) 'Values Behind the Market: Kant's Response to the *Wealth of Nations*', *History of Political Thought*, XVII(3): 379–407.

——(2005) 'Smith und der Kulrrelativismus', in Fricke, Christel and Schütt, Hans-Peter (eds) *Adam Smith als Moralphilosoph*, Berlin: Walter de Gruyter, 100–127.

Fontaine, Philippe (1997) 'Identification and Economic Behavior: Sympathy and Empathy in Historical Perspective', *Economics and Philosophy*, 13(2): 261–80.

Forman-Barzilai, Fonna (2005) 'Sympathy in Space(s): Adam Smith on Proximity', *Political Theory* 33(2): 189–217.

——(2006) 'Smith on 'Connexion', Culture and Judgment', in Montes, Leonidas and Schleisser, Eric (eds) *New Voices on Adam Smith*, London: Routledge: 89–114.

Fricke, Christel and Schütt, Hans-Peter (eds) (2005) *Adam Smith als Moralphilosoph*, Berlin: Walter de Gruyter.

Gordon, Robert (1995) 'Sympathy, Simulation and the Impartial Spectator', *Ethics* 105(4): 727–42.

Griswold, Charles (1999) *Adam Smith and the Virtues of Enlightenment*, New York: Cambridge University Press.

——(2000) 'Adam Smith and the Virtues of Enlightenment: A Discussion with Charles Griswold', *Ethical Perspectives* 7: 53–72.

Haakonssen, Knud (1981) *The Science of a Legislator*, New York: Cambridge University Press.

——(1996) *Natural Law and Moral Philosophy. From Grotius to the Scottish Enlightenment*, New York: Cambridge University Press.

Hanley, Ryan P. (2009) *Adam Smith and Character of Virtue*, New York: Cambridge University Press.

Hutcheson, Francis (2007) *A Short Introduction to Moral Philosophy*, Turco, Luigi (ed.), Indianapolis: Liberty Fund.

Montes, Leonidas (2004) *Adam Smith in Context*, New York: Palgrave Macmillan.

Montes, Leonidas and Schleisser, Eric (eds) (2006) *New Voices on Adam Smith*, London: Routledge.

Otteson, James (2002) *Adam Smith's Marketplace of Life*, Cambridge: Cambridge University Press.

Raphael, David D. (2007) *The Impartial Spectator*, New York: Oxford University Press.

Sherman, Nancy (1990) 'Sympathy, Respect and Humanitarian Intervention', *Ethics and International Affairs* 12: 103–19.

Smith, Adam (1982) *The Theory of Moral Sentiments*, Raphael, D. D. and Macfie, A. L. (eds), Indianapolis: Liberty Fund.

——(1987) *Correspondence of Adam Smith*, Mossner, E. C. and Ross, I. S. (eds), Indianapolis: Liberty Fund.

Sugden, Robert (2002) 'Beyond Sympathy and Empathy: Adam Smith's Concept of Fellow-feeling', *Economics and Philosophy* 18: 63–87.

Taylor, Charles (1989) *Sources of the Self. The Making of Modern Identity*, Cambridge, MA: Harvard University Press.

Tugendhat, Ernst (2004) 'Universalistic Approved Intersubjective Attitudes', *The Adam Smith Review* vol. 1: 88–104.

Villiez, Carola von (2006) 'Double Standard – Naturally! Smith and Rawls: A Comparison of Methods', in Montes, Leonidas and Schleisser, Eric (eds.) *New Voices on Adam Smith*, London: Routledge, 115–39.

Adam Smith's story of moral progress

Carola Freiin von Villiez

The Theory of Moral Sentiments is usually regarded as a fine work of moral psychology and/or sociology and, according to the predominant view, must be confined to being just that. Campbell is just one of a number of authors who argue that TMS must not be taken as a piece on (normative) moral philosophy.[1] The fact that in TMS Smith repeatedly claims to merely be explaining standard moral practice lends considerable credulity to their claim. The passage that is usually taken as conclusive in this regard reads: 'the present inquiry is not concerning a matter of right, […] but concerning a matter of fact' (TMS II.i.5.10). And, thus, it comes as no surprise that even his contemporaries accused Smith of merely justifying the moral status quo by declaring effective social practice appropriate moral practice.[2] Yet, the passage obviously lends itself to more than just this one interpretation. It could for instance be read as a rejection of first-principle, intuitionist and/or purely rationalist moral theories in favour of a procedural theory of morality where moral facts are established in human practice.[3] This, by itself, does not preclude a supra-positive conception of propriety.[4] Indeed, throughout TMS one can find evidence of a theory for the *justification* of moral norms, signalling a normative venture. Smith not only *de*scribes the socio-moral practices of his day, i. e. he does not merely give a detailed rendering of the normative beliefs effective in eighteenth-century Scottish communities. He also *pre*scribes the conditions for *appropriate* moral practice. He does not, however, do so in the manner of a rationalist moral philosopher, but against the backdrop of his empiricist beliefs. And this means that a normative theory of moral philosophy must to some extent be a candidate for validation through empirical findings and common sense. It must, to borrow Korsgaardian terminology, display explanatory (empirical) adequacy as well as justificatory (normative) adequacy.[5] It must sufficiently *explain* why people can be expected to adhere to the moral principles advanced by the theory (or, alternatively, simply demonstrate that they in fact generally do so) as well as convincingly *justify* these principles.

TMS went through six editions during Smith's lifetime, in the course of which he kept revising the original text. The 6th edition in particular 'contains very extensive additions and other significant changes'.[6] Of particular relevance to the present topic are the modifications made in response to the

The Adam Smith Review, 6: 30–45 © The International Adam Smith Society
ISSN 1743-5285, ISBN 0–415–66722–7

objections raised by the likes of Sir Gilbert Elliott.[7] In reaction to the critique that he had devised a theory that merely underlines existing socio-moral conventions, Smith modified one of his key concepts: the concept of the *well-informed and impartial spectator*. As I elsewhere argue, he did so in order to be able to further accommodate the normative intentions that were present in TMS from the beginning and can be retrieved from various points throughout the text.[8] In the following section, I will briefly introduce this concept as well as the other key concept of Smith's moral theory: his concept of *sympathy*. From this, it should already become clear that, according to Smith, intersubjectivity is the precondition for appropriate moral judgement. Thus, Smith develops a *social theory of morality*.[9] As I will be showing in the second section, he considers morality and communal moral standards natural side-effects of the interactions between individuals within social surroundings. His observations regarding moral development in individuals and in societies tend to produce a rather static picture of morality with a strong emphasis on custom and convention. And this, I believe, is what leads scholars like Sam Fleischacker to ascribe to him a culture-relativist stance on morality.[10] Yet, an analytic reconstruction of TMS shows that, despite his emphasis on the social foundations of morality, Smith conceives of morality as something that does not exhaust itself in effective social practice. Even though he does not explicitly pursue this idea in TMS, his procedural conception also accommodates a supra-positive standard of moral justification. This standard is essential to his theory of moral progress, since it enables assessments of communal standards from the internal perspective of their respective norm-cultures. His story of moral progress is one of moving from socio-moral conventions[11] to moral norms proper.[12]

Sympathy and the spectator

The two main elements of Smith's theory of moral sentiments are a concept of sympathy and his concept of a spectator. There are numerous passages in TMS that suggest a use of the term 'sympathy' in the sense of 'empathic receptivity'.[13] As such, Smith considers sympathy as a capacity common to all human beings. It is a capacity for being immediately affected and moved by the feelings of others. In social contexts, this basic capacity can become a disposition or *habitus*, the development and refinement of which depends on processes of moral learning and emotional education. The development of a sympathetic disposition is motivated by a natural desire for affective communication with and approbation of fellow human beings. It is motivated by a natural passion for an affectively and intellectually well-grounded 'correspondence of sentiments and opinions, […] a certain harmony of minds', on account of which we desire 'to feel how each other is affected, to penetrate into each other's bosoms, and to observe the sentiments and affections which really subsist there' (TMS VII.4.28, 337).

A major part of a person's emotional education thus consists in the active cultivation of two basic virtues to which Smith refers by the terms 'indulgent humanity' and 'self-command'. They are the instruments by which we can bring our feelings into tune, i.e. by which we can *sympathize.* From sympathy as a basic capacity of human nature and sympathy as a disposition, one may distinguish sympathy as a *modus* of feelings. As such it denotes the affective outcome of the act of sympathizing: i.e. concrete sympathetic feelings – feelings in the sympathetic mode.[14] It is essential to keep in mind that Smith does not use the term sympathy in the narrow sense of positive affinity, compassion or pity as we do today (and as, for example, his teacher Francis Hutcheson and his contemporary David Hume did).[15] Rather, the term sympathy can 'be made use of to denote our fellow-feeling with any passion whatsoever' (TMS I.i.1.5, 10). *Any* human emotion can be transposed into the sympathetic mode, so that there can be sympathetic joy or pain, sympathetic gratitude, etc., just as there can be sympathetic resentment, etc.

Human beings, according to Smith, have a natural interest in the affection and approbation of their fellow human beings along with their – equally natural and, thus, legitimate – self-centred interest in self-preservation. Sociability is not merely due to the cold calculation of advantage, as Hobbes or Mandeville would have us believe, but to genuinely social inclinations. Accordingly, the very frequently cited first sentence of TMS reads:

> How selfish soever man may be supposed, there are evidently some principles in his nature, which interest him in the fortune of others, and render their happiness necessary to him, though he derives nothing from it except the pleasure of seeing it.
>
> (TMS I.i.1.1, 9)

Man's selfish inclinations and natural partiality, which are essential for self-preservation (cf. TMS II.ii.2.1, 82–83) are accompanied by social inclinations and a natural propensity to impartiality, which serve to curb *excessive* self-love (= selfishness).[16] So it is not mere mutual dependency but mutual interestedness which allows and moves us to enter into affective communication, i.e. communication by means of and about our emotions. In Smith, affective communication constitutes the natural, i.e. innately human method of justification – *sympathetic justification.*

Sympathetic justification as such is enabled by our general empathic receptivity which allows us to grasp others in their emotionality. The idea that we possess this receptivity is indispensible for Smith, for only if we can be *affectively moved* by their situation will we be prompted to act in favour of others.[17] While thus enabled by empathic receptivity, sympathetic justification (beyond a very basic level) works primarily *via* acts of *imaginative transposition*, i.e. *conscious* identification with the Other by means of imagining ourselves in their situation and assessing the latter both affectively and cognitively from their inherent standpoint. It involves, that is, the role-reversal

I refer to in the second section, by which we try to discern what is appropriate in the situation at hand, with the capacity for imaginative transposition allowing us to sympathize even with the mentally deranged and with the dead (cf. TMS I.i.1.13, 13).

Sympathetic justification involves the following steps:

1 An action.
2 A reaction by a recipient of that action. This reaction, by which the recipient turns herself into an agent, importantly involves a judgement regarding the propriety of the feelings which motivated the action of the original agent.
3 A reaction by the original agent turned recipient, which itself again involves a judgement regarding the propriety of the feelings which motivated the original reaction.

In the course of acting and reacting, the participants in this affective communication about the propriety of feelings (and the physical actions to which they give rise ...) adjust their feelings – to some extent inadvertently. Thus the participants approach a common verdict on *proper feelings* (resp. justified actions): the closer the correspondences of feelings, the more correct the verdict. It is primarily this interaction which Smith has in mind when he talks about sympathy, although he uses the term indiscriminately to describe the very act of sympathizing as well as the intended outcome of sympathetic interaction – *sympathetic justification*.

In Smith's theory of justification there are no pre-given substantial standards of propriety to guide the participants to affective communication. Rather, the standards evolve in the process of justification itself, making for a procedural conception of propriety, which bears an intriguing methodological resemblance to the procedural conception of justice put forth by John Rawls more than 200 years later.[18] There is, however, a mediator to aid us in this quest for propriety, which Smith has given Gestalt in the persona of the (well-informed and impartial) spectator. Making use of a spectator-concept in a theory of moral justification is not a novelty, but picked up from his predecessors and contemporaries. However, Smith systematically develops the concept to accommodate a theory of justification that is vastly more refined (and more tenable) than those both of Hutcheson and of Hume.[19]

In their quest for that correspondence of feelings, which allows them to most effectively satisfy their social as well as their egoistical needs, the participants in the project of sympathetic justification naturally consult a spectator, for whose sympathy = approbation they contend. In TMS, this spectator appears in different guises. Smith makes use of the term sympathy to denote the workings of what I choose to call factual spectators, a virtual impartial spectator and an ideal impartial spectator. Obtaining these spectators' sympathies requires the fulfilment of increasingly demanding criteria. Each spectator is involved on a particular level of (both onto- and phylogenetic) human moral development and – on the normative side of the project – responsible for a particular level of sympathetic (moral) justification, so that an analytic reconstruction of these different guises allows for discerning three levels of justification in TMS. Sympathetic justification, as shall be discussed next, is a gradual concept tied to varying dimensions of impartiality.

Three levels of sympathetic justification

First level: empathy as criterion for natural justification

The immediate emotive interactions between people are decisive for the first and least demanding level of justification. Smith speaks of the emotions of one person being 'transfused' – 'instantaneously and antecedent to any knowledge of what excited them in the person principally concerned' (TMS I. i.1.6, 11) – to the bystander, thereby giving rise to the same type of emotion in the latter albeit in a somewhat weaker intensity.[20] On this level of justification, one might properly speak of empathy. The required correspondence of feelings comes about by means of an instinctive emotional adaptation and presupposes factual confrontations with fellow human beings, the basic human need for emotional and physical support naturally motivating mutual approximation.

Obviously in the case of instinctive emotional adaptation one can speak of 'justification' only in a very weak sense. Natural justification turns on mere empathy. And notwithstanding the fact that empathic *receptivity* functions as a precondition in human nature enabling us to engage in (factual or imaginary) affective interaction and, thus, justification, justification on the basis of mere empathy will only result in a very *imperfect sympathy* (cf. TMS I.i.1.9, 11). Imperfect sympathy – or *empathic sympathy* – can be revoked when unduly given, i.e. when not translatable into *well-considered sympathy*.[21] Translation depends on (affective *and* cognitive) imaginative transposition against the backdrop of the normative language that over time develops out of interpersonal interactions within social contexts, indicating the need for a more advanced form of sympathetic justification.

Second level: social consensus as criterion for conventional justification

According to Smith, nature has equipped man with a propensity toward instinctive mutual adaption. Yet as we act and react to each other, thereby continuously assessing each other's actions and motives and mapping out our spheres of interest, we sooner or later get entangled in disagreements. These are largely due to the fact that we initially assess things merely from our own perspective: initially, our sole concern is in the satisfaction of our own egoistical and social needs. Thus, we often perceive others' judgements as unfair assessments of our needs and motives, as not granting us our seemingly legitimate interests or at least not doing so to the extent we deem appropriate – we feel like we are not getting our fair share (of emotional and/or physical support, goods, etc.). Ardently pursuing our interests, however, we cannot help but realize that others have interests of their own which often conflict with ours and which they will equally persist on having satisfied. While we long for their love and affection, we have an equally strong drive to pursue our own interests even at the risk of offending those others. But we soon learn that, if we pursue self-centred interests beyond a certain point our fellows will react by withdrawing their emotional and physical support. Thus the perception of others judging us in a like manner as we do them leads us to reflect on our idiosyncratic standard of judgement. We find ourselves faced with the need to reconcile two competing natural needs: Our egoistical interests and our social interests must be brought into sync with one another in order to yield optimal results. So we develop a strategy to best satisfy both of these competing desires. By a method of trial and error,[22] we seek to anticipate the limits of the willingness of others to go along with our self-interest, as a side-effect cutting a path between self-interest and other-interestedness. For this purpose we must (by way of imaginative transposition) leave our own perspective and – as completely as possible – put ourselves in the position of the Other in order to assess the situation as she would assess it from her particular standpoint against the backdrop of her particular needs and her desire to protect her own sphere of interest. This procedure is, of course, understood to be a two-way street. Moreover, Smith conceives it as not being a purely intellectual procedure to discern rational interests, but also a sensual act to discern emotive interests. Uncovering the latter requires us to relate to the emotive constitution of the Other. And the cultivation of what I earlier on referred to as a 'sympathetic disposition' is prerequisite for this complete role-reversal, for it is precisely at this point that the active acquisition and continuous refinement of indulgent humanity and self-command comes in. In TMS, Smith gives a delightfully vivid description of this lifelong process of moral learning, a process which, as shall be demonstrated, leads us from complete self-partiality to an ever more comprehensive impartiality:

> A very young child has no self-command; but, whatever are its emotions, whether fear, or grief, or anger, it endeavours always, by the violence of its outcries, to alarm, as much as it can, the attention of its nurse, or of its parents. […] When it is old enough to go to school, or mix with its equals, it soon finds that they have no such indulgent partiality. It naturally wishes to gain their favour, and to avoid their hatred or contempt. Regard even to its own safety teaches it to do so; and it soon finds that it can do so in no other way than by moderating, not only its anger, but all its other passions, to the degree which its play-fellows and companions are likely to be pleased with. It thus enters into the great school of self-command, it studies to be more and more master of itself, and begins to

> exercise over its own feelings a discipline which the practice of the longest life is very seldom sufficient to bring to complete perfection.
>
> (TMS III.3.22, 145)[23]

This already indicates that the second level of moral justification turns on a more demanding form of identification. In human beings with an emotional constitution that lies within the normal range, empathy is always at work. Yet, the correspondence on the first level is only preliminary, and sympathy, before informed of the *actual causes* of the feelings expressed by a person, is always imperfect (cf. TMS I.i.1.9, 11). Sympathy, that is, 'does not arise so much from the view of the passions, as from that of the situation which excites it' (TMS I.i.1.10, 12), so that imaginative transposition can actually prompt us to revise the initial 'judgement' implicit in immediate empathy. Here, we ultimately judge the behaviour of others as well as our own by reflecting upon relevant features of the judgement-situation. On the basis of past experience, we soon start to classify types of actions and reactions. And as we do, so do our ever changing partners in the marketplace of life. Over time, the disparate interactions between people trying to anticipate each other's reactions and scoping out the boundaries of mutually acceptable – thus legitimate – self-interest lead to a certain conformity of behaviour. They crystallize in common rules effectively guiding social behaviour within a particular community, thus giving rise to what I call a *communal standard of moral justification*. This standard is simply the unintended outcome of the various interactions of people within a community over time. Born and raised within a normative community, moral education – aided, not least, by a functioning practice of social (and legal) sanctioning – leads us to acquire a working knowledge of the rules. We experience that, playing by the rules, we are most likely to achieve a reasonable amount of our self-centred goals while, at the same time, securing the love and affection of those around us, thus satisfying our social inclinations.

Although itself a valuable observation, the insight that we learn to optimally satisfy our self-centred and social interests by such a method of trial and error does not conclude the project Smith embarks on in TMS. For Smith is neither after a purely descriptive social psychology nor a purely normative moral philosophy of human behaviour, but pursues the twofold task of explanatory and justificatory adequacy. And the experience that our abiding by the rules of the communal standard leads to the greatest personal satisfaction is by itself sufficient in neither sense. It would be rather unorthodox, normatively speaking, to declare morality a mere function of advantageousness, and moral theories that turn on considerations of personal benefit have no convincing account for their own sustainability once implemented.

Theories of the individual advantageousness of morality as formulated by the likes of Hobbes and Mandeville usually counter the latter point with considerations of expected sanctions and/or of the longer-term benefits derived from being considered a trustworthy person. Neither, however, manages to go the last mile, for neither can reliably handle the free-rider problem. Traces of such explanations are surely present in TMS. On the whole, however, Smith has another story to tell about moral effectiveness. Nature, according to Smith, has not only equipped man with a need for the favourable regard of fellow human beings, but also with a notion of the rightful ascription of actions and motives. The natural desire for praise, that is, is complemented by a natural desire for being praise*worthy*. So it is not simply the fear of external sanctions which arouses the demons of guilt and shame that haunt us upon receiving undeserved praise and appreciation. Rather, according to Smith, we act on that mechanism of internal sanctioning commonly referred to as *conscience*, 'the ideal man within the breast' (TMS III.3.26, 147/III.2.32, 130). Conscience usually provides for so effective a control that the 'natural pangs of affrighted conscience' are likened to 'daemons, the avenging furies, which, in this life, haunt the guilty' and 'from which nothing can free them but the vilest and most abject of all states, a complete insensibility to honour and infamy, to vice and virtue' (TMS III.2.9, 117–18). The idea that the propensity for such an organ of normative reflection and control is a fact of human nature (within a healthy physical/emotional range) seems by now to be well enough supported by empirical findings. More interesting for the present context, however, is the question of how the standards guiding this reflection and control are established. According to Smith they are initially and primarily a function of our moral surroundings. He formulates a social theory of morality, according to which the various interactions of human beings within a community over time lead to the concretion of communal standards. Practices of both sanctioning and education are instrumental in the internalization of the communal standard to such an extent as to render subsequent external sanctions unnecessary in most instances.

Praise is bestowed by factual spectators – the man without, while praiseworthiness is a function of the man within (cf. TMS III.2.25, 126/2.32, 130–31). Initially and primarily, the man within has his eyes on the communal standard to fulfil his tasks (cf. e.g. TMS III.2.3, 114). In the shape of what I call the *virtual spectator*, he must be understood as a representative of factual spectators, upholding their fundamental moral convictions as manifest in the established rules of a moral community. The virtual spectator thus links individual conscience up with the moral surroundings. She ascribes praiseworthiness upon compliance with those rules, upon their impartial application in the face of opposing self-love. It is this impartial application of rules which I refer to as *first dimension impartiality*. And although we are quite good at conjuring up excuses exempting ourselves from the rules on certain occasions, we accept them as general guidelines for our own behaviour and expect others to comply.[24] The 'man within' will always scold us when we are being unduly partial to ourselves. Notwithstanding the fact that we often try to deceive ourselves as well as others, human beings are endowed with a capacity of impartial judgement. Our wish for being not only praised but actually praiseworthy comes to the fore in the impartial application of the prevalent rules of society. It is this communal standard that Smith seems to have in mind when he speaks of that standard of approximation to 'exact propriety and perfection […] which is commonly attained in the world, and which the greater part of our friends and companions, of our rivals and competitors, may have actually arrived at' (TMS VI.iii.23, 247, I.i.5.9, 26). Smith makes it perfectly clear that abiding by the judgement of the virtual spectator does not in the least require advanced theoretical moral capabilities, when he writes:

> The most vulgar education teaches us to act, upon all important occasions, with some sort of impartiality between ourselves and others, and even the ordinary commerce of the world is capable of adjusting our active principles to some degree of propriety.
>
> (TMS III.3.7, 139)

So to briefly sum things up: On the first level of *natural justification*, empathy serves as the basis of instinctive correspondence. Affective communication here turns on the correspondence of emotions filtered only by a certain pre-reflective aversion toward displays of the unsocial passions such as anger, resentment, etc.[25] On the second level of *conventional justification*, affective communication in the normative language of a particular community serves as basis of normative social consensus. The currency is here one of well-considered feelings and the criterion of their propriety lies in their compliance with the communal standard. The latter has come about on the basis of countless role-reversals where we, by help of imaginative transposition, try to discern what is appropriate in the situation at hand. On this level, the wish to ensure optimal satisfaction of our self-interest and social interests constitutes the motivation for actively bringing our emotions in tune with each other. The social foundations of morality may be said to have two benefits, there are benefits for those immediately engaged in individual interaction, and there are benefits for those peripherally affected *qua* members of the same community, the by-product of the manifold normative interactions of people being social harmony (cf. TMS I.i.4.7, 22). For under Smith's apparent assumption of ideal conditions, social interactions will yield a communal standard of justification that best reconciles both of these needs for *all* the members of the community.

In a nutshell, this was Smith's theory on the intersubjective foundations of (individual as well as collective) moral development as well as justification. Thus far, on the second level, justification must be considered a function of social consensus over a communal standard. The *normative validity* of the latter springs from its status as a by-product of human interactions within a given community, responsive to all of its members' needs. Its *effectiveness* in regulating the relations within society is owed to the mechanisms of internalization described above.

Yet, one has to realize that the workings of this invisible moral hand[26] are likely to be corrupted by distorting factors like normative monopolies, unequal communicative capacities and other descriptive inequalities setting people apart. And even upon the assumption of ideal conditions, the established communal standard can only be considered provisionally binding. Since it is ever evolving from the bottom up, it will never adequately encompass all the people within its normative reach, but will always lag one step behind, so that the mere *factuality* of social consensus cannot serve as the sole and conclusive criterion for its propriety. Smith himself acknowledges this when he sets up the impartial spectator as judge in a court of appeals, restoring the individual's integrity in the face of unjust verdicts by fellow human beings (cf. TMS III.2.32, 130–31) – even though factual restitution might have to be postponed to another world (cf. TMS III.2.33, 131). And it seems like, upon the adverse reactions of his contemporaries (if not earlier), Smith became sensitive to the fact that things can go wrong, prompting him to undertake revisions and specifications of his spectator concept in the 6th and final edition of TMS. This can be interpreted as responding to the need for a supra-positive standard, i.e. a standard that is to some extent external to the existing corpus of moral rules.[27]

Third level: universality as criterion for moral justification

Smith can be read as providing for a concept of *second dimension impartiality* which enables us to discern and counteract the shortcomings of the second level. On that third level of genuinely *moral justification* we free ourselves completely from the desire for the applause of our fellow human beings. We seek the approval neither of those factually present nor of the virtual spectator, that internalized representative of our normative community. Rather, we seek the sympathy of a spectator who does not assess things exclusively in light of the communal standard, but who at the same time critically reflects upon the *justificatory adequacy* of that very standard – and whom I refer to as the *ideal spectator*. This level implies a twofold distancing: that distancing from narrow self-interest for the sake of impartial application of the prevailing moral rules effectively guiding moral behaviour within a society which is characteristic for second level conventional justification; and a distancing from the agent's interest in social approval for acting in compliance with the communal standard. Here it is no longer primarily the propriety of personal behaviour in light of the accepted moral rules which is at stake. Rather, the validity of the social morality of a particular community at a particular time is under observation, or, more precisely, not the whole of social morality as such, but the legitimacy of particular rules. So that the sources of normativity, the sources of individual obligation, are no longer to be found in the mere social effectiveness of those rules as expressions of social consensus, but rather in the perception of their *legitimacy* in light of a *supra-positive standard* – the perception that they actually adequately reflect the interests of all those who are – actually or potentially – subjected to them.

Smith seems to pave the path to this further level of personal and collective moral development with his analysis of the dynamics of moral learning that lead to the development of the communal standard in the first place. It is to a large extent the perception of others treating us (factually or presumably as it may be) unjustly that leads us to question the authority of the particular perspective – both our own and that of others. It leads us to establish the imaginary person of an impartial spectator embodying the third-person perspective and insisting on the impartial application of the rules of our normative community as appropriate to the relevant features of a given situation. But the same should also hold true for those very rules. More than likely we will sometimes find that – even when applied impartially – they lead to unjustifiable results. The perception of collective misjudgement manifest in a socially effective rule then leads us to question its justificatory adequacy, the discrepancy between mere *effectiveness* and *legitimacy* marking the distinction between *socio-moral conventions* and *moral norms proper*. In the following, I will try to sketch a path from socio-moral conventions to moral norms proper in Smith's theory: the path of moral progress.

From socio-moral conventions to moral norms proper: Smith's story of moral progress

One of the keys to grasping the full potential of Smith's moral theory as developed in TMS is to understand him as using 'impartiality' not in the sense of a substantial concept, but of a *procedural disposition* requisite to correct moral judgement. Correct judgement, to Smith, is clearly a matter of the right perspective, and impartiality is the procedural disposition required for attaining that very perspective. In the quest for the right perspective – the *moral point of view* – there are no naturally privileged perspectives. The first-person perspective cannot be privileged. The fact that we are by nature more strongly affected by our own respective states of mind and body than by those of others leads to perspectivic distortions disqualifying it as a standpoint conducive to correct judgement. Neither can the second-person perspective – acquired by means of the first, mutual role-reversal – be naturally privileged, for what it ultimately amounts to is the first-person perspective of the Other, which leaves us with the *third-person perspective* as the perspective for correct judgement. Smith tells us to assume the perspective of a person quite candid and impartial when passing judgement on ourselves or on our opponents, thereby implying a *second role-reversal*.[28]

Now, there are passages in TMS where Smith seems to conflate this third-person perspective with the perspective of a casual bystander, such as when he comments on quarrels between nations. Remote nations, so Smith, are the only proper judges of the dispute between two adjacent nations in virtue of their not being affected by the outcome. One might think that their neutrality exempts them from having to engage in the second role-reversal. Yet, disinterestedness is only part of the story. The function of the second role reversal is to assure that the comprehensive information gathered in the first role-reversal be assessed neither from the first-person perspective nor from the second-person perspective, but from the third-person perspective. The latter must, however, *not* be understood as the *personal perspective* of the *bystander* either. It must indeed be understood as not exemplifying any particular perspective at all. Yet, at the same time, neither does it signify a 'view from nowhere'.

According to Smith, the third-person perspective must be entered into by *each and every* person involved in a judgement-process. Most notably this means that even a disinterested bystander, whom we might think of as being impartial simply by virtue of not having any personal stakes in the issue at hand, must engage in the second role-reversal for the sake of correct judgement. For, in order to fully grasp Smith's intentions, it is crucial to note that 'impartiality' must always be understood as *impartiality* with regard to a certain *dimension*. And the impartial perspective of any dimension is one that includes and gives adequate consideration to *all* the separate *perspectives* of all those within a *common dimension*. This is why, on the second level of justification, the impartial spectator can be considered an internal embodiment of a judge conscientiously applying the normative standard of her own community, the latter resulting from the continuous perspectivist interactions of the members of that community. As normative crystallization of previous perspectives, the communal standard can rightfully lay claim to normative validity. Yet, it itself turns into the particular perspective of a limited group at a certain point in time as soon as it has managed to establish itself as such. So that this normative validity is only ever bestowed under a *caveat*: namely that, over time, any socially effective rule may disclose itself to be merely a socio-moral convention rather than a moral norm proper in that it lacks the universal validity distinguishing the latter from the former. As a consequence, the communal standard must remain open to challenge by the current perspectives of those acting as builders of their moral community and seeking to not only be praised but to be praiseworthy in the eyes of the ideal impartial spectator. It is preliminary and must re-enter the process of moral communication with individuals, thereby undergoing gradual modification on the path from socio-moral conventions to moral norms. Understanding correct moral judgement as an ongoing process with an ideal end ensures that the rules of a particular community that might have been fully justified at a certain time, do not preclude adaptations to changing social circumstances and progressing moral insight once they are in place. The claim that Smith can ultimately be ascribed such an open-process view of (moral) normativity can be substantiated by recourse to the text. One example is his reference to the practice of abandoning infants in the chapter dealing with the influence of custom on moral sentiments. This practice – the gruesomeness of which is beyond doubt for Smith – might have been excusable in early societies under circumstances where the survival of the individual, family or society itself was at stake. Yet, its permissibility in the 'latter ages of Greece' – in a situation marked by increased material, intellectual and emotional resources, that is – out of far-fetched considerations of public utility, remote interest or convenience is to be most sternly condemned (cf. TMS V.2.15–16, 209–11). Its permissibility, that is, rested on a mere socio-moral convention that could never be a moral norm proper.

'Morality' in TMS is defined as a spatio-temporal phenomenon with a universal core, allowing for moral progress along both axes. We can – and we continually do – expand our narrow horizon of justification, moving from the closer circles to the more remote in space as well as time. This allows us in the long run to separate out those socially effective norms that have all the relevant properties of moral norms proper from those that as time goes by can be discarded as having been mere socio-moral conventions. And to do this, we need not even assume a standpoint that is strictly external to that of our own normative community. The path of moral progress is actually inscribed into the very foundational moral concepts we employ and the underlying moral principles by means of which we regulate our respective normative communities. Those concepts and principles – such as for example 'legitimacy', 'propriety', 'justice', 'impartiality', 'generality', 'equality' and many more – require us to justify exclusory social practices under recourse to criteria that can be shown to be *morally permissible* criteria for exclusion. Which is why, for example, a practice of 'general' suffrage which excludes groups of people on the basis of gender or skin colour could not stand scrutiny, but, in the long run, was disclosed as based on a socio-moral convention rather than on a moral norm proper. Upon this reading of TMS, 'The' moral standpoint is the well-informed, yet supra-temporal/-spatial and impartial comprehensive standpoint of the most inclusive dimension – a standpoint that *per definitionem* we can never entirely reach, but which we must always strive for in judgements laying claim to being grounded in moral norms. This clearly does not imply a wholesale invalidation of judgements correctly passed according to correct procedure from less comprehensive perspectives. And, in fact, Smith makes it quite obvious that we need the norms of our own space and time to effectively – and for all daily purposes legitimately – guide our everyday behaviour, when he distinguishes between the ideal standard of exact propriety and that common worldly standard of approximation governing the daily lives of most of us (cf. TMS VI.iii.23, 247, I.i.5.9, 26).[29] Yet, he is just as clear about the fact that some of those norms effectively governing our daily lives will in the long run turn out to have been mere socio-moral conventions rather than moral norms proper. A more detailed discussion of how effectiveness and legitimacy go together in Smith's story of moral progress from socio-moral conventions to moral norms, as well as of the idea of morality's 'universal core' will have to be postponed to a later paper.

Acknowledgement

I would like to thank the anonymous referee for helpful suggestions, and Christel Fricke for inspiring discussions.

Notes

1 Cf. Campbell (1971: 19).
2 Reeder's collection of contemporary responses to TMS (cf. Reeder 1997) is quite obvious in this regard.
3 This roughly resembles *moral constructivism* of the kind Rawls ascribes to Kant (cf. Rawls 1996: 99).
4 This passage is embedded in a discussion of the functions of reason and instinct in Smith's teleological view of nature. He uses the feeling of resentment – which he takes to be the foundation of justice – as an example of nature's measures in most effectively prompting unwitting man to both self-preservation and preservation of the species. This passage also contains in a nutshell the idea that mere factuality cannot serve as a sufficient basis for proper judgments.
5 Cf. Korsgaard (1996: 13).
6 Raphael and Macfie (1982: 1).
7 The relevant letter to Smith was lost but his original objection is reconstructed by D.D. Raphael in Raphael and Macfie (1982: 16).
8 Freiin von Villiez (2010).
9 This point has been sufficiently established in Morrow (1923a, 1923b and 1927).
10 Cf. e.g. Fleischacker (2005).
11 By this I mean that subgroup of social conventions or norms within the corpus of varied social conventions and norms in any given society which concern or, anyhow, lay claim to concerning morally relevant questions.
12 In this article I am not going to be preoccupied with arguing the point that there are (in one or another sense of the word 'are') indeed moral norms proper, i.e. norms whose authority stems from more than mere social effectiveness in the practices of a certain community at a certain time. This is not my main point and there are good enough reasons to warrant the assumption.
13 For well-informed discussions of this aspect of sympathy see Tugendhat (1997: 15th Lecture, particularly pp. 284ff.); and Solomon (2005).
14 For a full discussion of Smith's concept of sympathy, see Freiin von Villiez (2010).
15 Hume actually revised his original concept of sympathy as a transfusion of feelings from the *Treatise* to follow Hutcheson in the *Enquiry*. For detailed comparisons between the theories of Hutcheson, Hume and Smith see also Schrader (1984) and Rühl (2005).
16 This view immediately calls to mind Rousseau's idea of natural pity curbing excessive self-love (cf. Rousseau 2001: 140).
17 And it is after all in acting 'to promote by the exertion of his faculties such changes in the external circumstances both of himself and of others, as may seem favourable to the happiness of all' that man finds his destination (TMS II.iii.3.3, 106).
18 For a discussion of the similarities between Smith and Rawls, see Freiin von Villiez (2005, 2006, 2010).
19 For a more detailed discussion, see Freiin von Villiez (2010).
20 It is important to note that this transfusion does not include what Smith calls the 'unsocial passions'.
21 What I refer to as well-considered sympathy is roughly equivalent to Smith's 'sensible sympathy' (TMS I.i.1.9, 11).
22 See also Otteson (2005: 19) and Fricke (2005: 40).

23 While there are numerous passages in TMS indicating an overriding importance of self-command, '[o]ur sensibility to the feelings of others, so far from being inconsistent with the manhood of self-command, is the very principle upon which that manhood is founded' (TMS III.3.34, 152). Smith emphasizes that self-command and indulgent humanity are but two sides of one coin in the quest for human perfection, so that neither the perfect Stoic nor the 'whining and melancholy moralists' get it right (TMS III.3.8–11, 140–41).

24 This very much resembles Kant's (admittedly more systematic) reflection about our tendency to degrade *universalitas* to *generalitas*. Kant (1785: AA 4:424).

25 For a full discussion of Smith's doctrine of the passions, see Freiin von Villiez (2010).

26 This is only an allusion to his usage in the *Wealth of Nations*, not a term used by Smith himself.

27 For a more detailed discussion, see Freiin von Villiez (2010).

28 For an excellent discussion of perspectivity in Smith, see Darwall (2005).

29 In this he is actually in good company with Kant. For a nicely argued piece on the categorical imperative and Kant's vision of everyday morality, see Peter Herrisone-Kelly (2008).

Bibliography

Campbell, T. D. (1971) *Adam Smith's Science of Morals*, London: Allen & Unwin.

Darwall, S. (2005) 'Smith über die Gleichheit der Würde und den Standpunkt der 2. Person', in *Adam Smith als Moralphilosoph*, Ch. Fricke and H.-P. Schütt (eds), Berlin and New York: Walter de Gruyter, pp. 178–89.

Fleischacker, S. (2005) 'Smith und der Kulturrelativismus', in *Adam Smith als Moralphilosoph*, Ch. Fricke and H.-P. Schütt (eds), Berlin and New York: Walter de Gruyter, pp. 100–127.

Fricke, Ch. (2005) 'Genesis und Geltung moralischer Normen – ein Gedankenexperiment von Adam Smith', in *Adam Smith als Moralphilosoph*, Ch. Fricke and H.-P. Schütt (eds), Berlin and New York: Walter de Gruyter, pp. 33–63.

Fricke, Ch. and Schütt, H.-P. (eds) (2005) *Adam Smith als Moralphilosoph*, Berlin and New York: Walter de Gruyter.

Herrisone-Kelly, P. (2008) 'Situations, Incentives, and Reasons: Kant on Rational Agency and Moral Motivation', unpublished Ph.D. thesis, University of Central Lancashire.

Kant, Immanuel (1785) *Grundlegung zur Metaphysik der Sitten* (AA 04), in Kant, *Gesammelte Schriften*, vols 1–22, ed. Preussische Akademie der Wissenschaften; vol. 23, ed. Deutsche Akademie der Wissenschaften zu Berlin; from vol. 24, ed. Akademie der Wissenschaften zu Göttingen. Berlin, 1900ff.

Korsgaard, Christine (1996) *The Sources of Normativity*, Cambridge: Cambridge University Press.

Montes, L. and Schliesser, E. (ed.) (2006) *New Voices on Adam Smith*, London and New York: Routledge.

Morrow, G. (1923a) 'The Significance of the Doctrine of Sympathy in Hume and Smith', *The Philosophical Review*, 32: 60–78.

——(1923b) *The Ethical and Economic Theories of Adam Smith*, New York: Longmans.

——(1927) 'Adam Smith: Moralist and Philosopher', *Journal of Political Economy*, 35(3): 321–42.

Otteson, J. (2005) 'Adam Smith und die Objektivität moralischer Urteile: Ein Mittelweg', in *Adam Smith als Moralphilosoph*, Ch. Fricke and H.-P. Schütt (eds), Berlin and New York: Walter de Gruyter, pp. 15–32.

Raphael, D. D. and Macfie, A. L. (1982) 'Introduction', TMS.

Rawls, John (1996) *Political Liberalism*, Columbia University Press.

Reeder, J. (1997) *On Moral Sentiments: Contemporary Responses to Adam Smith*, Bristol: Thoemmes Press.

Rousseau, Jean-Jacques (2001) [1755] *Diskurs über die Ungleichheit. Discours sur l'inègalitè*, ed. Heinrich Meier, Stuttgart: UTB.

Rühl, U. (2005) *Moralischer Sinn und Sympathie. Der Denkweg der Schottischen Aufklärung in der Moral- und Rechtsphilosophie*, Paderborn, Germany: Mentis-Verlag.

Schrader, W. (1984) *Ethik und Anthropologie in der Englischen Aufklärung. Der Wandel der* moral-sense-*Theorie von Shaftesbury bis Hume*, Hamburg, Germany: Felix Meiner Verlag.

Solomon, Robert (2005) 'Sympathie für Adam Smith. Einige aktuelle philosophische und psychologische Überlegungen', in *Adam Smith als Moralphilosoph*, Ch. Fricke and H.-P. Schütt (eds), Berlin and New York: Walter de Gruyter, pp. 251–76.

TMS = Smith, Adam [1759, 1761, 1767, 1774, 1781, 1790] *The Theory of Moral Sentiments*, eds D. D. Raphael and A. L. Macfie, (1976, 1979), (=GE I), reprinted Indianapolis: Liberty Fund 1982.

Tugendhat, E. (1997) *Vorlesungen über Ethik*, Frankfurt am Main: Suhrkamp.

Villiez, Carola Freiin von (forthcoming 2010) *Dimensionen der Unparteilichkeit: Adam Smith auf der Suche nach dem moralischen Standpunkt*, Paderborn, Germany: Mentis-Verlag; revised version of 'Dimensionen der Unparteilichkeit: Adam Smith auf der Suche nach dem moralischen Standpunkt', *Habilitationsschrift*, University of Bremen, 2006.

——(2006) 'Double Standard – Naturally! Smith and Rawls: A Comparison of Methods', in *New Voices on Adam Smith*, L. Montes and E. Schliesser (eds), London and New York: Routledge, pp. 115–39.

——(2005) 'Sympathische Unparteilichkeit: Adam Smith's moralischer Kontextualismus', in *Adam Smith als Moralphilosoph*, Ch. Fricke and H.-P. Schütt (eds), Berlin and New York: Walter de Gruyter, pp. 64–87.

Adam Smith and 'the most sacred rules of justice'

Christel Fricke

Introduction

In his *Theory of Moral Sentiments*, Smith provides detailed and well-informed descriptions of the way people interact, of the way they emotionally respond to each other and make judgments about feelings and actions as morally good or bad. Scholars agree that his purposes include at least the following two: First, he wants to *provide evidence* for his claim that humans' natural dispositions include not only self-love or selfishness but also 'sympathy', a disposition to emotionally care for each other which plays a key role in a person's moral development. And second, his study of the dynamics of social interaction aims at *explaining* the way in which, through processes of interaction driven both by self-love and sympathy, people can, as individuals, acquire the capacity of self-command and moral conscience and, as members of a society, a state of mutual approval and respectful co-citizenship in accordance with moral standards. Self-command and moral conscience are, according to Smith, the characteristic features of the free and responsible moral agent. Respectful interaction in accordance with moral standards allows people to achieve a state of social harmony in which they still enjoy a great degree of individual liberty, a state which, according to Smith, is a condition for a happy life.

That people have by nature certain emotional dispositions in common neither implies that the societies in which they actually live are all the same, nor does it imply that all those societies are the same in which the conditions for a happy life are fulfilled to a high degree. Smith was fully aware of the fact that moral norms, understood as the non-conventional standards of propriety adapted by the members of a particular society, are subject to geographical and historical changes. But this does not mean that his project in TMS was exclusively sociological and psychological in kind, or that he only wanted to explain how different cultures (and, in particular, different moral cultures) come into existence even though all humans are intrinsically the same.[1] There is evidence enough that Smith's ambitions reached beyond social science, that he had a third purpose which was philosophical, namely normative in kind, that he wanted to *explore what was morally right and wrong from a pan-cultural or cosmopolitan point of view*, or rather: from the point of view of

The Adam Smith Review, 6: 46–74 © The International Adam Smith Society
ISSN 1743-5285, ISBN 0-415-66722-7

human nature as it prevails across all cultural differences. Smith's theory of sympathy, of the impartial spectator, his analysis of the morally good in terms of proper sympathetic feelings, judgments and actions, his account of moral conscience, as well as his description of the virtuous man, do indeed support a normative reading of the TMS.[2] But what was Smith's view of morality?

In this paper, I shall focus on Smith's third purpose, suggesting a new answer to this question. I shall try and defend the claim that Smith argues for there being some moral rules the authority of which is absolute, namely 'the most sacred rules of justice' (TMS II.ii.2.1, p. 84),[3] and that his argument is convincing. A rule prescribing how to act in a certain kind of way (in accordance with a certain norm) has absolute authority if all people of all times and cultures have an obligation to follow it and if this obligation is independent of any factual authority this rule might have, that is, if this obligation is independent of whether or not people in a particular social environment actually act in accordance with this rule (and the norm underlying it) or not. If the members of a society did not act in accordance with the rules of justice, they could never achieve any consensus on standards of proper behaviour that could be considered as having more than factual, namely justified or moral authority. The focus of my argument will be Smith's theory of the nature, function, origin and authority of the 'sacred rules of justice'.

Smith's normative moral theory: the state of the debate

In the literature, the answer to the question of what Smith's normative moral project actually was is highly controversial. Samuel Fleischacker reads Smith as a cultural pluralist and moral relativist: for Smith, moral thinking is common-sensical; he is aware of there being different, mutually incompatible moral cultures; any impartial spectator is himself informed by the moral thinking of the culture to which he himself belongs. But the impartial spectator does not have the means to identify and correct the prejudices inherent in this thinking. Whereas Fleischacker does not deny that there are some universalistic tendencies in Smith's argument, he does not find them convincing. Instead, he argues that different cultures as Smith understands them are equally morally justified and concludes that, according to Smith, there are no moral norms the authority of which reaches beyond the confines of a particular social group or culture.[4]

Charles Griswold reads Smith as an epistemic moral sceptic: the moral practices of actual societies provide the only evidence on which we can rely in order to answer questions about what we are morally obliged to do. Given the actual plurality and mutual incompatibility of moral cultures, we have no evidence for there being moral rules which have more than factual authority. Ordinary people within their cultural boundaries tend to be naïve moral realists and believe that their moral judgments are universally valid, that all people should act in accordance with them, independently of their cultural identity. But this is no more than the common-sensical way of distinguishing the authority of the moral norms underlying those judgments from that of merely contingent social norms. From the point of view of the philosopher, this common-sensical view cannot be justified.[5] According to Griswold, Smith avoids a more radical version of moral scepticism in so far as he assumes 'that the principles of human nature are constant through time'.[6]

James Otteson attributes to Smith the position of a moral absolutist. He reads the TMS as a divine command theory of the authority of moral norms according to which these norms should be endorsed by all people independently of their cultural identity because they have been prescribed by God. According to Otteson, Smith first provides an explanation of how the norms used in moral judgments arise in a society through an evolutionary process of communication and collective learning by trial and error. Smith's theory of sympathy plays a key role in this explanation. Sympathy, however, does not reach beyond the circle of those people with whom an individual person has acquired some degree of familiarity. In order to justify the claim that these norms should have authority over all people independently of their circles of familiarity, Smith ultimately relies on a transcendent source of these norms and their absolute authority, namely God.[7]

Carola Freiin von Villiez has suggested a Rawlsian reading of Smith's moral theory, accommodating moral pluralism with moral universalism. She distinguishes between three different levels of moral judgment which reflect different degrees of impartiality of the underlying norms: natural moral judgments, social moral judgments and well informed impartial moral judgments.[8] Only the latter can rightly claim to be universal and ultimately justified.[9] In the course of their socialization, people proceed from the first to the second level of moral judgment and their judgments thereby acquire a higher degree of impartiality or justification. But in order to make moral judgments that are not culturally biased, they have to move up to the third level. The third level is characterized by the exercise of moral conscience. Moral conscience allows a person to distinguish communal norms which represent an actual cultural consensus from moral norms proper (norms of praise from norms of praiseworthiness). According to von Villiez, the norms of praiseworthiness represent the point of view of ideal impartiality which has overcome any cultural bias.

Fonna Forman-Barzilai does not clearly distinguish between Smith's second and third purpose in the TMS – nor does Smith, as one might want to add. According to her reading of the TMS, what Smith provides in this work is 'a description of how moral culture develops and sustains itself, and not a theory of how we become conscious about that process or how we might transcend it when necessary'.[10] This means that Smith, according to Forman-Barzilai, reaches his second purpose. But what follows from this concerning his success or failure of reaching his third purpose, the purpose of providing a normative moral theory? Forman-Barzilai argues convincingly that Smith's theory of moral conscience and his distinction between praise and praiseworthiness by no means provide a psychologically realistic explanation of how an individual who has been socialized within a particular culture can learn to put the moral prejudices inherent in this culture into question, and to identify and use absolutely valid norms for her or his moral judgments.

According to the reading of the TMS I am suggesting here, Smith's theory of conscience does not play the central role in his normative moral theory. Thus, I disagree with both Forman-Barzilai and von Villiez in their understanding of the function of the theory of conscience within TMS. Contrary to von Villiez, Forman-Barzilai argues that Smith did not convincingly defend his claim that conscience provides the competence for making properly objective moral judgments. The claim I reject is that Smith's theory of conscience was at the heart of his normative moral theory: the target of Forman-Barzilai's criticism can therefore not be this theory. I agree with Otteson, according to whom Smith argues in favour of there being some moral norms which have absolute authority; but I reject Otteson's claim that Smith has to rely on transcendent sources for defending this view. Furthermore, I share Fleischacker's and Griswold's attributing to Smith a moral theory that leaves ample room for justified moral pluralism; but according to my reading of the TMS there is more to Smith's normative moral theory than either Fleischacker or Griswold are willing to admit.

The scholarly controversy over Smith's view of morality is explicable in terms of the fact that he has a somewhat ambivalent view both of the *history of civilization and moral progress* and of the *process of socialization of a child and this child's moral education* in particular. For Smith, civilization is both a process of collectively shaping the standards of propriety for moral judgments and, because this process is taking place simultaneously within different groups of people living under different external circumstances, a process in the course of which different sets of moral standards emerge, each of them confined to a particular culture. Thus, while being indispensable for any moral development, actual processes of civilization prevent this development from actually reaching its goal: the shaping of moral standards with absolute authority. And as far as the process of socialization of an individual child is concerned, Smith sees it not only as an essential part of a child's moral education but also as something that, typically and most frequently, hinders this child from actually reaching the ideal end of moral perfection, of becoming 'wise and virtuous' (TMS VI.iii.25, p. 247) beyond any kind of cultural bias: During his socialization, a child interacts with other people, including parents and teachers. He learns two things.[11] On the one hand, he learns to overcome his naturally overwhelming selfishness, to exercise self-control (at least to some extent), and he acquires a moral conscience. And in virtue of this, the process of socialization is an essential part of moral education. But on the other hand a child is, while being socialized, exposed to social pressure to adapt to the social rules which shape the society into which he is born; and these rules have, at least to some extent, been shaped by historically and culturally contingent factors. Socialization inevitably includes the endorsement of cultural prejudices. Because of this, the process of socialization, while being indispensable for a child's moral education, also prevents a child from achieving moral perfection, that is a culturally unbiased, strictly impartial point of view from where alone strictly objective moral judgments can be made. Not even the acquisition of moral conscience can provide a remedy against the moral disease of cultural bias: 'The violence and loudness, with which blame is sometimes poured out upon us, seems to stupify and benumb our natural sense of praise-worthiness and blame-worthiness.' Under such circumstances, we have to rely on our moral conscience in order to revive 'our natural sense of praise-worthiness and blame-worthiness' as it originates in our natural sympathy; but the standards of praiseworthiness have themselves been shaped by partly contingent factors and can therefore not be taken to have absolute authority (TMS III.2.33, p. 131).[12]

However, there is more to Smith's normative moral theory than his theory of conscience (the internalized impartial spectator); there is also his theory of the 'sacred rules of justice'. My questions are these: Do the rules of justice as Smith presents them in his TMS articulate obligations with absolute authority, with a normative authority over all people, across all times and places, independently of the contingent particulars of their socialization within a particular culture, independently of whether or not these rules are part of the social practice they have been taught to adopt? Can reflection on these rules help to make the voice of the 'natural principles of right and wrong' (TMS V.2.2, p. 200) heard even in the middle of the 'violence and loudness' of a majority (TMS III.2.33, p. 131)?

The place of the 'rules of justice' within the argument of the TMS

Norms, and the rules prescribing action in accordance with them, do not play the most prominent part in the TMS. Smith starts with an anthropological claim: he attributes to human beings both self-love or selfishness and an emotional disposition that he labels as 'sympathy'. Sympathy is a complex natural disposition, including a disposition to empathically respond to the sentiments of others, to desire the sympathy of fellow-humans and, in general, to desire a state of mutual sympathy with other people. Smith uses the notion also for describing those feelings we have when we actually share the feelings of another person. Underlying it is a view of human nature according to which humans are essentially social and moral beings whose happiness depends on their being members of a peaceful, free and flourishing society. Members of such a society enjoy relations of mutual sympathy. Mutual sympathy should, however, be based on mutual approval and thereby accord to impartial standards of propriety. Impartial standards of propriety are moral standards.

People are, however, not naturally endowed with a disposition to behave in a way that promotes their happiness most efficiently. Their sentiments, unconstrained by the effects of socialization, fail to provide proper moral guidance in a twofold way. On the one hand, people tend to behave in an overly selfish way and thereby provoke the resentment and antipathy of others rather than their gratitude and sympathy (TMS III.4.6, pp. 158–59). And on the other hand, they tend to empathically sympathize with every creature whose emotional state they witness; but sentiments of empathic sympathy as generated by a 'transfusion' of sentiments are 'extremely imperfect' (TMS I. i.1.6 and 9, p. 11).[13] Accordingly, in order to become moral judges and agents, people have, on the one hand, to learn to restrict their selfish passions in a process of socialization so that they can behave in a way that leaves a fair amount of space to others. And on the other, they have to learn to make their sympathy with the sentiments of others dependent on the propriety of these sentiments with respect to the circumstances under which they arise.

Smith's particular focus is on social interaction and the passions, emotions and reflections by which it is guided, rather than on instruction by institutionalized authorities.[14] He mainly distinguishes between two kinds of roles people can have in their interactions: they are either persons concerned by circumstances to which they respond emotionally (mainly by feelings of gratitude or resentment), or they are spectators of persons concerned. Spectators respond to persons concerned with evaluative feelings either of sympathy or of 'a want of sympathy' or 'antipathy' (TMS II.i.5.4, p. 75).

The spectator, observing a person concerned, observing how this person emotionally responds to certain circumstances, uses his sympathy with this person as a criterion for judging this person's emotional response (and the action motivated by this response) as being either right (proper) or wrong (improper). According to Smith, spectators do not blindly sympathize with those whom they observe, their sympathy is not simply empathic: they make their sympathy with a person concerned dependent on the *propriety* of these feelings and therefore pay a great deal of attention not only to the person concerned and her or his feelings but also to the circumstances to which this person emotionally responds (TMS I.i.1.10, p. 12; and I.i.3.1, p. 16).[15] Only those emotional responses of the person concerned which are proper with respect to the circumstances to which this person responds deserve the sympathy of the spectator.

Propriety is to be understood as moral propriety or as what is morally right. The spectator, by sympathizing with the feelings and action of a person concerned, morally approves of this person's feelings and action (TMS I.i.3.2, p. 17). What qualifies him to be the moral judge is that his sympathy is impartial and dependent on desert. The person concerned by circumstances responds to these circumstances in a way driven by selfish passions unconstrained by any concern about whether or not these passions actually deserve the sympathy of an impartial spectator. These passions make his response partial. He experiences the respective circumstances under a veil of selfishness, as I would like to put it. What makes the judgment of the spectator impartial is (a) that he is not himself either directly or indirectly concerned by the respective circumstances (negative impartiality), and (b) that his sympathy is well informed by all the relevant aspects of the respective circumstances which include the interests of all those persons who are, more or less directly, concerned by these circumstances and by the consequences of what anyone does under them (positive impartiality). This information allows him to make his sympathy dependent on considerations of desert – his sympathy is not just 'imperfect sympathy' or unconstrained empathy.

With respect to the condition of positive impartiality, one has to be aware of the possibility of understanding the 'all' in 'all the relevant aspects' and 'all those persons … concerned' in a more or less inclusive way. Impartiality comes in degrees, and the actual degree of impartiality of a spectator's judgment depends on how inclusive he understands the respective 'all'. Actual standards of impartial propriety are products of interactive processes which are the driving forces of both the socialization of an individual and the civilization of a society. Any real spectator has gone through a process of socialization within a society that has actually achieved a certain stage of civilization. Thus, what shapes his feelings of sympathy depends not only on his witnessing a person concerned and the respective circumstances directly rather than under the veil of selfishness. It also depends on which aspects of the respective circumstances and whose interests he actually takes into account before sympathizing and making a judgment. This is where less than ideally impartial standards of propriety come into the picture, shaped by individually and culturally biased feelings of sympathy and moral judgments. As mentioned earlier, the shaping of impartial standards of moral judgment is, according to Smith, an ambivalent affair: On the one hand, the spectator, in order to be impartial, has to rely on *proper* sympathy according to impartial standards of propriety rather than on *imperfect* sympathy. On the other hand, no real person in the position of a spectator is omniscient. An ideally impartial judgment which takes strictly all aspects of the respective circumstances and strictly all people who will, sooner or later, be concerned into account, is humanly impossible. A human being, when making a judgment as an impartial spectator, will always rely on standards of propriety which are less than ideally impartial.

It seems, however, that Smith assumes that proper sympathy is better than just imperfect sympathy, even if the respective standards of propriety are less than ideally impartial. Accordingly, he says about his enterprise in the TMS:

> We are not at present examining upon what principles a perfect being would approve of the punishment of bad actions; but upon what principles so weak and imperfect a creature as man actually and in fact approves of it.
>
> (TMS Iii.5.9)[16]

No real spectator is free from cultural prejudices, and such prejudices typically make him exclude certain people from those whose interests he takes into account when making his judgment. Cultural history is a history of exclusion of people from those whose interests count: women, racial or religious minorities, strangers, etc. Therefore, no real spectator's impartial standards of propriety as underlying his feelings of sympathy and moral judgments can be taken to be ideally impartial moral norms. The impartial standards of a real spectator will always represent a 'communal morality', to use a term von Villiez has brought into the discussion. Communal moral norms are not free from cultural bias: their authority does not reach beyond the confines of a particular society.[17]

The spectator's feelings of sympathy (or antipathy) with other people's emotions as Smith understands them are representational and evaluative, and their function is to provide evidence for making an evaluative judgment.[18] But the (positive or negative) sympathetic feelings of a spectator also have a motivational function. Whenever a spectator witnesses a person concerned by particular circumstances, one of two possible scenarios will occur: either the spectator actually sympathizes with the person concerned or he does not. In the former case, both the person concerned and his spectator feel confirmed in their respective feelings; after all, the spectator's sympathy implies moral approval of what the person concerned feels and encourages this person to act accordingly. But in the latter case, neither the spectator nor the person concerned will just state this lack of sympathy and moral agreement, they will not just leave it there and then walk off in opposite directions, hoping that they will never meet again. On the contrary, they will both make an effort to overcome their lack of mutual sympathy, and the motivation for this ultimately originates in their social nature and their wish to agree on impartial standards of propriety, on standards which, if not ideally impartial, they can at least share.

Thus, the spectator will make an effort to even better understand what the person concerned feels and what the circumstances are, implying that he might have overlooked something relevant when refusing to sympathize with this person and making a negative moral judgment about his performance. At the same time, the person concerned will make an effort and try to look at the circumstances affecting his emotions from the point of view of the spectator – as if the spectator was concerned and he himself the spectator. Simply by making this effort this person might already achieve the ability 'to bring down his emotions to what the spectator can go along with' (TMS I.i.5.1, p. 23), or he will at least calm down his emotions to some degree. In the latter case, he might be capable of looking at the circumstances and at himself as affected by them from the spectator's point of view; he then might find his emotional response improper and try to change it so that the spectator will finally be able to go along with it.

In the course of such a 'spectatorial process', as Vivienne Brown has called it,[19] both the person concerned and the spectator may experience a change of feelings. And as the spectator is the moral judge, a change of his feelings represents a change in the standards of propriety underlying his moral judgments. Thus, it is this spectatorial process that represents the motor of moral development and moral learning, both individually and collectively.[20] But this process alone cannot bring forth anything but communal moral norms.

The authority of these norms is both factual and justified: it is factual in so far as people actually rely on them in their decisions and actions, and without this factual authority these communal norms would not exist. Nevertheless, their authority is not exclusively factual, it is also justified, even though to a less than ideal degree. In so far as they have justified authority, they differ from all other social norms that regulate the behaviour of the members of the respective society, from all those norms the origin of which cannot be explained in terms of spectatorial processes. And the degree of justification of the communal moral norms depends on the degree of impartiality of the underlying spectatorial processes and spectatorial judgments.

Communal moral norms as they exist in the social practices of various societies do not differ only with respect to their degree of impartiality. They also differ according to the various cultural prejudices that informed the underlying spectatorial processes and judgments. And there is still another source of differences between communal moral norms as adapted by different societies: there may well be more than one answer to the question of what is, for a person concerned, the proper way of responding to circumstances of a certain kind. If pragmatically possible, a society can have a liberal attitude to the choice of one answer over the other and leave it to the taste of individuals which of these answers they choose. However, there may be pragmatic reasons which force people to actually make a choice and then collectively respect it. Such choices can bring forth further cultural differences. For example, in the latter case one may think of traffic rules and the difference between driving on the right hand or on the left hand side of the road.

Smith provides evidence for the claim that spectatorial processes actually take place within societies. He does not mention any counter-example and might have concluded inductively that such processes can be found in all societies.[21] His analysis of these processes can be read as a sociologically and psychologically convincing explanation of the way in which communal moral norms emerge and acquire factual and justified authority.[22] But, according to all evidence for cultural pluralism, including moral pluralism, these norms will neither have universal authority (factual authority within all societies) nor absolute authority (normative authority for all people across cultures, independent of their factual authority).

The rules of justice and their natural authority

In Smith's theory of the judgment about the propriety of a person's feelings and action – be it the judgment of an external or that of an internal spectator (the voice of moral conscience) – as it has been presented so far, norms of moral action and the corresponding rules to endorse them have not played a prominent role.[23] This can hardly be surprising as, according to Smith, a spectator, in order to judge the propriety of a person's feelings and action, relies on an evaluative *feeling* of sympathy as it arises in the context of a spectatorial process rather than on a conceptually explicit *norm*. It is only through such spectatorial processes that a social practice comes into existence which exhibits the kind of regularity characteristic of norm-guided behaviour. And only after such practices have come into existence can people use it as a source of data for extracting, via inductive generalization, the norms which correspond to the observed regularities.[24]

Smith takes a sceptical attitude to the question whether and to what extent the norms that emerge from observation of the regularities of a social practice and from inductive reasoning and the corresponding rules of behaviour can be made conceptually explicit. He rejects 'casuistic rules', as 'it is often impossible to accommodate to all the different shades and gradations of circumstance, character, and situation, to differences and distinctions which, though not imperceptible, are, by their nicety and delicacy, often altogether undefinable' (TMS VI.i.1.22, p. 227).[25] Thus, even where explicit norms are available for making judgments of propriety of feelings and actions, they cannot and should not replace the spectatorial process as a process to go through before making such judgments.

Only for the judgments of conscience (judgments of an internal spectator) does Smith consider the reliance on norms and rules as particularly useful. Where a person depends, for the judgment of the propriety of his feelings and actions, on his internal spectator alone, the danger of making a judgment based on appearances rather than reality, a judgment subject to the distortions of selfishness and self-deceit, is very great indeed; therefore, a person who, in his judgments of conscience, does not rely on explicit norms, cannot 'be much depended upon' (TMS III.5.2):

> Those general rules of conduct, when they have been fixed in our mind by habitual reflection, are of great use in correcting the misrepresentation of self love concerning what is fit and proper to be done in our particular situation.
>
> (TMS III.4.12, p. 160)

But the usefulness of the norms and rules for the judgments of conscience does not provide them with absolute authority, an authority which is ultimately independent of factual authority or existence in a social practice.

There are only a small number of rules which can be made explicit with accuracy and which have to be observed by all people, namely 'the sacred rules of justice' as Smith calls them (TMS VI.iii.11, p. 241). These rules are 'accurate in the highest degree, and admit of no exceptions or modifications' (TMS III.6.10, p. 175).[26] It is to these rules, I want to argue, that Smith attributes absolute authority. Which are the rules of justice? These rules are not numerous, and, within the TMS, Smith does not make the exact content of these rules very explicit:

> The most sacred laws of justice, therefore, those whose violation seems to call loudest for vengeance and punishment, are the laws which guard the life

> and person of our neighbour; the next are those which guard his property and possessions; and last of all come those which guard what are called his personal rights, or what is due to him from the promises of others.
>
> (TMS II.ii.2.2, p. 84)[27]

To put it briefly, the rules of justice include the rule not to kill or harm another, be it physically or psychically, not to steal, that is, to respect property, and to keep contracts. In one passage, Smith speaks about these rules in terms of the 'rules of fair play' (TMS II.ii.1, p. 83). Rather than positively prescribing to people what to do under circumstances of a certain kind, these rules prohibit certain kinds of action in order to prevent injustice. Smith characterizes his conception of justice accordingly, namely in terms of 'a negative virtue' (TMS II.i.9, p. 82).[28] In another passage, he describes the attitude of a person who actually acts in accordance with the rules of justice in the following way:

> We thus naturally lay down to ourselves a general rule, that all such actions are to be avoided, as tending to render us odious, contemptible, or punishable, the objects of all those sentiments for which we have the greatest dread and aversion.
>
> (TMS III.4.7, p. 159)

Given the perspective of the present paper, I am inquiring into the authority of the 'sacred rules of justice' within Smith's moral theory in general and within his theory of the spectatorial process in particular.[29] I take my starting point from a distinction between the basic motivation not to harm other people and the explicit endorsement of the rules of justice as normative principles. According to Smith, human beings are naturally disposed to emotionally respond to whatever affects them by feelings of gratitude or resentment. Our gratitude and resentment is not restricted to our fellow-humans, it includes non-human animals (TMS II.iii.1.3, pp. 94–95) and even inanimate objects (TMS II.iii.1.1, p. 93). But as with all feelings of resentment and gratitude, there is the question whether these feelings are proper. As it turns out, this question cannot only be asked from the point of view of a spectator (be it an external or an internal spectator). Before any spectator judgment comes in, a person can ask whether his feelings of gratitude or resentment are proper in the sense of addressing proper objects of such feelings. Only those objects can be proper objects of gratitude or resentment which can 'likewise be capable of feeling them' (TMS III.iii.1.3, p. 93). Non-human animals can be such objects (TMS II.iii.1.3, pp. 94–95). Such animals are, however, 'far from being complete and perfect objects, either of gratitude or resentment', and Smith argues for this in the following way:

> What gratitude chiefly desires, is not only to make the benefactor feel pleasure in his turn, but to make him conscious that he meets with this

> reward on account of his past conduct, to make him pleased with that conduct, and to satisfy him that the person upon whom he bestowed his good offices was not unworthy of them.
>
> (TMS II.iii.1.4, p. 95)
>
> … The object, on the contrary, which resentment is chiefly intent upon, is not so much to make our enemy feel pain in his turn, as to make him conscious that he feels it upon account of his past conduct, to make him repent of that conduct, and to make him sensible, that the person whom he injured did not deserve to be treated in that manner.
>
> (TMS II.iii.1.5, pp. 95–96)

In the context of the present argument, two aspects of our natural emotional dispositions have to be underlined: on the one hand, our emotional responsiveness is unrestricted, it can be triggered by anybody and even by non-human animals and inanimate things; and on the other hand there is a natural concern about the propriety of our emotional responses that precedes any interaction with an impartial spectator. Only fellow-humans are proper objects of our gratitude and resentment. Whenever we feel gratitude or resentment towards another human being, we address her or him as a fellow-human being, requesting her or his respect for us as fellow-human beings in return. Our natural social disposition brings into our emotional responses to other human beings a desire for recognition and respect as an equal human being. Smith is here anticipating an argument that Stephen Darwall developed when discussing Peter Strawson's famous essay on 'Freedom and Resentment':[30]

> Two ideas seem to be utterly essential to reactive attitudes. The first is that of a claim or demand, and the second is that of the corresponding statuses of addresser and addressee: The authority to address the demand and the standing to be thus addressed and, consequently, to have to answer to the addresser, to be accountable or responsible to her for acknowledging and discharging the demand. Beyond these two essential elements, however, everything else seems, in principle, up for normative discussion and debate.[31]

According to Smith's conception of human nature, humans, in so far as they are social beings, are originally disposed to address other humans as fellow-creatures rather than as competitors for scarce resources and as enemies who should be eliminated in the struggle for survival. And that means that they are naturally disposed not to harm or hurt each other. The request for recognition and respect as an equal human being is part of our natural emotional disposition; it is originally unrestricted by any cultural prejudices and antecedes all further 'normative discussion and debate', as Darwall rightly underlines. For Smith, this is the motivational basis of our human morality and, as I shall argue, the source of the absolute authority of the rules of justice. But it does not alone make our emotional responses to other people and the circumstances in which we interact with these people morally proper – for the reasons I have mentioned already: Our emotional request for recognition and respect as an equal human being comes from under a veil of selfishness and has to be properly shaped. The normative shaping of proper moral feelings and behaviour, however, has as its psychologically inevitable consequence the loss of our natural open mindedness and the introduction of culturally diverse prejudices about whose emotions we should care.

Someone who, in his dealings with another person, makes an effort not to harm this person, has to rely on certain assumptions as to what would represent a case of harm. Physical injury, unless undertaken for a medical purpose of healing, seems to represent a clear case of harm. But there are many ways of harming another person that cannot easily be accounted for in terms of the infliction of physical pain. Much of what it means to harm a person psychically, to damage or destroy his mental health or social status, underlies cultural determination and variation.[32] The motivation not to hurt or harm another person does not, however, depend on any specific determination of what counts as harm and what does not. And it is not by chance that Smith, at least within his moral theory, prohibits harm in such general terms. An agent is welcome to initially set his own, personal standards of harm. He would, by doing so, act in accordance with the 'Golden Rule' (a term, though, that Smith does not use himself in this context), an ethical principle of reciprocity which is part of many different cultures, according to which one should not do unto others what one would not have them do to oneself.[33]

Rather than assuming the monopoly of defining harm, an agent who intends to avoid harming another person and, given the lack of any generally accepted standards, sets his own standards of harm, thereby recognizes and respects the other person as a fellow human being. The agent simply assumes that what is harm towards him will be harm towards the other person in much the same way, implying that the other person is as vulnerable and sensitive to harm as he himself is. This assumption is an assumption of equality. The equality in question is to be understood in terms not only of the equality of physical and psychic vulnerability (which we share with the higher developed non-human animals) but also of equal accountability.[34] It is constituted by natural facts about human beings, their embodiment, and their natural emotional dispositions. There is the question whether and to what extent this equality of vulnerability and accountability is compatible with inequalities on other levels, like inequalities of social class or economic inequalities, but for the argument I want to make I can leave this open.[35]

It is because of our natural emotional dispositions as conceived by Smith, that we care about the feelings of others and try to avoid harming them. Thus, with his theory of human gratitude, resentment and sympathy Smith provides a naturalistic explanation of a universal human motivation to recognize all other people as equals, namely as equally vulnerable and equally accountable, and a universal human motivation to avoid harming each other.[36] Whenever we address other people as equals and hold them accountable, we expect their sympathy with us in return; we expect them not to harm us; and we are 'shocked as by the appearance of the contrary' (TMS I.1.2.1, p. 13). The recognition of equality gives rise to mutual expectations of respect and of abstention from harm. Our natural disposition to emotionally relate to other people, to care about them, to share their feelings if these seem to be proper and thereby rely on our own standards of propriety, is at the core of what Fleischacker has called 'Smith's normative egalitarianism'.[37] Human emotional dispositions as conceived by Smith are at the core of human morality. The recognition of the equal vulnerability and accountability of others to which we respond sympathetically and the expectation of their recognition of us as equals implies the recognition of them as moral persons whose interests are to be taken into account as much as our own.[38] We can conclude from Smith's normative egalitarianism that he endorsed an essentially natural, non-meritocratic understanding of human morality, a trait of his theory in which Fleischacker has recognized an anticipation of Kant's moral theory.[39]

In so far as the rules of justice in their most general form, namely as prohibitions of only minimally specified harm, articulate the normative standards which emerge from our behaviour as driven by our natural emotions, their authority for people is natural. The authority of these rules has its source in human nature and in human emotional nature in particular. In virtue of this, it reaches across all times and cultures, it is part of the motivational drives of all people. But in virtue of what do these rules also have normative authority?

One can read Smith's theory of human emotions in general and of sympathy in particular as an attempt at naturalizing the absolute moral duty to respect other people as equals. The examples of cases of sympathy that Smith uses at the very beginning of the TMS especially suggest such an interpretation:

> Upon some occasions sympathy may seem to arise merely from the view of a certain emotion in another person. The passions, upon some occasions, may seem to be transfused from one man to another, instantaneously and antecedent to any knowledge of what excited them in the person principally concerned.
>
> (TMS I.i.1.6, p. 11)

The phenomenon of a transfusion of emotions Smith describes here seems to anticipate recent findings about the working of mirror neurons.[40] Smith's examples for cases of transfusion of emotions include not only grief and joy (TMS I.i.1.6, p. 11), but first and foremost physical pain (TMS I.i.1.2, p. 9). And one might want to conclude that people will refrain from hurting other people just as much as they are subject to a transfusion of the physical and mental pain of the latter. Hume seems to have read Smith's theory of sympathy in terms of such a transfusion when he objected to him that his claim that 'all kinds of Sympathy are necessarily Agreeable' was inconsistent.[41] After all, the transfusion of physical or mental pain cannot be agreeable at all. In his response to Hume, Smith rejects this understanding of sympathy. He does not reduce the absolute duty to act in accordance with the rules of justice to a psychological condition that all humans naturally share, even though he refers to this condition in his psychological explanation of our habitual motivation to act in accordance with these rules, or rather to do so at least to some extent.

In one passage Smith says that 'we may often fulfil all the rules of justice by sitting still and doing nothing' (TMS II.ii.1.9, p. 82).[42] This sounds as if it takes little to follow the rules of justice.[43] But this is not the case. After all, given the lives most people live, sitting still and doing nothing is not very often an option. Of course, our absolute duty to follow the rules of justice in our interaction with other people, whoever they may be, does not imply that we have to constantly interfere in their everyday lives. And one should not overlook the 'often' in this phrase which limits its universal applicability. Smith's view of justice as a negative virtue is compatible with the claim that there are cases when 'sitting still and doing nothing' is not in accordance with the demands of justice, cases where lack of interference would be an expression of a lack of sympathy with regard to someone whose need of help we are witnessing. As far as I recall, Smith nowhere makes this point very explicit. But it is implicit in his universal rejection of infanticide. Infanticide does not only show a 'perversion of natural sentiment' (TMS V.2.13, p. 209) in those who actually abandon or kill newborn infants; it shows a similar perversion of sentiments in those who witness it and don't interfere or raise moral objections against it.[44] Refusing to help can be a violation of the rules of justice as much as actively hurting someone. In both kinds of cases the violator of the rules of justice will be an object of public disapproval:

> The violator of the more sacred laws of justice can never reflect on the sentiments which mankind must entertain with regard to him, without feeling all the agonies of shame, and horror, and consternation.
>
> (TMS II.ii.2.3, p. 84)[45]

Acting in accordance with the rules of justice means to care about the consequences of our actions for other people, to look at circumstances and possible outcomes of our actions from their point of view in order to avoid harming them in any improper way. Such an attitude expresses a desire not to be deprived of their sympathy and approval, a desire for recognition and respect as a moral person in Smith's sense of the term. And is not the disdain for the feelings of others and, in particular, for what they think and feel about us, the clearest indicator of our lack of respect for them? It is this respect as either paid or expected to be paid that motivates us to engage in spectatorial processes. Where, in the course of such a spectatorial process, we experience at some point mutual antipathy but continue with our engagement in this process nevertheless, our attitude exhibits our concern about this antipathy and the desire to overcome the moral disagreement underneath. And this desire is shared by the person principally concerned and his spectator because of their natural emotional dispositions.

Now, this still is no more than a psychological account of mutual respect as it is imposed on us by our natural emotional dispositions. It does not yet justify my claim that Smith convincingly attributes absolute authority to the rules of justice. In addition to his psychological explanation of the origin of respect for other people and the corresponding motivation to act in accordance with the rules of justice, Smith provides a functional account of the rules of justice:

> society cannot subsist unless the laws of justice are tolerably observed, … no social intercourse can take place among men who do not generally abstain from injuring one another …
>
> (TMS II.ii.3.6, pp. 86–87)[46]

But even though Smith endorses this functional account of the rules of justice, he rejects Hume's claim according to which our only motivation to follow the rules of justice originates in our selfishness, completed by instrumental reasoning about the fact that our respecting these rules represents a necessary condition for the well functioning of a society and thereby for our individual well being:

> so when a single man is injured, or destroyed, we demand the punishment of the wrong that has been done to him, not so much from a concern for the general interest of society, as from a concern for that very individual who has been injured. It is to be observed, however, that this concern does not necessarily include in it any degree of those exquisite sentiments which are commonly called love, esteem, and affection, and by which we distinguish our particular friends and acquaintance. The concern which is requisite for this, is no more than the general fellow-feeling which we have with every man merely because he is our fellow-creature.
>
> (TMS II.ii.3.10, p. 90)

According to Smith, human beings are naturally driven not to harm other people, to care about their well being, to respect them and to hold them accountable, quite independently of who they are. It is in light of this natural disposition that the impact of socialization within a particular culture is seen partly as a distortion, a distortion of our naturally egalitarian attitude to other people. And it is because of this disposition that people are motivated to act in accordance with the rules of justice in their intercourse with others. Cultural prejudice may restrict these others to those they recognize as members of their own culture. But this does not mean that their general motivation to act in accordance with the rules of justice undergoes a profound transformation.

By acting in accordance with the rules of justice, people also contribute to the well functioning of society; after all, the latter depends on the rules of justice being widely endorsed. But this is only a side-effect of their acting in accordance with the rules of justice – even though a side-effect which is most welcome. The functional account of the rules of justice is not supposed to replace the psychological account of the motivation to respect them in terms of natural human emotions.[47] Contrary to Hume, Smith can thus avoid the free-rider objection. Smith's examples of free-riding behaviour include a 'thief' who 'steals from the rich' and an 'adulterer' who 'covers his intrigue from the suspicion of the husband', both of whom imagine that they do 'no evil'. But they are wrong, and for this Smith provides a slippery slope argument: 'When once we begin to give way to such refinements, there is no enormity so gross of which we may not be capable.' (TMS III.6.10, p. 175).

Another point which Smith makes in the passage quoted above is that our willingness to respect others and to enter into sympathetic relations with them does not depend on our previously having established particular emotional relationships with them, relationships as they typically exist between family members, friends or lovers. Such emotional bonds between people may well grow out of frequent interaction and the engagement in spectatorial processes with each other. But whereas such bonds may be to some extent constituted by spectatorial processes, the respect for another person and the willingness to follow the rules of justice in all relations with this person cannot be constituted in this way.

The rules of justice and their absolute authority

Smith is aware of the anti-egalitarian and anti-cosmopolitan effects of socialization and acculturation: our natural 'sense of propriety and justice' (TMS III.3.3, p. 136) and the 'natural principles of right and wrong' implicit in it can be 'warpt', even though it 'cannot be entirely perverted' (TMS V.2.1, p. 200). Furthermore, our sentiments 'are … influenced by custom and fashion' (TMS V.2.1, p. 200) and may be 'altered by habit and education' (TMS V.2.1, p. 200). As a consequence, our motivation to respect all others as equals and to relate to all of them in accordance with the rules of justice may become restricted to the members of our own society or culture, to those with whom we enjoy at least some degree of familiarity. Spectatorial processes, given the contingent conditions under which they inevitably take place, tend to have an anti-cosmopolitan side effect: they restrict the kinds of people a person is willing to recognize as equals. But Smith provides a defence against it: there is a way to prevent our cultural prejudices from making us indifferent to all those with whom we have not had the opportunity of building up relations of familiarity. And with this argument we finally leave the realm of motivational psychology and enter the realm of moral motivation as guided by normative thought. According to Smith, engagement in spectatorial processes is common in all societies, and the more civilized a society is the more common this engagement is because the material and political achievements of civilization facilitate it. As we have seen, people who have been socialized in a particular society have acquired cultural prejudices, and this is a fact independent of how low or high a degree of civilization the respective society has acquired. All people tend to actually engage in spectatorial processes only with those who share their prejudices. This is because all cultures are essentially exclusive: they distinguish between those people who belong to it and those who don't. It is easier to recognize someone as an equal, as someone who deserves to be respected as such and about whose opinions about oneself one should care, if there is no cultural boundary to be crossed.

But even though habitual familiarity with someone makes it easier to care about this person and to engage in spectatorial processes with him, Smith explicitly says that familiarity is not a necessary condition for such an engagement. Acting in accordance with the rules of justice, however, is such a necessary condition – even though this does not mean that these rules have to be endorsed explicitly or intentionally; one can act in accordance with the rules of justice without even having heard of them. These rules do not restrict the obligation to respect people as equals and to refrain from harming those with whom we share our cultural prejudices. But whereas some ideally moral person who is disposed to act in accordance with the rules of justice anyway does not need to know and explicitly endorse them, a real person whose cultural prejudices induce him to restrict the number of people he is disposed to recognize as equals will have to think about these rules and actively endorse them. Otherwise, he would not be able to overcome his cultural prejudices. Anyone who is actually disposed to engage in spectatorial processes with some people cannot reasonably limit the possible participants in these processes to the members of his own culture or social community, even though he might be emotionally disposed to do so, due to his socialization and the then acquired cultural prejudices:

> [O]ur good-will is circumscribed by no boundary, but may embrace the immensity of the universe. We cannot form the idea of any innocent and sensible being whose happiness we should not desire, or to whose misery, when distinctly brought home to the imagination, we should not have some degree of aversion. The idea of a mischievous, though sensible, being, indeed, naturally provokes our hatred: but the ill-will which, in this case, we bear to it, is really the effect of our universal benevolence. It is the effect of the sympathy which we feel with the misery and resentment of those other innocent and sensible beings, whose happiness is disturbed by its malice.
>
> (TMS VI.ii.3.1, p. 235)[48]

The argument for the absolute authority of the rules of justice as implicit in Smith's account of the spectatorial process can be reconstructed as follows:

Driven by their natural emotional dispositions and by their natural sympathy in particular, people engage in spectatorial processes. It is through such processes as taking place among members of a society that communal moral norms come into existence. These norms acquire factual authority, and this authority is justified in virtue of the spectatorial processes that brought them about. Even though justified, the authority of these norms does not reach beyond the circles of those who have been involved in the processes of constituting them.

However, people who actually engage in spectatorial processes thereby already accept that they should act in a certain way, in a way that exhibits a kind of regularity as is typical for rule-governed behaviour. They act in accordance with the rules of justice, even though they may not be aware of this. The rules of justice represent those rules people have to endorse if they want to engage in spectatorial processes; they have to care about the Other and about the Other's opinion about what they are doing; they have to respect all the others as equally vulnerable and equally accountable and try not to harm them.

The rules of justice are the rules governing spectatorial processes; the authority of these rules cannot be constituted by people interacting in spectatorial processes; any constitution of communal moral norms with some degree of justified authority through spectatorial processes depends on people having previously endorsed the rules of justice. And even though this endorsement can be implicit or unconscious, it can take the form of an emotion-based recognition and respect. The rules of the spectatorial process are transcendental, even though not deducible from reason; rather, they are deducible from human nature and the emotional dispositions it includes. They represent the conditions of the possibility of constituting communal moral norms through spectatorial processes.[49]

Where a person concerned and his spectator have not achieved a state of mutual sympathy and one of them refuses to get further involved in the respective spectatorial process, this refusal implies a denial to respect the other as an equal, as someone with whom he wants to be in a state of mutual sympathy. But reflection will teach him that there is no good reason for such a refusal. A person who has acquired conscience and can rely on an internal judge of the propriety of his feelings and actions will have to conclude from internal reflection that the social tastes and preferences he has acquired during his socialization within a particular community, which make him inclined to disrespect certain people and refuse to engage in spectatorial processes with them, by no means provide an excuse for ignoring the feelings of these people; he has no excuse for just ignoring their resentment:

> It is he [the internal judge] who, whenever we are about to act so as to affect the happiness of others, calls to us, with a voice capable of astonishing the most presumptuous of our passions, that we are but one of the

> multitude, in no respect better than any other in it; and that when we prefer ourselves so shamefully and so blindly to others, we become the proper objects of resentment, abhorrence, and execration.
>
> (TMS III.3.4, p. 137)

Smith accords absolute authority to the rules of justice: every human being has an obligation to follow them, quite independently of his cultural identity and of his choice of friends. This obligation remains present in his motivational dispositions, even though the respective dispositions may have undergone a weakening of their motivational force in the process of socialization:

> we feel ourselves to be under a stricter obligation to act according to justice, than agreeably to friendship, charity, or generosity; that the practice of these last mentioned virtues seems to be left in some measure to our own choice, but that, somehow or other, we feel ourselves to be in a peculiar manner tied, bound and obliged to the observation of justice. We feel, that is to say, that force may with that utmost propriety, and with the approbation of all mankind, be made use to constrain us to observe the rules of the one, but not to follow the precepts of the other.
>
> (TMS II.ii.1.5, p. 80)[50]

In so far as the authority of the rules of justice is absolute, force may be used on people who do not otherwise respect them:

> There is, however, another virtue, of which the observance is not left to the freedom of our own wills, which may be extorted by force, and of which the violation exposes to resentment, and consequently to punishment. This virtue is justice: the violation of justice is injury: it does real and positive hurt to some particular persons, from motives which are naturally disapproved of. It is, therefore, the proper object of resentment, and of punishment, which is the natural consequence of resentment.
>
> (TMS II.ii.1.5, p. 79)[51]

Given that respect of the rules of justice is indispensible for the functioning of a society, any legislator will make them part of his legislation.[52] But whereas it is of crucial importance to impose the rules of justice in order to provide everybody's security, it is equally important that the legislator respects everybody's liberty:

> Of all the duties of a law-giver, however, this, perhaps, is that which it requires the greatest delicacy and reserve to execute with propriety and judgment. To neglect it altogether exposes the commonwealth to many gross disorders and shocking enormities, and to push it too far is destructive of all liberty, security, and justice.
>
> (TMS II.ii.1.8, p. 81)

The business of the lawgiver is, of course, not limited to the legislation of the rules of justice. But further specification of the rules which help a society to be peaceful and flourish is not the business of a moral theory:

> The wisdom of every state or commonwealth endeavours, as well as it can, to employ the force of the society to restrain those who are subject to its authority, from hurting or disturbing the happiness of one another. The rules which it establishes for this purpose, constitute the civil and criminal law of each particular state or country. The principles upon which those rules either are, or ought to be founded, are the subject of a particular science, of all sciences by far the most important, but hitherto, perhaps, the least cultivated, that of natural jurisprudence. Concerning which it belongs not to our present subject to enter into any detail.
>
> (TMS VI.ii.intro.2, p. 218)

Ideally, the legislation of the rules of justice by a legislator is not a top-down procedure. But in those societies in which the members do not even practice any kind of spectatorial process the legislator can only come as a stranger and impose the rules of justice from the top. In such cases, the habits people have adopted will favour neither their disposition to respect each other nor their disposition to act in accordance with the rules of justice. The legislator will have to rely on a strong police to impose the laws of justice by force. However, where the legislator addresses a society whose members habitually engage in spectatorial processes, his legislation can be a bottom-up procedure. The main function of the legislation in such a scenario is to institutionalize rules for which respect is already habitual in social practice. People would already be habitually motivated to act in accordance with the rules of justice anyway, and less force would be needed to impose their authority.

Our actual disposition to care more and more easily about those with whom we entertain relations of familiarity is explicable in psychological terms. But this culturally shaped psychological disposition does not affect our absolute duty to respect others as equals and to care about them, independently of who they are. Making these rules explicit and understanding their absolute authority cannot be a matter of sympathetic feelings alone; it depends on reasoning:

> It is by reason that we discover those general rules of justice by which we ought to regulate our actions …
>
> (TMS VII.iii.2.6, p. 319)

But this does not mean that Smith is here anticipating Kant's transcendental philosophy, the account of morality in terms of pure practical reason. In the passage quoted above, he continues by explaining that the kind of reasoning he has in mind is inductive in kind and that the data from which conclusions are drawn by inductive reasoning can only be found in human practice, in social interaction driven by the natural disposition of sympathy, that is, in spectatorial processes:

> The general maxims of morality are formed, like all other general maxims, from experience and induction. We observe in a great variety of particular cases what pleases or displeases our moral faculties, what these approve or disapprove of, and, by induction from this experience, we establish those general rules. But induction is always regarded as one of the operations of reason. From reason, therefore, we are very properly said to derive all those general maxims and ideas.
>
> (TMS VII.iii.2.6, p. 319)

> But though reason is undoubtedly the source of the general rules of morality, and of all the moral judgments which we form by means of them; it is altogether absurd and unintelligible to suppose that the first perceptions of right and wrong can be derived from reason, even in those particular cases upon the experience of which the general rules are formed. These first perceptions, as well as all other experiments upon which any general rules are founded, cannot be the object of reason, but of immediate sense and feeling.
>
> (TMS VII.iii.2.7, p. 320)

Inductive reasoning alone, however, cannot provide an argument for the absolute authority of the rules of justice. But, as I have argued above, there is a transcendental argument implicit in Smith's account of the rules of justice according to which they have absolute authority.

Conclusion

I have argued for the claim that Smith, in his TMS, provides a normative moral theory; the core part of this theory is his account of the 'sacred rules of justice'. According to Smith's conception of human nature, we are naturally disposed to act in accordance with these rules, quite independently of our actual knowledge and explicit endorsement of them. Socialization typically has the effect of restricting the realm of people with whom we are disposed to interact in accordance with the rules of justice. But reflection can make us aware of there being no good reasons for such a restriction.

The source of the absolute authority of the rules of justice is to be found in human nature as conceived by Smith, and in human beings' emotional nature in particular. Humans are by nature emotionally disposed to respect others as equals and to hold them accountable. At the same time, however, they are by nature too selfish, passionate and partly blind to relevant circumstances and therefore do not always properly understand what it means to judge and act in accordance with the rules of justice.[53] The rules of justice are the rules governing spectatorial processes; they have the status of absolute obligations;

their authority does not depend on their actually being respected by people. Thus, their authority differs from the authority of communal moral norms which are constituted by people as outcomes of spectatorial processes; the authority of communal moral norms is justified, but it depends on factual authority nevertheless. Even if there were no people in the world who had the opportunity of engaging in spectatorial processes with others and even if there was no practice in accordance with the rules of justice, the rules of justice would still have absolute authority. People would still be obliged to act and interact in accordance with these rules.

Whether people actually have the chance to participate in spectatorial processes or not depends on contingent factors. Even though they are naturally disposed to do so, there may be contingent factors that considerably reduce the opportunities to act in accordance with this disposition. Smith mentions the case of a person who is unfortunate enough to be born into a society where such processes are not common. But even a person who is unfortunate in this sense is not exempt from the rules of justice, because these rules are absolutely valid:

> In countries where great crimes frequently pass unpunished, the most atrocious actions become almost familiar, and cease to impress the people with that horror which is universally felt in countries where an exact administration of justice takes place. *The injustice is the same in both countries*; but the imprudence is often different.
>
> (TMS VI.i.16, p. 217, italics added)

Social stability and human happiness cannot be achieved without relying on spectatorial processes. Where these processes actually take place, the communal moral norms emerging from them acquire a certain degree of justification. Different communities, however, even though equally relying on spectatorial processes for their judgments of the propriety of feelings and actions, may constitute different sets of communal moral norms. All sets of communal moral norms whose origins are explicable in terms of spectatorial processes can be considered as justified, even though their degrees of justification may vary. These norms have been constituted in the same, the right way, the way that is most in accordance with human nature. But this does not provide them with universal authority. Thus, there is room for culturally induced moral pluralism in Smith's moral theory. Nevertheless, there are norms which all people have to respect, namely the norms underlying the rules of justice.

According to my reading of the TMS, Smith's answer to the moral question: 'What should I do?' does not anticipate the Kantian answer. In his moral theory, Kant relies on the assumption of there being a point of view – accessible to reason – from where to make moral judgments the normative standards of which are free from all kinds of perspectival constraints or cultural prejudices. Accordingly, Kant's answer to the moral question can – without relying on the conceptual details of his philosophy – be formulated like this:

'Find out what is proper from an ideally impartial point of view!' I do not see how a moral person as conceived by Smith, a person whose morality originates in his natural emotional attitude to other people and has taken particular shape in a process of socialization, could find an objectively true answer to this question. It seems to me that Smith's answer to the moral question 'What should I do?' should be phrased like this: 'Get engaged in spectatorial processes with as many people as possible who might – directly or indirectly – be concerned by the consequences of your action and make sure, with their help, that what you do does not harm anyone of them in any way. There are pragmatic limits to how many people's point of view you can actually take into account. But, in any case, you should never exclude from your consideration anyone of whom you can anticipate that his interests will be affected. Furthermore, you should be aware of the possibility of shortcomings of any of your moral judgments about what you should do, and listen to those who raise objections.'

Rather than relying on moral deliberation alone, the moral agent as conceived by Smith relies on interaction with others in spectatorial processes in order to answer the moral question. The rules of justice do not prescribe what to do under particular circumstances; they prescribe an attitude that the moral agent has to take towards other people, independently of who they are.[54]

Notes

1 Here, I disagree with the otherwise very informative readings of TMS as provided by Campbell (1971), Haakonssen and Winch (2006) and Raphael (2007).

2 I fully agree with Heilbroner who wrote that the TMS 'contains a number of distinct, although intertwined, themes'; his list of these themes only partly overlaps with mine, and even both lists taken together might not provide a complete account of the topics Smith deals with in the TMS. See Heilbroner (1982: 428).

3 Smith also uses two other, slightly different formulations: He speaks of 'the most sacred rules of morality' (TMSII.ii.3.8, p. 89) and of 'the most sacred rules of conduct' (TMS III.4.7, p. 159).

4 See Fleischacker (2005: 105–6, 107–15 and 125–27); in Fleischacker (1999), the focus is more on Smith's liberalism.

5 Griswold (1999: 155–73, 349–50).

6 Griswold (1999: 352).

7 Otteson (2002: chs 6 and 7).

8 See von Villiez (2006: 117).

9 See von Villiez (2006: 127).

10 Forman-Barzilai (2006: 94).

11 The child can just as well be a girl.

12 There is one passage which Smith added to the 2nd edition of TMS but then removed from the 6th edition in which he states this most clearly:

> But though this tribunal within the breast be thus the supreme arbiter of all our actions, though it can reverse the decisions of all mankind with regard to our character and conduct, and mortify us amidst the applause, or support us under the censure of the world; yet, if we inquire into the origin of its institution, its jurisdiction we shall find is in a great measure derived from the authority of that very tribunal, whose decisions it so often and so justly reverses.
>
> (TMS III.2, p. 129)

The distinction between praise and praiseworthiness actually does not solve this problem as it is unclear where the standards of praiseworthiness arise, if not as shared norms within a society or cultural group. Here, I agree with Haakonssen and Winch who attribute to Smith the view that 'the process known as civilization contained debit items as well as credits', a view according to which 'there is no guarantee that spontaneous social evolution will deliver the best outcome' (Haakonssen and Winch 2006: 377).

13 On the 'transfusion' of sentiments see also below, p. 00. Carrasco has characterized this kind of sympathy as 'mechanical sympathy'. See Carrasco (2010: 3).

14 See on this point Fleischacker (2004: 77).

15 Note that the impartial spectator does not have to be a man; any person can be in the role of an impartial spectator.

16 These are the sentences which immediately follow Smith's famous claim according to which his TMS 'is not concerning a matter of right … but … a matter of fact'. The passage is often referred to by those who deny that the author of the TMS had any normative ambitions. One of the more recent examples can be found in Haakonssen and Winch (2006: 386). However, the passage does not provide as much evidence for the adequacy of a merely sociological reading of the TMS as straightforwardly as some might wish. One should not overlook the sentence which immediately follows the one I quoted above: 'The principles which I have just now mentioned, it is evident, have a very great effect upon his sentiments; and it seems wisely ordered that it should be so.' This sentence clearly ends with a normative statement. What Smith rejects is an ideal moral theory that ignores the human condition, but this is compatible with the project of a more modest, empirically informed normative moral theory.

17 von Villiez (2011: 9).

18 See Griswold (1999: 116, 147); Otteson (2002: 3); Broadie (2006).

19 Brown (1994).

20 For a more detailed analysis of this process see Fricke (2005).

21 There is a passage in the TMS where Smith mentions societies 'where great crimes frequently pass unpunished' (TMS VI.i.16, p. 217, see more extensive quote below, p. 00). But even in such an unfortunate society some spectatorial processes might still take place on a small scale, that is, within very small groups of people.

22 Forman-Barzilai stresses this aspect of Smith's moral theory. See Forman-Barzilai (2006 and 2010: ch. 7).

23 Ryan Hanley speaks of Smith's 'ethical' rather than 'jurisprudential' approach to ethics, but he overlooks that the rules of justice as Smith understands them are part of his ethical theory. Hanley (2009: 65).

24 See TMS VII.iii.2.6, p. 319.

25 For another passage in the same spirit see TMS VII.iv.7, p. 329.

26 See also TMS VII.iii.3.17, p. 327.

27 See also TMS III.4.8, p. 159, VII.iv.1., p. 327 and VII.iv.7, p. 329.

28 See also TMS VII.ii.1.10, p. 269.

29 I exclude all further reaching questions concerning Smith's theory of jurisprudence. My focus will be on those of the rules of justice which forbid harming another person either physically or psychically. I shall not discuss Smith's theory of property rights and why he inserted the respect of a person's property into the list of things that are protected by the rules of justice. I do not read Smith as implying that the institution of property is an absolute moral requirement; rather, his claim seems to be that, if there is the institution of property, property should be considered as inviolable. For a discussion of Smith's theory of jurisprudence and his theory of property in particular see Fleischacker (2004: esp. part IV), Haakonssen (1981 and 1996: ch. 4), Haakonssen and Winch (2006), Winch (1978: esp. chap. 4) and Schliesser (2006).

30 Strawson (1968).
31 Darwall (2006: 82–83). Darwall refers back to Adam Smith in the context of this argument.
32 See Fleischacker (2004: 158).
33 On the cultural history of the Golden Rule see Wattles (1996). See also Darwall (2006: 115–17).
34 Here again, I read Smith as anticipating Darwall's account of equality as part of moral respect. See Darwall (2006: 146).
35 For a further discussion of this aspect see Fleischacker (2004: 78) and Griswold (2005).
36 Clearly, Smith's account of sympathy does not cover all motivational drives humans naturally have. Dispositions to aggression and cruelty seem part of human nature as much as sympathy is. There is the question whether all human behaviour which ignores the demands of sympathy can be explained in terms of human self-love or selfishness. I rather doubt it, but cannot go into this debate here.
37 See Fleischacker (2004: 80). A similar point has been made by MacIntyre; in the respective argument, MacIntyre refers back to Thomas Aquinas. See MacIntyre (1999: 125). On universal features of humans that prevail across cultures see also Haakonssen (1996: 131).
38 There is the question whether and to what extent we can and should include non-human animals into the realm of those whose vulnerability and interests we have a moral obligation to respect. From what Smith says about our natural disposition to emotionally respond to animals (see above, p.00), one would expect that, in the realm of human beings, the obligation to respect the vulnerability of the other is not conditional on the other's accountability. Furthermore, the moral obligation of respect extends beyond those mentally and emotionally healthy adults. According to MacIntyre, 'there is no significant difference in the case of the relationship of human beings to members of certain other animal species' (MacIntyre 1999: 15). But there is a long way to go from an emotional disposition to care which humans share with other kinds of animals to the attribution of moral obligations to non-human animals, and there may well be a gap impossible to bridge. And the way Smith describes the details of a spectatorial process through which a person concerned and his spectator have to go before they can reach a state of mutual sympathy in accordance to shared standards of propriety presupposes intellectual capacities (of imagination and reasoning) that we cannot expect non-human animals to share. Even humans have not all developed these capacities to the same amount of sophistication.
39 Fleischacker (2004: 74). Kant, however, disqualified a moral theory of the kind Smith develops in the TMS as 'tenuous' (Kant 1900–: AAVI, 216). He saw clearly that, within Smith's moral theory, any person who was not emotionally disposed to respect other people as equals and enter into spectatorial processes with them had to be considered as emotionally handicapped and could not be considered as morally accountable, even if this person was otherwise intelligent. It seems that Kant's account of moral accountability in terms of pure practical reason provides the only way of dealing with the amoralist: According to Kant, the amoralist's behaviour is internally contradictory in so far as he claims to speak in the name of rationality and refuses at the same time to do what is rationally required of him.
40 See Rizzolatti and Sinigaglia (2008).
41 See the quotation in the editorial note 2 in TMS, p. 46.
42 Forman-Barzilai (2010: 225).
43 See Forman-Barzilai (2010: 225).
44 See TMS V.2.15, pp. 209f.
45 See also TMS VI.ii.intro.2, p. 218 and VI.concl.1, p. 262.
46 Smith repeats this claim often. See II.ii.3.3, p. 86, II.ii.3.8, pp. 88–89, V.2.16, p. 211.

47 I am here in full accordance with D.D. Raphael who, in an early paper, explored and compared Hume's and Smith's accounts of justice. See Raphael (1972/73). See also Forman-Barzilai (2010: 224). Raphael draws attention to an inconsistency in Smith's account of justice: on the one hand, Smith rejects the utilitarian view of justice and says that no individual may be sacrificed for the sake of a sufficiently large number of people; on the other hand, he defends the death penalty for a sentinel who, while on duty, has fallen asleep as just – on utilitarian grounds. See Raphael (1972/73: 96–97). Rather than seeing the case of the sentinel as evidence for an inconsistency in Smith's theory, one can try and understand it in terms of a moral dilemma. Letting the sentinel sleep would imply exposing large numbers of people to great danger. Smith might have pointed out that, even though the rules of justice have absolute authority, how challenging it is for an agent to always act in accordance with these rules depends on how civilized, how peaceful and happy his social environment is (see further below). A state of war represents a particular challenge. Violations of the rules of justice under challenging external conditions are, even though not morally justifiable, explicable – and to some extent acceptable – in pragmatic and prudential terms.

48 See also TMS VII.ii.1.18, p. 274: 'Among those primary objects which nature had recommended to us as eligible, was the prosperity of our family, of our relations, of our friends, of our country, of mankind, and of the universe in general.'

49 Haakonssen has already drawn attention to the special status of the negative virtue of justice among the other virtues: 'the rules of justice arise from spectator disapproval of injustice, of the non-performance of the virtue'. (Haakonssen 1981: 86–87) Whether and to what extent I disagree with him depends on the interpretation of 'arise' here. People engaged in spectatorial processes act as if they explicitly followed the rules of justice. But their engagement in spectatorial processes does not depend on their having previous knowledge of these rules or on having explicitly endorsed them. And if knowledge of these rules is a condition for following them, then one can say that people have to engage in spectatorial processes and practise justice before they can know the rules of justice and explicitly follow them. But what I am arguing here is that the authority of the rules of justice does not depend on their factual authority, neither does it depend on these rules being known. On the particular status of the negative virtue of justice among the other virtues see also Lieberman (2006).

50 Smith attributes this thought which he endorses to 'an author of very great and original genius', and the editor suggests that the author Smith has in mind here is Henry Home, Lord Kames. (TMS II.ii.1.5, p. 80 and editorial note 1).

51 See also TMS VI.ii.intro.2, p. 218 and VII.ii.1.10, p. 269.

52 See TMS VII.iv.37, p. 341.

53 This is the reason why Smith rejects the claim that humans do, by nature, have a moral sense. See TMSIII.4.5, p. 158.

54 I would like to express my deep gratitude to Vivienne Brown, who has given me extensive feedback on a former version of this paper. Furthermore, I would like to thank Maria A. Carrasco, Peter Railton and an anonymous commentator for very inspiring criticism. This said, I underline that all errors and shortcomings in this paper are mine.

Bibliography

Ballestrem, Karl Graf (2001) *Adam Smith*. Munich, Germany: Beck.

——(2005) 'David Hume und Adam Smith. Zur philosophischen Dimension einer Freundschaft'. In Christel Fricke and Hans-Peter Schütt (eds) *Adam Smith als Moralphilosoph*. Berlin: de Gruyter, pp. 331–46.

Broadie, Alexander (2006) 'Sympathy and the Impartial Spectator'. In K. Haakonssen (ed.) *The Cambridge Companion to Adam Smith*. Cambridge: Cambridge University Press, pp. 158–87.

Brown, Vivienne (1994) *Adam Smith's Discourse: Canonicity, Commerce, and Conscience*. London and New York: Routledge.

Campbell, T. D. (1971) *Adam Smith's Science of Morals*. London: George Allen and Unwin.

Carrasco, Maria (2011) 'From Psychology to Moral Normativity'. *The Adam Smith Review* vol. 6. London: Routledge, pp. 9–29.

Clarke, Pete (2007) 'Adam Smith, Religion and the Scottish Enlightenment'. In G. Cockfield, A. Firth, and J. Laurent (eds) *New Perspectives on Adam Smith's Theory of Moral Sentiments*. Cheltenham, UK and Northampton, MA: Edward Elgar, pp. 47–62.

Cockfield, Geoff, Firth, Ann and Laurent, John (eds) (2007) *New Perspectives on Adam Smith's Theory of Moral Sentiments*. Cheltenham, UK and Northampton, MA: Edward Elgar.

Darwall, Stephen (2006) *The Second-person Standpoint: Morality, Respect, and Accountability*. Cambridge, MA: Harvard University Press.

Fleischacker, Samuel (1991) 'Philosophy in Moral Practice: Kant and Adam Smith'. *Kant-Studien* 82: 249–69.

——(1999) *A Third Concept of Liberty: Judgment and Freedom in Kant and Adam Smith*. Princeton, NJ: Princeton University Press.

——(2004) *On Adam Smith's* Wealth of Nations*: A Philosophical Companion*. Princeton, NJ and Oxford: Princeton University Press.

——(2005) 'Smith und der Kulturrelativismus'. In Christel Fricke and Hans-Peter Schütt (eds) *Adam Smith als Moralphilosoph*. Berlin: de Gruyter, pp. 100–127.

Forman-Barzilai, Fonna (2006) 'Smith on "Connexion", Culture and Judgment'. In L. Montes and E. Schliesser (eds) *New Voices on Adam Smith*. London and New York: Routledge, pp. 89–112.

——(2010) *Adam Smith and the Circles of Sympathy: Cosmopolitanism and Moral Theory*. Cambridge: Cambridge University Press.

Fricke, Christel (2005) 'Genesis und Geltung moralischer Normen. Ein Gedankenexperiment von Adam Smith'. In Christel Fricke and Hans-Peter Schütt (eds) *Adam Smith als Moralphilosoph*. Berlin: de Gruyter, pp. 33–63.

Fricke, Christel and Schütt, Hans-Peter (eds) (2005) *Adam Smith als Moralphilosoph*. Berlin: de Gruyter.

Griswold, Charles (1999) *Adam Smith and the Virtues of the Enlightenment*. Cambridge: Cambridge University Press.

——(2005) '*Fair Play,* Übelnehmen, und der Sinn für Gerechtigkeit'. In Christel Fricke und Hans-Peter Schütt (eds) *Adam Smith als Moralphilosoph*. Berlin: de Gruyter, 128–59.

Haakonssen, Knud (1981) *The Science of a Legislator: The Natural Jurisprudence of David Human and Adam Smith*. Cambridge: Cambridge University Press.

——(1996) *Natural Law and Moral Philosophy: From Grotius to the Scottish Enlightenment*. Cambridge: Cambridge University Press.

Haakonssen, Knud (ed.) (2006) *The Cambridge Companion to Adam Smith*. Cambridge: Cambridge University Press.

Haakonssen, Knud and Winch, Donald (2006) 'The Legacy of Adam Smith'. In K. Haakonssen (ed.) *The Cambridge Companion to Adam Smith.* Cambridge: Cambridge University Press, pp. 366–94.

Hanley, Ryan Patrick (2006) 'Adam Smith, Aristotle, and Virtue Ethics'. In L. Montes and E. Schliesser (eds) *New Voices on Adam Smith.* London and New York: Routledge, pp. 17–39.

——(2009) *Adam Smith and the Character of Virtue.* Cambridge: Cambridge University Press.

Heilbroner, Robert (1982) 'The Socialization of the Individual in Adam Smith'. *History of Political Economy* 14: 427–39.

Kant, Immanuel (1900–) *Gesammelte Schriften*. Ed. Royal Prussian (later German) Academy of Science. Berlin: Georg Reimer (later de Gruyter) (quoted as 'AA').

——(1996) *The Metaphysics of Morals.* Translated and edited by Mary Gregor with an introduction by Roger J. Sullivan. Cambridge: Cambridge University Press.

Lieberman, David (2006) 'Adam Smith on Justice, Rights, and Law'. In K. Haakonssen (ed.) *The Cambridge Companion to Adam Smith.* Cambridge: Cambridge University Press, pp. 214–45.

MacIntyre, Alsdair (1999) *Dependent Rational Animals. Why Human Beings Need the Virtues.* London: Duckworth.

Montes, Leonidas and Schliesser, Eric (eds) (2006) *New Voices on Adam Smith.* London and New York: Routledge.

Otteson, James R. (2002) *Adam Smith's Marketplace of Life.* Cambridge: Cambridge University Press.

Raphael, D. D. (1972/73) 'Hume and Smith on Justice and Utility'. *Proceedings of the Aristotelian Society* LXXIII: 87–103.

——(2007) *The Impartial Spectator. Adam Smith's Moral Philosophy.* Oxford: Clarendon Press.

Rizzolatti, Giacomo and Sinigaglia, Corrado (2008) *Mirrors in the Brain: How Our Minds Share Actions and Emotions.* English translation by Frances Anderson. Oxford: Oxford University Press.

Ross, Ian Simpson (1995) *The Life of Adam Smith.* Oxford: Clarendon Press.

Schliesser, Eric (2006) 'Articulating Practices as Reasons: Adam Smith on the Social Conditions of Possibility of Property'. *The Adam Smith Review* 2: 69–97.

Strawson, Peter F. (1968) 'Freedom and Resentment'. In *Studies in the Philosophy of Thought and Action.* London: Oxford University Press.

von Villiez, Carola (2005) 'Sympathische Unparteilichkeit: Adam Smiths moralischer Kontextualismus'. In Christel Fricke and Hans-Peter Schütt (eds) *Adam Smith als Moralphilosoph*. Berlin: de Gruyter, pp. 33–63.

——(2006) 'Double Standard – Naturally! Smith and Rawls: A Comparison of Methods'. In L. Montes and E. Schliesser (eds) *New Voices on Adam Smith.* London and New York: Routledge, pp. 115–39.

——(2011) 'Adam Smith's Story of Moral Progress'. *The Adam Smith Review*, vol. 6. London: Routledge, pp. 30–459.

Wattles, Jeffrey (1996) *The Golden Rule.* Oxford: Oxford University Press.

Winch, Donald (1978) *Adam Smith's Politics: An Essay in Historiographic Revision.* Cambridge: Cambridge University Press.

True to ourselves?

Adam Smith on self-deceit

Samuel Fleischacker

1

Adam Smith calls self-deceit 'the source of half the disorders of human life' (TMS III.4.6, 158). The remark has a hyperbolic quality, but Smith's great concern with seeing our selves correctly – as an impartial spectator would see us – suggests that he may have meant it literally. I propose to read it that way, to use it as a clue to Smith's moral philosophy as a whole. In particular, I will argue that Smith's entire account of the self can be understood as starting from the need, for moral purposes, to make sense of self-deception.

If this is right, Smith represents an approach to self-deception that can be found in a number of other eighteenth-century figures – Shaftesbury, Butler, and Kant, especially – but has largely disappeared from today's literature on that topic. Simply put, the eighteenth-century figures I have mentioned take self-deception as a moral phenomenon first and foremost, and then build an account of our psychological constitution, while philosophers today tend to start from a non-moral picture of our psychology and then try to account for self-deception. I suspect that this reflects a profound difference about what psychological theories should accomplish but will not address that issue here. Rather, I'll use the difference in orientation as a way of organizing an examination into how exactly self-deception functions for Smith.

2

I begin with three general remarks about self-deception.

First, those who emphasize the phenomenon tend to be drawn to a picture of the self as deeply divided. Almost 40 years ago, Herbert Fingarette identified the central problem in philosophical literature on self-deception, and his diagnosis remains accurate: 'Philosophical attempts to elucidate the concept of self-deception have ended [either] in paradox – or in loss of sight of the elusive phenomenon itself'.[1] The paradox concerns who exactly is deceiving whom. If I deceive myself, am I properly the deceiver or the deceived? And how *can* I be both – how can I fool myself into believing P if at the same time I believe not-P?

The Adam Smith Review, 6: 75–92 © The International Adam Smith Society
ISSN 1743-5285, ISBN 0-415-66722-7

One solution to this problem is to deny either that I really do believe both, or that I really bring about the deception under which I suffer. This is what Fingarette calls 'loss of sight of the … phenomenon' of self-deception, and it is a common philosopher's approach to the problem. For Fingarette, self-deception is necessarily something we do intentionally, but many philosophers deny that that is possible. Alfred Mele, for instance, has written an entire book denying that there is such a thing as intentional self-deception.[2] The main alternative approach to the paradox is to divide the self into parts, and hold that one part does the deceiving while the other is deceived. I favor this approach, but it has its problems too. For if my self consists of different parts, which one accounts for the unified agency that I take myself to have in deliberation? And if one part constitutes my agency, why should the other parts be considered part of 'me' at all? It is this worry that can throw one back to the dismissive approach to the problem that Mele represents.

We'll come back to these issues later. For the moment, I want just to stress the fact that philosophers who take self-deception seriously tend to give a divided picture of the self.

3

My other two general points concern the phenomenology of self-deception, the way it appears to us in ordinary life. First, we use the word 'self-deceit' and its cognates primarily in moral contexts and primarily with strong negative connotations. We *blame* people for self-deception; we say that a person who refuses to admit to obvious arrogance or laziness or cruelty 'really knows better', is really blinding himself to the truth about his own character. And it is in this moral context that we most need the notion of self-deception. Mele, and other contemporary writers, tend to choose examples of self-deception in which the phenomenon is morally neutral: people who can't accept the fact that they are seriously ill, or who have excessive confidence in their own charm or intelligence. In the eighteenth century, philosophers who discuss self-deceit almost always give moral examples of it: King David seducing Bathsheba and murdering her husband, for instance, while getting furious when he hears a story about a lesser exploitation of a weak person by a strong one.[3] They are right, I think, to put the phenomenon firmly in a moral context. In many of the cases that Mele gives us, we could accept his claim that the people in question are really just victims of ways in which human cognitive faculties malfunction. But we can't do that in the case of King David. Otherwise we couldn't blame him, couldn't hold him accountable for the wrongness of his actions. We might be able to do without the notion of intentional self-deception in descriptive psychology, but not in moral psychology. This is a point, as we will see, that Smith recognizes very well.

Second, we are all acquainted, I expect, with the phenomenon of being 'half-aware' that we shouldn't be doing something even as we try to excuse or justify doing it. I can't count the number of times the thought has floated through my mind that I'm getting too angry at someone even as I build myself into what seems like a justifiable tirade. Or I may consider several different views of something I'm doing, and be quite unsure, as I consider them, which of them I'm 'really' inclined to hold. Many thoughts float through my mind, in a blurry mélange, as I go about my deliberations, and I feel myself making efforts to concentrate on some and push others away. As I do this, I am uncertain which thoughts and which efforts represent 'the real me' or 'the best me' – I may decide on that later, or remain unsure of it even then. But *if* I decide, afterwards, that the real or best me was represented by the thoughts I pushed away, then I will regard myself as having engaged in self-deception.

The sense that our thoughts are a blurry mélange, and that we determine only in retrospect which of them we really hold, is not unique to cases of self-deceit. But self-deception draws attention to these phenomena and to the difficulties we therefore face if we try to determine exactly what constitutes our mind. Those who want a neat picture of the mind – suitable, say, for a respectably scientific psychology – may be inclined to dismiss the thoughts that just float through our minds and count as proper beliefs and desires only the more fixed attitudes on which we settle. Those willing to live without such a neat picture, on the other hand, need not find it implausible that our minds take an indefinite shape before they get around to believing and desiring in the strict sense of those terms. Our entire picture of mental contents can thus be radically altered by how we view the phenomenon of self-deception.

4

We're almost ready, now, to turn to Smith, but I'd like to get there via a few words on Joseph Butler. Smith almost certainly derives a fair bit of his account of self-deceit from Butler. Like Smith, Butler sees self-deceit as a central, grave threat to all moral reasoning,[4] and like Smith, he proposes a reliance on simple general rules as a way of finessing it. There are two points about self-deceit that are important for understanding Smith but appear explicitly only in Butler, however, and I want to begin with them.

The first is that it is hard to understand how there could be any such thing as self-deceit, even though it seems clear that there is. As we have seen, self-deception seems to be a contradiction in terms: how can I be deceived about something if I am also the one doing the deceiving? Yet we seem to be in this condition frequently. Butler brings out this point nicely. He describes the state of mind of the biblical character Balaam, whom he presents as a model of self-deception, as a 'paradox' and a 'contradiction in terms' which nevertheless 'is plainly a real one in life'.[5] He also says there is nothing 'more surprising and unaccountable' about human beings than self-deceit.[6] At one point he describes self-deceit as a mere hypothetical – '*if* there is such a thing in mankind, as putting half deceits upon themselves … ' – but then adds that 'there plainly is' such a thing.[7] So Butler wants to acknowledge the paradox of self-deceit even while insisting that we do engage in it.[8] I think this point of view is evident in Smith as well, who treats self-deceit as something remarkable but nevertheless takes its existence as a basic psychological datum. But Smith does not say as much explicitly.

The second point of interest in Butler is his claim that the phenomenon we are considering comes about when we 'put[…] half deceits upon [our]selves', are in 'half honesty', or adopt 'half-resolves'.[9] These are intriguing phrases, these 'half deceits' and 'half-resolves'. They suggest thoughts that are not wholly thoughts, a process or state of mind that lies below the level of fully formed belief or desire: mental contents on the order of the blurry mélange I described earlier.[10] I think the idea that our minds take this indefinite shape before they get to believing and desiring in the proper sense can be found in Smith as well, and it is a key of sorts to how self-deceit is possible. For there is a clear paradox in supposing that we both believe and do not believe a proposition P, both hold it true and hold it false.[11] So if we ever are in self-deceit, it will be helpful to find a mode of thinking that is not quite belief, a mode that involves something less than full commitment to a proposition, with which to analyze that condition. We'll come back to this idea in a while.

5

To come, now, to Smith. Smith's explicit treatment of self-deceit appears in Part III, chapter 4 of TMS,[12] and consists of two paragraphs, one on the way we deceive ourselves when we go into an action and one on the way we deceive ourselves when we reflect back on our actions. The paragraphs culminate in a wonderful remark comparing one who 'pull[s] off the mysterious veil of self-delusion' with a surgeon who operates on himself. I'll call this 'the canonical passage'. Here are some sentences from it on which I'd like to focus:

> When we are about to act, the eagerness of passion will seldom allow us to consider what we are doing, with the candour of an indifferent person. The violent emotions which at that time agitate us, discolour our views of things; even when we are endeavouring to place ourselves in the situation of another, and to regard the objects that interest us in the light in which they naturally appear to him, the fury of our own passions constantly calls us back to our own place, where every thing appears magnified and misrepresented by self-love.

Two notes on this passage: First, it suggests that self-deceit is a feature of *agency*, not just of human nature. The 'eagerness of passion' is what moves us into action at all, so overcoming it, however clear a view we might thereby gain, could make us lose our ability to act. People who see all sides of a question notoriously find it difficult to make a decision; recall the angels in Wim Wenders' *Wings of Desire*, whose impartiality makes them incapable of action. Smith shows here that he understands this fact. Self-deceit, he suggests, is not a trait to which humans just happen to be prone, but a feature built into any creature that reflects dispassionately but needs passion in order to act. We may be unable to overcome our tendency to self-deceit while retaining our ability to act. This represents a profound insight on Smith's part.

But there is a second, more troubling feature of the passage. This is the fact that Smith seems to bring a number of quite different things under the heading of self-deceit. Are we really self-deceived every time we are overcome by passion – every time we have a 'discolored' or 'partial' view of things? We may well be *deceived*, but why *self*-deceived? To be 'self-deceived' would seem to require our actively instigating our own deception, but it is not clear from what Smith says here that we actively place the discoloration or partiality into our views; some of the language in the passage indeed suggests that we are passive in this process, swept away by 'eagerness', 'fury', etc. Other language suggests otherwise: the idea that 'every thing appears magnified and misrepresented *by self-love*', above all, hints at what I think is Smith's deeper point, according to which an at least quasi-rational process, a deliberate effort of thought, brings us to self-deceit. 'Self-love' looks more like a principle, or at least a settled tendency, than a simple passion, so if *it* is doing the magnifying and misrepresenting, then we are not just being swept away. We are sweeping ourselves away, as it were. But Smith doesn't clearly say that that is what is going on.

This is one example of a running problem in Smith's account of self-deceit: he doesn't clearly distinguish among things we might want to keep apart. Being overcome by passion is one thing, most of us want to say, and deceiving ourselves another. There is also the phenomenon in which we are misled about values by our society, or perhaps by nature. Smith takes up socially induced illusion when he discusses religious fanaticism,[13] and seems to regard it as something other than self-deceit, but he doesn't quite say that. He is also unclear about whether naturally induced illusion is a form of self-deceit. Famously, he calls the idea that wealth is delightful a 'deception' that 'nature imposes on us'.[14] But is that to say that we are passive in relation to this deception, that we bear no blame for succumbing to it? Is the poor man's son, 'whom heaven in its anger has visited with ambition', deceived *by* God or nature, or is he deceiving himself? I don't think Smith makes this clear.

I'll argue in a bit that we get more illumination from Smith on the relation between being overcome by misleading passions and allowing ourselves to be so overcome. But in a full treatment of self-deceit, we would probably want more distinctions than Smith gives us.

6

The sentences I quoted from the canonical passage describe the central problem of self-deceit as a failure 'to place ourselves in the situation of another', or to see the situation in which we and the other are located 'with the complete impartiality of an equitable judge'. Smith will go on, shortly after the canonical passage, to sum up its teachings by describing self-deceit as the opposite of '[seeing] ourselves in the light in which others see us' (TMS III.4.6, 158). He thereby ties self-deceit to the theory of sympathy and the impartial spectator that forms the core of TMS. Indeed, he indicates in the same passage that his distinctive contribution to moral philosophy, by contrast with the views of his teacher Hutcheson, is validated in good part by its ability to account for self-deceit. The line about seeing ourselves as others see us comes immediately after, and the canonical passage comes immediately before, a paragraph criticizing Hutcheson's moral sense theory. In that paragraph Smith claims that one problem with Hutcheson's theory is that it does not explain why we see our own wrongdoing so much more poorly than we see the wrong in other people's conduct. If we had a true *sense* for moral qualities, it should perceive things close to it better than it sees things far away. But the widespread phenomenon of self-deceit shows that that is not the case. The best explanation of moral judgment will therefore not assume a direct sense for moral qualities, Smith says, but work via the complex interaction of agent-feelings and spectator-feelings he has proposed to replace that sense. Smith thus regards the ability of his spectator-theory to explain self-deceit to be one of its significant advantages.

I'd like to suggest something a bit stronger: that a great deal of Smith's spectator-theory looks as though it were *designed* to explain self-deceit. Smith's agent/spectator distinction gives us, after all, precisely the sort of divided-self view favored by philosophers who stress self-deceit. Smith explicitly describes the self as divisible into parts:

> When I endeavour to examine my own conduct, when I endeavour to pass sentence upon it, and either to approve or condemn it, … I divide myself, as it were, into two persons; and that I, the examiner and judge, represent a different character from that other I, the person whose conduct is examined into and judged of. The first is the spectator … The second is the agent, the person whom I properly call myself … The first is the judge; the second the person judged of. But that the judge should, in every respect, be the same with the person judged of, is as impossible as that the cause should, in every respect, be the same with the effect.
>
> (TMS III.1.6, 113)

Note that Smith makes clear *which* part of me, when I am divided, counts as 'the real me': the agent, in the spectator/agent division, is 'the person whom I properly call myself'. This makes good sense – for moral purposes, certainly, the true self is the active self – and it answers one of the questions about divided-self views that we canvassed in the beginning.

Note also that Smith does not describe the division in ourselves as a given, a psychological fact we might simply discover by introspection. Rather, he says that 'I *divide myself* … into two persons', and places an 'as it were' in the middle of this phrase for good measure, to hedge against anyone's thinking that the self might contain two separate compartments as a matter of empirical fact. The division in our selves is a device we use for moral judgment, not something that a scientific psychology might discover.

I suggest that Smith here anticipates the way Kant responds to Hume's dissolution of the self. Rather than try to demonstrate empirically, or from the perspective of speculative metaphysics, that there must be a continuous self, he *assumes* such a thing for moral purposes. And the kind of self he thinks we need, morally, is a divided one: because only a divided self can enable us to explain the morally crucial phenomenon of self-deceit.

7

Let's pause for a moment to compare Smith's account of the self with Hume's. Hume, famously, denied that we have any self that is identical across time.[15] All we have is a 'bundle or collection of different perceptions' (T 252), and the idea that there is some underlying unity to the bundle is a 'fiction' (T 254, 255, 259, 262). We 'feign a principle of union' in our various feelings and thoughts (T 263). I stress the words 'fiction' and 'feign' here, since what Hume does *not* say – but many wish he had – is that the notion of a self is a *social construct*, an idea that serves valuable purposes in our social lives, even if it cannot be derived from our experience. The idea might then be legitimated by the functions it serves. We find something close to this approach in Smith.
Smith never explicitly addresses Hume's deconstruction of the idea of the self but Book III of TMS depends heavily on the notion of a continuous, introspective self that can look back on its own actions and take responsibility for them.[16] It also suggests that we get the idea of such a self by way of our interactions with other people: that the idea is not a 'fiction', as Hume calls it, but a reasonable, even necessary, part of our social practices.

We first get the idea that we have selves, Smith says, by way of other people's judgments on our conduct:

> Were it possible that a human creature could grow up to manhood in some solitary place, without any communication with his own species, he could no more think of his own character, … of the beauty or deformity of his own mind, than of the beauty or deformity of his own face. All these are objects which he cannot easily see, which naturally he does not look at, and with regard to which he is provided with no mirror which can present them to his view. Bring him into society, and he is immediately provided with the mirror which he wanted before. It is placed in the countenance and behaviour of those he lives with, which always mark when they enter into, and when they disapprove of his sentiments; and it is here that he first views the propriety and impropriety of his own passions, the beauty and deformity of his own mind.
>
> (TMS III.1.3, 110)

Without this social 'mirror', Smith says, 'the objects of [our] passions, the external bodies which either please[…] or hurt [us], would occupy [our] whole attention'. We would not attend to 'the passions themselves'. We would have senses but no 'reflex senses', passions but no 'reflex' passions (TMS VII. iii.3.6, 322). We would live like other animals, conscious only of the world around us, rather than attending, also, to the consciousness that is so engaged. Hence we would be incapable of understanding how and why we act, and of taking responsibility for our acts, or holding other people responsible for theirs. Moral education would then be impossible, as would courtrooms and bureaucracies and social institutions of any kind: all such institutions need to apportion and scrutinize agency.

So society, which needs to regard us, and needs us to regard ourselves, as having a self, provides us with the 'mirror' by which we see those selves for the first time. Without this social mirror we would not become aware that we so much as had a self to scrutinize. Indeed, this puts the point too weakly. It is not just that, without the mirror provided by society, we would not be *aware* that we had a self; we would in fact *not have* a self. The metaphor of the mirror is misleading. I have a body before I see it in the mirror; the mirror gives me a way of becoming aware of my body, but my body exists whether I am aware of it or not. But, on the Lockean view of the self from which all eighteenth-century British philosophers begin, my self does not exist if I am not aware of it: the self, on these views, is *by definition* something that reflects on itself, that is self-aware.[17] So Smith's self cannot so much as exist until it is awakened to such reflection by society. Society brings the self into existence, and at the same time provides the standards guiding its characteristic act of self-reflection.

It's in this sense that for Smith the self is primarily a moral rather than a cognitive being: our ability to introspect arises first and foremost in the moral arena. The Lockean reflex senses are for Smith a product of moral practices first and foremost. The development of self-consciousness, for Smith, comes along with the development of norms and ideals, of judgments about how we have acted well and badly in the past, and how, consequently, we should strive to act in the future. These norms and ideals – this picture of who we are striving to be – gets grafted onto the more animal-like beings we were as young children. 'To a man who from his birth was a stranger to society', says Smith, 'the objects of his passions, the external bodies which either pleased or hurt him, would occupy his whole attention'.[18] Only after we begin to notice other people's approval and disapproval do we begin to attend to our 'desires and aversions, joys and sorrows' themselves. But as soon as we do attend to this, we derive 'new desires and new aversions, new joys and sorrows' from that very attention. Attending to our own passions immediately brings with it passions *about* those passions; reflection on our selves immediately leads us to be concerned about what our selves should be like, and whether we should change them.

Which is to say that the self is divided from the moment it comes into existence.[19] The very development of a self is for Smith the development of a divided self, of a creature who has outwardly-directed passions that want simply to be satisfied but also has higher-order passions about what sort of person she would like to be. And the higher-order passions can conflict with the first-order ones. It is no accident that the passage explicitly about the divided self – 'I divide myself, as it were, into two persons; ... [the] judge ... and [the person] judged of' – concludes the chapter about the self arising in response to a social mirror.

One consequence of this picture is that once we become self-reflective even our first-order passions are no longer concerned with external objects alone. Once I 'divide myself ... into two persons', my entire agential self – the person 'judged of' – becomes something that is in part trying to live up to my spectatorial (judging) self. *All* my passions, now, whether first- or second-order, are in part directed towards the approval of the impartial spectator. Self-consciousness, once present, pervades our mental life, and the consequence is that we act even on our most animalistic desires only after considering whether we *should* act on them. Hence, for one thing, we are capable of becoming the prudent creatures – the creatures who delay gratification, and exchange labor for goods – so important to Smith's economic theory. Smith sees the 'animal' aspect of ourselves as transformed by the awakening of self-consciousness: such that, above all, it no longer simply moves us but operates via the processes of imagination and reasoning by which our self as a whole, at this point, is guided.

But he also believes that the animal aspect of ourselves is always to some degree detached from the rest, never fully absorbed by the process of self-reflection. There is a constant tension between our passional and our reflective features, and it is this that makes self-deceit possible. The pre-reflective, outwardly directed passions, focused purely on 'external bodies', can always drag us away from the norm- or ideal-driven projects to which we are committed. They can even, as we'll see in a moment, use a moral vocabulary to justify their contribution to our deliberations. And if we accept that justification, against the call of our drive to uphold our norms and ideals, we fall into self-deceit. So the possibility of self-deceit appears immediately with the onset of selfhood, and is an ever-present threat to the project of trying to control our passions.

That said, neither the agent nor the judge in Smith's self resembles what gets derisively called, in today's literature on self-deceit, a 'homunculus' within our selves.[20] Rather, the ideal self, shaped out of our society's judgments upon us, amounts to little more than a *vocabulary* for moral judgment, a repertoire of standards on which self-conscious agents can draw. I make sense of my norms and ideals in terms of what an ideal self that I picture within me might say. The distinction between a passional and a reflective self is thus just a heuristic, just a way of making sense of my deliberations. 'I *divide myself*' into two persons, as Smith says, in order to sort out my moral thoughts. This mental division is itself an act for which I am responsible, and that alone should enable me to realize that I do not 'really' – as a matter of natural fact – have two parts within myself. Instead, I have a medley of conflicting thoughts whenever I try to make a decision, some of which can be categorized as the demands or promptings of my ideal self while others count as the promptings of my pre-reflective passions. I waver among these, often, when I try to make a difficult decision:

> At the very time of acting, at the moment in which passion mounts the highest, [the agent] hesitates and trembles at the thought of what he is about to do: he is secretly conscious to himself that he is breaking through those measures of conduct which, in all his cool hours, he had resolved never to infringe. He changes his purpose every moment; sometimes he resolves to adhere to his principle … and a momentary calm takes possession of his breast. … But immediately the passion rouses anew, and with fresh fury drives him to commit what he had the instant before resolved to abstain from. Wearied and distracted with those continual irresolutions, he at length, from a sort of despair, makes the last fatal and irrevocable step; but with that terror and amazement with which one flying from an enemy, throws himself over a precipice.
>
> (TMS III.4.12, 161)

A peculiarity about this passage is that, even though it concludes Smith's chapter on self-deceit, it reads more like a case of akrasia – weakness of the will.[21] We'll come back to that in a bit (§9). Setting it aside for the moment, note that the hesitations and doubts and irresolutions here nicely fit the Butlerian notion of 'half-thoughts' and 'half-resolves' mentioned earlier: mental contents that do not wholly belong to the agent until the point at which he makes a decision. Only when the agent 'throws him*self*' over the precipice do they become fully his. Which is to say, once again, that the contents of his 'real self' are determined only *from* a moral perspective, only insofar as he needs to be interpreted, by himself or others, as being committed to a certain view or principle for the purposes of holding him *accountable* for that commitment – for the purposes of judging him.

8

Rule-following is central to Smith's solution to self-deceit: we can get around our tendency to self-deceit, he says, by relying on moral rules. Nature has not let such an important and dangerous weakness go altogether without a remedy, for which reason she has built within us an inclination to form and follow moral rules:

> Some … actions shock all our natural sentiments. We hear every body about us express the like detestation against them. This still further confirms, and even exasperates our natural sense of their deformity. It satisfies us that we view them in the proper light, when we see other people view them in the same light. We resolve never to be guilty of the like, nor

> ever, upon any account, to render ourselves in this manner the objects of universal disapprobation. We thus naturally lay down to ourselves a general rule, that all such actions are to be avoided. … Other actions, on the contrary, call forth our approbation, and we hear every body around us express the same favourable opinion concerning them. … We become ambitious of performing the like; and thus naturally lay down to ourselves a rule of another kind, that every opportunity of acting in this manner is carefully to be sought after.
>
> (TMS III.4.7, 159)

The rules we form in this manner enter our deliberations as a corrective to 'the misrepresentations of self-love, concerning what is fit and proper to be done in our particular situation' (TMS III.4.12, 160). Smith gives the example of a man of 'furious resentment' who might regard the death of his enemy as an appropriate response to even a small insult if he listened to his passions alone, but will normally be kept from such a response by his respect for general rules. His past observations of other people's actions, says Smith, will have taught him the horrors of bloody revenges, and he will therefore have 'laid … down to himself as an inviolable rule, to abstain from them upon all occasions'. By way of general rules, that is, his *own* past reflections – the reflections he made in what Smith, again echoing Butler, calls 'his cool hours' – correct for the errors of his present reflections. Smith makes clear that these errors include, not just his present immoral impulses, but the tendency of those impulses to find a moral justification for themselves. The rule against bloody revenge 'preserves its authority with him' even in the heat of the present moment, '[y]et the fury of his … temper may be such, that had this been the first time in which he considered such an action, he would undoubtedly have determined it to be quite just and proper, and *what every impartial spectator would approve*' (my emphasis). So only by way of the general rule can this person, at the present moment, access the true impartial spectator. His past thoughts, encapsuled in a rule, must reach out to the present and block some of his sentiments, including what he might otherwise have taken to be his *moral* sentiments, if he is to deliberate properly.

Now we come to our moral rules by way of our reactions to particular cases: '[G]eneral rules of morality', says Smith, 'are … ultimately founded upon experience of what, in particular instances, our moral faculties … , approve, or disapprove of' (TMS III.4.8, 159). I must *feel* horror in reaction to instances of murder I hear about, for the societal rule against murder to become my own rule; I must feel admiration for paradigm acts of goodness if the rules commending such actions are to become mine. This fits with Smith's emotivism and particularism: rules arise out of the same impartial spectator procedure that leads us to particular moral judgments. It is just that one aspect of the impartial spectator procedure is sometimes needed to correct for other aspects; an impartial spectator reaction from a past cool hour can be needed to correct what I attribute to the spectator in a present 'hot' one.

Which is to say that rules play a specific, limited role in the moral life, for Smith. The chapter of TMS I have been discussing is followed by several chapters devoted to an explanation of when the moral life should and should not be governed by rules. Without a 'sacred regard to general rules', we are told, 'there is no man whose conduct can be much depended upon' (TMS III.5.2, 163). But Smith also says that the best of friends and spouses do not express gratitude, kindness, or loyalty out of respect for a rule (TMS III.5.1, 162; III.6.4, 172), and that truly virtuous people try to suit their sentiments and behavior to the particulars of each situation. An inclination to act purely out of regard for rules, and to follow rules without exception, is suited only to the rules of justice, we learn in Book III (TMS III.6.10, 175). Yet in Book VII we are told that 'it is impossible to determine' even what some aspects of *justice* require 'by any general rule that will apply to all cases without exception' (TMS VII.iv.12, 331).

So there is an ambiguity about the place of rules in Smith's moral thought – they are necessary, but can also be misleading. It is better to rely on rules than go without moral reflection, and it may be necessary to rely on rules when one would otherwise quibble with the requirements of justice. But it is a great mistake to suppose that rule-governed behavior could ever exhaust what virtue requires of us.

9

We now have in hand all the pieces by which to reconstruct Smith's overall picture of self-deceit, but before doing that, I'd like to return to the textual oddity I noted earlier: the fact that the passage I quoted from the end of Smith's chapter on self-deceit seems to merge self-deceit with akrasia. Smith talks of a person 'hesitat[ing] and doubt[ing]' whether or not to do something against which he already knows there is a moral rule, 'urged and goaded on' by a furious passion to violate a rule he has 'resolved never to infringe'. This sounds like akrasia. There is also language in the passage suited to self-deceit – the agent is only '*secretly* conscious to himself' not explicitly so, of the impropriety of his proposed action – but on the whole, it seems to concern akrasia.

This oddity goes with another one: the passage seems to undermine the role Smith has just given to moral rules. Why introduce worries about our ability to follow moral rules immediately after telling us that rules constitute the solution to the problem of self-deceit? How much of a solution can they offer, if passion can push us into violating them as easily as it can push us into deceiving ourselves?

One response to these difficulties is to say that Smith is simply moving on from self-deceit to akrasia. The agent Smith describes here is tempted to violate the law-based morality that is supposed to protect him from self-deceit. At that point, perhaps, akrasia becomes a greater danger than self-deceit. We might say that the chapter first discusses self-deceit, then offers a solution to it, then warns that that solution may fail if we fall prey to akrasia. Pre-rule deliberations will be threatened by self-deceit; post-rule, by akrasia.

The problem with this reading is that it attributes a preposterous view to Smith. Self-deceit vanishes after we have moral rules? And only then does akrasia pose a moral threat? The idea that we cease to deceive ourselves once we have moral rules is unrealistic; surely we are all acquainted with cases in which an agent self-deceptively argues to himself that a rule either doesn't apply to his circumstances or permits the action he wants to take. Fortunately, we do not have to saddle Smith with a view that would ignore these obvious points: elsewhere he gives examples, of a thief and an adulterer who rationalize their conduct by interpreting away the relevance of moral rules to their cases, that perfectly represent the self-deceit about rules I've just described.[22]

Smith says that anyone who thinks like his thief or adulterer – anyone who finds excuses to throw off the authority of moral rules – 'is no longer to be trusted, and no man can say what degree of guilt he may not arrive at. … When once we begin to give way to such refinements, there is no enormity so gross of which we may not be capable' (TMS III.6.10, 175). Similarly, in the precipice passage, the agent worries that violating a moral rule will lead him to 'the *highest* disapprobation' and 'corrupt the remaining part of his life with the horrors of shame and repentance'. I suggest that Smith's point, in separating off the temptation to violate rules from ordinary self-deceit, is that moral rules are our *last defense* against complete moral destruction. He doesn't deny that self-deceit can come in even when we are aware of a rule against our conduct, but stresses that if we then *do* violate the rule, we will enter a condition in which we can be tempted into the most evil of crimes. We will no longer be able to hold ourselves to moral standards at all anymore; nothing will be sacred to us. And as we consider whether to cross this line, the question of whether we can rationalize our conduct is less salient to us than our awareness that, rationalizable or not, what we plan to do would breach the most important of moral barriers. Hence the emphasis on akrasia rather than self-deceit.

Smith's considered view is I think the following: Sometimes we deliberate without a moral rule,[23] and sometimes we deliberate while aware that what we are inclined to do violates such a rule. In both cases we are in danger of self-deceit, but more so in the first case. In the second case, the 'awe and respect with which [we have] been accustomed to regard' the rule keeps us on the whole from quibbling with it, even if, in its absence, we could think of clever reasons for what doing what it forbids. That doesn't mean we will never quibble with it – Smith's thief and adulterer do. But the stakes of quibbling with moral rules are very high, and we are normally aware of this fact. We know that we will lose our grip on all our moral resources if we violate an important moral rule: all such rules will then lose their sacredness for us and we will be in danger of self-deceit and akrasia, in their gravest forms, all the time. Rules serve as the *best protection we can have* from self-deceit. Even they are not foolproof, but if we abandon them, we will have no protection at all.

If this is right, we have an explanation for why Smith devotes so much attention to self-deceit and so little to akrasia. Plunging over the precipice of gross immorality is a terribly self-destructive act, but it is not the source of the ongoing corruption of character that most threatens the moral life. Weakness of the will restructures our moral vision so that we can, for a moment, see the worse as the better reason, but this explains only our *momentary* moral lapses, not an ongoing *state* of bad character, which is what really interests Smith. The ongoing flaws that account for most of our failures to treat each other decently – that are 'the source of half the disorders of human life' – arise out of self-deception, not akrasia.

10

Putting all our pieces together, here is what I think goes on, for Smith, when we fall into self-deceit. Take the kinds of cases in which, according to Smith, we 'chicane with our … consciences' over the rules of justice (TMS III.6.10, 175; VII.iv.34, 339–40):

> The thief imagines he does no evil, when he steals from the rich, what he supposes they may easily want, and what possibly they may never even know has been stolen from them. The adulterer imagines he does no evil, when he corrupts the wife of his friend, provided he covers his intrigue from the suspicion of the husband, and does not disturb the peace of the family. When once we begin to give way to such refinements, there is no enormity so gross of which we may not be capable.
>
> (TMS III.6.10, 175)

Here we are in circumstances in which a strong passion inclines us to act badly. We know, from past experience and discussion with other people, that there are general rules against what we are contemplating, but we also know that moral rules have exceptions, and that truly virtuous people consider the particulars of their situations rather than blindly following a rule. We therefore appeal, against our impartial spectator of the past – the spectator of our cool hours, who has laid down rules to govern us in passionate moments like these – to our impartial spectator in the present, claiming that we have encountered a legitimate exception to the rules. We talk ourselves into thinking that the theft or adultery we are contemplating is justifiable, thereby enlisting the impartial spectator, the source of our moral judgments, on the side of our selfish passions. And we *can* do that because there is a division in our moral resources, a division between the past and present forms of the impartial spectator.

But to say that there is a division in our moral resources is to say that we are aware of a moral voice that *opposes* our course of action in these cases. And that voice may be reinforced by the comments of people around us.

The tug of war between these voices – within ourselves, as well as between us and the people around us – may give us pause. Wavering between several different opinions is characteristic of moral decision-making in the best of times – I try to figure out whether I should be angry or forgiving to my misbehaving child, and feel a twinge of conscience whatever I do – so I can tell myself that whichever voice I choose to squelch is the voice of temptation, or false morality, as opposed to the voice of conscience.

If I decide wrongly, other people will see me as having deceived myself. And if I come to see myself as these others see me, I will agree: I will recognize that I have misused my moral resources to lead myself into inappropriate moral opinions. Whether I am in self-deceit or not thus depends on whether what I do violates my own standards of right and wrong. This is not a wholly subjective matter – I cannot rightly see myself in self-deceit except if I really have violated my norms and ideals – but it is also not something that an external observer could discern without knowing what values I uphold. It is also not something that a *value-free* observer could discern. I am not in self-deceit if I waver over a decision that, in the end, I and everyone around me can agree was the right one: I am in self-deceit only if I *mis*-use my moral resources, and there is no way to cash that out without a judgment about what a proper use of those resources would look like. This goes with the general approach that I have been attributing to Smith, on which self-deceit is a moral notion, not a descriptive one.

11

I'd like to close with two broad conclusions that I think can be drawn from Smith's account of self-deceit. First, Smith does without any sharp partitioning of the self. There is one locus of agency in us, for Smith; it simply makes use of various *resources* as it comes to decisions. These resources include our passions, modes of instrumental reasoning, and norms or ideals drawn from the impartial spectator. They are divided up in many ways, come into various kinds of conflicts, and can be categorized for various purposes under such headings as 'the voice of self-love' and 'the voice of conscience'. Self-deceit occurs when the voice of self-love wrongly borrows resources from the voice of conscience in order to represent its actions under a moral rather than a selfish coloring. We are responsible for 'knowing better' because the considerations that could have led us to a more honest representation of our action were right before us and we glossed over or ignored them. We are also, however, prevented by our own reflective inadequacy from being able later on to correct ourselves easily. For the state of mind we are in, when we commit ourselves to one moral voice and resist the call of others, is the normal psychological condition even for people who are *not* in self-deceit. Nothing about that state of mind alone tells us it is faulty; nothing flags its deceptive quality. Rather, it is but one symptom of a mental division that comes with the very possibility of moral reflection.

But it goes with this moralized picture of self-deceit – and this is my second conclusion – that there may be no purely internal way of getting ourselves out of that condition. If there are no purely psychological marks of self-deceit, there is nothing that need awaken us to the possibility that we have fallen prey to it. We feel anxious and afraid we have done the wrong thing? But that is just the ordinary state of people who have made a difficult decision: we might feel that way even if we had done the *right* thing. We feel *guilty* about a decision we have made? But that too is natural when something can be said for both sides of a decision.

By the same token, and more commonly, we may feel calm and innocent even after we have made wrongful moral decisions. And we may tell ourselves they were not wrongful and thus put ourselves more deeply into self-deceit. On Smith's picture of this phenomenon, there is no reason to think we will come out of this state on our own, or notice that we are in it. *Because* there are no definitive introspective marks of self-deceit, we cannot solve the problem from within ourselves.

So we need an outside guide. This may be an impartial and honest friend or neighbor, as Smith often suggests,[24] or a therapist, as Freud suggests. Or we may read a novel or go to the theater, and be shocked into further reflection by the similarity of a quandary depicted there to a situation of our own.[25] Or, again, we may correct for self-deceit by way of general moral rules – but these incorporate, as Smith says, the views of the society around us: we endorse them only when 'we hear everybody about us express the like detestation' or approval of a particular action (TMS III.4.7, 159). In any case, we need somehow to get out of ourselves, to correct our internal deliberations by an outside voice. The idealized person within us is an internalization of other people's judgments upon us, a result of the thoughts we have when our society 'mirrors' our selves back to us. Consequently, we truly endorse that ideal only when we are willing to set aside our internal judgments of ourselves, to a considerable extent, and accept the word of outsiders instead.[26]

As we consider these solutions to the problem of self-deceit, we are brought back to the fundamental insight about the self driving Smith's response to Hume: that we get the idea of the self – even of our *own* selves – from *other* people in the first instance. We come into existence, as reflective personalities, when a mirror is held up to our conduct by the people around us – when they require of us that we become accountable for our conduct, and therefore regard that conduct as flowing from a continuous locus of agency. This creation of the self by the people around us means that we are divided, from the first moment of self-consciousness, between an idealized image of ourselves and the lesser being we are trying to transform into that image. And this division is the source of self-deceit. But the dependency of the self on other people makes it reasonable to expect that those others may also be the source of whatever cure there can be to self-deceit.[27] In my efforts to be what other people expect me to be, I often lie to myself. But I wouldn't be anyone at all, for Smith, if I stopped trying to live up to their expectations. So the Smithian solution to self-deceit is not, as current catch-phrases would have it, to try to 'be myself' independently of what other people think of me. It is instead to seek my true self in the judgments, and ideally with the help, of all those other people. In *The Love-Song of J. Alfred Prufrock*, a poem that struggles throughout with the danger of inauthenticity, TS Eliot worries that we merely 'prepare a face to meet the faces that [we] meet'. Smith, I suggest, thinks that we cannot be authentic in any sense – true to ourselves – *unless* we prepare a face to meet the faces that we meet. We will be true to ourselves only if we are true to others. And if we can face the 'face' implanted in ourselves by the judgments of others, we will have achieved all that we can achieve in the way of integrity. We overcome our internal divisions, and the self-deceit to which it leads – to the extent that we can – by recognizing that we are created in the image of others. We *are* the faces we prepare, to meet the faces that we meet.

Notes

1 Herbert Fingarette, *Self-Deception*, 2nd edition (Berkeley: University of California Press, 2000), p. 1.
2 Alfred Mele, *Self-Deception Unmasked* (Princeton, NJ: Princeton University Press, 2001).
3 One of Joseph Butler's two main examples of self-deceit (see note 5, below). Smith's examples include thieves, adulterers, and would-be murderers.
4 See Stephen Darwall, 'Self-Deception, Autonomy, and Self-Constitution', in B. P. McLaughlin and A. Rorty, *Perspectives on Self-Deception* (Berkeley: University of California Press, 1988).
5 Joseph Butler, *The Analogy of Religion to the Constitution and Course of Nature; Also, Fifteen Sermons*, ed. Joseph Angus (London: The Religious Tract Society,1855), 427, 424.
6 Ibid.: 457.
7 Ibid.: 429.
8 Compare also Kant: 'It is easy to show that man is actually guilty of many inner lies, but it seems more difficult to explain how they are possible; for a lie requires a second person whom one intends to deceive, whereas to deceive oneself on purpose seems to contain a contradiction.' I. Kant, *Metaphysics of Morals*, trans. Mary Gregor (Cambridge: Cambridge University Press, 1991), p. 226 (Ak 6:430).
9 Ibid.: 429, 463, 431.
10 Fingarette also employs a notion of consciousness below the level of belief. He even uses the language of 'half-thoughts': see pp. 25, 29.
11 See Mele, *Self-Deception Unmasked*, and the authors discussed in Fingarette, *Self-Deception*, chapter 2. Fingarette's account of self-deception makes use of a notion of consciousness below the level of belief that mirrors the point I am making about Butler. He even uses the language of 'half-thoughts': see pp. 25, 29.
12 The Glasgow editors note that this chapter originally formed the conclusion of III.1 – which would suggest even more strongly than its present placement does that Smith saw it as deeply connected to his divided picture of the self: see discussion of III.1 in §§5–6 below.
13 TMS 176–78. See also Book V.
14 TMS IV.i.10; 183.
15 David Hume, *Treatise of Human Nature*, ed. L. A. Selby-Bigge, revised by P. H. Nidditch (Oxford: Clarendon Press, 1978), p. 251. Henceforth: T.

16 See especially TMS p. 111, n [3]; III.2.4, pp. 114–19 and III.3.1–4, pp. 134–37.

17 I don't mean to say that the self is *nothing but* a process of self-reflection. That would be viciously circular – and Locke's view of the self has indeed been accused by some commentators of such circularity. I suspect the accusation is unfair even when applied to Locke, but in any case for Smith there is certainly more to the self than its capacity for self-reflection: there are, for starters, all the first-order ideas and feelings *on* which we reflect. It is just that these first-order sorts of awareness will not constitute a self unless and until the being that has them becomes aware *that* it has them, and begins to reflect on them: self-consciousness is a necessary but not sufficient condition of selfhood. (I am grateful to an anonymous reviewer for urging me to address this issue.)

18 All quotations in this paragraph from TMS III.1.3, pp. 110–11.

19 As we'll see in a moment, it would be more correct to say that the self *may be regarded as* divided from the moment it comes into existence. In the end, I don't think Smith is committed to a self that has parts. But I'll talk as if he did for a bit because it's cumbersome to put the relevant points differently.

20 See for instance Mark Johnston, 'Self-Deception and the Nature of Mind', in B. P. McLaughlin and A. Rorty, *Perspectives on Self-Deception* (Berkeley: University of California Press, 1988).

21 Jeff Weintraub pointed this out to me. I am indebted to him for extensive discussion of this issue.

22 TMS III.6.10, p. 175; see discussion below, §10.

23 Without being *aware* of one, that is, or without caring about one: we think the case we are considering isn't covered by the rules we know, or we have yet to appreciate the sacredness of the rules in question.

24 Smith emphasizes the way actual spectators on us can help us achieve the condition prescribed by the impartial spectator at, for instance, TMS I.i.4.3, pp. 19–20; I.i.4.9, pp. 22–23; III.2.16–24, pp. 122–26; and III.3.23–24, pp. 145–46.

25 On TMS 143, Smith presents imaginative literature as a better source of moral education than philosophy.

26 This does not eliminate the role of the impartial spectator within us, but makes clear *how*, especially in 'complicated and dubious' cases (TMS III.4.11, p. 160), we best relate to that internal voice: we need to be *more* scrupulous about our own actions than outsiders are, to use their judgments as a baseline below which the judgments of our internal conscience may not fall.

27 Bill Ruddick gives a lucid and deep account of the degree to which self-deceit is brought about by a social group in 'Social Self-Deception', collected in B. P. McLaughlin and A. Rorty, *Perspectives on Self-Deception* (Berkeley: University of California Press, 1988).

Propriety, persuasion and political theory[1]

Duncan Kelly

I

Most discussions of Adam Smith's *Theory of Moral Sentiments*, beginning with the famous assessments of Edmund Burke, David Hume and Gilbert Minto, overwhelmingly focus on the mechanism of sympathy at work in the book (see *Corr.* Letter 38 from Edmund Burke, 10 September 1759, in Smith 1987: 46; Smith 1976a, *Theory of Moral Sentiments*, I. iii. 1. 9: 45f. and notes; Raphael 2007: 7, 128f; cf. Anon. 1764: 152; Smith 1976a, TMS V. 2. 9: 206). Given that its opening chapters elaborate a specific concern with the propriety of action, however, it is surprising that relatively few interpreters examine the concept of propriety in the same detail (cf. Fleischacker 1999; Griswold 1999; Haakonssen 1989). One early response that does examine the concept, however, and upon which my discussion shall shortly build, explores its dramatic embodiment in the character of Cordelia, from Shakespeare's *King Lear* (Richardson 1788). Therefore, after first outlining some of the basic contours of propriety in *Theory of Moral Sentiments*, my discussion turns to how some of the central themes at issue in *King Lear* might in fact provide significant resources for understanding the broader and dramatically complex role played by propriety in Smith's work. This is because my principal aim is to show how central the standard of propriety is in Smith's work, and to explore its function as part of his wider moral and political theory of what might be termed persuasive agency. According to Smith, the propriety of agency or action is a measure of how persuasive its claims to our sympathy might be, particularly when seen from the vantage point of the spectator, and which is therefore a judgment of its suitability, rightness or otherwise.

II

Smith claims that the complete approbation of propriety requires an agent to feel perfect sympathy with the sentiments and the actions of another, and also to be aware that they 'perceive this perfect concord' at the same time (Smith 1976a, TMS II. i. 5. 11: 78). It is both a practical and an imaginative form of judgment, and propriety refers to the 'suitableness or otherwise' of an action in proportion to the 'cause or object which excites it' (Smith 1976a,

The Adam Smith Review, 6: 93–110 © The International Adam Smith Society
ISSN 1743-5285, ISBN 0-415-66722-7

TMS I. i. 3. 6: 18). This makes propriety both an expressive and a reactive judgment about the quality of an action, and an assessment of the motivations and sentiments behind it. Propriety is always a judgment of appropriateness in context, and it underscores our sympathy or disapprobation. Moreover, because sympathy upholds the strict standards of justice and decorum Smith elsewhere defends, propriety is both a necessary prerequisite for sympathy and therefore also for justice, yet it remains separable from judgments concerning the merit or demerit of action.

Thus, Smith writes that philosophers have typically concentrated on the intentional effects of action, and these are, he thinks, questions specifically pertaining to merit or demerit. Propriety, or fitness and fittingness, remains lexically prior in his system (Smith 1976a, TMS I. i. 3. 5: 18). Indeed, propriety rather than utility is the paramount guide to the judgment of action because Smith thinks that the value of 'the exact adjustment of the means for attaining any conveniency or pleasure', counts for more than 'the very conveniency or pleasure, in the attainment of which the whole merit would seem to consist' (Smith 1976a, TMS IV. 1. 3: 179f.).

In spite of this, Smith maintains a distinction between 'mere propriety' and virtue. The former indicates 'those qualities and actions' that 'simply deserve to be approved of', the latter focuses on those which should 'admired or celebrated' (Smith 1976a, TMS I. i. 5. 7: 25). There is, moreover, a natural propriety accorded both to 'mere justice' and to the 'sense of justice' (Smith 1976a, TMS II. i. 1. 10: 82; II. ii. 2. 1–4: 82–85). Natural sociability and our need for approbation make us 'anxious to be really fit' for society, and this anxiousness motivates individuals to act in ways that others deem to be praiseworthy. This requires propriety and justice both in our own judgment and action, and also in our judgment of the actions of others (Smith 1976a, TMS III. 2. 7: 117; cf. Smith 1976a, TMS III. 2. 2–5, 8–10: 114ff., 117f.; III. 2. 24: 126). The connections Smith proposes to explain this, between imagination and perception, sympathy and propriety, and between approbation and the judgment of the quality of agency, attest to both the complexity and 'agent-relative' character of his moral and political theory (Darwall 1998: 261–82). It is, though, his focus on the approbation of propriety that provides a clue as to the wider structure of the argument. Smith understands agency to be an exercise in persuasion geared towards the receipt of such sympathetic approbation, but recognizes that agency is instinctively motivated by a natural and competitive desire for approbation, esteem and even domination.

As Smith makes clear, in determining the degree of blame or applause we judge applicable to action, although we might look to a vision of perfect propriety, its very perfection renders it an ideal that is unavailable to ordinary agents. Alternatively, we may seek to ground our judgment in an assessment of how near or far from an intuitively grasped standard of perfection particular actions fall. If they are above our sense of an approximate mean, then they are worthy of applause. But should they fall below, we will commonly ascribe blame to them (Smith 1976a, TMS I. i. 5. 9: 26; Scanlon 2008: 165,

175, 179). This is the same, he thinks, of the aesthetic judgment provided by the critic, and the combination of aesthetic and moral judgment here implied makes it unsurprising in fact that a character like Cordelia might be seen as a theatrical presentation of propriety in Smith's sense of the term (Smith 1976a, TMS I. i. 5. 10: 26; see too Valihora 2001: 142f., 147ff., 160). In fact, the general example of *King Lear* offers keen insights into the character of Smith's moral and political theory, and for that reason my discussion now turns to it.

III

The theatricality of debates and discussions about selfhood and spectatorship, or sympathy and representation, in the eighteenth century is well known (cf. Wahrman 2004: 166f., 169, 171–74; Fried 1980). Smith himself literally toyed with Addisonian considerations of proximity, distance and spectatorship (Addison 1902, *The Spectator*, no. 10 (12 March 1711); no. 411 (21 June 1712: 19, 593; more generally, 'The Pleasures of the Imagination', *The Spectator*, nos. 411–21; Brewer 1997; Lomonaco 2002). He also engaged with debates about sympathy and judgment from Lessing and Hume onwards, concerning the interplay of visual with poetic or linguistic insight and *ekphrasis* (Lessing 1984: 76f.; Garsten 2005: esp. 24–129, 160f, 170f., 177ff., 188–92; Sheehan 2005: 164ff.).

As part of this general concern, visual representations of *King Lear* and its focal points of political rule, sibling rivalry and a fear of exposure to the natural world, had already reached high levels of emblematic or iconographic sophistication by the time of William Richardson's analysis of Cordelia's propriety (see Sillars 2008: 63, 78, 138, 157). Whether or not Smith was directly aware of this, Richardson presented the general point about propriety as follows:

> Cordelia, full of affection, feels for the distress of her father: her sense of propriety imposes restraint on her expressions of sorrow: the conflict is painful: full of sensibility, and of a delicate structure; the conflict is more than she can endure; she must indulge her emotions: her sense of propriety again interposes; she must vent them in secret, and not with loud lamentation … There are few instances in any poet, where the influences of contending emotions are so nicely balanced and distinguished.
>
> (Richardson 1788: 82f.)

It was a curiosity in contemporary receptions of *King Lear* that Cordelia's death should be seen as somehow heretical. In the opinion of Dr Johnson, Smith's contemporary, Shakespeare 'suffered the virtue of Cordelia to perish in a just cause, contrary to the natural ideas of justice' (Johnson 2008: 465). Yet as John Kerrigan notes, such a response is quite 'remarkable' in the face of Johnson's own faith, and his attempt to present Cordelia as a literal embodiment of Christ rather far-fetched (Kerrigan 1997: 139). In Kerrigan's view, what is really at issue in *King Lear* concerns the expression of rage and 'retribution' through language, as the only response left to a practically impotent King. Thus although his vengeance requires an outlet, its structure is much more obviously pagan and classical than Christian, even though an earlier and deleted scene from the play had depicted Cordelia as a pietist figure (Kerrigan 1997: 133, 136; cf. Foakes 2003: 142).

The natural and reactive character of the vengeful response points to certain obvious connections with classical tragedies, where what is often at issue is the interplay between nature and artifice, and the necessity of acting in line with our natural or reactive attitudes. Indeed, this classical focus still has considerable purchase in modern moral philosophy (see Strawson 1968; Williams 1993). Equally, although figures like T. S. Eliot might have overstated the unity of a Senecan Stoic worldview in Elizabethan England, conventional Senecan themes of anger, reciprocity and shame were certainly central to Shakespeare and were equally important for Smith (Eliot 1927/1951: 134f.; also Elster 2011: 152–171). Anger in particular is at the forefront in *King Lear*, and a climate of violence suffuses the play, beginning with the arbitrary power of the King, and soon descends into mindless and irrational physical violence in the blinding of Gloucester and the death of Cordelia. These acts are especially shocking because the perpetrators gain no obvious advantage from their actions (Foakes 2003: 143f.). In similar fashion, anger is also one of the first emotions tackled by Smith in his analysis of propriety, and he takes trouble to contrast the 'insolence and brutality of anger' with the approbation accorded to that 'noble resentment' which reacts to, and justifiably rejects as inappropriate, a misdirected attack on an agent's sense of dignity or rank (Smith 1976a, TMS I. i. 5. 4: 24; cf. Hampton and Murphy 1988: esp. 54, 56, 59ff.).

Little appears noble in Lear's early anger, of course, as he disowns and banishes Cordelia at the beginning of the play. He does so initially, it seems, because she cannot or will not act in accordance with the laws of polite, courtly rhetoric. Demanding of his daughters that they express their love for him in fulsome, ornate style, literally as payment for their territorial reward, Goneril and Regan fulfill their duties by speaking with propriety, at least as Lear seems to understand it. But Cordelia cannot undertake the 'glib and oily art' of rhetoric, and attempts instead to answer in line with both her nature and decorum (*King Lear*, Act I, Scene I, l. 227). When she intimates her love for Lear both to the audience and also to her suitor, the King of France, her lines recall the marriage vow. They give her expression double import, signaling a contract both with her father and her future husband (Danby 1948: 130f.). The King of France appears noble and magnanimous, refusing to let the loss of a territorial dowry come between them. He does so, moreover, just as Lear withdraws Cordelia's birthright, even though it is unclear whether Lear does so in a futile attempt at diplomatic maneuvering or simply from blind rage.

More broadly, Cordelia cannot answer as expected because her answers would be those Lear knows already to be true, and if it is the case (as writers like Stanley Cavell have claimed) that love equals truth in the play, then love cannot be stated as an epistemically knowable fact (Cavell 2004). Instead, it is simply natural and tied to the uniqueness of a person, which allows the exceptionally problematic relationship between politics and love to structure the tragedy of entire encounter (Hunter 1987: 136f; cf. Honneth 2009: 166, 170). If the sisters, Goneril and Regan, have no difficulty in expressing their designs it is because they are conventional, and being conventional or artificial they aim to dissimulate. Perhaps, then, Lear's rage is indeed focused around the fact that his love for Cordelia remains, but he cannot express it at court. He also knows (but cannot accept) that for her to speak as her sisters do is an impossibility, and recognizes that were she to do so, it would be at best a form of '*dissembled flattery*', which is to say that it would be a repudiation of the natural love he already knows her to have for him (Cavell 2004: 338f., quotation at 341; cf. Bruns 1990: 618f.; also Bate 1997: 148–51). The thoroughly problematic, and dramatic, quality of what constitutes fittingness or appropriateness in the play makes it a valuable point of entry into the wider sense of the term in Smith's writings.

IV

A concern with the relationship between propriety, persuasion and agency offers an intriguing point of reconciliation between Smith's work and Shakespeare's dramatic tragedy, even though Smith's direct use of Shakespeare is only minimal (cf. Smith 1976a, TMS I. ii. 3. 1: 34).[2] Because Lear's demands are, quite simply, too demanding, their fevered pitch inappropriate, his claims ridiculous and his response hyperbolic, we cannot properly put ourselves into his view, or in Smith's terms, bring his case home to ourselves. We cannot sympathize with him in the same way that we seem instinctively to be able to do with Cordelia. Equally, we can understand both the formal demerit of Cordelia's actions at the same time as we approve or sympathize with their conventional propriety. This paradoxical and theatrical situation falls clearly within Smith's angle of vision, when he writes that in order for the spectator to sympathize with the agent, passions must be expressed at a pitch one can go along with. Thus, 'the propriety of every passion excited by objects peculiarly related to ourselves, the pitch which the spectator can go along with, must lie, it is evident, in a certain mediocrity. If the passion is too high, or if it is too low, he cannot enter into it.' He continues, arguing that 'this mediocrity, however, in which the point of propriety consists, is different in some passions'. So 'if we consider all the different passions of human nature, we shall find that they are regarded as decent, or indecent, just in proportion as mankind are more or less disposed to sympathize with them' (Smith 1976a, TMS I. ii. Introduction. 1–2: 27).

His analysis of speech in the corresponding lectures on rhetoric says much the same. The 'true propriety of language' is, he says, to speak plainly and clearly, in the manner of what is expected, or in line with decorum and according to convention (Smith 1983, *Lectures on Rhetoric and Belles Lettres*, Lecture 11. 137: 56). Lear might seem to fail in this, but it is also his right to speak as he does, at least according to the wider tenets of Smith's political theory. For Smith suggests that authority and utility are the polestars of political theory, and his account of authority assumes a natural deference to superiority on the part of the majority, whether in terms of qualifications, age, fortune or birth. The argument leads him into a discussion of the major principles of political allegiance, namely authority and the common or general interest, which in turn mirrors a distinction between Tories (authority) and Whigs (utility) in his argument (Smith 1978, LJ (A), v. 123: 318f.; v. 123–24: 319f.; cf. Smith 1976a, TMS VI. ii. 2. 16: 233, and n. 7). And although Smith notes that 'lunacy, nonnage, or ideotism' will 'entirely destroy the authority of a prince', it is not yet clear where Lear sits on this continuum (Smith 1978, LJ (A), v. 126–27: 320f., 311–30). What matters is the extent to which propriety here is doing the groundwork in structuring how or why we sympathize, or fail to sympathize, with the characters and their actions in turn and with other agents in general. To make sense of this, one needs to see it as part of a concern with the persuasiveness of agency.

Sympathy is a judgment of gratitude and approbation, whilst its opposite is a judgment of disapproval and possibly resentment. Both senses, however, depend first upon as assessment of the propriety (that is, the rightness or the fittingness or otherwise) of the act and its claims to our sympathy (Smith 1976a, TMS I. ii. intro. 1: 27). Smith's positive account of propriety speaks of 'perfect concord', but the point is equally clear when he outlines the dangers of impropriety. For example, when

> to the hurtfulness of the action is joined the impropriety of the affection from whence it proceeds, when our heart rejects with abhorrence all fellow-feeling with the motives of the agent, we then heartily and entirely sympathize with the resentment of the sufferer.
>
> (Smith 1976a, TMS II. i. 4. 4: 74)

When writing about the foundations of agency, however, Smith states that natural ambition and self-interest, a 'desire of bettering our condition', lies at the heart of human motivation (Smith 1976b, WN, II. iii. 28: 341f.). This motivating desire nevertheless masks a more fundamental 'love of domination and authority', made manifest in the pleasure we have in getting others to carry out our will, and which can be more strongly expressed as a natural 'love of domination and tyrannizing' (Smith 1978, LJ (A), iii. 114: 186).

How these natural tendencies are tempered, particularly under commercial society, was a Montesquieuean problem that Smith investigated. They could be counterbalanced, he thought, by our equally deep-seated need for social acceptance and recognition, which means that the tasks of politics and economics are both related but distinct, and that the logic of the market must be tempered by the logic of the forum (see Elster 1986). A fear of shame, a reflex of the 'natural right' to preserve our 'reputation', underscores this tension, yet for Smith it tends naturally to result in politeness or decorum. And this general process is both a cause and a consequence of the division of labor, which produces opulence as well as drudgery, riches as well as poverty (Smith 1978, LJ (B), 8, 192: 399, 480f.; cf. Smith 1976b, WN, V. i. f. 51: 783f.; Smith 1978, LJ (B), vi. 6: 333; Berry 1997: 144ff.; Lamb 1973: 278). Given this imbalance, politics and economics can become vehicles either of enlightenment, entrapment or both simultaneously (Taylor 2004: 62ff., 79, 167; cf. Chowers 2004: 188, 193ff.; Force 2003). Part of the power of Smith's analysis, though, is his recognition that it is difficult in practice to distinguish between the effects of one from the other. The practical consequences of self-interest can, he suggests, mask the realities of our situation and when this is allied to a general sense of anxiety over our agency, it becomes difficult for us to choose rationally how best to act (Smith 1976a, TMS I. iii. 3. 2: 62). Rational agency therefore approximates to the mean of propriety, in order to guarantee at least a minimal chance of approbation through persuasion.

We cannot simply ignore the requirements of persuasive agency if we are to take our place as citizens who naturally feel 'love and admiration' for those whose 'character we approve of'. This relates back once again to an instinctual drive to better our condition, which is rooted in 'emulation, the anxious desire that we ourselves should excel', but which has its true origins in our attempts to compare ourselves with others. The desire to excel 'is originally founded in our admiration of the excellence of others', and it clearly matters because if we are to achieve success or 'the satisfaction this brings, we must become the impartial spectators of our own character and conduct. We must endeavor to view them with the eyes of other people, or as other people are likely to view them' (Smith 1976a, TMS III. 2. 3: 114). Here is Smith the theorist of a persuasive agency rooted in esteem, comparison and a desire for recognition and approbation, grounding a capacity to generate sympathy in the undertaking of actions that others view as fitting. Propriety is thereby a standard of suitability or appropriateness in agency, but it is ultimately motivated by a natural and competitive desire for approbation and esteem.

By 'rendering ourselves the *proper* objects of esteem and approbation', however, our self-interested justification for action 'cannot with any propriety be called vanity' (Smith 1976a, TMS VII. ii. 4. 8: 309, emphasis added. Cf. Fleischacker 2004: 104–18.) Only by acting well will we find tranquility, which is 'the principle and foundation of all real and satisfactory enjoyment'. We will only be able to do this if we can trade off the 'frivolous pleasures of vanity and superiority' and learn to see social life as an exercise in persuasion of a very particular sort, where persuasiveness is rewarded with sympathetic approbation. In order to be persuasive, there must be a standard of judgment in terms of agency, and my claim here is that this standard of judgment concerning the appropriateness of agency in Smith is propriety. In turn, these judgments motivate our sympathy or disapprobation with both the sentiments and actions of other agents (Smith 1976a, TMS III. 3. 31–32: 150; cf. Kalyvas and Katznelson 2008: 24f, 28, 30ff.). The fact that imagination, sympathetic engagement, practical reasoning and self-awareness are all interconnected in making judgments about propriety does suggest that it really is the bridge connecting sympathy with action. Nevertheless, the sheer complexity of what is at stake when considering propriety is indicated by Smith's rather ironic-sounding note that propriety includes everything that Plato says about virtue, but that Platonic virtue (indeed virtue in general) is certainly not propriety (Smith 1976a, TMS VII. ii. 1. 11: 270).

V

Smith's view of agency is in one sense quite simple, and in line with what Amartya Sen (making extensive use of Smith) calls agency-freedom. Put simply, this is the freedom to pursue choices you perceive to be important to you (Sen 1985: 203). Freedom for Smith in this sense is freedom to persuade in order to pursue the results of a system of natural liberty. In what form does the agent need to persuade though? Persuasion will be different in kind, certainly, whether it takes place in the market or in the forum, but Smith is quite clear that the need to persuade is general and stems from a natural 'disposition' towards 'trucking' and exchange, and from which the 'natural inclination every one has to persuade' develops. Indeed, the desire to 'persuade others to be of their opinion even when the matter is of no consequence to them' is a powerful motivational force, and its connections to trucking and bartering develop explicitly from the faculties of speech, reason and thus from a natural sociability (Smith 1978, LJ (A), iv. 56: 352; Smith 1976b, WN, I. ii. 1: 25, 27). As he elsewhere suggests, society is a mirror and our natural sociability helps us to learn quickly how to act appropriately in it. For although 'our first moral criticisms are exercised upon the characters and conduct of other people', unsurprisingly 'we soon learn that others are equally frank with regard to our own' (Smith 1976a, TMS III. i. 3–5: 111–12; Smith 1976a, TMS III. iii. 28: 148; cf. Campbell 1971: 95, 150f.; Schabas 2003: 272).

Furthermore, because 'a whole life is spent in the exercise of it, [persuasion, that is] a ready method of bargaining with each other must undoubtedly be attained', whether in the marketplace of ideas or of exchange (Smith 1978, LJ (B), 221: 493f.). To be successfully persuasive in terms of generating sympathy and approbation, one has to act with propriety. That means acting according to standards of appropriate conduct that are shared, conventional and which can then be strictly enforced according to the demands of justice. However, it is still the process of cultivating agency throughout the course of a life that gives meaning to the specific instances of persuasion in which individuals engage. This is itself a theme of considerable import to the contemporary philosophy of action, where self-cultivation allows one to engage more adroitly in persuasive, responsible and free agency (Frankfurt 2006).

Persuading others of the appropriateness (and hence of the mediocrity) of our claims to their sympathy is therefore the hallmark of action governed by propriety. Rather than the 'indirect' sympathy required in making judgments of merit, propriety depends upon a 'direct' sympathy with the motives of an agent and an agreeable approval of their actions in context (Smith 1976a, TMS II. i. 5. 1: 74). In other words, propriety is already also closely connected with justice as was earlier suggested. First, although fulfilling the basic minimum that justice demands might not lead to virtue, it remains the baseline of what propriety requires (Smith 1976a, TMA, II. ii. 1. 9–10: 81f.; II. ii. 3. 8: 89). Second, impropriety stems from a 'want of sympathy' or 'from a direct antipathy to the affections and motives of an agent', and demerit from 'indirect sympathy with the resentment of the sufferer', so that acting with impropriety might easily overlap with actions that are contrary to the propriety demanded by justice (Smith 1976a, TMS II. i. 5. 4: 75; also II. ii. 1. 6: 80; III. 6. 10–11: 175f.). This is what lies behind Smith's focus on the strict grammar of both justice and propriety (Smith 1976a, TMS VII. ii. i. 9–10: 269f.; II. ii. 3. 3–4: 86; III. 6. 10–11: 175f.). Moreover, one might add that by focusing on the necessity of regulating agency in accordance with both conventional propriety and justice, a line from Locke to the Scottish Enlightenment that is more direct than some have been willing to suppose appears here rather more clearly, though the context itself remains nothing if not complex (see Dunn 1985: 119; Griswold 1999: 272ff.; Harris 2003: 240f.; Smith 1976a, TMS III. 2. 12: 120f.; III. 3, 4: 137; III. 5. 3–4, 13: 163f., 170; Viner 1972).

The 'desire to be believed, the desire of persuading', which informs propriety, actually stems from speech and is the 'strongest of all our natural desires'. Speech 'is the great instrument of ambition, of real superiority, of leading and directing the judgments and conduct of other people.' This is why, Smith writes, it is 'always mortifying not to be believed, and it is doubly so when we are supposed to be unworthy of belief'. Indeed, the 'delightful harmony' or 'certain correspondence of sentiments and opinions' indicating sympathy only occurs when 'there is a free communication' between persons based on 'frankness and opennness' (Smith 1976a, TMS VII. iv. 25–26, 28: 336f.). Thus, although our capacity to learn appropriate conduct seems like a moral sense, in practice it is something that develops over time and according to the extent to which an agent learns to 'view his situation in a candid and impartial light', coming to see things as others see them as they try to persuade others of a just claim to their sympathy (Smith 1976a, TMS I. i. 4. 8: 22; cf. Sen 2002: 446f., 449ff., 455f.; Sen 1999). This capacity for self-observation as well as observation of others requires an increasingly strict and watchful eye to be placed over one's own conduct. It is this thought that lies, in part, behind his critical comments on both Mandeville and Rousseau over pity, conscience, and particularly human interdependence (Smith 1980, *Essays on Philosophical Subjects*: 243, 250; Rousseau 2002: 127, 152; Sonenscher 2008: 210; also Marshall 1988: 143ff.; Stewart 1855, vol. 6: 195).

By recognizing our natural interdependence, in fact, Smith makes a bold move. Noting first that what is assumed in modern theories of freedom is absence of dependence on traditional and arbitrary political power, without which none can be 'really free in our present sense of the word Freedom', he claims that such freedom allows for the cultivation of a hugely beneficial social shortcut towards persuasive agency (Smith 1976b, WN, III. iii. 5: 400; also Lewis 2000). In complex commercial societies individuals are unable in practice to fawn over persons of widely differing status to make certain they get what they want, but natural interdependence is clarified through the cultivation of appropriate conduct. The individual 'stands at all times in need of the cooperation and assistance of great multitudes, [even] while his whole life is scarce sufficient to gain the friendship of a few persons' (Smith, 'Early Draft of Part of the *Wealth of Nations*, ch. 2', in Smith 1978, LJ (B), 22: 571). This is the source of our appeal to the self-interest, properly understood, of those we rely on (Smith 1976b, WN, I. ii. 2: 26f.; also Tribe 2008: 514–25).

If persuasion takes place in an interdependent world of agents, and is predominantly expressed through speech, then our language will have to attune itself to the demands of propriety (Otteson 2003: 259–74). To put the point in Smith's terms once more, the language of modern commercial societies works best when it cultivates the 'plain stile'. Just as politics in the modern world is not about heroic leadership, neither is modern rhetoric a form of public warfare by other means. Ornate figures and tropes have been rendered otiose, and the language of political prudence similarly updated (Smith 1983, LRBL, Lecture 25, ii. 139: 148f.; cf. Phillipson 1993: 317ff.; Skinner 1996: 47). In sum, then, Smith claims that when language expresses your meaning with propriety it is as perspicuous as it can be. This sound of persuasive mediocrity, so to speak, is as important as the 'harmony and coincidence' that results from the 'perfect concords' of an original passion approved of by a spectator (see Smith 1983, LRBL, Lecture 6, i. v. iv: 26; *Corr.* Letter 40 to Gilbert Elliot, 10 October 1759, in Smith 1987: 48–57, at p. 51).

Smith takes this thought further, by asking what else might be at stake in the persuasive demand for sympathy, or the true demand of 'bringing your case home to myself'. He develops this idea through recognizing the truism that not only do we evaluate sympathy and propriety through speech, we also judge what we see, and by seeing things through the eyes of another, our sympathy can be transmitted through a process of envisioning and re-visioning (Smith 1976a, TMS VII. iii. 1. 4: 317; Gordon 1995: 741f.). He illustrates the resultant combination of imagination (as both perception and as moral judgment) and vision (as sight) necessary to understanding judgments of propriety in a discussion of painting. In fact, another early and anonymous review suggested that Smith's language is 'easy and spirited', indeed 'rather painting than writing' (Anon. 1759: 485; cf. Smith 1980, EPS: 152f.; Smith 1976a, TMS III. 3. 2: 134f.). However, because we cannot see everything that is visible to us in the image, we are required to use our visual sense in combination with our imagination in order to make judgments about it.

In practice, this looks rather like the way in which someone like Richard Wollheim famously discussed the idea of 'seeing-in' a picture (Wollheim 1996: 205–26). When applied to moral judgment, this combination helps us to make sense of the fact that we need to imagine the situation of another and to judge the context in which they act, as well as evaluate the action itself that we encounter in practice. We do so both in terms of our own immediate sense of and response to agency as seen, and also in terms of our own perception or judgment of ourselves as the judge of such action. Smith thinks that our visual sense alerts us to those objects or bodies that might either help or harm us (Smith 1980, EPS: 153–61, 168). Vision therefore becomes another important axis along a range of sensual responses to agency, and when it is understood as representational computation that is actually filtered through imagination and therefore already motivated by natural passions, Smith's attempt to synthesize vision and language into a general account of judgment and propriety takes on new scope. It serves also to amplify both the theatrical and performative character of his argument about agency and persuasion (Phillipson 2001: 77; Smith 1980, EPS: 152f.; Smith 1976a, TMS III. 3. 2: 134f.).

The centrality of imagination to perception is critical in this, because the analogy of visual perception and moral calibration allows us to consider the role of distance in making judgments. It helps us to gauge appropriate levels of sympathy relative to our position. For example, 'in the same manner, to the selfish and original passions of human nature, the loss or gain of a very small interest of our own, appears to be of vastly more importance' than the 'greatest concern of another with whom we have no particular connexion' (Smith 1976a, TMS III. 3. 3: 135; cf. Smith 1976a, TMS VI. ii. 1. 13: 223). Yet equally because of the progress of human societies through language and sociability, we learn over time to cultivate a more general value of sympathy and approbation towards strangers as well as friends and compatriots. This is partly what he has in mind, when he tells his readers how the 'humbler department' to which man is 'allotted' requires him to make arrangements first for the 'care of his own happiness, [then] of that of his family, his friends, his country' and so on (Smith 1976a, TMS VI. ii. 3. 6: 237 cf. Griswold 1999: 141ff.; Vivenza 2001: 192ff.).

Indeed, our continual development as a species actually requires us to conform to the 'constitution of human nature', and thereby to begin to identify personal situations and actions in the same way that an ideal or impartial spectator would do. In other words, to see ourselves as strangers see us. In cultivating this capacity, we come to internalize a certain way of thinking about moral judgment as embodying our own conscience, so that we can begin to imagine ourselves in the place of another (Smith 1976a, TMS VII. iii. i. 4: 317; cf. Smith 1976a, TMS VI. iii. 25: 247f.; Phillipson 2001: 78–82). It is this, which allows the agent to become the 'impartial spectator of his own situation' (Smith 1976a, TMS III. 3. 29–31: 148f.).

On the one hand, we learn (and it is important to remember that this is a process) how to see 'neither with our own eyes nor yet with his, but from the place and with the eyes of a third person' who can 'judge impartially between us' (Smith 1976a, TMS III. 3. 3: 135). On the other hand, however, any attempt at impartiality requires in the first place an effort of sympathetic interpretation of the situation, which is governed by considerations of proximity and which is always necessarily partial (Smith 1976a, TMS III. 3. 4: 136). This is a genetic characteristic of theories of sympathy. For Smith, however, the 'impartial spectator is the personification of that which is permanent, universal, rational natural in the phenomena of sympathy' (Morrow 1923: 72). Because we cannot literally see ourselves as others see us, nor see others in all their complexity without imaginative and sympathetic effort in the first place, literal envisioning is insufficient as a theory of judgment. Language combined with vision is one solution to the problem of judging propriety under conditions of uncertainty, and we might think of it as a claim that upholds his defense of the need for persuasive mediocrity (Smith 1976a, TMS VII. ii. 1. 12: 270).

VI

Smith says he has to 'divide myself, as it were, into two persons' to 'examine my own conduct', this 'I, the examiner and judge, represent[s] a different character from that other I, the person whose conduct is examined into and judged of'. Put in the terms of his general argument, the first person is the 'spectator, whose sentiments with regard to my own conduct I endeavour to enter into, by placing myself in his situation', whilst the 'second is the agent, the person whom I properly call myself, and of whose conduct, under the character of a spectator, I was endeavouring to form some opinion'. In different terms, the first person is the judge, the second, the 'person judged of' (Smith 1976a, TMS III. 1. 6: 113; cf. Hanley 2008: 137–58; 2006: 177–202).

In Smith's analysis, therefore, we cultivate our imaginative capacity for sympathetic judgment or moral approbation over time, mediating between the reality of actual spectatorship and the idealized form of the impartial spectator. That is to say, we cultivate this capacity in the muddy world of approximations, uncertainties, and proximity towards some sort of mean between extremes. And although judgments about sympathy that express approbation or disapprobation with the propriety of agency are always undertaken in public, Smith also wants to show how it is that we come to internalize this general point of view through the development of our conscience over time and in context. Put another way, he wants to show how the real external spectator in public can become the impartial spectator who judges our actions in private, so to speak, but as if we were in public (Darwall 1999: 142, 144). This move supports the wider interpretative claim that to the extent that they are rational creatures, agents will 'judge their own conduct from the vantage point of an impartial spectator' (Ignatieff 1986: 122; cf. Fleischacker 1999: 157). They may make mistakes, and self-deception or self-delusion is for Smith a 'fatal weakness of mankind', providing 'the source of half the disorders of human life' (Smith 1976a, TMS III. 4. 4. 6: 157f.; cf. Forman-Barzilai 2005: 193, 200–4). But a rational attempt to overcome these delusions requires a better understanding of the demands made by the impartial spectator upon us, the result of which can be seen in the development of conscience (the 'great demigod within the breast'), which provokes us into increasingly austere and complex self-judgment over time. This is why, according to Smith, our search for rational and persuasive agency is equivalent to the secular imitation of the 'work of a divine artist' (Smith 1976a, TMS VI. iii. 25: 247f.; cf. III. 5. 12–13: 170; see too *Corr.* Letter 40, to Gilbert Elliot, 10 October 1759, in Smith 1987: 51; discussion in Raphael 2007: 36–42; cf. Darwall 1995: 241 Hume, 1981: 320, 319; Hutcheson 1728: 10; Stewart 1855, vol. 7: 229f., 234f., 243f., 247, 263).

If we are therefore to understand judgments of propriety as judgments about the fittingness or otherwise of action, we must recognize that such judgments are themselves the culmination of an ever more refined awareness of the general rules of society that have developed over time. As Smith suggests, an appropriate understanding of these general rules is 'of great use in correcting the misrepresentations of self-love', in a claim that looks very much like an updated model of *oikeiosis* (Smith 1976a, TMS III. iv. 12: 160; see too Griswold 1999: 137; Vivenza 2001: 200 and n. 36, 204 and n. 62, 206).

The outward movement of the circles of sympathy is something that bears a family resemblance to ancient Stoicism, and has been much commented upon. However, like his illustration of painting, propriety is both an ethical and aesthetic category, as well as a simple term concerning fittingness or otherwise. It is therefore a form of social grammar, which although not exactly as burdensome as justice and also amenable to aesthetic and contextual transformations over time, retains its central importance to his system. Situated propriety (as the judgment of appropriateness in context) motivates our sympathy or otherwise, and it is that sympathy which in turn upholds the strict standards of justice and decorum (Griswold 1999: 183ff.). The individual who acts unjustly therefore fails to exhibit propriety in something like the way that a parent who feels nothing for their child lacks an appropriate capacity. Both have what Smith refers to as an 'extraordinary sensibility' (Smith 1976a, TMS III. 3. 14: 142f.).

Although propriety therefore looks at first glance like a rather weak, relative and potentially moralizing standard upon which to base a moral and political theory, Smith claims that without it there could be neither moral progress nor any way of assessing the basic validity of claims to sympathy and demands of justice it brings about. Propriety clearly matters as much to his attempt to provide historical grounding to his social and political theory as it does to his moral psychology. In order to reiterate the main point of my discussion, it consists in the 'suitableness or unsuitableness, in the proportion or disproportion, which the affection seems to bear to the cause or object which excites it' (Smith 1976a, TMS I. i. 3. 6: 18). To this extent, propriety is both an expressive and a reactive judgment about the quality of an action, as well as a measure or judgment concerning the motivations and sentiments behind it (cf. Raphael 2007: 12–26). This is a claim that supports a more general view, which is that what Smith offers us is a phenomenology of common life, showing how we take our emotional guide from spectators and situated judgments, and not from 'quibbling dialectic' (Smith 1976a, TMS III. 3. 20: 145).

By acknowledging how certain facts of our nature (our desire for approval, authority and reputation) lead us towards the 'general rules or morality', he claims that our judgments are 'ultimately founded upon experience of what, in particular instances, our moral faculties, our natural sense of merit and propriety, approve, or disapprove of'. This original approval or condemnation of actions does not relate to whether 'they appear to be agreeable or inconsistent with a certain general rule'. Instead, the general rule 'is formed, by finding from experience, that all actions of a certain kind, or circumstanced in a certain manner, are approved or disapproved of' (Smith 1976a, TMS III. 4. 8: 159).

That is to say, we can only come to be able to make judgments about morality in general, separable from social or conventional morality, as we move from being actual spectators ruled by conventional propriety, to thinking as impartial spectators judging ourselves in terms of an absolute or general propriety for each particular situation. This is our best chance of overcoming self-deception, while our best efforts at persuasive agency are simply our attempts to mediate between an ideal of impartiality and the reality of actual spectatorship. Presented in this way, situated judgments of a situational propriety are always more direct than judgments of merit or demerit, and always approximations to an ideal, made under conditions of uncertainty (Haakonssen 1989: 54–57, 58ff., 62; cf. Smith 1976a, TMS I. i. 3. 7: 18; III. 2. 16: 122).

As a mechanism of selection, propriety works to root out inadequate or unpersuasive agency, because our natural desire for emulation and approbation means that we simply cannot do without it. Failures in persuasive agency hurt, and they force us to react appropriately if we are to gain the recognition we seek. Precisely because we crave approbation, however, we might well be unable to recognize the threat it poses to propriety under certain conditions, nor act appropriately even when we recognize the cues for action. This confusion and uncertainty appears to be at play in the relationship between Lear and Cordelia, where the very real dangers of impropriety are clear for any spectator to see. If Lear's 'confusion of emotion can lead to a misapprehension of the self', and a demand for one form of emotion and approbation whilst expressing another, we recognize it clearly as an audience because the confusion and the malignant consequences are those we have all seen before (Barroll 1974: 222). How quick and easy is the slide towards despotism, injustice and resentment in Shakespeare's play makes Lear a supremely Smithian case study, pitting the politics of envy and resentment against the necessity of persuasive mediocrity in everyday judgments of propriety. It offers a lesson we should still pay attention to.

Notes

1 I should like to thank those involved in the Oslo conference on Adam Smith's *Theory of Moral Sentiments*, where an early version of this paper was first delivered in 2009, for their comments and questions. I am particularly indebted to Christel Fricke and Raino Sverre Malnes for their hospitality then, and their patience and forbearance since. I am equally grateful to Fonna Forman-Barzilai for her generous comments and also to an anonymous reader for this journal.

2 Some material in the following sections develops the argument in Kelly (2010).

Bibliography

Addison, J. (1902) *The Spectator: A New Edition Reproducing the Original Text, Both as First Issued and as Corrected by Its Authors*, ed. Henry Morley, London: Routledge & Sons.

Anon. (1764) 'Censure of Mr. Adam Smith ... By an American', *The General Magazine of Arts and Sciences*, 14, p. 252, London: W. Owen.

Anon. (1795) 'Review of Adam Smith, *The Theory of Moral Sentiments*', *The Annual Register*, 2nd edn, pp. 484–89, London: R. & J. Dodsley.

Barroll, J. L. (1974) *Artificial Persons: The Formation of Character in the Tragedies of Shakespeare*, Columbia: University of South Carolina Press.

Bate, J. (1997) *The Genius of Shakespeare*, London: Picador.

Berry, C. (1997) *Social Theory of the Scottish Enlightenment*, Edinburgh: Edinburgh University Press.

Brewer, J. (1997) *The Pleasures of the Imagination*, London: Fontana.

Bruns, G. L. (1990) 'Cavell's Shakespeare', *Critical Inquiry*, 16: 612–32.

Campbell, T. (1971) *Adam Smith's Science of Morals*, London: George Allen & Unwin.

Cavell, S. (2004) 'The Avoidance of Love: A Reading of *King Lear*', in *An Anthology of Criticism and Theory, 1945–2000*, ed. Russ McDonald, pp. 338–52, Oxford: Blackwell.

Chowers, E. (2004) *The Modern Self in the Labyrinth*, Cambridge, MA: Harvard University Press.

Danby, J. (1948) *Shakespeare's Doctrine of Nature: A Study of* King Lear, London: Faber and Faber.

Darwall, S. (1995) *The British Moralists and the Internal 'Ought': 1640–1740*, Cambridge: Cambridge University Press.

——(1998) 'Empathy, Sympathy and Care', *Philosophical Studies*, 89: 261–82.

——(1999) 'Sympathetic Liberalism', *Philosophy and Public Affairs*, 28: 139–64.

Dunn, J. (1985) 'From Applied Theology to Social Analysis: The Break between John Locke and the Scottish Enlightenment', in *Wealth and Virtue*, ed. I. Hont and M. Ignatieff, pp. 119–35, Cambridge: Cambridge University Press.

Eliot, T. S. ([1927] 1951) 'Shakespeare and the Stoicism of Seneca', in *Selected Essays*, pp. 126–40, London: Faber and Faber.

Elster, J. (1986) 'The Market and the Forum: Three Varieties of Political Theory', in *Foundations of Social Choice Theory*, ed. J. Elster and A. Hylland, pp. 103–32, Cambridge: Cambridge University Press.

——(2011) 'Two for One? Reciprocity in Seneca and Adam Smith', *Adam Smith Review*, vol. 6: 152–171. London: Routledge.

Fleischacker, S. (1999) *A Third Concept of Liberty: Judgment and Freedom in Adam Smith and Immanuel Kant*, Princeton, NJ: Princeton University Press.

——(2004) *On Adam Smith's* Wealth of Nations, Princeton, NJ: Princeton University Press.

Foakes, R. A. (2003) *Shakespeare and Violence*, Cambridge: Cambridge University Press.

Force, P. (2003) *Self-interest before Adam Smith*, Cambridge: Cambridge University Press.

Forman-Barzilai, F. (2005) 'Sympathy in Spaces: Adam Smith on Proximity', *Political Theory*, 33: 189–217.

Frankfurt, H. (2006) *Taking Ourselves Seriously and Getting it Right*, Stanford, CA: Stanford University Press.

Fried, M. (1980) *Absorption and Theatricality*, Chicago: University of Chicago Press.

Garsten, B. (2005) *Saving Persuasion*, Cambridge, MA: Harvard University Press.

Gordon, Robert M. (1995) 'Sympathy, Simulation and the Impartial Spectator', *Ethics*, 105: 727–42.

Griswold Jr, Charles L. (1999) *Adam Smith and the Virtues of Enlightenment*, Cambridge: Cambridge University Press.

Haakonssen, K. (1989) *The Science of a Legislator*, Cambridge: Cambridge University Press.

Hampton, J. and J. G. Murphy (1988) *Forgiveness and Mercy*, Cambridge: Cambridge University Press.

Hanley, R. (2006) 'From Geneva to Glasgow: Rousseau and Smith on the Theatre and Commercial Society', *Studies in Eighteenth-Century Culture*, 35: 177–202.

——(2008) 'Rousseau's Diagnosis and Smith's Cure', *European Journal of Political Theory*, 7: 137–58.

Harris, J. (2003) 'Answering Bayle's Question: Religious Belief in the Moral Philosophy of the Scottish Enlightenment', *Oxford Studies in Early-modern Philosophy*, vol. 1, ed. D. Garber and S. Nadler, pp. 229–53, Oxford: Oxford University Press.

Honneth, A. (2009) *Disrespect*, Oxford: Polity.

Hume, D. (1981) *Treatise on Human Nature*, ed. L. A. Selby-Bigge and P. H. Nidditch, Oxford: Clarendon Press.

Hunter, G. K. (1987) 'Shakespeare and the Traditions of Tragedy', in *The Cambridge Companion to Shakespeare Studies*, ed. S. Wells, pp. 123–42, Cambridge: Cambridge University Press.

Hutcheson, F. (1728) *An Essay on the Nature and Conduct of the Passions and Affections. With Illustrations on the Moral Sense*, London: P. Crampton.

Ignatieff, M. (1986) *The Needs of Strangers: An Essay on Privacy, Solidarity and the Politics of being Human*, New York: Penguin.

Johnson, Samuel (2008) *The Major Works*, ed. D. Greene, Oxford: Oxford University Press.

Kalyvas, A. and I. Katznelson (2008) *Liberal Beginnings: Making a Republic for the Moderns*, Cambridge: Cambridge University Press.

Kelly, D. (2010) *The Propriety of Liberty: Persons, Passions and Judgement in Modern Political Thought*, Princeton, NJ: Princeton University Press.

Kerrigan, J. (1997) *Revenge Tragedy: Aeschylus to Armageddon*, Oxford: Oxford University Press.

Lamb, R. (1973) 'Adam Smith's Concept of Alienation', *Oxford Economic Papers*, n.s. 25: 275–85.

Lessing, G. E. (1984 [1766]) *Laocoön*, trans. E. A. McCormick, Baltimore, MD: Johns Hopkins University Press.

Lewis, T. J. (2000) 'Persuasion, Domination and Exchange: Adam Smith on the Political Consequences of Markets', *Canadian Journal of Political Science*, 33: 237–89.

Lomonaco, J. (2002) 'Adam Smith's "Letter to the Authors of the *Edinburgh Review*"', *Journal of the History of Ideas*, 63: 659–76.

Marshall, D. (1988) *The Surprising Effects of Sympathy*, Chicago: University of Chicago Press.

Morrow, G. (1923) 'The Significance of the Doctrine of Sympathy in Hume and Adam Smith', *The Philosophical Review*, 32: 60–78.

Otteson, J. (2003) *Adam Smith's Marketplace of Life*, Cambridge: Cambridge University Press.

Phillipson, N. (1993) 'Propriety, Property and Prudence: David Hume and the Defence of the Revolution', in *Political Discourse in Early-Modern Britain*, ed. N. Phillipson and Q. Skinner, pp. 302–20, Cambridge: Cambridge University Press.

——(2001) 'Language, Sociability and History: Some Reflections on the Foundations of Adam Smith's Science of Man', in *Economy, Polity and Society*, ed. S. Collini, R. Whatmore and B. Young, pp. 70–84, Cambridge: Cambridge University Press.

Raphael, D. D. (2007) *The Impartial Spectator*, Oxford: Clarendon Press.

Rasmussen, D. (2008) *The Problems and Promise of Commercial Society: Adam Smith's Response to Rousseau*, University Park, PA: Pennsylvania State University Press.

Richardson, William (1788) *Essays on Shakespeare's Dramatic Character of John Falstaff and on his Imitation of Female Characters*, London: John Murray.

Rousseau, J. J. (2002) *Discourse on the Origin and Foundation of Inequality Among Men*, in *Rousseau: The Social Contract and Other Later Political Writings*, ed. V. Gourevitch, pp. 111–222, Cambridge: Cambridge University Press.

Scanlon, T. (2008) *Moral Dimensions*, Cambridge, MA: Harvard University Press.

Schabas, M. (2003) 'Adam Smith's Debts to Nature', *History of Political Economy*, 35: 262–81.

Sen, A. (1985), 'Well-Being, Agency and Freedom: The Dewey Lectures 1984', *Journal of Philosophy*, 82: 169–221.

——(1999) *Development as Freedom*, Oxford: Oxford University Press.

——(2002) 'Open and Closed Impartiality', *Journal of Philosophy*, 99: 445–69.

Sheehan, J. (2005) *The Enlightenment Bible*, Princeton, NJ: Princeton University Press.

Sillars, S. (2008) *The Illustrated Shakespeare 1709–1875*, Cambridge: Cambridge University Press.

Skinner, Q. (1996) *Reason and Rhetoric in the Philosophy of Hobbes*, Cambridge: Cambridge University Press.

Smith, A. (1976a) *The Theory of Moral Sentiments*, ed. D. D. Raphael and A. L. Macfie, Oxford: Clarendon Press; reprinted, Liberty Fund (1982).

——(1976b) *An Inquiry into the Nature and Causes of the Wealth of Nations*, ed. R. H. Campbell and A. S. Skinner, Oxford: Clarendon Press; reprinted, Liberty Fund (1981).

——(1978) *Lectures on Jurisprudence*, ed. R. L. Meek, D. D. Raphael and P. G. Stein, Oxford: Clarendon Press; reprinted, Liberty Fund (1982).

——(1980) *Essays on Philosophical Subjects*, ed. W. P. D. Wightman, Oxford: Clarendon Press; reprinted, Liberty Fund (1982).

——(1983) *Lectures on Rhetoric and Belles Lettres*, ed. J. C. Bryce, Oxford: Clarendon Press; reprinted, Liberty Fund (1985).

——(1987) *Correspondence of Adam Smith*, ed. E. C. Mossner and I. S. Ross, Oxford: Clarendon Press; reprinted, Liberty Fund (1987).

Smith, D. (2000) 'Persuasion, Domination and Exchange: Adam Smith on the Political Consequences of Markets', *Canadian Journal of Political Science*, 33: 273–89.

Sonenscher, M. (2008) *Sans-Culottes*, Princeton, NJ: Princeton University Press.

Stewart, D. (1855) *The Collected Works of Dugald Stewart*, vols 6–7, ed. Sir William Hamilton, Edinburgh: Thomas Constable & Co.

Strawson, P. F. (1968) 'Freedom and Resentment', in *Studies in the Philosophy of Thought and Action*, ed. P. F. Strawson, pp. 71–96, Oxford: Oxford University Press.

Taylor, C. (2004) *Modern Social Imaginaries*, Durham, NC and London: Duke University Press.

Viner, J. (1972) *The Role of Providence in the Social Order*, Philadelphia, PA: American Philosophical Society.

Tribe, K. (2008) '"Das Adam Smith Problem" and the Origins of Modern Smith Scholarship', *History of European Ideas*, 34: 514–25.

Valihora, K. (2001) 'The Judgement of Judgement: Adam Smith's *Theory of Moral Sentiments*', *British Journal of Aesthetics*, 41: 138–61.

Vivenza, G. (2001) *Adam Smith and the Classics*, Oxford: Oxford University Press.

Wahrman, D. (2004) *The Making of the Modern Self: Identity and Culture in Eighteenth-Century Britain*, New Haven, CT: Yale University Press.

Williams, B. (1993) *Shame and Necessity*, Berkeley: University of California Press.

Wollheim, R. (1996) *Art and its Objects*, Cambridge: Cambridge University Press.

Social distance and the new strangership in Adam Smith[1]

Lisa Hill

In his writings Adam Smith (1723–90) developed a sophisticated account of the new social physics he saw emerging to accommodate the material and economic changes that were taking place in his time. Like his Scottish contemporaries, he was absorbed with the dynamics of social change and was in a good position to notice the full force of the developments brought on by modernization.[2] Scotland became a commercial society during the second half of the eighteenth century (Strasser 1976: 53) and Smith was curious to understand the social impact of this process. Particularly relevant to this discussion are Smith's observations on the transition from social arrangements based on what might be termed mechanistic solidarity and homogeneity, to those characterized by organic solidarity and heterogeneity.[3] Such a transition involved the dissolution of clan and village life, the growth of cities, increasing refinement in task specialization and the growth of markets; it also saw the decline of arbitrary and dispersed forms of governance, the consolidation of rule of law and the accompanying rise of the modern state (Silver 1990: 1474–1504). These developments broke down traditional social and affective arrangements, thereby offering greater freedom to individuals and unleashing the enormous productive power of market agents. Smith's social theory focuses upon an expanding, increasingly differentiated society. He was, by his own account, concerned with 'the great society', the large, prosperous, differentiated world of commerce:[4] in other words, mass society.

Assemblies of strangers

Commercial strangership is, for Smith, an improvement on earlier social regimes partly because it is calmer and more predictable, generated as it is outside intensely emotional and exclusivistic units such as the family, *umma* and ethnic group. Little is lost in the passing of pre-commercial alliances based on intense and particularistic sentiments in favour of those animated by the cooler and more constant virtues of 'prudence' and 'justice': intense interactions and loyalties were increasingly less important than the new forms of amicable *strangership* peculiar to commercial society. Smith perceived that people were developing better and more sophisticated patterns of social

The Adam Smith Review, 6: 111–128 © The International Adam Smith Society
ISSN 1743-5285, ISBN 0–415–66722–7

distance in a civil society of amiably disposed strangers and that this way of living offered unprecedented levels of prosperity due to its capacity to unleash the full productive powers of self-interest and the division of labour. As Michael Ignatieff writes, for Smith 'only a society of strangers, of mediated and indirect social relations, has the dynamism to achieve progress' (Ignatieff 1984: 119). While not ruling out the possibility and value of benevolence in intimate relationships, this is not where Smith's primary focus lies in his social theory because his concern is to understand relationships between strangers. In James Otteson's words, 'Smith is thinking of people who are not family or friends. He envisions the marketplaces of exchange to coordinate the mutual satisfaction of interests among people who are largely unaware of and strangers to one another' (Otteson 2002: 299).[5]

Despite moments of pessimism, Smith's was a generally complacent – at times seemingly enchanted – vision of the new world of commerce and modernity. On his account, the transition towards large-scale commercial society, while sometimes a little lonely, was basically positive, displacing as it did a mean, stressful, insecure and alternately dull and conflict-riven world with one rich in possibilities for civility, mutual enablement, liberty, peace, dignity, independence and human flourishing.

Security, specialization and the breakdown of the extended family

An important part of Smith's story is the breakdown of the extended family. Whereas people in pre-commercial or 'pastoral' orders carefully maintained extended family networks for the purpose of 'common defence', in commercial states the evolution of an organized system of justice and defence offers adequate protection to even the 'meanest man in the state'; now, even a person devoid of friends, family and wealth could still be secure in 'his' person. With the security problem solved, families, over time, 'naturally separate and disperse' and 'in a few generations' cease to care for (or even remember) one another (TMS VI.ii.1.12–13); the longer a 'civilization' has been 'established', the less intense is its '[r]egard for remote relations' (TMS VI.ii.1.12–13). People are no longer anchored geographically to the extended family seat but may now move about more freely in a manner that enables them to best employ their increasingly specialized talents.

As workers become more and more specialized, and markets larger (thereby, in turn, enabling and hastening the process of specialization) the family becomes more dispersed. Increasing specialization is an extremely important part of the story of the transition to modernity, not only because it precipitates the breakdown of the extended family, and therefore the emergence of commercial society; it also resolves a longstanding obstruction to the development of commerce and civilization itself: the security problem. The internal security of states is solved by the establishment of a formal system of justice and the development of professional, 'well-regulated' standing armies to 'execute and maintai[n]' it. A 'standing army establishes, with an irresistible force, the law of the sovereign through the remotest provinces of the empire, and maintains some degree of regular government in countries which could not otherwise admit of any' (WN V.i.a.40).

An organized system of justice supported by regular armies affords 'to industry, the only encouragement which it requires, some tolerable security that it shall enjoy the fruits of its own labour' (WN I.xi.i).[6] When '[t]he natural effort of every individual to better his own condition' is unleashed under conditions of 'freedom and security' the society will be prosperous and happy. Smith noted with pride that '[i]n Great Britain', the most opulent, differentiated and commercially advanced nation in the world, 'industry is perfectly secure … [and, arguably] freer than in any other part of Europe' (WN IV.v. b.43).

Rather than damaging the social fabric (as Smith's contemporary Adam Ferguson had suggested), specialization generates unprecedented levels of mutuality. Now associations are increasingly voluntaristic, egalitarian and mutually beneficial; a matter of purely instrumental mutual 'good offices' (WN I.ii.2). The knot of intimate conspecifics celebrated by Ferguson and other romantic thinkers is, on Smith's alternative interpretation, restrictive, oppressive, precarious, intermittently traumatic but generally 'indolent', monotonous and dull[7] compared to the rich new 'strangership' of the commercial age, with its endless possibilities for social and material exchange, personal development, refinement, comfort and prosperity. While 'savage nations' are 'so miserably poor … they are frequently reduced … to the necessity … of directly destroying, and … abandoning their infants, their old people, and those afflicted with lingering diseases', among civilized and thriving nations 'all are often abundantly supplied' and 'may enjoy a greater share of the necessaries and conveniences of life than it is possible for any savage to acquire' (WN I.4: 10).

In the new universalistic society of specializers, exchange gradually displaces clan and familial displays of loyalty as the paradigmatic social interaction; it is 'by treaty, by barter, and by purchase, that we obtain from one another the greater part of those mutual good offices which we stand in need of'' (WN I.ii.1–3). Exchange is now a primary form and *purpose* of association,[8] the means by which, as Adam Seligman notes, 'the individual is constituted in his individuality' (Seligman 1992: 29). It is also, paradoxically, how the equally natural institution of society is held together (WN I.ii.1–3). Pursuing self-interest within an intricate web of specialization shifts the mechanisms of solidarity away from traditional sources like blood ties, security alliances, strategically arranged marriages and gifting to impersonal, non-particularistic exchange.

Now that specialization and a regular and impartial system of justice have dissolved the obligatory and particularistic constraints of rank, *umma,* clan and treaty, less intense forms of friendship can extend to almost anybody whom one has contact with in the course of the business day. Because impersonal and ubiquitous exchange is the paradigmatic social interaction in Smith's universe, amicable strangership displaces intense friendship and enmity as the archetypal affective orientation. Membership of 'in' groups is no longer indispensable to a person's survival; the new voluntaristic civil society is superior because it is not intense, obligatory and exclusivistic in the way that pre-commercial forms of solidarity were (for example, blood and fictive kinship and clientage).

'Dependency' and the new independence

One of the things Smith most disliked about the feudal age was the unavoidable dependence associated with the system of great landholders and retainers. 'Dependency' is destructive because it breeds servility and fosters asymmetrical and therefore unhealthy and unproductive social relations (WN III.iv.4–7; WN I.ii.2). There is nothing so likely 'to corrupt and enervate and debase the mind as dependency'; conversely 'nothing gives such noble and generous notions of probity as freedom and independency' (LJA vi.6).[9] (Smith also advocated high wages for workers in the name of independence: low wages are objectionable because they evoke feudal norms of behaviour, specifically, an attitude of subservience and deference towards employers [WN I. viii.48]).[10] The dissolution of the system of great landholders decentralized dependency relations and offered greater security to individual tradespeople: now '[e]ach tradesman or artificer derives his subsistence from the employment, not of one, but of a hundred or a thousand customers' and is therefore no longer in the precarious and potentially humiliating position of being 'absolutely dependent upon any one of them' (WN III.iv.12). A major disadvantage of 'menial' labour performed inside dependency relationships (and therefore outside market relations) is that it is unproductive, in other words, it does not result in 'vendible' or exchangeable commodities (Perelman 1989: 316). In addition, because of the 'the waste which attends rustick hospitality', productive labour is able to support greater numbers of people (WN III.iv.12). Specialization thereby generates more independence as well as more *inter*-dependence of the vastly superior impersonal kind while enabling the society to be increasingly more productive and prosperous. Smith thus perceives the division of labour as socially integrating – in the tradition of Spencer, Durkheim and Hayek – as opposed to someone like Ferguson, for example, who perceives it as having the opposite effect – in the tradition of Marx, Hegel and Comte.[11]

Cleaving desperately to in-groups, cultivating close alliances and courting the good favour of others might have been necessary in small-scale societies where food and military security were daily life-or-death matters, but this is no longer appropriate in mass societies of secure, differentiated and self-managing strangers. Whereas prior to the age of 'commerce and manufactures' people lived in 'servile dependency upon their superiors' (WN III. iv.4) and were forced to behave like a 'puppy fawn[ing] upon its dam', specializing strangers can now live with dignity as independent mutual enablers and exercisers of perfect rights. Although the busy commercial agent barely has time to 'gain the friendship of a few persons' throughout his whole life, 'he' nevertheless 'stands at all times in need of the cooperation and assistance of great multitudes'. But it would be a grave mistake to appeal to their benevolence for survival.

> He will be more likely to prevail if he can interest their self-love in his favour, and show them that it is for their own advantage to do for him what he requires of them. Whoever offers to another a bargain of any kind, proposes to do this. Give me that which I want, and you shall have this which you want, is the meaning of every such offer; and it is in this manner that we obtain from one another the far greater part of those good offices which we stand in need of. It is not from the benevolence of the butcher, the brewer, or the baker that we expect our dinner, but from their regard to their own interest. We address ourselves, not to their humanity but to their self-love, and never talk to them of our own necessities but of their advantages. Nobody but a beggar chooses to depend chiefly upon the benevolence of his fellow-citizens.
>
> (WN I.ii.2)

It is not benevolence but pragmatic mutual interest that makes the modern commercial economy function smoothly; this, and the steadying effect of an organized system of justice (to be discussed in more detail presently).

Emotional and moral life of commercial strangers

The world that absorbs Smith is one that has to be managed largely by and between strangers. Our 'ancestors' habitually 'considered strangers and enemies as one and the same thing' and had 'no knowledge' of 'other nations' except for 'what they have got when at war with them'; but commercialism allows modern citizens to appreciate 'the benefit of having foreigners coming amongst them' who can 'carry out what is superfluous of the product of the country' and import 'the superfluities' of their local region for the 'convenience' and enjoyment of the recipients (LJA v. 92–94). The turbulent passions attendant on feudal alliances are gradually displaced by tamer passions and virtues in which the golden mean is emotional equilibrium, not benevolent passion or patriotic enmity; impartial rationality, not personalism, particularism, philanthropy, charity or nepotism. Strangers are no longer default enemies but potential contractees or role-pair candidates,[12] therefore the exchange culture is and must be calm, open, rational, impersonal, polite, flexible, voluntaristic and rule-governed. In contrast to contemporaries like Rousseau, who voiced suspicion of those who 'smile contemptuously at such old names as patriotism and religion' (Rousseau 1973: 17)[13] and Ferguson, who lauded the 'simple passions' of 'friendship, resentment, and love' (Ferguson 1996 [1767], hereafter cited as *Essay*: 166) and wrote nostalgically of those '[s]mall and simple tribes' whose conflicts with out-groups were 'animated with the most implacable hatred' (*Essay*: 25), Smith regards emotions such as hatred, resentment, revenge and anger as 'unsocial' passions that 'poison … the happiness of a good mind'(TMS I.ii.37–38); as such, they needed to be reined in and kept within the bounds of civility and justice. Similarly, patriotic fervour provokes and prolongs war, isolating, segregating and desensitizing us to the world outside our own narrow sphere, thereby disposing us to us to dehumanize and mistreat strangers (WN V.iii.37).[14]

The spontaneous and intimate temper of clan, estate and village life is supplanted by the cool friendships of amiably disposed strangers. Under commercial conditions there is a greater general fund of goodwill from which everyone may benefit in an impersonal way, because everyone is a potentially useful or enabling stranger or else a stranger whose disapproval we do not wish to attract. In pre-commercial society, as Alan Silver puts it so well,

> [T]he space between friend and enemy was not occupied, as in commercial society, with mere acquaintances, or neutral strangers, but charged with uncertain and menacing possibilities. … strangers in commercial society are not either potential enemies or allies, but authentically indifferent co-citizens – the sort of indifference that enables all to make contracts with all.
>
> (Silver 1990: 1482–83)

Smith reflects on a social atmosphere suffused, not with the spontaneous vitality of benevolent affect or patriotic fervour, but with the constancy of legal rules and the sturdy constraints of social decorum (Mizuta 1976: passim). The new age of independence, competition and liberty is congenial to the cultivation of the cool, instrumental, practical and therefore highly desirable virtues of prudence, justice, propriety, self-command, frugality, sobriety, vigilance, circumspection, temperance, constancy, firmness, punctuality, faithfulness, probity, enterprise and industry (WN II.iii.36).[15] Though Smith lavishly praised those who exercised the higher, other-regarding virtues, in his social theory his moral focus is on the practical and more attainable forms of virtue that could and should be exercised by every market society actor. Smith's modest ideal is a character who can be relied upon, at the very least, to be negatively virtuous, industrious, 'bustling', self-governing, enterprising (TMS III.6.7; LJA v.124) and polite.

The 'soft spark' of beneficence could never support modern social life because advanced commercial societies are too large to be sustained by a drive so inconstant and contingent; in a mass society it would be unwise to rely on benevolence for our survival because it would be impossible to elicit the required degree of benevolence from those we live amongst, most of whom are strangers. In addition, benevolence is no longer sufficient to supply members of commercial society's increasingly multifarious wants.

> Benevolence may, perhaps, be the sole principle of action in the Deity … But whatever may be the case with the Deity, so imperfect a creature as

> man, the support of whose existence requires so many things external to him, must often act from many other motives.
>
> (TMS VII.ii.3.18)

The cooler, more temperate and reliable sentiments of prudence, probity, propriety and especially justice were best suited to that task.

Further, a society left to regulate itself by benevolence alone is untenable; ironically, such a society will be riven with conflict and mutual injury.

> All the members of human society stand in need of each others assistance, and are likewise exposed to mutual injuries … But though the necessary assistance should not be afforded from such generous and disinterested motives, though among the different members of the society there should be no mutual love and affection, the society, though less happy and agreeable, will not necessarily be dissolved. Society may subsist among different men, as among different merchants, from a sense of its utility, without any mutual love or affection; and though no man in it should owe any obligation, or be bound in gratitude to any other, it may still be upheld by a mercenary exchange of good offices according to an agreed evaluation. Society, however, cannot subsist among those who are at all times ready to hurt and injure one another. The moment that injury begins, the moment that mutual resentment and animosity take place, all the bands of it are broke asunder, and the different members of which it consisted are, as it were, dissipated and scattered abroad by the violence and opposition of their discordant affections. If there is any society among robbers and murderers, they must at least, according to the trite observation, abstain from robbing and murdering one another. Beneficence, therefore, is less essential to the existence of society than justice. Society may subsist, though not in the most comfortable state, without beneficence; but the prevalence of injustice must utterly destroy it.
>
> (TMS II.ii.3.1–3)

Justice ultimately makes social life between competitors possible. Benevolence is 'pleasing' but it is only the 'ornament which embellishes, not the foundation which supports' society. Bonds between people in commercial society are not bonds of passion or affection but are either bonds of contract or bonds of mutual enablement. Society can survive without deep affect, but without the temperate and dispassionate dispositions recommended to us by justice and prudence it is destroyed 'utterly' (TMS II.ii.3.3).

A key advantage of justice is its precision: society may justifiably use force to prevent the injury of one person by another, but it can hardly attempt to enforce by legal sanctions the exercise of the benevolent virtues. The 'offices' and 'actions required by' such classical virtues as 'charity … generosity. … gratitude … friendship … humanity, hospitality' and 'generosity' are too 'vague and indeterminate' and admit of too many 'exceptions and … modifications' to usefully guide our behaviour. But there is 'one virtue of which the general rules determine with the greatest exactness every external action which it requires. This virtue is justice.'

> The rules of justice are accurate in the highest degree, and admit of no exceptions or modifications, but such as may be ascertained as accurately as the rules themselves, and which generally, indeed, flow from the very same principles with them. If I owe a man ten pounds, justice requires that I should precisely pay him ten pounds, either at the time agreed upon, or when he demands it. What I ought to perform, how much I ought to perform, when and where I ought to perform it, the whole nature and circumstances of the action prescribed, are all of them precisely fixt and determined. Though it may be awkward and pedantic, therefore, to affect too strict an adherence to the common rules of prudence or generosity, there is no pedantry in sticking fast by the rules of justice. On the contrary, the most sacred regard is due to them.
>
> (TMS III.6.9–10)

Justice is the more dependable virtue because it can be treated with precision. Its rules are highly impersonal, impartial, predictable and accurate. No one need refer to her previous history or connection with a potential contractee or wrestle with the embarrassments and uncertainties of moral, social and emotional obligation. Instead, codified rules provide a reliable guide to right action and make life more predictable in at least some spheres of life.

Mobility, liberty and trust

In these passages Smith expresses what Adam Seligman has described as the early modern preoccupation with mutual promise-keeping as the new bond of 'generalized trust' to replace the dissolving 'bonds of primordial attachment to kith and kin', territory, and 'local habitus' (Seligman 2000: 15). Trust in persons 'built upon mutuality of response and involvement' is supplanted by trust in impersonal 'abstract systems' that offer 'the security of day-to-day reliability'.[16]

The increased mobility and liberty of commercial agents is partly a function of the fact that commercial societies are marked by greater levels of social capital than their stadial predecessors. Though agents no longer enjoy the complete trust of a handful of intimates they are amply compensated by the fact that there is now *more* trust (albeit of a diluted quality) between *more* people, the majority of whom are strangers. Commercial society is adept at manufacturing and strengthening trust via its superior capacity to generate security through rule of law.[17] Smith wrote that: 'Commerce and manufactures' introduces order and good government, and with them, the 'liberty and security of individuals … who had formerly lived almost in a continual state of war with their neighbours' (WN III.iv.4).

Trust between citizens and the state is also enhanced by the development of standing armies. A sovereign who enjoys the 'security' of an extensive, professional and well-armed military is unburdened of 'that troublesome jealousy' which causes less secure governors perpetually 'to watch over the minutest actions' and stand poised to 'disturb the peace of every citizen'. Paradoxically, the pre-modern, citizen militia-defended, state is also the oppressive, stifling state:

> Where the security of the magistrate, though supported by the principal people of the country, is endangered by every popular discontent; where a small tumult is capable of bringing about in a few hours a great revolution, the whole authority of government must be employed to suppress and punish every murmur and complaint against it. To the sovereign, on the contrary, who feels himself supported, not only by the natural aristocracy of the country, but by a well-regulated standing army, the rudest, the most groundless, and the most licentious remonstrances can give little disturbance. He can safely pardon or neglect them, and his consciousness of his own superiority naturally disposes him to do so. That degree of liberty which approaches to licentiousness can be tolerated only in countries where the sovereign is secured by a well-regulated standing army. It is in such countries only, that the publick safety does not require, that the sovereign should be trusted with any discretionary power, for suppressing even the impertinent wantonness of this licentious liberty.
>
> (WN V.i.a.41)

Nathan Rosenberg has noted that for Smith (provided conditions of competition prevail) commerce also increases the sum of *moral* capital (Rosenberg 1990: 8). The rise of the bourgeois or 'merchant' class creates a new and more enduring moral order characterized by 'probity and punctuality', which are 'the principal virtues of a commercial nation' and unknown in the 'rude' (LJB 326–28). In fact, the more commercially advanced is a nation, the more are its people 'faithfull to their word' (LJB 327).

Smith's new 'civil society' is more pacific, orderly and predictable than its stadial predecessors (the hunting, herding and agricultural stages) partly because its regulating mechanisms are generated *outside* intensely emotional and exclusivistic social units like the family, the village, the *umma* or the feudal estate. Notwithstanding the persisting importance of the nuclear family, social behaviour is now learned more diffusely and impersonally through interaction with the world at large, among our 'rivals and competitors' (TMS VI.iii.23) and in 'societies', 'associations', 'companies', coffee houses, 'clubs' and dining societies[18] where students of civility congregate. Hostility and suspicion are defused by all this friendly, superficial interaction and the particularistic alliances bred by sectarianism, 'custom, corporate group, station, and estate are dissolved' (Silver 1989: 274–79). Politeness and civility is the new lingua franca, our passport to the 'great society' and our way of signifying to the world at large that we have freed ourselves from the maladaptive jealousies of a pre-modern in-group/out-group mentality; that we are ready to interact – and especially trade – with all. Richard Boyd detects similar sentiments in Hume's thought:

> Just as being civil obliges us to look past the different beliefs and identities that separate us from others, our prejudices against other nations, religions or races should not interfere with our ability to engage in trade. Understanding national, ethnic, or religious differences as incidental or irrelevant to a more fundamental interest in buying low and selling dear amounts to a kind of education or strengthening of reason and tolerance. (Boyd 2007: 78)

Mass market society is natural and beneficial, first, because it results from the innate 'propensity to truck, barter, and exchange' (WN I.ii.1), and second, because it embodies the cosmopolitan ideal; commerce progressively enlarges markets and therefore the concentric circles of instrumental friendship or commercial 'strangership'. Although Smith is no moral cosmopolitan he is quite definitely an economic cosmopolitan.[19]

Modular 'man' and social distance

In the new civil society of amiable strangers, citizens are no longer bound together by total forms of governance and religious obligation, the exigencies of security, or the restrictive ties of place and tradition, but move about freely, anonymously and in a modular fashion. Personal mobility seems to have been an extremely important concern for Smith and is central to his conception of individual liberty. People must be permitted the freest possible use of their bodies, minds and properties, provided that there are no violations of either the public interest or the system of natural liberty. Agents have a 'natural right' to 'free commerce' (including 'the right to freedom in marriage') (LJA i.12–13) and to enjoy their 'liberty free from infringement' (LJB 11; LJA i.24). Smith tells us that '[t]he property which every man has in his own labour' is 'the original foundation of all other property' and therefore 'the most sacred and inviolable' (WN I.x.c.12; IV.v.b.43). Humans are constitutionally disposed to specialize their economic effort, therefore it is their 'natural' right to exchange any resulting vendibles with the products of the specialized effort of others. It follows, then, that provided 'there is no injury to [one's] neighbours' (WN I.x.c.12), there can be no legitimate interference with exchange either by private persons or public bodies. England's poor laws were to Smith the most pernicious constraint on the right to 'commerce' and were more destructive than corporation laws because they disproportionately disadvantaged the poor (WN I.x.c.44–45). Similarly, the laws of apprenticeship were egregious, not only because they were an impediment to the mobility of labour, but also because of their tendency to discourage industry and commercial effort.[20] In short, they were an intolerable obstruction to our necessary participation with commercial strangers.

In Smith's ideal universe, the archetypal agent is 'modular man'; social links have moved 'from situs to contract' and are now 'flexible, specific [and] instrumental'.[21] Unlike Ferguson or Rousseau, Smith finds little romance in the necessitous and compelled relations of socially intimate societies, but embraces instead the possibilities unleashed by interactions unanchored in place or time: impersonal, interchangeable, voluntaristic, deracinated, cosmopolitan and mobile.[22] The modular agent is not completely immobilized by tradition, caste or ritual, while the switching of alliances is catastrophic neither for the social structure nor for the individual person concerned. Ernest Gellner describes the modern modularity extremely well and his observations can be easily applied to Smith's thinking here. Unlike pre-commercial forms of association, in the new commercial world agents always have the capacity to exit without being vulnerable to the 'accusation of treason'; similarly, agents can withdraw their 'cognitive' convictions without fear of being charged with 'apostasy' or any of the other fearful consequences that accompany such withdrawal in the mechanistic society (for example, ostracism, civil death, imprisonment, excommunication and even execution). In the new civil society of modularity, contract is the primary mechanism of association, the means by which obligations and commitments are made and kept. Associations are 'entered and left freely, rather than imposed by birth' and are made binding by sober and dispassionate legalism, as opposed to 'awesome ritual' enacted in an artificially heightened 'atmosphere'. Modular agents are individuated, separative, interchangeable and mobile and their associations and institutional affiliations are neither 'total, many-stranded, underwritten by ritual [nor] made stable through being linked to a whole inside set of relationships' (Gellner 1994: 103–4). This is why justice is the superior virtue for Smith: it is rational, dispassionate, predictable, transparent, objectively measurable and enforceable, and yet it does not preclude the potential for a clean exit should the contracting parties desire it.

In contrast to the classical approach – where citizens owe almost everything, including their lives if necessary, to the community – Smith seems to have had a comparatively thin conception of what each citizen owed to the other and to the society in general. In the normal course of daily life market agents owe each other little more than a decent measure of honesty, civility and propriety exercised within a spirit of fair competition and justice. Most importantly, they should respect each others' autonomy and extend reciprocal non-interference, not compassion or benevolence.[23] Justice between individuals consists in mutual forbearance, rather than blind loyalty to a sacramental community, or the exercise of filial or religious piety, beneficent charity or even common-or-garden philanthropy. Similarly, just institutions (especially the state) will avoid interfering with the autonomy and mobility of individual agents which, if left to follow their natural tendencies, will, in orderly fashion, secure their own happiness and prosperity as well as that of the society in general (WN IV.v.b.43). As Smith wrote: 'Little else is requisite to carry a state to the highest degree of opulence from the lowest barbarism, but peace, easy taxes, and a tolerable administration of justice; all the rest being brought about by the natural course of things'.[24] He famously advocated government restraint, limiting legitimate government activity to three functions only: justice, defence and public works. Intrusive and paternalistic forms of governance not only corrupt individual moral character but subvert the prosperity and well-being of nations.

Smith's reservations about the commercial age and the new strangership

It is important to acknowledge that Smith was by no means oblivious to the drawbacks of the commercial age. He recognized the problems of isolation and alienation that accompanied urbanization (WN V.i.g.12), appreciated the alienating effects of the division of labour, thought that commercialism undermined education (LJB, 329–30), and noted that commercial labour involved inequality and even exploitation (WN I.viii.14).[25] But there is no sustained nostalgia for the rude state of comparative equality; the privations of the 'savage' age are contrasted with the 'general security and happiness which prevails in the ages of civility and politeness' (TMS V.2.8–9). Despite Smith's references to the negative aspects of commercialism, he sees them as regrettable but tolerable (and in most cases ameliorable) by-products – even *symptoms* – of material prosperity that could be addressed within existing social arrangements. He ultimately rejects intimate, 'rude' or simple social forms in favour of large scale, non-particularistic communities based on civilized strangership, calculation, 'probity', 'self-interest', contract and impartial justice.[26]

Though it is sometimes suggested that Smith was actually hostile to commercialism[27] and even that he perceived in 'capitalism' the seeds of its own inevitable destruction,[28] it seems clear that he both approved of and was optimistic about its future. Commercial societies are more orderly than their 'rude and barbarous' predecessors and this is mainly due to the diffusion of 'probity and punctuality' that 'always accompan[ies]' the development of commerce. Smith is not suggesting here that commercial society is morally superior to earlier forms; simply that commercial agents are more orderly and pacific because more prudent and circumspect in their dealings with others. In fact, the relative civility of commercial society is all 'reducible to self interest, that general principle which regulates the actions of every man, and which leads men to act in a certain manner from views of advantage … A dealer is afraid of losing his character, and is scrupulous in observing every engagement' (LJB 327). For Smith, as Fonna Forman-Barzilai puts it, 'individual utility calculation sociologically emulated the effects of morality, permitting society to thrive in the absence of genuine love and affection among men and without anachronistic forms of moral policing' (Forman-Barzilai 2000: 405).

The interaction between sympathy and the impartial spectator plays an important role here. Making sympathetic judgements from the standpoint of the impartial spectator allows us to be 'more disciplined, in "command" of ourselves, proper, sociable and polite' (Forman-Barzilai 2005: 207).[29] By this process, observes Knud Haakonssen, we are continually 'weeding out' behaviour that 'is incompatible with social life' (Haakonssen 1989: 58).

Drawing upon the *doux commerce* thesis popularized by Montesquieu (and carefully tracked by Albert O. Hirschman [Hirschman 1977]), Smith argues that commerce is synonymous with (or at least a necessary 'requisite' for) civilization and refinement in the arts, sciences and manners of a people. Indeed, the 'desires of elegance and refinement' are innate and therefore an irresistible spur to industry (LJB 24).[30] The art of prose composition is especially improved under commercialism because it is 'naturally the Language of Business; as Poetry is of pleasure and amusement' (Smith 1983: 137). David Hume, whose optimism about the positive effects of commerce was far less qualified than Smith's, also noted that 'industry and refinements in the mechanical arts' are inevitably accompanied by refinements in the 'liberal' arts. 'The same age, which produces great philosophers and politicians, renowned generals and poets, usually abounds with skilful weavers, and ship carpenters.' Wherever commerce is well established, '[p]rofound ignorance is totally banished, and men enjoy the privilege of rational creatures, to think as well as to act, to cultivate the pleasures of the mind as well as those of the body' (Hume 1987 [1777]: 270–71). The more opulent and refined a civilization, the more industrious, knowledgeable and humane is the culture and the less 'excess[ive]', licentious and self-indulgent are its individual members (Hume 1987 [1777]: 271–72). Dismissing Ferguson's nostalgic picture of an intimate pre-commercial 'knot of friends' united by beneficence and common interest (Ferguson 1996 [1767]: 208), Hume regards the barbarous age as a dreary state of 'solitude' in which each is compelled to live with their fellows in a 'distant manner'. The barren affective climate of pre-commercial life pales in comparison to the coruscating sociality of commercial society where people 'flock into cities [and] love to receive and communicate knowledge' (Hume 1987 [1777]: 270–71).

Commercial society has a number of other benefits to recommend it, says Smith. The entire system of commercialism generates higher levels of liberty and independence for all members of society, including the working poor.[31] Further, the commercial age is the age of greater security, as we have seen. Perhaps most importantly, this stage – and its characteristic mode of production (specialization) – is the source of almost all of the progress and prosperity enjoyed by commercial agents[32] and radically improves the lives of every person, regardless of class location (LJB 26–28).[33] This is significant because, for Smith, the happy society is the prosperous, materially abundant society (TMS I.ii.2.1).[34] Referring to the 'natural joy of prosperity' (TMS III.3.9) he invites his reader to compare the 'serenity' and 'happiness' of the wealthy with the 'misery and distress' of the poor (TMS I.iii.2.1).

Concluding remarks

The social changes that made thinkers like Rousseau and Ferguson so anxious, gave Smith cause for complacency and optimism. Market society – and its typical mode of production, specialization – transforms social interaction dramatically and for the better in a number of ways: it purges relationships of their intensity and potential fearfulness and makes possible less intense but more universal, ubiquitous, diffuse and pacific forms of instrumental association. Pre-commercial friendship and strangership were defined in terms of the problem of security; but now the modern commercial state provides security from external threat and regulates conflict between strangers. Particularistic cleavages are broken down and a more universalistic and moderately civil society established. Since all strangers are now potential contractees or role-pair candidates and not potential enemies, the exchange culture is one of calm amity among distant strangers. The general quantity of trust and goodwill is increased, even though it is of a relatively tepid and diluted quality compared with organic societies.

Smith's vision is basically modern: he describes and endorses a mass society held together by voluntaristic mechanisms, in which the obligatory and total aspects of monolithic institutions like the church, feudal estate, extended family and corporation have been broken down. Independent agents are now self-governed by cool virtues and the conventions of friendly commercial strangership, while their interactions are regulated and sustained by the division of labour, exchange relations and a regular system of justice. Smith embraces the de-personalization and impartiality of the commercializing state, and welcomes a society that is increasingly neutral, impartial, legalistic and inhabited by moderate, tolerant, dispassionate, reasonable and self-governing agents. Such agents will also enjoy more mobility and liberty than has been possible at any other stage of history.

Notes

1 The inspiration for this article comes from Alan Silver's earlier work on the topic. See: Silver 1990: 1474–1504; and Silver 1989: 274–97. The author wishes to thank the anonymous referees for their constructive comments on an earlier version of this article. She also thanks the Australian Research Council whose generous funding made its completion possible, and Kelly McKinley for her able editorial assistance.

2 In Smith's time, Scotland was 'a living museum of stages or modes of existence' while the lowlands were the 'economic wonder region of Europe' (Eriksson 1993: 251–76).

3 Mechanical and organic solidarity refers to 'the distinction drawn by Emile Durkheim (1893) between two types of social solidarity; mechanical … based on the similarity between individuals, the form … predominant in simple. … societies, and organic. … based on the division of labour and complementarities between individuals … ideally occurring in modern advanced societies' (Jary and Jary 1991: 389).

4 For Jeremy Shearmur it means 'the extended liberal social order – akin to Karl Popper's "Open Society"' (Shearmur and Klein 2004: 14).

5 For a full discussion of the concept of interest in moral discourse up to and including the eighteenth century see: Hirschman 1986.

6 See also WN I.xi.g.

7 'The life of a savage, when we take a distant view of it, seems to be a life either of profound indolence, or of great and astonishing adventures' (Smith 1980: 251).

8 'Each man thus lives by exchanging, or becomes in some measure a merchant, and the society itself grows to be what is properly a commercial society' (WN VI.1).

9 See also: LJB 205 and 326.

10 See Perelman 1989: 320–1. Smith also advocated high wages because they encouraged 'the industry of the common people' (WN I.viii.44) and boosted population growth. For a fuller discussion here see: Firth 2002.

11 For further discussion see: Hill 2007: 339–66.

12 For example, seller and buyer, lawyer and client, teacher and pupil, or doctor and patient.

13 For a comparative assessment of Smith's and Rousseau's attitude to modernity, see Ignatieff 1984:108–28.

14 See also TMS VI.ii.2.3.

15 See also TMS VII.ii.3.15; TMS III.5.8.

16 To quote Anthony Giddens (1990: 114). Seligman invites us to distinguish between a premodern 'trust in people' and a modern '*confidence* in system' (Seligman 2000: 19, my emphasis).

17 'Commerce and manufactures can seldom flourish long in any state which does not enjoy a regular administration of justice, in which the people do not feel themselves secure in the possession of their property, in which the faith of contracts is not supported by law, and in which the authority of the state is not supposed to be regularly employed in enforcing the payment of debts from all those who are able to pay' (WN V.iii.7).

18 Clubs were extremely important to the social and intellectual life of Smith's milieu. Though some 'were little more than glorified drinking clubs others were highly formal, highly institutionalized organizations' (Phillipson 1981: 19, 27, 31–2).

19 For a fuller discussion see: Hill 2010.

20 'During his apprenticeship the young man perceives [correctly] that there is no connection between his effort and his reward [as would exist under piecework], and habits of slothfulness and laziness are therefore encouraged' (Rosenberg 1960: 561; WN I.x.c.14–16). The laws of settlement are a similar and therefore unjust restriction on mobility (WN I.x.c.58–9).

21 As Gellner has noted, though not with direct reference to Smith but rather to the ideal liberal agent generally (Gellner 1994: 99–100).

22 Indeed, Smith seems to have anticipated Gellner's (and of course Durkheim's) view that '[t]he modularity of modern man was probably a precondition of the industrial miracle' (Gellner 1994: 103).

23 'In the race for wealth, and honours, and preferments, he may run as hard as he can, and strain every nerve and every muscle, in order to outstrip all his competitors. But if he should justle, or throw down any of them, the indulgence of the spectators is entirely at an end. It is a violation of fair play, which they cannot admit of' (TMS II.ii.2.1).

24 'As reported by Dugald Stewart from a document no longer in existence in his *Account of the Life and Writings of Adam Smith* in his *Collected Works*, ed. Sir William Hamilton, 1858, vol.x, p.68' (Winch 1978: 4 n.2).

25 'The poor labourer who has the soil and the seasons to struggle with, and who, while he affords the materials for supplying the luxury of all the other members of the commonwealth, bears, as it were, upon his shoulders, the whole fabric of human society, sees himself to be buried out of sight in the lowest foundation of the

building' ('Early Draft of Part of the *Wealth of Nations*', in LJ: 564. See also: LJA 26).

26 LJB 303: 528. See also: Berry 1992: 80–2; WN I.ii.3; WN I.ii: 26; and Hill 2007.

27 For example, Vivienne Brown has denied that Smith's discourse constitutes 'the classical statement of liberal capitalism'. Instead, she argues that it 'marks out the moral impatience of Stoic moral philosophy for material goods and worldly ambitions' (Brown 1994: 7).

28 See, for example: Winch 1997: 384–402; Rosenberg 1965: 127–39; Alvey 1998: 1425–41; and Alvey 2003: 1–25.

29 Forman-Barzilai nicely problematizes the relationship in Smith between sympathy and proximity in this article.

30 Montesquieu wrote that 'it is an almost general rule that everywhere there are gentle mores, there is commerce; and everywhere there is commerce, there are gentle mores' (Montesquieu 1990: XX.i: 338).

31 See for example, LJA vi.45–49; and WN III.iv.12.

32 See, for example, WN I.i.10–111.

33 See also WN I.viii.1–2.

34 WN I.Viii.36: 'No society can surely be flourishing and happy of which the far greater part of the members are poor and miserable'.

Bibliography

Alvey, J. (1998) 'Adam Smith's three strikes against commercial society', *International Journal of Social Economics*, 25: 1425–41.

——(2003) 'Adam Smith's view of history: consistent or paradoxical', *History of the Human Sciences*, 16(2): 1–25.

Berry, C. J. (1992) 'Adam Smith and the virtues of commerce', *Nomos*, 34: 69–88.

Boyd, R. (2007) 'Manners and morals: David Hume on civility, commerce, and the social construction of difference', in *David Hume's Political Economy*, C. Wennerlind and M. Schabas (eds), pp. 65–85, London: Routledge.

Brown, V. (1994) *Adam Smith's Discourse*, London: Routledge.

Eriksson, B. (1993) 'The first formulation of sociology: a discursive innovation of the eighteenth century', *Archives Europeennes de Sociologie*, 34: 251–76.

Ferguson, A. (1996) [1767] *An Essay on the History of Civil Society*, F. Oz-Salzberger (ed.), Cambridge: Cambridge University Press.

Firth, A. (2002) 'Moral supervision and autonomous social order: wages and consumption in eighteenth-century economic thought', *History of the Human Sciences*, 15: 39–57.

Forman-Barzilai, F. (2005) 'Sympathy in space(s): Adam Smith on proximity', *Political Theory*, 33: 189–217.

——(2000) 'Adam Smith as a globalization theorist', *Critical Review*, 14: 391–419.

Gellner, E. (1994) *Conditions of Liberty: Civil Society and Its Rivals*, London: Penguin Books.

Giddens, A. (1990) *The Consequences of Modernity*, Stanford, CA: Stanford University Press.

Haakonssen, K. (1989) *The Science of the Legislator*, Cambridge: Cambridge University Press.

Hill, L. (2007) 'Adam Smith, Adam Ferguson and Karl Marx on the division of labour', *Journal of Classical Sociology*, 7: 339–66.

——(2010) 'Adam Smith's cosmopolitanism: the expanding circles of commercial strangership', *History of Political Thought*, 31: 449–73.

Hirschman, A. O. (1986) 'The concept of interest', in *Rival Views of Market Society and Other Recent Essays*, pp. 35–55, New York: Viking.

——(1977) *The Passions and the Interests*, Princeton, NJ: Princeton University Press.

Hume, D. (1987) [1777] 'Of refinement in the arts', in *Essays Moral, Political, Literary*, E. Miller (ed.), Indiana: Liberty Classics.

Ignatieff, M. (1984) *The Needs of Strangers*, London: Chatto and Windus.

Jary, D. and Jary, J. (eds) (1991) *The Collins Dictionary of Sociology*, Glasgow: HarperCollins.

Mizuta, H. (1976) 'Toward a definition of the Scottish Enlightenment', *Studies in Voltaire*, 154: 1459–64.

Montesquieu, C. (1990) *The Spirit of the Laws*, trans. A. M. Cohler, B. C. Miller, and H. M. Stone (eds), Cambridge: Cambridge University Press.

Otteson, J. (2002) *Adam Smith's Marketplace of Life*, Cambridge: Cambridge University Press.

Perelman, M. (1989) 'Adam Smith and dependent social relations', *History of Political Economy*, 21: 312–29.

Phillipson, N. (1981) 'The Scottish Enlightenment', in *The Enlightenment in National Context*, R. Porter and M. Teich (eds), Cambridge: Cambridge University Press, pp. 19–40.

Rosenberg, N. (1990) 'Adam Smith and the stock of moral capital', *History of Political Economy*, 22: 1–17.

——(1965) 'Adam Smith on the division of labour: two views or one?', *Economica*, 33: 127–39.

——(1960) 'Some institutional aspects of the *Wealth of Nations*', *Journal of Political Economy*, 68: 557–70.

Rousseau, J.-J. (1973) [1762] 'A discourse on the moral effects of the arts and sciences', in *The Social Contract and Discourses*, trans. G. D. H. Cole, rev. J. H. Brumfitt and J. C. Hall (eds), London: Dent (Everyman's Library).

Seligman, A. (2000) *The Problem of Trust*, Princeton, NJ: Princeton University Press.

——(1992) *The Idea of Civil Society*, Princeton, NJ: Princeton University Press.

Shearmur, J. and Klein, D. B. (2004) 'Good conduct in a great society: Adam Smith and the role of reputation'. Online. Available HTTP: http://lsb.scu.edu/~dklein/papers/goodConduct.html (accessed 7 September 2005).

Silver, A. (1990) 'Friendship in commercial society: eighteenth-century social theory and modern sociology', *American Journal of Sociology*, 95: 1474–1504.

——(1989) 'Friendship and trust as moral ideals: an historical approach', *European Journal of Sociology*, 30: 274–97.

Smith, A. (1983) *Lectures on Rhetoric and Belles Lettres*, J. C. Bryce (ed.), Oxford: Clarendon Press.

——(1980) 'Letter to the *Edinburgh Review*', in *Essays on Philosophical Subjects*, I. S. Ross (ed.), Oxford: Clarendon Press.

——(1979) *An Inquiry Into the Nature and Causes of the Wealth of Nations*, R. H. Campbell and A. S. Skinner (eds), Oxford: Clarendon Press.

——(1978) *Lectures on Jurisprudence*, R. L. Meek, D. D. Raphael and P. G. Stein (eds), Oxford: Clarendon Press.

——(1976) *The Theory of Moral Sentiments*, D. D. Raphael and A. L. Macfie (eds), Oxford: Clarendon Press.

Stewart, D. (1858) *The Collected Works of Dugald Stewart*, Sir William Hamilton (ed.), Edinburgh: Thomas Constable.

Strasser, H. (1976) *The Normative Structure of Sociology: Conservative and Emancipatory Themes in Social Thought*, London: Routledge and Kegan Paul.

Winch, D. (1997) 'Adam Smith's problem and ours', *Scottish Journal of Political Economy*, 44: 384–402.

——(1978) *Adam Smith's Politics*, Cambridge: Cambridge University Press.

The political economy of recognition

John O'Neill

Smith's often noted ambivalence about commercial society in part turns around claims about the virtues and pathologies of recognition in commercial society. On the one hand, for Smith commercial society is a sphere in which actors mutually recognise each other as independent agents, each acting towards the other neither as benefactor nor as dependent. On the other, he acknowledges particular pathologies of recognition in commercial society: the social invisibility of the poor, the divorce of recognition from its proper object; the absence of limits on the pursuit of goods desired for appearance. For all the ambivalence apparent in the acknowledgement of these pathologies, Smith in the end defends commercial society. He does so partly in response to the contemporary egalitarian criticisms of commercial society in the work of Rousseau.[1] Many of the themes in the debate between Smith and Rousseau reappear in later arguments between defenders of commercial society and their egalitarian critics. Hegel's discussion of civil society as a sphere of mutual recognition, along with his sensitivity to pathologies of misrecognition, echo Smithian themes. The pathologies of recognition are central to later critics of commercial society – in particular the early writings of Marx. So also is a less often noted theme in egalitarian thought – the claim that defenders of commercial society fail to acknowledge unavoidable dependence and the forms of non-commercial networks of social support that this requires.

These classical debates contrast with more recent work on recognition in which the political economy dimensions of recognition have largely disappeared and recognition focuses on the valuation of different identities in the cultural sphere. In the first section, I introduce the significance and distinctiveness of the classical debate on recognition in political economy through a contrast with more recent discussions of recognition and the particular reading of Hegel they assume. In the remainder of the paper, I explore these virtues and pathologies of recognition in more detail. In the second section, I outline Smith's account of commercial society as a sphere in which actors recognise each other as independent agents. In the third section, I examine the pathological forms of recognition and Smith's defence of commercial society in the light of these pathologies. In the fourth section, I consider later egalitarian responses to the pathologies. In the final section, I develop a version of

The Adam Smith Review, 6: 129–151 © The International Adam Smith Society
ISSN 1743-5285, ISBN 0–415–66722–7

the arguments from unacknowledged dependence at more length. A proper understanding of the virtues of independence needs to be more Aristotelian. The virtues of independence need to be contrasted not only with vices of deficiency, but also those of excess, of arrogant self-sufficiency and hubris. Both defenders and many critics of commercial society tend to be blind to the vices of excess.

Recognition and political economy

One of the major influences on recent work on recognition has been Hegel. In much of this recent work, Hegel's account of recognition has been read through a particular identity model, in which recognition and misrecognition tend to be characterised in cultural terms and treated independently of traditional problems of distribution in the economic realm. Questions of recognition and misrecognition have been associated with an identity politics, which is concerned with the ways in which different groups in society have been culturally devalued (O'Neill 2010). More specifically, a particular reading of Hegel's discussion of the master–slave relationship is often taken to be the starting point for this account. The development of full self-consciousness requires mutual recognition: 'They recognize themselves as mutually recognizing one another' (Hegel 1977: para. 184). The failures of mutual recognition involved in the master–slave relationship are taken to provide a general model for the relationship between superordinate and subordinate groups.

> Proponents of the identity model transpose the Hegelian recognition schema onto the cultural and political terrain. They contend that to belong to a group that is devalued by the dominant culture is to be misrecognized, to suffer a distortion in one's relation to one's self.
>
> (Fraser 2000: 109)

Recognition is understood in Hegelian terms – 'identity is constructed dialogically, through a process of mutual recognition' (Fraser 2000: 109). Correspondingly 'to be denied recognition – or to be 'misrecognized' – is to suffer both a distortion of one's relation to one's self and an injury to one's identity' (Fraser 2000: 109).[2]

This reading of Hegel is distant from Hegel's own treatment of the realisation of mutual recognition in modern society. Hegel's work on recognition grounds the conditions for mutual recognition in relations of property and contract in civil society. The pathologies of recognition turn on poverty on the one hand and the unlimited acquisition of goods on the other. In contrast to the picture of his work that dominates much recent discussion of recognition, his work belongs to a tradition of writing in political economy on recognition that goes back to Smith and Rousseau, and leaves its own legacy in subsequent debates between socialist critics and liberal defenders of commercial society.

The central theme in the discussion of lordship and bondage in the *Phenomenology of Mind* – that the full development of self-consciousness requires mutual recognition – reappears initially in the *Philosophy of Right* in the sections on private property and contract. Within the contractual sphere of exchange in civil society, individuals develop an abstract personality as rights-holders.[3] Mutual recognition of personhood is realised through contract. 'Contract presupposes that the parties entering it recognise each other as persons and property owners. It is a relationship at the level of mind objective, and so contains and presupposes from the start the moment of recognition.' (Hegel 1967: 71R) In contractual relations between property owners we enter into relations with each other as self-subsistent rights-holders, who through property have independence and standing. The master–slave relationship reappears in this context (Hegel 1967: 57R) as a failure of mutual recognition of persons as independent persons who are their own property. Slavery involves a failure to recognise an individual as a person, as a self-consciousness 'who takes possession of himself and becomes his own property and no one else's' (Hegel 1967: 57). The achievement of contractual exchange relations between property holders in modern economies is the realisation of mutual recognition of individuals as persons who are rights-holders. This abstract personality realised in civil society is still insufficient. It is in the sphere of citizenship in the state that the full realisation of identity is achieved (Hegel 1967: 260). However, it is a necessary condition for the form of freedom realised in modern society. The market sphere is understood as a sphere in which actors mutually recognise each other as independent rights holders.

The distributive problems of poverty in this context become primarily problems about recognition. Poverty potentially undermines the conditions for achieving independent standing. The difficulties it creates for Hegel are well explored. On the one hand, poverty is taken to be an inevitable consequence of the workings of civil society. However, on the other, the direct alleviation of poverty by welfare payments from public sources of income or the wealthy would lead to a dependency that is incompatible with the principle of civil society: 'the needy would receive subsistence directly, not by means of their work, and this would violate the principle of civil society and the feeling of individual independence and self-respect in its individual members' (Hegel 1967: 245). Central to Hegel's solution is the alleviation of poverty through corporations based on particular skills. Since membership of the association already involves recognition of an individual's standing, corporations can alleviate poverty without a loss of independence and self-respect. In a corporation 'his nexus of capability and livelihood is a *recognised* fact, with the result that the Corporation member needs no external marks beyond his own membership as evidence of his skill and his regular income and subsistence, i.e. as evidence that he is a somebody' (Hegel 1967: 253 emphasis in the original). Through the associations of skill that form corporations, aid no longer involves an absence of recognition.[4] There are problems with Hegel's solution even on Hegel's own terms. Thus, Hegel himself notes that those who are most vulnerable to poverty, unskilled day labourers, are excluded from corporations (Hegel 1967: 252A).

The passages on corporations also introduce a distinct pathology of recognition in commercial society. Recognition associated with membership of a corporation is contrasted with the forms of recognition pursued by those in civil society who are members of no association of skill and who gain instead recognition through the acquisition of market goods. The pursuit of goods for such recognition is without limits: '[H]is isolation reduces his business to mere self-seeking ... Consequently, he has to try to gain recognition for himself by giving external proofs of success in his business, and to these proofs no limits can be set' (Hegel 1967: 253A).

The view of commercial society as a sphere of mutual recognition does not start with Hegel. Neither does the appreciation of the relationship between the distribution of material goods and forms of misrecognition. While the language in which the debate is conducted shifts,[5] the themes are central to the work of the classical political economists that formed the basis of Hegel's account of civil society, in particular the work of Smith.[6] An understanding of commercial society as a sphere in which actors mutually recognise each other as independent agents of standing is already to be found in Smith.[7] So also is the acknowledgement of the pathologies of recognition in commercial society.

Commerce, recognition and dependence

Consider Smith's much quoted passage about the limits of benevolence of commercial society in *The Wealth of Nations*:

> It is not from the benevolence of the butcher, the brewer, or the baker that we expect our dinner, but from their regard to their own interest. We address ourselves, not to their humanity but to their self-love, and never talk to them of our own necessities but of their advantages. Nobody but a beggar chooses to depend chiefly upon the benevolence of his fellow-citizens.
>
> (WN I.II)

The passage makes two distinct claims which are central to Smith's account of commercial society. The first is a negative claim that is developed in *The Theory of Moral Sentiments* and is standard in commentaries – that commercial society is consistent with the limited benevolence we can expect in the wider communities of strangers (TMS VI.ii.1). Bonds of benevolence cannot be expected to extend to or be extended from the local communities of families and friends to the wider 'assembly of strangers' with whom our lives are related (TMS I.i.4.9). Through market exchange, individuals who are not directly motivated by concern for each others' needs can still serve each others' necessities.

> Society may subsist among different men, as among different merchants, from a sense of its utility, without any mutual love or affection; and though no man in it should owe any obligation, or be bound in gratitude to any other, it may still be upheld by a mercenary exchange of good offices according to an agreed valuation.
>
> (TMS II.ii 3.2)

The rules and sentiments of justice governing negative responsibilities to avoid harming others are a necessary condition for this social order. However, sentiments of beneficence are not necessary conditions for society.

The second claim of the passage concerns not self-love and benevolence, but rather a related theme that emerges in the final sentence, that of dependence and independence. To call chiefly on the benevolence of others is to render oneself dependent upon them. In contrast, to appeal to their advantage is to approach others as an independent agent among other independent agents. Agents in commercial society do not engage with others though 'servile and fawning attention to obtain their good will' (WN I.II.2), but rather though exchange as independent property holders. The argument here for commercial society turns not merely on the negative point that market exchange is consistent with limited benevolence. It is rather the positive point that by stripping away reliance on the gift of others, the market fosters social independence:

> Nothing tends so much to corrupt and enervate and debase the mind as dependency, and nothing gives such noble and generous notions of probity as freedom and independency. Commerce is one great preventative of this custom.
>
> (LJ vi.6.)

Commercial society realises the Stoic virtues of independence and self-sufficiency: 'Every man, as the Stoics used to say, is first and principally recommended to his own care; and every man is certainly, in every respect, fitter and abler to take care of himself than of any other person' (TMS VI. ii.1.1). Through market relations we recognise others as independent agents of standing, towards whom we act neither as benefactor nor as dependent. Agents are recommended to their own care and we mutually recognise each other as individuals who are best able to care for themselves.

The claim that commercial society fosters these virtues of independence is central to Smith's account of the achievements of commercial society over pre-modern societies in *The Wealth of Nations*:

> commerce and manufactures gradually introduced order and good government, and with them, the liberty and security of individuals, among the inhabitants of the country, who had before lived almost in a continual state of war with their neighbours and of servile dependency upon their

> superiors. This, though it has been the least observed, is by far the most important of all their effects.
>
> (WN III.IV.4)

Markets free individuals from the forms of dependency that the gift in pre-commercial economies involves. In pre-commercial society the poor are rendered dependent on the wealthy through the power of patronage and gift.[8] Commercial society breaks these ties of personal dependence. Through exchange and the division of labour, the interdependence of individuals is disassociated from personal dependence. Since the income of each worker is not tied to that of any particular individual, the ties that the rich previously exercised over their workers is broken. 'Though [the wealthy person] contributes, therefore, to the maintenance of them all, they are all more or less independent of him, because generally they can all be maintained without him' (WN III.IV.11).[9] The division of labour mediated by exchange relations is taken to allow the combination of the interdependence of individuals through the division of labour in the production of the necessities and luxuries of life with social independence.

The pathologies of recognition

Smith's account of commercial society as a sphere of independent agents who mutually recognise each other as such is combined with an appreciation of particular pathological forms that the desire for differential recognition can take within commercial society.[10] Commercial society is also a sphere in which individuals seek differential standing and attempt to gain recognition of having a particular rank among others of equal rank. The desire for recognition in this differential sense is taken to be the psychological drive for the accumulation of wealth in commercial society. The desire for respect and standing, rather than to satisfy bodily needs, moves the accumulation of wealth.

> Though it is in order to supply the necessities and conveniencies of the body, that the advantages of external fortune are originally recommended to us, yet we cannot live long in the world without perceiving that the respect of our equals, our credit and rank in the society we live in, depend very much upon the degree in which we possess, or are supposed to possess, those advantages. The desire of becoming the proper objects of this respect, of deserving and obtaining this credit and rank among our equals, is, perhaps, the strongest of all our desires, and our anxiety to obtain the advantages of fortune is accordingly much more excited and irritated by this desire, than by that of supplying all the necessities and conveniencies of the body, which are always very easily supplied.
>
> (TMS VI.i.3)

Smith takes the desire for differential recognition of having a particular rank to be the source of growth in commercial society. However, at the same time the desire corrupts the character and is the source of central vices that mark commercial society. Smith's ambivalence towards commercial society in part turns on the conflict between the civilising effects of accumulation and the independence of the labourer on the one hand and the corrupting consequences of desire for differential recognition for its own sake on the other. The poor are not properly recognised, wealth not virtue becomes the object of recognition, and the desire for recognition through the display of wealth is pursued without limits.

Poverty

Consider first the problem of poverty. The claim that markets are spheres of mutual recognition for Smith as for Hegel faces a problem in the existence of poverty – of those without property who are excluded from the sphere of recognition. The social invisibility of the poor is a theme that runs through the work of Smith: 'The poor man goes out and comes in unheeded, and when in the midst of the crowd is in the same obscurity as if shut up in his own hovel' (TMS I.iii.2.1: 51). Hence Smith's social account of the necessaries of life as those goods that are minimally required to give them social standing within a particular society: 'By necessaries I understand, not only the commodities which are indispensably necessary for the support of life, but whatever the custom of the country renders it indecent for creditable people, even of the lowest order, to be without' (WN V.11.k: 869). At the same time the centrality of the Stoic value of independence underpins Smith's own rejection of the traditional view that claims of need gave rights to call upon the property of others. The priority of the virtues of self-command over claims of need reveals Smith's Stoicism at its strongest.[11]

The social invisibility of the poor for Smith is understood in the context of a wider problem of misrecognition in commercial society, that is the divorce of recognition from its proper object. The obverse of the social invisibility of the poor is the social recognition that wealth draws to itself. The desire for the differential recognition that wealth brings that ultimately drives accumulation in commercial society. Hence the following oft quoted passage:

> For to what purpose is all the toil and bustle of this world? What is the end of avarice and ambition, of the pursuit of wealth and power, and preeminence? Is it to supply the necessities of nature? The wages of the meanest labourer can supply them ... From whence, then, arises that emulation which runs through all the different ranks of men, and what are the advantages which we propose by that great purpose of human life which we call bettering our condition? To be observed, to be attended to, to be taken notice of with sympathy, complacency and approbation, are all the advantages which we can propose to derive from it. It is vanity,

> not the ease, or the pleasure, which interests us. But vanity is always founded upon the belief of our being the object of attention and approbation. The rich man glories in his riches, because he feels that they draw upon him the attention of the world …
>
> (TMS I.iii.2.1: 50)

The vanity that moves the desire for accumulation involves a mistaken desire for recognition for its own sake divorced from features of character for which recognition is properly deserved.

The divorce of recognition from its proper object

Central to the moral theory of Smith's *The Theory of Moral Sentiments* is the distinction between 'the love of praiseworthiness' and 'the love of praise'. To desire to be praiseworthy is to desire those characteristics for which praise is owed: 'to be that thing which, though it should be praised by nobody, is, however, the natural and proper object' (TMS III.2.1). The desire for praise itself is properly parasitic on the desire for praiseworthiness: it is a good where it confirms our worth and it can only do so where we believe that those who proffer praise are themselves competent to do so:

> Their praise necessarily confirms our own self-approbation. Their praise necessarily strengthens our sense of our own praiseworthiness. In this case, so far is the love of praiseworthiness from being derived altogether from that of praise: that the love of praise seems, at least in a great measure, to be derived from that of praiseworthiness.
>
> (TMS III.2.3)

Vanity is defined as the love of praise for its own sake, divorced from this relationship to the characteristics that deserve praise: 'To be pleased with groundless applause is a proof of the most superficial levity and weakness. It is what is properly called vanity … ' (TMS III.2.4). Vanity is recognition for its own sake, divorced from independent worth.

Both the attention accorded to the wealthy and the social invisibility of the poor are based then on forms of misrecognition. They are the same time both the driving force of accumulation and the principal cause of the corruption of the moral sentiments. Its corrupting influence lies in the divorce of recognition from its proper object.

> The disposition to admire, and almost to worship, the rich and powerful, and to despise, or at least, to neglect persons of poor and mean condition, though necessary to establish and to maintain the distinction of ranks and order of society, is, at the same time, the great and most universal cause of corruption of our moral sentiments. That wealth and greatness are often regarded with the respect and admiration which are

> due only to wisdom and virtue; and that the contempt, of which vice and folly are the only proper objects, is often most unjustly bestowed upon poverty and weakness …
>
> (TMS I.iii.3.1)

The mistake lies in a confusion of sentiments where the respect that is owed to real excellences of character is mistakenly transferred to a different object.

> The respect which we feel for wisdom and virtue is, no doubt, different from that which we conceive for wealth and greatness; and it requires no very nice discernment to distinguish the difference. But notwithstanding that difference, those sentiments bear a very considerable resemblance to one another. In some particular features they are, no doubt, different, but, in the general air of the countenance, they seem to be so very nearly the same, that inattentive observers are very apt to mistake the one for the other.
>
> (TMS I.iii.3.3)

Smith's arguments about the divorce of recognition from its proper object draw on a theme about the confusion of appearance and real character that appears in Rousseau's *A Discourse on Inequality.* On Rousseau's account of the origins of inequality, a crucial moment in the fall from original independence and freedom occurs at the point at which the individual starts to see himself in the eyes of others and where appearance is consequently divorced from character:

> To be and to appear to be, became two things entirely different; and from this distinction arose imposing ostentation, deceitful guile, and all the vices which attend them. Thus man, from being free and independent, became by a multitude of new necessities subjected in a manner, to all nature, and above all to his fellow creatures, whose slave he is in one sense even while he becomes their master; rich, he has occasion for their services; poor, he stands in need of their assistance; and even mediocrity does not enable him to live without them.
>
> (Rousseau *Discourse on Inequality*, Smith translation, 'Letter to the Edinburgh Review', in *Essays on Philosophical Subjects*, p. 119).

The translation of Rousseau here is that of Smith, and one can see in the distinction between being and appearance at least one source of his account of the corrupting influence of the disposition to admire riches. The upshot for Rousseau is the loss of the virtues of independence. Smith takes the argument in a different direction.

Smith is not a Rousseauian egalitarian. While the conflict between the corruption of the sentiments on the one hand and the maintenance of ranks and order and the accumulation of wealth on the other runs through

The Theory of Moral Sentiments, in the end it is decided in favour of the latter.

> Nature has wisely judged that the distinction of ranks, the peace and order of society, would rest more securely upon the plain and palpable difference of birth and fortune, than upon the invisible and often uncertain difference of wisdom and virtue. The undistinguishing eyes of the great mob of mankind can well enough perceive the former: it is with difficulty that the nice discernment of the wise and the virtuous can sometimes distinguish the latter.
>
> (TMS VI.ii.1.21)

The errors have their origin in human psychology, in our cognitive limits to properly discern virtue on the one hand and in our psychological dispositions with respect to joy and sorrow on the other. It is in virtue of 'our propensity to sympathize with joy is much stronger than our propensity to sympathize with sorrow' (TMS I.iii.1.5) that our admiration for wealth ultimately arises: 'It is because mankind are disposed to sympathize more entirely with our joy than with our sorrow, that we make parade of our riches, and conceal our poverty' (TMS I.iii.2.1).

The failures of proper recognition are in the end for the best: 'The peace and order of society, is of more importance than even the relief of the miserable' (TMS VI.ii.1.21). The mistake that underpins the disposition to admire the rich and powerful is corrupting but 'necessary to establish and to maintain the distinction of ranks and order of society'.

Moreover the forms of misrecognition engendered by wealth lead in the end to the improvement in the human condition:

> The pleasures of wealth and greatness, when considered in this complex view, strike the imagination as something grand and beautiful and noble, of which the attainment is well worth all the toil and anxiety which we are so apt to bestow upon it … It is this deception which rouses and keeps in continual motion the industry of mankind. It is this which first prompted them to cultivate the ground, to build houses, to found cities and commonwealths, and to invent and improve all the sciences and arts, which ennoble and embellish human life; which have entirely changed the whole face of the globe, have turned the rude forests of nature into agreeable and fertile plains, and made the trackless and barren ocean a new fund of subsistence, and the great high road of communication to the different nations of the earth.
>
> (TMS IV.1.9–10)

As the editors of the Glasgow edition of *The Theory of Moral Sentiments* note, the passage echoes Smith's own earlier translation of another passage from Rousseau's *A Discourse on Inequality*:

> But from the instant in which one man had occasion for the assistance of another, from the moment that he perceived that it could be advantageous to a single person to have provisions for two, equality disappeared, property was introduced, labour became necessary, and the vast forrests of nature were changed into agreeable plains, which must be watered with the sweat of mankind, and in which the world beheld slavery and wretchedness begin to grow up and blosom with the harvest.
>
> (Rousseau, DI, translated by Smith, EPS: 252)

Smith's invocation of the consequences of misrecognition inverts the critical force of Rousseau's arguments. The passage that appears in the opening of the paragraph that ends in appeal to the metaphor of the invisible hand makes its appearance as a link between the 'natural selfishness and rapacity' of the rich and the realisation of 'nearly the same distribution of the necessaries of life, which would have been made, had the earth been divided into equal portions among all its inhabitants' (TMS IV.1.10). Smith's attitude to commercial society is ambivalent – but the ambivalence in the end is resolved in a defence of commercial society.[12] The same ambivalence and the same resolution are evident in his account of the limitless nature of the acquisition of goods in commercial society.

The absence of limits

A central theme in a number of traditions of classical philosophy which Smith takes up in *The Theory of Moral Sentiments* is the limit to the goods a person requires for well-being. The claim is made thus by Epicurus: 'Natural wealth is both limited and easy to acquire. But wealth [as defined by] groundless opinions extends without limits' (Epicurus, *Principal Doctrines* 15, Inwood and Gerson 1988: 27). To desire goods without limit is a mistake founded upon false beliefs:

> The stomach is not insatiable as the many say, but rather the opinion that the stomach requires an unlimited amount of filling is false.
>
> (Epicurus, *Vatican Sayings* 59, Inwood and Gerson 1988: 31)

Smith in *The Theory of Moral Sentiments* echoes Epicurus's claims:

> It is to no purpose, that the proud and unfeeling landlord views his extensive fields, and without a thought for the wants of his brethren, in imagination consumes himself the whole harvest that grows upon them. The homely and vulgar proverb, that the eye is larger than the belly, never was more fully verified than with regard to him. The capacity of his stomach bears no proportion to the immensity of his desires, and will receive no more than that of the meanest peasant.
>
> (TMS IV.1.10; cf. WN I.xi.c.7)

The unlimited desires of the wealthy are founded upon an error about the goods that are required for happiness. The goods required for happiness, properly understood, are limited.

In the Aristotelian tradition and an important thread in civic republicanism, the arguments about limits were tied to a criticism of commercial society. The discussion of limits is introduced in the context of the influential distinction in book I of the *Politics* between two modes of acquisition: the economic associated with the household economy, and the chrematistic associated with the market economy. The forms of economic acquisition with the household are recognisably limited: '[T]he amount of household property which suffices for a good life is not unlimited, nor of the nature described by Solon in the verse "There is no bound to wealth stands fix for men". There is a bound fixed … ' (Aristotle, *Politics*, book 1, ch. 8). The forms of acquisition that aim to meet needs that are characteristic of the household economy are contrasted with the forms of acquisition that are characteristic of the commercial world in which wealth is pursued for its own sake. It is within the particular institutional setting of the market that acquisition appears to lack limits: 'There is no limit to the end it seeks; and the end it seeks is wealth of the sort we have mentioned [i.e. wealth in the form of currency] and the mere acquisition of money' (Aristotle, *Politics*, book 1, ch. 8). Within this tradition the claim that the wealth required for a good life is limited is tied to a criticism of commercial society. Its spread leads to the mistaken acquisition of goods without limit.

Smith's employment of the argument about limits departs significantly from this tradition. In Smith the error is a benign one. It leads indirectly to the improvement of welfare and the distribution of wealth to the poor. Hence the appeal to the invisible hand in the passage that follows the discussion of limits in *The Theory of Moral Sentiments*:

> The rich only select from the heap what is most precious and agreeable. They consume little more than the poor, and in spite of their natural selfishness and rapacity, though they mean only their own conveniency, though the sole end which they propose from the labours of all the thousands whom they employ, be the gratification of their own vain and insatiable desires, they divide with the poor the produce of all their improvements. They are led by an invisible hand to make nearly the same distribution of the necessaries of life, which would have been made, had the earth been divided into equal portions among all its inhabitants, and thus without intending it, without knowing it, advance the interest of the society, and afford means to the multiplication of the species.
>
> (Smith TMS IV.1.10; cf. WN I.xi.c.7)

Again the classical argument that the acquisition of goods without limit in market society is founded upon error is turned back in a defence of commercial society. The desire for appearance associated with wealth leads to the general improvement of the human condition and the independence of the worker.[13]

Egalitarian responses

Smith's defence of commercial society treats the economy as a sphere of recognition. In commercial society, actors mutually recognise each other as independent agents. At the same time, the desire for recognition takes pathological forms: the poor go unrecognised; recognition does not track its proper object in virtue; goods desired for recognition are accumulated without limit. However, the vices associated with misrecognition drive the civilising effects of commercial society. For all Smith's ambivalence, he is offering a defence of commercial society, including from the egalitarian criticisms of Rousseau. At the same time they also leave his defence of commercial society vulnerable to internal empirical and normative objections. Empirically it is far from obvious that commercial society has the distributional consequences he claims for it – even his own analysis in *The Wealth of Nations* does not sustain the strong claims he makes in these passages of *The Theory of Moral Sentiments* that the invisible hand leads to 'nearly the same distribution of the necessaries of life, which would have been made, had the earth been divided into equal portions among all its inhabitants'. Normatively, his account involves a systematic tension between the corrupting effects of such forms of misrecognition that move accumulation and beneficial consequences that might flow from it, which opens up a space for egalitarian criticism (O'Neill 1998: ch. 4).

While it would be too strong to talk of a Smithian legacy in subsequent work on political economy and recognition, it is the case that many of the themes that Smith addresses are pursued in later writing on the subject. I have already noted some of the parallels with Hegel's work. Civil society as a sphere of mutual recognition, the problems of poverty, the pursuit of goods without limits for the sake of recognition in markets, all of these themes reappear in Hegel. However, there are significant differences. Hegel's response to the problems has an associational dimension that is noticeably absent in Smith. The corporations as associations of skill provide a form of recognition that is tied to skills and capacities that are properly recognised as against the limitless acquisition of external goods. The associations are taken to remove humiliation from the alleviation of poverty – although, as we noted earlier, the solution fails on Hegel's own terms. There is nothing in Smith that corresponds to this associational form of recognition that Hegel describes. Smith was deeply sceptical of the kinds of association within the economy to which Hegel's solution appeals. Professional associations, trade associations, and guilds are treated primarily as conspiracies against the public, concerned with the pursuit of sectional interests at the expense of those of consumers. They represent barriers to the free movement of labour, particularly through the practice of the extended apprenticeship. 'It is to prevent [the] reduction of price, and consequently of wages and profit, by restraining free competition which would most certainly occasion it, that all corporations … have been established' (WN I.x.c.17).

It is not just in Hegel's work that we see Smith's themes pursued, but also in subsequent egalitarian responses to market society. The social invisibility of the poor and the divorce of recognition from its proper object form the starting point for a significant strand of egalitarian thought which inverts Smith's position. Marx's account of alienation, for example, in part turns on the separation of appearance and real character in commercial society. Character founded on the actual dispositions, skills, and relationships an individual has is divorced from the social identity defined by what can be bought: 'The properties of money are my, the possessor's properties and essential powers. Therefore what I *am* and what I *can do* is by no means determined by my individuality' (Marx 1974: 377). The promise of communism on this account is that it closes the gap of appearance and real worth:

> If we assume *man* to be *man*, and his relation to the world to be a human one, then love can only be exchanged for love, trust for trust, and so on … Each of your relations to man – and to nature – must be a *particular expression* corresponding to the object of your will, of your *real individual* life.
>
> (Marx 1974: 379)

Questions about the divorce of recognition from character are also to be found in the very different moral economy tradition of writers such as Tawney. The need to properly recognise persons 'for what people are' rather than 'for what they own' is taken to provide a ground for economic equality (Tawney 1964: 87). Equality in economic and social standing is a condition for differential recognition to track real virtues.[14]

Similarly, criticism of the limitless nature of the goods pursued in commercial society has remained a significant line of argument amongst critics of commercial society. The Aristotelian version of the argument is developed in a structural form in Marx's (1970) account of the absence of limits on expansion of capital accumulation (Marx, *Capital* I: ch. 4). Specific questions of social recognition and limits have been central to more recent discussions that have focused on the self-defeating nature of the collective pursuit of goods desired for differential social recognition. The pursuit of positional goods that signal status and relative standing is self-defeating since their worth to a person is affected by the consumption of the same goods by others. The promise to each individual that a good will make them better off will not be realised, since collective consumption of that good will mean that no one will be better off (Hirsch 1977). Increased income and consumption is not matched with any increase in life satisfaction in market societies (Lane 2001).[15]

The arguments around the pathological forms of recognition for differential standing that Smith identifies remain important themes in consequent egalitarian thought and remain central to current debates on the limits to growth. One source of the continuing power of the debates lies in the tensions that Smith identifies between the benefits of accumulation and the corrupting consequences of misrecognition in commercial society. One central Smithian argument for resolving the tension in the direction commercial society lies in the claim that commercial society is not just the condition for accumulation but also for social independence (Rasmussen 2006b). In the final section, I want to return to the core claim found in Smith: that commercial society is a social order in which independent agents mutually recognise each other as such.

Independence and the problem of unacknowledged dependence

For Smith a central achievement of commercial society lies in its fostering of the virtues of social independence. Agents do not relate to each other through 'servile and fawning' demands on the benevolence of others or through 'servile dependency upon their superiors'. In commercial society agents recognise each other as independent agents of standing, each able to look after their own interests. These achievements of commercial society are again echoed in later social theory. Hegel's defence of commercial society turns on the mutual recognition of independent standing of agents as rights-holders. Later socialist theorists, and Marx in particular, accept this account of the achievements of commercial society: 'In the money relation, in the developed system of exchange … the ties of personal dependence … are in fact exploded, ripped up. … and individuals *seem* independent' (Marx 1973: 163). For Marx this dependence is in the end illusory, in the sense that agents remain in a state of 'objective dependency' on the impersonal workings of market.[16] Moreover, the worker, while independent of any individual capitalism, is dependent on the employment of some capitalist. However, for all these limits Marx concurs with the classical political economists in celebrating the ways in which commercial society liberates individuals from personal dependence.

Marx's arguments concern the conditions for social independence. There is a distinct line of egalitarian thought that is concerned rather with the characterisation of the virtues of independence that is assumed by liberal defenders of commercial society. Various forms of unavoidable dependence are unacknowledged (MacIntyre 1999). The result is a mischaracterisation of the virtues of independence, self-sufficiency and autonomy. One way of capturing the point is Aristotelian. The virtues are typically characterised in terms of contrast with vices of deficiency. Independence is contrasted with dependence. Autonomy is contrasted with heteronomy. The vices of excessive dependence on others, the defects of heteronomy, can and should be recognised as vices. However, the virtues of the autonomous character need to be contrasted not only with vices of deficiency, but also those of excess. The point is made thus by Benson:

> The virtue of autonomy is a mean state of character with regard to reliance on one's own powers in acting, choosing and forming opinions. The

> deficiency is termed heteronomy, and there are many terms which may be used to describe the heteronomous person, some of which suggest specific forms of the vice: credulous, gullible, compliant, passive, submissive, overdependent, servile. For the vice of excess there is no name in common use, but solipsism might do, or arrogant self-sufficiency.
>
> (Benson 1983: 5)

Benson's point that there is no term for the vices of excess is a telling one. The existence of these vices is often unrecognised and, as I have argued elsewhere, often celebrated as virtues (O'Neill 1998: chs 5–7). Forms of human dependence and the limits of self-sufficiency go unacknowledged.

MacIntyre presses the charge of failure to acknowledge dependence against Smith in particular (MacIntyre 1999: chs 1 and 10). Smith is taken to assume the standpoint of 'self-sufficiently superior'. He is 'unable to give due recognition to affliction and to dependence' (MacIntyre 1999: 7). However, in choosing Smith as his antagonist to develop his account of the virtues of acknowledged dependence and their relation to the virtues of independence, MacIntyre does not choose well. His account depends upon a somewhat caricatured account of Smith. Smith's account of the virtues of independence and self-sufficiency display his customary ambivalence to commercial society. On the one hand, he does acknowledge the necessary existence of 'affliction and dependence'. On the other, he concedes and ultimately defends the ways in which commercial society develops on the basis of self-deception about its existence.

Smith's core account of independence is sensitive to the limits of human self-sufficiency and dependence. Smith's claims about the development of personal independence afforded by commercial society are married with a recognition of the inescapable fact of human dependence that is grounded in our biological nature: 'All the members of human society stand in need of each others assistance, and are likewise exposed to mutual injuries' (TMS II.ii.3.1). Mutual dependence is a consequence of our biological frailties that even wealth and social power cannot in the end overcome. We enter the world in complete dependence on others: 'In the natural state of things … the existence of the child, for some time after it comes into the world, depends altogether upon the care of the parent' (TMS VI.ii.1.3). Further, in passages that MacIntyre himself cites, Smith acknowledges that we spend periods of life, and usually exit the world, in a similar condition of dependence.

> In the languor of disease and the weariness of old age, the pleasures of the vain and empty distinctions of greatness disappear … Power and riches appear then to be, what they are, enormous and operose machines contrived to produce a few trifling conveniences to the body, consisting of springs the most nice and delicate, which must be kept in order with the most anxious attention. … They keep off the summer shower, not the winter storm, but leave him always as much, and sometimes more

> exposed than before, to anxiety, to fear, and to sorrow; to diseases, to danger, and to death.
>
> (TMS IV.1.8)

However, while Smith clearly acknowledges that all agents are dependent upon others, he takes commercial society to depend upon agents being self-deceived about the limits of their self-sufficiency.

The development of commercial society relies on a form of self-deception in which the truths of this 'splenetic philosophy' go unrecognised.

> But though this splenetic philosophy, which in time of sickness or low spirits is familiar to every man, thus entirely depreciates those great objects of human desire, when in better health and better humour, we never fail to regard them under a more agreeable aspect. ... The pleasures of wealth and greatness ... strike the imagination as something grand and beautiful and noble, of which the attainment is well worth all the toil and anxiety which we are so apt to bestow upon it ... It is this deception which rouses and keeps in continual motion the industry of mankind.
>
> (TMS IV.1.9–10)

As elsewhere, Smith displays an ambivalence that is in the end resolved in a defence of commercial society. The error is a happy one. The passages on unacknowledged dependence appear in the lead-up to the invisible hand. This self-deception has socially beneficial outcomes – the improvement of the condition of the poor.

There is a current of egalitarian thought which is contemporaneous with Smith that runs in the opposite direction to Smith's about the benign nature of the self-deception involved in commercial society. A good society is one which starts from the premises of splenetic philosophy – in the acknowledgement of mutual vulnerability and dependence. One theoretical expression of this line of argument is to be found in Rousseau's *Emile*:

> Why have kings no pity on their people? Because they never expect to be ordinary men. Why are the rich so hard on the poor? Because they have no fear of becoming poor. Why do the nobles look down upon the people? Because a nobleman will never be a commoner ... So do not train your pupil to look down from the height of his glory upon the sufferings of the unfortunate, the labours of the wretched, and do not hope to teach him to pity them as long as he considers them as far removed from himself. Make him clearly thoroughly aware of the fact that the fate of these unhappy persons may one day be his own, that his feet are standing on the edge of an abyss, into which he may be plunged at any moment by a thousand unexpected irresistible misfortunes ...
>
> (Rousseau 1911, *Emile*, Book IV: 185)

Rousseau, in defending these claims, starts from a strong assumption about the nature of the emotion of pity, that the belief that a like calamity could befall oneself is constitutive of the emotion of pity. The passage opens with the maxim: 'we never pity another's woes unless we may suffer in like manner ourselves' (ibid.). The claim that pity is constituted by the possibility that like woes could befall one is not original to Rousseau. Versions of the claim are defended, for example, by Aristotle and Hobbes.[17] However, while it might be contingently true that the possibility of calamity may foster the emotion of pity, it is not at all obvious that the belief is a necessary condition for the emotion. The counter-examples offered by Smith have some force: 'A man may sympathize with a woman in child-bed; though it is impossible that he should conceive of himself as suffering her pains in his own proper person and character' (TMS VII.iii.1.4). There maybe some epistemic limits on fellow-feeling in cases like this. Imagination is not a substitute for the direct experience of a particular condition for which one feels fellow-feeling. However, the possibility of compassion or pity as such is not ruled out. Similarly to return to Rousseau's example, while kings, the rich, and nobleman may seldom feel pity for those in a subordinate position, it is possible for them to do so.

There is, however, a distinct claim that an egalitarian like Rousseau might make here that concerns the social meaning of attitudes of pity. Consider the distinction that Rousseau draws in these passages of *Emile* between the expression of pity in contexts in which vulnerabilities are equally distributed, and those in which they are not. Pity in a social context in which 'tomorrow, any one may himself be in the same position as the one he assists is in today' (Rousseau 1911, *Emile*: Book IV: 185) is contrasted with the context in which the benefactor does not share the same vulnerabilities. Expressions of pity take on different social meanings in the different contexts. In conditions of equality in vulnerability, expressions of pity can be understood as expressions of solidarity or fellow feeling. In conditions of inequality it cannot be thus understood and hence can take on properties of condescension and charity. On the one hand, the benefactor appears to 'look down from the height of his glory upon the sufferings of the unfortunate', and on the other, the beneficiary is transformed into an object of a sympathetic gaze from above.

The assumption of an equality of vulnerabilities as a basis for proper expressions of fellow feeling underpins the forms of mutualist egalitarianism that were developed in the institutions of mutual aid that developed in the eighteenth- and nineteenth-century working-class communities (Thompson 1968: ch. 12; cf. Tawney 1964: 40ff. and Titmuss 1967). Hence something close to what Smith characterises as splenetic philosophy finds a formal expression in the rules of the unions, benefit and friendly societies of the period. In the Rules and Orders of the Honourable Society of Workington, February 2nd, 1792, one finds the following:

> When we look upon mankind as being subject to an innumerable train of evils and calamities, resulting either from pain or sickness, or the

> infirmities of old age, which render them unable to procure even a scanty subsistence, when at the same time they are made capable of the noblest friendship, common prudence induces us so to form ourselves into society, that the insupportable condition of the individual may, by the mutual assistance and support of the whole, become tolerable …
>
> (cited in Gray 2001)

Or consider again the following from the Rules of the Sociable Society in Newcastle, 1812:

> We, the members of this society, taking into our serious consideration, that man is formed a social being … in continual need of mutual assistance and support; and having interwoven in our constitutions those humans and sympathetic affections which we always feel at the distress of our fellow creatures …
>
> (cited in Thompson 1968: 461)

In conditions of equality of vulnerability, acknowledged dependence on others and the receipt of assistance are not associated with the asymmetries of power or the loss of social standing as an independent agent which Smith properly criticises as features of patronage in pre-commercial society. In conditions of equality, the existence and recognition of common vulnerability to evil and calamity robs the fact of dependency of its potentially humiliating condition. The argument remains an important strand of egalitarian thought.

None of this is to deny the virtues of social independence. Nor is it to deny the vices of servile dependency that Smith properly criticises in pre-commercial society. It is, however, to criticise a particular conception of those virtues of independence in which they are contrasted only with vices of deficiency and ignore vices of excess that leave the facts of dependence unacknowledged. Smith, of all the theorists of commercial society, is at the same time both sensitive to the existence of dependence and of the ways in which commercial society develops on the basis of self-deception about its existence. As with his discussion of the pathologies of recognition, Smith's ambivalence is a strength of his account which at the same time leaves his defence of commercial society open to internal criticism. This ambivalence is part of the enduring interest of his work, for critics as well as defenders of commercial society.

The problems of addressing needs in a world of strangers in a way that does not humiliate the recipients and undermine their social independence remain central to public policy (Titmuss 1966, 1967; Ignatieff 1990; Wolff 1998; O'Neill 2006b). An appreciation of those problems requires an understanding of the economy as a sphere of recognition and of the ways in which social recognition is tied to different distributions of goods within the economy. They are questions that are obscured by accounts of recognition that treat it as a purely cultural problem and accounts of distributional justice that abstract from questions of social standing and respectful treatment. Whatever view is ultimately taken of his answers, the problems of recognition that Smith addressed retain their importance. Many still stand in need of institutional solutions.[18]

Notes

1 For recent discussions of the relationship between Smith and Rousseau see Force (2003), Hanley (2008) and Rasmussen (2006a).

2 For Fraser's own critical response to this account of recognition see Fraser (1995, 2000) and Fraser and Honneth (2003). I discuss her response in O'Neill (2010).

3 'Personality essentially involves the capacity for rights and constitutes the concept and the basis (itself abstract) of the system of abstract and therefore formal right. Hence the imperative of right is: "Be a person and respect others as persons"' (Hegel 1967: 35).

4 'Within the Corporation the help which poverty receives loses its accidental character and the humiliation wrongfully associated with it. The wealthy perform their duties to their fellow associates and thus riches cease to inspire either pride or envy, pride in their owners, envy in others. In these conditions rectitude obtains its proper recognition and respect' (Hegel 1967: 253R).

5 In particular, the term 'recognition' itself is one that becomes prevalent after Hegel. It is not the term that is used in Smith's writing on the themes discussed in this paper.

6 For a detailed discussion of the relation of Hegel and Smith, see Waszek (1988).

7 There is more clearly a general sense in which the picture of the self as constituted by mutual recognition is also shared by Smith. Moral identity is constituted through seeing ourselves through the eyes of others we ourselves recognise as moral agents:

> Were it possible that a human creature could grow up to manhood in some solitary place, without any communication with his own species, he could no more think of his own character, of the propriety or demerit of his own sentiments and conduct, of the beauty or deformity of his own mind, than of the beauty or deformity of his own face. All these are objects which he cannot easily see, which naturally he does not look at, and with regard to which he is provided with no mirror which can present them to his view. Bring him into society, and he is immediately provided with the mirror which he wanted before.
>
> (Smith 1759: III.1.3)

For a useful discussion see Griswold (1999: ch. 2).

8 '[The great proprietor] is at all times … surrounded with a multitude of retainers and dependants, who, having no equivalent to give in return for their maintenance, but being fed entirely by his bounty, must obey him … Before the extension of commerce and manufacture in Europe, the hospitality of the rich, and the great, from the sovereign down to the smallest baron, exceeded everything which in the present times we can easily form a notion of' (WN III.IV.5–6).

9 The wage worker is 'more or less' independent. The independence is not complete. In the *Wealth of Nations* Smith makes much of the distinction between the fully independent artisan and the dependent servant and wage-worker (WN I.viii.48). In entering the wage contract the worker lays down a portion of 'his ease, his liberty, and his happiness' (WN I.v.7).

10 For a useful discussion see Khalil (1996).

11 Smith follows Cicero on the limits of claims of need to the property of others:

> for one man to take from another and to increase his own advantage at the cost of another's disadvantage is more contrary to nature than death, than poverty, than pain and than anything else that may happen to his body or external circumstances.
>
> (Cicero, *On Duties*, III.21).

Smith explicitly echoes the Cicero's claim:

> The poor man must neither defraud nor steal from the rich, though the acquisition might be much more beneficial to the one than the loss could be hurtful to the other. The man within immediately calls to him, in this case too, that he is no better than his neighbour, and that by this unjust preference he renders himself the proper object of the contempt and indignation of mankind; as well as of the punishment which that contempt and indignation must naturally dispose them to inflict, for having thus violated one of those sacred rules, upon the tolerable observation of which depend the whole security and peace of human society. There is no commonly honest man who does not more dread the inward disgrace of such an action, the indelible stain which it would for ever stamp upon his own mind, than the greatest external calamity which, without any fault of his own, could possibly befal him; and who does not inwardly feel the truth of that great stoical maxim, that for one man to deprive another unjustly of any thing, or unjustly to promote his own advantage by the loss or disadvantage of another, is more contrary to nature, than death, than poverty, than pain, than all the misfortunes which can affect him, either in his body, or in his external circumstances.
>
> (TMS III.ch.3)

For a discussion of these claims see Salter (1999). For a more general discussion of the status of claims of necessity in *The Wealth of Nations* see Hont and Ignatieff (1983). For a contrasting view to the one presented here see Fleischacker (2004: ch. 10).

12 For a contrasting view of how Smith resolves the ambivalences in his attitudes to commercial society see Brown (1994).

13 For a discussion of these themes see Winch (1996).

14 I discuss these egalitarian responses in more detail in O'Neill (1998: ch. 4).

15 The argument has been taken to offer grounds for the possibility of decoupling increased consumption from improving well-being (Jackson 2009). I discuss the difference between Epicurean and Aristotelian versions of this claim in O'Neill (2006a and 2008).

16 Compare Kant:

> [M]oney makes one independent, one gains respect by the possession of it; one has worth, needs no one and depends on no one. But in making us independent of others, money in the long run makes us dependent on itself; it frees us from others in order to enslave us.
>
> (Kant 1979: 177)

17 Pity may be defined as a feeling of pain caused by the sight of some evil, destructive or painful, which befalls one who does not deserve it, and which we might expect to befall ourselves or some friend of ours, and moreover to befall us soon.

(Aristotle, *Rhetoric* II.8 85b12ff.)

> *Griefe*, for the Calamity of another, is PITTY; and ariseth from the imagination that the like calamity may befall himselfe; and therefore is called also COMPASSION, and in the phrase of this present time a FELLOW-FEELING …
>
> (Hobbes, *Leviathan* I.6: 126)

18 An earlier version of the paper was read at *Adam Smith on the Conditions of a Moral Society*, University of Oslo, Norway, 27–29 August 2009. I would like to thank the participants at that conference for their comments and criticisms. I would also particularly like to thank Richard Christian, Russell Keat, Terry Peach and John Salter for their comments and conversations on earlier versions of the paper. The paper benefited a great deal from the reading group on *The Theory of Moral Sentiments* that met at Manchester University, 2008–9. It also benefited from the helpful comments of the journal's editors and referees.

Bibliography

Aristotle (1946) *Rhetoric*, W. Roberts (trans.), Oxford: Clarendon Press.

——(1948) *Politics*, E. Barker (trans.), Oxford: Clarendon Press.

Benson, J. (1983) 'Who Is the Autonomous Man?' *Philosophy* 58: pp. 5–17.

Brown, V. (1994) Adam Smith's Discourse: Canonicity, Commerce, and Conscience, London, Routledge.

Cicero (1991) *On Duties*, M. T. Griffin and E. M. Atkins (eds), Cambridge: Cambridge University Press.

Fleischacker, S. (2004) *On Adam Smith's* The Wealth of Nations*: A Philosophical Companion*, Princeton, NJ: Princeton University Press.

Force, P. (2003) *Self-Interest Before Adam Smith: A Genealogy of Economic Science*, Cambridge: Cambridge University Press.

Fraser, N. (1995) 'From Redistribution to Recognition? Dilemmas of Justice in a "Post-Socialist" Age', *New Left Review* I, 212: pp. 69–93.

——(2000) 'Rethinking Recognition', *New Left Review* II, 3: pp. 107–20.

Fraser, N. and Honneth, A. (2003) *Redistribution or* Recognition*? A Political-Philosophical Exchange*, London: Verso.

Gray, P. (2001) *A Brief History of Friendly Societies*, http://web.archive.org/web/20011225144332/http://www.afs.org.uk/research/researchpgrayhistorypage.htm

Griswold, C. (1999) *Adam Smith and the Virtues of the Enlightenment*, Cambridge: Cambridge University Press.

Hanley, R. P. (2008) 'Commerce and Corruption: Rousseau's Diagnosis and Adam Smith's Cure' *European Journal of Political Theory* 7: pp. 137–58.

Hegel, G. (1967) *Philosophy of Right*, T. Knox (trans.), Oxford: Oxford University Press.

——(1977) *Phenomenology of Spirit*, A. Miller (trans.), Oxford: Oxford University Press.

Hirsch, F. (1977) *Social Limits to Growth*, London: Routledge and Kegan Paul.

Hobbes, T. (1968) *Leviathan*, Harmondsworth: Penguin.

Hont, I. and Ignatieff, M. (1983) 'Needs and Justice in *The Wealth of Nations*', in I. Hont and M. Ignatieff (eds) *Wealth and Virtue: The Shaping of Political Economy in the Scottish Enlightenment*, pp. 119–36, Cambridge: Cambridge University Press.

Ignatieff, M. (1990) *The Needs of Strangers*, London: Hogarth Press.

Inwood, B. and Gerson, L. (eds) (1988) *Hellenistic Philosophy*, Indianapolis: Hackett.

Jackson, T. (2009) *Prosperity Without Growth?* London: Earthscan.

Kant, I. (1979) *Lectures on Ethics*, London: Methuen.

Khalil, E. (1996) 'Respect, Admiration, Aggrandizement: Adam Smith as Economic Psychologist', *Journal of Economic Psychology* 17: pp. 555–77.

Lane, R. (2001) *The Loss of Happiness in Market Democracies*, New Haven, CT: Yale University Press.

MacIntyre, A. (1999) *Dependent Rational Animals*, London: Duckworth.
Marx, K. (1970) *Capital I*, London: Lawrence and Wishart.
——(1973) *Grundrisse*, Harmondsworth: Penguin.
——(1974) *Economic and Philosophical Manuscripts*, L. Colletti (ed.) *Early Writings*, Harmondsworth: Penguin.
O'Neill, J. (1998) *The Market: Ethics, Knowledge and Politics*, London: Routledge.
——(2006a) 'Citizenship, Well-being and Sustainability: Epicurus or Aristotle?' *Analyse und Kritik* 28: pp. 158–72.
——(2006b) 'Need, Humiliation and Independence', in S. Reader (ed.) *The Philosophy of Need: Royal Institute of Philosophy Supplement, 57*, Cambridge: Cambridge University Press.
——(2008) 'Living Well Within Limits: Well-being, Time and Sustainability', Thinkpiece for the Sustainable Development Commission, available at: www.sd-commission.org.uk/publications/downloads/John_ONeil_thinkpiecel.pdf
——(2010) 'Recognition and the Market', *Renewal* 19: pp. 13–22.
Rasmussen, D. (2006a) 'Rousseau's "Philosophical Chemistry" and the Foundations of Adam Smith's Thought', *History of Political Thought* 27: pp. 620–41.
——(2006b) 'Does "Bettering Our Condition" Really Make Us Better Off? Adam Smith on Progress and Happiness', *The American Political Science Review* 100: pp. 309–18.
Rousseau, J. J. (1911) *Emile*, B. Foxley (trans.), London : Dent.
Salter, J. (1999) 'Sympathy with the Poor: Theories of Punishment in Hugo Grotius and Adam Smith', *History of Political Thought* 20: pp. 205–24.
Smith, A. [1756] (1982) 'Letter to the Edinburgh Review', in *Essays on Philosophical Subjects*, Indianapolis: Liberty Press.
——[1759] (1982) *The Theory of Moral Sentiments*, Indianapolis: Liberty Press.
——[1762–64] (1982) *Lectures on Jurisprudence*, Indianapolis: Liberty Press.
——[1776] (1981) *An Inquiry into the Nature and Causes of the Wealth of Nations*, Indianapolis: Liberty Press.
Tawney, R. (1964) *Equality*, London: Unwin.
Titmuss, R. [1965] (1987) 'Social Welfare and the Art of Giving', in *The Philosophy of Welfare: Selected Writings of Richard M. Titmuss*, B. Abel-Smith and K. Titmuss (eds), London: Allen and Unwin.
——[1966] (1987) 'Social Policy and Economic Progress', in *The Philosophy of Welfare: Selected Writings of Richard M. Titmuss*, B. Abel-Smith and K. Titmuss (eds), London: Allen and Unwin.
——[1967] (1987) 'Universal and Selective Social Services', in *The Philosophy of Welfare: Selected Writings of Richard M. Titmuss*, B. Abel-Smith and K. Titmuss (eds), London: Allen and Unwin.
——(1987) *The Philosophy of Welfare: Selected Writings of Richard M. Titmuss*, B. Abel-Smith and K. Titmuss (eds), London: Allen and Unwin.
Thompson, E. P. (1968) *The Making of the English Working Class*, Harmondsworth: Penguin.
Waszek, N. (1988) *The Scottish Enlightenment and Hegel's Account of Civil Society*, Dordrecht: Kluwer.
Winch, D. (1996) *Riches and Poverty*, Cambridge: Cambridge University Press.
Wolff, J. (1998) 'Fairness, Respect, and the Egalitarian Ethos', *Philosophy and Public Affairs* 27: pp. 97–122.

Two for one?

Reciprocity in Seneca and Adam Smith

Jon Elster

Introduction

In recent behavioral economics, the idea of *strong reciprocity* has become central, both as an explanans and as an explanandum. On the one hand, it is used to *account for altruistic behavior* in experimental and non-experimental settings. On the other hand, it is explained as the *outcome of natural selection* possibly operating at the group level. In the development of these arguments, the work of Ernst Fehr and his network of collaborators has been especially important.

In this paper I look at some of the antecedents of this work in *The Theory of Moral Sentiments*. This work examines both the role of negative reciprocity, or resentment, and that of positive reciprocity, or gratitude. I shall also discuss the writings of Seneca, notably *On Anger* and *On Benefits*, which deal with respectively negative and positive reciprocity. The book *On Mercy* is also relevant with regard to punishment. Adam Smith was deeply influenced by the Stoics, devoting more than 20 pages of TMS to their philosophy. Although he does not often cite Seneca, and never (in TMS) these two works, we may assume he was familiar with them. I shall not, however, make a strong argument for an influence of Seneca on the treatment of reciprocity in TMS. Rather, by drawing attention to some striking similarities and equally striking differences between the two writers I believe we can get TMS into better focus.

We can look at the phenomena of resentment and gratitude from two different perspectives. First, from a normative point of view, what is the proper degree of these emotions and, especially, of the actions they inspire? When someone has hurt you, how much should you hurt the offender in return? When someone has helped you, how much should you help the benefactor in return? Second, from a positive point of view, what are the spontaneous action tendencies (Frijda 1987) of these emotions? (There is also a subsidiary set of normative questions: if someone punishes too harshly or returns too little, compared to the normative standard, what punishment – if any – would be appropriate?) Seneca and Adam Smith address both the normative and the positive questions. By contrast, behavioral economics has not explicitly addressed the question of the appropriate degree of retaliation for an offense

The Adam Smith Review, 6: 152–171 © The International Adam Smith Society
ISSN 1743-5285, ISBN 0-415-66722-7

or return for an act of benevolence. I believe, however, that there may be some implicit pointers.

I shall proceed as follows. I first discuss Seneca in the second section, then Adam Smith (third section), to conclude (fourth section) by suggesting some connections between their work and current behavioral economics. In an Appendix I discuss Smith's treatment of negative reciprocity in his *Lectures on Jurisprudence.*

Seneca[1]

Seneca was a playwright as well as a philosopher. His revenge plays, notably *Thyestes*, had an immense influence on the Elizabethan revenge tragedies. In particular, the sentence 'Scelera non ulcisceris, nisi vincis' – *a wrong not exceeded is not avenged* – was the direct inspiration of many plays of the period (Mercer 1987). This sentence suggests that the spontaneous action tendency of anger is not 'an eye for an eye' but 'impose a greater harm than the one you suffered' or, in a shorthand expression, 'two eyes for an eye'.

In his philosophical and normative writings, however, Seneca was an anti-retributivist. Citing Plato (*Laws* XI, 934 A), he writes that 'A sensible person does not punish a man because he has sinned, but in order to keep him from sin; for while the past cannot be recalled, the future may be forestalled' (*On Anger* I. 19). More generally, he makes a distinction between the appropriate reactions of the Prince to offenses against himself (second-party punishment) and reactions to offenses against others (third-party punishment). In his opinion, the Prince ought to show *more clemency towards offenders against himself* than towards offenders against third parties (*On Mercy* I. 20). Concerning the punishment of third parties, he distinguishes three reasons: 'either to reform the man that is punished, or by punishing him to make the rest better, or by removing bad men to let the rest live in greater security' (ibid.: I. 22). The second of these reasons, as Seneca makes clear elsewhere (*On Anger* I. 19), is that of general deterrence. The third corresponds to the idea of incapacitation.

In a more general statement, Seneca first draws a contrast between positive and negative reciprocity and then a distinction within the second category:

> 'But of course there is some pleasure in anger', [his interlocutor says], 'and it is sweet to return a harm'. Not at all; for it is not honorable, as in acts of kindness to requite benefits with benefits, so to requite injuries with injuries. […] 'Revenge' is an inhuman word and yet one accepted as legitimate, and 'retaliation' is not much different except in rank [*ordine*]; the man who returns a harm commits merely the more pardonable sin.
>
> (*On Anger* II. 32)

According to one authority (Veyne 1993: 148) 'retaliation' here refers to *lex talionis*, 'an eye for an eye'. By contrast, revenge would be closer to 'two eyes for an eye'. Seneca rejects both, but finds the former more excusable. Elsewhere (*On Mercy* I. 7) he excuses private revenge on the grounds that an offended individual 'is afraid of being scorned, and, when one is injured, the failure to make requital seems a show of weakness, not of mercy'.

Seneca also offers several tests to distinguish between desires inspired by anger and those grounded in judgment. Emotions abate quickly whereas reason is constant (*On Anger* I. 17). Hence if you delay action, and 'the delay produces no change, that proves that we were obeying our judgment, not anger' (ibid.: III. 12). Another test relies on the inappropriately personal nature of anger: it 'does not merely wish the hated person to be harmed, but to harm him' (ibid.: III. 5). A reasonable person would be indifferent with regard to the agent of punishment, and might even prefer that someone else punish the one who harmed him. A third test relies on the tendency of anger to cloud the mind and therefore to undermine the very end it seeks. 'No passion is more eager for revenge than anger, and for that very reason is unfit to take it; being unduly ardent and frenzied, as most lusts are, it blocks its own progress to the goal toward which it hastens' (ibid.: I. 12). This is why, for instance, 'Pyrrhus, the most famous trainer for gymnastic contests, made it a rule, it is said, to warn those whom he was training against getting angry; for *anger confounds art* and looks only for a chance to injure' (ibid.: I. 14; my italics). Also, anger may undermine instrumental rationality by inducing wishful thinking: 'rather than choosing easy tasks [the angry man] wishes to find easy the tasks he chooses' (ibid.: III. 7).

In the main Seneca wants punishment to be a matter for the courts. By contrast, he rejects the idea of having gratitude enforced by the laws. Except for Macedonia, he claims, 'in no state has the ungrateful man become liable to prosecution' (*On Benefits* III. 6). In fact, ingratitude 'is the only crime for which we have provided no law, as if Nature has taken sufficient precautions against it' (ibid.: IV. 17). These precautions, it turns out, consist in the natural attractions of virtue. Elsewhere, however, Seneca affirms that the ungrateful are the object of 'public hate', constantly 'under the public eye or believing themselves to be so' (ibid.: III. 17), and suggests that no punishment could be worse.

One reason for leaving ingratitude to the spontaneous ostracism of the citizens is the risk of giving publicity to ingratitude by penalizing it.

> 'More men', you say, 'will become ungrateful if no action can be brought against ingratitude'. No, fewer men, because benefits will be given with a greater discrimination. Then, too, it is not advisable that all men should know how many are ungrateful, for the multitude of the offenders will remove the shame of the thing, and what is a general reproach will cease to be a disgrace.
>
> (ibid.: III. 16)

Another reason is that to assess the degree of ingratitude, one first has to determine the value of the gift. The latter, however, is highly context-dependent in a way that defies codification (ibid.: III. 7). A third reason is the difficulty of establishing the correct relation between the value of the gift and the severity of punishment for ingratitude. While a punishment smaller than the benefit would seem unjust, a punishment equal to the gift would, contrary to moral intuition, compel the death penalty for a person who was ungrateful towards the person who saved his life (ibid.: III. 10).

Although the law may be unable to determine the value of the gift, the recipient presumably knows what it was worth to him. Hence the question arises: how much should he return? Speaking broadly (and too precisely), the recipient should return two for one. He is not

> merely to equal, but to surpass in deed and spirit those who have placed us under obligation, for he who has a debt of gratitude to pay never catches up with the favor unless he outstrips it; the [donor] should be taught to make no record of the amount, the [recipient] to feel indebted for more than the amount.
>
> (*On Benefits* I. 4)

Moreover,

> I must be far more careful in selecting my creditor for a benefit than a creditor for a loan. For to the latter I shall have to return the same amount that I have received, and, when I have returned it, I have paid all my debt and am free; but to the other I must make an additional payment.
>
> (Ibid.: II. 18)

As the second passage makes clear, the demand to return more than you received does not reflect the need to pay interest.

Hence the *normative analysis of gratitude* and the *positive analysis of resentment* lead to the same conclusion: the norm or the tendency to return two for one. As we saw, the *normative analysis of resentment* as a retributive emotion denies it any validity at all, although the *lex talionis* (one-for-one) is somewhat excusable in private matters. Seneca also offers some elements towards a *positive analysis of gratitude*, such as the observations on the spur of public contempt. He also notes that gratitude is more likely to be forthcoming if the gift is a durable one, which will constantly, by its presence, remind the recipient of the benefit he received (*On Benefits* I. 12, III. 2).

Seneca insists on the importance of intention in the target agent in anger as well as in gratitude. Although sheer frustration of our desires may cause 'mock anger, like that of children who, if they fall down, want the earth to be thrashed' (*On Anger* I. 2), it is not really anger. There is also mock anger when 'we see the people grow angry with gladiators, and so unjustly deem it an offence that they are not glad to die' (ibid.: I. 3).

Conversely, real anger can arise simply because we know that another person wants to hurt us, even if no actual harm has been done (ibid.). Similarly for gratitude:

> There is a great difference between the matter of a benefit and the benefit itself; and so it is neither gold nor silver nor any of the gifts which are held to be most valuable that constitutes a benefit, but merely the good will of him who bestows it.
>
> (*On Benefits* I. 5)

In fact, I owe gratitude to an attempt to benefit me that failed (ibid.), but not to a benefit that I received by accident (ibid.: VI. 7).

These distinctions reflect traditional distinctions with regard to wrongdoings. Just as deliberately inflicting harm 'adds insult to injury', the intentional bestowing of a benefit causes two goods: 'a material good and an act of good will' (ibid.: VII. 15). In fact, the donor takes pleasure both from the good of the recipient and from knowing that he is the one to cause it (ibid.: II. 22). Each of the goods separately calls for gratitude. Good will is repaid with a show of a pleasure for the gift (ibid.: II. 23); the material gift with a (greater) material gift. Seneca asks whether an expression of thankfulness might not be enough to repay both debts if the recipient is unable to return the gift, and replies as follows:

> In the case of every question, let us keep before us the public good; *the door must be closed to all excuses*, to keep the ungrateful from taking refuge in them and using them to cover their repudiation of the debt. 'I have done all in my power', says he. Well, keep on doing so. Tell me, do you suppose that our forefathers were so foolish as not to understand that it was most unjust to consider a man who wasted in debauchery or gambling the money he had received from a creditor to be in the same class with one who lost the borrowed property along with his own in a fire, or by robbery, or some other major mishap? Yet they accepted no excuses in order to teach men that a promise must be kept at all costs; in their eyes it was better that a few should not find even a good excuse accepted than that all should resort to excuse.
>
> (Ibid.: VII. 16; my italics)

One might think, though, that a mere verbal expression of gratitude might be sufficient in the following kind of case: 'If I have rescued a friend from pirates, and afterwards a different enemy seized him and shut him up in prison, he has been robbed, not of my benefit, but of the enjoyment of my benefit' (ibid.: I. 5). To my knowledge, Seneca does not address the issue whether the friend is under an obligation to reimburse me for the ransom I paid in my unsuccessful attempt to rescue him.

Adam Smith[2]

In *The Theory of Moral Sentiments*, Adam Smith proposes two separate ideas of reciprocity. The first is the standard one: 'To reward, is to compensate, to remunerate, to return good for good received. To punish, too, is to recompense, though in a different manner; it is to return evil for evil that has been done' (TMS III.i.1.2). The second idea is expressed in the following passage:

> As every man doth, so shall it be done to him, and *retaliation seems to be the great law which is dictated to us by Nature*. Beneficence and generosity we think due to the generous and beneficent. Those whose hearts never open to the feelings of humanity, should, we think, be shut out, in the same manner, from the affections of all their fellow-creatures, and be allowed to live in the midst of society, *as in a great desert where there is nobody to care for them, or to inquire after them*. The violator of the laws of justice ought to be made to feel himself that evil which he has done to another; and since no regard to the sufferings of his brethren is capable of restraining him, he ought to be over-awed by the fear of his own. The man who is barely innocent, who only observes the laws of justice with regard to others, and merely abstains from hurting his neighbours, can merit only that his neighbours in their turn should respect his innocence, and that the same laws should be religiously observed with regard to him.
>
> (TMS II.ii.1.10; my italics)

Setting punishment aside for a moment, these two passages make two very different propositions about benevolence, i.e. doing good to others. First, 'To him who does good to others, good will be returned.' Second, 'To him who does no good to others, no good will be done.' We spontaneously tend to *avoid* those who violate the norms of beneficence, just as we tend to *punish* those who violate the norms of justice. However, since being ostracized – 'to live as in a great desert' – is a horrible fate, it can also be seen as punishment in a broad and collective sense. It is, as it were, civic death by a thousand cuts.

Hence reward has two antonyms: punishment (in the strict and narrow sense) and avoidance (an aspect of punishment in a broad sense). Avoidance is the action tendency of contempt, the emotion triggered by the belief that another person is intrinsically inferior or worthless. Although the many references to contempt in TMS do not seem to reflect a unitary concept, the following passage suggests something like the idea of living in a 'great desert':

> Human virtue is superior to pain, to poverty, to danger, and to death; nor does it even require its utmost efforts do despise them. But to have its misery exposed to insult and derision, to be led in triumph, to be set up for the hand of scorn to point at, is a situation in which its constancy is

> much more apt to fail. Compared with the contempt of mankind, all other external evils are easily supported.
>
> (TMS I.iii.2.11)

As we shall see shortly, contempt can sustain the desire to punish. As we have just seen, it can sustain ostracism of those who do not benefit others. Although Adam Smith does not say so, it seems reasonable that contempt might also sustain ostracism of those who fail to return the benefits of others. *Lack of proper resentment, lack of beneficence and lack of gratitude may all trigger contempt.*

Consider now resentment. Most of the time Adam Smith uses 'resentment' for a generic concept with two separate species:

> The insolence and brutality of *anger*, in the same manner, when we indulge its fury without check or restraint, is, of all objects, the most detestable. But we admire that noble and generous resentment which governs its pursuit, of the greatest injuries, not by the rage which they are apt to excite in the breast of the sufferer, but by the *indignation* which they naturally call forth in that of the impartial spectator.
>
> (TMS I.i.5.2; my italics)

Although there are some exceptions to this usage, I shall ignore them. The substantial point is that Adam Smith distinguishes consistently between resentment as the spontaneous emotion of the victim of wrongdoing and resentment from the perspective of an outside observer. Descartes (1978: §65), who to my knowledge was the first to make this distinction, referred to these emotions as *colère* and *indignation* respectively. Remarkably, and perhaps not accidentally, Smith uses the very same terms. As in the following passage, 'indignation' is often referred to as 'just': 'this just indignation is nothing but anger restrained and properly attempered to what the impartial spectator can enter into' (TMS VI.iii.9).

Exactly how do anger and indignation differ? There is both a qualitative and a quantitative difference. Qualitatively, the emotion is transformed by the internalization of the impartial spectator. Quantitatively, it is attenuated so as to call for a punishment that is 'proportionable' (TMS II.i.4.4) to the offending action. That remark, however, prompts the question, proportional to what? The only hint comes from a manuscript passage, not reproduced in the published version, which refers to 'improper punishment, punishment which is either not due at all or *which exceeds the demerit of the Crime*' (TMS 390; my italics). I suggest, therefore, that proper punishment corresponds to the *lex talionis*, 'an eye for an eye', and improper or excessive punishment to 'two eyes for an eye'.

The idea of proportional punishment, however defined, reflects the idea of merit-based or backward-looking retributive justice. Adam Smith's friend David Hume, by contrast, adopted a utilitarian – forward-looking – argument for punishment. As emphasized by the editors of the Glasgow edition of *The Theory of Moral Sentiments*, Adam Smith 'found himself in a cleft stick' on this issue (TMS p. 394). The counter-example that got him into trouble was that of the sentinel who falls asleep on his post:

> A centinel, for example, who falls asleep upon his watch, suffers death by the laws of war, because such carelessness might endanger the whole army. This severity may, upon many occasions, appear necessary, and, for that reason, just and proper. When the preservation of an individual is inconsistent with the safety of a multitude, nothing can be more just than that the many should be preferred to the one. Yet this punishment, how necessary soever, always appears to be *excessively severe*. The *natural atrocity* of the crime seems to be so little, and the punishment so great, that it is with great difficulty that our heart can reconcile itself to it. Though such carelessness appears very blamable, yet the thought of this crime *does not naturally excite any such resentment, as would prompt us to take such dreadful revenge*. A man of humanity must recollect himself, must make an effort, and exert his whole firmness and resolution, before he can bring himself either to inflict it, or to go along with it when it is inflicted by others. It is not, however, in this manner, that he looks upon the just punishment of an ungrateful murderer or parricide. His heart, in this case, applauds with ardour, and even with transport, the just retaliation which seems due to such detestable crimes, and which, if, by any accident, they should happen to escape, he would be highly enraged and disappointed. The very different sentiments with which *the spectator* views those different punishments, is a proof that *his approbation of the one is far from being founded upon the same principles with that of the other*. He looks upon the centinel as an unfortunate victim, who, indeed, must, and ought to be, devoted to the safety of numbers, but whom still, in his heart, he would be glad to save; and he is only sorry, that the interest of the many should oppose it. But if the murderer should escape from punishment, it would excite his highest indignation, and he would call upon God to avenge, in another world, that crime which the injustice of mankind had neglected to chastise upon earth.
>
> (TMS II.ii.3.11; my italics)

Adam Smith's general strategy in TMS is to argue that actions – including punishments – that are not directly motivated by the general good, nevertheless tend to serve it. 'Nature, *antecedent to all reflections upon the utility of punishment*, has in this manner stamped upon the human heart, in the strongest and most indelible characters, an immediate and instinctive approbation of the sacred and necessary law of retaliation' (TMS II.i.3.1; my italics). Or again,

> Though man, therefore, be naturally endowed with a desire of the welfare and preservation of society, yet the Author of nature has not entrusted it

> to his reason to find out that a certain application of punishments is the proper means of attaining this end; but has endowed him with *an immediate and instinctive approbation* of that very application which is most proper to attain it.
>
> (TMS II.i.5.9; my italics)

In the case of the sentinel, however, we have to apply *reason* to find the proper degree of punishment.

The paradox, then, is that the impartial spectator may sometimes impose less severe punishment than what we spontaneously tend to require, and sometimes more severe. Or to put it differently, the requirements of unrestrained passion and those of utility might coincide, and both stand in opposition to the ideal of passion tempered by reason. If the natural tendency of passion is to require two eyes for an eye, a utilitarian might, on a given occasion, reach the same conclusion. For instance, even if more-than-proportionate reprisals are against the laws of war, they might be justified on utilitarian grounds. In the reminder of the paper (except in the Appendix) I shall disregard utilitarian arguments for punishment and consider only the backward-looking tendency to punish, whether tempered or not by an impartial attitude.

In addition to the indirect benefits to society of resentment, Adam Smith cites 'the utility of those passions to the individual, by rendering it dangerous to insult or injure him' (TMS I.ii.3.4). He would seem to deny, however, that these 'remote effects' (ibid.) enter into the motivations of revenge. Although Adam Smith cites tit-for-tat arguments for retaliation (among states) in the *Wealth of Nations* (WN IV.2), they are absent from TMS.

The (proper degree of) spontaneous punishment also constitutes a norm. One may be ostracized for failing to take revenge:

> How many things are requisite to render the gratification of resentment completely agreeable, and to make the spectator thoroughly sympathize with our revenge? The provocation must first of all be such that we should become *contemptible*, and be *exposed to perpetual insults, if we did not, in some measure, resent it.*
>
> (TMS I.II.3.8; my italics)

Adam Smith here reflects the codes of honor that we usually associate with Mediterranean countries, where failure to take revenge triggers the most violent contempt (Elster 1999: 234). Although Adam Smith at one place says that '*resentment is not disapproved of*' when 'brought down to the level of the sympathetic indignation of the spectator' (TMS II.1.5.6; my italics), he also holds the stronger view that *not resenting an affront is disapproved of.*

Whereas a person who reacts too weakly to an insult is subject to the contempt of his fellow citizens, one who reacts too much is the proper object of their resentment. A 'too violent resentment [i.e. anger], instead of carrying us along with it, becomes itself the object of our resentment and *indignation*' (TMS II.i.5.9; my italics). Logically, anger might itself be the object of anger, that is, of excessive resentment. Adam Smith does not mention this case. He does mention, however, that because resentment is 'excessive a hundred times for once that it is moderate', we tend to consider it 'odious and detestable' even when it is in fact of an appropriate degree (TMS ibid.).

Before proceeding to the role of gratitude in TMS, let me compare Seneca and Adam Smith on the topic of resentment. Both distinguish between excessive revenge ('two eyes for an eye') and proper (TMS) or excusable (Seneca) retaliation ('one eye for an eye'). To distinguish between them, Seneca appeals to 'the test of time' and other criteria, whereas Adam Smith appeals to the approval of the impartial spectator. Both note the role of social norms in triggering revenge. Adam Smith defends and Seneca rejects (with the 'excusable' modification) a retributive justification of punishment. Seneca defends and Adam Smith rejects (with the 'sentinel' modification) a proximate consequentialist justification. Adam Smith argues that punishment for retributive motives nevertheless has an ultimate explanation and justification in terms of consequences.

I shall now consider some aspects of the treatment of gratitude in TMS, beginning with the relation between gratitude and benevolence. Conceptually, a previous act of benevolence is a *condition* for an act of gratitude. A somewhat ambiguous statement may be read as saying that the expectation of gratitude is also the *motive* of benevolence: 'Nature […] exhorts mankind to acts of beneficence by the pleasing consciousness of deserved reward' (TMS II.ii.3.3). Later, it is said that gratitude is merely the *effect* of disinterested benevolence:

> Nature […] renders every man the peculiar object of kindness, to the persons to whom he himself has been kind. […] No benevolent man ever lost altogether the fruits of his benevolence. If he does not always gather them from the persons from whom he ought to have gathered them, he seldom fails to gather them, and with a tenfold increase, from other people.
> (TMS VI.ii.1.19)

In the discussion leading up this claim, however, the cause of benevolence is sympathy, rather than 'the pleasing consciousness of deserved reward'. Because of the vague nature of the first statement, not too much should be made of this apparent inconsistency. It seems clear, though, that nature shapes the attitudes of the dispensers of benevolence, of the recipients, and of third parties. Just as the non-benevolent person is generally avoided, the benevolent one is generally rewarded.

In the continuation of the first passage, Adam Smith asserts that Nature

> *has not thought it necessary to guard and enforce the practice of [beneficence] by the terrors of merited punishment in case it should be neglected.*

> It is the ornament which embellishes, not the foundation which supports the building, and which it was, therefore, sufficient to recommend, but by no means necessary to impose. Justice, on the contrary, is the main pillar that upholds the whole edifice. […] In order to enforce the observation of justice, therefore, Nature has implanted in the human breast that consciousness of ill-desert, those terrors of merited punishment which attend upon its violation, as the great safe-guards of the association of mankind, to protect the weak, to curb the violent, and to chastise the guilty.
>
> (TMS II.ii.3.3; my italics)

The italicized statement is correct if we think of punishment in the narrow sense, but not, as we saw, if we take it in a wider sense that also includes avoidance with the concomitant loss of welfare. While Adam Smith does not think the law would be an appropriate instrument for enforcing benevolence, he does not even raise the question whether gratitude could be so enforced. Nor, as noted, does he mention the plausible idea that gratitude, like benevolence, could be enforced by social norms.

He does, however, make an important normative claim about gratitude. It requires us 'to make a return of equal, and *if possible of superior value* to the services we have received would seem to be a pretty plain rule' (TMS III.6.8; my italics). On reflection, however, he finds that the circumstances of gratitude are so context-dependent that 'no general rule can be laid down' (ibid.). At the same time the rules which determine the duties of gratitude are 'more accurate' than those which regulate the duties of friendship, humanity, hospitality and generosity (ibid.). Smith does not say why, when the context is sufficiently unambiguous, we should return more than we have received. Conjecturally, he may have been influenced by the fact that loans are repaid with interest. Alternatively, he may have thought that a supererogatory act of beneficence must be matched by a supererogatory act of gratitude.

Adam Smith has much to say about the role of intention and accident in gratitude and resentment. He affirms that according to our general moral intuition, 'fortune' – good or bad luck – ought not to influence our views on the merits or demerits of actions (TMS II.iii.intro.3, II.iii.3.2). Yet by an 'irregularity of sentiment' (TMS II.iii *passim*) we are nevertheless sensible to fortune or accident. Attempted crime is punished less severely than successful crime. Great projects not brought to fruition for reasons outside the control of the agent do not command the same sentiments as successful ones. In the spirit of behavioral economics, Adam Smith first inquires into the efficient or proximate causes of this deviation from moral intuition (TMS II.iii.1). In the spirit of evolutionary economics, he then tries to identify its final or ultimate causes or functions, essentially offering an incentive argument (TMS II.iii.3.).

If I love or hate another person, I naturally wish that good or ill befall him, but I do not care whether I am instrumental in bringing it about (TMS II.i.1.2). By contrast, if I feel gratitude or resentment I want to be myself the means by which the target of my emotion is rewarded or punished. 'What gratitude chiefly desires, is not only to make the benefactor feel pleasure in his turn, but to make him conscious that he meets with this reward on account of his past conduct' (TMS II.iii.1.4). Similarly, 'Resentment would prompt us to desire, not only that he should be punished, but that he should be punished *by our means* and on account of *that particular injury which he had done to us.* (TMS II.i.1.7; my italics).

Hence the phenomenology of the desire for retribution has the following components: when A has offended B, B will desire (1) that A suffer, (2) that A suffer because of what he did to B, (3) that A suffer at B's hands. Although Adam Smith does not say so in TMS, we might add (see the Appendix) that B will tend to desire (4) that A *know* (2) and (3). If A suffers an accident that hurts him as much as the punishment B wanted to inflict on him, only (1) is satisfied. If C punishes A for what A did to B, only (1) and (2) are satisfied. If B punishes A for what A did to B but A ignores or misidentifies the causal source of his suffering, only (1), (2) and (3) are satisfied.

Let me conclude by comparing again Seneca and Adam Smith on some of the points covered above. They both assert, but Adam Smith more tentatively, that gratitude requires us to return a good greater than the gift. They both agree that while gratitude for unsuccessful attempts to help may seem to be as obligatory as gratitude for actual assistance, the wisdom of our ancestors (Seneca) or nature (Adam Smith) have created an asymmetry in this regard. Both insist on the personal nature of resentment and punishment, in the sense that the punisher wants to inflict the punishment himself and the target to know why and by whom he is being punished. Whereas Seneca underlines the personal nature of benevolence, Adam Smith emphasizes the personal nature of gratitude. Seneca admits, however, that in some cases, the benefactor should hide his identity out of concern for the donor. Whereas Seneca argued against enforcing gratitude by the law, Adam Smith argued against legal enforcement of benevolence (the cause of gratitude). Both assert, however, alternative mechanisms: Seneca argues for the importance of social norms in sustaining gratitude, and Adam Smith for their role in sustaining benevolence.

Some comments

I conclude by assessing some of the arguments and claims canvassed above from the perspective of modern social science.

Seneca and Adam Smith both argued for the asymmetric nature of positive as well as negative reciprocity. In stylized form, 'return two for one'. What they actually say, of course, is 'return more than you got'.

In assessing their claims, I begin with negative reciprocity. It seems widely accepted that the *lex talionis* served to limit the extent of revenge rather than to create an obligation to take revenge (Parisi 2001). It forbids the taking of two eyes for an eye or of an eye for a tooth. The Koran, too, says that 'If you want to take revenge, the action should not exceed the offense' (Sura XVI). In this perspective, the *lex talionis* serves to counteract a spontaneous tendency to excessive revenge.

Is there in fact such a tendency? Kalyvas (2006: 59) cites one example of two-for-one from the American Civil War and two from contemporary Lebanon. Mazover (2001: 346) notes that in Greece in 1944, after an attack by left-wing groups on the right-wing leader Nikolaos Papageorgiou, 'two young men were found dead in the road where the original attack had taken place; placards round their necks read: "Papageorgiou – 2 for 1".' When the French government used the one-for-one principle in executing members of the 1871 Paris Commune, the latter responded by adopting a policy of three-for-one (Antonetti 1991: 307). As noted above, it is possible, however, that some of these excesses were intended to have a deterrent effect.

Neurophysiological experiments (Shergill et al. 2003) also suggest a tendency towards excessive retaliation. When instructed to apply the same force on another participant as the latter had applied to them, subjects escalated on average 38 per cent in each round. The explanation is that the perception of force is attenuated when the force is self-generated. Although this mechanism may well explain, as the authors suggest, escalation in fighting among children, it would not apply to less direct forms of interaction.

In an experiment by de Quervain et al. (2004), subjects played a trust game with the payoffs shown below in Figure 1.

In the 'costless' condition of the experiment, the investor could attach, at no cost to himself, up to 20 'punishments points' to the trustee, each point causing the trustee to lose 2 monetary units (MU). When the trustee chose no back transfer, most investors punished maximally, leaving the trustee with a net benefit of 10 MU. We do not know whether these investors were retaliating for the loss of their initial endowment (10 MU) or for the sum of that loss and the income forgone (10+15 MU). Perhaps, as suggested by the theory of loss aversion, the subjective loss was somewhere between these two magnitudes. On any of these hypotheses, the loss inflicted on the trustee (40 MU)

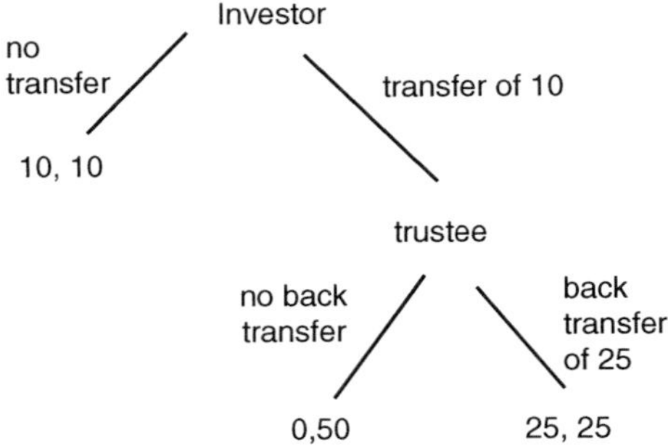

Figure 1 de Quervain et al.'s trust game with the payoffs shown.
Source: de Quervain et al. (2004).

was substantially larger than the loss inflicted on them by the trustee. Ernst Fehr (personal communication) informs me that most subjects would probably have punished even more if they had not been constrained. The Bible (Psalm 79: 12) urges seven-fold retaliation.

With respect to asymmetry in positive reciprocity, Seneca and Adam Smith offer only normative analyses. They make no positive claim that there is an actual spontaneous tendency to return more than one received. To my knowledge, little is known about this issue. It makes some intuitive sense that a recipient who wants to match the generosity of the donor, and not simply return equal for equal, has to show his gratitude through a surplus payment. As noted above, however, it may be hard to distinguish 'gratitude overpayment' from ordinary interest payment.

Some evidence comes from studies of the potlatch, in which gifts were typically expected to be returned with an interest between 30 and 100 per cent (Mauss 1967: 40). As an alternative, the gift could be destroyed. The latter fact, and many other aspects of the potlatch, suggest that giving and returning gifts was a matter of power and humiliation rather than of benevolence and gratitude. This interpretation is confirmed by the tendency in potlatch societies to reject 'hyperfair' offers in the Ultimatum Game (Henrich et al. 2004: ch. 8).

A theoretical argument for overpayment might come from loss aversion. For the donor, the gift is an outright loss. If at some later time he receives an equal-sized return gift from the recipient, it is a windfall gain whose value to him is about half that of the loss. To compensate the donor fully, in subjective terms, the recipient ought therefore to return twice as much as he received. While this may or may not be an appealing normative idea, its positive value as an explanation for behavior is reduced by the fact that we do not seem to impute loss aversion to other people (van Boven et al. 2001).

As noted, both Seneca and Adam Smith distinguished between appropriate and excessive punishment. In commenting on this distinction, I shall follow Adam Smith and limit myself to appropriate and excessive *retribution* – motivated respectively by indignation and anger – and ignore the forward-looking arguments for punishment.

Most experimental studies of punishment are in fact designed to capture effects of the retributive emotions, by eliminating repeated interactions that might induce forward-looking punishments. The general strategy of these experiments is to measure the strength of the desire for punishment of unfair behavior by the willingness to pay for punishment. In the 'costly' condition of the experiment by de Quervain et al. (2004), every punishment point attached to the trustee cost the investor 1 MU and the trustee 2 MU. Not surprisingly, the average subject imposed fewer punishment points (about 22) in this condition than in the costless one, although some punished maximally. However, there was no difference between the costly and costless conditions with regard to the intensity of the desire to punish, as determined by answers to a questionnaire rather than by behavior. As we would expect, these desires are very close to actual behavior in the costless condition.

I conjecture that compared to indignant subjects, angry subjects would both express a desire for stronger punishment and be more willing to pay for punishment. Comparisons of second-party and third-party punishments (Fehr and Fischbacher 2004) confirm the latter conjecture. The former idea is probably what Adam Smith had in mind. Although it has not been tested, as far as I know, it seems plausible. A testable question is whether variations in behavior and in preferences are independent of each other. Consider an experiment comparing anger and indignation, and suppose that some angry subjects and some indignant subjects express the same desire for the punishment of similar offenses. Although the angry will on average tend to prefer stronger punishments, the more moderate among them will align themselves with the less moderate among the indignant. The testable question is whether these individuals will (on the same cost schedules) also behave similarly. Anger might have a separate effect on punishment behavior over and above the impact on punishment preferences.

We might also expect that angry subjects would express a desire for stronger punishment and be more willing to pay for punishment immediately after the offending action than some time later, when the emotion has cooled off. By contrast, the strength of indignation may be expected to remain more nearly constant over time. The relation between these two pairs – second-party and third-party punishment on the one hand and immediate versus delayed punishment on the other hand – seems worth exploring. Over time, the agent might in fact come to consider his former self at the time of the offense as something like a third party.

A complication arises from the fact that since the agent buys revenge in the experiments, the costs are certain and paid up front. Outside the laboratory, however, the costs mostly take the form of uncertain downstream risks that the agent might incur in carrying out the revenge. The offender might fight back, or his relatives might do so, or the plan might fall through for some other reason. Yet these risks may not enter appropriately into the ex ante decision to pursue revenge. As Seneca noted, the angry man does not calculate well. The forced trade-offs in the experiments may not, therefore, reflect how anger actually works.

In the case of indignation, however, we might expect a trade-off between costs and benefits. As Adam Smith tells us, indignation is a 'cool' and 'calm' state that allows for this kind of balancing. First, the impartial spectator determines what would be an appropriate punishment for the offense. This is a matter of *justice*. Assuming that the agent internalizes this assessment, he will then determine the appropriate action. This is a matter of *prudence*, a character trait that Adam Smith valued highly. Although he would certainly not have admitted that commutative and distributive justice might have to be tempered by prudence, he might have accepted a trade-off in the case of retributive justice. If my anger tells me to impose a punishment of 10 and my indignation a punishment of 8, my prudence might reduce it still further to 6.

The distinction between second- and third-party punishment pertains to the offended party: A punishes B for what B did to A or for what B did to C. One might also make a similar distinction with regard to the punishing party: A punishes B for what B did to A or C punishes B for what B did to A. As noted, both Seneca and Adam Smith argued that the offended person A might prefer to punish B personally rather than having a third party (e.g. a court of law) do so. In an experiment by Singer et al. (2006) a subject was brain-scanned while watching a painful shock being inflicted on two persons (confederates of the experimenter) who had interacted with the subject in a trust game, one of them behaving fairly and one unfairly. When the subject observed the fair player being punished, the brain scan showed activation of pain-related brain areas ('I feel your pain'). Observing the punishment of unfair players caused less activation in pain-related areas but increased activation in pleasure-related areas ('Schadenfreude').

In a variant of this experiment, one might compare the activation of pleasure-related areas in the brain that occurs when the punishment is inflicted on the unfair player by the subject with the activation that occurs when the punishment is imposed by a third party. To my knowledge, that experiment has not been done, but it is clearly feasible. One might also, along the lines sketched above, manipulate the beliefs of the offended party concerning the beliefs of the punished party. In principle, the alleged personal nature of benevolence and of gratitude could also lend itself to experimental analysis.

In experiments, the somewhat unfocused idea of benevolence has been sharpened to that of cooperation in public goods games. Whereas no experiments (to my knowledge) have tried to assess the gratitude-motivated rewards to cooperators, many have considered punishment of non-cooperators in the form of inflicting actual losses on them. This modeling may not, however, be very realistic. When members of a cooperative fail to do their part of a common chore, they are rarely fined: they are ostracized or excluded. I take Adam Smith to be arguing that non-cooperators are subject to avoidance, which hurts them by blocking their access to the gains from joint ventures.

Maclet (2003) shows the importance of exclusionary behaviors of this kind, some of them spontaneous and others motivated by strategic thinking. He cites the observations of Francis (1985: 269) on ostracism among British miners during a strike in 1984: 'To isolate those who supported the "scab union", cinemas and shops were boycotted, there were expulsions from football teams. "Scabs" witnessed their own "death" in communities which no longer accepted them.' No doubt some of the scabs had their windows broken or cars set on fire, just as some loyalists during the American Revolution were tarred and feathered. Yet although punishment and ostracism often go together, the conceptual distinction is clear enough. In modern societies, where private punishment is rare, fear of avoidance may be the more potent or frequent cause of cooperation.

In the cases of Seneca and Adam Smith, as in that of Tocqueville (Elster 2009), I believe that the classics not only anticipated findings of modern social science, but that some of their insights remain to be fully explored. Because they did not have the formal skills of the modern social scientist, they were forced to pay close attention to psychological and sociological facts that may, today, be examined using the tools they lacked. In this paper I have tried to draw attention to some ideas that struck me as particularly suggestive.

Appendix: negative reciprocity in the *Lectures on Jurisprudence*[3]

The *Lectures on Jurisprudence* (LJ) are relevant partly because they offer a supplement to TMS and partly because they provide evidence of the tension in Smith's thinking between consequentialist and non-consequentialist arguments for retribution.

In LJ it is hard to tell when Adam Smith is explaining and when he is justifying the various principles of punishment that he cites. Before I discuss some relevant passages, let me first cite a statement about the need for an injured person to know that the offender knows why and by whom he is punished:

> the resentment of the offended person leads him to correct the offender, as to make him feel by whom and for what he suffers. Resentment is never compleatly, nor as we think nobly gratified by poison or assassination. This has in all nations and at all times been held as unmanly, because *the sufferer does not by this means feel from whom, or for what*, the punishment is inflicted.
>
> (LJ p. 105, my italics; see also pp. 108, 476)

In light of this passage, we are justified in imputing to Adam Smith the fourth component in the phenomenology of the desire for revenge that I discussed above.

In TMS, if I have read it correctly, Adam Smith uses 'resentment' as a generic concept that has two species, anger and indignation. Whereas anger is hot and impulsive, indignation is calm and collected. Anger leads to excessive punishment, indignation to appropriate retaliation. When he affirms that 'barbarous nations punish crimes according to the degree of resentment they excite, and when the thief was catched *in the act* their resentment was very high, and consequently disposed them to punish him severly' (LJ p. 48; my italics), it would seem that he refers to anger. In civilized nations, by implication, the irrelevant fact of being caught in the act should not make a difference.

Yet the tailoring of punishment to the 'resentment of the moment' turns out to be much more general:

> We may observe that the form of process in criminall causes is always very different from that in civil. The process of criminall causes is always very short. The jury bring in their verdict, being all enclosed together. A

triall of life and death needs but one hearing; the crime is alledged, and the witnesses brought on both sides, and sentence is passed at once; nor is there any appeal from this sentence. – But for the value of 40sh in England one may be sued first before a Justice of Peace, and there may demand abatements, delays, etc. and may put off the sentence for 3 or 4 months, and if he is not satisfied he may carry it from thence to the sheriffs court; from thence to the Court of Common Pleas; from that again by a writ of error to the Court of Kings Bench; and from that again to Parliament; and may in this manner delay the sentence for a very long time. *We should naturally think that the triall should be longer in a case of life and death*, and greater time allowed for the examination of the cause, as the life of a man is a thing to him invaluable, than for the pityfull sum of 40sh. But we see the contrary has always been the case, and the reason is plain from what I have already observed to be the foundation of punishment. *The whole of criminal law is founded on the fellow feeling we have with the resentment of the injured person.* Revenge, as we commonly say, is a hasty passion: it wont wait for a delay of its gratification but demands it immediately, and the prosecution dictated by our fellow feelings partakes of the rapidity of the passion they were excited by. But there does not appear to be any thing so urgent in a demand for 40 shs.

(LJ p. 277; my italics)

Consider also the following passage from a discussion of Roman law:

Punishment is always adapted originally to the resentment of the injured person; now the resentment of a person against the thief when he is caught in the fact is greater than when he is only discovered afterwards and the theft must be proved against him, which gives the persons resentment time to cooll. The satisfaction he requires is much greater in the former than in the latter case. We see too that there was the same odds made in the punishment of other crimes. The murderer who was caught rubro manu was punished much more severely than he against whom the murder was afterwards proven.

(LJ p. 129; my italics)

The puzzle is why a rational punishment – one that could be approved by the impartial spectator – would be sensitive to the demand for immediate gratification of the desire for revenge and to the demand for greater punishment of the thief or murderer who is caught in the act. Perhaps Adam Smith is offering only an explanation of the criminal justice system without also endorsing it. Yet as the following passage makes clear, LJ is not in any way value-neutral:

The laws of all countries in their secondary state have introduced retaliation in place of the pecuniary compensation. This was at first brought

> in when the delinquent was not able to pay the forfeit, in the same manner as capitall punishment for murder was introduced in place of the compensation, when the murderer or his friends were not able or would not pay the composition. – And in the same manner as revenge requires that the death of the person should attone for the death of the friend, so it will require that the delinquent should be as much hurt and in the same way as the offended person. Thus the Jewish law says eye for eye and tooth for tooth, and the laws of the Twelve Tables quicunque, etc. nisi pacit cum eo, detur talio. Laws still posterior to these gave damages to the injured person instead of retaliation. *Retaliation is without doubt a barbarous and inhuman custom, and is accordingly laid aside in most civilized nations.*
>
> (LJ p. 118; my italics)

Smith argues that retaliation represents an intermediate stage in the reaction to violent crimes. In the 'most antient laws of all countries' (LJ p. 117), these were regulated by pecuniary compensation. In 'civilized nations', too, damages are preferred to retaliation. It is difficult to square this with the praise of retaliation in TMS or with the claim (LJ p. 277, cited above) that the fellow feeling with the desire for revenge is the basis of all punishment.

Notes

1 I cite Seneca from the translation in the Loeb Classical Library. The Introductions and editorial comments in Veyne (1993) are invaluable.

2 *The Theory of Moral Sentiments* is cited from the Glasgow edition in the *Works and Correspondence of Adam Smith*, Oxford University Press, 1976.

3 Page numbers refer to the Glasgow edition in the *Works and Correspondence of Adam Smith*, Oxford University Press, 1978. I have tacitly incorporated the suggested interpolations and amendments proposed by the editors.

References

Antonetti, G. (1991) *Histoire contemporaine politique et sociale*, Paris: Presses Universitaires de France.

de Quervain, J. F., Fischbacher, U., Treyer, V., Schellhammer, M., Schnyder, U., Buck, A. and Fehr, E. (2004) 'The neural basis of altruistic punishment', *Science* 305: 1254–58.

Descartes, R. (1978) *Passions of the Mind*, in John J. Blom, *Descartes: His Moral Philosophy and Psychology*, trans. Blom, Hassocks, Sussex: Harvester Press.

Elster, J. (1999) *Alchemies of the Mind*, Cambridge: Cambridge University Press.

——(2009) *Alexis de Tocqueville: The First Social Scientist*, Cambridge: Cambridge University Press.

Fehr, E. and Fischbacher, U. (2004) 'Third-party punishment and social norms', *Evolution and Human Behavior* 25: 63–87.

Francis, H. (1985) 'The law, oral tradition and the mining community', *Journal of Law and Society* 12: 267–71.

Frijda, N. (1987) *The Emotions*, Cambridge: Cambridge University Press.

Henrich, J., Boyd, R., Bowles, S., Gintis, H., Camerer, C. and Fehr, E. (eds) (2004) *The Foundations of Human Sociality*, Oxford: Oxford University Press.

Kalyvas, S. (2006) *The Logic of Violence in Civil War*, Cambridge: Cambridge University Press.

Maclet, D. (2003) 'Ostracism in work teams: A public goods experiment', *International Journal of Manpower* 24: 867–87.

Mauss, M. (1967) *The Gift*, New York: Norton.

Mazover, M. (2001) *Inside Hitler's Greece*, New Haven, CT: Yale University Press.

Mercer, P. (1987) *Hamlet and the Acting of Revenge*, Iowa City: University of Iowa Press.

Parisi, F. (2001) 'The genesis of liability in ancient law', *American Law and Economics Review* 3: 1340–53.

Shergill, S. Bays, P. M., Frith, C. D. and Wolpert, D. M. (2003) 'Two eyes for an eye: The neuroscience of force escalation', *Science* 301: 187.

Singer, T., Seymour, B., O'Doherty, J. P., Stephan, K. E., Dolan, R. J. and Frith, C. D. (2006) 'Empathic neural responses are modulated by the perceived fairness of others', *Nature* 439: 466–69.

Van Boven, L., Dunning, D. and Loewenstein, G. (2001) 'Egocentric empathy gaps between owners and buyers: Misperceptions of the endowment effect', *Journal of Personality and Social Psychology* 79: 82–123.

Veyne, P. (1993) Translation of and editorial comments in *Sénèque*, Paris: Robert Laffont.

Intersubjectivity, *The Theory of Moral Sentiments* and the Prisoners' Dilemma

Vivienne Brown

I

One of the remarkable transformations in Adam Smith scholarship since the publication of the Glasgow Edition of the works and correspondence of Adam Smith initiated in the 1970s is the high and growing level of interest in *The Theory of Moral Sentiments* (TMS 1976). It might have been expected that philosophers would be drawn to this work, but economists and other social scientists have been discovering its insights and have applied them to a range of social and economic issues. Coinciding with new developments in behavioural economics, game theory, institutional economics and evolutionary biology – and perhaps even contributing to some of them – this new interest in TMS has also stimulated attempts to rethink and even attempt to overcome some of the institutionalized disciplinary boundaries between the human sciences.

In this essay I would like to take up just one aspect of this wider application of the TMS to social and economic issues – the simultaneous one-shot Prisoners' Dilemma game. This game was first formally developed in 1949/50 although some scholars argue that there are important precursors in the writings of, for example, Hobbes and Hume.[1] The game has been taken to express in stark form the conflict between individual and collective interest: individual rationality construes cooperative play as self-sacrificial and so rational players do not cooperate, even though both players are worse off not cooperating than if they had both cooperated. As an *n*-person game it has come to represent the class of 'social dilemmas' in which society loses out because the application of individual rationality leads individuals not to cooperate, even though all would benefit from cooperation. Important examples of social dilemmas include the arms race, degradation of the environment, and human contribution to climate change. The basic two-person Prisoners' Dilemma game has thus come to symbolize the wider significance of social dilemmas in an increasingly interconnected world.

The Prisoners' Dilemma is also controversial amongst game theorists. Critics argue that game-theoretic reasoning fails both normatively and

The Adam Smith Review, 6: 172–190 © The International Adam Smith Society
ISSN 1743-5285, ISBN 0-415-66722-7

explanatorily for the simultaneous one-shot Prisoners' Dilemma, in that it recommends strategies that lead to a Pareto-inefficient outcome and it fails to explain why a significant proportion of players do in fact cooperate (e.g. Bacharach 2006; Gold and Sugden 2007). Defenders respond that such criticism misses the point of the game, which is that it illustrates how individual rationality can lead to Pareto-inefficiency. They thus insist that cooperative play is irrational in a simultaneous one-shot Prisoners' Dilemma even though it leads to beneficial results if both players cooperate (e.g. Binmore 1994). It is into this controversy that TMS has been introduced by the critics in order to provide refinements on the way that preferences and choices are modelled in the Prisoners' Dilemma game, and to show thereby how cooperation might be explained as rational in terms of this more rounded view of human behaviour and motivation (e.g. V. L. Smith 2010). If defenders of the Prisoners' Dilemma game are correct, however, such applications of TMS miss their mark and suggest that TMS is being put to service in a losing argument.

These are the issues that I wish to take up in this essay. I consider the debate between critics and defenders of the traditional logic of the simultaneous one-shot Prisoners' Dilemma game together with the place of TMS in this debate. I argue that what is needed for this debate is a new approach to individual practical reasoning and that existing applications of TMS to the Prisoners' Dilemma have neglected a fundamental aspect of TMS which can help to provide conceptual resources for developing such an approach. I thus enrol TMS on the side of the critics, in that I try to show that cooperation can be rational, but I also aim to develop a new and better response to the defenders of the Prisoners' Dilemma. I thus hope to provide a new way of dissolving what otherwise seems to be a dichotomy between individual and collective interests.

Section II describes the Prisoners' Dilemma game and critically examines how the insights of TMS have been brought to bear in explaining how cooperation might be conceived as rational behaviour, and Section III argues that the resources of TMS suggest a new approach that answers the criticisms raised in Section II. Section IV concludes the essay.

II

In this essay I shall focus on a two-person simultaneous one-shot Prisoners' Dilemma. The game is often illustrated in terms of two prisoners taken in for interrogation in connection with a crime that they are suspected of having committed together, but the logic of the game is quite general and that is how I'd like to consider it here.

In this simple version the game is played just once and with two players, whom I'm calling Player 1 and Player 2. The aim of the game for each player is to maximize the payoff. Each player has a choice of two strategies which I'm calling *cooperate* and *not cooperate*. As there are two possible strategies

Table 1 The Prisoners' Dilemma (payoff structure)

		Player 2	
		cooperate	*not cooperate*
Player 1	*cooperate*	b, b	d, a
	not cooperate	a, d	c, c

a > b > c > d; b > (a+d) / 2

for each of the two players, there are four possible pairs of strategies altogether: (*cooperate*, *cooperate*), (*not cooperate*, *cooperate*), (*cooperate*, *not cooperate*) and (*not cooperate*, *not cooperate*), where the first strategy listed in the pair is that of Player 1 and the second is that of Player 2. The payoffs are symmetrical for the two players and give the value of each player's chosen strategy given the other player's chosen strategy. The standard assumptions of rationality and common knowledge apply, so each of the players knows all the payoffs and knows that the other player knows them, and each of the players knows that the other knows that he knows them, and so on. The players choose their strategies simultaneously. The structure of payoffs is given in Table 1, with Player 1 as the row player and Player 2 as the column player; and some illustrative values are provided in Table 2.

According to a form of reasoning employed in game theory and decision theory, known as the principle of dominance, Player 1 reasons as follows: 'If Player 2 chooses *cooperate*, my payoff for *not cooperate* is higher (4) than for *cooperate* (3); and if Player 2 chooses *not cooperate*, my payoff for *not cooperate* is higher (2) than for *cooperate* (1). Thus, whichever strategy Player 2 chooses, my payoff to *not cooperate* is higher than my payoff to *cooperate*. Therefore I choose the strategy *not cooperate*.' Player 1's strategy *not cooperate* is said to be the (here, strictly) dominant strategy because it yields a better (that is, not just a no-worse) payoff regardless of which strategy Player 2 chooses. Playing *cooperate* is thus construed as 'self-sacrificial'. As the game is symmetrical, Player 2 reasons along the same lines and chooses the strategy *not cooperate*. Thus, *not cooperate* is the strictly dominant strategy for both players: no rational player would choose to cooperate. If both play *not cooperate* the outcome is the strategy pair (*not cooperate*, *not cooperate*), with payoffs (2, 2). This is the Nash equilibrium at which each player's chosen strategy is a best reply to the other player's chosen strategy (neither would

Table 2 The Prisoners' Dilemma (illustrative payoffs)

		Player 2	
		cooperate	*not cooperate*
Player 1	*cooperate*	3, 3	1, 4
	not cooperate	4, 1	2, 2

regret the strategy chosen, given the other player's chosen strategy). If both players had chosen (*cooperate, cooperate*), however, the payoffs would have been (3, 3). In the Prisoners' Dilemma game, the Nash equilibrium is not Pareto-efficient: reasoning individually according to the dominance principle does not result in the best outcome for the players.

This reasoning is unaffected by a player's 'trust' in the other to cooperate, or by prior communication between the players. Even if a player trusts the other to cooperate, or even if there is prior communication or a prior agreement with the other player to cooperate, it is still the case that *not cooperate* yields a higher payoff to that player. Neither player therefore has any reason to trust the other to cooperate, and prior communication is merely 'cheap talk' as it has no effect on which strategy gives the higher payoff and hence no effect on the conclusion to play *not cooperate.*

Applications of this game are manifold. Construed in terms of an *n*-person game, we can see examples of it in terms of the arms race, environmental resource use, environmental recycling, and voting behaviour. These are situations in which players benefit if all play cooperatively, but an individual player benefits even more – so the reasoning goes – if all others play cooperatively and he is the only one not to. The trouble is that if all players reason and act in that way, the outcome is worse for everyone.

The Prisoners' Dilemma game has been widely debated on account of this apparent conflict between individual and collective interests. How can it be that rational behaviour leads to a Pareto-inefficient outcome whereas it is irrational behaviour that leads to Pareto efficiency? Furthermore, there is significant evidence that a substantial proportion of people do behave cooperatively. There is everyday evidence that individuals do cooperate to some degree in many contexts; for example, many people do take the trouble to vote, many people do take the trouble to recycle their rubbish, and so on. There is also a large experimental literature on the Prisoners' Dilemma. Here the consensus seems to be that players cooperate about half the time in simultaneous one-shot Prisoners' Dilemma games (Camerer 2003: 46). Must we conclude that these cooperators are behaving irrationally?

This simultaneous one-shot version of the game is both the simplest version of the game and the hardest in terms of explaining why the experimental evidence shows a substantial level of cooperation. It is harder to explain cooperation in a simultaneous one-shot game than in a repeated game because punishment and reputation effects, which can explain cooperation in repeated play as rational, have no bearing if the game is played just once since their effectiveness relies on there being future rounds of play. Defenders of the traditional logic of the game argue that cooperative play in a simultaneous one-shot game is irrational, and that players' cooperation in such games is to be explained either by a lack of experience at playing such a game or by the players' importing norms of cooperation from everyday life where threats of future punishment provide incentives to current cooperation (Binmore 1994, 2006). For critics, the challenge is to explain how cooperative play in the simultaneous one-shot Prisoners' Dilemma can be justified or explained in some way. They argue that the standard approach misconstrues the nature of human preferences and motivations, and hence mis-specifies the payoffs of the game. Traditionally, payoffs in game theory have been construed in terms of material payoffs that answer to players' self-interest. Critics of this traditional approach to game theory argue that this is too narrow in overlooking the relevance of non-material payoffs and the significance of attitudes towards other players' payoffs (e.g. Camerer 2003: ch. 2 for survey). They re-theorize the objects of preference to include not only material benefits to a player, but also non-material items involving social or moral considerations such as positive or negative feelings associated with cooperating or not, sympathetic feelings for other players, and moral or psychological factors concerning fairness or social norms. Players may thus be other-regarding as well as self-regarding, and utility maximization becomes maximization of 'social utility' (or 'social preferences') such that players attach value to a range of factors, including even cooperation itself. The resulting payoff transformation in the case of the Prisoners' Dilemma implies that *cooperate* can dominate *not cooperate*, thus making *cooperate* the dominant strategy. For such maximizers of social utility, it is rational to cooperate when such payoff transformation makes *cooperate* the dominant strategy.

It is in developing this payoff transformation approach to the Prisoners' Dilemma that some theorists have found inspiration in the rich account of social and moral life in TMS, and in the account of sympathy and the moral sentiments presented there. Robert Frank (1988, 2004, 2007) focuses on the moral sentiments and argues that moral sentiments such as guilt provide 'pre-commitment' for cooperative behaviour by changing the structure of payoffs. For example, a person who would feel guilty from not cooperating would experience a lower real payoff to *not cooperate* than would otherwise be the case because the negative feeling of guilt would have to be set against the material payoff. If this guilt effect were sufficiently substantial it would result in a lower payoff to *not cooperate* than to *cooperate*. This is illustrated in Table 3 where the payoff to *not cooperate* is reduced by 2 as compared with Table 2.

Applying the principle of dominance, each player reasons as follows: 'If the other Player chooses *cooperate*, my payoff for *cooperate* is higher (3) than for *not cooperate* (2); and if the other Player chooses *not cooperate*, my payoff for *cooperate* is higher (1) than for *not cooperate* (0). Thus, whichever strategy the

Table 3 Payoff transformation: reduced payoff from *not cooperate* arising from (negative) moral sentiment of guilt

		Player 2	
		cooperate	*not cooperate*
Player 1	*cooperate*	3, 3	1, 2
	not cooperate	2, 1	0, 0

other Player chooses, my payoff to *cooperate* is higher than my payoff to *not cooperate*. Therefore I choose the strategy *cooperate*.' Payoff transformation thus changes the dominant strategy from *not cooperate* to *cooperate*, so it now becomes rational to cooperate. The outcome (*cooperate, cooperate*) is the new Nash equilibrium.

Thus, Frank argues, moral emotions facilitate mutual cooperation even in a simultaneous one-shot Prisoners' Dilemma, and in this are consistent with, perhaps even necessary for, the pursuit of self-interest. In addition to the importance of moral sentiments, Frank also argues that the forging of sympathetic bonds, for example in pre-play communication, is important in communicating intentions and influencing cooperative behaviour. In an experiment that he reports, almost 74 per cent of people cooperated in a one-shot Prisoners' Dilemma when they had spent 30 minutes talking to each other prior to the game (Frank 2007: 206). This is in contrast to the standard game-theoretic view that prior communication is 'cheap talk' in not affecting the rational strategy of not cooperating.

David Sally (2000) draws on the TMS to argue that the Prisoners' Dilemma game is changed by how it is perceived by the players. If it is perceived as a game played with others who are similar, familiar or valued positively – with others for whom sympathy is felt – then it is played with an enlarged sense of self and a correspondingly broader range of payoffs. Whether or not Sally's notion of sympathy is the same as Adam Smith's – Sally goes on to identify sympathy in terms of 'reading the mind of another' (pp. 570, 572) – what he draws from TMS is a socialized picture of human communication that lends psychological support to his argument that the payoffs of the game need to register an 'enlarged self-interest' that includes others' interests too (e.g. pp. 571, 574, 575). Sally argues that the process of interpersonal identification 'loosens the boundary of the self' and leads to 'an expansion of the self' so that there is 'some overlap' with another person (pp. 571, 574). This overlap of the sympathetic self with another implies a 'sympathetic utility function' such that 'other-oriented action may be motivated by the same basic self-concern as most other actions. Simply put, I help another because the other is part of myself' (pp. 574, 599–604). This implies that the payoff to *cooperate* is increased because in helping another I help myself. As with Frank, changing the preferences leads to a different payoff matrix (pp. 570, 575). This is illustrated in Table 4 where the payoff to *cooperate* is increased by 2 as compared with Table 2.

Table 4 Payoff transformation: additional benefit from *cooperate* arising from other-regarding sympathy

		Player 2	
		cooperate	*not cooperate*
Player 1	*cooperate*	5, 5	3, 4
	not cooperate	4, 3	2, 2

Again, with payoff transformation *cooperate* is the dominant strategy and so individual reasoning according to the dominance principle results in the (*cooperate*, *cooperate*) outcome. Each player finds that, whichever strategy is chosen by the other player, *cooperate* has a higher payoff than *not cooperate* (5>4; 3>2). Again, the outcome (*cooperate*, *cooperate*) is the new Nash equilibrium.

Both Frank and Sally thus provide instances of payoff transformation inspired by Smith's TMS. According to these interpretations, adding more objects of preference – in connection with mutual sympathy, moral emotions or social norms – supports cooperation where payoff transformation makes *cooperate* the dominant strategy. These interpretations thus introduce additional behavioural complexity into game theory and emphasize the importance of non-material items in players' utility functions. They might also shed some light on experimental results where players are working to an expanded set of preferences: if players are cooperating because their non-material together with their material preferences result in *cooperate* being the dominant strategy, then such players are being rational in cooperating. Postulating that players are maximizing social utility preserves the traditional logic of the game whilst providing an explanation of apparent experimental anomalies.

But the theoretical weakness of such payoff transformation is that it does not answer to the challenge of the Prisoners' Dilemma game because payoff transformation changes the game so that it is no longer an instance of the Prisoners' Dilemma (Binmore 1994: 102–14). Arguing that players are rational in cooperating when *cooperate* is the dominant strategy thus does not bear on the question whether it is rational to cooperate in a Prisoners' Dilemma game; and integrating moral sentiments and sympathy into the Nash equilibrium, as Sally explicitly recommends (2000: 575), cannot constitute a challenge to thinking about the game in terms of the Nash equilibrium. The payoff transformation approach to the Prisoners' Dilemma therefore does not challenge the traditional logic of the game, and incorporating Smith's insights from the TMS does not alter that.

This is also evident in another influential adoption of TMS in explaining cooperative behaviour. Herbert Gintis et al. (2005a, 2005b) draw on the insights of TMS to explain cooperation, but here it is recognized that doing so goes beyond the Prisoners' Dilemma. Gintis et al. argue that Smithian sympathy is important in understanding cooperation in human evolution and that this can be modelled using game theory. They argue that cooperation can be explained by the presence of players who are 'strong reciprocators', that is, players who are altruistically predisposed to cooperate with others whom they expect to cooperate, but who will punish, even at a cost to themselves, those who do not cooperate in reiterated play. The altruism of such 'conditional cooperators' is thus held to explain cooperation even in simultaneous one-shot games. This reasoning accords with the standard logic of the Prisoners' Dilemma that it is self-sacrificial to cooperate, even if the other player is expected to cooperate, but Gintis et al. argue that some players are predisposed to such 'altruistic behaviour'. These theorists, however, recognize that this changes the game, in this case from a Prisoners' Dilemma game to a coordination game with two equilibria (*cooperate, cooperate*; *not cooperate, not cooperate*) (Fehr and Fischbacher 2005).[2] In such a coordination game, if strong reciprocators believe that the other player will cooperate, then (*cooperate, cooperate*) is the equilibrium outcome.

As with Frank and Sally, Gintis et al.'s attempt to explain cooperation accepts the standard logic of the Prisoners' Dilemma game that it is self-sacrificial to cooperate if *not cooperate* is the dominant strategy. To challenge the standard logic of the game that it is self-sacrificial to cooperate we need to show how a *different form of individual reasoning* could lead players to cooperate.[3]

III

How might we show this? It seems to me that this is where the conception of human agency in TMS has something important to teach us that is not picked up by Frank, Sally or Gintis et al. TMS is generally understood primarily in terms of its account of sympathy, moral sentiments and the making of moral judgments. From this perspective its account of human sympathy is essentially an exploration of the sympathetic dimension of social relations and the ways in which this influences the nature of morality and the making of moral judgments. But the investigation into social life in TMS also presents a distinctive view of the nature of individual human agency itself. A core aspect of TMS is that the nature of individual human agency is constituted by the spectatoriality of social life. In TMS all are spectators to each other: each person is a spectator to others, and these others are at the same time spectators to that person. Human agency is thus construed in terms of an overarching spectatoriality in which mankind lives 'in the eyes of the world', 'in the view of the public', and 'open to the eyes of all mankind' (TMS I.iii.1.15, II.iii.3.2, I.iii.2.1, V.2.10, I.iii.2.1). The notion of spectatorship might seem to be a passive one in that it denotes onlookers rather than agents, but in TMS it is an active notion in denoting the way that all are simultaneously spectators and spectated upon. All human life – from the immediate family, to circles of friends and acquaintances, to public life – is presented as an arena within which individuals live in the eye of others.

This omnipresent spectatoriality has important implications for the theorization of the individual in that it provides an *intersubjective* account of individuality.[4] According to this spectatorial model, an individual human being is incomplete without others since, if human beings live 'in the eyes of the world', without the eyes of others the life that is lived is not fully human. Without those eyes there is a lack of something that is constitutive of human life. We can see the importance of this intersubjective individuality in three main areas of TMS.

First, social emulation and material self-betterment is presented in terms of the need to appear well in the eyes of the world. Smith asks from whence 'arises that emulation which runs through all the different ranks of men, and what are the advantages which we propose by that great purpose of human life which we call bettering our condition?' (I.iii.2.1). The answer is: 'To be observed, to be attended to, to be taken notice of'. It is 'vanity', Smith says, 'not the ease, or the pleasure, which interests us'. But, he adds, 'vanity is always founded upon the belief of our being the object of attention and approbation'. Social emulation and material self-betterment thus presuppose intersubjectively constituted individuality.

Second, sympathetic responses to others are construed in terms of spectatorial relations among intersubjectively constituted individuals. Fellow-feeling or sympathetic responses by spectators are presented as a necessary part of socialized human nature, a fundamental component of the pleasures of social life and human interaction. Spectators experience pleasure in sympathizing with others and in having those others, as their spectators, sympathize with them in turn; and because of this human need to experience the sympathy of spectators, those being looked upon try to modulate their feelings to elicit the sympathy of their spectators, and they do this by imagining how their spectators view them. The outcome is a series of sympathetic and modulated feelings which provide the basis for the sociality and relational pleasures of human life.

Third, morality is made possible by society since it is society that provides the initial moral looking-glass by which people are able to evaluate themselves. Without this moral mirror of society, morality and critical self-awareness would not be possible (III.1.3). People would be as unaware of the moral qualities of their mind and character as they would of the aesthetic qualities of their facial features. It is by viewing themselves 'with the eyes of other people' that they are able to judge themselves (III.1.2, 4, 5; III.2.3). The possibility of moral agency is thus constituted intersubjectively, both in first-person and third-person cases. In first-person cases, the person imagines the extent to which an impartial spectator to himself would be able to share and, hence, approve his sentiments and conduct. To the extent that the agent is able to imagine that such a spectator would share and hence approve his sentiments and conduct, to that extent he is able to judge favourably of his own conduct (III.1.6). Moral judgment is construed in terms of a spectatorial relation in which the imagined spectator is invested with a degree of impartiality that would otherwise be unavailable to the agent in scrutinizing himself. This model of moral judgment is applied in the case of third-person judgments; a spectator judges another to the extent that he can share the sentiments of the other and hence sympathize with what he imagines are those sentiments (I.i.3, 4). To the extent that the spectator is able to exercise impartial judgment upon himself, rather than simply reflect conventional mores, to that extent he is also able to exercise considered moral judgment on others. There is thus both a social gaze as well as a moral gaze.[5] The social gaze reflects conventional values including the ambitious emulation of spectators in society. The moral gaze embodies impartial moral sentiments and is the foundation of moral judgment proper.[6] The portrayal of the impartial spectator as a metaphor of moral judgment thus builds upon the portrayal of the spectatoriality of human life; it is only in being imagined as impartial that the moral judge is different, not in being a spectator to oneself.

An intersubjective conception of individuality is presupposed in these accounts of self-awareness, sentiments and judgment. This intersubjectivity is an existential characteristic of individuals in TMS and so it is registered at a more fundamental level than the formation of specific sentiments and sympathies. It is thus present whether or not agents experience particular moral sentiments on particular occasions (such as Frank's sentiment of guilt in situations of non-cooperation), whether or not agents feel that other players are especially valued (as in Sally's account of enlarged self-interest and expansion of the boundaries of the self for especially valued others), and whether or not agents are predisposed towards altruism (as in Gintis et al.'s strong reciprocity). The intersubjectivity that I am identifying would still be present even in cases of inappropriate sentiments, low valuation of other players, or absence of any predisposition to altruism; that is, it would be present even in the absence of what scholars have suggested to be the specific preference adjustments that would sustain payoff transformation in the case of the simultaneous one-shot Prisoners' Dilemma. It is thus independent of any particular preference formation or moral (or immoral) qualities, and for this reason it pertains even in cases of the narrowest and most selfish self-interest. It is in this sense that I characterize such intersubjectivity as an existential characteristic of human individuality in TMS.

It seems to me that this conception of intersubjectivity introduces the possibility of theorizing individuality in a different way. This conception of intersubjectivity is in contrast with the classical liberal notion of the individual agent who lives in a sort of external relation to society and to others. This may be illustrated by comparing the classical liberal metaphor of the individual with that of Smith's spectatorial metaphor. The classical liberal metaphor is that an individual agent occupies a 'space' of thought and action that is intimately his own and which is to be protected against others. In clarification of this, it might be said that individual preferences and self-images – as given within the domain of the 'private' – are in fact influenced by the individual's association with others, and that it is only within the 'public sphere' that the image of the separable individual really comes into play as one who claims ownership of that individual space. By contrast, however, Smith's spectatoriality of human life erodes notions of separateness or spatial distance in that individuals' spectatorially-based conceptions of themselves are not independent of how they imagine others are viewing them. It nibbles away at the distinction between the private and the public sphere by making both susceptible to the eyes of others, whether the eyes are of family members or acquaintances, or indeed 'the eyes of the world' or 'the eyes of all mankind'. Thus the classical liberal notion of 'association with others' is displaced by the notion of spectatoriality which erodes somewhat the distinctions of inside and outside, private and public, which the classical liberal notion of individuality tends to rely upon.[7] By this means, Smith's account in TMS facilitates an understanding of individuality that repositions it within the inter-relatedness of all human life, the most private and personal as well as the most public. This is not to detract from another aspect of classical liberal thinking, which is evident in Smith's writing, that the 'freedom' of the individual is something to be respected and preserved. Furthermore, Smith's account of moral judgment and moral behaviour in TMS is premised upon freedom of individual choice (Brown 2009). Yet, the individual whose freedom is so important to Smith's analysis is one who is constituted intersubjectively in TMS.[8]

Smith's account of intersubjectivity thus provides conceptual resources for moving beyond the dichotomy of the 'individual' and the 'collective' that runs through much of liberal thought and much of game theory too. It holds out the promise of developing a conceptual space for understanding a form of individual agency that is compatible with cooperation in pursuing individual interests; and this holds whether those individual interests are construed in terms of self-regarding or other-regarding behaviours.

This intersubjective approach to individual agency suggests that for game-theoretic purposes we need a different mode of individual *reasoning*, not a different set of individual *preferences*. In developing such a mode of reasoning, I adapt the notion of a schema of instrumental practical reasoning as presented in Gold and Sugden's edited version of Michael Bacharach's uncompleted manuscript, *Beyond Individual Choice* (Gold and Sugden 2006, 2007; Bacharach 2006).[9] Such a schema of instrumental practical reasoning generates normative statements of what should be done as the conclusion derived from a series of premises; the validity of such a schema is construed in terms of its success in generating the best outcome for the reasoning player. Schema 1 gives a schema of practical reasoning in the case of individual rationality construed in terms of what 'I' as an agent should do in trying to achieve the best outcome (Gold and Sugden 2006: 156–57). As I present it, this schema also includes the possibility of broad payoffs (material plus non-material payoffs) as well as narrow payoffs (material payoffs), thus including the possibility of a social payoff function including, for example, other-regarding factors. I include these here to show that the schema of reasoning is independent of the actual content of preferences.

Schema 1: individual rationality

(P1) I must choose either A or B.
(P2) If I choose A, the outcome will be O_1 (narrow or broad payoff).
(P3) If I choose B, the outcome will be O_2 (narrow or broad payoff).
(P4) I want to achieve O_1 more than I want to achieve O_2.

(C) I should choose *A*.

Schema 1, individual rationality, is set up in terms of what 'I' should do to achieve 'my' objective: 'I' am an agent in pursuit of 'my' objective *O*, (where O_1 is more preferred than O_2), and this holds whether or not objectives include non-material or other-regarding ones. It is irrelevant whether objectives are formed as a result of social influences, affective relations, or moral criteria. As choosing *A* yields the more preferred outcome for 'me', then *A* is what 'I' should choose. If this reasoning is applied to the Prisoners' Dilemma, the agent aims to maximize the payoff, *P* (narrow or broad), and the reasoning is consistent with the principle of dominance. This is shown in Schema 2:

Schema 2: individual rationality in the Prisoners' Dilemma game

(P1) I must choose either *cooperate* or *not cooperate.*
(P2) If the other player chooses *cooperate,* the outcome will be P_1 (narrow or broad payoff) if I don't cooperate and P_2 (narrow or broad payoff) if I cooperate.
(P3) If the other player chooses *not cooperate,* the outcome will be P_3 (narrow or broad payoff) if I don't cooperate and P_4 (narrow or broad payoff) if I cooperate.
(P4) I want to achieve P_1 more than I want to achieve P_2, and I want to achieve P_3 more than I want to achieve P_4.

(C) I should choose *not cooperate.*

The conclusion that 'I' should choose *not cooperate* holds even if the payoffs are construed broadly to include non-material or other-regarding benefits, as long as the payoff structure is consistent with the Prisoners' Dilemma. Cooperative behaviour would thus require changing *P* to make *cooperate* the dominant strategy; this is Frank's and Sally's approach.

Smith's account of intersubjectivity is suggestive of a different form of individual reasoning because it has a different conception of individual agency. In TMS individual agency is formed 'in the eye of others' and this implies that individuality presupposes omnipresent others whatever the agent's preferences or dispositions: for each individual 'I' there is always another 'I' (or other 'I's) already present. When individual agents aim to maximize on individual objectives, each maximizing 'I' acknowledges the presence of 'You', who is another maximizing 'I' (or other maximizing 'I's). Thus when reasoning to maximize on individual objectives, the individual 'I' includes 'You' within the practical reasoning employed. Schema 3 attempts to capture this alternative mode of individual reasoning for the Prisoners' Dilemma where individual rationality explicitly takes account of intersubjectivity:

Schema 3: intersubjective rationality in the Prisoners' Dilemma game

(P1) I must choose *cooperate* or *not cooperate,* and you must choose *cooperate* or *not cooperate.*

(P2) I want the best outcome for myself, and you want the best outcome for yourself.
(P3) The outcome for me of my choice of strategy depends upon your choice of strategy, just as the outcome for you of your choice of strategy depends upon my choice of strategy.
(P4) The best outcome for me, given that you are a maximizing agent, is when you and I cooperate; and the best outcome for you, given that I am a maximizing agent, is when you and I cooperate.

(C) I should choose *cooperate*, and so should you.

Schema 3 provides an example of intersubjective rationality in the case of the Prisoners' Dilemma. The agent who reasons and maximizes here is an individual 'I'. Nonetheless, this 'I' acknowledges that there is a 'You', who also has to choose a strategy (premise 1) and who also aims to maximize on individual objectives (premise 2). With this inclusion of 'You', the 'I' acknowledges not only the constraints on what either can achieve (premise 3) but also the existence of some congruence of individual interests between them (premise 4). Intersubjective rationality therefore concludes that 'I should choose *cooperate*, and so should you', because that is what yields the best that a player can achieve individually given the presence of another maximizing 'I'.

Schema 3, intersubjective rationality, makes possible what I term 'instrumental cooperation'. As with Schemata 1 and 2, Schema 3 is posed in terms of individual reasoning and individual maximization, but unlike Schemata 1 and 2 it can exploit the individually beneficial potential for cooperation. Importantly, this shift in agential focus construes instrumental cooperation in terms of realizing the potential benefits afforded by congruence of individual interests, instead of construing individual cooperative behaviour as 'self-sacrificial'. Cooperative behaviour is thus re-theorized as instrumentally beneficial instead of being self-sacrificial. Concluding that 'I and you' – that is, 'each of us' – should cooperate is thus not to gift the other player an advantage, but to reason to the best possible individual payoffs given the structure of the game.

According to Schema 3, then, it is rational to cooperate: cooperation is the strategy that is recommended by the instrumental practical reasoning of Schema 3. This is in contrast to the standard interpretation of the Prisoners' Dilemma where individual practical reasoning recommends non-cooperation. This difference may be illustrated by considering the issue of 'trust', where trust is the subjective probability that a player will cooperate. Intersubjective practical reasoning promotes cooperation because it facilitates *mutual trust* between the players. The reason for this is that, as intersubjective reasoning concludes that it is in the individual interest of each of the players to cooperate, both players have good reason to trust that each of them will indeed cooperate. It is because it is individually rational for each to cooperate that mutual trust between them is facilitated. By contrast, in the case of the traditional interpretation of the Prisoners' Dilemma, individual rationality concludes that it is self-sacrificial to cooperate. In concluding that it is irrational to cooperate, it promotes distrust.

Schema 3 thus rationalizes instrumental cooperation and thereby promotes mutual trust between the players. In asking, 'what is the best strategy for me, given that you and I each have to choose whether to cooperate?', it seeks a solution that takes due account of the fact that each of the players is reasoning instrumentally in the presence of both constraints and some congruence of interests. This is in contrast to the traditional game-theoretic approach to individual reasoning in the Prisoners' Dilemma, which, in asking, 'what is the best strategy for me, given the other player's strategy?', fails to take into account the implications of having both players reasoning this way, a failure that leads to a Pareto-inefficient outcome. Schema 3 is thus superior to Schema 2, as evidenced by the fact that its conclusion implies higher payoffs for the players.

Normatively, intersubjective rationality thus performs better than individual application of the dominance principle in yielding better payoffs. *Explanatorily*, intersubjective rationality can provide new insights into the existing evidence on cooperative behaviour in experimental situations. One aspect of the experimental evidence that has received considerable support is that prior communication tends to result in greater cooperation, as both Frank (2007: 206) and Sally (1995: 80; 2000: 612–13) report. This is inexplicable in rational terms according to standard game theory according to which such communication is mere 'cheap talk' that does nothing to dislodge *not cooperate* as the rational strategy. The significance of this prior communication may be explained, not in terms of preference adjustment, but in terms of promoting intersubjective rationality which leads players to the conclusion that 'each of us' should cooperate. Experimenters also argue that players are more likely to cooperate if they believe the other player will cooperate, even though this also goes against the standard interpretation, as Frank (2007: 206) and Fehr and Fischbacher (2005: 165) report. This result could be explained in terms of players assuming that the other player is also intersubjectively rational. Experiments and wider social observations also note the importance of norms of cooperation in influencing outcomes in Prisoners' Dilemma games. A difficulty with making sense of this in terms of the traditional understanding of the game is that such norms would have to outweigh what is deemed to be the self-sacrificial nature of cooperation, but if such norms are understood as conducing towards intersubjective rationality they can readily be theorized in explaining cooperative behaviour.

In positing socialized agents as beings that live outside themselves to some degree – in the eyes of the world that are looking on them – Adam Smith's TMS provides a model of agency that supplies conceptual resources for supporting the intersubjective rationality of Schema 3.[10] Smith's spectatorial account of human agency illustrates how individual human agency internalizes the presence of another 'I': individuals view themselves from the standpoint of others as well as viewing others from their own standpoint, a multiperspectival viewpoint that facilitates intersubjective rationality. Intersubjectivity is thus a characteristic of human individuality; it makes morality possible, just as it makes immorality possible too, according to Smith's account.

Instrumental cooperation in the Prisoners' Dilemma is independent of issues of fairness or morality. Neither Frank's emphasis on the function of moral sentiments, nor Sally's emphasis on the significance of sympathy for those other players who are especially valued, has any essential part in the intersubjectivity being explored here. Schema 3 works to resolve the Prisoners' Dilemma by introducing a different mode of individual reasoning. It is therefore not reliant on any moral considerations or sentiments, or on any sympathetic feelings, that would change the value of the payoffs. Indeed, the instrumentally cooperative outcome of the Prisoners' Dilemma game might be contrary to the public interest or contrary to morality: for example, if they were to cooperate, the prisoners in the original Prisoners' Dilemma game would be acting so as to minimize punishment for their crime. Instrumental cooperation is thus not intrinsically moral. The approach of many theorists, including Frank, Sally, and Gintis et al., tends to regard cooperative behaviour as intrinsically moral or prosocial in some sense. But the account of instrumental cooperation developed in this essay shows that cooperation is beneficial for the players in the sense of achieving an outcome that is Pareto-superior to the Nash equilibrium in terms of players' payoffs. This is separate from the question whether it is beneficial or 'good' in some other or wider sense for the players' payoffs to be thus increased. Cooperation amongst criminals or, say, amongst collusive oligopolists, is clearly a different matter from cooperation amongst citizens to vote and do their recycling: agents may cooperate to further many different kinds of ends, not all of which are socially beneficial or even legal.

Of course, this is not to suggest that there are not many socially beneficial forms of cooperation which are motivated by moral or social concerns or by feelings of friendship and sympathy; such cooperation is clearly important in human life, but if it is explained by payoff transformation it doesn't address the theoretical problems posed by the Prisoners' Dilemma. Neither is it to underestimate the importance of societal norms in predisposing people to one conception of agency, or one mode of reasoning, over another. The analysis of modes of reasoning presented in this essay thus does not detract from the importance of such norms in social and economic life.[11] Notwithstanding these wider considerations, however, what the essay does argue is that, in the specific case of the simultaneous one-shot Prisoners' Dilemma, achievement of the cooperative outcome can be an instance of instrumental cooperation motivated by the pursuit of individual interest, whether or not pursuit of that individual interest might be thought to involve self-regarding or other-regarding behaviours, or to involve material or non-material objectives, or to conduce towards a moral, amoral or immoral orientation. I suggest that recognition that cooperation can be individually rational provides a challenge to arguments which purport to show that cooperation by individual agents in the simultaneous one-shot Prisoners' Dilemma is self-sacrificial and hence irrational. Given the importance of such dilemmas in an increasingly interdependent world, this conclusion seems worth taking seriously.[12]

IV

In this essay I've argued that the resources of TMS suggest, or at least are consistent with, a new mode of individual practical reasoning along the lines of Schema 3's intersubjective rationality. In contrast with the notion of individual agency that is characteristic of game theory and decision theory, this notion of the individual agent incorporates an intersubjectivity that recognizes the presence of another 'I'. According to the intersubjective mode of individual practical reasoning presented in Schema 3, it is because the individual 'I' is premised upon the presence of another 'I' that it is able to pursue individual objectives by means of instrumental cooperation. This intersubjective mode of reasoning thus dissolves the dichotomy between 'individual interest' and 'collective interest' that has characterized much of the debate about the Prisoners' Dilemma, thus enabling recognition of the way that some individual players can exploit congruent individual interests by adopting cooperative strategies.

The intersubjective mode of individual practical reasoning presented in Schema 3 does not rely on moral principles or on moral motivation for agents: even the most selfish, although not only the selfish, can reason their way to instrumentally cooperative choices. Its aim is efficiency (for the individuals concerned, not necessarily for society) not morality; and that is why it provides resources for challenging the traditional logic of the Prisoners' Dilemma. This is not inconsistent with Smith's approach either. In many respects Smith was not optimistic about the prospects for moral excellence. He inclined to the view that the basic safety and well-being of society are more likely to be assured if (in addition to the public works he argues for) society relies upon the pursuit of individual interest, suitably restrained by the laws of justice and conventional rules of decent behaviour, rather than on voluntary benevolence or the demanding morality of the impartial spectator.

Acknowledgements

Versions of this essay were presented at: 'Adam Smith on the Conditions of a Moral Society', an interdisciplinary conference commemorating the 250th anniversary of the publication of Adam Smith's *Theory of Moral Sentiments*, University of Oslo, Norway, August 2009; 'Workshop on *The Theory of Moral Sentiments* 1759 on its 250th anniversary', Institute of Advanced Study, University of Bologna, Italy, December 2009; the Cambridge Seminar in the History of Economic Analysis, Clare Hall, Cambridge, UK, February 2010; and HET conference, Kingston University, UK, September 2010. I am grateful for discussion on these occasions and in particular I thank Nahid Aslanbeigui, Luigino Bruni, James Konow, John O'Neill and Roberto Scazzieri. I also thank Lisa Herzog for discussion and comments. This essay was completed whilst I was an Academic Visitor at the Faculty of Philosophy, Oxford; I am grateful for the hospitality provided. I am indebted to an anonymous referee for very helpful comments.

Notes

1 For a history of the game see Poundstone (1992) and http://ask.metafilter.com/126323/Prisoners-Dilemma-citation.

2 See also Rabin (1993) for the argument that the Prisoners' Dilemma should be understood as a coordination game.

3 Schick (1997) argues that, as both selfishness and altruism are consistent with the Prisoners' Dilemma (hence the possibility of an altruists' dilemma), 'the problem is rationality' (p. 96). But it seems to me that Schick forgets this when he later argues that sociality or friendship may be (even, is) sufficient to overcome the dilemma. His later argument is that if a player is influenced by the other player's *wanting* him to cooperate, the player will cooperate:

> Suppose that Adam and Eve are social vis-à-vis each other. Each then wants to do what the other wants him or her to do. Each knowing what the other wants, each will here take S [*cooperate*], and that will yield (S, S), which is the cooperative outcome. That is, if Adam and Eve are social, they will both cooperate, and this though rationality directs them both to T [*not cooperate*] … sociality implies cooperation. And in a one-round Prisoners' Dilemma, social people cooperate and rational people don't.
>
> (pp. 121–22)

But, as with Frank's and Sally's attempts to integrate Smith's sympathy, Schick's sociality yields this outcome by payoff transformation so that *cooperate* becomes the dominant strategy because it includes the payoff of pleasing the other. I am indebted to Raino Malnes for drawing my attention to this work by Schick.

4 This interpretation builds on that of Brown (1994). I am grateful to Christel Fricke and Dagfinn Føllesdal for stimulating my interest in the intersubjectivity of TMS by inviting me to the Adam Smith–Edmund Husserl workshops, CSMN, 2007 and 2008.

5 This distinction is introduced in Brown (1997).

6 The initial explanation of third-person moral judgments in Part I thus needs to be understood in the light of the later explanation of first-person moral judgments in Part III.

7 This raises some questions as to whether what is taken as the canonic liberal representation of individuality is actually true to the writings of what are taken to be the canonic liberal philosophers; but that is another story.

8 See Brown (1994: ch. 8), for a discussion of some issues relating to Smith and freedom.

9 Bacharach argues in favour of a collective/team notion of agency and rationality as a means of solving a number of problems in game theory, including the Prisoners' Dilemma; and so Gold and Sugden contrast Schema 1's 'individual rationality' with schemata showing 'team rationality' in terms of the agent 'We' construed as a team. I do not address Bacharach's arguments in this essay.

10 This is not to suggest that the intersubjectivity of TMS is the only model of individuality that could support intersubjective rationality, although it was in thinking about TMS that I first developed the intersubjective rationality of Schema 3.

11 For the argument that competitive economic efficiency (as specified in the First Fundamental Theorem of Welfare Economics) requires moral normative constraints, see Schultz (2001).

12 It does not imply, of course, that public policy responses to such dilemmas are thereby made redundant. The aim of this essay is only to argue against the proposition that cooperation in the specified circumstances is self-sacrificial and, hence, irrational.

Bibliography

Bacharach, M. (2006) *Beyond Individual Choice: Teams and Frames in Game Theory*, N. Gold and R. Sugden (eds), Princeton, NJ: Princeton University Press.

Binmore, K. (1994) *Playing Fair*, vol. 1 of *Game Theory and the Social Contract*, Cambridge, MA: MIT Press.

——(2006) 'Why do people cooperate?', *Politics, Philosophy and Economics*, 5: 81–96.

Brown, V. (1994) *Adam Smith's Discourse: Canonicity, Commerce and Conscience*, London: Routledge.

——(1997) 'Dialogism, the gaze and the emergence of economic discourse', *New Literary History*, 28: 697–710.

——(2009) 'Agency and discourse: revisiting the Adam Smith problem', in the *Elgar Companion to Adam Smith*, Jeffrey T. Young (ed.), Cheltenham: Edward Elgar, pp. 52–72.

Camerer, C. F. (2003) *Behavioral Game Theory: Experiments in Strategic Interaction*, Russell Sage Foundation, New York; Princeton, NJ: Princeton University Press.

Fehr, E. and Fischbacher, U. (2005) 'The economics of strong reciprocity', in *Moral Sentiments and Material Interests: The Foundations of Cooperation in Economic Life*, H. Gintis, S. Bowles, R. Boyd and E. Fehr (eds), Cambridge, MA: MIT Press, pp. 151–91.

Frank, R. (1988) *Passions Within Reason: The Strategic Role of the Emotions*, New York: W. W. Norton.

——(2004) 'Introducing moral emotions into models of rational choice', in *Feelings and Emotions: The Amsterdam Symposium*, A. S. R. Manstead, N. H. Frijda and A. Fisher (eds), Cambridge: Cambridge University Press, pp. 422–40.

——(2007) 'Cooperating through moral commitment', in *Empathy and Fairness*, G. Bock and J. Goode (eds), Novartis Foundation Symposium 278, 2006, New York: John Wiley, pp. 197–208, discussion pp. 208–15.

Fudenberg, D. and Tirole, J. (1991) *Game Theory*, Cambridge, MA: MIT Press.

Gintis, H., Bowles, S., Boyd, R. and Fehr, E. (eds) (2005a) *Moral Sentiments and Material Interests: The Foundations of Cooperation in Economic Life*, Cambridge, MA: MIT Press.

——(2005b) 'Moral sentiments and material interests: origins, evidence, and consequences', in *Moral Sentiments and Material Interests: The Foundations of Cooperation in Economic Life*, H. Gintis, S. Bowles, R. Boyd and E. Fehr (eds), Cambridge, MA: MIT Press, pp. 3–39.

Gold, N. and Sugden, R. (2006) Introduction and Conclusion to M. Bacharach, *Beyond Individual Choice: Teams and Frames in Game Theory*, Princeton, NJ: Princeton University Press.

——(2007) 'Theories of team agency', in *Rationality and Commitment*, F. Peter and H. B. Schmid (eds), Oxford: Oxford University Press, pp. 280–312.

Poundstone, W. (1992) *Prisoner's Dilemma*, New York: Doubleday.

Metafilter (2009) http://ask.metafilter.com/126323/Prisoners-Dilemma-citation.

Rabin, M. (1993) 'Incorporating fairness into game theory and economics', *American Economic Review*, 83: 1281–302.

Sally, D. (1995) 'Conversation and cooperation in social dilemmas: a meta-analysis of experiments from 1958 to 1992', *Rationality and Society*, 7: 58–92.

——(2000) 'A general theory of sympathy, mind-reading, and social interaction, with an application to the Prisoners' Dilemma', *Social Science Information*, 39: 567–634.

Schick, F. (1997) *Making Choices: A Recasting of Decision Theory*, Cambridge: Cambridge University Press.

Schultz, W. J. (2001) *The Moral Conditions of Economic Efficiency*, Cambridge: Cambridge University Press.

Smith, A. (1976) *The Theory of Moral Sentiments*, D. D. Raphael and A. L. Macfie (eds), Oxford: Clarendon Press: Liberty Press reprint, 1982.

Smith, V. L. (2010) 'What would Adam Smith think?', *Journal of Economic Behavior and Organization*, 73: 83–86.

The moral sentiments of *Wealth of Nations*[1]

Karl Ove Moene

Introduction

Looking back, it is clear that Adam Smith has been kidnapped. It happened some time after his death in 1790 as *Wealth of Nations* was turned into an Employers' Gospel by right-wing economists and ideologists. As Beatrice Webb wrote in her diary, 30 July 1886:

> The Political Economy of Adam Smith was the scientific expression of the impassioned crusade of the 18th century against class tyranny and the oppression of the Many by the Few. By what silent revolution of events, by what unselfconscious transformation of thought, did it change itself into the 'Employers' Gospel' of the 19th century?

After a while the kidnapping was supported by the political left. Both ends of the political spectrum now have a vested interest in maintaining his captivity. In popular writing Adam Smith is involved in an ends-against-the-middle battle. He has not yet been released in spite of courageous individual attempts to free him.

Indeed, there is a growing literature that challenges the traditional perception of Adam Smith. Emma Rothschild (2001, from where the quote from Beatrice Webb is taken) offers an excellent historical and theoretical treatment of how Adam Smith's works contrast with conservative economics and relate to the French Enlightenment. Likewise, Iain McLean (2006) nicely defends Adam Smith as a radical and egalitarian; Ashraf et al. (2005) strongly recommend Adam Smith as a modern behavioral economist; while Gavin Kennedy (2005, 2008) and Amartya Sen (1984, 2000, and 2009) fight against the unbalanced view on Adam Smith on a broad set of issues.[2]

My aim is more modest. I wish to demonstrate how Smith considered unequal power, unequal opportunities, and unequal pay to be closely related, and how these disparities have devastating effects on the utilization of human resources and on economic development. Smith's commitment to progress through equity, I claim, is the real moral sentiment of *Wealth of Nations*.

The Adam Smith Review, 6: 191–206 © The International Adam Smith Society
ISSN 1743-5285, ISBN 0-415-66722-7

More is at stake, however, than Smith's reputation. One issue is whether markets need to be complemented by social intervention in order to work well, and whether social interventions need to be disciplined by market competition in order to achieve their intended goals. While conservative followers of Adam Smith claim that the discipline of markets would be eroded by social reforms, left-leaning opponents claim that partial social victories would continually be eroded by market forces.

While the left-leaning opponents of Smith make 'the invisible hand' stronger than Adam Smith would admit, the conservative followers make it weaker. Both refer to an imagined version of *Wealth of Nations* – the conservative followers for ideological support, the left-leaning opponents as an ideological warning.

In contrast, the real version of *Wealth of Nations* is morally concerned about equity in society as well as the basic needs of its workers. 'It is but equity, besides', Smith insists, 'that they who feed, cloath and lodge the whole body of the people, should have such a share of the produce of their own labour as to be themselves tolerably well fed, cloathed and lodged' (WN I.viii, p. 88).

Adam Smith considered the huge inequalities around him as a form of oppression that required social intervention. 'For one very rich man', he says, 'there must be at least five hundred poor, and the affluence of the few supposes the indigence of the many' (WN V.i, p. 232). Yet, he was skeptical of governments simply because they tended to favor the rich over the poor: 'We have no acts of parliament against combining to lower the price of work; but many against combining to raise it' (WN I.viii, p. 74).

To change the structure of power and influence Smith advocated not only more market competition, but also institutions and policies that could complement markets and mitigate income differentials. Unlike what most conservatives prefer to see, his arguments favor social interventions that could allocate social opportunities more fairly, empowering the poor and distributing incomes more equally. Unlike what most radicals prefer to see, his arguments point to how markets could be used to achieve social goals such as equity and poverty alleviation.

Perhaps Smith should be considered a 'libertarian' in his skepticism against the government and a 'socialist' in his sympathies for the lower ranks in society. He resembles modern social reformers today, for instance modern European social democrats, who wish to establish a business-friendly environment in order to raise the real incomes of the majority in society. One major difference, however, is that Smith in *Wealth of Nations* is less naive about capital owners' motives than social democrats normally are. In any case the book emphasizes how more equality in the labor market would induce higher economic growth to the benefit of the majority in a way that resembles the North European experience.

I proceed by a discussion of Smith's views on unequal power, unequal opportunities, and unequal pay, making a case for a reinterpretation of his efficiency wage considerations. I then turn to how more equality of earnings would fuel the process of modernization and economic growth, before I conclude by a brief discussion of how Smith's arguments shed light on the Scandinavian development strategy of the second half of the twentieth century.

Unequal opportunities and power

Smith considers common workmen as a huge productive source not only in routine production, but also in inventions and innovations if the labor force has the opportunity to participate in developing local improvements. As he observes in the beginning of *Wealth of Nations*:

> A great part of the machines made use of in those manufactures in which labour is most subdivided, were originally the inventions of common workmen who, being each of them employed in some very simple operation, naturally turned their thoughts towards finding out easier and readier methods of performing it. Whoever has been much accustomed to visit such manufactures, must frequently have been shewn very pretty machines, which were the invention of such workmen.
>
> (WN I.i, p. 13)

More independence of working groups would also raise worker productivity and power. The rewards to society of worker independence and empowerment are so obvious and important to Smith that he uses strong words:

> Nothing can be more absurd […] than to imagine that men in general should work less when they work for themselves, than when they work for other people. A poor independent workman will generally be more industrious than a journeyman who works by the piece. The one enjoys the whole produce of his own industry; the other shares it with his master.

And he continues: 'The superiority of the independent workman over those servants who are hired by the month or by the year […] is likely to be still greater' (WN I.viii, p. 93).

Less dependence on their masters could be achieved by empowering the workers, first of all by creating more equal opportunities for all. One important example was to allow free migration between trades and between districts. Smith's vivid protests against the English poor laws should be viewed in this light.

Smith's protests are in reality concerned with the restrictions the poor laws imply for free movements of labor. He is not against public support for the poor per se, as the conservative interpretation would have it. He emphasizes rather how the poor are to lose from poor laws that make them unable to search for employment outside their parish. He concludes that this law is the cause of the very unequal price of labor in England (see the long discussion in I.x, pp. 151–57).

Second, less dependence could be achieved by more power over wage setting. The wages of labor, Smith emphasizes, depend on 'the contract usually made between those two parties, whose interests are by no means the same. The workmen desire to get as much, the masters to give as little as possible' (WN I.viii, p. 74).

In such bilateral bargaining, the one who can tolerate a conflict the best has an edge. He can pose more severe credible threats; he is less vulnerable to threats from the opponent; and he is thus the most powerful of the two. Smith recognizes this bargaining logic, as when he claims: 'the workman may be as necessary to his master as the master is to him, but the necessity is not as immediate' (WN I.viii, p. 75). The employer can hold out longer; he can subsist for a year or two without a single employee, while many workers cannot subsist for a week without employment. It is therefore not difficult, says Smith, 'to foresee which of the two parties must […] have the advantage in the dispute, and force the other into compliance with their terms' (WN I. viii, p. 74).

The employers have this advantage not only because they have more financial resources, however, but also because they more easily can utilize their collective monopsony power. 'Masters are always and every where in a sort of tacit, but constant and uniform combination, not to raise the wages of labour above their actual rate.' Masters sometimes combine 'to sink the wages of labour even below this rate' (WN I.viii, p. 75). Of course, Smith clearly recognizes that masters could not reduce the wages below a certain subsistence level for long.

Yet, employers' monopsony power is important, as wages could fluctuate over their lower bound. It is a consequence in part of unequal wealth and in part of unequal political influence. 'We rarely hear, it has been said, of the combinations of masters, though frequently of those of workmen. But whoever imagines, upon this account, that masters rarely combine, is as ignorant of the world as of the subject' (WN I.viii, p. 75). These are clear examples of how the government in Smith's view tended to favor the rich.

In sum, the power of employers is so strong that in most cases Smith considers them as de facto wage setters. He does not openly support labor unions or other combinations of workmen, but he points to the unbalanced power between employers and employees that easily emerges without them, and hence the need for countervailing powers in the labor market.

Smith's emphasis both on common workmen as a potentially huge productive source, and on the prevailing inequalities of opportunities and power that hampered the utilization of the workmen, are important for the interpretation of his theory of effort inducing wages, or simply efficiency wages – to which I now turn.

Unequal efforts

Smith observes how a higher pay may lead people to work harder both because they get better nourished and thus become stronger, and because they are better motivated. He talks about how employers use piece rates to raise work efforts and how they use fixed wage payments as rewards for higher effort and stronger commitment to their work tasks.

Positive and negative encouragements

Smith states that in general '[t]he wages of labour are the encouragement of industry, which, like every other human quality, improves in proportion to the encouragement it receives' (WN I.viii, p. 91).

Smith emphasizes that high wages may have a positive encouragement, and low wages may have a negative encouragement: 'The liberal reward of labour, as it encourages the propagation, so it increases the industry of the common people […] Where wages are high, […] we shall always find the workmen more active, diligent, and expedious, than where they are low' (WN I.viii, p. 91).

This is in some contrast to the modern use of efficiency wage arguments, where the mechanism indicates that both wages and effort are 'higher' than they otherwise would have been. According to the modern use, it simply pays for the employer to raise wages to induce higher effort (see Shapiro and Stiglitz 1984; Weiss 1990; Bowles and Gintis 1993). In Smith's exposition, however, he imagines a certain prevalence of less 'active, diligent, and expeditious' workers where wages are low (WN I.viii, p. 91).

Could smart employers benefit from setting a low wage knowing that it would lead to a less active workforce? If so, why are they not always doing that? It is in the answer to questions like these that the difference between Smith's efficiency wage story and the traditional one becomes clear. The key is the importance that Smith attaches to unequal power in the workplace.

It matters how much local influence workers have over working speed and the quality of work; how secure their employment is; what kind of protection they can garner against their employers; and so on. It is decisive who can 'force the other into compliance with their terms'.

If low-paid and worn-out workers can be easily replaced, for instance, it indicates a low level of worker control. The distribution of power and control may therefore also reflect the general conditions in the labor market – workers' monopoly power when labor is scarce and employers' monopsony power when labor is abundant.

The main point to be emphasized is the possibility of a divergent work performance between high- and low-productivity enterprises: A high pay and a high effort constitute a form of high-wage leverage, an outcome of positive reciprocity within high-productivity enterprises. Low pay and low effort can constitute a form of low-wage trap, an outcome of negative reciprocity within low-productivity enterprises.

Both reciprocity and fairness considerations are important sentiments in the *Theory of Moral Sentiments.* The mechanism I suggest is in that spirit. It is also inspired by Matthew Rabin's (1993) influential discussion of how fairness can be incorporated into game theory. Rabin also discusses similar mechanisms, emphasizing that efficiency may require a balance of power.

A simple model of the low wage trap and the high wage leverage

To be more precise, let me set up a simple model where jobs and workplaces may differ in their 'productivity', denoted p, depending (in Smith's case) on the level of specialization and the type of production technique that employers apply. An employer with a given degree of specialization earns a profit

$$\pi = pe - w \tag{1}$$

where his workforce (normalized to size 1) puts in an effort e and is paid a wage w. An efficiency wage relationship is simply a link between effort and wages: $e = e(w)$ with $e'(w) > 0$. The traditional efficiency wage mechanism is to increase wages to induce higher efforts till the marginal benefit of higher efforts equals the marginal costs, i.e. till $pe'(w) = 1$. This is indeed the equilibrium outcome when productivity p is sufficiently high relative to how strongly workers respond to higher and lower wages.

In jobs with low productivity relative to worker control, however, there may be no wage where the first order condition is satisfied. In that case $pe'(w)$ is less than the marginal wage cost of 1 for all wage levels w, implying that the employer would benefit from lowering the wage until it reaches the level of the participation constraint h.

Reciprocity can account for both cases that I for simplicity denote good and bad jobs, to use a metaphor by Acemoglu (2001).

In good jobs there is positive reciprocity: Employers raise wages above the norm, and workers respond by a work effort above the norm. How much the work effort is raised depends on their retaliation power.

In bad jobs there is negative reciprocity: Employers reduce wages below the norm, and workers respond by a work effort below the norm. The reason why wage reductions are profitable in these jobs is that the retaliation power is low relative to the productivity of the jobs.

I shall now derive a specific relationship e(w) to demonstrate how the outcome may depend on worker control and retaliation power. The social work norm is an effort level equal to q which is given. Workers consider a wage equal to w_f to be fair in order to put in the effort level q. The pay-off to a worker is

$$U(w, e) = w - \frac{1}{2}(q - e)^2 + re \ln\left(\frac{w}{w_f}\right) \tag{2}$$

Here the first term just states that the worker 'desires' higher wages to lower wages. The second term indicates that it is costly for the worker to deviate from the work norm q. The third term indicates the worker's desire for fairness. It captures the worker's ability to reciprocate in his choice of effort with a strength r – his retaliation power. The reciprocity is positive when $w > w_f$ and negative when $w < w_f$. The particular functional forms are chosen to get an explicit solution in a simple manner.

Given the wage w, a worker determines his effort to maximize U(w, e) in (2). This yields an effort level equal to

$$e(w) = q + r \ln\left(\frac{w}{w_f}\right) \tag{3}$$

As seen, the worker puts in an effort level equal to the work norm q, when he receives what he consider a fair wage w_f. When he is paid less, his effort is lower than q; when he is paid more, his effort is higher than q. This is so since

$$\ln\left(\frac{w}{w_f}\right)\begin{cases} \leq 0 \text{ when } & w \leq w_f \\ > 0 \text{ when } & w > w_f \end{cases} \tag{4}$$

The employer then chooses the wage level w that maximizes his profits π = pe – w, taking the worker response into account:

$$\max_{w}\left[p\left(q + r\ln\left(\frac{w}{w_f}\right)\right) - w\right] \quad \text{s.t } w \geq h \tag{5}$$

The solution can be expressed as

$$w = \max[h, pr] \tag{6}$$

There are two rather different possibilities:

High wage leverage: When pr is sufficiently high, the wage is determined by pr = w > h. These are good jobs since workers get more than what is required for them to participate and workers' effort is high. Starting from w = h, the rise in employers' revenues in good jobs is higher than the rise in wage costs, implying that profits go up as wages are raised until the equilibrium is reached where w = pr. Thus, there is a gain to the employer of inducing higher efforts by paying a higher wage than h, either because high effort is particularly valuable, p is high, or because workers have sufficient power to punish employers by a low effort if they instead were paid a low wage.

Low wage trap: When pr is sufficiently low, a strict inequality pr < w = h applies. These are bad jobs since workers get no more than what is required for them to participate and effort is low. In bad jobs the gain to the employer of paying higher wages, to induce higher efforts, does not pay off as the increase in revenues in the job is lower than the rise in wage costs. The employer would therefore, instead, lower the wage as much as possible. By so doing, efforts decline. Yet this decline is less than the corresponding decline in wage costs, implying that profits go up as wages are reduced. The gain to the employer of inducing higher efforts does not support the higher wage costs, either because productivity p is low, or because the workers have little power r to punish employers by a low effort in response to a low wage.

For a given (intermediate) level of p there can be either good or bad jobs depending on the relative power of workers and employers. Good jobs may be characterized by a high degree of worker control over the work process; a high willingness and ability of workers to harm 'unfair' employers; a high vulnerability of employers to such effort adjustments. Bad jobs have powerless workers who as a consequence are not very 'active, diligent and prosperous'.

I have shown how powerful employers can generate a low wage trap. They can exercise monopsony power without the usual reduction in labor demand. They gain from obtaining a larger share of a smaller pie. Thus the low wage trap can be costly not only to the workers, but also to society at large. Production goes down and poverty increases, as profits go up. Employers simply gain by employing human resources inefficiently. It is an example of a behavior that 'comes from an order of men, whose interests are never exactly the same with that of the public, who have generally an interest to deceive and even oppress the public, and who have, upon occasion, both deceived and oppressed it' (WN I.xi, p 278).

The inefficiency is associated with inequality. As the two cases above demonstrate, there can be unequal pay for equal work depending on distribution of power between workers and employers. The wage gap between good and bad jobs, for instance, can magnify with differences in r. More worker influence over their own work performance and over contract negotiations would generate more equal wages, and less inefficient use of resources, since 'the low wage trap' becomes easier to escape.

There may obviously be jobs below a certain threshold productivity p* that cannot become good jobs even if workers were all-powerful. To improve performance in these cases one has to rely on new investments and structural change. The wage equalization effect of empowering workers and leveling the playing field is likely to induce this kind of change as well (see the following two sections).

Unequal pay

Smith's labor market mechanisms easily lead to unequal pay for equal work. Depending on the distribution of bargaining power and retaliation power over different enterprises, similar workers may obtain very different wages. In some instances or locations employers may effectively utilize their collective monopsony power, in other cases they may be less effective. In some instances, the low wage trap applies, in others the high wage leverage applies.

In a few instances or locations workers may have some bargaining power, in other cases they may have none. In some cities, workers may have better outside options than in others, and so on. All this would lead to wage differentials across more or less identical workers.

Smith also discusses inequalities in pay that arise from the nature of the employment in itself. He discusses how wages depend on the 'agreeableness or disagreeableness of the employments themselves' (WN I.x, p. 112), on the cost of learning the trade, on the insecurity of the job, on the expected trust, and of the probability of success in the occupation. Most of these causes of inequality would today go under the name of compensating wage differentials. The last one – the probability of success in the occupation – deserves some remarks as Smith here comes with some rather intriguing observations.

After mentioning how men have 'an over-weening conceit [...] of their own abilities' – an ancient evil remarked by the philosophers and moralists of all ages – he goes on: 'Their absurd presumption in their own good fortunes, has been less taken notice of' (WN I.x, p. 120). Here Smith gives a precise account of a risk behavior that today goes under the name of overconfidence: 'The chance of gain is by every man more or less over-valued, and the chance of loss is by most men under-valued' (WN I.x, p. 120).

This bias in the perception of good fortunes implies inequality in pay, as Smith hints at. The general principle seems to be this: In risky occupations where workers are remunerated for their successes only, actual pay becomes lower with the bias as workers are too willing to take these jobs. In occupations where workers are remunerated with a fixed pay independent of success and failure, actual pay becomes higher as their employers have a presumption of the good fortunes of the enterprise increasing their willingness to pay for the labor services they employ.

More important than overconfidence, according to Smith, is the political economy in favor of the rich and wealthy. Smith discusses how 'exclusive privileges given to corporations, which require long apprenticeships and limit the number of apprentices' (WN I.x, p. 133) lead to high wage inequality. He points out that these arrangements reap monopoly gains and insists that 'corporations were established to keep up prices and consequently wages and profits' (WN I.x, p. 138). It is in this connection he comes with the famous statement: 'People of the same trade seldom meet together, even for merriment and diversion, but the conversation ends in a conspiracy against the public, or in some contrivance to raise prices' (WN I.x, p. 144).

The corporation laws further obstruct social mobility again to the disadvantage of poor workers: 'It is every-where much easier for a wealthy merchant to obtain the privilege of trading in a town corporate, than for a poor artificer to obtain that of working in it' (WN I.x, p. 151).

Lifting the restrictions of free movements of labor would affect all the wage setting mechanisms that I have mentioned. It would tend to eliminate monopoly rents in protected occupations associated with guild privileges and production monopolies by increasing the competition for these jobs. It would raise the outside options in local wage negotiations and limit the profitability of employers by reducing both wages and the corresponding worker efforts.

Empowering workers means more retaliation power in cases where employers try to gain by exploiting negative reciprocity. It would lead workers to leave low-productivity jobs and to enter higher-productivity jobs. While the pay for the jobs that workers leave would rise, the pay in the jobs that they enter would decline.

In all cases empowerment by providing more equal opportunities for all workers would tend to equalize wages by leveling the playing field. Low wages in bad jobs would rise and high wages in good jobs would decline, but as more workers would be employed in good jobs, average wages would tend to go up. The more equal worker opportunities are (combined with increasing competition in the product markets), the stronger the rise in the average wage.

Unequal growth

In *Wealth of Nations* it is possible to identify a two-way link between wages and economic growth: Economic growth affects the wage distribution and the wage distribution affects economic growth. Combined, they can explain why economic growth is unequal across countries and across segments of each society.

The first linkage goes from prosperity to wage increases. For Smith as for so many economists after him, a booming labor market is considered the workers' best friend. Nothing could improve the living conditions for workers more than progressive economic growth. It would reduce poverty as the mass of people at or below subsistence would decline.

Smith emphasizes that it is not the wealth of nations that makes the average wages high, but its increase that leads to a higher demand for labor and thus to wages that are persistently above subsistence levels. Thus high average wages are caused by the increase, not the actual size, of national wealth: 'It is not', Smith explains, 'in the richest countries, but in the most thriving, or in those who are growing rich the fastest, that the wages of labour are highest' (WN I.vii, p. 78). He compares England to the less affluent North America. Wages in North America were higher since economic growth was higher there than in the England.

The second linkage goes from the distribution of wages to the rate of growth and structural change: Wage equalization would tend to increase economic growth which in itself would stimulate the demand for workers. Smith's description of the mechanisms of economic growth is simple but powerful. The most important source of growth and of improvements in the productive powers of labor is seen to be in the division of labor and the corresponding gains from specialization. A process of increasing division of labor is like a production process with increasing returns to scale. The larger the scale, the wider the division of labor can be, and the higher the productivity per worker can become. Smith provides several examples, of which the best known is his case study from simple pin making.

He then goes on to explain how the division of labor is limited by the extent of the market where the size of the market again depends on the level of the division of labor. Economic growth also requires fixed capital investments. Markets expand by the higher incomes that further division of labor and capital investments generate. Division of labor becomes wider the more the market expands. This mutual dependence between market size and division of labor is crucial for continuous economic growth.

First, growth slows down if further division of work is restricted by the monopoly practices of reducing output to reap high prices. Smith calls this capitalists' tendencies 'to levy, for their own benefit, an absurd tax upon the rest of their fellow-citizens' (WN I.xi, p. 278). The extent of the market then stagnates, which in turn hampers further division of labor in other branches of industry.

Second, growth slows down if further division of work is not profitable because of wage premiums to local workers associated with guilds, unnecessary long apprenticeships, and restrictions on free labor mobility. This would be particularly harmful to growth when the sectors with the highest potential for further division of labor must pay the highest wage premiums.

Smith does not elaborate much on the second aspect, but there are hints. He says for instance that '[p]rofits are less unequal than wages, and their inequality is often only due to the inclusion of wages' (WN I.x, p. 124). He also observes that '[w]ages are generally higher in new than in old trades' (WN I.x, p. 128), indicating that rising industries where the potential for further division of labor must be particularly great, can be hampered by low profitability. Old or declining industries where specialization gains have already been fully exploited, pay low wages. These industries may have both low productivity p and low worker power r, in terms of the model sketched out in the third section above. The wage gaps can obviously lead to development traps that one could have escaped with more equal wages across new and old trades.

Leveling the playing field by increasing competition both in the output market and in the labor market would therefore stimulate growth. Thus fewer worker privileges to insiders with high wage premiums and fewer monopoly positions in the output market would generate a more equitable growth. In tandem with higher growth, this would over time increase average wages, reduce poverty and improve the circumstances of the lower ranks in society.

There would be winners and losers from more egalitarian developments. Privileged insiders among masters and workers may lose, while disadvantaged outsiders would gain. Smith asks: Is 'improvement in the circumstances of the lower ranks of the people to be regarded as an advantage or an inconveniency to the society?' (WN I.viii, p. 88). High real wages to workers are an advantage, he answers, since 'what improves the circumstances of the greater part can never be regarded as an inconveniency to the whole. No society can surely be flourishing and happy, of which the far greater part of the members are poor and miserable' (WN I.viii, p. 88).

Smith under the Northern Lights

The Scandinavian model is to some extent Smithian. It is characterized by a market-based free-trade economy distinguished by comprehensive labor market organizations, a large welfare state and a system of routine consultation among government and representatives of interest groups. The typical policies are wage compression, lowering high wages and raising low wages; the provision of basic goods for all citizens as a right of citizenship; and a government commitment to full employment. In fact, these aspects of the Scandinavian model of social democratic development owe more to Adam Smith than to Karl Marx.

The intellectual inspiration is not direct. The similarity is caused by the same social sympathies and a similar quest for feasibility. Both Adam Smith and social reformers of Northern Europe were ardent defenders of the poorest groups in society. Both saw modernization and the expansion of markets as the key to escaping poverty. Both saw the primary task as being one of removing the obstacles to rapid modernization. Adam Smith viewed the primary obstacles to modernization as restrictions on the free movement of labor and capital, such as guild privileges and monopolies that limited the size of the market and the extent of specialization.

The social democrats, in effect, saw the primary obstacle to modernization as strong local unions whose wage premiums restricted the expansion of the most productive sectors. What distinguished the social democrats from more conservative followers of Adam Smith like Margaret Thatcher was their solution to the problem of restricting the power of local unions. While Thatcher's solution was to weaken unions as institutions, the social democratic approach was to strengthen unions as institutions and to structure collective bargaining in a highly centralized manner that reduced the influence of high-paid workers in the wage setting process.

The oppressing nature of economic inequality, as Smith saw it in *Wealth of Nations*, was to some extent remedied by empowering weak groups in the labor market and of course by extending the franchise.

Equalizing opportunities: Like in most European countries, democracy in Scandinavia extended opportunities for people, especially the lower ranks in society that Smith was so concerned about. Public education, health care and other programs of the welfare state made each person less dependent on their parents' income and wealth. Social mobility went up. Restricting workers' geographical movements was not an issue. On the contrary, the Scandinavian countries utilized active labor market programs, pioneered by the Swedes in the 1950s, with the explicit goal of increasing the mobility of labor without increasing wage differentials. Social insurance by the welfare state also enables workers to seek employment in the best paying sectors even when the prospects are risky.

Equalizing power: To escape the unequal power between employers and employees that Smith emphasized, one might wonder whether it is possible to increase union power at the local level without increasing the bargaining power of the best paid workers. This is a challenge, as higher bargaining power among high-wage workers can lead to a profit squeeze in the most productive enterprises, limiting economic growth for the whole economy. In Scandinavia this challenge is resolved by an encompassing union movement that includes strong local unions with a mandate to coordinate wage setting with an employers' association at the central level. The strong employer associations are equally important as the union movement. Together the two tend to take wages out of competition by way of collective centralized wage negotiations.

Equalizing efforts: Union power and the presence of welfare state benefits are important remedies to escape Smith's low-wage trap. The employer strategy that leads to the trap is profitable only when declining wages raise profits in spite of lower worker efforts. When workers are able to retaliate backed by local union power, and when welfare benefits set a lower bound on how low wages can become, the strategy that leads to the trap becomes less attractive to employers. Thus both worker empowerment and safety nets help eliminate Smith's low-wage trap, implying that both the lowest wages and the lowest effort levels go up together with social efficiency.

Equalizing pay: In the imagined version of *Wealth of Nations* the performance of markets is often associated with the way they are described in the economics textbooks of today. As I have tried to illustrate, the real version of *Wealth of Nations* is different. Here Smith provides an assessment of labor markets far from the textbook idealization.

Surprisingly, however, the results of centralized wage setting in Scandinavia come closer to the outcomes in the idealized textbook description. First of all the union movement insists on 'equal wages for equal work' eliminating the wage differentials between homogeneous workers. Second, centralization of wage bargaining takes wage setting out of the hands of the unions representing relatively high-paid workers and puts wage setting in the hands of leaders of the union movement as a whole, which includes almost everyone. This all-encompassing nature of the union movement (strongly emphasized by Mancur Olson [1990]) implies a strong commitment to full employment, implying that average wage costs are constrained by a preference for low unemployment.

As a consequence, close to full employment combined with an almost uniform wage for similar workers (the textbook result) are more realistic under quite opposite assumptions to those that dominate the textbooks. Employers may also gain from higher aggregate profits by reducing wage inequality relative to the wage schedule associated with decentralized bargaining, and even relative to the wage schedule associated with a real competitive labor market where employers set wages unilaterally (as demonstrated in Moene and Wallerstein 1997).

Efficiency and equity: In Scandinavia the main concern of unions and employer associations was not equality, but rather macroeconomic efficiency by way of encouraging structural change through investment in good modern jobs. Equal pay for equal work achieved exactly that and became the first step towards the coordinated wage bargaining that was institutionalized in the 1950s. This policy is the world's most dramatic instance of union-sponsored wage equalization. In both Norway and Sweden, an ambitiously egalitarian wage policy was adopted by the central blue-collar confederation and pursued steadily for decades. Solidaristic bargaining, as the policy was named, called for the equalization of workers' pre-tax income by eliminating or reducing the wage differentials that existed between plants within the same industry, between industries, between regions, and ultimately between occupations (Moene and Wallerstein 1995, 1997).

Equalizing growth: Wage compression does in fact stimulate innovation and economic growth, as firms with advanced new technologies do not have to pay excessive wage premiums. While wage inequality operates as though high-productivity firms are taxed and low-productivity firms are subsidized as wages adjust to local conditions, wage compression works in the opposite way: it is as though high-productivity firms are subsidized and low-productivity firms are taxed. As a result, wage equality implies that inefficient firms close down earlier as newer and more productive firms appear, contributing to the process of structural change that Schumpeter (1942) called 'creative destruction'.[3] In terms of the small model in the third section above, low p enterprises are destroyed as more high p enterprises are created.

The main beneficiaries of solidaristic bargaining are to be found in the tails of the income distribution, among low-paid workers and capitalist employers; the losers are highly skilled middle-class workers. Solidaristic bargaining was initially supported by important actors opposed to redistribution. Efficient and innovative enterprises gained from wage setting with small wage differentials. A compressed earnings distribution was supported by a coalition of numerous workers and influential capital owners. Such concurrent interests, typically categorized as alliances of ends against the middle, may explain the viability of the Scandinavian model and why it is associated with high economic growth.

All in all the Scandinavian experience shows how obstacles to rapid modernization can be removed by equalizing opportunities, power and pay in a way that resembles Smith's claim of progress through equity.

Free Adam Smith

In *Wealth of Nations* Adam Smith is openly impressed by capitalists' achievements, but not by their motives. In his *Theory of Moral Sentiments* of 1759 he had already warned '[o]f the corruption of our moral sentiments, which is occasioned by this disposition to admire the rich and the great, and to despise or neglect persons of poor and mean condition' (TMS I.iii, p. 84). Finishing *Wealth of Nations* 17 years later, one might wonder whether he failed to follow this impartial spectator who was looking over his shoulder, scrutinizing every sentence he wrote.

He did not fail. *Wealth of Nations* is much more pro poor, pro labor, and pro majority interests than both conservatives and radicals today are willing to see. Freeing Adam Smith from his ideological captivity by the right and the left would enable a better discussion of how markets and social policies can be fruitfully combined to the benefit of the majority of workers – those with incomes below the mean. In my view it is the political left that holds the key. It should abandon the false proposition that markets and free trade cannot complement social interventions, strong unions and a generous welfare state on an egalitarian development path.

Notes

1 This paper is part of a larger project at the ESOP Research Center, Department of Economics, University of Oslo, sponsored by the Norwegian Research Council. I wish to thank Astrid Jorde Sandsør for valuable assistance. Thanks also to the referees and editor for constructive suggestions, and to Christel Fricke for encouraging advice.
2 See also earlier treatments in Karl Polanyi (1944) and Robert Heilbroner (1953).
3 See also Moene and Wallerstein 1995, 1997, and 2001.

References

Acemoglu, Daron (2001) ‘Good Jobs versus Bad Jobs’, *Journal of Labor Economics*, 19: 1–22.

Ashraf, N., Camerer, C. and Loewenstein, G. (2005) ‘Adam Smith, behavioral economist’, *Journal of Economic Perspectives*, 19(3): 131–45.

Bowles, Samuel and Gintis, Herbert (1993) ‘The Revenge of Homo Economicus: Contested Exchange and the Revival of Political Economy’, *Journal of Economic Perspectives*, 7: 83–102.

Heilbroner, Robert (1953) *The Worldly Philosophers*, New York: Simon and Schuster.

Kennedy, Gavin (2005) *Adam Smith's Lost Legacy*, Basingstoke: Palgrave.

——(2008) *Adam Smith: A Moral Philosopher and His Political Economy*, Basingstoke: Palgrave Macmillan.

McLean, Iain (2006) *Adam Smith, Radical and Egalitarian*, Edinburgh: Edinburgh University Press.

Moene, Karl and Wallerstein, Michael (1995) ‘Solidaristic Wage Bargaining’, *Nordic Journal of Political Economy*, 22: 79–94.

——(1997) ‘Pay Inequality’, *Journal of Labor Economics*, 15: 403–30.

——(2001) ‘Inequality, Social Insurance and Redistribution’, *American Political Science Review*, 95(4): 859–74.

Olson, Mancur (1990) *How Bright are the Northern Lights? Some Questions about Sweden*, Institute of Economic Research, Lund University, Sweden.

Polanyi, Karl (1944) *The Great Transformation*, Boston, MA: Beacon Press.

Rabin, Matthew (1993) ‘Incorporating Fairness into Game Theory and Economics’, *American Economic Review*, 83: 1281–1302.

Rothschild, Emma (2001) *Economic Sentiments: Adam Smith, Condorcet and the Enlightenment*, Cambridge, MA: Harvard University Press.

Schumpeter, Joseph (1942) *Capitalism, Socialism and Democracy*, New York: Harper and Row.
Sen, Amartya (1984) *Resources, Values and Development*, Oxford: Basil Blackwell.
——(2000) *Development as Freedom*, New York: Alfred A. Knopf.
——(2009) *The Idea of Justice*, London: Allen Lane.
Shapiro, Carl and Stiglitz, Joseph (1984) 'Unemployment as a Worker Discipline Device', *American Economic Review*, 74: 433–44.
Smith, Adam (1977}[1776] *An Inquiry into the Nature and Causes of the Wealth of Nations*, Chicago: University of Chicago Press.
——(2000) [1759] *The Theory of Moral Sentiments*, New York: Prometheus Books.
Weiss, Andrew (1990) *Efficiency Wages*, Princeton, NJ: Princeton University Press.

Shaftesbury

Das Shaftesbury Problem

Douglas J. Den Uyl

I am about to engage in some speculation which, so far as I know, is all one can finally do with the problem I am about to discuss. Perhaps there are historians of the era who know relevant details of which I am unaware that could be brought to bear on the issue. I certainly do not claim any special expertise and think of myself only as an interested observer trying to make sense out of something that has struck a number of people as unusual. It might be said that I will attempt to persuade you of some things as we go along, but I have no illusions that I will be offering any proofs or in any other way settling the issue I address. As unanchored as my speculations might be, I am nevertheless hoping that there would still be value to the exercise itself. I am hoping, in other words, that some general questions of interest would arise from what follows even if the topic seems at first narrowly construed.

The problem I wish to discuss is Adam Smith's treatment of Shaftesbury in his *Lectures on Rhetoric and Belles Lettres* (LRBL).[1] The problem is not that Smith might disagree with Shaftesbury on some things or that the treatment of Shaftesbury is harsh. Smith disagrees with many people, and he can be quite merciless in his diagnosis of their mistakes and misconceptions. One is immediately reminded in this connection of his discussion of Bernard Mandeville at the end of TMS. But virtually all readers of Smith see something a good deal more scathing, indeed arguably unfair, in his discussion of Shaftesbury. Indeed, I could be wrong again, but Shaftesbury is the only person I can recall about whom Smith uses ad hominem attacks. Even more remarkably, these attacks upon Shaftesbury are not reserved with regard to some substantive doctrine in economics or morals, but rather over Shaftesbury's writing style! So let's begin with a quick reminder of what Smith does say about Shaftesbury.

The main principle Smith uses to evaluate writing is as follows:

> the perfection of stile consists in Expressing in the most concise, proper and precise manner the thought of the author, and that in the manner which best conveys the sentiment, passion or affection with which it affects ... him and which he designs to communicate to his reader.
>
> (LRBL i.133)

The Adam Smith Review, 6: 209–223 © The International Adam Smith Society
ISSN 1743-5285, ISBN 0–415–66722–7

With this general principle or 'Rule' as Smith calls it, in mind, the problem with Shaftesbury is that

> the author seems not at all to have acted agreably to the Rule we have given above but to have formed to himself an idea of beauty of Stile abstracted from his own character, by which he proposed to regulate his Stile.
>
> (LRBL i.138)

The problem with being abstracted from his own character is that the style Shaftesbury adopts is, according to Smith, directed to the object or purpose of his writing rather than to the expression of Shaftesbury's own thoughts. This abstracted approach, where the author's own position is somewhat obscure, in turn means for Smith that there is finally no restraint upon the style at all because the object itself cannot provide it. Consequently,

> polite dignity is the character he aimed at, and as this seems to be best supported by a grand and pompous diction that was the Stile he made choise of. This he carried so far that when the subject was far from being grand, his stile is as pompous as in the most sublime subjects.
>
> (LRBL i.146)

So far so good. Smith does not like Shaftsbury's style because it violates his principle Rule and because in doing so it leads to an overly ornate use of language and pomposity. Such use of language is an impediment to understanding the thoughts and feelings of the author which simply obfuscates the author's intention. If this were the whole story we might move on or simply formulate our own opinions on whether and to what extent Shaftesbury violates Smith's Rule. Yet within this plausible criticism of Shaftesbury's style we find a number of other not so plausible 'arguments' in support of it. The first is that because of his father (Smith might mean his grandfather as well) and tutor (John Locke), Shaftesbury had no 'very strong affection to any particular sect or tenets in Religion' (LRBL i.138). Shaftesbury would thus prattle on about freedom of religion and philosophizing but 'without being attached to any particular man or opinions' (LRBL i.138). If Shaftesbury had any inclinations at all in this regard, it was away from the established church and towards those sects which themselves allow freedom of speech and thought. The suggestion here is that (a) Shaftesbury's style is unfocused because he has no real substantive commitments, (b) that he is a kind of ideologue who chooses his friends on the basis of some abstract commitments rather than genuine sentiment, and (c) that he is not completely trustworthy because he is drawn to fringe groups rather than the common core of the established church.

But that is not all. Shaftesbury was in fact a shallow and weak reasoner according to Smith. Why: because Shaftesbury was

> of a very puny and weakly constitution, always either under some disorder or in dread of falling into one. Such a habit of body is very much connected, nay almost continually attended by, a case of mind in a good measure similar. Abstract reasoning and deep searches are too fatiguing for persons of this delicate frame.
>
> (LRBL i.139)

Such men, Smith goes on to point out, tend toward the fine arts because these subjects demand little with respect to reasoning. They can indulge their sensibilities, in other words, without taxing their minds or constitutions. Needless to say, pointing to Shaftesbury's health problems and his choice of interests are both ad hominem arguments for rejecting Shaftesbury's style and disparaging his powers of reasoning. On the surface, Smith's next claim, namely that Shaftesbury was unacquainted with 'Naturall philosophy' or what we would now call 'science', seems at first less in this ad hominem vein. But instead of making the case directly about Shaftesbury's ignorance of science, Smith claims that Shaftesbury 'shews a great ignorance of the advances [science] had then made and a contempt for its followers' because 'it did not afford the amusement his disposition required and the mathematicall part particularly requires more attention and abstract thought than men of his weakly habit are generally capable of' (LRBL i.140–41).

If Shaftesbury had had some training in science, perhaps his reasoning would have been better and his style clearer. But because he did not have such training, or did not have the fortitude to go through with training were he to pursue it, Smith's conclusion seems to be that Shaftesbury lacked substance and effectively knew nothing but his own sensibilities. We are told, for example, that men like Shaftesbury are often enthusiasts and much 'disposed to mysticall contemplations'. But in Shaftesbury's case, knowing only Puritan sects, he was offended by the 'grossness of their conduct' which 'shocked his delicate and refined temper and in time prejudiced him against every scheme of revealed religion' (LRBL i.142). The point here is that at least revealed religion would have given some content to Shaftesbury's reflections. Yet since even that was absent, Shaftesbury is left only with his sensibilities.

The same could be said for schools of philosophy such as those of Hobbes and (probably) Locke, which Smith describes as 'selfish and confined systems' (LRBL i.142). These too were too disagreeable to Shaftesbury's delicate constitution, so he does not give himself content in this way either. What he does instead, according to Smith, is to form his own plan (LRBL i.143). I take it here that Smith's point is that Shaftesbury had pretenses towards producing a philosophy, but without it being anchored in any substantive knowledge, Shaftesbury is left only with his sensibilities and pretensions. With no means of regulating his writing style through content and because he ignores Smith's

Rule, the pompous style makes it seem like he's saying something deep when in fact he is not. Consequently, 'as he was of no great depth in Reasoning he would be glad to set off by ornament of language what was deficient in matter' (LRBL i.143). It is hard to imagine a less charitable analysis!

At this stage one would be correct to ask what exactly the problem is? True Smith was less than charitable towards Shaftesbury, but Smith no doubt believes what he says, and lack of charity is at best a moral failing, not an intellectual problem. As we noted at the outset, however, Smith's attacks do seem out of character for him, and the vehemence with which he attacks Shaftesbury's style suggests that something more is at stake. I want to first explore the idea that something more is at stake with what could be called the 'proximity thesis'. The proximity thesis holds that the closer someone's thoughts are to one's own (or the more one derives one's own ideas from another), the more need there is to find a way to differentiate oneself from that other. A corollary would be that the force with which one does so is directly proportionate to the distance one is from the other's ideas (the closer one is or the greater the debt, the more force). In short, if Smith's ideas were close to or owed a good deal to Shaftesbury, he would feel compelled to look for ways to differentiate himself from Shaftesbury. If the ideas are really close, perhaps a verbal 'lashing out' could be expected. Of course, the proximity thesis might be false or the wrong explanation here, or perhaps only part of the explanation. Let us keep it for the moment, however, as our working assumption.

First, if the proximity thesis is to have any plausibility we would have to say something about the connection between Smith and Shaftesbury. As you can imagine, this is a task well beyond the scope of this paper. Fortunately, two recent papers give us a basis upon which to say a few things in summary fashion about the possible connection between Shaftesbury and Smith. One paper, by Jim Otteson, is explicitly about the connection between the two thinkers, but is not especially focused on our issue here. The other paper, by Ryan Hanley, explicitly addresses the matter of Smith's treatment of Shaftesbury, though the paper itself is about Smith and Swift.[2] Swift's style, I might add, is a style Smith admires and which he believes adheres to his Rule.

Let us begin with Otteson. Otteson opens his direct comparison of Shaftesbury and Smith in the following way:

> There are numerous intriguing similarities between Shaftesbury and Adam Smith – so many, in fact, that on reading the works side by side one might think that the latter one simply adopted some of the ideas, arguments, and perhaps even phrasing of the earlier.
>
> (ASR 123)

Otteson then notes that this phenomenon is all the more remarkable given Smith's contemptuous attitude towards Shaftesbury that we have been discussing above. The first main area of comparison between Shaftesbury and

Smith that Otteson discusses is the anti-Hobbesian theory of human nature, or, put more positively, the thesis of natural human sociality. Of course, on this score Shaftesbury was *generally* influential on the Scots through Hutcheson, so by the time Smith was writing about such matters, the move away from Hobbes was already well under way. Second, Otteson argues that Shaftesbury, to varying degrees, advances evolutionary spontaneous-order accounts of human sociality – more as one finds it in TMS than in WN. These accounts are not consistent, or nearly as well worked out, as one finds them in Smith, but the rudiments of this way of looking at human sociality are clearly evident in Shaftesbury. Third, Shaftesbury and Smith have similarities when it comes to the development of moral judgments, both with respect to the evolutionary aspect of such development, and also as a function of the interior dialogue that both precedes and constitutes moral reflection. Otteson claims that Shaftesbury is inconsistent on this score, because his attraction at times to fixed moral principles runs counter to his evolutionary tendencies. Without necessarily endorsing this criticism, it does seem fair to say that both men recognized the need for some stability in the evolutionary process, otherwise there would be a complete moral relativism. Smith handles this with his impartial spectator, and no doubt fixed moral principles would be doing the same thing for Shaftesbury as well. Finally, Otteson argues that Smith, along with other Scottish Enlightenment figures, followed Shaftesbury in linking politeness with liberty. Shaftesbury's metaphor of stones being polishing by bumping into one another was a standard image for drawing this connection. But Shaftesbury, Otteson claims, notices only the connection, but does not provide the account of what it is about liberty that causally encourages the development of politeness. Of course, the explanation has a lot to do with detailing how the sentiments – first identified by Shaftesbury as important to morality – play off each other to produce patterns of politeness and moral norms.

I would concur with Otteson that Shaftesbury does indeed provide a basis from which a number of doctrines associated with Smith seem to emerge. It is not clear, however, that in saying this we get anything more than generic support for our proximity thesis. Because a number of Scots from Hume onward were working with the same generic paradigms, it seems unlikely that Smith would need to struggle to differentiate himself from Shaftesbury any more than the next person. In addition, it is probably true to say that Smith was closer to Hume in many of his views suggesting that if there was a need to differentiate, it would be even more pronounced there. We do not, however, see any such worry on Smith's part with respect to his intellectual proximity to Hume. What would be more compelling would be evidence of positions Smith might claim as original with him which could nonetheless be found in Shaftesbury. The differences between Smith and Hume seem somewhat evident because Smith is careful to point them out. But what would support the proximity thesis more directly would be a set of differences that seem unique to Smith but which upon inspection can be found elsewhere. An author, whether consciously or not, who sensed such similarities might be particularly harsh towards their source, especially if it was not clear how one's contributions were really offering much of an advancement. Here is where I believe Hanley's paper proves so useful. In my view, Hanley attributes to Smith positions which I would argue are actually held by Shaftesbury.

Hanley's paper is devoted to exploring some of the central reasons for Smith's admiration of Jonathan Swift. One of the central reasons given, and the one that concerns us here, is that Smith admired Swift's 'plain style' (ASR 88–89). It is clear from what we said at the outset that Shaftesbury as Smith regards him could not be farther away from the plain style. In this respect, I am in complete accord with Hanley that Smith's aversion to Shaftesbury is due to his dislike of Shaftesbury's style and his preference for the plain style. Where I differ with Hanley is in the interpretation he gives to this dispute over style. In my view, doctrines Hanley attributes to Smith which are designed to separate him from Shaftesbury are actually doctrines Shaftesbury embraces. We would seem to be left with either something close to the proximity thesis or the notion that Smith really did not understand what was going on in Shaftesbury.

Hanley begins by noting a version of Smith's 'rule' as we described it above. It is interesting, however, that Hanley's citing of the rule is slightly, though very significantly, different from my own. Hanley cites Smith saying when it comes to style 'the expression ought to be suited to the mind of the author' (ASR 91). What I cited earlier stated that that basic rule of style consisted in 'Expressing in the most concise, proper and precise manner the thought of the author'. My claim would be that Shaftesbury's style was indeed quite suited to 'the mind of the author' in the sense of carrying out the author's intention in writing, but that that intention did not always include what Shaftesbury himself thought about a given subject, and that was quite deliberate on Shaftesbury's part. Thus on Hanley's way of stating the rule, Shaftesbury could possibly qualify as a good stylist, whereas on the way I formulated the matter above, he could not. Why it was that Shaftesbury chose to hide himself is an issue I shall come back to in a moment, but the general claim here is that Shaftesbury's style should be interpreted in light of the author's own purposes in writing. As it turns out, these are purposes Smith either does not share or fails to appreciate.

In another place, Hanley notes that Smith (along with Swift) offers 'one of his most important, if sweeping, indictments of modern moral philosophy' (ASR 92). As it turns out what is wrong with modern moral philosophy is that it is (quoting Smith) 'inclined to abstract and speculative reasons which perhaps tend very little to the bettering of our practice' (ASR 92). Hanley points out in commenting on this position that 'Smith proved to be sympathetic to Hutcheson's attempt to recover the importance of practical judgment and common sense' (ASR 92). Readers of Shaftesbury know full well that this project of restoring practical judgment in the face of abstract speculation was fully Shaftesbury's own. Apart from Shaftesbury's Socratic turn in writing about morals and his depiction of modern philosophers as 'bubble blowers' (and thus out of contact with the practical world) in one of the images that serve as a frontispiece for the essay 'The Moralists' in the *Characteristicks*,[3] there is abundant evidence that the practical turn did not begin with Hutcheson. In short, what Hanley says about Smith and Swift could first be said about Shaftesbury; to wit, Shaftesbury's 'larger project [was to] reorient modern moral discourse to the practical judgments and dispositions of classical morality and the practical methods of plain speech that accompany it' (ASR 93). No doubt Smith thinks of the plain style as a manifestation of this attack on abstraction and speculation in morals, but it does not follow from this that it is the only way to attack this tendency in modern philosophy. Indeed, I would hold that Shaftesbury was also interested in the production of plain speaking even if his own style did not exhibit it. That has much to do with the purposes of writing that we have yet to mention. If I am right, Smith either fails to understand this feature of Shaftesbury's philosophy or, in the manner of the proximity thesis, he sees the deeper point and seeks to differentiate himself by disputing its manifestation in style.

Hanley also points out in his discussion that Smith admires Swift for his use of humor to reform the manners and morals of mankind. No mention here is made by Hanley, nor do I recall any mention made by Smith, of Shaftesbury's very famous and extended defense of 'raillery' and ridicule which, I would argue, are put forward for precisely the same ends as Hanley attributes to Swift.[4] In this regard Hanley even mentions the 'gentlemanliness' that this approach for the reformation of manners and morals seeks to accomplish. Needless to say, few terms are more associated with Shaftesbury's own goals than 'gentlemanliness'.[5] Finally, it is the exposition of vanity that moves both Swift and Smith in their use of (or admiration for) ridicule and humor in bringing to light hidden vices. Again, one of the foremost images of Shaftesbury's writing is the masked ball where the whole question of the hidden characters of people is the object of the essay. Noting these similarities does nothing to lessen Swift's genius or originality. My point is only to say that if Hanley is right, Smith does not acknowledge being in accordance with purposes that he shares with Shaftesbury, but only seems to admire them when expressed by Swift.

In his conclusion of what is wrong with Shaftesbury, Hanley claims that 'Shaftesbury is thus condemned by Smith for his penchant for both abstract moral theorizing characteristic of the moderns, and then also for his embrace of the convoluted prose characteristic of such an approach' (ASR 93). I shall not dispute Hanley's claim as to Smith's dislike of Shaftesbury as just described. But if this is accurate we simply come back to the problem of Smith either grossly misunderstanding Shaftesbury or Smith being so much like him that he feels the need to lash out as a means of differentiation. In saying this I am, of course, saying that the option Hanley prefers, namely that Smith is right about Shaftesbury being a modern, is in fact mistaken. But are these really our only options?

I take it that Shaftesbury's purpose as a writer is stated most centrally and forcefully in his *Soliloquy.* I have argued elsewhere that the *Soliloquy* is in fact Shaftesbury's central text;[6] but even if that is mistaken it can still serve for our purposes here, for my claim is that this is the text that tells us what writing is all about for Shaftesbury and thus the text to use in finding a principle to assess his style. My claim is quite simple: Shaftesbury deliberately does *not* write so that the 'thought of the author' is immediately or easily conveyed. If the thought of the author is what the reader wishes to know, the reader will have to work at it when reading Shaftesbury. In any case, conveying the thought of the author is not what writing should be about for Shaftesbury, though it would be wrong to say that such a purpose is completely absent. Rather there is a more important goal to achieve in writing which, as we shall see, involves obscuring the author's intentions somewhat.

Let us begin, however, by noting what is wrong with the writers of Shaftesbury's era.

> Our modern *Author*s, on the contrary, are turn'd and model'd (as themselves confess) by the publick Relish, and current Humour of the Times. They regulate themselves by the irregular Fancy of the World; and frankly own they are preposterous and absurd, in order to accommodate themselves to the Genius of the Age. In our Days *the Audience* makes *the Poet;* and *the Bookseller the Author:* with what Profit to *the Publick,* or what Prospect of lasting Fame and Honour to *the Writer,* let any one who has Judgment imagine.
>
> (CTS I.164)

The two points worth nothing from this passage are that modern authors pander to their audiences and do little to improve the public in the process. From this we can infer, and numerous other passages support it, that whatever good writing is for Shaftesbury, it would not involve simply supplying the reader with what the reader wishes to hear, finds agreeable, or is conveyed in a manner the reader finds convenient. For our purposes, another way of putting this point is to say that a good writer for Shaftesbury demands something from the reader, and this in turn demands something from the author, namely some reflection on how to write so that the appropriate demands on the reader are properly executed. The 'thought of the author' is no more the point than the thought of the reader. Good writing engages both in some sort of exchange, and is not merely the process of conveying the ideas of one to the other. In fact, the problem with modern authors is that they 'write in their own person'.

> An author who writes in his own Person, has the advantage of being *who* or *what* he pleases. He is no certain Man, nor has any certain or genuine Character: but sutes himself, on every occasion, to the Fancy of his

> readers, whom as the fashion is now-a-days, he constantly caresses and cajoles.
>
> (CTS I.124)

To avoid pandering and to actually provide some benefit to the reader, an ideal form of writing for Shaftesbury would be the dialogue form. Dialogues – and here the dialogues of the ancients are the model – neither make the intentions of the author immediately clear nor leave the reader to passively soak in that author's intentions. Dialogues also have the advantage of engaging both author and reader simultaneously and doing something to improve the characters of both.

But Shaftesbury tells us we cannot use the dialogue form today:

> Thus dialogue is at an end. The Antients cou'd see their own Faces; but we can't. And why is this? Why, but because we have less Beauty: for so our Looking-Glass can inform us … Our Commerce and manner of Conversation, which we think the politest imaginable, is such, it seems, as we our-selves can't endure to see represented to the Life.
>
> (CTS I.127)

For an author to write a dialogue, he must be of 'a certain and genuine character'. This, as we have seen, is not the modern pandering author. The modern reader is no better. Both are subject to 'a thousand shifts' and characterized by 'affected Habits' (CTS I.128). Dialogues would expose all this, so we cannot bear to see them employed. Like Smith, Shaftesbury is concerned with the veneer that masks the true self, but that veneer is not vanity alone, but whatever habits serve to hide the fact that there is no genuine character underneath. Modern man cannot face the fact the he is all veneer and no substance.

So although I have not shown, nor will I, that Shaftesbury is a good stylist, it seems abundantly clear that he is a thoughtful one, and it seems reasonable to assume that he is carrying out his intentions in writing the way he does, whatever those intentions may be. Of course one option Shaftesbury would have would be to adopt something like the plain and simple style Smith so admires. But Shaftesbury seems to conclude that this path is largely closed as well. In speaking of various sorts of writing styles, Shaftesbury says:

> *The Simple* Manner, which being the strictest Imitation of Nature, shou'd of right be the completest, in the Distribution of its Parts, and Symmetry of its Whole, is yet so far from making any ostentation of Method, that it conceals the Artiface as much as possible: endeavouring only to express the effect of Art, under the appearance of the greatest Ease and Negligence. … The Authors indeed of our Age are as little capable of receiving, as of giving Advice, in such a way as this: So little is the general Palat form'd, as yet, to a Taste of real SIMPLICITY.
>
> (CTS I.160)

Thus simplicity, like the dialogue, would be a suitable form of writing if there were any genuine characters out there to receive it or authors to deliver it, since it best depicts the nature of things in such a way that the art of it does not impede the message. 'Real simplicity' just is this genuine character, but both modern authors and readers lack it. Consequently, since authors and their readers do not do well at giving and receiving advice – and here we are discovering that this has something to do with what writing is all about, rather than about conveying the authors' intentions – artful simplicity of style will not serve that purpose. It does not seem unreasonable, therefore, to conclude that however one describes the ornate style Shaftesbury chooses to use in his own writing, he does so with the full knowledge that there are other ways to write, and he rejects them as faulty for the purposes he regards as essential to the relationship between author and reader.

What then is the purpose of writing for Shaftesbury? I have suggested that whatever rule Shaftesbury is following, it is not Smith's. In addition, I have suggested that Shaftesbury seeks to improve the reader – at least by his lights – as well as himself by the method of writing he uses. Style is somehow a reflection of that purpose of improvement. My thesis, then, is that Shaftesbury is trying to bring both himself and his reader to philosophy understood in precisely the same way as Socrates understands it – as a process of self-examination towards truth. I believe there is plenty of evidence to support this in the *Soliloquy* alone. As but one simple example, one need only consider the epigraph for this particular essay: 'And you need not have looked beyond yourself.' But we have other evidence as well. In commenting on his own writing (Shaftesbury is the 'author' referred to below), particularly as it applies to the *Soliloquy*, Shaftesbury gives us most of the picture we need.

> BY this time, surely, I must have prov'd my-self sufficiently engag'd in the Project and Design of our *Self-discoursing Author*, whose Defence I have undertaken. His Pretension, as plainly appears in this third Treatise, is to recommend Morals on the same foot, with what in a lower sense is call'd *Manners;* and to advance Philosophy (as harsh a Subject as it may appear) on the very Foundation of what is call'd *agreeable* and *polite.*
> (CTS III.100)[7]

Besides telling us that the purpose of his writing – and thus the writing he admires – is to advance philosophy and moral perfection, Shaftesbury also indicates the foundation upon which such writing is to be built, namely manners. Shaftesbury wishes to write in such a way and with such a style that 'agreeable and polite' people would find it attractive. The connection between Shaftesbury and politeness has been noted by all commentators, but it seems reasonable to say here that Shaftesbury must have thought of his own style as being of such a nature that it would appeal to the polite or gentlemanly class of his day. Indeed he tells us that, 'nothing, according to our Author, can so well revive this *self-corresponding* Practice, as the same Search and Study of the highest Politeness in modern *Conversation*' (CTS III.96). It thus is neither his failings as a thinker or a man that explains the style to which Smith objects. Rather, whether well or badly executed, Shaftesbury's style is a function of his purpose in writing and the audience to whom he wishes to appeal. Shaftesbury must have regarded the gentlemanly class as most amenable to, and most important for, the purposes he had. Perhaps reforming them first would be the means to a general reformation of society. I shall not speculate further on that issue here.

It seems clear to me, and is certainly arguable, that the sort of philosophy that Shaftesbury inclines towards, and thus was trying to induce in himself and his readers, is Socratic in nature, which means coming to truth through self-examination. The epigraph for his *Miscellaneous Reflections* is, 'He was favorable to Virtue only, and to her friends', suggesting strongly again that the use of language for Shaftesbury was put to the end of improving character. In his own case, Shaftesbury's *Miscellany* – being commentaries on his own writing – is further evidence of self-examination and transforms his corpus as a whole into a dialogue. In the case of the reader, Shaftesbury's style, form, and mode of discussion we must presume were also designed to stimulate self-examination. I suspect that Shaftesbury saw his ornate style as a means of attracting the reader, but as anyone who has read Shaftesbury knows (Smith included), it is easy to get lost in the words and have to double back to get the meaning. That was perhaps exactly Shaftesbury's intention.

If this is Shaftesbury's intention, he is remarkably subtle about it. Smith, apparently, sees only the style and not the point behind it, for example. But Shaftesbury is also – if one looks for it – remarkably forthright too about what he is doing.

> THUS HAVE I endeavour'd to tread in my *Author's* steps, and prepare the Reader for the serious and downright Philosophy, which even in this last commented Treatise, our *Author* keeps still as a Mystery, and dares not formally profess. His Pretence has been to *advise Authors,* and polish *Styles;* but his Aim has been to correct *Manners,* and regulate *Lives.* He has affected Soliloquy, as pretending only to censure Himself; but he has taken occasion to bring others into his Company, and make bold with *Personages* and *Characters* of no inferior Rank. He has given scope enough to Raillery and Humour; and has intrench'd very largely on the Province of us *Miscellanarian* Writers. But the Reader is now about to see him in a new aspect, 'a formal and profess'd *Philosopher,* a *System*-Writer, a *Dogmatist,* and *Expounder'*. – *Habes consitentem reum.*[8]
>
> (CTS III.114–15)

In this passage he tells us that he has hidden himself a bit from the reader and that he is not beyond keeping his intentions deliberately away from the reader when he writes. This, of course, is simply further evidence that the main point of Smith's Rule is not exactly to Shaftesbury's purpose. The passage also reinforces my other claims about Shaftesbury's purposes in pursuing philosophy. Smith, as we noted, recognizes something of this claim, but puts it in the category of pretention to philosophy rather than philosophy itself. In any case, it does seem clear that Smith has failed to evaluate Shaftesbury's style of writing in terms of its purposes and underlying assumptions about audience, the nature of philosophy as Shaftesbury understands it, and the possibilities of writing in the modern age.

All this, then, brings us back to the proximity thesis. We could, of course, say that Smith understood Shaftesbury and his purposes perfectly well, and in order to divert the reader's attention from the substantive similarities of their doctrines, he chooses to attack the style and call into question Shaftesbury's credentials as a thinker. The problem with such a thesis, however, is that it requires us to speculate about Smith's psychology, and it puts Smith in an entirely negative light. One could say, for example, that Smith is unfair to Shaftesbury without thereby accusing him of malicious intent, as the proximity thesis seems to demand. That benefit of the doubt, I believe, we owe Smith. Moreover, as we noted above, Smith is quite 'proximate' to Hume. Why does he not lash out in some way there as well if the proximity thesis is true?

However, I also do not think it is much better to take the opposite side of the proximity thesis and claim that Smith was, after all, clueless about what Shaftesbury was doing, so that his remarks are simply ignorant and unfair because of that ignorance. I wish to close, therefore, with a thesis that attempts to avoid both these conclusions. Smith and Shaftesbury both agree that style matters, but I would speculate that Smith sensed something about Shaftesbury's style that represented some significant difference of doctrine or approach between them. Perhaps Smith only sensed that difference and could not fully articulate it at the time. Whatever may be the case with articulating the differences, there are, I believe, two differences between Smith and Shaftesbury that should be noted in this context. Smith more or less articulates the first, somewhat less substantive, difference, but only hints at the second.

The first difference is a version of Smith's claim that Shaftesbury does not know any science. I take this as the basis for reformulating that complaint into a broader disagreement between them, namely, that the problem with Shaftesbury is that he was appealing to the wrong audience. Shaftesbury wrote for the gentleman, where Smith writes for the intellectual. The gentleman, let us suppose, is attracted by the flowery edifying style that Shaftesbury himself exhibits. The modern intellectual, by contrast, sees science as being at the center of modern intellectual life. Science is clear, exact, logical, and discursive – qualities that would be most suited to the plain style Smith admires. If, therefore, the class of people who really mattered, not just to ideas themselves, but also to the reformation of culture were intellectuals rather than gentlemen, then perhaps Smith is quite right to complain of Shaftesbury's style. Shaftesbury, as we have seen, complains about the nature of modern philosophy which is suited to this scientific temperament. He is thus not disposed to use a style that imitates it. But more importantly, he concludes for some reason that gentlemen are the holders of the future of morals, manners, culture, and politics and suits his style to them. The opinions of both our authors could be right for their respective times. But my point is that Smith differs from Shaftesbury on which audience one should be writing for, and this difference may reflect a deeper difference over the forces that significantly influence the conduct of a society.

Second, and I think more profoundly, the two may differ over the foundations of morals and the shaping of character, and style is reflective of that difference. For Smith, moral norms and the shaping of character are essentially social in nature. Our propensity to correspond our sentiments with others gives rise to the norms themselves and even to our understanding of who we are as individuals. Writing according to Smith's Rule is critical to this process of correspondence because the author's intentions, like any agent's, must be clear if the correspondence is to take place. Moreover, the author may not be any settled character prior to the author's engagement with others, as perhaps Shaftesbury would like in his ideal author. In any case, to move towards correspondence a simple and plain style is most appropriate, because the reader clearly knows where the mark is for sympathizing with the author. The author too, in being clear about the author's meaning and intentions, is doing what is necessary for correspondence between author and reader by meeting the reader 'half way'. The social links that are thus needed for there to be solid correspondences of sentiment among individuals are more easily secured with the plain style and obedience to Smith's Rule than any alternative.

As I read Shaftesbury, his concept of character formation and the foundation of morals is significantly different from Smith's, being what I would call Socratic. The development of character is not, in the end, social but is rather a process of looking within oneself for the truths that lie buried there. The development of character comes through self-dialogue and internal reflection, not correspondences of sentiment. Of course, Shaftesbury is the one who developed the metaphor of the stones polishing each other, and Smith's impartial spectator does not arise without internal reflection. But the aid of others in one's reflections and development of character does not contradict the basic Socratic moral paradigm. Socrates was certainly a gadfly who would improve those willing to be improved, but there was always the understanding that the truths were pulled from within oneself by oneself. And although Smith's impartial spectator is certainly only possible through dialogical exercises the moral agent must employ, impartiality is something exercised among or between agents for Smith. I am suggesting, therefore, that whatever similarities exist between our two thinkers, Shaftesbury's end is self-perfectibility whereas Smith's is social propriety. If I am right, this is a difference of some significance philosophically.

Of course we do not have the luxury here of turning back to Otteson's project of seeing just how similar Smith and Shaftesbury really are. My point is that if my thesis has any plausibility, it might explain why Smith was so harsh towards Shaftesbury. There may be much they shared, but Smith did not want to get pulled into what I suspect from his point of view was an antiquated Platonism. He sought to be part of the modern world and not a member of a remnant hanging on to antiquity, however much he drew from it. Moreover, the audience he respected and to whom he wished to appeal was quite different from Shaftesbury's. Smith himself actually seems to hint at much of what I have been suggesting:

> His [Shafesbury's] acquaintance with the ancients inclined him to imitate them; and if he had any one particularly in view it was Plato. As he copied him in his Theology and in a great measure in his philosophy so he seems to have copyed his Stile and manner also, tempering it in the same manner so as to make it more suitable to the times he lived in. Theocles in his Rhapsody is exactly copied from Socrates. But as Socrates humour is often too coarse and his sarcasms too biting for this age he has softened him in this respect and made his Theocles altogether polite and his wit such as suits the character of a gentleman.
>
> (LRBL i.145)

About the only thing missing from this passage connected to our closing argument is a direct confirmation of the claim that the foundations and ends of what they were doing in ethics finally fall out quite differently. Despite the fact that Smith respected and employed many facets of ancient ethics, he was not in the end an ancient in ethics. Ethics for him was about the norms governing the relations among persons. Shaftesbury, by contrast, did align himself with the ancients, seeing ethics as primarily about the problem of self-perfection. The scientific disposition of the modern world tells against the ancient approach to ethics because it rejects teleology. Smith, I believe, wants to play in the modern world intellectually.[9] Shaftesbury, I believe, was struggling to find a way to keep antiquity alive in the face of the modern forces against it.[10] But they both agree that the style with which one writes does in fact say something significant about an author's larger projects or commitments. I have only extended that insight a bit to suggest that with our two authors their styles too are indicative of such commitments, some of which they do not share. That may not explain Smith's ad hominems, but it might help explain the sense of frustration they exhibit.

Acknowledgements

I wish to thank those present at the 2008 ASECS panel on Shaftesbury, especially William Levine, for helpful comments when a version of this paper was delivered. I wish also to thank Ryan Hanley for some helpful suggestions as well.

Notes

1 Smith, Adam (1985) *Lectures on Rhetoric and Belles Lettres*, J. C. Bryce (ed.), Indianapolis: Liberty Fund Inc.

2 Both papers can be found in volume 4 of *The Adam Smith Review* (New York: Routledge, 2008) (henceforth ASR). I do not mean to suggest that these are the only two papers one might find of relevance to our issue. In a recent paper, for example, one commentator says that 'Smith develops his moral theory from Shaftesbury's authorial theory, and he also develops his linguistic theory from Shaftesbury's insistence on the sociability of humankind.' Tom Jones, 'Language, Origins and Poetic Encounters in Rousseau, Shaftesbury, Smith and Ferguson', *Modern Language Studies* 42(4): 395–411. Jones cites the authority of Isabel Rivers in making this claim.

3 Shaftesbury, Third Earl of (Anthony Ashley Cooper) (2001) *Characteristicks of Men, Manners, Opinions, Times* (henceforth CTS), Douglas J. Den Uyl (ed.), Indianapolis: Liberty Fund Inc. References in text state volume number (I–III) and page.

4 I shall leave off for the moment the issue of whether Shaftesbury does it well as Smith would conceive it. I assume not.

5 In this respect see Klein, L. E. (1994) *Shaftesbury and the Culture of Politeness: Moral Discourse and Cultural Politics in Early Eighteenth-Century England*, Cambridge: Cambridge University Press.

6 Den Uyl, D. J. (1998) 'Shaftesbury and the Modern Problem of Virtue', *Social Philosophy and Policy* 15: 275–316.

7 In the *Soliloquy* Shaftesbury says:

> there can be no kind of writing which relates to Men and Manners, where it is not necessary for the Author to understand *Poetical* and *Moral* TRUTH, *the Beauty* of Sentiments, *the Sublime* of Characters; and carry in his Eye the Model or Exemplar of that *natural Grace*, which gives to every Action its attractive Charm. If he has naturally no Eye, or Ear, for these *interior Numbers*; 'tis not likely he shou'd be able to judg better of that *exterior Proportion* and *Symmetry* of Composition, which constitutes *a legitimate Piece.*
>
> (I.206)

8 Probably to be translated as: 'You have a defendant who has confessed.' I thank Tom Martin for help on this. He pointed out that that the 's' in *consitentem* in the Liberty Fund edition is probably an 'f' and was misread when the work was put together. This mistake is, obviously, my fault!

9 Largely I believe this because I see its roots in Smith's *History of Astronomy.*

10 In this regard, he seems utterly unsympathetic to the benefit of modern philosophy for ethics:

> 'Tis hardly possible for a Student, but more especially *an Author*, who has dealt in *Ideas*, and treated formally of *the Passions*, in a way of *natural Philosophy*, not to imagine himself more wise on this account, and knowing in his own Character, and the Genius of Mankind. But that he is mistaken in his Calculation, Experience generally convinces us: none being found more impotent in themselves, of less command over their Passions, less free from Superstition and vain Fears, or less safe from common Imposture and Delusion, than the noted Headpieces of this stamp.
>
> (I.180)

Response to Douglas J. Den Uyl's 'Das Shaftesbury Problem'

James R. Otteson

Professor Forman-Barzilai, editor of *The Adam Smith Review,* has generously offered me space to post a brief reaction to Professor Den Uyl's intriguing and provocative essay, 'Das Shaftesbury Problem'. I thank the latter for the provocation and the former for the opportunity.

I am willing to be persuaded by Den Uyl that 'Smith has failed to evaluate Shaftesbury's style of writing in terms of its purposes and underlying assumptions about audience' (p. 220). Yet I wonder whether Den Uyl is right to locate Smith's difficulty in the fact that he and Shaftesbury 'differ over the foundations of morals and the shaping of character' (p. 221). In my paper on Smith and Shaftesbury, I argue that the similarities between their accounts of morality run through several details, and, as Den Uyl rightly reminds us, it is after all Shaftesbury who suggests that 'All Politeness is owing to Liberty. We polish one another, and rub off our Corners and rough Sides by a sort of *amicable Collision*' (I.42[1]). Den Uyl suggests that Shaftesbury subscribes to a 'basic Socratic moral paradigm' (p. 221) in which moral truths come more from within oneself than from a process of social construction, though that is hard to square with Shaftesbury's polishing metaphor. Regardless, where I think I may disagree with Den Uyl is when he concludes that whereas Shaftesbury's 'end is self-perfectibility,' Smith's by contrast 'is social propriety' (p. 221).

I think this misdescribes what Smith is doing in TMS. As Den Uyl recounts, Shaftesbury's 'Aim has been to correct *Manners,* and regulate *Lives*' – not, as Shaftesbury says, 'to advise *Authors,* and polish *Styles*' (III.114–15). If that is true, then I think a difference between Shaftesbury in *Characteristicks* and Smith in TMS is that whereas the former is attempting to correct manners, the latter is trying to account for them. Smith is interested in TMS to understand and describe the processes by which amoral infants transition into moralized adults and by which people's moral judgments come to overlap to greater or lesser extents with those of their loved ones, peers, and community. If Smith in TMS is engaged in a project we today might consider moral psychology, then it seems entirely appropriate that his style would adhere to his 'Rule' of expressing thoughts 'in the most concise, proper and precise manner' possible (LRBL i.133). Note that Smith elsewhere in LRBL

The Adam Smith Review, 6: 224–227 © The International Adam Smith Society
ISSN 1743-5285, ISBN 0-415-66722-7

claims, 'The Didacticall method tho undoubtedly the best in all matters of Science, is hardly ever applicable to Rhetoricall discourses' (LRBL ii.135). He goes on to suggest that under some circumstances, we 'are to conceal our design and beginning at a distance bring them [i.e. our audience] slowly on to the main point and having gained the more remote ones we get the nearer ones of consequence' (LRBL ii.137). But Smith argues that this is a rhetorical device appropriate only when an 'orator' finds himself addressing an audience that is 'prejudiced against the Opinion to be advanced' (ibid.). Perhaps, then, this gives us some insight into Smith's criticism of Shaftesbury: Shaftesbury adopts this 'Rhetoricall' method when his subject matter – human morality – requires instead the 'Didacticall' method.

If I am right, it would lend credence to Den Uyl's claim, with which I agreed above, that perhaps Smith misunderstood Shaftesbury's project. Smith might have taken Shaftesbury to have intended to write a descriptive, even 'scientific,' account of the characteristics of men, manners, opinions, and times, which would therefore have required the 'Didacticall method' – in which case Smith would have been disappointed to see Shaftesbury employing a 'Rhetoricall' method instead. Smith might thus have concluded that Shaftesbury either does not understand the nature of his own project or is simply not up to the task. Scientific reasoning, and its appropriate didactic writing style, are, after all, more difficult, Smith might have thought, than what by contrast requires a rhetorical style; hence if Shaftesbury did not adopt it, perhaps it was because he was unable to.

Is there any other reason Smith might have had to think that Shaftesbury was not up to the task? Perhaps Shaftesbury on Descartes provides an instance. Shaftesbury mentions Descartes only twice, as far as I know: once is a passing reference, without analysis, to Descartes's *Passions of the Soul* (I.182); the other is a discussion of 'the seeming *Logick* of a famous Modern [i.e. Descartes]' who says, '"*We Think:* therefore *We are*"' (III.118). Note the word 'seeming': Shaftesbury is not impressed with the Cartesian argument. He first mocks it: 'a notably invented Saying, after the Model of that philosophical Proposition; That '*What is, is.*' – Miraculously argu'd! "If *I am; I am.*" – Nothing more certain!' (III.118). Shaftesbury proceeds to tell us that he, apparently unlike Descartes, is willing to take his existence '*upon Trust*' (ibid.), and, Descartes's argument notwithstanding, 'there is no Impediment, Hinderance, or Suspension of *Action,* on account of these wonderfully refin'd *Speculations*' (III.119). According to Shaftesbury, radical Cartesian doubt is entirely otiose, issuing in no practical difference in people's lives. It may provide entertainment or diversion for the metaphysician, but in real life people must still act – and even argue and debate (ibid.). The fact that we might prove our own existence 'a thousand times', even to the satisfaction 'of our *Metaphysical* or *Pyrrhonean* Antagonist' (ibid.), yet still without making any concrete difference in our lives, demonstrates the futility of engaging in these metaphysical speculations.

From this Shaftesbury concludes: 'This to me appears sufficient Ground for a *Moralist.* Nor do I ask more, when I undertake to prove the reality of

VIRTUE and MORALS' (III.119). As Den Uyl reminds us, Shaftesbury sees himself as a 'moralist'; indeed, Den Uyl suggests that perhaps this is Shaftesbury's principal interest – namely, in 'improving character' (p. 219). Can this be a place Smith might have seized upon, in forming his opinion that Shaftesbury was 'no great reasoner'? I suggest this possibility because I can imagine – though of course I cannot prove – that Smith might have read Shaftesbury's discussion of Descartes here and come away cold, thinking it is the analysis of a philistine, not a philosopher. There are many moralists indeed who presume to declaim upon vice and virtue but who have little conception of the foundations on which their positions rest. I suspect Smith is suspicious of such endeavors, and that he strove, by contrast, to base whatever moral exhortations he would make on a thorough and firm explanation of the origin and nature of moral sentiments. He might then have expected Shaftesbury should do the same. When he discovers, therefore, that Shaftesbury does not, but instead – despite a few tantalizing remarks – proceeds to moralize without philosophizing, Smith concludes that Shaftesbury must simply not be up to the task.

Yet perhaps we have not gotten to the bottom of why Smith is *so* hostile to Shaftesbury. Smith recognizes, for example, the appropriateness in some contexts of a 'Socratick method' in which one 'keep[s] as far from the main point to be proved as possible, bring on the audience by slow and imperceptible degrees to the thing to be proved' (LRBL ii.135). If Den Uyl is right that Shaftesbury adopts a 'basic Socratic moral paradigm' and perhaps its accompanying method, why would Smith not have noticed as much – and, then, approved Shaftesbury's style as appropriate to its intentions? Den Uyl claims that whereas 'Shaftesbury wrote for the gentleman', 'Smith writes for the intellectual' (p. 220), which Den Uyl suggests might account for the fact that Smith is more impressed by science than rhetoric. Den Uyl further argues that because for Smith 'moral norms and the shaping of character are essentially social in nature' (p. 221), Smith understandably prizes transparency and clarity, not raillery, in writing. But this presumes that Smith is interested in TMS in reforming morals, that Smith in one way or another wants to be a 'moralist'. If that is a concern of Smith's, I think it is at best secondary. Thus I think the more straightforward explanation of Smith's relatively clear, transparent, and simple style in TMS is not that it is a rhetorical device but that he believes it is appropriate to his subject matter. Den Uyl argues that 'Shaftesbury's end is self-perfectibility whereas Smith's is social propriety' (p. 221). I agree with the former but question the latter: Whereas Shaftesbury was arguably interested in encouraging self-perfection among his readers, Smith was, I suggest, far less interested in fostering social propriety than he was in correctly describing human moral sentiments.

I think Den Uyl is correct that if Smith believed he discovered 'an antiquated Platonism' (p. 222) in Shaftesbury, this certainly would have rankled him, and thus perhaps explained some of the venom in his dismissals of Shaftesbury. My claim is that Smith might additionally have believed that

Shaftesbury was in fact no very great reasoner, which is why Shaftesbury was led to raillery and wit instead of science and philosophy. Since the latter is what his subject required, Smith's conclusion might have been that Shaftesbury was too dense to understand the nature of his own project – which would make him very dense indeed. A dismissal of the implications of Cartesian skepticism might have confirmed this negative judgment in Smith's mind. Now, if Den Uyl is correct that it is in fact Smith who misunderstood Shaftesbury's project, instead of Shaftesbury's having misunderstood his own, then Smith's venom is quite unjustified. But justifying a judgment is different from explaining it. My intention has been to suggest only that Smith might have had reasons to suspect Shaftesbury's project, reasons that might have seemed weighty to Smith if not to us.

Note

1 Here and throughout, the reference to Shaftesbury's *Characteristicks* is to the 2001 Liberty Fund edition, edited by Douglas J. Den Uyl, by volume number and page. All italics are in the original. Shaftesbury, Third Earl of (Anthony Ashley Cooper) (2001) *Characteristicks of Men, Manners, Opinions, Times.* Douglas J. Den Uyl (ed.), Indianapolis: Liberty Fund Inc.

Another response to Douglas J. Den Uyl's 'Das Shaftesbury Problem'

Ryan Patrick Hanley

It was very kind of the editor to invite me to submit a response to Douglas J. Den Uyl's thought-provoking essay. I shall keep it brief – just long enough to offer additional evidence for two of Den Uyl's claims, and to call attention to a side of Smith's critique of Shaftesbury not discussed by Den Uyl – but which is, I think, of great interest and import.

The first point for which I want to offer further evidence concerns what Den Uyl calls the 'proximity thesis' (p. 212). Den Uyl's intriguing suggestion on this front is that Smith's hostility to Shaftesbury may owe to his recognition of the need to distinguish himself from a thinker whose substantive claims resemble his own or may have served as the source of his own. The suggestion is all the more intriguing, I think, given the pattern of Smith's engagement with other near-contemporary thinkers from whom he is known to have drawn. In several cases, this engagement follows precisely the trajectory that is here considered by Den Uyl, namely critique of style and appropriation of substance. Smith's engagements with Mandeville and Rousseau are especially obvious examples. In his few explicit invocations of Mandeville and Rousseau in his published corpus, Smith notably emphasizes their 'eloquence,' and particularly insists that such eloquence conceals a set of substantively problematic doctrines (e.g. LER 11–12; TMS VII.ii.4.6; cf. Imitative Arts 2.24–25). Yet for all this, and as at least two generations of scholars have demonstrated, Smith's critiques hardly prevented him from drawing liberally upon, and in certain cases, explicitly appropriating, certain substantive positions and locutions from both Mandeville and Rousseau. Seen thus, Smith's engagement with Shaftesbury may be unique for its vehemence, but in fact fits an established pattern in his thought – attention to which may be of benefit in future (and much-needed) scholarship on Smith's sources.

Den Uyl's second principal claim is that Smith may simply have 'misunderstood' Shaftesbury (p. 215). On this front, Den Uyl's primary suggestion is that the nature of Shaftesbury's project compelled him to employ a less direct manner of writing in order to better accomplish certain of his purposes, and indeed a manner antithetical to the plain or simple styles admired by Smith. In this light, Shaftesbury's choice of style can be seen to emerge from his awareness of the nature of his ends and his audience, and led him further to employ a

The Adam Smith Review, 6: 228–231 © The International Adam Smith Society
ISSN 1743-5285, ISBN 0-415-66722-7

method of communication that, in Den Uyl's words, involves obscuring the author's intentions somewhat (p. 216). If so, it seems quite reasonable to suggest that this would have failed to resonate with Smith. In a notorious footnote to his 'History of the Ancient Logics and Metaphysics', Smith rejects the very possibility of esotericism or a 'double doctrine', deriding it as a 'strange fancy' which 'the writings of no man in his senses ever were, or ever could be intended to do' (HALM 3n). Given Smith's hostility to concealment in Plato, it would hardly be surprising if he were disinclined to recognize it in Shaftesbury.

But with this we reach what is to my mind the most interesting aspect of Smith's engagement with Shaftesbury – though one which, so far as I know, has yet to be noticed. This concerns Smith's account of Shaftesbury's orientations to antiquity and modernity. On Den Uyl's reading, Shaftesbury is an 'ancient' and Smith a 'modern', a formulation that leads him ultimately to describe Shaftesbury's attachment to a vision of philosophy understood in precisely the same way as Socrates understands it (p. 218). This itself demands scrutiny; Shaftesbury's claim that 'to philosophize, in a just signification, is but to carry good breeding a step higher' is arguably something less than precisely Socrates' understanding of philosophy. Smith himself, at any rate, insists on a difference between the two; thus his central comment on Shaftesbury's debts to Plato:

> His acquaintance with the ancients inclined him to imitate them; and if he had any one particularly in view it was Plato. As he copied him in his Theology and in a great measure in his philosophy so he seems to have copyed his Stile and manner also, tempering it in the same manner so as to make it more suitable to the times he lived in. Theocles in his Rhapsody is exactly copied from Socrates. But as Socrates humour is often too coarse and his sarcasms too biting for his age he has softened him in this respect and made his Theocles altogether polite and his wit such as suit the character of a gentleman.
>
> (LRBL 1.145–46)

Shaftesbury's is thus a 'softened' or 'tempered' Platonism, one that aims to minimize or negate the fundamental classical distinction between the philosopher and the gentleman.

But even this doesn't go quite far enough. To say that Shaftesbury's is merely a Platonism softened or tempered suggests him to be engaged merely in a familiar effort to accommodate ancient doctrines to modern conditions. But Smith's deeper point is much more interesting. Shaftesbury is engaged in something decidedly more radical than mere accommodation. Smith gives us some hint as to what might be at stake in his account of Shaftesbury's 'modernization', which adds a crucial element to the more moderate claim above:

> The system which of all others best suited his disposition was that of the Platonists. Their refined notions both in Theology and Philosophy were

> perfectly agreeable to him, and accordingly his Philosophy and Theology is the same in effect with theirs but modernized a little and made somewhat more suitable to the taste then prevailing. In these he intermixes somewhat of the Philosophy of Hobbes and his preceptor Locke ... But tho he endeavours to run down these philosophers yet he sometimes takes their assistance in forming his own plan.
>
> (LRBL 1.142–43)

Shaftesbury is hardly a conventional ancient. So far from a conservator of the traditions of antiquity, his aims were fundamentally Hobbesian – and indeed more so than Hobbes' own! Thus Smith's arresting claim: 'Such is Lord Shaftesburys Undertaking to overturn the Old Systems of Religion and Philosophy as Hobbes before him had done but still more, which Hobbes never had attempted to do, to erect a new one' (LRBL 1.144). This striking critique reaches its head in Smith's comparison of Shaftesbury to Lucian:

> In the Choise of his subject he was allmost the same as Lucian. The design of both was to overthrow the present fabric of Theology and Philosophy but they differed in this: Lucian had no design of erecting another in its place. Whereas Shaftesbury not only designed to destroy the Structure but to build a new Aedifice of his own in its room.
>
> (LRBL 1.146–47)

Taken collectively, these remarkable allegations help to explain Smith's interest, noted by Den Uyl, in Shaftesbury's education among men who 'cried up freedom of thought and Liberty of Conscience in all matters religious or philosophical' (LRBL 1.138). They also help explain his interest in the experiences which 'prejudized [Shaftesbury] against every scheme of revealed religion' (LRBL 1.142). But most importantly, they suggest that Smith's attacks on Shaftesbury's style and his character may be mere preludes to his fundamental concern: namely Shaftesbury's irreligion. Smith's vehement denunciation of such naturally invites speculation on his motives. This task is of course well beyond the scope of this brief response, and here the most we can say is that Smith's engagement with Shaftesbury would seem to represent a key if underappreciated moment not simply in his conception of literary style but in his conception of revealed religion.

One final point deserves notice. Den Uyl's article ends with an important claim concerning the fundamental difference between Shaftesbury and Smith: namely that the end of the former is 'self-perfectibility' whereas the latter's is 'social propriety' (p. 226). But this strikes me as overstated. Much of TMS, it seems to me, is best understood as an attempt to set forth a normative morality at once responsive to the moral challenges of commercial society and capable of furthering the genuine flourishing of the individual. But having argued this elsewhere (Hanley 2009), rather than repeat it here I'd prefer to end with a point concerning Smith's view of Shaftesbury on perfection.

Specifically: Smith's critique of Shaftesbury is not that he organized his theory around 'some Model or Ideal of perfection'. Rather, what seems to have concerned Smith is Shaftesbury's method of apprehending this ideal. As Smith three times insists, far from seeking the ideal of beauty somewhere 'out there' – as far-too-roughly might be said of the Platonic Forms or the Aristotelian *kalon* so well known to Shaftesbury himself – Shaftesbury was governed by an ideal of beauty that he 'abstracted from his own character' (LRBL 1.137–38). Shaftesbury, that is, was less dedicated to understanding the transcendent Forms than to 'forming some system to himself more agreeable to his own inclinations and temper' (LRBL 1.142 and cf. 1.144). Read alongside his critique of Shaftesbury's theological ambitions, Smith's suggestion here reinforces our sense that he regarded Shaftesbury as a strikingly modern philosophical revolutionary.

Now, whether such an account of his project is fair to Shaftesbury himself is of course another question altogether, one itself deserving of further consideration. In the meantime, Den Uyl's stimulating analysis of Smith's remarkable and underappreciated critique of Shaftesbury has done scholars the crucial service of reminding us that 'we are only beginning to scratch the surface of what sources might be considered when thinking of potential influences on Adam Smith' (Den Uyl 2008: 4).

References

Den Uyl, Douglas J. (2008) 'Introduction: Adam Smith's Sources', *Adam Smith Review* 4: 3–7.

Hanley, Ryan Patrick (2009) *Adam Smith and the Character of Virtue*, Cambridge: Cambridge University Press.

Anglo-American capitalism

Guest editor: Sandra Peart

Introduction

Sandra Peart

The call for papers in this special issue asked whether there is a future for the robust sort of capitalism favoured by Adam Smith or whether we have reached a limit to Anglo-American capitalism as the engine of human betterment. Contemporary events loomed large late in 2008 and it seemed appropriate to consider whether Anglo-American capitalism was passing away. We were particularly interested in contributions that viewed current economic events through a lens informed by Smith's teaching on institutions, money and economic growth.

It will come as no surprise that these essays on Adam Smith and Anglo-American capitalism interpret both the notion of 'Anglo-American capitalism' and Smith's take on capitalism rather differently. He was complex and arguably the most subtle of the classical political economists. So, his insights are discovered and reinterpreted in this journal and elsewhere. A new set of research questions and a new Adam Smith emerged after the rediscovery of his *Theory of Moral Sentiments* by philosophers and economists in the latter part of the twentieth century.

The papers that follow on Smith's capitalism are situated along a spectrum of economic to intellectual history. Hugh Rockoff presents a fascinating examination of the crisis of 1772 in the context of Smith's monetary metaphors, the highway through the air supported on Daedalian wings. He asks the good question whether adopting Smith's regulatory framework might have reduced the probability of and ameliorated the effects of a repetition of the 1772 crisis. Like Rockoff, Maria Pia Paganelli focuses on banking and banking policy; she uses Smith's insights regarding the incentives to commit financial fraud and the bias in perceiving the odds of success to shed light on the recent banking crisis. Alessandro Roncaglia, by contrast, claims that the theoretical foundations of Anglo-American capitalism, a faith in the strong form of the invisible hand argument, simply fail to pertain in today's economic setting. Robert Urquhart, too, takes issue with the empirical content of the order linked to Smith's writing and finds Smith's economic order to be 'a political and commercial society' as opposed to a capitalist mode of production. Urquhart rightly focuses on the centrality of the propensity to exchange in Smith's framework. Jonathan Wight holds that Smith's policy

The Adam Smith Review, 6: 235–236 © The International Adam Smith Society
ISSN 1743-5285, ISBN 0–415–66722–7

recommendations for economic development were pragmatic. Rather than recommending a single institutional framework, Smith recognized that multiple sorts of institutions might accomplish the job reasonably well. Niall Ferguson takes up the issue of how one might contain the influence of large banks while not simply transferring economic and political power and influence from private to public institutions. That concern is much in line with Smithian priorities.

What might we take away from such a variety of viewpoints? Three themes emerge from even a cursory reading of this collection. First, Smith was on the whole optimistic about the capacity of ordinary people for bettering their condition. Though institutions might develop and sometimes fail, the course of human history strongly suggests that humans will emerge from the crisis with better banking habits and better banks. The real question is whether governments, too, will emerge with improved spending habits and here the record yields less evidence.

Second, however, there is rigidity in the Smithian system caused by partial sympathy, by what Smith would have referred to as factions. As Smith saw things, factions, group allegiances that count those outside the group differently from those inside the group, were the most pressing problem of democratic politics. One way to think about factions in the context of the current economic climate is that regulators and policy makers align their interests more tightly with current generations, hence bailing out today's voters at the expense of distant future voters. Here, too, however, there is some reason for hope. Factions, though sluggish, may change over time. When it became clear in the nineteenth century that British law wrongly excluded some groups from political decision making, institutions of the day were altered. Women were granted the right to own property even though this reform meant a decrease in the available property to be owned by men. Similarly, we may hope that the institutional reforms which may well be forthcoming in the near future will proceed along lines that protect interest politics and political factions less and investors, large and small, more.

Upon Daedalian wings of paper money

Adam Smith and the crisis of 1772

Hugh Rockoff

A wagon-road through the air[1]

> The commerce and industry of the country … cannot be altogether so secure when they are thus, as it were, suspended upon the Daedalian wings of paper money as when they travel about upon the solid ground of gold and silver.
> (WN II.ii.86)

Rather than being a model builder in the modern mathematical style, Adam Smith was a metaphor builder. We can discover how Smith reached the conclusions that he did about money and banking by focusing on his most important metaphor for money, a highway, and his most important metaphor for banking, a highway through the air supported on Daedalian wings of paper money. Smith is not unique in relying on metaphors to explain the nature of money. Milton Friedman (1969), for example, begins his collection of essays entitled the *Optimum Quantity of Money* by explaining that the theory of money is like a Japanese garden: simple on the surface, but filled with subtleties that emerge after contemplation. And the lead essay in that volume begins by asking what would happen if a helicopter flew over an economy and dropped $1,000 on it, a story made famous more recently by Ben, 'Helicopter Ben', Bernanke. Smith is not even unique in using the classical tale of Daedalus and Icarus to illustrate the dangers of a financial bubble. Levy and Peart (2010) found two images of Icarus in *The Great Mirror of Folly*, an eighteenth-century Dutch collection of cartoons illustrating the South Sea and Mississippi bubbles. What is unique about Smith, and perhaps some of the other economists of the classical era, is that he used his metaphors not only as a way of communicating ideas, but also, as I will try to show here, as a tool of analysis.

Here is the passage from the *Wealth of Nations* that contains Smith's metaphor:

> The gold and silver money which circulates in any country may very properly be compared to a highway, which, while it circulates and carries to market all the grass and corn of the country, produces itself not a single pile of either. The judicious operations of banking, by providing, if

The Adam Smith Review, 6: 237–268 © The International Adam Smith Society
ISSN 1743-5285, ISBN 0-415-66722-7

> I may be allowed so violent a metaphor, a sort of waggon-way through the air, enable the country to convert, as it were, a great part of its highways into good pastures and corn-fields, and thereby to increase very considerably the annual produce of its land and labour. The commerce and industry of the country, however, it must be acknowledged, though they may be somewhat augmented, cannot be altogether so secure when they are thus, as it were, suspended upon the Daedalian wings of paper money as when they travel about upon the solid ground of gold and silver. Over and above the accidents to which they are exposed from the unskillfulness of the conductors of this paper money, they are liable to several others, from which no prudence or skill of those conductors can guard them.
>
> (WN II.ii.86)

This was not the only metaphor that Smith used to analyze money. He also likened money to a great (water) wheel that provided the motive force for commerce, but the wagon-road in the air was the most extraordinary metaphor. It captures both the benefits of banking and the dangers. We know what happened to Daedalus. He made wings of feathers held together by wax. Daedalus used them wisely, but his son Icarus flew too close to the sun, the wax melted, and Icarus plunged into the sea. A meltdown – clearly Smith has a wonderful metaphor for the crisis of 1772, or for that matter, the crisis of 2008.[2]

Smith's use of this metaphor can be traced in some detail because we have a preliminary draft of part of the *Wealth of Nations* and lecture notes from his course in jurisprudence. The preliminary fragment, which is said to have been written before April 1763, contains an early version of the metaphor; it has the wagon-road through the air, but no Daedalian wings.[3]

> They [banks] enable us, as it were, to plough up our high roads, by affording us a sort of communication through the air by which we do our business equally well. That therefore, to confine them by monopolies or any other restraints, except such as are necessary to prevent frauds and abuses, must obstruct the progress of public opulence.
>
> (Smith 1978, *Early Draft*, 36)

In the Lecture on Jurisprudence given on 8 April 1763 Smith used the high road metaphor, but in that lecture, assuming the student's notes were accurate, everything was strictly on the ground.

> The high roads may in one sense be said to bear more grass and corn than any ground of equall bulk, as by facilitating carriage they cause all the other ground to be more improved and encourage cultivation, by which means a greater quantity of corn and grass is produced. … Now if by any means you could contrive to employ less ground in them by straightening them or contracting their breath without interrupting the

> communication, so as to be able to plow up 1/2 of them, you would have so much more ground in culture and consequently so much more would be produced, viz a quantity equall to what is produced by 1/2 the road. … Paper money is an expedient of this sort.
>
> (LJA vi.128)

In the lecture on banking in the course on jurisprudence given in the following academic year, Smith returned again to the metaphor, but again, everything is on the ground (LJB 245). Indeed, Smith goes on to explain to the class that a banking crisis could not do much damage in Scotland. Imagine, says Smith, the extreme case:

> all the money of Scotland was issued by one bank and it became bankrupt, a very few individuals would be ruined by it, but not many, because the quantity of cash or paper that people have in their hands bears no proportion to their wealth.
>
> (LJB 250)

Smith then draws the conclusion that competition that divided the banking system would reduce the effects of a single failure still further. Conclusion: Do not worry about bank failures. One interesting aspect of this thought experiment, one that Smith apparently did not consider, is that if the total of cash and paper money is small relative to total wealth, then the social savings from replacing more or all of the hard money in circulation with paper is going to be small relative to total wealth as well. The amount of additional land that could be brought into production, in other words, by building wagon-roads through the air will be small relative to the total amount in production.

The question, clearly, is what had happened to change Smith's mind about the dangers of paper money between the *Early Draft* and the *Lectures on Jurisprudence*, on the one hand, and the *Wealth of Nations*, on the other. I believe that the change was the result of the shocks hitting the Scottish banking system in the interim, especially the crisis of 1772. The idea that Smith's view of banking was transformed by the events that he experienced, I should hasten to add, is not new. The most compelling evolutionary treatment of Smith's views come from Checkland (1975b) and Gherity (1994). My paper is in that tradition, but I think that by using quantitative data to frame the experiences that were shaping Smith's thinking, by relying on some analogies with American banking history with which I am familiar, and by uncovering some hidden gems in Smith's work, I have been able to add something of value to their interpretations.

Smith's metaphor shows how bank-issued paper money increases a society's real income. To fix ideas, let's first consider a very simple example. Suppose the stock of money in circulation is £100, all gold and silver. That means that at some time in the past £100 worth of labour and capital were used to dig gold out of the ground, if there were domestic gold or silver mines, or that £100 of labour and capital were used to produce goods for export that were exchanged for gold or silver. Now suppose that the gold and silver is replaced by paper and that the gold and silver is invested abroad in assets that provide a real return. Then the total income of the economy would be higher since the economy would have the return from the assets purchased abroad while the paper money would be fulfilling all the duties that the gold and silver had fulfilled previously. The innovation of paper money would create a 'social savings' to use the term that became standard after Robert Fogel used it to describe his estimate of the contribution of the railroad to American economic growth.

In this example, the gold and silver could be replaced by bank notes or fiat paper money. But Smith considers seriously only a bank-issued paper currency. Although he mentions John Law and legal tender paper money issues in the American colonies, he appears to have seen little benefit in fiat paper money issues as a way of saving real resources or as a way of stimulating a slumping economy (Paganelli 2006).

Smith was not content to simply make the theoretical case that paper money created a social savings. Like any modern economist, Smith attempted to go further and compute the social savings.[4] But here I think Smith ran into a problem: the social savings implied by Smith's metaphor were not as large as Smith's intuition told him they should be. In the *Wealth of Nations* (II.ii.30) Smith imagines a country in which the circulation consists of £1,000,000 sterling (gold or silver).[5] This money is now replaced by a paper currency of £1,000,000 in notes for which the banks hold one-fifth, £200,000 in reserve.[6] This frees £800,000 that can be used to purchase consumption or investment goods abroad. The paper money, Smith points out, would not have been accepted abroad, but the gold and silver replaced by paper in the Scottish circulation would be. The money could be invested in various ways, for example in the 'carrying trade' (transporting goods from one place to another).

A modern economist would then finish the social savings calculation by dividing an estimate of the profits in the carrying trade by an estimate of the net domestic product. (We usually use gross domestic product, but as Smith pointed out, net is better.) Suppose that the carrying trade produced a profit of 10 per cent per year;[7] a good return in an economy where long-term bonds were yielding 4 per cent. Then the £800,000 invested in the carrying trade would yield £80,000 per year.

What would be the neat revenue, to use Smith's spelling, or annual product, appropriate to this hypothetical example? Smith thought that it was difficult to determine the proportion that the circulating medium bore to the annual produce, and pointed out that estimates ranged from one-fifth to one-thirtieth (WN II.ii.40). If we take one-fifth, the assumption most favorable to the role of banking, then the increase in annual produce that we could attribute to banking, measured as a percentage of the total annual product, would be

1.60 per cent [80,000/(5*1,000,000)]. If we use the least favorable estimate of the ratio of money to annual product, the result would be 0.27 per cent. Even the larger figure, 1.60 per cent, is relatively small. The conclusion would be that replacing gold and silver with bank notes would have a positive impact, but not a major impact, on the standard of living.

But Smith did not finish the calculation in this way. Instead he followed another path and concluded that the effect was large (WN II.ii.40). Smith argued that only a small part of the annual produce is 'ever destined to the maintenance of industry'. If the sterling freed by the introduction of banking is compared with this small amount we reach the conclusion that banking can make a very considerable addition to 'the annual produce of land and labour'. What does Smith have in mind? I believe that it must have been something like the following. Suppose that the annual produce of a farm is 100,000 tons of grain. Then it would be a mistake to consume the full 100,000. Some part must be retained to provide seed for the next year. Suppose that we require 10,000 tons of seed to produce a crop of 100,000 tons. Then the annual produce will be (net) 90,000 tons of grain. Year after year the economy will produce 100,000 tons, consume 90,000, and save 10,000. Suppose that by buying grain from abroad with hard money consumption can be maintained at 90,000 while a stock of 20,000 tons is made available to be planted next year. The harvest will therefore increase to 200,000 tons. If consumption is increased to 180,000 tons and 20,000 saved then production can be maintained year after year at nearly twice what it was before! Alchemy!

Here, I believe, Smith nodded. Smith is implicitly assuming a very high rate of return to investments in agriculture. In my example the return is 900 per cent (90/10). Clearly the returns to agriculture can't be that high. To increase output much more investment besides the investment in seed will be required. Land must be cleared and manured, farm implements must be purchased, houses must be built for workers, roads must be built, and so on. We simply don't observe the high returns necessary to make Smith's calculation yield a large social savings.

There is an interesting juxtaposition of descriptive phrases in the passage which contains the Daedalian wings metaphor. In the second sentence of the metaphor Smith tells us that the effect of replacing gold and silver with paper would be to 'increase very considerably the annual produce of its [a nation's] land and labour'. But in the very next sentence Smith tells us that commerce and industry 'may be somewhat augmented'. The two phrases are not necessarily in contradiction, and the use of two different phrases is probably simply an example of 'elegant variation'. However, the use of two phrases that lean in different directions may reflect some underlying doubts about the size of the social savings from banking. Smith, to put it somewhat differently, may have been conflicted about the role of banking because his wagon-road metaphor, and the social savings calculation based on it, do not lead to the conclusion that banking was crucial to Scottish economic development if carried through logically. On the other hand, Scotland had made enormous economic progress in the eighteenth century, and Scotland's banking system, with its system of branches, had also made enormous progress. Surely, one feels, there must have been some connection. There must have been something the banks were doing to promote economic development. But it is not easy to say precisely what it was, and move on to a quantitative calculation. Rondo Cameron (1967) wrestled with precisely this problem in *Banking in the Early Stages of Economic Development*. Cameron was able to show in detail how the Scottish economy and its banking system had progressed over the course of the eighteenth century, and in this and other studies was able to establish a relationship between banking and industrialization. He was able, moreover, to identify many of the possible causative connections between banking and economic development. But he did not carry out the exercise that Smith recognized was important and quantify the contribution of banking to economic development in Scotland.

The sanguine views of banking that Smith held at the time his *Lectures on Jurisprudence* were recorded were altered by a series of shocks that hit the Scottish banking system in the following decade. The first was a wave of small (less than £1) notes issued by banks and individual merchants: the small note mania.

The 'small note mania'

When the small note mania took place has been described in various ways. Checkland (1975b: 508), for example, writes broadly of the 'small notes mania of the 1750s and 1760s', but others, including Smith, have described it, narrowly, as the early 1760s. With the aid of James Douglas's (1975) catalogue of Scottish bank notes we can be more specific. Douglas's catalogue was compiled for numismatists, and attempts to describe all notes known to have been issued by the Scottish banks, by date of issue. With a few exceptions it does not include the notes issued by individuals, the merchants Smith referred to as 'beggarly bankers'. Nevertheless, it appears to be a very carefully compiled and thorough list and should give us some idea of the timing of events. The first note for less than £1 issued by a Scottish bank (as opposed to an individual entrepreneur) appears to have been a 10 shilling note issued by the British Linen Bank in 1750. The first note for less than £1 issued by the Bank of Scotland appears to have been a 10 shilling note that bears the date 15 May 1760. Figure 1 shows new issues of Scottish bank notes in denominations of less than £1 each year from 1725 to 1810. On the basis of this evidence it appears that the small note mania reached its zenith in 1763 and 1764. Smith was probably right – it was a phenomenon concentrated in, if not confined to, a few years.

The notes that we have been discussing were issued by banks. It appears that in addition many small notes were issued by local merchants. Apparently notes for as little as 1 shilling Scots (1 penny) were issued (Kerr 1902: 86–88; Munro 1928: 122). These small notes, moreover, were mocked by the issue of

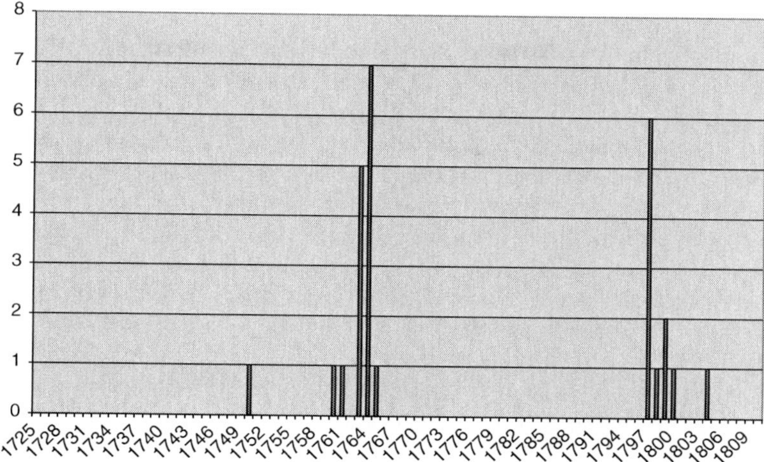

Figure 1 New issues of Scottish bank notes with face values less than £1, 1725–1810.
Source: Compiled from Douglas (1975).

bogus notes. According to Munro (1928: 122) and other sources, one of the best of these was the Wasp note: 'One penny sterling or in the Option of the Directors three Ballads six days after a Demand'. It was elegantly printed in Glasgow, had an ornamental border of wasps, bore the motto 'We swarm', and was signed 'Daniel Mcfunn'.

Why there should have been a small note mania is also unclear. One possibility, of course, is that it was, as the name suggests, a mania: People saw an opportunity to make some short-term profits by issuing small denomination notes, and they simply got carried away. If my neighbor can get into banking and issue notes, why can't I? This interpretation has been advanced by a number of Scottish banking historians. Another possibility that has a substantial body of adherents is that a shortage of small denomination coins created a market for small denomination bank notes.[8] The two explanations, mania and scarcity of small denomination coins, of course, are not mutually exclusive. It is possible that there was a shortage of small coins, that banks and individuals rushed in to fill the gap with small denomination paper notes, and that some people were carried away and issued too many notes.

My guess is that the shortage of small denomination coins was the most important factor, and that it was the result of a familiar process: wartime inflation that raises the value of coins as foreign exchange or as a raw material above their value as coins. The Seven Years' War (1756–63) produced a net drain of specie from Britain. It was a world war and Britain was forced to send funds abroad to support British military actions and those of its foreign allies (Kerr 1902: 88; Graham 1911: 86; Munro 1928: 121). Scotland, moreover, seems to have suffered a balance of payments crisis with England and the rest of the world in 1762 (Hamilton 1953). This was partly the result of the winding down of the war. Until that time Scotland had benefited from the war because its chief export, linen, had benefited from the absence of European competition. The end of the war produced a decline in Scottish linen exports. However, this was not the only factor; a shift of investment toward London financial markets also undermined the Scottish balance of payments. The balance of payments deficit in turn must have been covered by an outflow of specie, including, presumably, small coins.

Moreover, like most big wars, the Seven Years' War was accompanied by inflation, although the amount was small by the standard of the Napoleonic and the First and Second World Wars: Britain was not forced off the specie standard in the Seven Years' War as it would be in subsequent 'world wars'. Clapham (1945: vol. 1, 240–41), it is true, perhaps because of the absence of massive inflation, suggests that there was little connection between the banks' efforts to finance the war and the small note mania, but as he also notes (Clapham 1945: vol. 1, 236), the government strained to finance the war, and this must have at least added to the inflationary pressures that contributed to the shortage of small denomination coins.

The market prices of gold and silver (in £s/ounce), are shown in Figure 2 for the years 1730–90. The price of gold is measured on the left vertical axis and the price of silver, because it was worth much less per ounce than gold, is measured on the right vertical axis. Both series rose during the Seven Years' War. The price of silver, moreover, reaches its highest point in the sixty years shown in the figure in 1760, just at the onset of the small note mania. The price of silver, of course, was crucial for the small note mania because the

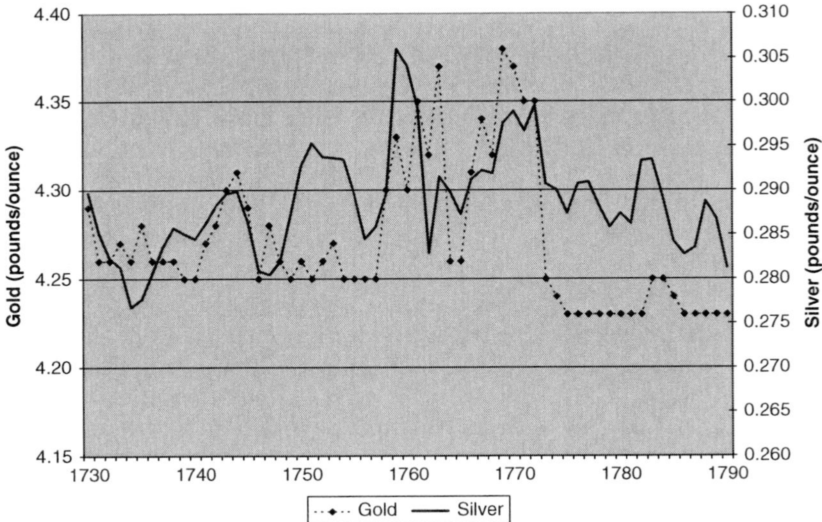

Figure 2 Market prices of gold and silver in London, 1730–1790.
Source: Officer (2009b).

notes would replace silver shillings. If the price of silver was high enough shillings would be hoarded for export.

The increases in the price indexes (Figure 3) were not, as I noted previously, of the extreme nature that characterized subsequent major wars. But there was a sustained rise after 1760. As shown in Figure 3, Gilboy's index of the cost of living in London rises by nearly 10 per cent in 1762. In 1764 there was a parliamentary inquiry into the causes of the high prices of provisions (WN I.xi.b.17). There were, undoubtedly, non-monetary forces at work. There was an unparalleled drought in 1762, and poor harvests that drove up agricultural prices (Hamilton 1953: 355; Kindleberger 1978: 48). The price indexes (Figure 3) confirm that the inflation was concentrated in agricultural prices: The consumer price index net of cereals and the producer price index do not increase very much. Nevertheless, it seems likely that monetary expansion contributed to the inflation. In the absence of monetary accommodation the increase in the real price of cereals might have been accomplished through a fall in non-cereal prices that left the more complete consumer price indexes unaffected.

It is common, incidentally, for wartime inflation to produce hoarding or melting of small coins, creating a vacuum in the circulation that can be addressed by the issue of small notes. This is what happened, for example, in the United States during the Civil War. The silver coinage disappeared from circulation, spent about fifteen years on a working vacation in Canada, Central and South America, and the West Indies, and returned after the war

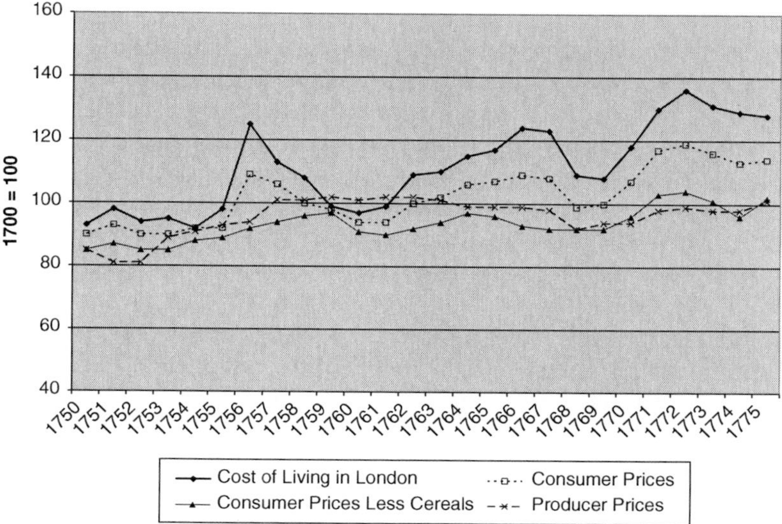

Figure 3 Prices in Britain, 1750–1775.
Sources: Cost of living in London: Gilboy (1936: 137). Consumer prices, consumer prices less cereals, and producer prices: Schumpeter (1938: 35).

(Carothers 1967 [1930]: 259)! Another piece of evidence along the same lines suggesting that the small note mania was a wartime phenomenon is shown in Figure 1. Evidently, there were two periods during the eighteenth century when the Scottish banks issued small notes: in the early 1760s during the Seven Years' War and in the late 1790s during the Napoleonic Wars, when a ban on small notes, discussed below, was temporarily lifted. It is well known that there was a shortage of small coin during the latter period. Indeed, it was the shortage of small change that gave rise to the innovations in the production of small coins introduced by Matthew Boulton (Selgin 2008). Boulton, of course, is famous now as the business partner of Scottish engineer James Watt, although Boulton was responsible for the production of coins. Although Boulton is famous for his association with Watt and their innovative technologies, the solution to the problem of small coins, as Selgin shows, was more prosaic and was solved by a number of issuers: the selling of coins at cost plus and the offer to redeem quantities of them on demand in banknotes. We are probably observing a similar shortage of small coins arising from similar causes in the 1760s. Indeed, Selgin (2008: 34–35) suggests that legislation limiting the issue of small notes passed in response to the small note mania made the production of a high-quality small change even more important than it otherwise would have been.

Unfortunately, we do not have data on the Scottish money supply for this era. Thanks to Checkland, however, we do have balance sheets for the Bank of Scotland, one of the two dominant banks in the Scottish system. Table 1 shows notes and deposits of the Bank of Scotland from 1747 to 1810. There was a very rapid increase in notes and deposits between 1753 and 1764, one year before the Seven Years' War – if we take the nine-year definition of the Seven Years' War (!) which includes the actions in North America – until one year after. The note issue increased by a factor of more than 2.5, an annual rate of 8.5 per cent per year; deposits increased by a factor of almost 3.3, an annual rate of 10.8 per cent per year. The Bank did not significantly increase its capital during these years. Instead, as Table 1 shows, it increased its leverage. If other banks in Scotland were following a similar trajectory, the inflationary pressures must have been substantial.

Figure 4 shows the circulation (total bank notes issued and not returned) of the Bank of England, the Bank of Scotland, and for part of the period, the Ship Bank of Glasgow. The Scottish banks were dwarfed by the Bank of England so the circulation of the Bank of England is measured on the left vertical axis and the circulations of the Scottish banks are measured on the smaller scale of the right vertical axis. All three series show a strong upward thrust during the Seven Years' War.

Something similar was happening in the American colonies. The Seven Years' War (for Americans the French and Indian War) was financed in several colonies by issues of legal tender paper money, probably producing some inflation, although there has been some debate about the degree of inflation. The American system, it might be said, was more 'modern' than the British

Table 1 The Bank of Scotland, key features of the balance sheet, selected years, 1747–1810.

	Notes, 1,000£	*Deposits, 1,000£*	*Paid-Up Capital, 1,000£*	*Surplus, 1,000£*	*Reserve ratio (notes), %*	*Leverage ratio*
1747	26	39	50	5	3.85	1.18
1750	58	41	50	11	5.17	1.62
1753	64	31	50	17	4.69	1.43
1756	83	43	60	11	4.82	1.77
1759	58	40	60	15	5.17	1.65
1762	138	42	60	23	3.62	2.27
1764	163	102	60	23	4.29	3.24
1766	87	116	60	23	4.60	2.45
1768	79	111	60	22	3.80	2.99
1771	60	108	70	16	3.33	2.19
1775	25	240	177	7	8.00	1.49
1780	289	92	200	32	4.84	1.87
1792	80	191	300	77	33.75	0.81
1797	852	293	803	144	4.69	1.21
1800	937	242	989	110	4.80	1.11
1802	867	430	1000	124	4.84	1.15
1805	650	334	1000	148	4.77	0.90
1810	730	388	1000	174	5.07	1.04

Source: Checkland (1975a: tables 34 and 36).

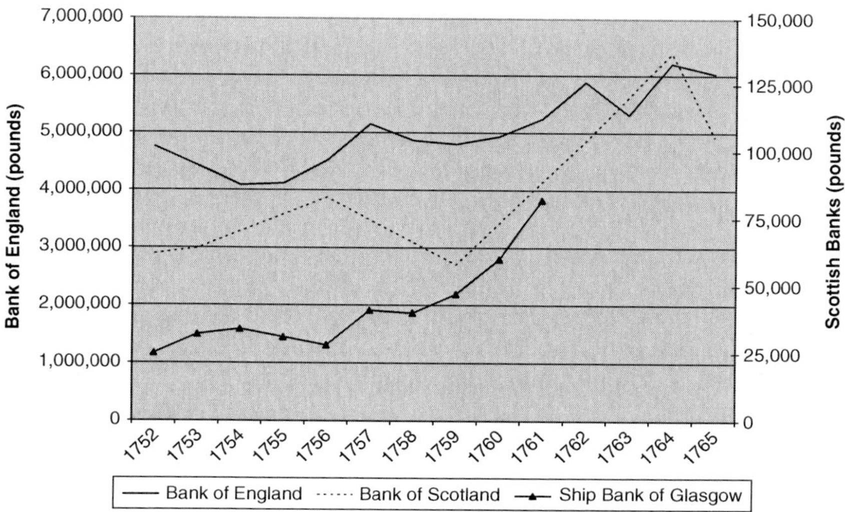

Figure 4 The stock of bank notes in circulation during the era of the Seven Years' War. *Sources*: Bank of England: Clapham (1945: vol. 1, appendix C); Bank of Scotland: Checkland (1975a: table 34); Ship Bank of Glasgow: Munn (1981: appendix A).

system in the sense that in the colonies the government moved directly to the printing press. These issues led Parliament in 1764 to extend a ban on colonial paper money issues from the northern colonies to the middle and southern colonies (Wicker 1985).

The high price of silver produced by the forces outlined above meant that the mint was not producing shillings, a key denomination, that could be replaced by small notes. George III ascended the throne in 1760, but it was not until 1787 that the mint struck shillings with his face on them in volume. The one exception was the 'Northumberland shilling', a small issue, undertaken by the Duke of Northumberland in 1763, to celebrate his appointment as Lord Lieutenant of Ireland (Mays 1982: 78–82). The issue of copper tokens by the mint in 1762 and 1763 is also evidence that the shortage of small denomination coins was a problem (Redish 2000: 124). Somewhat later, privately produced underweight coins known as 'evasions' were produced, mainly copper halfpennies. Evasions were similar to coins issued by the mint, but were distinguishable so that they would not violate the laws against counterfeiting. They were put into circulation by being sold at half-price to wholesalers (Redish 2000: 123–24).

In his *Lectures on Jurisprudence* (LJA vi.126) Smith noted the shortage of small denomination silver coins, attributing it to a mistake in the bimetallic ratio: silver would purchase more gold abroad than at home; so little silver was brought to the mint. He also noted that underweight foreign shillings were tolerated because of the lack of domestic coinage. Although Smith was clearly aware of the shortage of small change, he does not seem to have been deeply concerned about it, and left it unaddressed (Checkland 1975b: 515).

A number of additional shocks were hitting the Scottish banking system between 1763 and 1776 that might have changed Smith's thinking about the risks of banking. The growth of the system might itself have led to some rethinking about the costs of a major failure. But the decisive event in reshaping Smith's thinking about banking, I believe, was the failure of the Ayr Bank (Douglas, Heron, and Company 1778) and more generally what became known as the crisis of 1772.[9]

The crisis of 1772

Andreadēs (1966: 157) describes this crisis as the first modern banking panic to be faced by the Bank of England. It was international in scope, affecting London, Edinburgh, Europe, and the Americas. Even so, Edinburgh and the Ayr Bank were at the heart of the story. Smith presents his history of the Crisis in the *Wealth of Nations* (II.ii.66–77). His analysis breaks the speculative period leading up to the Crisis into three stages.[10] First, Smith describes a wave of investment by projectors (entrepreneurs trying to carry out ambitious schemes) which they financed by drawing and redrawing bills of exchange, that is financing long-term investments by rolling over short-term debt. Smith does not name the projectors he had in mind.[11] He simply notes that

> Many vast and extensive projects, however, were undertaken and for several years carried on without any other fund to support them besides what was raised at this enormous expense. The projectors, no doubt, had in their golden dreams the most distinct vision of this great profit. Upon their awaking, however, either at the end of their projects, or when they were no longer able to carry them on, they very seldom, I believe, had the good fortune to find it.
>
> (WN II.ii.69)

In the second stage, the banks responded to the boom. Smith recognizes that the banks may initially have had trouble distinguishing between real and fictitious bills, but argues that they eventually realized the danger. By the time they began to understand how deeply they were involved, however, it was not easy for them to cut back. Suddenly cutting off credit to the projectors might have ruined the banks along with their borrowers. The banks did, however, attempt to gradually cut back on their discounting, a process that raised howls of protest from the projectors.

The third stage of the boom was marked by the entry of the Ayr Bank. Smith, following his usual policy of not identifying the objects of his criticism by name, does not name the Ayr Bank or its principals.[12] He says merely 'in the midst of this clamour and distress a new bank was established in Scotland for the express purpose of relieving the distress of the country' (WN II.ii.73). But it is clear which bank he was describing. The rise of the Ayr Bank was remarkable. Founded in 1769, by 1772 the bank supplied 25 per cent of the notes in circulation by Scottish banks, 25 per cent of total deposits, and 40 per cent of total Scottish bank assets. The public banks, a category that includes the Bank of Scotland and the Royal Bank of Scotland, accounted for only 21 per cent of total assets. In three years the Ayr Bank had become a colossus (Checkland 1975a: 237).

Smith then describes the imprudent policies of the Ayr Bank (WN II.ii.73–77). (1) The bank had advanced loans for long-term capital investments, violating the key principle of the real bills doctrine, described below. (2) Instead of raising the full amount of its capital, the bank lent money to its investors, so it was more highly leveraged than its books would suggest. (3) The bank had made unwise acquisitions of other banking firms. (4) The bank had tried to force its notes into circulation, only to find them returning and depleting its reserves. And finally (5) the bank had tried to replenish its reserves by drawing on London, and then redrawing when its drafts came due, thus piling up a large short-term debt in London. The bank had expanded at a remarkable pace, but it was clearly heading for a fall.

The failure of the Ayr Bank proved to be the crucial spark that ignited the crisis of 1772. Alexander Fordyce, a London speculator, was one of the key figures. Fordyce had financed a large short position in English East India stock with loans from his bank, Neale, James, Fordyce, and Downe, which in turn was heavily indebted to the Ayr Bank. Early in 1772 the Bank of England tried to limit over-trading by selectively limiting credit. Fordyce, for example, was denied accommodation on a bill drawn on Amsterdam. Conceivably, he could have made it through the squeeze on his credit if his speculations had worked out. However, when the price of East India shares failed to fall as he had expected, Fordyce went bankrupt and fled to France on 9 June 1772. This event set off a financial panic in London; a number of firms would close by the end of the month. On 12 June a horseman reached Edinburgh with news of Fordyce's bankruptcy and the alarm in London. A run on the Ayr Bank began, and on 22 June it was forced to stop payment on its notes. A genuine banking panic in Edinburgh ensued. Fifteen private bankers in Edinburgh went bankrupt during the crisis (Saville 1996: 162). On 27 June 1772 David Hume wrote to Smith.

> We are here in a very melancholy Situation: Continual Bankruptcies, universal Loss of Credit, and endless Suspicions ... even the Bank of England is not entirely free from Suspicion. Those of Newcastle, Norwich, and Bristol are said to be stopp'd: The Thistle Bank has been reported to be in the same Condition: The Carron Company [an iron works, and pioneer of the industrial revolution] is reeling, which is one of the greatest Calamities of the whole; as they gave Employment to near 10,000 people. Do these Events any-wise affect your Theory?
>
> (Smith 1987: 131)

Soon after, a related crisis gripped Amsterdam. The story was similar: excessive speculation in British East India stock had left speculators and their financiers in a precarious position. This time, however, a number of Dutch firms were betting on a rise in the stock of the East India Company when discouraging news arrived from India (Wilson 1939). In the first week of January 1773, trade and finance between London and Amsterdam came to a halt. Although the crisis was centered in London and Amsterdam, it spread to the continent. Hamburg, Stockholm, and St. Petersburg all felt the effects of the crisis. The colonies, including the future United States, were also hit (Sheridan 1960).

The Bank of England came to the rescue. On 10 January 1773, a Sunday, the Bank allowed gold and silver to be drawn against notes and government bonds. One Dutch banker, it is said, received £500,000 (Kindleberger 1978: 184); William Alexander and Sons, a Scottish firm, received £160,000. The bank, however, discriminated among its borrowers. The Ayr Bank – the Lehman Brothers of the day – approached the Bank of England for a loan, and the Bank offered £300,000, but the terms were so stiff that the deal was never completed. The Bank of England was not the only lender of last resort in the crisis. In Scotland, the Bank of Scotland discounted bills of Carron and

Company (the object of concern in Hume's letter to Smith) to help it get through the crisis (Saville 1996: 164). In Amsterdam, in January 1773 the city opened a loan office backed up by the Bank of Amsterdam (Clapham 1945: vol. 1, 248). In Sweden, the Bank of Stockholm intervened, and in St. Petersburg, Catherine the Great secured the British merchants (Andreadēs 1966: 157). These banks, all of which enjoyed privileged relations with the state, may not have been lenders of last resort by way of formal legislation, but they all understood their role in a financial crisis.

The financial crisis was accompanied by a real decline in economic activity and high unemployment. It sounds, of course, a lot like the crisis of 2008. As Hamilton (1956) showed, the decline in real activity had a number of sources, but it seems probable that the financial crisis intensified the downturn. The history of the business cycle suggests that recessions are worse when they are accompanied by a financial crisis.

Smith was intimately involved with the Ayr Bank in the aftermath of the failure. The young Duke of Buccleuch, who Smith traveled with as advisor and tutor, was one of the principals of the bank. The Duke was probably one of the people that Smith strove to extricate from the mess (Ross 1995: 242).[13] In July 1776 a committee of inquiry was established to examine the affairs of the Ayr Bank, and I think it is fair to say, to see if there was anyone connected with the bank that the owners could sue (Douglas, Heron, and Company 1778). The report was issued in November 1778, and it is damning, even when one takes into account the obvious interest of the inquirers. In case after case the report uses phrases like 'clearly illegal', 'cash advances made without proper authority', and so on, and gives specific details that have the ring of truth. The principals were clearly 'unskillful conductors', to use the term Smith used in his metaphor, and it was to prevent this sort of thing from happening in the future that Smith advocated what has come to be called the 'real bills doctrine'.

Unfortunately, there appears to be little quantitative data, at least by modern standards, with which to trace the course of the crisis of 1772. Nevertheless, what little we have suggests that the recovery was relatively quick; it appears to have been a V-shaped recession, to use the modern jargon. Figure 5 shows British bankruptcies from 1755 to 1780. Evidently, bankruptcies rose abruptly in 1772, peaked in 1773, but then fell to the pre-crisis norm in 1774. Figure 6 shows British imports from 1766 to 1776. Imports are likely to be a function of national income, and are probably the best available proxy for national income that we have for this era. Imports fall abruptly between 1772 and 1773, but then recover their pre-crisis level in 1774. Part of the explanation for the rapid recovery may have been that the speculative mania was confined mainly to the Ayr Bank and its partners; at least this appears to have been the case in Scotland (Kerr 1902: 110). In this respect, the crisis of 1772 may be counted a partial success for the Scottish system. The Ayr Bank was an upstart. The more experienced Scottish bankers recognized the danger and avoided entanglements with the

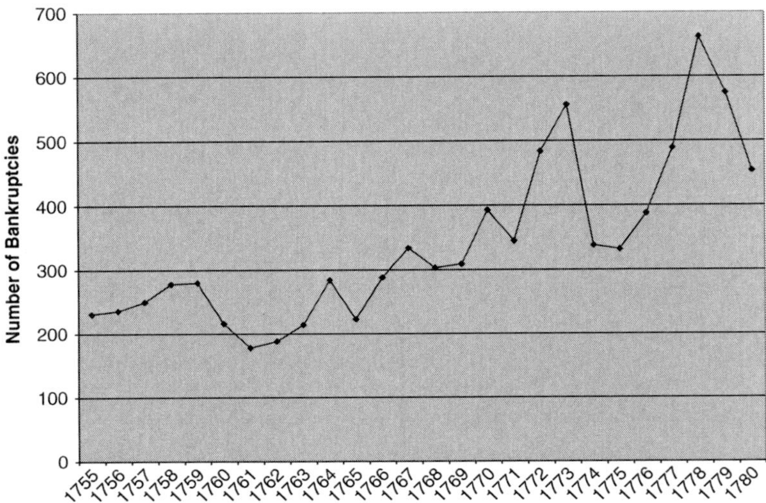

Figure 5 British bankruptcies, 1755–1780.
Source: Mitchell (1988: 694).

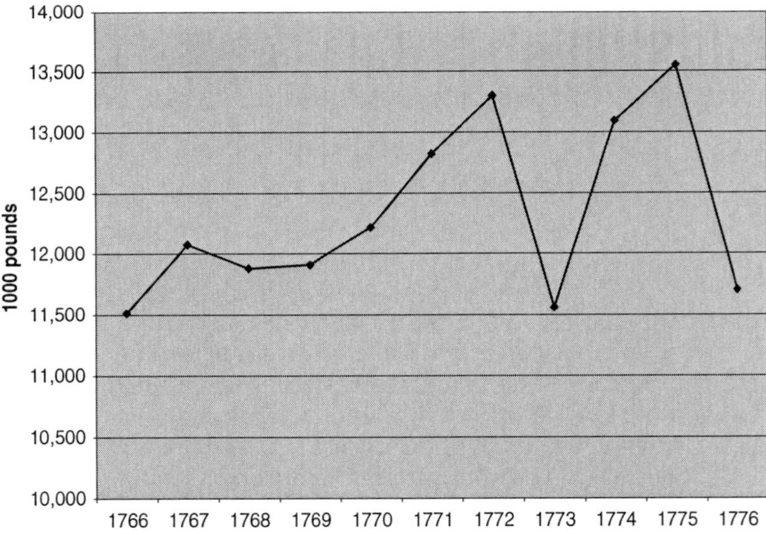

Figure 6 The value of British imports, 1766–1776.
Source: Mitchell (1988: 449).

Ayr Bank. As a result, the system as a whole was able to recover quickly. The V-shaped recovery may have influenced Smith. Had a long depression ensued he might have recommended more draconian measures to prevent banking crises.

While the crisis of 1772 accounts for much of Smith's views on money, it cannot do so completely. Smith's thinking was shaped by his understanding of banking and monetary history as well as by the events that were in the news, and with which he was intimately involved, while he was composing the *Wealth of Nations*. In his metaphor, a wagon-road in the air, Smith explains that they [the holders of paper money] are liable to several other accidents, from which 'no prudence or skill of those conductors can guard them'. Smith, however, gives only one example of these other accidents: an unsuccessful war 'in which the enemy got possession of the capital' (WN II.ii.87).

The enemy captures the financial center

It is easy to understand the danger to the monetary system of the nation as a whole that would follow if an enemy got control of the capital city. The capital was normally the home to the main bank or banks in the country. They would supply most of the bank notes used in the countryside. Bank notes that were payable in the capital might become irredeemable if the enemy captured the capital and its banks, and the countryside that relied on those notes would be reduced to barter. Gherity (1994: 439) wondered why Smith chose 'a rather far-fetched hypothetical illustration instead of using an actual and recent historical event'. It was, as Gherity says, only an example, but it was not far-fetched or hypothetical. Something like this happened during the 'Forty-Five' when the army of Prince Charles Edward Stuart took control of Edinburgh.

When Prince Charles and his army made the fateful decision to leave the Highlands, and cross the 'Forth at the Fords of Frew', the banks in Edinburgh immediately moved to protect their reserves (Graham 1911: 99–100; Munro 1928: 91–107; Checkland 1975a: 71–74). As the rebels approached the city, the Bank of Scotland and the Royal Bank stopped payment on their notes and moved their gold and silver coins, bank notes, and other items of value to Edinburgh's formidable castle for safekeeping. Although Prince Charles and his army captured the city, they never took the castle. The banks, and especially the Royal Bank, with its Whig sympathies, however, were still vulnerable. By taxing the citizens of Edinburgh the rebels acquired notes issued by the Royal Bank. The officials of the Royal Bank were then given access to the castle where they acquired the gold needed to pay the notes. While in the castle they also took the occasion to burn or tear into pieces most of the Royal Bank notes stored there, so that they could not fall into rebel hands. Thus, according to Munro, the historian of the Royal Bank, it was gold and silver from the Royal Bank that financed the remainder of the rebellion. After occupying Edinburgh and refitting, Prince Charles's army of mountaineers (to use Munro's term) headed south on its ill-fated invasion of England, igniting new fears and another incipient banking panic: The Bank of England paid in sixpences to slow withdrawals (Clapham 1945: vol. 1, 71; Andreadēs 1966: 150–51).

Smith, of course, was intimately familiar with the history of the 'Forty-Five' as any Scotsman of the era would be. He also discussed another case that he would know only from history: the French invasion of the Dutch Republic in 1672 (WN IV.iii.b.13). Smith notes that although the French were at Utrecht, the Bank of Amsterdam was able to pay out so regularly 'as left no doubt of the fidelity with which it had observed it engagements'. The point for Smith was that the Bank of Amsterdam was founded on, and very likely was maintained on, the principle of 100 per cent reserve backing for its notes: one guilder in coin for each guilder in notes circulating. Presumably, high or 100 per cent reserves prevented a disaster that might have occurred had the French been at Utrecht, and had the Bank of Amsterdam been a fractional reserve bank. Then a run, like the one that hit the Bank of England when Prince Charles entered England, might have forced the Bank of Amsterdam to stop payment on its notes, and trade would have been disrupted. Smith chose the example of an enemy capturing the capital because it was a clear example of an exogenous shock, but it was not a fanciful example.

Smith might have recommended any number of measures to prevent future crises. The Utrecht example suggests 100 per cent reserves, a recommendation later made famous by Henry Simons and Milton Friedman (Friedman 1992 [1960]). Instead, however, he proposed a series of milder reforms.

The real bills doctrine

Bankers, of course, had an understanding of the rules of prudent banking before Smith. But it seems that it was Smith who was the first to write down a set of rules of prudent banking and relate them to larger issues in monetary policy. Lloyd Mints (1945: 25) identified Smith as 'the first thoroughgoing exponent of the "real bills" doctrine'.

Smith's exposition of the real bills doctrine begins with the assertion that a banker can prudently lend to a borrower only the amount that the borrower would otherwise keep in a cash reserve. Long-term capital investments were out as far as banks were concerned. The capital that 'the undertaker of a mine employs in sinking his shafts' cannot rightly be supplied by a bank because the returns would come after a period of many years, 'a period far too distant to suit the conveniency of a bank' (WN II.ii.64). But how was a bank to know that it was lending an amount that the firm would otherwise keep in a cash reserve and not supplying long-term capital? Smith offers two practical rules, one for discounting bills of exchange,[14] and one for the cash accounts[15] typically used by Scottish banks for lending.

For bills of exchange the rule was: discount only 'a real bill of exchange drawn by a real creditor upon a real debtor, and which, as soon as it becomes due, is really paid by that debtor … ' (WN II.ii.59). It is hard to miss the origin of the term 'real bills'. One can imagine how this would work in practice. The names on the paper could be examined and checked to see that the bill was genuine, associated documents such as bills of lading could be examined, and the bank, of course, would know if it received payment as scheduled. For cash accounts the rule was simply to follow the activity in the account. If the borrower regularly paid the amounts borrowed, there was no problem. If the debts were rolled over, and if they mounted over time, the bank should not provide more accommodation.

The real bills doctrine was not intended by Smith to be part of the regulatory structure erected by the state. These rules were advice for bankers. If only Smith's protégé, the Duke of Buccleuch, had insisted on these rules at the Ayr Bank, much of the troubles at the bank, including those of the Duke, might have been avoided. It was not implausible, moreover, given the close-knit structure of Scottish society, that prudent rules, clearly formulated by one of the leading Scottish philosophers, would have an impact. Indeed, there is some evidence that the Scottish banks did come around to real bills (Munn 1981: 122–26). Although Smith seems to have viewed these rules as advice to bankers, they could be incorporated to some degree in bank charters, and could even be the basis for legislation. A prohibition on mortgage loans for banks, to take a simple example, would be a way of trying to implement real bills, which could be written into bank charters by the owners of the bank or written into banking laws.

The real bills doctrine has been criticized frequently because it doesn't provide a rule for monetary policy. As Mints (1945) pointed out, in an inflationary economy the nominal value of the bills being offered to banks would rise with the price level, hence inflation could continue even though every bank, including the central bank, was following real bills.[16] It is true, as Mints shows, that subsequent theorists and policy makers made the mistake of thinking of the real bills doctrine as a rule for the conduct of monetary policy. But as Laidler (1981) argues, Smith never made this mistake. In Smith's model the price level is anchored by adherence to the specie standard; the real bills doctrine is designed to prevent imprudent banking. In the short run imprudent banking could lead to the overissue of notes by one bank or even the overissue of notes by the entire banking system. However, this would lead to return of notes by the overissuing bank or banks for redemption in specie, which would check the initial overissue (Selgin 2001). Even in the unlikely case that a general overissue persisted for some time, the price level could not permanently diverge from the limits set by Hume's price-specie-flow mechanism. Smith might have been clearer about the limits of the real bills doctrine, but it is unfair to place much of the blame on him for the future misuse of his idea.

The usury laws

Smith was an advocate of usury laws: maximum legal interest rates. The usury laws applied to banks as well as other lenders, although Smith did not discuss them in his chapter on banking, but rather in the chapter on 'Stock Lent at Interest'.[17] The belief that maximum interest rates should be set by the government, of course, was a major exception to Smith's defense of 'natural liberty', a free market, and has attracted the attention of many scholars attempting to understand Smith's views (Jadlow 1977; Levy 1987; Paganelli 2003; Rockoff 2009).[18] One aspect of usury laws that made them relatively attractive to Smith as a form of regulation was that they did not require a government bureaucracy to enforce them. The usury law simply created a legal defense that could be raised by a borrower who was being sued for nonpayment.

Smith's argument for usury laws was subtle, and closely related to the issues of concern here. The legal maximum (a level which Smith thought reasonable) was then at 5 per cent, where it had been for most of the century. Smith thought that substantially increasing the maximum rate, or eliminating it, would encourage investors to channel funds to the wrong sort of person.

> The legal rate, it is to be observed, although it ought to be somewhat above, ought not to be much above the lowest market rate. If the legal rate of interest in Great Britain, for example was fixed so high as eight or ten per cent., the greater part of the money which was to be lent, would be lent to prodigals and projectors, who alone would be wiling to give this high interest. Sober people, who will give for the use of money no more than a part of what they are likely to make by the use of it, would not venture into competition.
>
> (WN II.iv.15)

Smith's belief in the efficacy of usury laws, I suspect, was strengthened by his analysis of the boom leading up to the crisis of 1772, although there is no direct evidence. One bit of suggestive evidence is his repeated use of the term projectors in his discussion of the Ayr Bank, and his use of the term in making his case for the usury laws. Even if the Ayr Bank had succeeded in its dream of becoming the dominant bank in Scotland, it would have been likely, Smith thought, that its borrowers would be mere 'chimerical projectors' (WN II.ii.77). Another suggestive bit of evidence is that the *Lectures on Jurisprudence*, which provides a remarkably broad and deep survey of British and Scottish law, including commercial law, rather surprisingly, does not include a detailed discussion of the usury laws, even though Smith incorporated a rather lengthy history and discussion of the usury laws in the *Wealth of Nations*. There could be many explanations for this difference between the *Lectures* and the *Wealth of Nations*, but I have a hunch that Smith's attention was drawn to negative consequences of excessive lending to projectors during the boom of 1769–1771 and the crisis of 1772.

The option clause

One of the most intriguing features of the Scottish banking system in the eighteenth century is that many Scottish bank notes bore the 'option clause'.

The option clause is best explained with an example. A Bank of Scotland note issued in 1750 read as follows:

> The Governor and Company of the Bank of Scotland constituted by Act of Parliament do hereby oblige themselves to pay to Bearer One Pound Sterling on Demand *or* in the Option of the Directors One pound Six pence at the end of six months after of the demand and for ascertaining the demand and option of the directors the accomplant and one of the tellers of the bank are hereby ordered to mark and sign this note on the back thereof.
>
> (Douglas 1975: 25)

The conventional part of the note is the part before the '*or*' [my italics]. If the note holder went to the office of the bank and demanded hard money, the teller would pay it on demand. The option clause, the part after the *or*, however, allows the bank to delay payment, if it chooses to do so. If it chooses to delay payment, however, the bank agrees to pay interest at an annual rate of about 5 per cent (the legal maximum). The option clause has attracted the attention of monetary historians because it might be a device for reducing the threat of runs on a bank: Instead of being forced to close by a run, a bank could exercise its option and would then have up to 6 months to raise cash (Rockoff 1986). Perhaps the mere presence of option clauses could prevent runs on individual banks from turning into panics. Gherity (1995) showed that the runs were the result of specific attacks from other banks that had accumulated the notes of a rival. In other words, they were the result of a commercial tactic, rather than a panic. A comment by Selgin and White (1997) establishes that earlier writers had noted the origin of the option clause in raids by competing banks rather than panics by bank note holders, and stresses that whatever the origin of the option clause it might have reduced the potential for panics.

Contemporaries, perhaps including Smith, had a very different concern. The option clause might encourage banks to issue too many notes. For example, a bank that held £10 in reserve and had issued, say, £100 in demand notes, might believe that it could safely keep £150 in circulation when it issued notes bearing the option clause, thus adding £50 to its loan portfolio, while it held the same £10 in reserve.

Figure 7, based on Douglas's catalog of new issues, shows the progress of the option clause. Although the option was never universal, and although the use of the option clause was not as concentrated in time as the issue of small notes, it is clear that the use of the option clause became pronounced in the early 1760s, about the same time that the flood of small notes was hitting. Given the timing of the widespread adoption of the option clause, and the apparent incentive for banks that issued notes with option clauses to expand their circulation, it is easy to see why contemporaries blamed the option

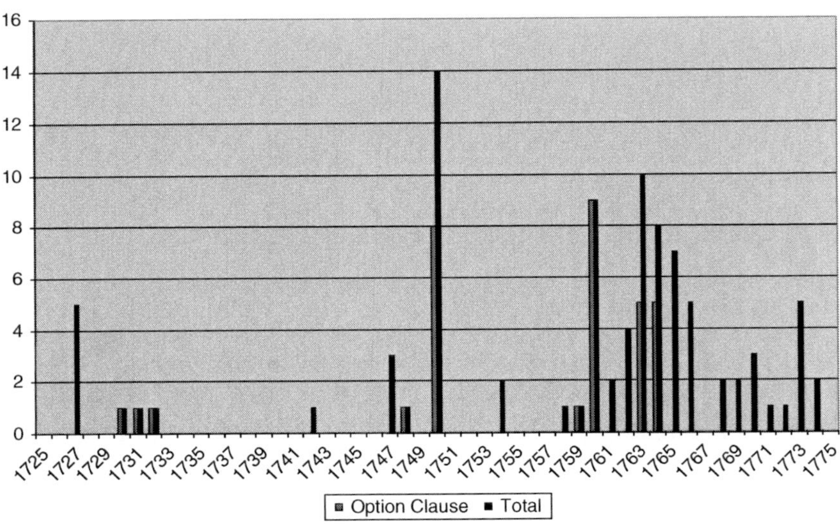

Figure 7 All new issues of Scottish bank notes and new issues bearing the option clause, 1725–1775.
Source: Compiled from Douglas (1975)

clause for the small note mania (Rait 1930: 34–35). Since Smith supported the prohibition of the option clause, he may have shared this concern.

In any case, the option clause was prohibited well before the crisis of 1772 (Checkland 1975a: 253–55). In 1764 London received requests from Scotland to do something about the Scottish banking system. The local banking companies wanted to end competition from the informal note issuers. The Bank of Scotland and the Royal Bank, on learning about the pressure to limit the issue of small notes, countered with a different proposal: that they be the sole issuers of notes in exchange, possibly, for an agreed annual sum to be used for public purposes. The Privy Council, which included friends of Smith, received detailed notes on Scottish banking from Sir James Steuart, and, it has been conjectured, may have consulted Smith, who was in London at the time (Checkland 1975a: 529). In the end the Privy Council rejected the push by the Bank of Scotland and the Royal Bank for a monopoly of the note issue. But it did recommend elimination of the option clause and of notes less than £5 (Smith's idea?). The legislation, which took effect in 1766, eliminated the option clause, but only eliminated notes less than £1.

Although Smith favored banning the option clause, as Gherity (1995: 720) points out, Smith never mentions the option clause in his detailed discussions of the banking problems of the 1760s and 1770s in the *Wealth of Nations*. Smith's main concern was with preventing or ameliorating the effect of crises like that of 1772, and that was to be addressed with the restriction on banking that had not yet been adopted: the £5 minimum.

The £5 minimum

Smith's main recommendation for preventing falls from the wagon-road in the air, or at least for ameliorating their consequences, was to limit the minimum bank note to £5. Smith chose the sum of £5 carefully. In London, Smith tells us, the use of bank notes was limited to the £10 Bank of England notes. These circulated mainly among businesses (say between wholesalers and retailers) while gold and silver were used in transactions between retailers and the public. Smith thought that this was a desirable state of affairs and that a limit of £5 would accomplish the same task elsewhere. Smith tells us that when the issue of very small notes is allowed, many 'beggarly bankers' enter the field, and their frequent failures may be the source of a great 'calamity to many poor people' (WN II.ii.90). This passage seems to refer to the small notes issued in the early 1760s. These notes, notes for less than £1, had been prohibited by legislation in 1766. But I suspect that Smith had other targets in mind when he called for raising the limit from £1 to £5: the Ayr Bank had issued £1 and one guinea (£1.05) notes. It would have had more trouble expanding its circulation, and may not have failed, or at least would have done less damage when it did fail, if it had been forced to issue notes in denominations of £5 or higher.[19]

Attempts to put such sums into today's money are always bedeviled by index number problems. If we use a retail price index to inflate £5, we get a figure of £540 in 2007 (Officer 2009a), a denomination that would not be in general circulation today. Indeed, the denominations common in Smith's day are still in common use today. The reason may be that the role of the bank note has changed drastically from the business-to-business role it played in Smith's day (where the checkable deposit has supplanted it) to the business-to-consumer role filled by coins in Smith's day.

Smith's idea addresses the problem of asymmetric information. If the notes are large-denomination, the knowledgeable merchants will put in the time and effort to ensure that the banks whose notes they use are in good shape. Banking will be safe. However, if there are small denominations, people who are less informed will use them and fewer people will have an incentive to check up.

Smith's proposal, at least in intention, bears some resemblance to traditional bank deposit insurance. Traditionally, deposit insurance was limited to some particular amount, say the first £100,000. One purpose of the limit was to minimize the government's exposure in the event of a failure. The main idea, however, was to protect the poor while trusting the rich to watch the affairs of the bank and get their money out in time, and even to impose, thereby, some discipline on the bank. Smith's idea was similar. The poor would be protected in the case of a banking crisis because they would have been forced to use coins in their everyday transactions. The rich would be vulnerable, but they could watch out for themselves, and they would impose some discipline on the banks, because they would convert their notes into

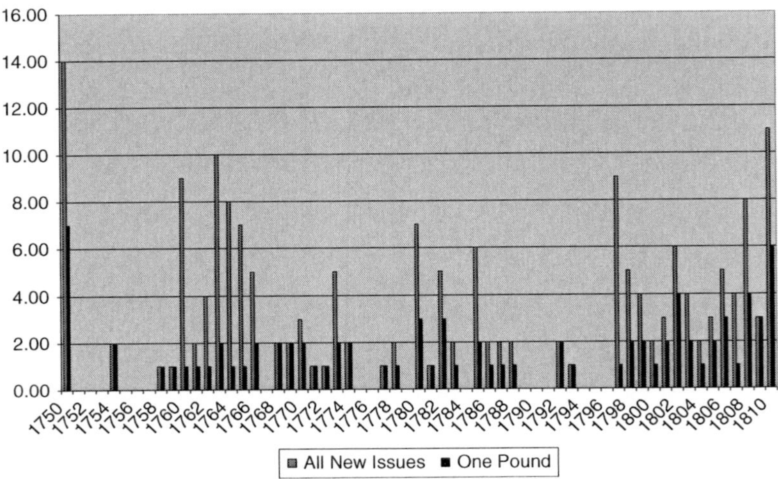

Figure 8 All new issues of Scottish bank notes and all new issues for one pound or one Guinea, 1750–1810.
Source: Compiled from Douglas (1975).

gold or silver when they had information that the bank was in trouble. In effect, to go back to Smith's wagon-road-in-the-air metaphor, Smith was proposing to dismantle some of the wagon-roads and force the poor, for their own good, to use the safer wagon-roads on the ground.

The prohibition of the option clause and the prohibition of notes less than £5 were, Smith acknowledged, a violation of 'natural liberty'. He argued, however, in another celebrated metaphor, that the restrictions on banking he was recommending could be compared to the requirement that builders install firewalls between apartments (WN II.ii.94).

Despite Smith's advocacy, the £5 minimum was never adopted in Scotland either in law or in practice. Figure 8 shows all new issues of Scottish bank notes, and new issues of one pound or one guinea notes, from 1750 to 1810. Even after the publication of the *Wealth of Nations* most of the new issues were one pound or one guinea notes. Indeed, the Scots became rather proud of their £1 notes. Later when an attempt was made to ban the £1 note, Sir Walter Scott came to their defense (Munn 1981: 80–81).

Was Smith's regulatory framework sufficient?

Would adopting Smith's regulatory framework have reduced the likelihood of, or at least ameliorated the effects of a repetition of the Ayr Bank crisis? Smith advocated, let us recall, four restrictions on banking: (1) adoption of a reasonable usury law, (2) prohibition of the option clause in bank notes, (3) adoption of the real bills doctrine as part of the culture of banking, and

(4) prohibition of notes in denominations less than £5. Let us take them in turn. The first two were already in place when the crisis of 1772 hit. They didn't prevent the Ayr Bank failure and it is unclear that they could contribute much to preventing recurrences. The usury law had been unchanged for many years and its presence had failed to discourage imprudence at the Ayr Bank. Perhaps some blame for the crisis, however, could still be attached to the option clause. The prohibition of the option clause did not go into effect until May 1766 and the ill effects on the banking system from the use of the option clause may have lingered. In Smith's story of the crisis he emphasizes that the older banks (which had made use of the option clause) were able to extricate themselves from their overextended positions in part because of the rise of the Ayr Bank. So it is conceivable that if the option clause had been banned earlier, the Scottish banks might never have made so many risky loans. They might then have looked at the Ayr Bank as a dangerous competitor, rather than as a vehicle for siphoning off risky investments, and done more to restrain it. Still, neither the usury laws nor the prohibition of the option clause had prevented the crisis of 1772, so they could not be counted upon to prevent or reduce the likelihood or impact of future crises of the same sort.

The adoption of the real bills doctrine would, undoubtedly, have helped prevent individual failures, and perhaps as a result reduced the likelihood of another banking panic, or the damage caused by one. However, the rules of prudent banking were well understood before Smith. The failure of the Ayr Bank was not caused by a failure to understand the rules of prudent banking, but rather by a determination to ignore them. After the failure of the bank, as I noted, a detailed investigation was carried out at the request of the owners. Admittedly the investigators were under pressure to find a particular result: The proprietors wanted to find cases in which the managers had broken rules of conduct laid down in the bank's charter in order to lay the basis for lawsuits. Nevertheless, one can't read the report without being impressed by the sheer quantity of detailed misbehaviors that they uncovered. Either the authors were very imaginative, or there were a lot of problems at the Ayr Bank. There were three branches – at Ayr, Edinburgh, and Dumfries – and the problems were worst at Ayr. At one point the managers at Edinburgh wrote to the managers at Ayr complaining about the latter's lax standards; but the committee of inquiry found abuses at all three branches. The main problem was not sophisticated mistakes, but rather excessive insider lending. Given the nature of the failure of the Ayr Bank it is hard to see how the adoption of Smith's rules of prudence, as helpful as they would often be, could have prevented the failure of the bank, although it is conceivable that they might have done so. Most of the charter regulations violated by the managers of the Ayr Bank were procedural rules, such as the number people required to make a quorum for decisions. It is just conceivable that had real bills restrictions been written into the charter, the managers would have been less likely to violate them.

Finally, we come to (4), the limitation on the size of notes to £5 or more. This might have had a substantial effect if it had been in effect before 1769, because it would have forced the Ayr Bank to rely on a more limited and sophisticated class of note holder for its funds. The Ayr Bank issued, as I noted, one pound and one guinea (£1.05) notes. It had trouble keeping these notes circulating; it would have had more trouble keeping £5 notes circulating. Without the one pound note, it may never have expanded to the extent that it did, although the Ayr Bank did manage to expand its portfolio to an even greater extent by drawing bills on London. Expansion of portfolios by short-term borrowing, of course, is familiar to students of the crisis of 2008. By inhibiting repetitions of the rise and fall of speculative banks like the Ayr Bank, the £5 note limit might have lessened the likelihood of repetitions of the crisis of 1772. But, as we noted previously, Smith's recommendation was not put into practice.

The real end to banking crises in Britain (until now) was brought about not by the adoption of any of Smith's recommendations, but rather by the assumption by the Bank of England of the role of lender of last resort. What did Smith think about this? Smith discussed the Bank of England, which he claimed 'acts, not only as an ordinary bank, but as a great engine of state' (WN II.ii.85) in several places in the *Wealth of Nations.* In particular he noted one occasion in the crisis of 1763 when the bank acted as lender of last resort;[20] indeed, when the bank may have (Smith is cautious) advanced £1,600,000 in bullion in a week.[21] However, while Smith describes the special powers and role of the Bank of England – Edwin G. West (1997: 127) describes Smith as appearing deferential – Smith does not explicitly endorse the use of these powers as a means of ameliorating or preventing crises. This idea came later and is usually associated with Bagehot (1924 [1873]), although Bagehot's views on the role of the lender of last resort were more complex than they are usually portrayed.[22] As Anna J. Schwartz (1987: 276–77) pointed out, there were no banking crises in England after 1866; that is after the Bank of England fully assumed the role of lender of last resort. The answer to the problem of Daedalian wings, it seems, was a central bank helicopter that could swoop in and keep the wagon-road through the air afloat while Daedalus and Icarus cooled off and got their wings working again. (I know – I did my best.)

Speculative booms followed by financial crises and recessions are an old story. Adam Smith, the founding father of economics, wrestled with just such a crisis, the crisis of 1772, when he wrote the *Wealth of Nations.* Some students of Smith, for example West (1997), have been troubled by the apparent contradiction between Smith's willingness to trust the market in most sectors of the economy while advocating restrictions on banks. The answer appears to be that Smith was an empiricist, willing to modify his views on the basis of contemporary and historical experience. Smith's willingness to examine the crisis of 1772 in detail and to modify his views based on his understanding of it can be a model for economists trying to respond to the crisis of 2008.

A chronology of Scottish banking in Adam Smith's time

1730	
19 November	The Bank of Scotland begins issuing £5 notes bearing the option clause.
1745	
23 July	Prince Charles Edward Stuart lands in Scotland.
13 September	Prince Charles and his army cross the Forth at the Fords of Frew.
13 September	The Bank of Scotland and Royal Bank store their assets at Edinburgh Castle.
17 September	Prince Charles and his army enter Edinburgh.
31 October	Prince Charles and his army leave Edinburgh and head south.
1763	
10 February	The Treaty of Paris ends the Seven Years' War.
8 April	Adam Smith delivers a lecture on banking to his class in Jurisprudence.
1766	
15 May	Prohibition of the option clause in Scottish bank notes.
1 June	Prohibition of bank notes in denominations less than £1.
1769	
6 November	Douglas, Heron, and Company (Ayr Bank) opens.
1772	
8 June	Alexander Fordyce's bank, which has extensive dealings with Ayr Bank, fails after Fordyce loses on speculations in East India Company stock.
9 June	Fordyce flees England.
12 June	News of Fordyce's failure reaches Edinburgh.
25 June	The Ayr Bank suspends payment of gold and silver.
27 June	David Hume writes to Smith: How do these events affect your theory?
28 September	The Ayr Bank reopens with a promise to pay notes in full.
1773	
January	Lines of credit between Amsterdam and London snap. Trade halts.
	The City of Amsterdam, backed up by the Bank of Amsterdam, opens a loan office to provide emergency aid.
10 January	The Bank of England comes to the rescue; bullion may be withdrawn on the presentation of notes and government bonds.
12 August	The proprietors resolve to wind up the Ayr Bank.
1776	
10 July	A committee is appointed to investigate the affairs of the Ayr Bank.

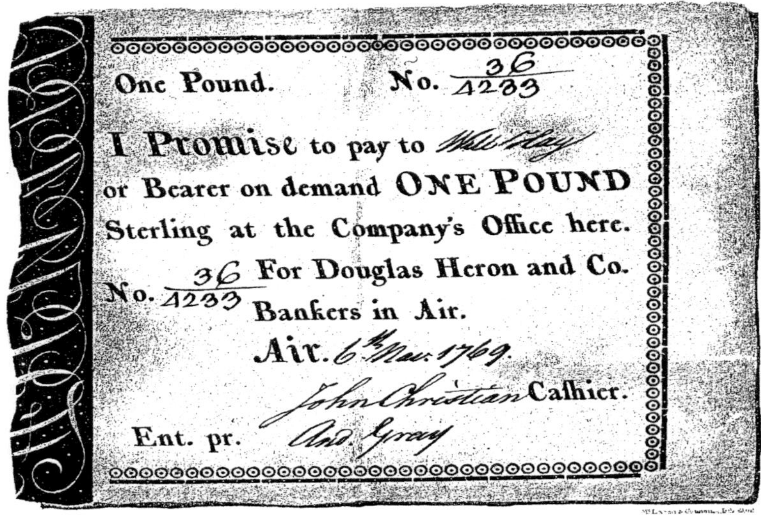

Figure 9 A note issued by the Air (Ayr) Bank.
Source: Graham (1911).

1778
23 November Report of the Committee of Inquiry of the Ayr Bank is printed.

Acknowledgements

I must thank Simone Pollilo, Brad Pasanek, and the participants in the conference they organized, 'After the Crash, Beyond Liquidity', which was held at the University of Virginia on October 30, 2009, for a number of ideas that I have incorporated. David Levy, Maria Pia Paganelli, Sandra Peart, George Selgin, and Eugene White read a subsequent draft and made a number of suggestions that I have incorporated. The remaining errors are solely my responsibility.

Notes

1 After completing an early draft of the paper I encountered Paganelli (2006), a fine paper that also uses the Daedalian wings metaphor in its title. However, it is such a wonderful metaphor, one that deserves to be better known, so I felt there is a justification for using it again.
2 Smith had given considerable thought to the construction of metaphors; he discusses them in his *Lectures on Rhetoric and Belles Lettres*, in lecture 6 'On What Is Called Tropes and Figures of Speech'. One fascinating part of that lecture described why some hyperbolic metaphors succeed and others do not (Smith 1983 [1763]: 31–32).
3 Some of the key dates are collected in the chronology which follows the main text.
4 Lawrence White (1999: 42–49) offers a comprehensive modern discussion of the resource costs of a commodity currency. Milton Friedman (1986) in a famous paper argued that fiat money could also impose resource costs.

5 At a later point in the text, Smith estimates the actual circulation of Scotland to be about £2,000,000; £500,000 in coin and £1,500,000 in paper (WN II.ii.30).
6 Smith considers the adjustment process from the old equilibrium to the new one in detail. It is clear that he has a version of Hume's price-specie-flow mechanism in mind.
7 In Scotland, Smith thought, 'the ordinary profits of stock in the greater part of mercantile projects are supposed to run between six and ten per cent … ' (WN II.ii.69).
8 White (1992: 163–64) summarizes the positions of the Scottish banking historians.
9 Although Ayr is the current spelling, the contemporary spelling, as the facsimile below shows, was Air. Inevitably, the 'Bankers in Air' were the victims of many puns (Rait 1930: 167).
10 Hamilton (1956) provides a modern treatment of the failure of the Ayr Bank; it provides more detail, but generally agrees with Smith.
11 Rait (1930: 165) lists investments in agricultural improvements, land in the West Indies, and Edinburgh's new town. Hume, in a letter to Smith cited below, expresses concern about the Adelphi project in London, an ambitious London development undertaken by the Scottish architects Robert, James and John Adam, and expresses special concern for Robert who has a 'projecting turn'. This may be one of the 'projects' Smith had in mind.
12 Smith, famously, does not mention his rival Sir James Steuart, or Steuart's treatise, *An Inquiry into the Principles of Political Oeconomy*, by name.
13 The student of metaphors will notice another parallel. Daedalus used his wings wisely, but his son Icarus soared too close to the sun, the wax holding his feathers together melted, and he fell into the sea. If we continue the metaphor, Smith is wise Daedalus and his protégé, the Duke of Buccleuch, is the impetuous Icarus.
14 A bill of exchange is simply an order to a debtor to pay a certain sum of money to a third party on a certain date. A bank check is an example.
15 A cash account was similar to a credit card: borrowers would make use of the facility when they chose to do so.
16 When I was a graduate student at the University of Chicago in the 1960s the doctrine was always referred to as the 'fallacious real bills doctrine'.
17 Most analysts do not discuss the usury laws as part of Smith's regulatory architecture for banking. Checkland (1975b: 517) is an exception.
18 Paganelli (2003) provides a recent guide to the literature along with her own explanation of how usury laws fit into Smith's system.
19 There were repeated attempts to suppress the issue of small notes in antebellum America, based partly on Smith's authority (Bodenhorn 1993; White 1995).
20 Although the Bank of England acted as a lender of last resort in the crisis of 1763, the crisis was centered in Amsterdam, and does not appear to have had a major impact on Smith's thinking about banking.
21 Clapham (1945: vol. 1, 240), addresses this passage in the *Wealth of Nations* and concludes that Smith is right not to put too much weight on the story, but to quote it as the sort of thing that might have happened.
22 Bagehot's demand that the Bank of England formally adopt the mantle of the lender of last resort was, as Bagehot (1924 [1873]: 66) pointed out, based on the then current institutional structure of the British banking system in which the Bank of England enjoyed a privileged position of long standing. Bagehot's preference if one could start de novo was for a free banking system along Scottish lines.

Bibliography

Andreadēs, A. M. (1966) *History of the Bank of England, 1640–1903*, 4th edn. London: Cass.

Bagehot, W. (1924) [1873] *Lombard Street: A Description of the Money Market*, London: John Murray.

Bodenhorn, H. (1993) 'Small-denomination banknotes in Antebellum America', *Journal of Money, Credit and Banking*, 25(4): 812–27.

Cameron, R. (1967) 'Scotland, 1750–1845', in *Banking in the Early Stages of Industrialization: A Study in Comparative Economic History,* R. Cameron, pp. 60–99, New York: Oxford University Press.

Carothers, N. (1967) [1930] *Fractional Money: A History of the Small Coins and Fractional Paper Currency of the United States*, New York: John Wiley & Sons.

Checkland, S. G. (1975a) *Scottish Banking: A History, 1695–1973*, Glasgow: Collins.

——(1975b) 'Adam Smith and the bankers', in *Essays on Adam Smith*, A. S. Skinner and T. Wilson (eds), pp. 504–23, Oxford: Clarendon Press.

Clapham, J. H. (1945) *The Bank of England: A History*, 2 vols, Cambridge: Cambridge University Press.

Douglas, Heron, and Company. Committee of Inquiry (1778) *The Precipitation and Fall of Mess. Douglas, Heron, and Company, Late Bankers in Air, With the Causes of Their Distress and Ruin, Investigated and Considered, by a Committee of Inquiry Appointed by the Proprietors*, Edinburgh: publisher unknown.

Douglas, J. (1975) *Scottish Banknotes*, London: Stanley Gibbons.

Friedman, M. (1992) [1960] *A Program for Monetary Stability*, New York: Fordham University.

——(1969) *The Optimum Quantity of Money: And Other Essays*, Chicago: Aldine.

——(1986) 'The resource cost of irredeemable paper money', *Journal of Political Economy*, 94: 642–47.

Gherity, J. A. (1994) 'The evolution of Adam Smith's theory of banking', *History of Political Economy* (Fall): 423–41.

——(1995) 'The option clause in Scottish banking, 1730–65: a reappraisal', *Journal of Money, Credit and Banking*, 27(3): 713–26.

Gilboy, Elizabeth W. (1936) 'The cost of living and real wages in eighteenth century England', *The Review of Economics and Statistics*, 18(3) (August): 134–43.

Graham, W. (1911) *The One Pound Note in the History of Banking in Great Britain*, Edinburgh: J. Thin.

Hamilton, H. (1953) 'Scotland's balance of payments problem in 1762', *The Economic History Review*, 5(3): 344–57.

——(1956) 'The failure of the Ayr Bank, 1772', *The Economic History Review*, 8(3): 405–17.

Hoppit, J. (1986) 'Financial crises in eighteenth-century England', *The Economic History Review*, 39(1): 39–58.

Jadlow, J. M. (1977) 'Adam Smith on usury laws', *Journal of Finance*, 32(4): 1195–1200.

Kerr, A. W. (1902) *History of Banking in Scotland*, London: A& C Black.

Kindleberger, C. P. (1978) *Manias, Panics, and Crashes: A History of Financial Crises*, New York: Basic Books.

Laidler, D. (1981) 'Adam Smith as a monetary economist', *The Canadian Journal of Economics/Revue Canadienne d'Economique*, 14(2): 185–200.

Levy, D. M. (1987) 'Adam Smith's case for usury laws', *History of Political Economy*, 19(3): 387–400.

Levy, D. M. and Peart, S. P. (2010) 'Economists, crises, and cartoons'. Available HTTP: http://ssrn.com/abstract=1547886

Mays, J. O. (1982) *The Splendid Shilling: The Social History of an Engaging Coin*, Ringwood, United Kingdom: New Forest Leaves.

Mints, L. W. (1945) *A History of Banking Theory in Great Britain and the United States*, Chicago: University of Chicago Press.

Mitchell, B. R. (1988) *British Historical Statistics*, Cambridge: Cambridge University Press.

Munn, C. W. (1981) *The Scottish Provincial Banking Companies, 1747–1864*, Edinburgh: J. Donald.

Munro, N. (1928) *The History of the Royal Bank of Scotland, 1727–1927*, Edinburgh: R. & R. Clark.

Officer, L. H. (2009a) 'What were the UK earnings and prices then? A question-and-answer guide', in *The Annual RPI and Average Earnings for the United Kingdom, 1264–2007*, MeasuringWorth. Available HTTP: www.measuringworth.org (accessed 17 November 2009).

——(2009b) ' The price of gold, 1257–2008', in MeasuringWorth. Available HTTP: www.measuringworth.org/gold (accessed 17 November 2009).

Paganelli, M. P. (2003) 'In medio stat virtus: an alternative view of usury law in Adam Smith's thinking', *History of Political Economy*, 35(1): 21–48.

——(2006) 'Vanity and the Daedalian wings of paper money in Adam Smith', in *New Voices on Adam Smith*, E. Schlieser and L. Montes (eds), pp. 271–89, London and New York: Routledge.

Rait, R. S. (1930) *The History of the Union Bank of Scotland*, Glasgow: John Smith & Son Ltd.

Redish, A. (2000) *Bimetallism: An Economic and Historical Analysis*, Cambridge: Cambridge University Press.

Rockoff, H. (1986) 'Institutional requirements for a stable free banking regime', *Cato Journal* (Fall): 617–34.

——(2009) 'Prodigals and projectors: an economic history of usury laws in the United States from colonial times to 1900', in *Human Capital and Institutions: A Long-Run View*, D. Eltis, F. D. Lewis and K. L. Sokoloff (eds), pp. 285–323, Cambridge: Cambridge University Press.

Ross, I. S. (1995) *The Life of Adam Smith*, Oxford and New York: Clarendon Press and Oxford University Press.

Saville, R. (1996) *Bank of Scotland: A History, 1695–1995*, Edinburgh: Edinburgh University Press.

Schubert, E. S. (1997) 'Crises of 1763 and 1772–73', in *Business Cycles and Depressions: An Encyclopedia*, D. Glaser (ed.), pp. 122–23, New York: Garland.

Schumpeter, Elizabeth Boody (1938) 'English prices and public finance, 1660–1822', *The Review of Economics and Statistics*, 20(1) (February): 21–37.

Schwartz, A. J. (1987) 'Real and pseudo-crises', in *Money in Historical Perspective*, M. D. Bordo (ed.), pp. 271–88, Chicago: University of Chicago Press.

Selgin, G. (2001) 'In-concert overexpansion and the precautionary demand for bank reserves', *Journal of Money, Credit and Banking*, 33(2): 294–300.

——(2008) *Good Money: Birmingham Button Makers, the Royal Mint, and the Beginnings of Modern Coinage, 1775–1821*, Ann Arbor: University of Michigan Press.

Selgin, G. and White, L. W. (1997) 'The option clause in Scottish banking', *Journal of Money, Credit and Banking*, 29(2): 270–73.

Sheridan, R. B. (1960) 'The British credit crisis of 1772 and the American colonies', *The Journal of Economic History*, 20(2): 161–86.

Smith, A. (1976) *An Inquiry into the Nature and Causes of the Wealth of Nations*, R. H. Campbell and A. S. Skinner (eds), Oxford: Clarendon Press.

——(1978) *Lectures on Jurisprudence*, R. L. Meek, D. D. Raphael and P. G. Stein (eds), Oxford: Clarendon Press. Reprinted Liberty Classics, 1982.

——(1983) *Lectures on Rhetoric and Belles Lettres*, J. C. Bryce (ed.), Oxford: Clarendon Press.

——(1987) *Correspondence of Adam Smith*, E. C. Mossner and I. S. Ross (eds), Oxford: Clarendon Press.

West, E. G. (1997) 'Adam Smith's support for money and banking regulation: a case of inconsistency', *Journal of Money, Credit and Banking*, 29(1): 127–34.

White, E. (1995) 'Free banking, denominational restrictions, and liability insurance', in *Money and Banking: The American Experience,* George Edward Durell Foundation (ed.), pp. 99–117, Fairfax, VA: George Mason University Press.

White, L. H. (1992) 'Free banking in Scotland before 1844', in *The Experience of Free Banking*, K. Dowd (ed.), pp. 157–86. London: Routledge.

——(1999) *The Theory of Monetary Institutions*, Oxford: Blackwell.

Wicker, E. (1985) 'Colonial monetary standards contrasted: evidence from the Seven Years' War', *The Journal of Economic History*, 45(4): 869–84.

Wilson, C. H. (1939) 'The economic decline of the Netherlands', *The Economic History Review*, 9(2): 111–27.

Is a beautiful system dying?

A possible Smithian take on the financial crisis

Maria Pia Paganelli

Adam Smith is often considered the father of capitalism or a passionate promoter of free markets. The invisible hand of self-interest generates prosperity everywhere it is left to work without interference. But then we have 2008. The financial system of the United States seems to break down. All major European economies struggle to remain above water. Iceland, praised for its embrace of free markets in the last few decades, goes down. Alan Greenspan is cited over and over again saying that markets have failed, and nobody knows why. Adam Smith is wrong!

But is Adam Smith wrong? Or is the caricature of Smith wrong?

In this paper I show that Adam Smith is indeed right, even if his caricature is not. The reading of Smith that I present here does not make him seem an optimistic describer of a providential order moved by an always-successful invisible hand. Rather, I will present some of the more pessimistic analyses of Smith, which, unfortunately, seem to be most appropriate to describe and analyze our current affairs. This reading of Smith may provide an explanation for the events that started in the fall of 2008. I fear that the pessimism that one can read in certain parts of Smith may apply to today's situation.

To show how we can look at the financial crisis of today with Smithian tools, I will focus only on a few relevant stylized facts, without any pretence of completeness. Homeowners and other borrowers took on loans too big to be repaid. Accounting frauds generated large profits for some at the expense of many. Many banks and institutions grew too big to fail. And the attempts to mitigate the breakdown of the system generated a large amount of public funds available for grabbing. Smith, in his own time, described this combination of factors which today have weakened the commercial system to a worrying degree.

The 'beautiful system of natural liberty' that Smith describes is a system that may be achieved only under rare circumstances. Smith recognizes systematic biases in human behaviours, ranging from overestimation of probability of success to almost blind admiration for the rich. He recognizes the dangers of concentrated interests. He recognizes the fundamental role of justice and morality in a well-functioning society, so that laws should serve the general population, not the interest of a few at the expense of the many.

The Adam Smith Review, 6: 269–282 © The International Adam Smith Society
ISSN 1743-5285, ISBN 0-415-66722-7

Smith makes a few policy recommendations, suggesting that the beautiful system that results from human actions but not human design would be threatened otherwise. Dismissing or failing to recognize its potential weaknesses may lead to it crumbling into ruins.

With this I am not claiming that Smith does not believe that a natural system of liberty is not possible at all. But simply that its achievement is not to be taken for granted. Smith does present the idea of a natural system of liberty which develops with and allows for the further development of economic growth. This point is well known and does not need to be challenged or developed further here. In fact, the strength of Smith's claim is notorious. Smith notices that our nature is not perfect. Perfection is not to be expected for individuals and for institutions. Our bodies are not perfect, and do not need to be perfect for us to live relatively well. Similarly, our institutions are not perfect and do not need to be perfect to direct us toward the natural system of liberty. We are able to achieve an economic system that leads to prosperity and liberty even with our imperfect means. This point has recently been made by Tony Aspromourgos (2009: 245), who claims that 'Smith expresses here a conviction that even under second-best (or worse) constitutions, regimes, and policies, "nature" is still in play, working away for the good'. Smith indeed tells us that:

> Some speculative physicians seem to have imagined that the health of the human body could be preserved only by a certain precise regimen of diet and exercise, of which every, the smallest, violation necessarily occasioned some degree of disease or disorder proportioned to the degree of the violation. Experience, however, would seem to show that the human body frequently preserves, to all appearance at least, the most perfect state of health under a vast variety of different regimens; even under some which are generally believed to be very far from being perfectly wholesome. But the healthful state of the human body, it would seem, contains in itself some unknown principle of preservation, capable either of preventing or of correcting, in many respects, the bad effects even of a very faulty regimen. Mr. Quesnai, who was himself a physician, and a very speculative physician, seems to have entertained a notion of the same kind concerning the political body, and to have imagined that it would thrive and prosper only under a certain precise regimen, the exact regimen of perfect liberty and perfect justice. He seems not to have considered that in the political body, the natural effort which every man is continually making to better his own condition, is a principle of preservation capable of preventing and correcting, in many respects, the bad effects of a political economy, in some degree, both partial and oppressive. Such a political economy, though it no doubt retards more or less, is not always capable of stopping altogether the natural progress of a nation towards wealth and prosperity, and still less of making it go backwards. If a nation could not prosper without the enjoyment of perfect liberty and perfect justice, there is not in the world a nation which could ever have prospered. In the

> political body, however, the wisdom of nature has fortunately made ample provision for remedying many of the bad effects of the folly and injustice of man; in the same manner as it has done in the natural body, for remedying those of his sloth and intemperance.
>
> (WN IV.ix.28)

The parallels between our natural body and the living body of society are frequent. But they are not always as upbeat. Our body can get sick. And bad policies can make a social and economic body sick. They can even kill it.

> The whole system of her industry and commerce has thereby been rendered less secure [by the monopoly of the colony trade]; the whole state of her body politick less healthful, than it otherwise would have been. In her present condition, Great Britain resembles one of those unwholesome bodies in which some of the vital parts are overgrown, and which, upon that account, are liable to many dangerous disorders scarce incident to those in which all the parts are more properly proportioned. A small stop in that great blood–vessel, which has been artificially swelled beyond its natural dimensions, and through which an unnatural proportion of the industry and commerce of the country has been forced to circulate, is very likely to bring on the most dangerous disorders upon the whole body politick. The expectation of a rupture with the colonies, accordingly, has struck the people of Great Britain with more terror than they ever felt for a Spanish armada, or a French invasion. … The blood, of which the circulation is stopt in some of the smaller vessels, easily disgorges itself into the greater, without occasioning any dangerous disorder; but, when it is stopt in any of the greater vessels, convulsions, apoplexy, or death, are the immediate and unavoidable consequences.
>
> (WN IV.vii.c.43)

Smith seems, therefore, to be both optimistic and pessimistic about the power of nature to generate and sustain a healthy natural system of liberty. On the one hand, nature seems to be powerful enough to allow us to achieve it, however imperfectly. On the other hand, there is nothing that can guarantee the emergence or sustainment of an economic system that generates and maintains prosperity and freedom. History indeed seems to show how rare that emergence is and how difficult its maintenance is. It may not be an accident that Smith was over-pessimistic regarding the possibility of eliminating restrictions from the inland trade in Britain and about the voluntary emancipation of slavery. It turned out that he was wrong, but, nevertheless, he had little reason to be otherwise.

The tendency toward the development of an order of natural liberty, for Smith, is not necessarily linear, or necessary at all. Human history is convoluted and its path zigzags. The natural system of liberty interacts with accidents of history, as well as all of our natural yet at times destructive human passions. Pratap Bhanu Mehta (2006: 255) may be right when he states that

> The bulk of *The Wealth of Nations* is devoted to the thought that for much of their history human beings have not acted on their interests; at least, they have set up systems of regulation and restraints such that only the interests of a few were served. Most important … the interests of humans are in conflict. For Smith, there is in a sense, nothing natural about the 'system of natural liberty'. If mankind had by degrees, unevenly and uncertainly, emerged from tutelage, it was less of a testament to the power of interest than to unanticipated consequences of actions or to fortuitous combinations of interests.

Smith indeed points out that the system of natural liberty in a sense is not that natural. That is, that what is natural is not the norm. For example, in the introductory chapter of Book III of the *Wealth of Nations*, titled 'Of the Natural Progress of Opulence', Smith explains the 'natural order of things' that brings the progress of opulence to different countries. 'The cultivation and improvement of the country, therefore which affords subsistence, must necessarily, be prior to the increase of the towns, which furnishes only the means of conveniency and luxury' (WN III.i.2): exactly the opposite of what he illustrates in chapter 4, 'How the Commerce of the Towns Contributed to the Improvement in the Country'. In fact, three of the four chapters of Book III tell the story of how the natural order of things was inverted! Smith explicitly warns his readers of this inversion of the natural course of things at the end of the first chapter: 'But though this natural order of things must have taken place in some degree in every society, it has, in all modern states of Europe, been, in many respects, entirely inverted' (WN III.i.9).

Joseph Cropsey (2001 [1957]: 73) describes this idea in the following way:

> there is nothing in the nature of things which will or might 'inevitably' lead to the coming into being of the natural or the most expedient social arrangement, indeed since history is not the rational expression of nature but in principle may conflict with nature, there arises the need for a statement of the strictly natural, which of course is the substance of the *Wealth of Nations*, a book that delivers the truth about nature.

It is possible therefore to read current events as being in conflict with and threatening the development of the natural system of liberty that Smith describes.

The paper develops as follow. In the next section I present the problem in the loan markets generated by what Smith would have described as our systematic overestimation of the probability of success. The analysis of the motivations that lead us to big commercial frauds follows. The third section describes how Smith envisions a stable decentralized banking system, a vision that is absent today. The fourth section describes the major threat for Smith's time and ours, the power of lobbies. A section on the solutions that Smith proposes, which unfortunately are weak, is followed by some conclusions.

Overestimation of the probability of success

Today's financial crisis is often attributed to excess lending. Adam Smith, too, worried about problems in lending markets. For Smith, a properly functioning lending market has to take into account some characteristics of human behaviour. Smith worried that if lending practices are based on an assumption of human behaviour that is different from actual behaviour, lending markets will not function properly and will therefore cause a misallocation and/or destruction of resources rather an increase in them. The problem described by Smith is unfortunately, in part, what we experience today.

For Adam Smith, human beings are systematically biased. In particular, any man in reasonable health would overestimate his probability of success. It is 'the presumptuous hope of success [that] seems to act here as upon all other occasions' (WN I.x.b.33) that causes miscalculation of the probability of success. A man thinks others may fail, but not him. He will therefore overestimate the probability of his success and underestimate the probability of his failure.

> The over-weening conceit which the greater part of men have of their own abilities, is an ancient evil remarked by the philosophers and moralists of all ages. Their absurd presumption in their own good fortune, has been less taken notice of. It is, however, if possible, still more universal. There is no man living who, when in tolerable health and spirits, has not some share of it. The chance of gain is by every man more or less overvalued, and the chance of loss is by most men under-valued, and by scarce any man, who is in tolerable health and spirits, valued more than it is worth.
>
> (WN I.x.b.26)

This implies that any project that has a probability of failure that is more than zero would be incorrectly seen as a potential success in the eyes of its proposer. Smith explains the 'irrational' decision of going into certain high-risk professions in terms of this systematic overestimation of success. For example, people who decide to get into smuggling are attracted by the high rate of profits of the successful smugglers and underestimate the very high rate of failure of this profession. They seem to think that the high probability of failure applies to others, not to themselves (WN I.x.b.33). Similarly, gamblers persist in their failures because they systematically overestimate their good luck. Lotteries are, for Smith, a basically sure form of revenue for the state (WN I.x.b.27) exactly because of this reason. Markets where risk is involved, such as the lending market, are markets that have to deal with this systematic perception bias (Bentham 1952 [1787]).

I do not think it is accidental that Smith proposes regulation in the lending market (Paganelli 2003). If a borrower systematically overestimates his probability of success and he is wrongly convinced he will be able to repay his debt, the lending market may have a problem: too many loans that will not be repaid may be given out. This is particularly true when the lender is lending out someone else's money. And if we add a potential reward for each loan given out, and a lack of punishment in case of failure to get the loan repaid, the problem of moral hazard not only emerges but lacks any obvious remedy.

For Adam Smith, an economic system that disregards, or even worse promotes, the systematic perception bias of our probability of success is a system that can neither prosper nor last.

Overweight on wealth

The second problem we hear blamed for today's crisis seems to be financial fraud. Ponzi schemes, insider trading, creative accounting, or questionable practices are so often in the news that it seems that the success of markets is just an illusion. Smith, again, warns us against fraudulent practices because they may undermine the system of natural liberty of which he is so fond.

Smith believes that mankind is driven, among other things, by the desire to receive the approbation of others. We receive approbation in two ways: by behaving morally and by parading wealth. Wealth glitters while virtue is modest. That is to say that wealth is easily recognizable, while virtue is not. An increase in wealth, like an increase in virtue, generates approbation. A decrease in wealth, like a decrease in virtue, generates disapprobation. But because we can easily see the wealth, and we can recognize virtues only with difficulty, a large increase in wealth would generate more approbation than the approbation lost due to the immoral means used to generate that wealth (Paganelli 2009). Smith indeed tells us:

> We frequently see the respectful attentions of the world more strongly directed towards the rich and the great, than towards the wise and virtuous. We see frequently the vices and follies of the powerful much less despised than the poverty and weakness of the innocent. … Two different roads are presented to us, equally leading to the attainment of this so much desired object [respect and admiration of mankind]; the one, by the study of wisdom and the practice of virtue; the other, by the acquisition of wealth and greatness. Two different characters are presented to our emulation; the one, of proud ambition and ostentatious avidity; the other, of humble modesty and equitable justice. Two different models, two different pictures, are held out to us, according to which we may fashion our own character and behaviour; the one more gaudy and glittering in its colouring; the other more correct and more exquisitely beautiful in its

> outline: the one forcing itself upon the notice of every wandering eye; the other, attracting the attention of scarce any body but the most studious and careful observer. … The great mob of mankind are the admirers and worshippers, and, what may seem more extraordinary, most frequently the disinterested admirers and worshippers, of wealth and greatness.
>
> (TMS I.iii.3.2)

In Part VI of TMS, Smith repeats the same claim: the great mob of mankind is more fascinated by the greatness of the rich than by the wise and virtuous, because the glitter of wealth is more visible and more easily recognizable.

> [Our] fascination of greatness … is so powerful, that the rich and the great are too often preferred to the wise and the virtuous. … The undistinguishing eye of the great mob of mankind can well enough perceive the [plain and palpable difference of birth and fortune]: it is with difficulty that the nice discernment of the wise and the virtuous can sometimes distinguish the [invisible and often uncertain difference of wisdom and virtue].
>
> (TMS VI.ii.1.20)

Indeed 'the same principle' that makes 'the great mob of mankind … look up … with a wondering … and foolish admiration' at 'wealth and greatness' makes us admire the success of great conquerors. We do not distinguish between 'such splendid characters as those of a Caeser or an Alexander … [and] that of the most brutal and savage barbarians, of an Attila, a Gengis, or a Tamerlane' because they are all successful (TMS VI.iii.30).

So Smith gives a description of the incentives to commit *large* financial frauds: the gains in approbation from the increase in wealth are more than the losses generated by the decrease in virtue. In TMS I.iii.3, a chapter titled 'Of the corruption of our moral sentiments, which is occasioned by this disposition to admire the rich and the great, and to despise or neglect the persons of poor and mean condition', and written after the completion of the *Wealth of Nations*, Smith tells us that

> The candidates for fortune too frequently abandon the paths of virtues … They often endeavour, therefore, not only by fraud and falsehood, the ordinary and vulgar arts of intrigue and cabal; but sometimes by the perpetration of the most enormous crimes, by murder and by assassination, by rebellion and civil war, to supplant and destroy those who oppose or stand in the way of their greatness.
>
> (TMS I.iii.3.8)

We have a plausible explanation for why financial scandals are in the billions of dollars rather than just in the hundreds. Smith seems to indicate that this kind of behaviour is more observable where there are large 'profit' opportunities. A poor society does not have the opportunity to generate as many incidents like these, simply because there is not much to possess. But when we have a large economic expansion, probably starting from a real change such as the IT revolution, we have large opportunities for monetary gain. Everybody is making millions. Why aren't you?

If we take Smith's argument seriously, is our economic situation sustainable? Are laws and regulations really enough to constrain our innate desire to receive the approbation of others, even if that implies doing the wrong thing? Are stricter laws really going to prevent another Madoff from arising if the opportunity for material gains is so large? Or does our wealthy system contain the seeds of its destruction, since trust in other individuals as well as in institutions and in the system itself will eventually crumble, as many accusations we hear today seem to indicate?

Overconcentration of banking

A third factor that seems to have challenged the stability of the system before the fall of 2008 is the presence of banks and financial institutions that are too big to fail. When we read what Smith considers a successful banking system, we read the opposite of what we observe today. For Smith, a successful banking and financial system is a system composed of many small banks rather than few large banks. Smith's rationale is the following.

Banks may be short-sighted and may have the tendency to over-issue credit to try to increase their profits (WN II.ii.43). So not only are creditors, because of their overestimation of the probability of their success, tempted to ask for over-issuing of credit, as we saw above, but banks are also tempted to over-issue credit.

In addition, Smith tells us that certain commercial activities may have high profits. When they do, they attract merchants' attention. Merchants ask for money to participate in these profitable trades. But as more and more merchants enter these markets, profits are eaten away (over-trading) and with them the resources to pay the banks back (over-issuing). When wise banks reject a credit extension, traders use 'shift of drawing and redrawing' to raise the money used to over-trade (WN II.ii.65). That is to say, 'over-trading of some bold projectors … was the original cause of … excessive circulation of paper money' (WN II.ii.57). This story is not that different from what we have read in the newspapers in the past few years.

Over-issuing of credit for Smith is dangerous. Banks have to be ready to fulfil their obligation at all times. But if they over-issue, they might not be as ready. And if they signal hesitation or difficulties, they might generate bank runs (WN II.ii.48). Furthermore, if a bank that has over-issued tries to fulfil its promises, it faces an outflow of funds larger than its inflow. The acquisition of reserves to fulfil its demand might quickly become very expensive. It is therefore in the bank's interest not to over-issue, because, to keep its coffers ready, it would have to spend what it would gain, if not more, by over-issuing.

And the bank, losing profits, would decrease the amount of issuing (WN II.ii.49–51). The implication is that neither merchants nor banks should over-issue, as it may bring all into bankruptcy.

But this does not prevent banks from over-issuing (WN II.ii.41–87). One reason for over-issuing, besides the problems just mentioned, says Smith, is the bank's ignorance – banks do not always understand what they are doing and what is best for them (WN II.ii.53). Indeed Smith tells us more than once that 'every particular banking company has not always understood or attended to its own particular interest, and the circulation has frequently been overstocked with paper-money' (WN II.ii.56).

Smith explains that banks may not understand what they are doing because projectors fool banks when traders draw and redraw upon one another. If they do it from the same banks, the bank may realize what is going on. But traders use different banks, and might add more projectors to the circle. Distinguishing between a 'real bill of exchange' and a 'fictitious' one becomes more difficult. And when a banker realizes he is discounting 'fictitious bills', it is too late (WN II.ii.72). Additionally, banks, like everybody else, tend to overestimate their probability of success and underestimate their probability of failure. They tend to overestimate the inflow of money and underestimate their outflow (WN II.ii.76). This, again, is not a story unique to the eighteenth century....

Smith seems to maintain an optimistic attitude as long as there are *many small* competing banks, as competitive markets are generally good teachers (Cowen and Kroszner 1994; White 1995). Many small competing banks should be able to constrain the tendency to over-issue because if depositors fear over-issuing, they can withdraw their deposits and bring them to more prudent banks. Additionally, and most importantly, the advantage of competing banks is that they are many and small. This means that if one of them fails because its behaviour was indeed imprudent, the effects will be limited. The consequences of the failure of a small bank will be small, unlike the potentially catastrophic consequences of the failure of a big bank (Paganelli 2006).

> The late multiplication of banking companies in both parts of the United Kingdom, an event by which many people have been much alarmed, instead of diminishing, increases the security of the publick. It obliges all of them to be more circumspect in their conduct, and, by not extending their currency beyond its due proportion to their cash, to guard themselves against those malicious runs, which the rivalship of so many competitors is always ready to bring upon them. It restrains the circulation of each particular company within a narrower circle, and reduces their circulating notes to a smaller number. By dividing the whole circulation into a greater number of parts, the failure of any one company, an accident which, in the course of things, must sometimes happen, becomes of less consequence to the publick.
>
> (WN II.ii.106)

So a bank should fail, if it behaved imprudently. The bankruptcy of a bank is a very powerful lesson to its banker and to other banks. By allowing a bank to fail, the market teaches its participants what should be done and what should not be done. Once banks understand what they have 'not always understood', they will not over-issue. And because every man is driven by his desire to better his condition, there is no reason to believe that banks will forever 'not attended to [their] own particular interest' (Skaggs 1999). Unfortunately, this face of the market does not seem to be allowed to show itself today. If we are not learning from our mistakes, can we ever learn at all?

Perhaps even if there is a possibility of learning from our mistakes, David Hume (1985 [1752]: 363) was correct when he claimed:

> So great dupes are the generality of mankind, that, notwithstanding such a violent shock to public credit, as a voluntary bankruptcy in ENGLAND would occasion, it would not be long ere credit would again revive in as flourishing a condition as before. … And though men are commonly more governed by what they have seen, than by what they foresee, with whatever certainty; yet promises, protestations, fair appearances, with the allurement of present interest, have such powerful influence as few are able to resist. Mankind are, in all ages, caught by the same baits: the same tricks, played over and over again, still trepan them.

Lobbying

Another factor that Smith sees as fundamental for the sustaining of a system of natural liberty is a functioning system of justice. This, for Smith, implies that the laws that are passed are laws that favour the majority of the people, not just a small group. If that is not the case, the system of justice becomes a system of monstrous injustice, poisoning the beautiful system of natural liberty.

We are indeed told in TMS that 'Sometimes the interest of particular orders of men who tyrannize the government, warp the positive law of the country from what natural justice would prescribe' (TMS VII. iv.36), and in WN that

> To hurt in any degree the interest of any one order of citizens, for no other purpose but to promote that of some other, is evidently contrary to that justice and equality of treatment which the sovereign owes to all the different orders of his subjects.
>
> (WN IV.viii.30)

But, unfortunately this is exactly what some great merchants and manufacturers do when there are large profit opportunities generated by government-granted monopolies. A system of justice, when taken over by lobbies, degenerates. The government grants favours to organized interests at the expense of the rest of society, causing the most severe injustices:

> The cruellest of our revenue laws, I will venture to affirm, are mild and gentle, in comparison of some of those which the clamour of our merchants and manufacturers has extorted from the legislature, for the support of their own absurd and oppressive monopolies. Like the laws of Draco, these laws may be said to be all written in blood.
>
> (WN IV.viii.17)

Smith indeed accuses big merchants and manufacturers of conspiring against the public, explaining that they are 'an order of men whose interest is never exactly the same with the public, who generally have an interest to deceive and even oppress the public, and who accordingly have, upon many occasions, both deceived and oppressed it' (WN, I.xi.10).

The virulent dangers of lobbying are many, such as, but not limited to, those in WN, IV.i.10: IV.ii.38; and IV.iii.c.10 (Stigler 1971; Evensky 2005). An additional source of worry for Smith is that lobbies are able to convince others that special organized groups are not enemies of society but defenders and promoters of the wealth of the country (e.g. WN IV.iii.c.13).

The cupidity of interest groups springs and grows the more wealth there is to grab through the protection of the government. And unfortunately this is what seems to be the case today, with the stimulus money. We have an undreamt of sum of money available for those who lobby the most.

Solutions?

Is there hope, then? Or is the Western-style economic system as we know it about to become a part of history? Smith, in attempting to address the problems of his day, appeals to both the self-organizing forces of markets as well as to the feeble public spirit of the legislator. But if markets are suffocated by regulations, and if hell is indeed paved with good intentions, we are left with little hope to hold onto.

Commerce itself seems to be able to generate some remedies (WN IV.vii.c.47–54. See also Rosenberg 1990), as does our weak civic spirit (TMS IV.1.11). The legislator should not fall for the flattery of the lobbyists but should preserve the system of natural liberty out of reverence toward its beauty. Unfortunately, this seems to be just a dream.

The glimmers of wealth presented by organized interest groups seem to overwhelm political leaders, like everybody else.

> The external graces, the frivolous accomplishments of that impertinent and foolish thing called a man of fashion, are commonly more admired than the solid and masculine virtues of a warrior, a statesman, a philosopher, or a legislator. All the great and awful virtues, all the virtues

> which can fit, either for the council, the senate, of the field, are, by the insolent and insignificant flatterers, who commonly figure the most in such corrupted societies, held in the utmost contempt and derision.
>
> (TMS I.iii.3.6)

Even if commerce seems to provide large enough benefits to compensate for its downsides, the damages of rent-seeking are going to last. Once privileges are granted, they will not be taken away. Indeed Smith is convinced that the 'formidable' powers merchants and manufacturers have 'intimidate the legislature' (IV.ii.43) so much that

> To expect, indeed, that the freedom of trade should ever be entirely restored in Great Britain, is as absurd as to expect that an Oceana or Utopia should ever be established in it. Not only the prejudices of the publick, but what is much more unconquerable, the private interests of many individuals, irresistibly oppose it.
>
> (WN IV.ii.43)

The damage great merchants and manufacturers inflict upon society is permanent (Tullock 1975).

That the system of natural liberty so much wished for is not the norm is confirmed by the different levels of growth that we observed. Smith tells us indeed that an economy that has been in an expansionary state may not be expansionary forever. It may become sedentary or even recede. North America, in Smith's time, was an example of an expansionary economy, China of a sedentary one, and Bengal of a declining one. The reason for these differences is, for Smith, based both on accidents of history and, especially, on differences in the quality of the government. When the government falls into the hands of interest groups an economy may very well decline:

> The difference between the genius of the British constitution which protects and governs North America, and that of the mercantile company which oppresses and domineers in the East Indias, cannot perhaps be better illustrated than by the different state of those countries.
>
> (WN I.viii.26)

All major forms of civilization eventually perished, either deliberately by human hands or inadvertently as a side effect of other events. If the feudal system and the temporal power of the church have been brought down by the silent revolution of commerce and the childish vanity of the nobles and the high clergy, why can't the capitalist system be brought down by the loud attacks of lobbies and the vanity of those who claim to have perfect knowledge of human rationality and to be able to control the economy and correct the 'mistakes' of the market?

It may very well be that, as Mehta (2006: 257) claims,

> Establishing the 'system of natural liberty' under which every man is 'left perfectly free to pursue his own interest his own way' is thus for Smith a *task*, rather than something that comes naturally (WN IV.ix.51). The paradox is that the very motive, self-interest, that allows that system to produce the beneficial consequences it does, constantly threatens to undermine it. It is the pursuit of their interests that leads merchants to demand monopolies and privileges that harm society; yet, those very same interests can, under the right institutional conditions, produce beneficial outcomes. *The Wealth of Nations* is an account of how the interests of all might be harmonized, not a claim that they are always, or naturally, in harmony.

Conclusions

Adam Smith describes the beauty of a natural system of liberty, which later has often been associated, correctly or not, with capitalism. This beautiful system of natural liberty is robust under certain conditions but fragile under other conditions, as Smith recognizes. It is robust in the sense that as a system that emerged spontaneously over centuries, it enjoys the strengths of a system that is not limited by the design of human reason. On the other hand, it is subject to shocks as a result of human hubris. The belief that we are better than everybody else, either because of our presumptuous hope of success or because of our vain parade of wealth, may lead us to disregard some structural foundations of the system of natural liberty, undermining it. Combining our systematic perception biases with perverse incentives that motivate us to disregard the precepts of justice and favour ourselves at the expense of others or of society may cause structural cracks to an otherwise solid system. Excess borrowing, excess lending, excess concentration in the banking industry, excess lobbying, and excess fraudulent activities are all worries that Adam Smith had for his time. And the same worries may apply to our time as well.

Acknowledgements

I would like to thank an anonymous referee as well as the Japanese Society for the Promotion of Science, thanks to which I was able to present this work at Keio University.

References

Aspromourgos, T. (2009) *The Science of Wealth: Adam Smith and the Framing of Political Economy*, London and New York: Routledge.

Bentham, J. (1952) [1787] 'Defence of usury', in *Jeremy Bentham's Economic Writings*, W. Stark (ed.), London: George, Allen & Unwin.

Cowen, T. and Kroszner, R. (1994) *Explorations in the New Monetary Economics*, Cambridge, MA and Oxford: Blackwell.

Cropsey, J. (2001) *Polity and Economics*, South Bend, IN: St. Augustine's Press.

Evensky, J. (2005) *Adam Smith's Moral Philosophy*, Cambridge: Cambridge University Press.

Hume, D. (1985) *Essays: Moral, Political, and Literary*, Indianapolis: Liberty Fund.

Mehta, P. B. (2006) 'Self-interest and other interests', in *The Cambridge Companion to Adam Smith*, K. Haakonssen (ed.), pp. 246–69, New York: Cambridge University Press.

Paganelli, M. P. (2003) 'In Medio Stat Virtus: an alternative view of usury in Adam Smith's thinking', *History of Political Economy*, 35(1): 21–48.

——(2006) 'Vanity and the Daedalian wings of paper money in Adam Smith', in *New Voices on Adam Smith*, L. Montes and E. Schliesser (eds), pp. 270–89, London and New York: Routledge.

——(2009) 'Approbation and the desire to better one's condition in Adam Smith: when the desire to better one's condition does not better one's condition and society's condition … ', *Journal of the History of Economic Thought*, 31(1): 79–92.

Rosenberg, N. (1990) 'Adam Smith and the stock of moral capital', *History of Political Economy*, 22(1): 1–17.

Skaggs, N. T. (1999) 'Adam Smith on growth and credit: too weak a connection?' *Journal of Economic Studies*, 26(6): 481–96.

Smith, A. (1981) *An Inquiry into the Nature and Causes of the Wealth of Nations*, R. H. Campbell and A. S. Skinner (eds), Indianapolis: Liberty Fund.

——(1984) *The Theory of Moral Sentiments*, D. D. Raphael and A. L. Macfie (eds), Indianapolis: Liberty Fund.

Stigler, G. (1971) 'Smith's travels on the ship of the state', *History of Political Economy*, 3(2): 265–77.

Tullock, G. (1975) 'The transitional gain trap', *Bell Journal of Economics*, 6(2): 671–78.

White, L. (1995) *Free Banking in Britain: Theory, Experience, and Debate, 1800–1845*, London: IEA.

What do we mean by 'Anglo-American capitalism'?

Alessandro Roncaglia[1]

Before discussing the perspectives of Anglo-American capitalism, we need to be sufficiently clear about what we mean by it. In the presentation to this Symposium, it is equated with 'the robust sort of capitalism' favoured by Adam Smith. My opinion is, rather, that in recent decades – more or less since the times of Thatcher and Reagan – Anglo-American capitalism has moved away from the sort of capitalism favoured by Adam Smith, and this move has, on the whole, had negative consequences.

Faced with such a vast issue to deal with in a brief presentation, I can only sketch out this viewpoint in broad terms. This I shall attempt by discussing separately some of the elements that go into it. First of all, how can we characterize contemporary (immediately pre-crisis) Anglo-American capitalism? In what respects does it differ from 'European' capitalism, and from the capitalism prevailing in the United States and the United Kingdom in the 1950s and 1960s? Second, what sort of capitalism was close to Adam Smith's heart? Third, what are the merits and demerits of the recent variety of Anglo-American capitalism, in the light of the recent crisis? What are the perspectives?

First things first. A recent book by Giorgio Ruffolo (2008) has the provocative title *Il capitalismo ha i secoli contati*, to the effect that, contrary to what some hasty commentators ventured to suggest immediately after the financial crisis exploded, capitalism's residual life span can still be measured in centuries. By capitalism Ruffolo simply means, in accordance with a long tradition, a market economy with private ownership of means of production.[2] This definition leaves room for a wide spectrum of varieties of capitalism; in one variety or another, the market economy will be with us for an indefinite, but certainly not short, future.

Varieties of capitalism may appear in sequence, as the economy and its institutional, cultural, political, and social framework change over time; or, with different countries experiencing different historical developments, may be present side by side at the same time. Thus, Berle and Means (1932) hailed the rise to dominance of a 'managerial capitalism' quite different from an original entrepreneurial capitalism, when the entrepreneur was also commonly the owner of the firm; under managerial capitalism, by contrast, corporations have many shareholders, so that the top managers were often

The Adam Smith Review, 6: 283–289 © The International Adam Smith Society
ISSN 1743-5285, ISBN 0-415-66722-7

able to guide the company without being its proprietors.[3] Kenneth Galbraith (1967) advanced the idea of a 'new industrial state' dominated by a 'technostructure': the paradigm of perfectly competitive equilibrium is wholly inappropriate for the interpretation of contemporary economies, the evolution of which is mainly determined by interactions among the leading players such as the government (especially the military), the largest corporations, and the trade unions. Many commentators, in the aftermath of the financial crisis, signalled the 'revolving door' custom by which government jobs and managerial roles in big corporations are held in rapid sequence by the same persons, with Goldman Sachs acquiring in recent years the role which was held in Kenneth Galbraith's times by Exxon or General Motors. James Galbraith, the son of Kenneth, criticizes the 'Bush regime', which, under the cover of the myth of the competitive market economy, brought the methods and mentality of big business to public life, thus giving rise to a 'predator state', with its 'systematic abuse of public institutions for private profit' and its 'drive to divert public resources to clients and friends' (Galbraith 2008: xiii). Previously, Hyman Minsky (1993) had signalled, with some apprehension, the rise of a 'money manager capitalism', characterized by the dominance of finance within the economy, of financial markets over financial intermediaries, and as a consequence of the very short time span adopted for crucial economic decisions compared with the long-run view of managerial capitalism.[4]

Minsky's view signalled a tendency present all over the world, but more markedly apparent in the United States and the United Kingdom. The direction of movement, towards a 'money manager capitalism', is imposed worldwide by the international character of financial markets; however, a financial intermediaries-based economy (so-called 'Rhine capitalism') can still be seen in Germany and other European countries, although the scope of such intermediaries as banks is now much wider than before, due to closer interconnection with the financial markets.[5]

In the USA and the UK, too, the move in this direction required some active policy intervention to drive the economy away from regulated international and national monetary and financial systems. The abandonment of the Bretton Woods international monetary arrangements in 1971 and the abandonment of a monetary policy aiming at stabilizing the interest rate in the USA in 1979, favoured the explosion of speculative (including covered) dealings in currencies and financial assets, and the development of booming derivatives markets. Concomitantly came the deregulation policy, culminating in the Gramm-Leach-Bliley Act of 1999. Thus a whole system of rules constraining financial activity in order to contain financial fragility and avoid systemic crises was dismantled, and the door was open to the development of the 'money manager capitalism' described by Minsky (1993). The derivatives markets reached a size nine times that of world GDP; the financial sector came to absorb up to 40 per cent of total corporate profits in the USA, and still higher shares in other countries. Deregulation, and with it the dominance of the financial markets and the concomitant decline of financial intermediation, was also favoured by the laissez-faire attitude adopted towards fiscal and regulatory paradises, competition from which drove all the developed countries to slacken their reins on all sorts of financial activity.[6]

The rise of financial markets, as opposed to a traditional set-up based on financial intermediaries (banks), was considered by many commentators – but by no means all – as a particularly superior feature of Anglo-American capitalism, before the crisis exploded. We may take as an example the book by Rajan and Zingales (2003), where certain episodes of historical narrative and some of the literature are cited in support of the argument, but the contrary opinions (from Keynes to Minsky, from Kindleberger to Godley, from Sylos Labini to Kregel) are not discussed at all. The dramatic financial crisis, whose evolution is still far from complete, is now prompting second thoughts on deregulation policy and the relative role of the financial markets in our economies (for fuller illustration of these points, see Roncaglia 2010). How economic institutions will change in the future remains to be seen.

The different varieties of capitalism are not to be distinguished solely in terms of their financial structure. For instance, we may reasonably suppose (although reliable statistics are not available) that both in the USA and the UK the proportion of goods and especially services going through the market is higher than in most European countries, Japan, China, India and so on, where self-provision within the family is more important. Political institutions and industrial relations should also be considered, and as far as they are concerned the differences between the US and UK are indeed great. For instance, as far as the role of the welfare state is concerned, the United Kingdom is closer to the other European countries, even after the Thatcher era, than to the United States.[7] In one sense, the difference in the welfare state is simply a matter of the decision of a political community (a country) to have certain services provided by the state (be it the central government or local authorities), paying a somewhat higher proportion of taxes in order to cover the costs. In another sense, however, it is a decision that reveals a different culture, with a more pronounced leaning towards individualism in the USA, while in Europe recognition of individual rights combines with the preference for some services to be managed by the state, the idea being that in this way the interests of the poorest and the most needy strata of society are better taken care of. (Incidentally, in the United States the opposite view is supported, in clearly non-competitive markets, with widespread and well-financed lobbying influencing both government and public opinion: the popular opposition to the Obama drive for a more comprehensive public health system is a testimony to this, incomprehensible as it may appear to the European observer.[8])

This brings us to the other two issues, namely the theoretical foundations of Anglo-American capitalism and its alleged Smithian roots, and the relative validity of this variety of capitalism compared to the European variety.

In a nutshell, the theoretical foundations of Anglo-American capitalism can be reduced to the Chicagoan faith in 'the invisible hand of the market', or in other words the idea that the supply and demand market mechanism is able, if the right conditions are ensured, to lead the economy to an optimal equilibrium characterized by full employment of resources, labour included. The right conditions include as much freedom as possible from any sort of constraints, and the development of markets for all sorts of commodities, including the contingent commodity world of which the derivatives markets are a natural implication.

To endow it with a certain nobility, this view is attributed to Adam Smith (George Stigler, one of the leaders of the Chicago school, was the first to state this attribution, cf. Stigler 1951). But the attribution is unfounded (cf. Rothschild 1994, 2001). In all his published writings, Smith only utilizes the expression 'invisible hand' three times, never referring to 'the market'. One of the references is ironical (primitive people attribute to 'the invisible hand of Jupiter' the natural phenomena that they cannot explain, Smith 1980, 'Astronomy', III.2) and one – the only occurrence in *The Wealth of Nations*, and the only case in which a matter of economics is discussed (WN IV.ii.9) – considers an example of non-competitive markets (because of the preference of entrepreneurs for internal to external investments). Smith's 'natural prices', his theoretical variable, are not determined by supply and demand; 'market prices' – which are *influenced* by supply and demand, not *determined* by a market-clearing mechanism – are simply the empirical correlate of the theoretical variable. Nor are wages and profits determined by a market-clearing mechanism. What is more, Smith's 'self-interest' is something different from mere selfishness: it requires subjects able to take into account societal constraints and endowed with an ethics of 'sympathy', meant as the ability and willingness to share the feelings of others (cf. Roncaglia 2005a: ch. 5). Smith attributes great importance not only to social rules and their enforcement, but also to the disparities of income, wealth, and power inevitable in a market economy. In his opinion, public interventions are required not only to check monopoly power, but also in support of the lower strata of the population: his proposal of elementary public education for all (WN, V.i.f.52–57) was, for his times, truly ground-breaking, pointing to the need to reduce the distance between the higher and the lower strata of society. While others at the time were opposed to public charity (Necker, subsequently Malthus), Smith – like Condorcet and Turgot in France – favoured it (cf. Roncaglia 2005b: chs 5 and 9).

At the time the economy, and especially the financial sector, were much less developed than nowadays, and it is therefore useless to look to Smith for keys to interpret our current problems subsequent to the crisis. (We may simply observe, in passing, that the dominance of the financial markets is associated with a redistribution of income in the direction of greater inequality; cf. for instance Sylos Labini 2003; Galbraith and Garcilazo 2004.) But the idea of the invisible hand of the market, when taken up in mainstream macroeconomics, implies theoretical errors which should by now be generally recognized, having been illustrated by Keynes, Sraffa, and their followers. Here again I must content myself with a couple of unsubstantiated observations, offering only a few references for the reasoning that underlies them. First, contrary to a basic tenet of mainstream macroeconomics, there is no automatic tendency to full employment in a competitive market economy: the inverse relationship between wage rate and demand for labour on which it relies has been disproved by the 'reswitching controversy' following publication of Sraffa 1960 (cf. Roncaglia 2009a: ch. 6). Second, contrary to the idea prevailing in the past couple of decades (and supported by the Nobel Memorial prize commission) that uncertainty within the financial world can be reduced to computable risk, the Keynesian views on uncertainty need be taken up again, with the implications indicated by Keynes himself on the need to avoid any domination of finance over the productive sectors.[9]

Thus, in conclusion, if by Anglo-American capitalism we mean that variety of capitalism in which the financial markets dominate over the real economy, its unfettered persistence bodes for us a future marked by ever more dramatic economic crises, possibly greater income inequalities, and – should it spread to Europe – the fiscal crisis of the welfare state. Whether the resulting society would be better than the society open to us with a 'European' variety of capitalism is, I believe, quite doubtful.[10]

Notes

1 Dipartimento di studi sociali, economici, attuariali e demografici, La Sapienza Università di Roma. E-mail: alessandro.roncaglia@uniroma1.it. Financial support from MIUR is gratefully acknowledged. Sincere thanks are due to an anonymous referee for her/his thought-provoking remarks.

2 Adam Smith does not utilize the term 'capitalism' but his notion is the same. He contrasts modern society with a somewhat mythical construct, 'that early and rude state of society which precedes both the accumulation of stock and the appropriation of land' which is then utilized, by contrast, in the analysis of a modern economy where 'stock has accumulated in the hands of particular persons' and 'the land of any country has all become private property' (WN I.vi.1–8).

3 For a theory of managerial capitalism, cf. Marris 1964.

4 Big corporations, such as the East India Company, already existed (though under different rules) in Smith's times – but were very few – active in foreign trade and colonization. Smith refers to them frequently in the pages of the *Wealth of Nations* (cf. for instance WN IV.vii), condemning their monopoly power and their political influence in his analysis of the 'mercantile system' (which is an analysis of a policy system rather than interpretation of a stage in the development of market economies). Obviously, he could not have foreseen the precise nature of future developments of the market structure of modern economies, and the phenomena discussed above are consequently extraneous to his analysis; this especially holds true for the financialization of the economy and Minsky's money manager capitalism. However, this does not mean that the theoretical structure developed by Smith and other Classical authors cannot be utilized – with the necessary additions – in analysis of contemporary capitalism; indeed, the flexibility of Smith's (and in general the Classical economists') analytical structure with its openness to consideration of social and political factors, can provide a much better basis for such analysis than

the neoclassical/marginalist structure focused on scarcity of resources and consumers' preferences (on this, cf. Roncaglia 2005a).

5 The dichotomy between a financial intermediaries-based economy (or 'Rhine' model) and a financial markets-based economy (or Anglo-Saxon model) is a rather impressionistic notion. In a few words and with drastic simplification, in the 'Rhine' model financial intermediaries such as commercial banks traditionally collect sight or short term deposits from the general public and make loans to individuals or firms or, in the case of investment banks, hold equity participation in firms; this model is thus characterized by an arms-length relationship between financial intermediaries and their clients, which favours more informed evaluation of clients' requests for financing. In the Anglo-Saxon model, the financial intermediaries organize the issue of claims by the deficit spending unit and their sale to the general public; such claims are then traded in the financial markets, with financial intermediaries actively participating in the trade.

6 For more extensive illustration of these issues, cf. Roncaglia 2010.

7 Comparative statistics on the relative size of the state and the welfare state in different countries (as provided for instance by the OECD, cf. in particular its *Social Expenditure Database*) call for great caution; for fuller analysis of the available information and an authoritative assessment of the situation, cf. Lindert 2004.

8 Inter-country differences in life expectancies are commonly associated with per capita income. If we consider deviations from this regression, we may analyze the effects of other factors, such as the relative weights of public and private health expenditure, on life expectancies. My bet is that the welfare-state countries fare better. Obviously life expectancy is also affected by other factors, such as dangerous behaviour (for instance obesity or violence); control for such factors is needed in order to evaluate the robustness of the relationship between life expectancy and the welfare state. We may add that the scale and degree of dangerous behaviour have socio-cultural roots, including the role of the state, through – for instance – public education or the public provision of psychiatric help, and (as Smith, WN V.i.b.1ff. stressed) 'an exact administration of justice'.

9 Cf. Roncaglia 2009b, 2010. It is the Keynesian notion of uncertainty rather than Knight's (1921), that Minsky relies on, as evidenced by his treatment of uncertainty in Minsky (1975: Knight is not even mentioned), and by his evaluation of Knight in a beautiful recollection of his formative years (Minsky 1985).

10 If we consider the dichotomy illustrated above between selfishness and self-interest, we cannot say that American or British culture and society are characterized by selfishness and European culture and society by self-interest. Putnam's (1993, 2000) thorough enquiries, respectively surveying Italy and the USA, testify to a more complex picture. What we can say is that, in so far as culture can change under the influence of the economy and economic ideology, the Anglo-American model of capitalism and the ideological celebration made of it tend to drive towards selfishness rather than Smithian self-interest.

Bibliography

Berle, A. A. and Means, G. (1932) *The Modern Corporation and Private Property*, New York: The Commerce Clearing House.

Galbraith, J. K. (1967) *The New Industrial State*, Boston: Houghton Mifflin.

——(2008) *The Predator State*, New York: Free Press.

Galbraith, J. K. and Garcilazo, E. (2004) 'Unemployment, inequality and the policy of Europe: 1984–2000', *BNL Quarterly Review*, 57: 3–28.

Knight, F. H. (1921) *Risk, Uncertainty and Profit*, Boston: Houghton Mifflin.

Lindert, P. H. (2004) *Growing Public: Social Spending and Economic Growth since the Eighteenth century*, 2 vols, Cambridge: Cambridge University Press.

Marris, R. (1964) *The Economic Theory of 'Managerial' Capitalism*, London: Macmillan.

Minsky, H. (1975) *John Maynard Keynes*, New York: Columbia University Press.

——(1985) 'Beginnings', *BNL Quarterly Review*, 38: 211–21; reprinted in J. A. Kregel (ed.) *Recollections of Eminent Economists*, vol. 1 (1989), pp. 169–79, London: Macmillan.

——(1993) 'Schumpeter and finance', in *Market and Institutions in Economic Development*, S. Biasco, A. Roncaglia and M. Salvati (eds), pp. 103–15, London: Macmillan.

Putnam, R. D. (1993) *Making Democracy Work: Civic Traditions in Modern Italy*, Princeton, NJ: Princeton University Press.

——(2000) *Bowling Alone: The Collapse and Revival of American Community*, New York: Simon & Schuster.

Rajan, R. G. and Zingales, L. (2003) *Saving Capitalism from the Capitalists*, New York: Random House.

Roncaglia, A. (2005a) *The Wealth of Ideas: A History of Economic Thought*, Cambridge: Cambridge University Press.

——(2005b) *Il mito della mano invisibile*, Roma-Bari: Laterza.

——(2009a) *Piero Sraffa*, Basingstoke: Palgrave Macmillan.

——(2009b) 'Keynes and probability: an assessment', *The European Journal for the History of Economic Thought*, 16: 489–510.

——(2010) *Why Economists Got It Wrong: The Crisis and Its Cultural Roots*, London: Anthem Press.

Rothschild, E. (1994) 'Adam Smith and the invisible hand', *American Economic Review. Papers and Proceedings*, 84: 319–22.

——(2001) *Economic Sentiments: Adam Smith, Condorcet and the Enlightenment*, Cambridge, MA: Harvard University Press.

Ruffolo, G. (2008) *Il capitalismo ha i secoli contati*, Turin: Einaudi.

Smith, A. (1976) *An Inquiry into the Nature and Causes of the Wealth of Nations*, R. H. Campbell and A. S. Skinner (eds), Oxford: Oxford University Press.

——(1980) *Essays on Philosophical Subjects*, W. P. D. Wightman (ed.), Oxford: Oxford University Press.

Sraffa, Piero (1960) *Production of Commodities by Means of Commodities*, Cambridge: Cambridge University Press.

Stigler, G. (1951) 'The division of labor is limited by the extent of the market', *Journal of Political Economy*, 59: 185–53.

Sylos Labini, P. (2003) 'Prospects for the world economy', *BNL Quarterly Review*, 56: 179–206.

Freedom, efficiency, and concern

Smith's future, and ours

Robert Urquhart

Smith and his time

One of the many peculiarities around Adam Smith is that he is linked, seemingly indissolubly and forever, to an economic order that he himself never knew: the order we may most simply name *capitalism*. The commercial society of Smith's time was, indeed, well on the way towards capitalism, and by the time of his death in 1791 had probably passed the point of no return. But, first, the objective conditions for capitalism were far from complete. Large-scale machine industry was at best in its infancy: the crucial development of a machine tools industry – making machines with machinery – necessary to complete the internal dynamic of industrial production had not yet occurred (Marx 1977: 504–5). Wage-labour had not yet fully emerged as the dominant, potentially universal, form of productive activity; and a proper capitalist class had not yet coalesced around the principle of unlimited accumulation of capital.

Second, even the extent of actual change was not recognized. This is seen in *The Wealth of Nations* itself. Smith's account of the social order is traditional, with the landlords, however stupid, on top. He sees this order as natural and necessary (Smith 1976b, WN I.xi.7), even if he argues against some of its main supports – primogeniture, for example (WN III.ii.6). Of those who receive revenue in the form of profit, the merchants are the senior partners, and given the most attention, for all Smith's concern with production. The master manufacturers are masters of *manufactories*, where the typical form is that of a detail division of labour still employing handcraft techniques (as in the famous pin manufactory). Smith includes facilitating the introduction of machinery in his account of how division of labour improves the productive powers of labour. But, as Marx points out, he ranks this only as the third reason. Furthermore, 'machinery' here, in normal eighteenth-century usage, means any kind of implement, not specifically large-scale artificially powered machinery. The problem with the division of labour in Book V (see below) is with the monotony of pulling out the wire in the pin manufactory, not that of subservience to a vast, steam-powered machine. Agriculture remains primary: America is advancing more rapidly than Europe because of its agrarian nature (WN I.viii.23).[1]

The Adam Smith Review, 6: 290–308 © The International Adam Smith Society
ISSN 1743-5285, ISBN 0–415–66722–7

When Smith looks forward, he is pessimistic: his distinction among advancing, stationary, and declining states suggests an overall movement from the first state through the second to the third, although he does think that a stationary state can last for a long time (China is the great example). He has a more specific set of claims as well, however: the course of human prosperity rarely lasts more than 200 years; this is not long enough for a nation to acquire sufficient capital for the full development of the three main methods of its employment (agriculture, manufactures, foreign trade); anyway, England has already had more than two hundred years of prosperity (WN II.v.22, III.iv.20). In considering the possibilities of development, Smith names Egypt, India, and China as outstandingly wealthy, and even they only managed two out of the three methods – agriculture and manufactures (WN II.v.22). Note, also, that Smith's criterion for advance is always, and only, simply wealth.

China is a particularly interesting example. It is richer than any part of Europe (WN I.xi.e.34). Smith does say that with other laws and institutions it could have been richer still (WN I.ix.15). But on occasion, he compares China favourably to Europe, precisely on grounds of it allowing greater freedom to the natural course of things (WN I.x.c.24). China is distinctive not only for its great wealth, but also for the length of time that it has remained in a stationary state. It has not, indeed, advanced for ages, but it has staved off decline. The emphasis Smith gives to this implies the normal expectation that the declining will supersede the stationary state.

On the one hand, Smith sees no fundamental difference between Europe and the rest of the world: along with other eighteenth-century writers, he sees China, in particular, as in some ways more advanced than Europe. Differences are in laws, institutions, policy, which impede 'the natural course of things' to a greater or lesser extent: and it is by no means the case that Europe is unequivocally superior in this regard. Such a view is in accord with Smith's account of the natural origins of the division of labour in the propensity to exchange, which should be the same for everyone everywhere.

On the other hand, he has no anticipation of a fundamental change to come. Europe may grow more wealthy, but it may also be running out of time. In any event, the same processes have been at work in human history since the beginning as are at work today. Smith is representative of his time in not seeing just what the industrial revolution was doing. He was representative also in describing what may be called – and *was* so called – a *polite and commercial society*,[2] and not a capitalist mode of production.

Karl Polanyi says of Smith's natural propensity to exchange: 'no misreading of the past ever proved more prophetic of the future' (Polanyi 2001: 45). We may expand on this. Smith finds what he wants looking backward over the course of history, discerning in this a 'natural course of things'. Although it is possible, even inevitable, for nations to deviate from it, there is only one true course. When he looks forward from his own modern Europe, all he sees is more of the same, with the likelihood of decline sooner or later. He neither sees nor expects the economic order that still takes him as its prophet. Yet, as Polanyi implies, there is good reason to link Smith to it: we rightly orient Smith towards the future, even if he did not. Polanyi is also right to see the propensity to exchange as central. The enormous and continuing prestige of the free market idea depends upon privileging the exchange relation above all others. I want to discuss three ideas that come out of this.

First, exchange and the market define an account of individual freedom as the freedom to pursue an economically determined self-interest.[3] Second, exchange relations in a free market are understood to realize economic processes with maximum efficiency. Third, the market order as a whole promotes the good of society without individuals having to concern themselves with it directly: concern, that is to say, is built into the system impersonally. Whether for good or ill, these ideas of freedom, efficiency, and concern have played a huge role not only in the development of economic thought, but also in the shaping of modern economic life. But Smith's value in reflecting on the current state of economic affairs comes from his willingness to make things difficult for his own ideas. To get a sense of this value, I want to think about Smith's view of the three ideas – freedom, efficiency, concern – first through three well-known passages, two from *The Wealth of Nations*, one from *The Theory of Moral Sentiments*; and then by placing the results in the context of more recent ideas, and of the current situation.

Three passages

The first passage is from the end of Book IV of *The Wealth of Nations*:

> All systems either of preference or of restraint, therefore, being thus completely taken away, the obvious and simple system of natural liberty establishes itself of its own accord. Every man, as long as he does not violate the laws of justice, is left perfectly free to pursue his own interest his own way, and to bring both his industry and capital into competition with those of any other man, or order of men. The sovereign is completely discharged from a duty, in the attempting to perform which he must always be exposed to innumerable delusions, and for the proper performance of which no human wisdom or knowledge could ever be sufficient; the duty of superintending the industry of private people, and of directing it towards the employments most suitable to the interest of the society.
>
> (WN IV.ix.51)

Left to itself, the system of natural liberty establishes itself automatically. This system, that works itself out through division of labour and exchange, is beyond our understanding. It will establish itself if we do not get in its way, but it does not require – would be impeded by – deliberate human coordination.

This is one of the grand statements of the free market theory of economics. It follows straightforwardly the main line of thought laid down in Books I and II. The freedom of the individual is compressed into one simple and powerful phrase – 'to pursue his own interest his own way'. Efficiency lies in the working of the 'obvious and simple system of natural liberty', which, once all artificial preferences or restraints are removed, directs 'the progress of the society towards real wealth and greatness' (WN IV.ix.50). It is the automatic result of the complex interplay of division of labour and exchange, which, in Smith's view, can only be understood as two parts of a single whole. Concern for the progress, the prosperity, the good, 'the interest of the society', insofar as it is a concern felt by individuals, can only be truly expressed by a kind of self-denial. All deliberate attempts at coordination for the social good must be given up. True concern must simply trust in the obvious and simple system itself, since something beyond human wisdom or knowledge is now the real concernful entity. The great strength of this passage comes from its claim that freedom, efficiency, and concern are all accounted for and brought together in a single, simple set of relations. Freedom and concern may reliably depend on efficiency.

The second passage is from Book V:

> In the progress of the division of labour, the employment of the far greater part of those who live by labour, that is, of the great body of the people, comes to be confined to a very few simple operations; frequently to one or two. But the understandings of the greater part of men are necessarily formed by their ordinary employments. The man whose whole life is spent in performing a few simple operations, of which the effects too are, perhaps, always the same, or very nearly the same, has no occasion to exert his understanding, or to exercise his invention in finding out expedients for removing difficulties which never occur. He naturally loses, therefore, the habit of such exertion, and generally becomes as stupid and ignorant as it is possible for a human creature to become.
>
> (WN V.i.f.50)

This passage has been much discussed (for example, West 1964; Rosenberg 1965). But whatever one's view of it, it ought to come as a shock. It is not entirely unprepared (WN I.x.c.14, for example), but the overwhelming sense of *damage* done to so many is quite different to any earlier passage. The problem that arises here is not at all accidental. It is the necessary result of a successful development of the division of labour, and can only get worse as time goes on – at least insofar as a society continues advancing.

In describing the way in which this development makes people stupid, Smith says: 'A man, without the proper use of the intellectual faculties of a man, is, if possible, more contemptible than even a coward, and seems to be mutilated and deformed in a still more essential part of the character of human nature' (WN V.i.g.61). This is the most arresting formulation: one part of human nature, the propensity to exchange, destroys another. Smith has no doubt that something must be done about the problem. People cannot be left to suffer in this way, even if nothing more than their suffering is at stake, yet clearly more is at stake – this is a *social* problem of the first magnitude.

What we have here is a problem of efficiency: the demands of productivity come into conflict with those of freedom and concern. The latter is at issue because the damage done to labourers should be a matter of concern to all, on which action must be taken to counter the results of a system that was itself supposed to make such action unnecessary. The former, because freedom is supposed to reside in pursuing one's own interest one's own way: but how can it be seen as being in the labourers' self-interest to submit themselves to such damage?

Smith's commitment to the primacy of productivity increases ('improvements in the productive powers of labour') as cause of increases in the wealth of a nation, asserted in the first sentence of the first chapter of *The Wealth of Nations*, is one of the most distinctive features of his economic theory. This primary commitment to what we may call, somewhat anachronistically, economic efficiency, sets him against an important line in eighteenth-century thought. Montesquieu is only the most influential of those who argued that the development of machinery could lead to depopulation, and so could be pernicious (Montesquieu 1961: XXIII, XV). Tucker respectfully disagrees with Montesquieu on this, but nonetheless argues that factory production has negative effects because of its oppressive regimentation of workers (Tucker 1758: 20–25). Ferguson condemns division of labour as fatal to civic virtue (Ferguson 1980: 218–20).[4] All these writers see economic development (again, speaking anachronistically) as necessarily problematic, even when desirable. The main argument of *The Wealth of Nations* is a huge assault on their claims. Yet here, Smith echoes their concerns.

For all Smith's concern for labourers, however, he never recommends a change in what they will actually do: they will have to remain imprisoned in the terrible monotony of the advancing division of labour. His solution is to do with what happens before they become labourers: elementary education of labourers' children, enforced by government (WN V.i.f.52–56). The manifest inadequacy of this solution – how could a few years' schooling outweigh a lifetime of debilitating monotony? – contradicts Smith's concern, and reveals another current of pessimism in his thought. Understanding and intelligence increase with the variety of objects considered (WN I.x.c.24, LJ (B) 328), but advancing division of labour will necessarily diminish the variety of objects. Even with some education, the intelligence of most people will decline as society advances.

The third passage is from the beginning of Part III of *The Theory of Moral Sentiments*:

> Were it possible that a human creature could grow up to manhood in some solitary place, without any communication with his own species, he

> could no more think of his own character, of the propriety or demerit of his own sentiments and conduct, of the beauty or deformity of his own mind, than of the beauty or deformity of his own face. All these are objects which he cannot easily see, which naturally he does not look at, and with regard to which he is provided with no mirror which can present them to his view. Bring him into society, and he is immediately provided with the mirror which he wanted before. … To a man who from his birth was a stranger to society, the objects of his passions, the external bodies which either pleased or hurt him, would occupy his whole attention. The passions themselves, the desires or aversions, the joys or sorrows, which those objects excited, though of all things the most immediately present to him, could scarce ever be the objects of his thoughts. The idea of them could never interest him so much as to call upon his attentive consideration.
>
> (Smith 1976a, TMS III.i.3)

Not only moral sense, but also individuality and a sense of self are impossible without the mirroring presence of others within an established social order.[5]

This is the heart of the argument of *The Theory of Moral Sentiments*, though it had virtually no influence on later thought, and even with the revival of interest in Smith's philosophy has not received its due. The case of Smith's influence on recent economics is particularly relevant here. In the last few decades many mainstream economists[6] have struggled to develop a concept of the individual beyond the straitjacket of the atomistic, methodological individualist view of standard neoclassical economics.[7] In so doing, some have sought help in the revived, and revised, view of Smith: for instance, V. L. Smith (1998); and Ashraf et al. (2005).[8] These writers sense that Smith truly does have something important to tell them, yet it is unclear that they have found what it is. A main reason for this is that they want Smith to validate positions that they have already adopted. The approach is clear from the title of Ashraf et al.'s paper, which simply looks in Smith for anticipations of recent work. A similar outcome occurs through Vernon Smith's broadening of the propensity to exchange to include virtually any kind of personal or social interaction, based on any motivation (Smith 1998: 1). He takes this as permitting him to fold the entirety of *The Theory of Moral Sentiments* into the propensity, without any further argument. The effect, in both cases, is to shut off discussion just at the point at which it needs to begin, on the question of what an individual is.

So, to see the possibilities for economics still in Smith, and, especially, in this passage, we must turn elsewhere, to important lines in twentieth-century philosophy, psychology, and neurophysiology, with which he has no direct connection, but which share with him the concept of *plural individuality*: that it is only possible to be an individual among other individuals.[9] The connection, invisible as it is, gives Smith's authority for the claim that these modern lines of thought are crucial for the development of economics (I will return to this below). In the terms developed here, what is most important is the deepening of the idea of concern, though through it, freedom and efficiency also will be substantially affected. In the other two passages the idea of concern amounts to little more than a generalized assertion that we somehow ought to be concerned with the good of society and the welfare of others. The first passage, indeed, can be vague because the market will take care of the social good. In any event, no basis for the assertion is given. The mirror passage, by contrast, claims that unless we have a concern that is in the end truly social, we cannot even *be* individuals. Concern now has an ontological basis.

The word 'concern' always indicates a particular form of relation, though this relation appears in two different modes. On the one hand, I may speak of how mathematics is concerned with numbers; or of our judgments concerning our own sentiments; or of the question concerning technology: so, a relation between two contents that are in some way objectively identifiable. On the other, I might say that I am concerned about your health; or you are not paying attention to my concerns; or this is a matter of concern for all of us: so, a subjective attitude of a particular kind. But in both modes, two things are separate but joined, and what joins them is in some way significant or meaningful. This is particularly appropriate for the mirror passage. I can only be an individual, separate from others, because I am joined with them, each reflecting back the other: separate and joined.

Smith uses 'concern' and its variants often, but unemphatically: it is simply a useful word for speaking of the kinds of relations with which he is concerned. He gives it nothing like the stature of such technical terms as 'sympathy' in *The Theory of Moral Sentiments*, or 'self-love' in *The Wealth of Nations*. But he does use it, and in both ways – one of my examples of the first is from the title of Part III of *The Theory of Moral Sentiments*. He also speaks of the idea of good or bad fortune creating 'some concern for the person who has met with it' (TMS I.i.1.8), and gives a kind of intermediate case: 'the person principally concerned' (TMS I.i.1.4). Given the way in which the mirror idea fits our notion of concern, it seems fair to use it, in the grand sense, as denoting a major theme in Smith's thought.

Smith is very anxious to bring thought down from the grand abstractions of philosophy to our own limited experience.[10] In *The Theory of Moral Sentiments*, especially, this means placing thought within the realm of the senses, especially sight and sound. So the mirror passage is not at all metaphorical: he is speaking of what happens when a (prospective) individual actually sees, hears, and feels those around him (he always uses the masculine pronoun). Here, he is distinct, and seeks to distinguish himself from his contemporaries, notably Hume. It is not unreasonable to apply the term *phenomenological* to this line in Smith's thought; and phenomenology is one of the twentieth-century lines of thought, mentioned previously, with which he has an invisible link.[11]

In this regard, my choice of the word 'concern' here is influenced by its use as the English translation of the German 'Besorgen' in Heidegger's *Being and*

Time. Heidegger introduces the idea of concern in working out the *Being-in* part of Dasein's (the human being's) Being-in the-world. Being-in, he says, 'is not a "property" which Dasein sometimes has and sometimes does not have, and *without* which it could *be* just as well as it could with it' (Heidegger 1962: 84). There can be no final distinction between inner and outer, subjective and objective, Dasein is always and completely inner and outer. Smith, in turn, allows much to inner states, thoughts, sentiments. But these states are never simply apart, they are always bound in dynamic tension with outer things. Smith's world is very much a moral one, though with necessary materiality, but individuals are what they are only through *being in* this world. So, we may repeat with more assurance that in the mirror passage concern comes to have an ontological basis.

This discussion already begins to bring Smith into our time, but it also shows that considerable tensions exist among, and even within, the three passages. In the first, freedom, efficiency, and concern fit easily together, all realized automatically, simply by the removal of obstacles. Yet, if we look a little closer, this is not quite right. Concern never really figures here at all, since no one ever has to be concerned for others, or for the order as a whole. Freedom is here, but only as a negative: the absence of barriers to individuals' pursuit of their own interest their own way. Nothing else is required of them. So efficiency is what does the work, and it is the fullest working out of the division of labour and exchange. Efficiency, also, must get the most credit: it allows freedom, and relieves everyone of the need for concern.

We may put this another way, starting from self-interest. Each individual is free 'to pursue his own interest his own way'. This suggests that each individual has a particular interest of his own, and is able to pursue it through economic activity: on the whole, then, individuals can realize their own purposes in the market. This is an enormously influential view, accepted, for example, by both neoclassical and Austrian economists, as a foundation of methodological individualism. Von Mises sums it up succinctly when he says: 'Seen from the point of view of the individual, society is the great means for the attainment of all his ends' (von Mises 1966: 165). But there is something very odd about it. Who, for example, can really be said to have an *interest* in pulling out the wire in the pin manufactory? Smith sometimes behaves as though workers are independent artisans exchanging with one another (WN I.i.10); but the logic of the division of labour is exemplified in the pin manufactory; and he says later that in Europe, for one independent workman, twenty work for a master (WN I.viii.10). When he comes to speak of classes ('the great original and constituent orders') he makes clear that the merchants and master manufacturers are the employers of the labourers (WN I.xi.p.10). The 'interest' of the labourers, then, lies simply in the possibility that they may be able to work for others. Such labouring activity has no relation to the particular interest of any individual engaged in it. A labourer's interest is only *his* insofar as the natural course of things has seen fit to place him in the class of labourers: for Smith rejects the comforting conservative notion (still held by von Mises) that the division of labour is caused by differences in natural talent.[12] Rather than turning the economy to their own interests, labourers at least are constrained by its structure to perform specific functions. Since Smith assumes that labourers are poor, ignorant, and work very long hours, we can say that, even on his own showing, the benefits of the obvious and simple system of natural liberty are going to be quite limited for the great majority of people.

We get this far simply from Smith's main line of argument itself. When we turn to the Book V passage, a much larger problem arises. The choice faced by labourers in the advanced division of labour is between subjecting themselves to an order that will destroy essential parts of their own nature, or withdrawing from that order altogether. It is not clear whether Smith thinks that the second course is even possible; it is certainly not open to many. To say that someone faced with such a choice is free 'to pursue his interest his own way' would be a vicious joke.[13] Moreover, one 'bred to' this kind of work, according to Smith, would seem to be incapable of formulating any accurate sense of his own condition. He can neither have a unified interest, nor understand what it would be like to act on it. To say that such an individual is free is simply absurd. The Book V passage raises this problem, but clearly does not provide anything even approaching a solution for it. It leaves us with a view of the system of division of labour and exchange as a vast structure of domination from which there is no escape: at least, no escape within its terms and that of the first passage. For although the two passages seem so much at odds, the second does not offer any alternative insofar as thinking about individuals, interest, and freedom is concerned.

The third passage does offer something else, however. For in its far more profound account of concern, it puts forward a different view of what it is to be an individual, of individual freedom, of relations among individuals, and between individuals, economy, and society. In this view, freedom and concern are indissolubly linked, and set the terms for efficiency. With this in mind, we must turn to our own time.

Smith in our time

Towards the end of the last chapter of *The General Theory*, Keynes offers a remarkable summary: what is necessary is 'to indicate the nature of the environment which the free play of economic forces requires if it is to realise the full potentialities of production' (Keynes 1964: 379). In a highly compressed way, this is a formidable critique of the free market theory, the core of which is the claim that 'the free play of economic forces' alone, once all barriers are removed, will automatically realize 'the full potentialities of production'. We have already seen Smith's version of this claim. Keynes's crucial move is not to reject 'the free play of economic forces', but rather to reject the claim that they alone are sufficient. A much more complex environment is required, he says, and it must be constructed deliberately, it will not come about automatically and by nature. No other agency but government can do this, for it must be outside the economic order, encompassing all interests, not following any one.

In this line of thought, Keynes is close to Steuart, and very far from Smith. But two things can be said right away. First, Keynes argues that the existing system – call it the capitalist system – does better than any other available, and does so particularly in directing resources to the best uses. The need is for *more* employment, not for employment of any particular kind (Keynes 1964: 379). That is, Keynes does not demand that government seek 'to superintend the industry of private people'. Second, he certainly does not deny that the working of the economy is beyond human wisdom or knowledge: indeed he goes beyond Smith in his insistence on uncertainty.

What Keynes does insist on, however, is the need for action in the face of uncertainty. Here we find an odd affinity with, at least, the Smith of *The Theory of Moral Sentiments*, for both appeal to irrationality to explain what it is that makes people get up and do the world's work. Keynes says, on the one hand, that 'practical men' will have to pretend that the future is much more predictable than reason, correctly, tells us that it is (Keynes 1937: 214); on the other, not that much investment would result from 'cold calculation' alone (Keynes 1964: 150). Smith ascribes 'all the toil and bustle of this world' on the one hand, to the motive of self-betterment prompted by the desire to be admired by others (TMS I.iii.2.1);[14] on the other, to 'an irregularity of [our] sentiments' implanted in us by nature, which makes us judge according to the results of actions rather than the intentions of the actors (TMS II.iii. intro. 3–6; 3.3).

Keynes's critique of the market does indeed distinguish him from Smith, but it links him to Mill in that both are what may be called 'critical liberals'; and an exploration of critical liberalism will lead us back, oddly enough, to Smith. Both Keynes and Mill accept the free market as the best available economic system within the framework of a liberal morality of individual freedom. But they refuse to accept the automatic functioning of the market as sacrosanct. Keynes, of course, explicitly denies the capacity of the market to function adequately on its own, and makes government intervention a requirement of individual freedom. Mill, first, denies the continued legitimacy of wage labour, and argues for competitive worker cooperatives instead (Mill 1987: IV, vii). Second, he argues that the requirements of individual freedom (through self-development) can only be fully realized by representative democracy (Mill 1912a: III, 1912b: III). Both, then, tie individuality and freedom to the political. This, on the one hand, requires them to see a positive role for the political sphere. On the other, it sets them against the emptying out of the idea of the individual and of freedom found in classical utilitarianism, neoclassical, and Austrian economics, all linked by methodological individualism.[15] The simple negative view of freedom as the absence of external obstacles to the pursuit of self-interest,[16] realizing itself in choice among external alternatives, is inadequate for both.[17]

As long as the liberal view remains shackled to the narrow free market theory, founded on methodological individualism, it cannot do justice to its own very real and substantial concerns.[18] This appears particularly clearly in the problem of freedom. If the economy has a definite structure that imposes itself on individuals, then the negative view of freedom is fatally inadequate both in defining freedom and in defining the individual whose freedom is supposed to be at issue. To this may be added the apparent dishonesty of a view that insists that individuals meet on equal terms in exchange, in spite of the vast disparities of the hierarchy of wealth. Keynes and Mill can show a way for liberalism to break out of its theoretical and practical isolation through real, critical public debate (which both see as necessary for social development) with other lines of thought with which it has more affinity than one might think. Let us consider some of the topics, and also the lines of thought that might participate in such a debate.

Keynes himself already laid out the groundwork for understanding basic macroeconomic problems, especially concerned with aggregate effective demand. This work has been very well developed by the post-Keynesians, who have also extended the analysis of money and shown how the inherent instability of the capitalist economy is exacerbated by the growth of the financial sector. (Hyman Minsky's work is particularly noteworthy here.) But the central Keynesian issue of unemployment is enormously complicated by the process of development and the so-called North–South problem: this is manifested by the cruel dilemma in which relatively well-paid jobs are lost in the developed 'North', but the gain in the developing 'South' is bought at the cost of exploitation that matches the worst conditions of the early industrial revolution: starvation wages, and lack of the most basic civil and political rights. The problem of freedom arises in the developed as well as the underdeveloped world, however.

Such problems are clearly not simply *economic*, and neither 'the free play of economic forces' nor strictly economic policy alone will ever solve them. Bound up with them is the even broader and fundamental problem of environmental sustainability. Even such a cursory review poses the question of the continued viability of capitalism. Within this question one thing that looms large is the dominant form of business enterprise in advanced capitalism, the corporation (using the term rather loosely). It can be said that corporations have both too much and too little power. Too much, because their concentrated wealth and hierarchical structure are clear threats to democracy both in the economic and political spheres. Too little, because for all their wealth, they cannot, on their own, ensure economic stability. Moreover, as *capitalist* enterprises, they cannot escape the law of accumulation which, as Marx says, imposes itself on them as an objective necessity. In turning to approaches, we will keep the corporation in the forefront.

Keynes's proposals for the coordination (or 'socialization') of the investment process remain cogent. But since growth itself is in question in relation to the problem of environmental sustainability, they need to be placed in a wider context, one that recognizes the possibility of modifying the business enterprise itself. We can think of this through earlier transformations of the business enterprise. The traditional individually owned capitalist firm, at least in laissez-faire ideology, competes as a price-taker in the market on an equal footing with all other firms and individuals. It neither can, nor should be expected, to take responsibility for anything but itself. The corporation, in an oligopolistic market, sets prices and plays an important role in shaping the conditions of the market.[19] That it therefore must undertake a *social* responsibility was recognized, at least in principle, by the early corporate leaders themselves (Williams 1988: 346–62).[20] This can be the basis for important modifications, such as the requirement in Germany, for example, that the public be represented on all boards of directors.

How much can be achieved by such measures in a global capitalist economy is unclear.[21] At the other end of the spectrum is the claim that, however modified, capitalist enterprises can neither permit economic democracy, nor operate within the limits of environmental sustainability. David Schweickart argues for this view, and for the necessity on these grounds, of replacing capitalist enterprises with competitive worker cooperatives within a system of coordinated aggregate investment (Schweickart 2002: chs 3, 5). The framework of Schweickart's analysis is unabashedly socialist, and Marxist in particular. But his approach to aggregate investment draws heavily on Keynes. More strikingly, his account of worker cooperatives sounds a lot like Mill (though he does not mention Mill in this regard). Both think that worker cooperatives have become the only fully legitimate form of enterprise; but they both also think that such cooperatives must continue to compete in the market. Critical liberalism needs to find the confidence to engage with views such as Schweickart's, rather than writing them off because they fall outside of the assumptions of orthodox economic theory, as it should also engage with other approaches to the problem of the corporation.

So, Richard Sennett uses the term 'corrosion of character' as an overall description of the new issues raised by *flexible capitalism*, in contrast to the relative stability of the so-called *Fordist* regime of the post-war period (Sennett 1998: 9–12). The problem is manifested most clearly in one of the main slogans of flexible capitalism: 'No long term' (Sennett 1998: 22). This slogan seems to proclaim as a goal what Sennett sees as particularly corrosive, the impossibility, not only for workers, but even for managers, of formulating a coherent life plan. Success in such a system comes by conforming to a particular pattern of behaviour, projecting an image – as a 'team player', for example – that has little to do with ability, or with an authentic sense of self. Beyond the workplace, Sennett sees corrosion as spreading to the sphere of private life, and so revealing an increasing invasion of the private by the economic. Such corrosion affects not only what individuals can do, but also what they can think and feel, so it also affects what they *are*.

Individuals come to be shaped for the economy and its structure, not for themselves; yet they can want for themselves what the economy demands because their individuality itself has been distorted: they can see themselves as simply pursuing their own self-interest. Here, Sennett is close to our Book V passage, which he mentions. Theodor Adorno gives a broader conceptual formulation in arguing that individual subjectivity necessarily contains objective elements coming from an oppressive social order, and internalized by the individual. The more individuals assert their pure subjectivity, the more are they subject to the objective structures of domination (Adorno 1973: 176–80; Horkheimer 2004: 94).

The methodological individualist response to this, most cogently made by the Austrian economists, is to assert that it is always a denial of freedom to make a judgment concerning an individual that questions the choice made *by* the individual (for example, von Mises 1966: 19). But this is simply to prohibit any discussion of what individuals are. Here, Smith's Book V claim about damage done to the individual is especially important, first, simply because of his impeccable free market credentials. More substantially though, he gives a very precise account of a way in which individuals can be damaged, where the damage will alter all their intellectual and moral capacities, and therefore, obviously, also their choices. This manifestation of an invasion of private life by the economic is not something that can be properly recognized in neoclassical or Austrian economics, because neither can make a clear, theoretical distinction between the two. The danger here can be understood through the growing importance of the idea of *human capital*, both in economic theory and in actual practice, and of the way in which the idea completes a necessary tendency in methodological individualism.

For Sennett, Adorno, and even the Smith of the Book V passage, human capital must require a complete self-alienation in which no part of my individuality can any longer be my own. To maximize my capital, my individuality in its entirety must be up for sale. Individual agency must now entirely align itself with market outcomes over which it has no control at all. We must all now destroy ourselves, just as Smith saw the division of labour destroy labourers. But this self-destruction takes place under the banner of self-interest. The methodological individualist individual, sovereign in his or her own pure subjectivity, is revealed as nothing more than a function of the objective order of the market. Human capital has gone beyond theory to become a real force in determining the actions of individuals, and in persuading them to empty themselves of any truly individual content.[22] So Adorno's sense of a bitter consolation in failure applies here: 'He who offers for sale something unique that no one wants to buy, represents, even against his will, freedom from exchange' (Adorno 2005: 68).

For Adorno, the principle of exchange itself, governed by the law of value, is the great dominating force: flattening out all differences; emptying things of content and meaning; isolating individuals in their own blind adherence to 'self-interest'. But Smith, so important in the rise of the dogma of self-interest as over-riding motive for exchange, has an alternative view – though he never mentions it in *The Wealth of Nations.* In the *Lectures on Jurisprudence* he says that exchange and division of labour arise from the desire to persuade, which he sees as a universal human trait (Smith 1978, LJ (A) vi.56, (B) 221–22). In *The Theory of Moral Sentiments* he had already described the 'desire of being believed, the desire of persuading' as 'one of the strongest of all our natural desires', and as also lying behind the faculty of speech (TMS VII.iv.25).[23] This desire is so strong that the 'man who had the misfortune to imagine that nobody believed a single word he said' would be likely 'to die of despair' (TMS VII.iv.26).

The claim about the desire to persuade or be believed belongs to the central line of thought in *The Theory of Moral Sentiments*, and it is fair to link exchange as persuasion to it. We can trace this line back to the mirror passage itself. But there is another link along the way, in which Smith names another basic desire: 'the chief part of human happiness arises from the consciousness of being beloved, as I believe it does' (TMS I.ii.v.1).[24] Whether or not Smith saw this line as consonant with the exchange for self-interest view,[25] his work has split in two since his time, on the one hand as a major influence on the main, methodological individualist line in economics (though even in *The Wealth of Nations* he is not a methodological individualist); on the other, standing as an invisible precursor of twentieth-century views that see individuality as necessarily requiring many individuals, the position of plural individuality. At root, then, the question between the two views is: what is an individual? The new path suggested here is anything but a return to collectivism, pre-modern or modern. It will be, rather, the proper working out of what it is to be an individual, after the unfortunate detour of methodological individualism.

For the methodological individualist individual, centred on a self-interest for which society (including other individuals) is just a means, concern is always abstract and optional: one may or may not choose to take it as a concern. But such proudly self-interested individuals have only a very odd freedom: if efficiency goes against them, there is nothing to be done, any more than there is for concern. Standard economics preaches passive obedience to the absolute dictates of the market, whose sovereign will is law. Of course, individuals are keener on this when they are preaching to the unfortunate than when they are unfortunate themselves.

For the line we find in Smith's mirror/persuasion passages, and for modern plural individuality, concern is not only unavoidably built into social life, but also into individuality itself. Sennett speaks of 'the dangerous pronoun', *we*, seeing in it the only force that might counter the corrosion of character in flexible capitalism. In invoking the *we*, he specifically rejects a communitarian approach, based on shared values. He insists rather on the value and strength of disagreement and argument within a *we* (Sennett 1998: 139–45). Smith, in *The Theory of Moral Sentiments*, and modern theories of plural individuality, provide a deep foundation for this insight.

So Smith's position is surprising. His is a trusted liberal voice, but one that has been invoked largely in defence of a narrow view of the free market. Yet here he appears as a link between critical liberals and much more radical views with whom they may fruitfully debate. Moreover, his alternative interpretation of the ideas of freedom, efficiency, and concern indicate the necessity of a reaching out by economics beyond its normal boundaries, in a way that truly accepts non-economic thought, on its own terms, as valuable for economics. I would say that two lines, themselves in disagreement, are of particular value here as critical and rigorous versions of plural individuality: phenomenology, and the critical theory of the Frankfurt school. In addition to these, recent developments in neurophysiology in the study of so-called *mirror neurons*, have a striking resemblance to the central line of thought in *The Theory of Moral Sentiments* (Rizzolatti 2004). Including these lines in a real and open, public, critical debate is of vital importance as a way to prepare for significant change in economics and society.

In the mainstream view (to which Smith also contributed) the economy enforces the separateness of individuals as a principle of individualism. Apart from this, even a simple description of modern capitalism must see it as imposing its order on individuals and on any non-economic pursuits that remain to them. There is no arguing with efficiency. But if Smith, in *The Theory of Moral Sentiments*, is broadly right about individuality, as I believe he is – and if he is right about persuasion and exchange – then there is something fundamentally wrong with all this simply as a matter of what individuals naturally *are*. So he leads us to the very obvious conclusion that it was absurd to imagine that individual freedom and the social good (with which we should be concerned) would come from the economic sphere alone, especially from an economic sphere dominated by production geared to the goal of unlimited accumulation. At the very least, we can say that this was a serious departure from the natural course of things.

The idea of a system based on nothing more than the pursuit of individual self-interest originally seemed insane, to which free-market theorists, Smith among them, replied: this is human nature. But in some way this had to be taken as *authoritative* before it could work: and the authority of large-scale, steamed-powered machinery was very convincing even with fourteen-hour working days. The claim for plural individuality in the other Smith, in phenomenology, critical theory, and contemporary neurophysiology, also asserts itself as how individuals are. It can expect to be manifested in actual social relations, but existing social structures will be in its way, just as the structures of traditional society were in the way of the capitalist market economy. Yet the working out of plural individuality can only occur through transforming the economic order. If efficiency is subordinated to freedom and concern, not only in social and individual relations, but also in the technical conditions of sustainability, then the working out is possible. If not, it is not.

The future is as opaque to us as it was to Smith; and he turns out to have been right, for good or ill, about something that he did not foresee – self-interest as motive for exchange in capitalism. We sense, more than Smith did, that we are at a historical turning-point, though this gives us no more ability to predict. Still, we might say that the idea of exchange as a mediation between otherwise unconnected individual interests has had a good run for its money, and that it is time to try something else, though oddly enough something else also suggested by Smith. If we do not move in this new direction, it does seem safe to say that the 200 years since the Industrial Revolution are about all the prosperity – with all its attendant poverty and misery – that we are likely to get. Thus, to evaluate with critical sympathy what Smith did and did not understand about a future that became our past, may allow us to be more insightful and resolute in the face of our own unknown future.

Notes

1 The primacy of agriculture remains in Ricardo.

2 Paul Langford (1992) emphasizes this phrase, and its common use, in his book *A Polite and Commercial People: England, 1727–1783*.

3 Generally, in *The Wealth of Nations*, what Smith says is that exchange is motivated by individual self-interest. As we will see, his account of exchange in the *Lectures on Jurisprudence* is significantly different in ways that link it to *The Theory of Moral Sentiments*. It is possible to argue that in *The Wealth of Nations* he is silently incorporating the other account in that based on self-interest. I have my doubts about this (see below, including note 25).

4 Marx sees Ferguson's influence in the Book V passage (Marx 1977: 483, n. 47).

5 Smith's distinction between passions as immediately present, and passions as the objects of thoughts by the one experiencing them, is strikingly similar to the distinction made by Charles Taylor between first- and second-order desires, and the 'strong evaluation' associated with the latter (see Taylor 1985a: 23–26, 1985b: 220–23).

6 I take the term 'mainstream economics' from John Davis (2003). For Davis, mainstream economics refers to a variety of recent developments, including game theory, behavioural, and experimental economics, that, to one degree or another, have pushed beyond the standard assumptions of neoclassical economics, but without clearly establishing an alternative theoretical foundation.

7 For an excellent account of this struggle see John Davis (2010).

8 I am grateful to an anonymous referee for suggesting these papers.

9 See Urquhart (2010: 184) for a somewhat fuller discussion of this.

10 See Griswold (1999: 141–42, 127) for a good description of this.

11 See, for example, Merleau-Ponty (1962: II, 4). Emmanuel Levinas' view of the fundamental significance of an individual's concern for the other, captured in the title of one of his late works, *Ethics as First Philosophy* (*Éthique comme philosophie première*) (Levinas 1998) also expresses this invisible connection.

12 Smith does say that in the tribe of hunters, one is better than the others at making bows and arrows. But in the next paragraph he makes the general claims that differences in natural talents are not very great, and that the division of labour is more the cause than the effect of perceived differences (WN I.ii.3–4). In any event, it makes no more sense to think of anyone as having a natural talent for pulling out the wire in a pin manufactory than to say that they have an interest in doing it. For von Mises, see (1966: 158).

13 This line of thought is heavily indebted to conversations with Vincent Menella, and I thank him for his help in developing it.

14 His account of self-betterment in *The Wealth of Nations* is quite different, resting on individual self-interest alone.

15 For the centrality of the 'atomistic individual' for modern mainstream economics, but also for its incoherence as an idea of the individual, see Davis (2003: ch. 2).
16 The methodological individualist idea of self-interest is quite malleable. Alongside proud (Mandevillean) assertions of it as narrowly understood, Lionel Robbins claims that economic subjects can be egoists, altruists, ascetics, sensualists, or mixtures of these (Robbins 1935: 95). Von Mises, in his usual way, treats selfishness as formal, in that even actions for the sake of others are undertaken for the satisfaction of the individual agent (von Mises 1966: 242). What is common across the whole range of views is that a choice is of, by, and for the chooser alone, whatever the range of its effects.
17 See the discussion of Mill in Taylor (1985b: 212).
18 See an eloquent expression of this idea in Taylor (1995: 144–45).
19 See Chandler (1960) for the classic account of this transformation. Chandler adopts the phrase 'modern business enterprise' as the technical term for what he is describing. The corporation is one particular form of modern business enterprise.
20 For this responsibility as taking the form of a new feudalism, and thus threatening democracy, see Williams (1988: 357–59).
21 For a somewhat sceptical appraisal of the possibilities, stressing the need for legislation – and corporate recognition of its value – see Vogel (2005).
22 A recent article in the *New York Times* offers a telling example, regarding changes in the choice of college majors, and in the teaching of all majors, so that they may become 'relevant'. In the annual survey by UCLA of incoming freshmen, in '1971, 37 per cent responded that it was essential to be "very well-off financially", while 73 per cent said the same about "developing a meaningful philosophy of life"', in contrast to 78 per cent and 48 per cent respectively, in 2009. Some colleges are 'integrating workplace lessons into capstone research seminars for humanities majors'. For example, in one, students are asked 'to develop a 30-second commercial on their "personal brand"' (Zernike 2009). Comment is really superfluous, except to note how the reference of the word 'relevant' has changed since the 1960s; and how strongly this brings to mind the original meaning of 'branding': applying a piece of red-hot iron to a cow's hide. I am grateful to Yavuz Yaşar for showing me this article.
23 All that is left of the link between exchange and persuasion in *The Wealth of Nations* is the possible origin of the propensity to exchange in the faculty of speech (WN I.ii.2).
24 The unusual personal assertion – 'as I believe it does' – is important. This is why I have chosen this version of the claim over others.
25 I see a very real difference between them, see Urquhart (2010), but now is not the time to bring that up.

Bibliography

Adorno, T. (1973) *Negative Dialectics*, trans. E. B. Ashton, New York and London: Continuum Publishing Company.

——(2005) *Minima Moralia: Reflections from Damaged Life*, trans. E. F. N. Jephcott, London and New York: Verso.

Ashraf, N., Camerer, C. F. and Loewenstein, G. (2005) 'Adam Smith, Behavioral Economist', *Journal of Economic Perspectives*, 19: 131–45.

Chandler, A. (1960) *The Visible Hand: The Managerial Revolution in American Business*, Cambridge, MA: Harvard University Press.

Davis, J. B. (2003) *The Theory of the Individual in Economics*, London and New York: Routledge.

——(2010) *Individuals and Identity in Economics*, Cambridge: Cambridge University Press.

Ferguson, A. (1980) *An Essay on the History of Civil Society*, New Brunswick and London: Transaction Books.

Griswold, C. (1999) *Adam Smith and the Virtues of Enlightenment*, Cambridge: Cambridge University Press.

Heidegger, M. (1962) *Being and Time*, trans. John Macquarrie and Edward Robinson, New York and Evanston, IL: Harper & Row.

Horkheimer, M. (2004) 'Rise and Decline of the Individual', in *Eclipse of Reason*, London and New York: Continuum.

Keynes, J. M. (1964) *The General Theory of Employment, Interest, and Money*, New York and London: Harcourt.

——(1937) 'The General Theory of Employment', *The Quarterly Journal of Economics*, 51: 209–23.

Langford, P. (1992) *A Polite and Commercial People: England 1727–1783*, Oxford and New York: Oxford University Press.

Levinas, E. (1998) *Éthique comme philosophie première*, Paris: Éditions Payot et Rivages.

Marx, K. (1977) *Capital*, vol. I, trans. B. Fowkes, New York: Vintage Books.

Merleau-Ponty, M. (1962) *Phenomenology of Perception*, trans. C. Smith, London: Routledge.

Mill, J. S. (1912a) *On Liberty*, in *On Liberty, Considerations on Representative Government, The Subjection of Women*, Oxford: Oxford University Press.

——(1912b) *Considerations on Representative Government*, in *On Liberty, Considerations on Representative Government, The Subjection of Women*, Oxford: Oxford University Press.

——(1987) *Principles of Political Economy*, Fairfield, NJ: Augustus M. Kelley.

Montesquieu, C. L. de Secondat, Baron de la Brède et de (1961) *De L'Esprit des Lois*, 2 vols, Paris: Garnier.

Polanyi, K. (2001) *The Great Transformation: The Political and Economic Origins of Our Time*, Boston, MA: Beacon Press.

Rizzolatti, G. (2004) 'Understanding the Actions of Others', in *Functional Neuroimaging of Visual Cognition, Attention and Performance XX*, N. Kanwisher and J. Duncan (eds), Oxford: Oxford University Press.

Robbins, L. (1935) *An Essay on the Nature and Significance of Economic Science*, 2nd edn, London: Macmillan.

Rosenberg, N. (1965) 'Adam Smith on the Division of Labour: Two Views or One?', *Economica*, 32: 127–39.

Schweickart, D. (2002) *After Capitalism*, London and New York: Rowman and Littlefield.

Sennett, R. (1998) *The Corrosion of Character: The Personal Consequences of Work in the New Capitalism*, New York and London: W. W. Norton.

Smith, A. (1976a) *The Theory of Moral Sentiments*, D. D. Raphael and A. L. Macfie (eds), Oxford: Oxford University Press; reprinted, Liberty Press (1982).

——(1976b) *An Inquiry into the Nature and Causes of the Wealth of Nations*, 2 vols, R. H. Campbell, A. S. Skinner, and W. B. Todd (eds), Oxford: Oxford University Press; reprinted, Liberty Press (1981).

——(1978) *Lectures on Jurisprudence*, R. L. Meek, D. D. Raphael and P. G. Stein (eds), Oxford: Oxford University Press; reprinted, Liberty Press (1982).

Smith, Vernon L. (1998) 'The Two Faces of Adam Smith', *Southern Economic Journal*, 65: 1–19.

Taylor, C. (1985a) 'What Is Human Agency?', in *Human Agency and Language: Philosophical Papers 1*, Cambridge: Cambridge University Press.

——(1985b) 'What's Wrong with Negative Liberty', in *Philosophy and the Human Sciences: Philosophical Papers 2*, Cambridge: Cambridge University Press.

——(1995) 'Irreducibly Social Goods', in *Philosophical Arguments*, Cambridge, MA: Harvard University Press.

Tucker, J. (1758) *Instructions for Travellers*, Dublin: William Watson.

Urquhart, R. (2010) 'Adam Smith's Problems: Individuality and the Paradox of Sympathy', *The Adam Smith Review*, 5: 181–97.

Vogel, D. (2005) *The Market for Virtue: The Potential and Limits of Corporate Responsibility*, Washington, DC: Brookings Institution Press.

von Mises, L. (1966) *Human Action: A Treatise on Economics*, 3rd revised edn, Chicago: Henry Regnery Company.

West, E. G. (1964) 'Adam Smith's Two Views on the Division of Labour', *Economica*, 31: 23–32.

Williams, W. A. (1988) *The Contours of American History*, New York and London: W. W. Norton.

Zernike, K. (2009) 'Making College "Relevant"', *New York Times*, 29 December.

Institutional divergence in economic development

Jonathan B. Wight[1]

Introduction

The Anglo-American capitalist model (AACM) encompasses a set of theories and policies that advance the classical objectives of individual autonomy, wealth acquisition, and economic growth. In the twentieth century, the neoclassical goal of short-run Pareto efficiency was added yet remains in possible tension with these other aims. The AACM generally upholds the primacy of markets as the means for achieving its normative ideals through private, decentralized actions, with some exceptions. In the modern political arena this ideology is associated with the Reagan-Thatcher revolution of the 1980s and provides a framework for many who oppose statist solutions to social problems (Steger and Roy 2010). The AACM has come under attack from a variety of perspectives because of its assumptions of perfectly rational traders, competitive markets, incentive compatibilities, low transaction costs, informational symmetries, and no externalities (Stiglitz 2007; Kay 2004). This paper examines a different critique arising from the a-historical and a-institutional manner in which the AACM has been adopted by some neoclassical policy makers. This criticism, incidentally, also applies to statist models adopted in the 1950s that likewise ignored institutional constraints and path dependency issues.

While the AACM ideology traces back in various forms to Smith, Ricardo, and other writers of the classical era, its principles are widely known in Latin American and other developing countries by the label *neoliberalism* – associated with neoclassical economic policies adopted during the last two decades of the twentieth century. After the Second World War, virtually all developing countries had embraced statist ideologies and economic interventions in order to overcome perceived market deficiencies. While state planning and protectionism resulted in rapid industrialization and GDP growth in many countries, these policies often increased inequality and ultimately proved to be unsustainable, as evidenced by Latin America's debt crisis of 1982. The neoliberal economic revolution, known as the 'Washington Consensus', arose to provide a coherent set of policies used to restructure countries experiencing external debt crises (Williamson 1990). The first fundamental welfare theorem (the so-called 'invisible hand' theorem) that

The Adam Smith Review, 6: 309–326 © The International Adam Smith Society
ISSN 1743-5285, ISBN 0-415-66722-7

developed in neoclassical economics during the 1950s supported the view that laissez-faire markets could maximize the satisfaction of all feasible consumer preferences. While neoclassical economists make numerous assumptions and qualifications in deriving this result, in simplified form the first fundamental welfare theorem seemed to validate the simplistic and stereotypical view of Adam's Smith's non-interventionist approach to development. For Smith, however, economic analysis and institutions are deeply intertwined; hence, the neoliberalism of the 1980s and 1990s was in many ways quite different from Adam Smith's conception of the invisible hand or the development process he envisioned.

In particular, Smith did not emphasize short-run efficiency but rather long-run growth. Moreover, Smith did not insist that long-term growth required any particular set of policies or institutions, such as those promulgated in the Washington Consensus. While Smith would share much in common with the ideology of neoliberalism, this paper develops the thesis that Smith's approach to policy making is informed by and imbedded in culture, ethical norms, power structures, and other institutions. Smith, who chided François Quesnay (the 'speculative physician') for a similar mistake, argued that diversity of institutions is both expected and desirable for the unfolding of development. Attempting to implement an ideal or perfect system would be a fool's errand, because history and path-dependency can suggest acceptable alternatives that work reasonably well, and often better than those derived from pure theory. Smith's rhetoric was soaring and ideological, but his policy prescriptions were incremental and context specific, reflecting concern for justice and process.

The following section outlines the fall of AACM as a credible ideology during the first half of the twentieth century and its replacement with statist development thinking. The third section explores the rise of the neoliberal model in Europe in the 1930s, and its application to the neoclassical model in the 1980s. The fourth section demonstrates that Smith's AACM model is nuanced and substantially different from the neoliberal model in terms of policy implementation. The final section provides conclusions on the usefulness and survivability of the AACM.

The fall of AACM and the rise of development planning

By mid-twentieth century, the Anglo-American capitalist model was in serious disarray following the Great Depression and World War II (Plehwe 2009; Lewis 1969). The depression had shown the fallacy of Say's Law that markets would self-correct, and had been replaced by Keynesian counter-cyclical fiscal policies to combat falling aggregate demand. The world war, meanwhile, had demonstrated the capacity of central planning in the Pentagon to mobilize vast resources for investment, production, and distribution. The Soviet Union also emerged from the war using a growth model that seemed superior due to high rates of investment. In this post-war milieu, many developing countries gained their independence (such as India) and others concluded civil wars (such as China). Other countries in Latin American, which had been independent since the early nineteenth century, sensed an opportunity to break neocolonial relationships with Great Britain and the United States. The world was ripe for economic experimentation using the levers of central government authority to force along the development process.

Since the late nineteenth century, a number of economists had been preparing the intellectual groundwork for the movement away from AACM through arguments known today as the "socialist calculation debate" (Levy and Peart 2008). Could a planned economy replicate the efficiency of a market system? More importantly, could it do better? The AACM relied upon the epistemological belief that no policy maker could ever amass or process enough information to make centralized interventions sensible (Hayek 1945). According to this view, millions of consumers and producers – acting in their own best interests – would generate the superior wisdom of the decentralized market process. However, in addition to theoretical work on planning, Wassily Leontief's research on input-output models in the 1930s and 1940s seemed to supply policy makers with the practical information needed for planning execution. Not coincidentally, the Second World War produced a shift in economics research toward interventionism because economists – no longer simply theorists – were given wartime positions in government. One of the founders of linear programming recalls how many economists came away from this applied experience with the notion that development was a mechanical process that could be controlled through central planning:

> Linear programming can be viewed as part of a great revolutionary development which has given mankind the ability to state general goals and to lay out a path of detailed decisions to take in order to 'best' achieve its goals when faced with practical situations of great complexity.
>
> (Dantzig 2002: 42)

Even as computers and linear programming were in their infancy, developing countries optimistically adopted socialist approaches to address wealth creation and poverty mitigation. In 1951, Prime Minister Jawaharlal Nehru of India released the first Five-Year Plan that led to government investments in dams and other agricultural infrastructure. In 1956, India's second Five-Year Plan pushed government investments into steel and other heavy industries – following the lead of Stalinist and Maoist development plans. A subsequent Five-Year Plan nationalized banks and imposed price controls in key sectors.

In Latin America, meanwhile, prominent economists contested the notion that trade based on comparative advantage would lead to greater wealth in the long run. Argentine economist Raúl Prebisch became in 1948 the director of the Economic Commission for Latin America at the United Nations and, in 1964, the founder and first secretary-general of the UN Conference on Trade and Development (UNCTAD). These positions offered a bully pulpit in which he highlighted the key failings of the Ricardian trade model upon which the AACM relied.

In *The Economic Development of Latin America and its Principal Problems* (1950), Prebisch outlined the theory which became widely known as the Prebisch-Singer hypothesis. According to this view, rich Western countries export industrial products that experience rapid technological innovation. These products also have high income elasticities of demand. By contrast, developing countries export agricultural and mineral commodities with low income elasticities of demand and low potential for technological innovation. As world income rises, industrial good demand grows much faster than commodity demand. In addition, industrial producers can gain market power through oligopolies and patents while it is more difficult for commodity producers to acquire any long-lasting leverage, given high price elasticities of supply. The prediction that emerges from this structural analysis is that the terms of trade for developing countries will inevitably fall over time (Prebisch 1950: 9). Empirical evidence in the 1950s and 1960s supported the terms of trade pessimism that developing countries had to export more commodities each year simply to retain the same level of real imports as they had previously; in other words, developing countries were riding a downward economic escalator. Prebisch urged them to jump off, by rejecting the AACM in favor of protectionism.

Other researchers argued along different lines that developing countries had been *forced* to acquire a comparative advantage in commodities as part of a deliberate imperialistic strategy by developed countries. For example, British merchants financed, built, and then operated the railroads in Argentina in order to open up the pampas for beef and wheat exports (Wright 1974). The emphasis was entirely on enhancing exports and not on developing an integrated transportation network that would lead to balanced growth. A hodgepodge of rail lines emanated from Buenos Aires to the hinterland, but these were often of different gauges and could not interact with each other (Duncan 1937). The introduction of railroads substantially altered the production possibilities curve for Argentina in favor of agriculture and away from industry because rural areas could trade only with the port city, but not laterally with each other. The lack of planning and uncoordinated competitive efforts that led to this outcome are cited as a major failure of Argentine development in this period (Duncan 1937: 578). Similar examples of 'export-enclave' production investments were made throughout Latin America and Africa. Hence, the view that comparative advantage arose from historical accidents of climate and natural resource endowments needs to be reconsidered, especially since some resource endowments were not accidents at all – they were designed by imperial powers.

The anti-trade conclusions of Prebisch's structural approach also coincided with those of dependency theorists such as Paul Baran, Paul Sweezy, and Andre Gunder Frank (Frank 1966). Dependency theory posits that 'center' countries use their power to exploit 'periphery' areas for resources and to provide markets for finished industrial products. Both Britain and the United States intervened overtly and covertly (with the complicity of local elites) to thwart political efforts to create balanced developmental policies, thereby creating dependency according to critics (Lewellen 1995). Disruptions to the global trading system during World War I, the Great Depression, and World War II revealed that developing countries could naturally develop industries in the absence of free trade (Frank 1966). Dependency theory became a major intellectual counterpoint to the AACM in major universities in Latin America and elsewhere in departments of political science, sociology, and anthropology. The narrative story of colonial and neocolonial oppression in Latin America and Africa fueled the belief – along with Prebisch's empirical evidence – that the AACM was simply an ideological tool adopted by those who stood to gain from it.

With these factors as the intellectual backdrop, the AACM had few adherents in the early 1950s in the Latin American capitals of Rio, Buenos Aires, and Mexico City – or, for that matter, in Delhi, Djakarta, and other Asian political centers. In their quest to jump-start growth, governments established or nationalized public monopolies in telecommunications, petroleum, airlines, and other strategic investments; stimulated infant industry manufacturing for domestic consumption via high tariffs (Import Substituting Industrialization or ISI); fixed exchange rates (generally overvalued); imposed capital controls; forced private and public banks to loan at below-market interest rates to selected industrial borrowers; set price controls on basic goods; and provided substantial tax subsidies for investments.

ISI in Latin America involved successive waves of industrial planning and promotion using imported capital and technology (Franko 2007). In Stage 1, high tariff barriers were imposed on finished consumer products such as automobiles. In Brazil, almost all the major American and German manufacturers (GM, Ford, Volkswagen, Mercedes, and others) jumped the tariff wall to set up assembly plants, using capital and parts imported with no duties. In Stage 2, high tariffs were placed on intermediary inputs (steel, glass, tires, and motors) to encourage Firestone, Pirelli, and other suppliers to similarly make the jump. In Stage 3, high tariffs on machinery gave infant industry protection to Brazil's nascent capital goods industry. While private foreign direct investments and infrastructure loans from the World Bank supplied the initial capital, by the mid-1970s commercial banks from around the world were pouring hundreds of billions of petrodollars into Latin America and earning high returns in these markets.

On the surface at least, Latin America's rejection of the AACM had paid off. Today, Brazil is a major exporter of industrial products, from cars to commercial airplanes. Yet the cost of this accomplishment was high. Because ISI emphasized the domestic manufacture of products previously imported, it *ipso facto* meant disregarding the insights of comparative advantage for lowest cost production. Industrial products were initially of poor quality and commanded high prices in the domestic market, often exceeding world prices by more than 100 per cent (Franko 2007: 63). Huge government deficits run up by state-owned companies swamped fiscal budgets, leading to bouts of hyperinflation. Fixed or pegged exchange rates were not able to adjust, and vastly overvalued currencies resulted. The high price of domestic currency impaired the traditional export market for agricultural commodities, resulting in a diminished ability to earn hard currency. Meanwhile, the huge value of imports required to maintain the burgeoning domestic industry meant that most countries used state favoritism to allocate scarce foreign exchange. Bribery and corruption followed. When world interest rates climbed steeply because of US monetary contractions in the early 1980s, Latin America went into a deep financial crisis. The 'lost decade' of the 1980s in Latin America is a testament to the problems of state intervention and the ultimate collapse of ISI (Franko 2007: ch. 4).

Many East Asian countries followed similar interventionist policies in the 1950s, yet are credited with being much quicker to switch to export-led strategies (World Bank 1993). East Asian countries also tended to have more balanced fiscal budgets, so that inflation was less of a concern. In addition, East Asian societies generally financed investment from domestic savings and were less prone to external financial shocks (but there are exceptions, such as South Korea in the 1970s and the East Asian crisis in 1998). Starting in 1978, China gradually began to free resources for private use and for international trade, while India remained highly interventionist until 1991. One by one, developing countries that had discarded the AACM found themselves returning to the fundamental doctrines of global trade, fiscal stewardship, and wealth creation through markets. We turn now to this transformation with a focus on Latin America.

The rise of neoliberalism

The AAC ideology had been a dominant feature of many Latin American countries in the nineteenth and early twentieth centuries under the neocolonial influence of the United States and Great Britain. Economic collapse in the 1980s forced the reintroduction of the AACM to policy making (under the label neoliberalism) – using the visible hand of the World Bank and IMF as levers. These institutions provided advice and emergency funds, and were the score keepers whose adjustment loans provided a signal to private investors that reforms were underway. Before addressing neoliberalism in this modern usage it is necessary to briefly consider the origins and transformation of the term (for a thorough discussion, see the essays in Mirowski and Plehwe 2009).

Alexander Rüstow, the German economist credited with coining the term 'neoliberal' in 1938, was disillusioned with Germany's hierarchical, corporatized economy that restricted liberties; at the same time, he rejected the failed laissez-faire policies he associated with Adam Smith (Hartwich 2009: 6). The German imperial economy at the start of the twentieth century had been highly protectionist and cartelized, serving the interests of heavy industry and the Kaiser's political and military objectives. The goal of catching up and surpassing Britain required the antithesis of the AACM: in Germany the invisible hand of markets was thought to produce the chaos of 'ruinous competition' (Hartwich 2009: 11). By contrast, state-led (or 'organized') capitalism was thought to produce methodical and predictable progress. Three decades later, Hitler's obsession with state-led industrialization and militarizing represented continuity with this past.

Rüstow and other German economists such as Ludwig Erhard, Walter Eucken, Wilhelm Röpke, and Alfred Müller-Armack proposed a new liberalism, a 'Third Way', which was a mix of the best parts of free markets and socialism. In line with the AACM, government would provide and enforce the economic rules, but would otherwise not pick the winners. In line with socialism, the state would provide various safety nets, such as unemployment insurance, wage subsidies, and various types of redistributions, such as free public education and high taxes on inheritance. The state would also ensure competition by preventing monopolies (Hartwich 2009: 17). These neoliberal economists participated in the Mont Pèlerin society, provoking serious arguments with Ludwig von Mises and others (Hartwich 2009: 21). The envisioned 'Third Way' eventually became West Germany's 'Social Market Economy' after the Second World War (Ptak 2009).

As originally invoked, neoliberalism is indeed quite different from the AACM, and equally different from the neoclassical efficiency programs pushed by the Washington Consensus in the late twentieth century. Moreover, the term 'neoliberal', in its modern pejorative incarnation, has often come to mean the *imposition* of AACM policies in developing countries. Imposition implies coercion, and one must ask, to what extent were Latin American countries in the debt crisis of 1982, and East Asian countries in the crisis of 1998, forced to adopt neoliberal policies against their wills? From an AACM perspective, coercion would not be possible in a situation of secure property rights, freedom to engage in or refrain from trade, and other basic liberties. Yet from a dependency theory perspective, none of these basic rights was assured.

The Third World debt crisis of 1982 was mainly a Latin American crisis, since the predominance of commercial bank loans had been to this region, amounting to more than $300 billion (Franko 2007: 79). Much of this was dollar-denominated floating rate debt, tied to world spot rates. The rapid rise of interest rates in the early 1980s pushed up debt servicing payments to unsustainable levels. In addition, Latin American commodity exports had collapsed in the world-wide recession. When Latin American countries could no longer earn the foreign exchange needed to service their loans, these bank assets were technically in default. But Latin American borrowers were 'too big to fail' because writing off these loans would have essentially bankrupted all of the world's major banks, who did not have sufficient reserves to cover these losses. To keep the world financial system afloat, major banks were pressured by regulators to issue new loans so as to keep debtor accounts afloat.

As the lenders of last resort, the IMF and World Bank played important roles in bringing commercial banks to the bargaining table. Without this clearinghouse, each bank would have been left to muddle along by itself. It is likely that the world's major multinational banks would have quickly gone bankrupt had they individually and simultaneously tried to negotiate loan restructuring with the multitude of debtor countries. Competition among banks would lead to a Prisoners' Dilemma: private banks would have little incentive individually to cooperate and release new funds unless all banks cooperated. As the convener and enforcer of loan conditions, the IMF had huge bargaining power to enforce cooperation.

By being cajoled to band together under the aegis of the IMF, commercial banks could thus act as a banking cartel. The terms and conditions imposed on debtor countries were unilateral and could be considered coercive given the circumstances. From the perspective of the poor in developing countries, the rolling over of old loans with new loans constituted 'involuntary' borrowing since the benefits accrued to banks and elites, but the obligations for repayment fell to workers (Franko 2007: 91). It is ironic that the conditions imposed (later known as the Washington Consensus) would be associated with the AACM, since the terms were created by a closed process of financial elites acting in collusion. Little wonder that the neoliberal revolution came to acquire a solidly derogatory connotation, at least in the 1980s and 1990s in debtor developing nations. In the East Asian crisis of 1997–98, for example, neoliberal policies were again used by the IMF playing the role of a financial gatekeeper. The image of this coercive power was visually captured by IMF Director-General Michel Camdessus (with folded arms) overseeing Indonesian President Suharto's signing of a letter of agreement in 1998 (Chang 2008; Getty Images 1998).

The three pillars of the Washington Consensus were to stabilize, liberalize, and privatize markets in countries experiencing fiscal deficits, inflation, and current account deficits. Stabilizing the macro economy required cutting government spending and reducing monetary growth. As real income fell and real interest rates rose, the induced recession would lower imports and constrain wages, making imports less attractive and exports more attractive. Rising real interest rates would stem capital outflows and potentially attract capital inflows. The second pillar of reform was to liberalize markets by reducing tariffs, eliminating price controls on food, currency, and other sectors, and by opening up financial markets to the free flow of capital (although not labor). The third pillar addressed the privatization of government-owned enterprises (GOES). Injecting the profit motive in GOES would in theory reduce costs by eliminating bloated payrolls, increase product and service qualities by responding to consumer demands, and attract foreign investment and technology, thereby alleviating the external disequilibrium.

It is hard to imagine that Adam Smith would object to any of these policies as guiding principles. But what he likely would have questioned is the rigid implementation, ignoring time and circumstance. We turn now to this discussion.

Smith's pragmatism in development policy

Viner (1927) noted the numerous ways in which Smith veered from a dogmatic adherence to laissez-faire policy making. That is, while Smith's rhetoric soared in defense of the inalienable rights of persons to seek their own fortunes through individual effort, he did not assume that actually bringing about a system of perfect liberty would ever be feasible or desirable. Moreover, there were specific instances in which individual liberty needed to be restrained by the state in order to promote the goals of stability or growth. This section develops these points in the areas of financial markets, labor markets, international trade, and the path dependent nature of the development process.

Financial markets

Financial market liberalization was a key tenant of the Reagan-style AACM in the 1980s and played an importunate role in the neoliberal reforms endorsed by the IMF and World Bank. Larry Summers, former chief economist at the World Bank (and subsequently Secretary of the Treasury), believed that free markets in capital and foreign exchange improved the overall efficiency of global markets. While there were occasional currency collapses, Summers equated these to the infrequent but spectacular crash of a Boeing 747. Efficiency would dictate that we keep flying such planes because the risks were low and the benefits large. In what seems paradoxical today (given the USA's present reliance on Chinese and Brazilian capital inflows) Summers noted in 1999 that 'there are few things with as great a potential to raise human welfare as the creation of a safe and sustainable system for the flow of capital from the developed world to the developing one' (cited in Wolf 2002: 46).

A plethora of critics attacked this fundamental tenet of AACM. The analogy of free capital flows to flying a jumbo jet is mistaken: developing countries have thin financial markets and an appropriate analogy is that of flying a single propeller Cessna: the death rate in such small planes is tenfold higher than in jumbo jets. Joseph Stiglitz, who was also chief economist of the World Bank, notes that in practice capital market liberalizations have not worked as advertised to stimulate investment and growth. Stiglitz posed this question:

> Given the overwhelming theory and evidence against capital market liberalization, one wonders: how could the major international organization responsible for promoting growth and stability have promoted a policy that seemed so contrary to its objectives?
>
> (Stiglitz 2002: 221)

The answer, according to Stiglitz, is that the directors of the IMF were instilled with AACM ideology and became blinded to facts. Ideology trumped science. Wolf states the problem astutely and with prescience for the great global contraction of 2008: 'Too many countries have been devastated by financial crises that have resulted from throwing open poorly regulated financial systems under-pinned by comprehensive government guarantees. While liberalization is desirable, *it has to be done in the right way*' (Wolf 2002: 51, emphasis added).

Adam Smith had similar reservations about liberal financial markets. Britain had endured the South Sea Bubble of 1720 and the Scottish banking crisis of 1772 (Rockoff, this volume). Smith was thus concerned about financial speculation as a cause of imprudent lending and financial melt-down. In *The Wealth of Nations* Smith advocated government regulations that would prevent speculators from squandering capital that could be better employed. Institutional regulations were needed (in this case) to harmonize private passions with the public interest. Smith noted that the natural flow of capital will largely be toward investments creating the greatest individual opulence, which when summed over the nation produce the greatest national opulence. Private and public interests thus converge. But some lenders can make more money offering loans to 'profligates' whose activities contribute more to consumption than to growth. Smith thus favored an interest rate ceiling of 5 per cent that would create a shortage of loanable funds (Smith 1976b, WN II.iv.14–15). Since risk-taking would be constrained by lower returns, banks would advance credit only to their most trustworthy clients, weeding out speculative borrowers whose private aims were not in keeping with society's objectives. Smith also advocated limiting paper bank notes issues to £5 and higher, which would restrict their circulation to wealthier merchants (Rockoff, this volume). Such mild paternalism would keep the poor from suffering 'a very great calamity' in the case of bank failure (WN II.ii.90) but clearly would violate the modern principle of Pareto efficiency.

In a related discussion in which the invisible hand appears, Smith considered the problem of capital flight. He theorized that security concerns would lead merchants to congregate funds domestically, hence no regulations on capital exports would be needed to harmonize private with public interests (WN IV.ii.3–6). The preference for home country investments is not a necessary feature of all economies, however. That is, the incentives that give rise to the trust, character, and legal system required to create such preferences are idiosyncratic to the confluence of events, institutions, and individuals populating a time and place. Were Smith to offer advice to Latin American countries with weak existing financial markets, poor legal systems for protection of property, and a long history of capital flight, it is at least debatable as to whether he would have recommended some controls on short-run capital flows to discourage speculation. The two preceding points make clear that Smith was not promoting global market efficiency but rather dynamic growth in the *home* country. Smith was willing to sacrifice some freedom and some short-run efficiency to promote this end.

Labor markets

In the area of labor markets, Smith's aims and those of AACM coincide in theory and only partially in practice (Levy and Peart 2009). Smith called attention to the plight of workers facing monopsony employers:

> We rarely hear, it has been said, of the combinations of masters [employers], though frequently of those of workmen. But whoever imagines, upon this account, that masters rarely combine, is as ignorant of the world as of the subject.
>
> (WN I.viii.13)

To some extent the neoliberal reforms called for by the World Bank address the problems of monopsony in labor markets. In *Why Africa Had to Adjust*, the World Bank (1994) highlighted numerous government marketing boards that produce a large wedge between the world price of commodities and the price paid to peasant producers. Special interests, notably government leaders, earn this rent and use it to solidify their power to block reforms. Smith would have both understood this situation and applauded the Bank's attempts to redress it.

Yet the neoliberal reforms in Latin America of the 1980s were largely perceived to be anti-union and anti-labor. Moreover, they failed to address land reform, perhaps the key issue in the region at that time: huge hereditary estates (*latifundios*) held by 1 per cent of the population controlled 72 per cent of the land under cultivation (Todaro 2000: 373). Adam Smith labeled large European feudal landholdings 'barbarous institutions' that formed only in response to disorderly times. As with estates in Latin America, Smith predicted that large landholdings would produce lower yields than smallholdings:

> To improve land with profit, like all other commercial projects, requires an exact attention to small savings and small gains, of which a man born to a great fortune, even though naturally frugal, is very seldom capable. The situation of such a person naturally disposes him to attend rather to ornament which pleases his fancy, than to profit for which he has so little occasion.
>
> (WN III.ii.7)

Evidence for lower productivity in Latin America's *latifundios* has been found by numerous researchers (Todaro 2000).

Because neoliberal reforms emphasized a return to commodity exports, they increased the demand for rural labor and would in theory raise real wages. But in situations where labor markets are uncompetitive, land distribution highly skewed, and indigenous property rights weak, such reforms often produced unintended negative consequences for the poor that Smith would have found objectionable (Wight 2001). Military rulers in Guatemala, for example – like those in other Latin America countries – often used state violence to suppress worker organizations and to expropriate peasant lands for mining and other purposes controlled by elites. A tight oligarchy dominated political and economic life (Viscidi 2004). Acemoglu and Robinson (2008: 20) note that:

> The conclusion … seems to be that to change the political equilibrium there needs to be changes in both de jure and de facto power. For instance, if there is an elite that is structuring institutions to its benefit with adverse aggregate effects, then to engineer a transition to a better equilibrium both their de jure and de facto power must be simultaneously reformed.

When Adam Smith wrote that 'The natural effort of every individual to better his own condition … is so powerful a principle that it is alone … capable of carrying on the society to wealth and prosperity. … ' he added the key qualifying phrase, 'when suffered to exert itself with freedom and security' (WN IV.v.b.43). By security Smith meant the legal reforms introduced by Magna Carta, the English Revolution, and other institutional safeguards of justice. A key property right was to one's person:

> That security which the laws in Great Britain give to every man that he shall enjoy the fruits of his own labour is alone sufficient to make any country flourish, notwithstanding these and twenty other absurd regulations of commerce.
>
> (WN IV.v.b.43)

If Smith were advising Latin American countries in the 1980s, it is unthinkable that he would proceed without first devoting considerable attention to the history of property and labor rights. Smith's reforms would proceed according to what the circumstances would permit, not according to ideological or theoretical beliefs about ideal market situations.

International trade

Adam Smith was well aware of the nuances of the gains and losses from opening to trade. Smith's defense of free trade is well-known, exemplified by this quote:

> By means of glasses, hotbeds, and hot walls, very good grapes can be raised in Scotland, and very good wine too can be made of them at about thirty times the expense for which at least equally good can be brought

> from foreign countries. Would it be a reasonable law to prohibit the importation of all foreign wines merely to encourage the making of claret and burgundy in Scotland?
>
> (WN IV.ii.15)

As with labor markets, however, Smith's trade policies were not constructed in isolation. They addressed existing realities of the time, place, and institutions. Smith cynically remarked: 'To expect, indeed, that the freedom of trade should ever be entirely restored in Great Britain is as absurd as to expect that an Oceana or Utopia should ever be established in it' (WN IV.ii.43). In particular, Smith was sensitive to injustices that could arise from a rapid re-introduction of free trade (or 'shock therapy' in modern parlance). Smith argued for gradualism:

> Humanity may in this case require that the freedom of trade should be restored only by slow gradations, and with a good deal of reserve and circumspection. Were those high duties and prohibitions taken away all at once, cheaper foreign goods of the same kind might be poured so fast into the home market, as to deprive all at once many thousands of our people of their ordinary employment and means of subsistence. The *disorder* which this would occasion might no doubt be very considerable. It would in all probability, however, be much less than is commonly imagined. …
>
> (WN IV.ii.40, emphasis added)

As if following Smith's advice, Chinese communist rulers (fearing political disorder) proceeded cautiously to open select markets after 1978, 'fording the river by feeling for the stones'. Smith also noted his concern for owners of capital who would be hurt by new trade rules:

> The undertaker of a great manufacture who, by the home markets being suddenly laid open to the competition of foreigners, should be obliged to abandon his trade, would no doubt suffer very considerably. … The equitable regard, therefore, to his interest requires that changes of this kind should never be introduced suddenly, but slowly, gradually, and after a very long warning.
>
> (WN IV.ii.44)

In these passages Smith makes two points: that efficiency should be balanced with justice for workers and for investors; and that maintaining order is a social objective worthy of important consideration.

Developmental process

Smith's policy making is thus incremental, geared to allowing slow and achievable progress rather than radical revolution. Policy making should not be driven by ideological purity, but by pragmatic considerations of what would, at the margin, move society forward with equity and the least disruption. Hence, in commenting on an export revenue bounty, Smith writes:

> With all its imperfections, however, we may perhaps say of what was said of the laws of Solon, that, though not the best in itself, *it is the best which the interests, prejudices, and temper of the times would admit of.* It may perhaps in due time prepare the way for a better.
>
> (WN IV.v.b.53, emphasis added)

In *The Theory of Moral Sentiments* Smith explicitly addresses the character of a virtuous leader who contents himself with moderating laws and regulations, consistent with the prejudices of the times. A virtuous leader would 'respect the established powers and privileges' of individuals and orders, and content himself with restraining 'what he often cannot annihilate without great violence' (Smith 1976a, TMS VI.ii.2.16). While a general idea of the 'perfect' policy is necessary to inform the statesman, 'to insist upon its establishing, and upon establishing all at once, and in spite of all opposition, every thing which that idea may seem to require, must often be the highest degree of arrogance' (TMS VI.ii.2.18). Smith's reserved approach could easily have inspired Abraham Lincoln, who abhorred slavery yet argued that it should be 'tolerated and protected only because of and so far as its actual presence among us makes that toleration and protection a necessity' (Lincoln 1860). One should not infer that Smith would himself be as tolerant of slavery.

These points highlight the role that process plays in Smith's conception of economic development. Seen from the perspective of millennia, the advance of society from hunting and gathering to herding, then to agriculture, and finally to industry appears as a seamless advance. Yet at any point in time there are wrenching institutional changes to be experienced. The invisible hand does not produce perfect results because human instincts work within human institutions that must constantly evolve. 'Ghost institutions' linger, serving no purpose (Wilson 2007). Smith provides two examples of feudal property rights – primogeniture and land engrossing – that anachronistically survived for centuries and failed to adapt to the needs of the present (WN III.ii.3–4). Hence, while human instincts for betterment lie behind the invisible hand, human institutions sometimes 'thwarted those natural inclinations' (WN III.i.3). Historical circumstances and path dependency limit how well the invisible hand can work at any particular point in time (Nozick 1994: 314).

As noted by a number of authors, the beneficial spin ascribed to the invisible hand is thus premised on specific institutional, social, and ethical constructs (Wight 2007; Grampp 2000; Evensky 1993; Persky 1989). In considering limitations of time and place, Smith observed that 'If a nation could not prosper without the enjoyment of perfect liberty and perfect justice, there is not in the world a nation which could ever have prospered' (WN IV. ix.28). Policies work through imperfect institutions, and Smith was unwilling to promote reforms derived merely from ideology and abstracted from local context.

Smith's concerns have been borne out by the widespread disillusionment with the cookie-cutter restructuring carried out by the IMF under the guise of AACM (Stiglitz 2003). Dani Rodrik writes that 'What [countries] need is not a laundry list [of reforms], but an explicitly diagnostic approach that identifies priorities based on local realities' (Rodrik 2007: 5). History, culture, and politics flatten a path and limit the range of options and potential methods that can be used effectively. Rodrik thus distinguishes between ideal principles and practical policies:

> First-order economic principles – protection of property rights, market-based competition, appropriate incentives, sound money, and so on – do not map into unique policy packages. Reformers have substantial room for creatively packaging these principles into institutional designs that are sensitive to local opportunities and constraints.
>
> (2007: 6)

Adam Smith, who greatly respected the Physiocratic reformers in France who advocated laissez-faire, gently chided their leader (Dr. François Quesnay) for advocating doctrinaire policies. Smith was ideologically supportive but pragmatically distant:

> Some speculative physicians seem to have imagined that the health of the human body could be preserved only by a certain precise regimen of diet and exercise. … Mr. Quesnai, who was himself a physician, and a very speculative physician, seems to have entertained a notion of the same kind concerning the political body, and to have imagined that it would thrive and prosper only under a certain precise regimen, the exact regimen of perfect liberty and perfect justice. He seems not to have considered that, in the political body, the natural effort which every man is continually making to better his own condition, is a principle of preservation capable of preventing and correcting, in many respects, the bad effects of a political economy. …
>
> (WN IV.ix.28)

General principles are guiding lights, but when applied unthinkingly can do harm. Smith is equally critical of command economy dictators ('the man of system') (TMS VI.ii.2.17) as he is of laissez-faire. The linking of Adam Smith to the general aims of the AACM is obvious at the surface but troubling for reasons of policy design and implementation elaborated in this section.

Conclusion

Adam Smith's soaring rhetoric was written for all ages, yet his explicit policy proposals were grounded in the reality of circumstance. This paper offers evidence that Smith would have found good and bad aspects of the AACM as it was applied to neoliberal policies in the late twentieth century. Smith would likely be critical of economic reforms that focused on short-run efficiency and failed to address issues of justice. Smith was also an incremental reformer; he understood the problem of path dependency, which blocks the implementation of perfect states. He would have found it unacceptable to design economic policies in the absence of a careful elaboration of historical, cultural, and political constraints.

Smith's physiologic-based critique of Dr. Quesnay in *The Wealth of Nations* provides a metaphor for understanding why, despite his rhetorical flourishes, Smith avoided utopian economic policies. Time and place create a context in which particular policies need to be crafted. Ideology inspires one's principles, but practicality grounds one's practice. The human instinct for betterment remains stable over time but institutions must evolve to address changing circumstances. However, a particular institution suitable for one period can be assumed to become obsolete. Ghost institutions act as a brake on progress and carve out a number of different evolutionary solutions. Smith's model supports the view that diverse approaches to mixed-market capitalism are feasible and desirable given different historical, cultural, and political circumstances.

This understanding provides two possible responses to the question, 'Is the Anglo-American style capitalism passing away?' The response is yes, if by this we mean the blind application of neoclassical theory without regard to context. The response is no, if we consider the dedication to freedom and justice that lie behind Smith's version of the AACM.

Note

1 Professor of Economics and International Studies, Robins School of Business, University of Richmond, VA 23173. jwight@richmond.edu. The author acknowledges valuable suggestions from an anonymous referee.

References

Acemoglu, D. and Robinson, J. (2008) 'The Role of Institutions in Growth and Development', Working Paper no. 10, Commission on Growth and Development, Washington, DC: World Bank.

Chang, H. J. (2008) 'The Economics of Hypocrisy', *Guardian* (October 20).

Dantzig, G. B. (2002) 'Linear Programming', *Operations Research*, 50(1): 42–47.

Duncan, J. S. (1937) 'British Railroads in Argentina', *Political Science Quarterly*, 52(4): 559–82.

Evensky, J. (1993) 'Ethics and the Invisible Hand', *Journal of Economic Perspectives*, 7(2): 197–205.

Frank, A. G. (1966) 'The Development of Underdevelopment', *Monthly Review*, 18(4): 17–31.

Franko, P. (2007) *The Puzzle of Latin American Economic Development*, 3rd edn, Lanham, MD: Rowman and Littlefield.

Getty Images (1998) Available HTTP: www.daylife.com/photo/0bMcgTFgVt2hs (accessed 30 January 2010).

Grampp, W. D. (2000) 'What Did Smith Mean by the Invisible Hand?', *Journal of Political Economy*, 108(3): 441–64.

Hartwich, O. M. (2009) 'Neoliberalism: The Genesis of a Political Swearword', The Center for Independent Studies, CIS Occasional Paper 114 (May). Available HTTP: www.cis.org.au/temp/op114_neoliberalism.pdf (accessed 27 November 2009).

Hayek, F. A. (1945) 'Use of Knowledge in Society', *American Economic Review*, 35(4): 519–30.

Kay, J. (2004) *Culture and Prosperity: The Truth About Markets – Why Some Nations Are Rich But Most Remain Poor*, New York: HarperBusiness.

Levy, D. M. and Peart, S. J. (2009) 'Adam Smith, Collusion and "Right" at the Supreme Court', *Supreme Court Economic Review* 16 (June). Available HTTP: http://ssrn.com/abstract=1022829

——(2008) 'Socialist calculation debate', *The New Palgrave Dictionary of Economics*, 2nd edn, S. N. Durlauf and L. E. Blume (eds), pp. 685–92, New York: Palgrave Macmillan.

Lewellen, T. C. (1995) *Dependency and Development*, Westport, CT: Bergin & Garvey.

Lewis, W. A. (1969) [1949] *The Principles of Economic Planning*, 3rd edn, London: George Allen & Unwin.

Lincoln, A. (1860) 'Cooper Union Address', New York City, 27 February. Available HTTP: http://showcase.netins.net/web/creative/lincoln/speeches/cooper.htm

Mirowski, P. and Plehwe, D. (eds) (2009) *The Road from Mont Pèlerin: Making of the Neoliberal Thought Collective*, Cambridge, MA: Harvard University Press.

Nozick, R. (1994) 'Invisible-hand explanations', *American Economic Review*, 84(2): 314–18.

Persky, J. (1989) 'Retrospectives: Adam Smith's Invisible Hand', *Journal of Economic Perspectives*, 3: 195–201.

Plehwe, D. (2009) 'The Origins of the Neoliberal Economic Development Discourse', in *The Road from Mont Pèlerin: Making of the Neoliberal Thought Collective*, Mirowski, P. and Plehwe, D. (eds), pp. 238–79, Cambridge, MA: Harvard University Press.

Prebisch, R. (1950) *The Economic Development of Latin America and its Principal Problems*, New York: The United Nations Economic Commission for Latin America.

Ptak, R. (2009) 'Neoliberalism in Germany: Revisiting the Ordoliberal Foundatations of the Social Market Economy', in *The Road from Mont Pèlerin: Making of the Neoliberal Thought Collective*, Mirowski, P. and Plehwe, D. (eds), pp. 98–138, Cambridge, MA: Harvard University Press.

Rockoff, Hugh (2011) 'Upon Daedalian Wings of Paper Money: Adam Smith and the Crisis of 1772', *The Adam Smith Review*, vol. 6.

Rodrik, D. (2007) *One Economics, Many Recipes: Globalization, Institutions, and Economic Growth*, Princeton, NJ: Princeton University Press.

Smith, A. (1976a) *The Theory of Moral Sentiments*, D. D. Raphael and A. L Macfie (eds), Oxford: Clarendon Press; reprinted, Liberty Press (1982).

——(1976b) *An Inquiry into the Nature and Causes of the Wealth of Nations*, R. H. Campbell and A. S. Skinner (eds), Oxford: Clarendon Press; reprinted, Liberty Press (1981).

Steger, M. B. and Roy, R. K. (2010) *Neoliberalism: A Short Introduction*, Oxford: Oxford University Press.

Stiglitz, J. E. (2007) *Making Globalization Work*, New York: W. W. Norton & Co.

——(2003) *Globalization and Its Discontents*, New York: W. W. Norton & Co.

——(2002) 'Capital Market Liberalization and Exchange Rate Regimes: Risk Without Reward', *Annals of the American Academy of Political and Social Science*, vol. 579, Exchange Rate Regimes and Capital Flows (January): 219–48.

Todaro, M. P. (2000) *Economic Development*, 7th edn, Reading, MA: Addison-Wesley Longman.

Viscidi, L. (2004) 'A History of Land in Guatemala: Conflict and Hope for Reform', Interhemispheric Resource Center, 17 September. Available HTTP: http://americas.irc-online.org/pdf/focus/0409guatland.pdf

Viner, J. (1927) 'Adam Smith and Laissez Faire', *Journal of Political Economy*, 35(2): 198–232.

Wight, J. B. (2007) 'The Treatment of Smith's Invisible Hand', *The Journal of Economic Education*, 39(3): 341–58.

——(2001) 'Does Free Trade Cause Hunger? Hidden Implications of the Free Trade of the Americas Area', *Richmond Journal of Global Law and Business*, 2(2): 167–81.

Williamson, J. (1990) 'What Washington Means by Policy Reform', in *Latin American Adjustment: How Much Has Happened?* J. Williamson (ed.), pp. 5–20, Washington, DC: Institute for International Economics.

Wilson, D. S. (2007) *Evolution for Everyone*, New York: Delacorte.

Wolf, M. (2002) 'Exchange Rates in a World of Capital Mobility', *Annals of the American Academy of Political and Social Science*, vol. 579: Exchange Rate Regimes and Capital Flows (January): 38–52.

World Bank (1993) *The East Asian Miracle: Economic Growth and Public Policy*, Washington, DC: World Bank.

——(1994) *Why Africa Had to Adjust: Reforms, Results, and the Road Ahead*, Washington, DC: World Bank.

Wright, W. R. (1974) *British-owned Railways in Argentina*, Austin: University of Texas Press.

Too big to live?

Why we must stamp out state monopoly capitalism[1]

Niall Ferguson

I

For conservatives, the financial crisis that began in the summer of 2007 has posed a major problem. We had grown rather accustomed to singing the praises of free financial markets and the institutions that flourish in them. The crisis threatens to discredit the very idea of capitalism – even to vindicate the old Marxists who, we had assumed, were about to fade into extinction. It is therefore vital that we understand the true character of the crisis, and do not fall into the trap of accepting that it was the result of deregulation and market failure.

In reality, this was a crisis born of a highly distorted financial market, in which excessive concentration, excessive leverage, spurious theories of risk management and, above all, moral hazard in the form of implicit state guarantees, combined on both sides of the Atlantic not only to create property bubbles, but also to erect huge inverted pyramids of securities and pseudo-securities upon the bubbles. Unanticipated losses on US subprime mortgages were merely the catalyst for an implosion that was bound to come sooner or later. The greatest danger we currently face is that the emergency measures adopted to remedy the crisis have made matters even worse by increasing concentration, scarcely reducing leverage, leaving the spurious theories in place and making the state guarantees explicit.

It has often been said since the crisis began that an institution that is 'too big to fail' (TBTF) is too big to exist.[2] I agree. The question is how we can best get rid of the 'TBTFs' without increasing the power of government in the economy still further. This should be among the first priorities of any Western leader committed to free market principles.

II

It was almost exactly eleven years ago that the Federal Reserve Board approved Travelers' takeover of Citibank. Slightly more than a year later, on 4 November 1999, both Houses of Congress retrospectively legalized the creation of 'Citicorp' by repealing the Glass-Steagall Act, passed during the Great Depression to separate commercial and investment banking. It has

The Adam Smith Review, 6: 327–340 © The International Adam Smith Society
ISSN 1743-5285, ISBN 0–415–66722–7

been suggested that this legislative change paved the way for the financial crisis that began two years ago and reached its nadir in the months following the bankruptcy of Lehman Brothers in September 2008 (Kaufman 2009). But in truth the repeal of Glass-Steagall merely facilitated a trend that can be dated back to the mid-1980s. It was a trend that was not confined to the US, but rather occurred in nearly all the major economies of the Western world. That trend was for certain financial institutions to get much too big.

The past two decades witnessed an unprecedented concentration in the traditionally fragmented US financial services sector. With the creation of behemoths like Citigroup and Bank of America, a few institutions came to control an astonishingly large proportion of commercial bank deposits and loans. These same institutions also became involved in asset management, credit cards, insurance, leasing, mortgages, mutual funds, securities trading, and underwriting. Between 1990 and 2008, the share of financial assets held by the ten largest US financial institutions rose from 10 per cent to 50 per cent, even as the number of banks fell from over 15,000 to around 8,000 (see Figure 1). With the exception of retail banking and mutual funds, concentration increased across the board: in mortgage origination, credit cards, corporate lending, custody banking, and investment banking (Walter 2004: 82).

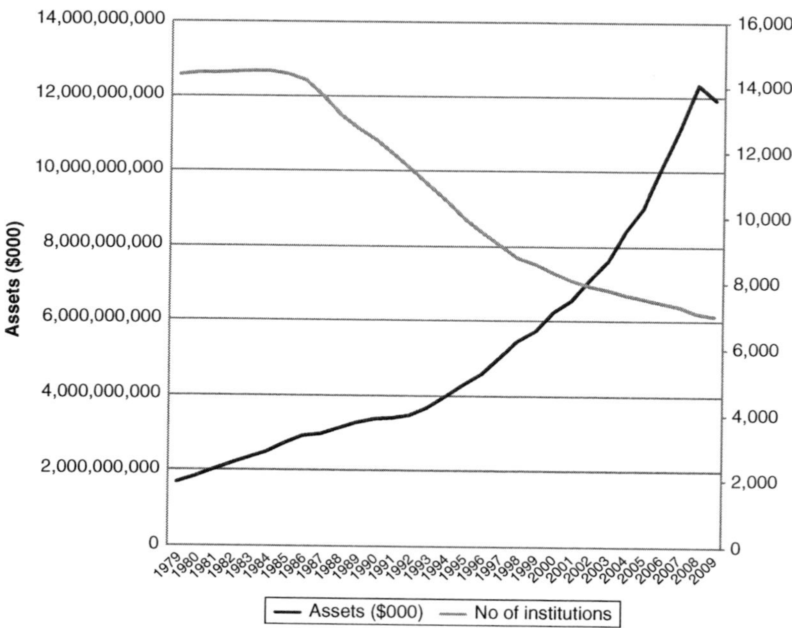

Figure 1 The number and assets of US commercial banks, 1979–2009.
Source: Federal Deposit Insurance Corporation.

But it was not only the scale and scope of financial institutions that changed. The growth of securitization of mortgages and other forms of consumer debt (pioneered by Salomon Brothers in the 1980s), the explosion of derivatives traded on exchanges or sold 'over-the-counter', the doubling of turnover on the stock market, and, above all, the vast increase of leverage on bank balance sheets – all these changes added to the concentration of the financial system, and thereby increased its vulnerability. Contrary to the self-serving cliché of the time, which maintained that risk was being optimally distributed to 'those best able to bear it', risk was in fact being dangerously concentrated on (and off) the balance sheets of about fifteen institutions and their 'shadow bank' satellites.

By the end of 2007, these megabanks, with combined shareholder equity of $857 billion, had total assets of $13.6 trillion and off-balance-sheet commitments of $5.8 trillion – an aggregate leverage ratio of 23 to 1. They also had underwritten derivatives with a gross notional value of $216 trillion – more than a third of the total.

It is not convincing to blame 'deregulation' for the crisis, though this is fast becoming the orthodox interpretation.[3] It was not the least regulated parts of the financial system – hedge funds and private equity partnerships – that proved to be the problem, but the most regulated: precisely the megabanks described above, not to forget the even more regulated mortgage market-makers, Fannie Mae and Freddie Mac, both of which were 'government sponsored entities' under direct Congressional oversight. There are, after all, international rules governing bank capital adequacy. They are set out in the Basel I and Basel II accords and applied with varying degrees of rigour by a host of national regulators. It was the Basel system of weighting assets by their supposed riskiness that permitted the 'Enronization' of bank balance sheets, so that (for example) the ratio of Citigroup's tangible on- and off-balance-sheet assets to its common equity reached a staggering 56 to 1 at one point in 2008. It was also the Basel system that helped to enshrine the credit rating agencies as semi-official arbiters of risk, despite the obvious incentive these agencies have to please the issuers of securities who pay their fees. Banks were encouraged by regulators to use credit ratings when calculating their capital requirements. The more assets could be rated AAA, the less capital they needed to hold. By January last year the agencies had conferred triple-A ratings on more than 64,000 structured financial instruments, at a time when just twelve corporations qualified for that rating.

In short, it was not so much deregulation that caused the crisis as excessive concentration, combined with regulatory capture or regulatory arbitrage as the big banks schmoozed and bamboozled their supposed supervisors or shopped around for the softest touch.

This phenomenon was far from being a purely American phenomenon. On the contrary, precisely the same tendencies were in evidence in Europe. As is well known, British banking has long been more concentrated than US banking. There has never been an equivalent of Glass-Steagall to prevent the big 'high street' banks from extending their operations beyond deposit-taking and loan-making. But the reforms of the City of London known as 'Big Bang' created a wide range of new opportunities for big banks in the hitherto tightly regulated and institutionally fragmented stock market.

The rise of Royal Bank of Scotland to become at one time the world's largest financial institution in terms of assets epitomized the 'supersize' mania that gripped British finance in recent years. By the end of 2007, the RBS Group had assets of £1.9 trillion – a sum larger than the gross domestic product of the entire United Kingdom – and equity of just £91 billion, implying a leverage ratio of 21:1 (Lanchester 2009). The merger of the Halifax with RBS's traditional rival, Bank of Scotland, was another sign of the bloated times. Between 1989 and 2003 there was a clear trend towards financial sector concentration, by almost any measure, including the widely used Herfindahl-Hirschman Index (HHI).[4] By 2003 the five largest banking groups in the UK accounted for 71 per cent of deposits and 75 per cent of loans. The HHI for deposit concentration rose markedly in 1995 and 2000–2001 (Logan 2004: 129–35).

Yet it was not only in the English-speaking world that outsized institutions came to the fore in the years before 2007. To be sure, the German banking system remains relatively decentralized and the 2005 HHI scores were even lower for Austria, Spain, and Italy. But other continental countries – notably Belgium, Denmark, Finland, the Netherlands and Sweden – have an even higher level of banking concentration than the UK (Masciandaro 2005: 320f.). And all the major continental economies saw significant increases in concentration after 1997 (Cipollini and Fiordelisi 2008).

Concentration is, of course, not unique to financial services. There are many countries in which other economic sectors are more concentrated (Baumol and Blinder 2008: 269f.). By the standards of the Office of Fair Trading, the HHI score for UK banks is not exceptionally high; adjusted for the impact of building society de-mutualizations, it was still only around 1,600 in 2003, whereas 1,800 is regarded by the OFT as the threshold above which a sector is defined as 'highly concentrated' (Logan 2004: 133).

Nor is it self-evident that even a highly concentrated banking system is likely to be a source of economic instability. The empirical evidence on this score is ambiguous. Canada has a far more concentrated banking sector than the US. Yet Canada's banks have been among the world's least troubled and troublesome in the past two years. One study using data from 79 countries over the period 1980–97 concluded that crises were less likely in more concentrated banking systems (Beck et al. 2003). Since many of the countries in the sample were less developed economies with primitive banking systems, the result seems of limited value, however. A more recent analysis of the European experience between 1997 and 2005 shows that concentration in the commercial banking sector increases the probability of financial distress (Cipollini and Fiordelisi 2008).

The best explanation for this is that concentration in banking in most developed economies – including Canada – has not gone so far as to eliminate competition. On the contrary, banking remains a highly competitive business. Indeed, it was precisely this competition that encouraged bank executives aggressively to pursue economies of scale, to increase leverage (see Figure 2) and to take on increasingly risky positions. To some extent, the excessive risks taken in the period leading up to 2007 can be blamed on defective mathematical models of risk assessment such as those based on the concept of 'Value at Risk' (VaR).[5] As the experience of Lehman Brothers in 2007 and 2008 made abundantly clear, things can go much more wrong than these models predict (Triana 2009). However, another explanation is that big financial institutions had reason to believe they enjoy a privileged and in some measure protected position.

Economic theory since the time of Milton Friedman, if not Walter Bagehot, has held that bank failures pose a 'systemic' economic risk, because failed banks are associated with monetary contractions and financing difficulties for the economy as a whole. There is therefore a presumption that, should they encounter difficulties, they may be bailed out in some way by the action of the central bank or government. Despite much pious talk of 'moral hazard' prior to 2007, little was done to disabuse big financial institutions of this notion. They could and did assume that they enjoyed an implicit government guarantee.

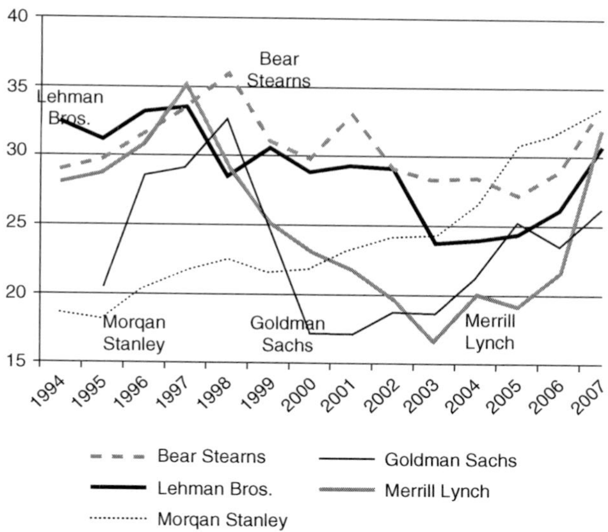

Figure 2 US investment banks' leverage (assets/equity), 1993–2007.
Source: 1993–2002: Bob Lockner, Chapman and Cutler LLP, private communication, 10 March 2009; 2003–07: http://en.wikipedia.org/wiki/File:Source_Data_-_Leverage_Ratios.png

III

The crisis that began with defaults in the US subprime mortgage market implied calamity for virtually all the big financial institutions on both sides of the Atlantic. This was for three reasons. First, the liabilities side of their balance sheet was highly vulnerable to a liquidity crisis. When the market for inter-banking lending and commercial paper essentially froze in mid-2007 and again in September–October 2008, the most highly leveraged, least reputable firms struggled to roll over their short-term debt. Second, at the same time, the big banks' large proprietary holdings of mortgage-backed securities and collateralized debt obligations were collapsing in value as US house prices fell steeply. Third, the banks began to lose faith in the insurance-like instruments they had bought to protect themselves against a financial crisis, such as credit default swaps. 'Counter-party risk' was a euphemism for the fact that, without massive government aid, they might all go down together.

To an extent that is truly astonishing, the greater part of the losses suffered by financial institutions over the past two years were due to grotesque miscalculations by the biggest banks. In the US, 80 per cent of losses were accounted for by just ten institutions. The equivalent figure for the top ten losers in Europe was 60 per cent. In view of the magnitude of the losses suffered since the financial crisis began – an estimated $626 billion in the US and $456 billion in Europe (including the UK) – the culpability of the biggest institutions is great indeed. Governments on both sides of the Atlantic have at the time of writing committed $361 billion to recapitalizing the Western banking system. Yet there are more losses still to come: perhaps as much as $323 billion. At this rate, total financial losses could approach $1 trillion, with around twenty institutions responsible for about three-quarters of the damage (Steinberg et al. 2009). By the end of 2008 the US government alone had been forced to make a total potential commitment to the financial system of nearly $11 trillion (Moss 2009: 6).

Beginning with the British government's takeover of Northern Rock in 2007 and culminating in the US government's injections of capital into Citigroup and other big banks, the Western world has witnessed a succession of government interventions in the banking system unprecedented other than in time of war. These measures can be justified on the ground that without them there would have been a banking crisis comparable with that of 1931, which did as much as the 1929 stock market crash to plunge the world into a Great Depression. In many ways, central bankers and finance ministers have done exactly what Milton Friedman would have recommended: they have injected liquidity with every conceivable means to prevent a chain reaction of bank failures and monetary contraction.

But there is a danger that justifiable emergency measures give rise to unjustifiable permanent conditions. It is far from clear that it is time to start discussing an 'exit strategy' in terms of macroeconomic stimulus. It is certainly high time we started discussing an exit strategy from state monopoly capitalism.

IV

The sequence of events described above provided a belated vindication for one of the central tenets of Marxism-Leninism. It was the German Social Democrat theorist Rudolf Hilferding whose 1910 book *Finanzkapital* predicted that increasing concentration of financial capital would lead ultimately to crisis, followed by the socialization of the banking system. The idea appealed to Lenin, who recycled it in his *Imperialism: The Highest Stage of Capitalism*. Here is how Lenin put it:

> As banking develops and becomes concentrated in a small number of establishments, the banks grow from modest middlemen into powerful monopolies having at their command almost the whole of the money capital of all the capitalists and small businessmen and also the larger part of the means of production and sources of raw materials in any one country and in a number of countries. This transformation of numerous modest middlemen into a handful of monopolists is one of the fundamental processes in the growth of capitalism into capitalist imperialism. … Scattered capitalists are transformed into a single collective capitalist. … banks greatly intensify and accelerate the process of concentration of capital and the formation of monopolies in all capitalist countries, notwithstanding all the differences in their banking laws. …
>
> In other words, the old capitalism, the capitalism of free competition … is passing away. A new capitalism has come to take its place, bearing obvious features of something transient, a mixture of free competition and monopoly. The question naturally arises: into what is this new capitalism 'developing'?
>
> (Lenin 1963: ch. 2)

The answer, Lenin argued, was that a 'financial oligarchy' was becoming increasingly powerful not only economically but also politically, establishing 'a close network of dependence relationships over all the economic and political institutions of present-day bourgeois society without exception' and promoting foreign policies based on imperialism – the export of finance capital to the less developed world (Lenin 1963: conclusion). However, this concentration of power was merely the prelude to that takeover of capitalism by the state, which Lenin believed would be the next stage of the historical process. Later East German authorities would coin the phrase 'State Monopoly Capitalism' (Stamokap for short) to describe this way-station on the road to 'real existing socialism'.

It is not often that I quote Lenin approvingly. But one of the lessons of the recent – and in my view continuing – financial crisis is that not everything the Marxists said was wrong, even if the normative conclusions they draw from their observations certainly were. As a believer in what Lenin disapprovingly called 'the capitalism of free competition', I regard the emergence of excessively large, government-guaranteed financial conglomerates in a very different light – not as a prelude to socialism but as a massive distortion of the market, similar to that which Adam Smith deplored when he considered the role of quasi-governmental monopolies like the East India Company in his own time, or warned against unregulated monopolies in banking (Rockoff 2009). But I wholly share Lenin's view that the rise to power of a financial oligarchy is undesirable and should be as far as possible a transient phenomenon. The question is how we can extricate ourselves from Stamokap and return to the capitalism of free competition. It will not be easy.

V

The crisis has made the problem of excessive concentration worse in two ways. First, it wiped out three of the biggest US investment banks – Bear Stearns, Merrill Lynch and Lehman Brothers – while at the same time condemning more than 180 (at the time of writing, and still counting) smaller regional and local banks to oblivion. Second, because the failure of Lehman was so economically disastrous, it established what had previously only been suspected – that the survivors were Too Big To Fail and were effectively guaranteed by the full faith and credit of the US. In other words, it became official: heads, they win; tails, taxpayers lose. And in return, taxpayers – in their capacity as bank customers – get a $35 charge if they inadvertently run up an overdraft with their debit card. They also face higher taxes and a greater likelihood of losing their jobs, savings, and homes. Meanwhile, J. P. Morgan and Goldman Sachs senior executives have resumed awarding themselves multimillion-dollar bonuses.

That glaring injustice is a consequence of policy. The money available to big banks from the Federal Reserve is virtually free. The spreads on most forms of bank lending are therefore well above average. Meanwhile, having been branded TBTF, the big banks can afford to take on even more risk than in the past. In the second quarter of this year, according to Value at Risk measures (for what little they are worth), the top five US banks stood to lose up to $1 billion on an average day in the second quarter – an 18 per cent increase in VaR compared with the same period last year and a 75 per cent increase on the first half of 2007 (Enrich and Paletta 2009). In rallying financial markets – such as we have seen since March 2009 – higher risk translates into higher reward: hence the large second-quarter profits reported by a number of big banks, most of which was derived from proprietary trading, rather than providing financial services to customers.

The lesson has apparently not been learned that VaR is a highly unreliable measure of risk. But why worry? None of the survivors is going to go the way of Lehman. The system, in other words, is more unstable than ever. This is moral hazard run mad – a system in which a few giant banks get to operate as hedge funds with a government guarantee that if they blow up, their losses will be socialized.

None of the regulatory reforms proposed so far do anything to address the central problem of the TBTFs. Consider, for example, the proposals outlined by Treasury Secretary Timothy Geithner in the summer of 2009:

- The Federal Reserve should become the 'system risk regulator' with power over certain institutions identified as 'systemically important', a.k.a. TBTFs. But wasn't it that already?
- The originators of securitized products should be required to retain 'skin in the game' (5 per cent of the securities they sell). What, the way Bear and Lehman did?
- There should be a new Consumer Financial Protection Agency. So what were the other regulatory agencies doing? Presumably protecting the TBTFs.
- There should be a new 'resolution authority' for the swift closing down of big banks that fail. But such an authority already exists and was used when Continental Illinois failed in 1984.
- And 'federal regulators should issue standards and guidelines to better align executive compensation practices of financial firms with long-term shareholder value'. It is hard to believe that a better system could be devised to achieve such an alignment than the system of compensating executives with shares or options to buy shares in their own companies. Yet not even the ownership of $1 billion of Lehman Brothers' stock deterred Dick Fuld from blowing up his own firm.

Among many omissions, it was especially striking that these proposals made no mention of the egregious role of the ratings agencies in supplying the banks with bogus AAA-rated securities.

Admittedly, Secretary Geithner went several steps further in his Congressional testimony of 23 September 2009:

- There will be a new National Bank Supervisor, merging the Office of the Comptroller of the Currency and the Office of Thrift Supervision. However, it appears that responsibility for regulating the TBTFs will lie elsewhere, by implication with the Federal Reserve or the Treasury, the institutions that have dominated the government response to the financial crisis.
- The administration intends to 'tighten constraints on leverage ... by requiring that all financial firms hold higher capital and liquidity buffers'. But TBTFs will be asked to do more, in at least two respects:
    - First, following a suggestion by the Governor of the Bank of England (King 2009), they will be asked to prepare 'living wills' – plans for how they should be 'dismantled in case of failure ... in a way that protects taxpayers and the broader economy while ensuring that losses are borne by creditors and other stakeholders'. These plans will be subject to 'careful evaluation ... on an ongoing basis' by 'supervisors'.

- Second, they will also be subject to 'very strong government oversight' in the form of a 'common framework of supervision and regulation'. The 'tough rules' would include not only the aforementioned increases in capital but also a 'comprehensive regulation' of the over-the-counter derivative markets to encourage the use of exchanges.

Some, though not all, of these proposals have found their way into the bill sponsored by Senator Christopher Dodd, which is now under discussion in the Senate. Lawmakers in both parties maintain that the legislation will not institutionalize Too Big To Fail institutions. It remains to be seen, however, whether the final bill will accept Paul Volcker's call for a return to the separation of commercial banking and investment banking along the lines of Glass-Steagall, which could mean banning banks from running proprietary trading desks, private equity partnerships, or hedge funds (Volcker 2009).

The regulatory debate in Europe has been different. Speaking in the House of Commons on 8 July 2009, Chancellor of the Exchequer Alistair Darling declared that he feared 'the consequences of telling a large bank that it is too big. In response to that, the bank might say, "We're too big, so we'll go somewhere else"' (UK Parliament 2009). Although prepared to countenance tighter regulation for big financial institutions, the British government made it clear in its White Paper of the same date that it was 'not persuaded that artificial limits should be placed on firms to restrict their size or complexity' (HM Treasury 2009). This sounds like a manifesto for the preservation of TBTF.

An alternative approach, floated by the head of the UK Financial Services Authority, Lord Turner, would be to levy a low but pervasive tax on all financial transactions (sometimes known as a 'Tobin tax'), a little like the stamp duty paid when a house changes hands, though at a much lower rate. Earlier in 2009 Lord Turner produced a different set of proposals for regulatory reform that focused on reducing bank leverage as well as varying rules on bank capital adequacy to make them counter-cyclical rather than pro-cyclical (Financial Services Authority 2009). A case could also be made for tightening anti-trust rules for the financial services sector, on the ground that the degree of concentration that has been attained in the banking system is inimical to financial stability, if not to competition. This is roughly the position of the EU Commissioner Neelie Kroes. Finally, a few economists on both sides of the Atlantic have begun arguing for 'narrow' or 'limited purpose' banking, which would limit the ability of deposit-taking institutions to engage in risky business.[6]

The post-crisis debate on financial regulation is now in full swing. There is, however, a danger that the essential goal – the euthanasia of the TBTFs – will vanish from sight as the number of proposals increases. So let us dismiss the various red herrings:

- Politicians like to focus on bankers' bonuses, because everyone can be shocked by the fact that Lloyd Blankfein, the Goldman CEO, gets paid

2,000 times what Joe the Plumber gets. But that differential is a symptom, not a cause, of the deep-rooted problem. The TBTFs are able to pay big bonuses because they reap all the benefits of risk-taking without running the ultimate risk of going bust. Regulating excessive compensation is certainly the most inefficient way of attacking the TBTFs.

- Raising transactions costs in the financial sector by means of a Tobin tax, even if there were a successful international agreement to do so in all markets, would help rather than hinder the TBTFs. It would be the biggest firms, exploiting economies of scale, who could most easily cope with such a change.
- Also a herring, though less red in hue, is Secretary Geithner's pledge to regulate the big banks more tightly at the level of the federal government. It is impossible to be impressed by such pledges when, as we have seen, it was the most regulated institutions in the financial system that were the most disaster-prone. It is more than a little convenient for America's political class to blame this financial crisis on deregulation and the resulting excesses of the free market. Not only does that neatly pass the buck. It also creates a justification for … more regulation. The old Latin question is apposite here: *quis custodiet ipsos custodes?* Who regulates the regulators? Until that question is answered, calls for more regulation are symptoms of the very disease they purport to cure.
- The most appealing fish on offer – but still a herring – is the idea of narrow or limited purpose banking. The problem with this is that it would turn the clock back not to the 1930s but to the 1650s – to the period before fractional reserve banking began to spread through the Western world. Though I am attracted to the intellectual elegance of the limited purpose model, in the end I am unpersuaded that we need to jettison so much of what financial evolution has achieved over three and a half centuries.

There is in fact one simple insight, buried in Secretary Geithner's testimony last year, upon which we need to build. Instead of trying to regulate each banker's compensation or to tax every dollar that moves in financial markets, governments merely need to clarify that public insurance applies only to bank deposits and that bank bondholders will no longer be fully protected, as they generally have been in this crisis. In other words, when a bank goes bankrupt, the creditors should take the hit, not the taxpayers. This is in fact the key to Secretary Geithner's testimony. As he clearly understands, the real aim of government should be to give the TBTFs 'positive incentives … to shrink and to reduce their leverage, complexity, and interconnectedness' (Geithner 2009). The best way of creating such incentives is to reiterate this key point: in case of failure, 'the largest, most interconnected firms' should in future be wound up 'in a way that protects taxpayers and the broader economy while ensuring that *losses are borne by creditors and other stakeholders*' (emphasis added). That was the principle that was thrown overboard in the crisis, when it was decided to prevent the holders of bank bonds (apart from those of Lehman Brothers) from losing their money or even suffering a 'haircut'.

Increasing the big banks' cost of capital by removing their TBTF status would at a stroke undermine their raison d'être. We can already see how this would work. At the recent G20 finance ministers' meeting there was an unequivocal call for the big banks to raise more capital and become less leveraged, albeit 'once recovery is assured', whenever that might be. Even this elicited protests from the bankers. Before the ink was dry on the G20 communiqué, J.P. Morgan published a report warning that proposed regulatory changes would reduce the profitability of the investment-banking operations of Deutsche Bank, Goldman, and Barclays by as much as a third. Such a reduction is in fact highly desirable.

There are of course various ways in which increasing the cost of capital might be achieved. David Moss has proposed having tighter capital adequacy, leverage, and liquidity standards for systemically important firms, as well as making them pay insurance premiums against future federal bailouts. They might also be required to hold a significant proportion of their debt in the form of convertible instruments, which would switch from debt into equity in a serious financial crisis. The aim, as Moss rightly says, should be to 'provide financial institutions with a strong incentive to avoid becoming systemically significant' (Moss 2009). The problem of course remains that a resolution fund, even if paid for by the banks, would quickly come to be regarded as a bailout fund.

In my view, the ideal must be to get rid of the TBTFs with less rather than more government intervention in the financial system. Explicit denial of future bailouts for bank bondholders ought to suffice, though Moss's penalties for TBTFs may be necessary to accelerate the process. The problem clearly remains that very large financial institutions can be very profitable for considerable periods of time before their risky strategies drive them into insolvency. Even after explicit changes to the rules, firms may be tempted to call the government's bluff, on the ground that posing a systemic risk should ensure a bailout. Despite being rivals, the TBTFs are also partners in crime, since the failure of one (as the case of Lehman made clear) threatens the survival of all.

VI

Having blinked once in the face of a systemic banking crisis, Western governments have a long fight on their hands to establish the credibility of 'no bailout' rules in the eyes of bank creditors. Yet that is not an argument for fatalism. It is an argument for emphatic action. The economies of the developed world simply cannot be left at the mercy of a gang of super-sized, government-sponsored megabanks. During the crisis it was often said that officials at the Federal Reserve and Treasury would do 'whatever it takes' to avoid a Great Depression. Now they must do whatever it takes to address one of the key causes of the financial crisis: the existence of financial institutions that consider themselves too big to fail – but which are run in such a way that they are bound sooner or later to do so. Such institutions not only pose a threat to the functioning of the free market system. By saddling taxpayers with mind-boggling bailout bills, they also pose a threat to its very legitimacy.

Notes

1 I am grateful to my colleagues at Harvard Business School for comments on earlier drafts and to one anonymous reader. All errors that remain are my own.
2 See for example Johnson (2009).
3 For the best statement of this case, see David Moss (2009), 'An Ounce of Prevention: The Power of Public Risk Management in Stabilizing the Financial System', Harvard Business School Working Paper, 09–087. The case against deregulation has been made more crudely by Paul Krugman in his *New York Times* column.
4 The HHI is the sum of banks' squared market shares (whether of deposits, assets or capital). The higher the value the greater the concentration. Typically it lies between a notional minimum of zero and a notional maximum of 10,000.
5 For a given portfolio, probability and time horizon, Value at Risk is a threshold value commonly expressed in the following way. A one-day 95 per cent VaR means that there is a 5 per cent probability that the portfolio will fall by more than, say, $1 million over a one-day period.
6 See for example Laurence J. Kotlikoff and John C. Goodman (2009), 'Solving Our Nation's Financial Crisis with Limited Purpose Banking', Boston University Working Paper', 15 April. See also John Kay (2009) 'Narrow Banking: The Reform of Banking Regulation', Centre for the Study of Financial Innovation.

References

Baumol, W. J and Blinder, A. S. (2008) *Economics: Principles and Policy*, India: Cengage Learning.

Beck, T., Demirgüç-Kunt, A., and Levine, R. (2003) 'Bank concentration and crises', NBER Working Paper 9921. Cambridge, MA: National Bureau of Economic Research.

Cipollini, A. and Fiordelisi, F. (2008) 'The impact of bank concentration on financial distress: The case of the European banking system', EMFI Working Paper 2. Denver, CO: Emerging Markets Finance International.

Enrich, D., and Paletta, D. (2009). 'Finance overhaul falters as '08 shock fades', *Wall Street Journal*, 9 September 2009.

Financial Services Authority (March 2009) *The Turner Review: A Regulatory Response to the Global Banking Crisis.* Available HTTP: www.fsa.gov.uk/Pages/Library/Corporate/turner/index.shtml

Geithner, T. F. (2009) 'Written Testimony on Financial Regulatory Reform', House Financial Services Committee, 23 September 2009.

HM Treasury (July 2009) *Reforming Financial Markets.* Available HTTP: www.hm-treasury.gov.uk/d/reforming_financial_markets080709.pdf

Johnson, S. (2009) 'The quiet coup', *Atlantic Monthly Online*, 1–4. www.theatlantic.com/doc/200905/imf-advice

Kaufman, H. (2009) *The Road to Financial Reformation: Warnings, Consequences, Reforms*, Hoboken, NJ: John Wiley & Sons.

Kay, J. (2009) 'Narrow banking: The reform of banking regulation', London: Center for the Study of Financial Innovation.

King, M. (2009) 'Blaming individuals is no substitute for acknowledging the failure of a system', *Financial Times*, 17 June.

Kotlikoff, L. J. and Goodman, J. C. (2009) 'Solving our nation's financial crisis with limited purpose banking,' Working Paper, Boston, MA: Boston University.

Lanchester, J. (2009) 'It's finished', *London Review of Books*, 31: 3–13.

Lenin, V. I. (1963) [1917] 'Imperialism, the highest stage of capitalism', in V. I. Lenin, *Collected Works*, vol. 22, Moscow: Progress Publishers.

Logan, A. (2004) 'Banking concentration in the UK', Bank of England, *Financial Stability Review*, 16: 129–35.

Masciandaro, D. (2005) *Handbook of Central Banking and Financial Authorities in Europe: New Architectures in the Supervision of Financial Markets*, Cheltenham: Edward Elgar.

Moss, D. (2009) 'An ounce of prevention: The power of public risk management in stabilizing the financial system', Working Paper 09-087, Cambridge, MA: Harvard Business School.

Rockoff, H. (2009) 'Upon Daedalian wings of paper money: Adam Smith and the crisis of 1772', Working Paper 15594, Cambridge, MA: National Bureau of Economic Research.

Steinberg, B., Dobrin, P., and Karniol-Tambour, K. (2009) 'A scan through the European banking picture', *Bridgewater Daily Observations*, 14 September.

Triana, P. (2009) *Lecturing Birds on Flying: Can Mathematical Theories Destroy the Financial Markets?* Hoboken, NJ: John Wiley & Sons.

UK Parliament (2009) *Parliamentary Business, 8 July 2009*. Available HTTP: www.parliament.the-stationeryoffice.co.uk/pa/cm200809/cmhansrd/cm090708/debtext/90708-0005.htm

Volcker, P.A. (2009) 'Statement before the Committee on Banking and Financial Services of the House of Representatives', 24 September.

Walter, I. (2004) *Mergers and Acquisitions in Banking and Finance: What Works, What Fails, and Why*, New York: Oxford University Press.

Book reviews

Tony Aspromourgos, *The Science of Wealth: Adam Smith and the Framing of Political Economy*

Routledge Studies in the History of Economics
London: Routledge, 2009, 396 pp.

ISBN Hardback: 978-0-415-46385-0

Reviewed by Jeffrey T. Young

Professor Aspromourgos's book is a welcome addition to contemporary Smith scholarship, particularly the almost forgotten realm of Smith's analytical economics. As economists and philosophers alike have discovered the richness and appeal of Smith's philosophical output in general and the moral philosophy in particular, interest in recent years has decidedly shifted in this direction. We have been more interested in the totality of Smith's works and the place of the WN within this larger system of social thought, and old controversies over the meaning of productive and unproductive labour, for example, have receded into the background. While recognizing the embeddedness of WN in his system of thought, Aspromourgos, nonetheless, insists that Smith's political economy, or science of wealth, is a 'distinct and separate intellectual discipline' (i). However, this book is more than just a critical review of Smith the economist. It is a major study of the totality of Smith's work from the perspective of an interpretation of his economics, both its scientific, analytical side, and its normative, policy making concerns. The author's method is to isolate thirteen key words and phrases (e.g. 'political economy', 'wealth', 'price', 'capital', etc.), group them into their appropriate place in the structure of WN, and then thoroughly investigate the meanings, historical genesis, and Smithian usage of these concepts. After a short introductory chapter, these four constitute the subject matter of the chapters of the book.

Given the scope of the project, it is not surprising that there are at least three books here, although at 396 pages the total is not excessive. There is an interpretation of Adam Smith as a 'surplus' theorist (more on this below). There is what I would call a 'word study' on the historical genesis of these terms and their evolution into the meanings they had in Smith as well as a study of their occurrence throughout all of Smith's known works. Lastly there is a parallel text in the 82 pages of endnotes, which can get quite tedious, as I found myself frequently having to flip back to the notes, read an extensive comment, and then discover that I had lost my place when I returned to the

The Adam Smith Review, 6: 343–358 © The International Adam Smith Society
ISSN 1743-5285, ISBN 0–415–66722–7

text itself. It is here, for example, that we find the invisible hand, which in my opinion exhibits good sense (although I would not relegate the associated concept of unintended consequences to the endnotes).

As an historian of economics, and as one who was once quite sympathetic to the surplus approach, I found the discussions of Smith's theories of value, distribution, and growth to be the most important part of the book. To understand the perspective which informs the author's understanding of Smith we must jump ahead to the year 1960. For it was in that year that Piero Sraffa of Trinity College, Cambridge, and one time colleague of John Maynard Keynes, published an enigmatic little book, *The Production of Commodities by Means of Commodities; Prelude to a Critique of Economic Theory.* While mainstream economists did not quite know how to react to it, Ronald Meek immediately recognized it as a 'rehabilitation of classical economics' (Meek 1961). Historically, then, the book pointed in both directions: to the past as an interpretation of Classical economics and to the future as an alternative to Neoclassical approaches to value, distribution, and growth. Sraffian economics quickly gained a following among Marxists, such as Maurice Dobb, and Post-Keynesians, such as Joan Robinson, and heated debates ensued between the Sraffians and mainstream Neoclassical economists such as Paul Samuelson and Robert Solow. The issues were technically complex, the competing articles mathematically rigorous, and the Sraffians I would say won the technical battle, but lost the war. Mainstream value and distribution theory are still anchored in axioms of rational choice under conditions of scarcity, and the concept of an aggregate production function still rules much of growth theory. Needless to say we cannot rehearse all of this in a short review in a journal such as the *Adam Smith Review.*

In brief the Sraffian model of an economic system is based on the idea of the social economy as continually reproducing itself with a surplus. Commodities produce commodities. If the commodity output exceeds the commodity input there is a surplus. In agriculture, for example, we might imagine workers producing food, which in turn becomes their subsistence for the next production cycle. If they produce more than they eat, there is a surplus to feed non-agricultural labour. If they work with fixed capital, tools, then the system must reproduce two commodities, food and tools. If the food and tools produced exceeds the food and tools needed to maintain labour and tools used up, then again there is a surplus. Production is a circular affair, the commodities are physical entities, and relation between input and output (how much food is needed to maintain the number of units of labour it takes to produce a unit of food, for example) is given. Under these conditions the technically determined relation between the commodity inputs and the commodity outputs determines the rates of exchange in a system where the food producers get their tools by selling food and buying tools in a market, and *vice versa* for the tool producers. Commodities such as food and tools in this simple example are called 'basics' since they enter into the production of all other commodities. Commodities which are produced but not used as means of production are 'nonbasics'. Now the significant feature of such a model is that the exchange ratios, values, are determined by the technical conditions of production. Demand plays no role, as evidenced by the fact that mathematically the system has no demand equations. Thus, the axioms of rational choice, the foundation of Neoclassical theory, play no role. This is why the Sraffian theory is said to be an 'objective' theory of value, while the Neoclassical is 'subjective'.

The affinity between this conception and a labour theory of value suggests the connection with Classical economics, especially Ricardo and Marx, while the idea of an agricultural surplus suggests the circular flow models of the French Physiocrats. If we think in terms of the labour time directly and indirectly embodied in each commodity, then under certain assumptions these technically given input requirements will determine the exchange ratios between goods. The surplus will be the difference between output measured in labour time and input measured in labour time, which Marx uses to develop his theory of exploitation of labour under capitalism. Once again there is no room for demand and rational choice; the technical requirements of production determine exchange ratios. The assumptions are fairly stringent and both Ricardo and Marx struggled to generalize the model. For Ricardo this meant finding a measure of absolute value that would be independent of the relative distribution between wages and profit, and for Marx it led to the famous 'transformation problem': the relationship between the technically determined labour embodied values and long run market prices under competitive capitalist conditions. According to Aspromourgos, Sraffa developed a 'genuinely satisfying formulation of the classical approach' (133). Meek also claimed that Sraffa had essentially solved the problems inherent in the labour theory approach, by doing away with labour embodied in favour of the physical quantities of commodities (Meek 1977: 133). I recognize that I have glossed over significant technical details of the analysis. I hope to at least to have conveyed some meaningful sense of some of the fundamentals.

The Sraffian system should be seen as a form of static general equilibrium model in which commodity inputs produce the same commodity output with a surplus. Once an institutional datum is brought in, such as an exogenously determined wage rate, prices are determined as is the distribution of the surplus between labour and capital. Its Classical pedigree can be found in the labour theories of Ricardo and Marx, as well as in the circular flow models of Quesnay's *Tableau Economique*, first published in 1758. Here we introduce another aspect of the Sraffian, Classical, and Marxian paradigm, namely the distinction between productive and unproductive labour. If the annual reproduction generates a surplus, then it would seem to make sense to suggest that the activities that are surplus-producing are 'productive' while those that are merely surplus consuming are 'unproductive'. Thus, we have a series of interconnected analytical concepts, which radically differentiate this approach from mainstream economics as it is taught and practised in most of the world today: a distinction between productive and unproductive labour, a concept of necessary vs. surplus production, an 'objective' vs. 'subjective' theory of value, and technically determined production requirements vs. rational actors on both the supply side and the demand side of the market.

That this constitutes a radically different conception of the economic system is not in doubt. A number of historians of economics, however, have disputed the Sraffian interpretation of Ricardo. Among these that of Samuel Hollander is probably the most extreme (Hollander 1979, 1987).[1] Marxists have generally been quite receptive to the Sraffian revision of the labour theory. Indeed Sraffa developed his model at least partly in an attempt to solve the Ricardian problem of a standard of value, and the very similar Marxian problem of the relation between value and price.[2] However, while Smith searched for a standard of value, his problem (converting nominal into real quantities) is not technically the same problem as Ricardo's, and Marx's problem of transforming labour values into prices of production finds no counterpart in Smith. Thus, placing Smith into this version of the Classical tradition in economics is problematic.

Let's consider two aspects of the interpretation Aspromourgos offers us in this book. First, consider the concept of the social surplus and the related problem of productive and unproductive labour. Second, consider the theory of natural price.

Smith's debt to the Physiocrats has been thoroughly explored in the secondary literature. There can be little doubt that WN Book II on capital accumulation and growth owes almost its entire existence to Smith's encounter with Physiocracy during his visit to France, 1764–66. Here we do indeed encounter the idea of a circular system of reproduction with a surplus, which if saved and invested in new fixed and circulating capital generates an upward spiral of rising national output. This is a profoundly important development in the history of economics, as ever since economic growth has been characterized as essentially a process of capital accumulation. The idea of net revenue is 'the important scientific development for economic theory in the eighteenth century' (156).

Moreover, in Book II we also find his famous, conflicting, definitions of productive labour as producing a material good, which endures after the act of creation, and producing value added. If services, such as those of an opera singer add value to the materials with which they work, they are productive in the value sense, but not in the material sense. However, there does seem to be a kernel of truth in the distinction. Workers who produce food seem to contribute something to the production process that servants of the rich do not. Perhaps Smith is really getting at the distinction between consumption and capital accumulation.

This is a real intellectual quagmire, which Aspromourgos proposes to solve using the Sraffian distinction between basics and nonbasics, which he defends against the charge of anachronism. The method of rational reconstruction, namely using later theoretical concepts and mathematical techniques to clarify and expound earlier theoretical work, is a matter of some controversy and considerable discussion among historians of economics. However, since modern approaches and techniques clearly came from somewhere there must be a sense in which such reconstructions do indeed help us grasp earlier analysis. In this case the problem is not so much an interpretive one. We know Smith's categories are contradictory, but we may want to salvage the productive/unproductive distinction in order to maintain the surplus concept. This is what Aspromourgos is doing here, showing that we can render the distinction coherent with Sraffa's concept of a basic.

> The coherent distinction is between commodities (and the associated labour) which are inputs to production in general, and commodities which contribute only to final (above-necessary or luxury) consumption. The labour of opera singers, and of Smith's menial servants, State personnel and so on, does not contribute to production of the former.
>
> (172)

This is true, provided that, 'attending opera performances is not itself part of necessary consumption or other inputs' (170). Aspromourgos concludes that,

> To the question – what kind of employments are capable of enabling the growth of national produce? – the answer, 'labour producing basics in the sense of Sraffa', is conceptually and analytically superior to the answer, 'productive labour in the sense of Smith'.
>
> (172)

Within the confines of the surplus approach this seems reasonable. I do not doubt that Smith was working within this conceptual framework in WN Book II, and I have no problem with the author's proposed reconstruction. I do not believe that this salvages the approach itself. The above quote begs the question, what do we include in 'national produce'? And what do we exclude? Are luxury goods and services part of output? If they are part of output the distinction disappears. If they are not, we are in the danger of making a circular argument. Basics contribute to the production of output, and output is defined as basics. As Helen Boss has argued, every economic theory must decide what constitutes output, i.e. what activities are considered part of the economic system, and what activities are outside of the system (Boss 1990: 5). Exchanges within the system are exchanges of equivalents, while exchanges from within to those without are transfer payments. Modern national income accounting, for example, treats government pension payments as transfers. Marx's theory of exploitation, based on the class monopoly of the capitalists over the means of production treats property income as transfer payments. Note that in each case there is a coercive institutional structure that accomplishes the transfer, since voluntary exchange presumably entails exchange of equivalents in some sense. Thus, voluntary exchange and one-way transfers do not seem to sit well together.

I do not think that the Sraffian categories have really solved the problem of services. If they are considered to be part of the national product, then producing them has to be productive by definition. If they are not part of the national product, the income of service producers must be treated as transfer payments. What is the transfer mechanism? If it is voluntary exchange then we are back into the conundrum. Services are immaterial, but value-creating.

Does this mean the surplus concept itself must be discarded? No, modern national income accounts distinguish between gross and net product, where the latter subtracts depreciation of physical capital. The difference between this and the surplus concept we have been discussing is that Classical surplus theory also subtracts off something for the maintenance of labour. This was the Classical concept of the subsistence wage, which is also included in Sraffa's basics. The idea is of a bundle of physical goods, food, necessary to maintain labour and allow for reproduction of the population. While Classical economists including Marx all conceived of this bundle as socially determined, not bare biological subsistence, the important point for the structure of Classical theory was that this was exogenously given, a sort of technical coefficient of the production process. Absent such a fixed constant, at the macroeconomic level the Classical surplus is no different from the standard definition used today in macroeconomic accounting as well as in Neoclassical growth models.[3] The idea that there is this separate and radically different 'surplus' approach seems to break down.

Consider the opera singer again. If consuming the services are part of the bundle of necessary consumption of those who produce the basics, then on the argument outlined above, opera singing is productive, a basic commodity. The question is absurd in a Classical world where the positive checks to population growth hold the population in equilibrium. However, in the modern world where government-determined poverty levels might be seen as constituting the socially determined subsistence bundle, this bundle is hardly just the material goods of food, clothing, and shelter. Nearly everyone below the poverty line has a television set, many have computers with internet access, and I'm sure they go to the movies once in awhile. Services do indeed enter into any conception of necessary consumption in modern economies. Whatever portion of the national income is used to 'maintain labour', it must be very small relative to the total income, and contain a wide variety of goods and services, such that it would be impossible to determine how much of the consumption of the services of television and movie actors, for example, is necessary and how much is not. Moreover, once we allow that some service production is productive, we must admit that all service production is also productive. Eliminating the concept of a subsistence standard of living was not a retrograde development in the history of economics.

What about Adam Smith? He certainly understood the Malthusian population dynamics under subsistence conditions, i.e. where the positive checks dominated. 'It is not uncommon, I have been frequently told, in the Highlands of Scotland for a mother who has borne twenty children not to have two alive' (WN I.viii.38, p. 97). Then after explaining the population dynamics he concludes that, 'It is in this manner that the demand for men, like that for any other commodity, necessarily regulates the production of men; quickens it when it goes on too slowly, and stops it when it advances too fast' (WN I.viii.40, p. 98). However, Smith does not have a fully developed Classical subsistence wage theory. The long-run trajectory for labour's real standard of living depends on whether the stationary, progressive, or declining state scenario prevails. Moreover, at a point in time there is nothing like a socially determined subsistence wage toward which actual wages are converging. Rather there is a whole structure of relative wages, which depends on differential investments in human capital, differential risks of success in various occupations, social status of occupations, and so on.

Now this structure is natural in the sense that these differentials would exist even in the absence of policy interventions in the labour market. It would also seem to be determined by the interaction of supply and demand, and, furthermore, inherently subjective elements, such as risk assessment enter into the decision to acquire education.[4]

This leads us into a consideration of Smith's price theory, and Aspromourgos's interpretation of it. Here I will try to be brief, as I have published elsewhere much of what I would want to say here (Young 1997). Recall that in Sraffian economics relative prices, or values, are determined by given technical requirements of a circular system of reproduction in which 'equilibrium' prices are those which insure the reproductive viability of the system. Mathematically there is a determinate set of prices, given the wage, in the absence of any specification of consumer demand preferences. Smith is placed within this conceptual universe. 'In relation to the role of demand [in the adjustment of market price to natural price], it is important that his competitive process does not depend upon such onerous assumptions as are entailed by demand functions' (133). Now there seems to me to be a very subtle, and complicated point of interpretation. No less an authority on Smith than Andrew Skinner (1974: 92) has used a supply and demand *graph* to explain the logic of Smith's adjustment process. But Aspromourgos is talking about supply and demand *functions* derived from the axioms of Neoclassical consumer theory. I certainly agree that such a theory of rational behaviour cannot be ascribed to Smith. However, I would make two points. First Smith's text implicitly assumes that higher prices entail fewer sales, and *vice versa* all other things unchanged. When set in graphical form there is a downward sloping demand curve. Second, Smith's text also implicitly assumes that natural price does not vary with output, so the supply curve is flat. The independence of price from demand rests on this implicit assumption, which Neoclassical theory treats as a special case. It does not arise from a Sraffian notion of reproduction with given technical coefficients.

Recall that the true historical antecedent to Sraffian price theory is the labour theory of value. It is not surprising, then, that the place where we do find technical requirements of production determining relative prices is in Smith's depiction of the early and rude state.

> In that early and rude state of society which precedes both the accumulation of stock and the appropriation of land, the proportion between the quantities of labour necessary for acquiring different objects seem to be the only circumstance which can afford any rule for exchanging them for one another. If among a nation of hunters, for example, it usually costs twice the labour to kill a beaver which it does to kill a deer, one beaver should naturally exchange for or be worth two deer. It is natural that what is usually the produce of two days or two hours labour, should be worth double of what is usually the produce of one day's or one hour's labour.
>
> (WN I. vi.1, p. 65)

The technical requirement of one hour to hunt a deer and two to hunt a beaver determines the exchange ratio, independently of demand. However, Smith immediately qualifies what he just said.

> If the one species of labour should be more severe than the other, some allowance will naturally be made for this superior hardship and the produce of one hour's labour in the one way may frequently exchange for that of two hours labour in the other.
>
> (WN I.vi.2, p. 65)

Severity of labour introduces a subjective element, which in turn undermines the idea that technical requirements will alone be sufficient data to determine relative prices.[5] However, the subjectivity that is involved here is not that of the rational utility maximizer. In the previous chapter Smith talks of 'toil and trouble' in the context of justifying his labour command standard of value (WN I.v.2, p. 47), and 'time and pains' (LJA i.37, p. 17) appears in his explanation of the origin of property rights. Now, I would claim that the subjectivity here has to do with the judgments of the impartial spectator who sympathetically enters into the labourer's claim to a right of possession in this context, and the claim to be rewarded for greater 'severity' of labour, as well as to an equivalent reward for deer compared to beaver hunting. These thoughts take us way beyond the scope of a book review into alternative readings of the value theory material in Smith. Suffice it to say at this point that, I believe there is an interpretive pathway through Smith, which is both non-Sraffian and non-Neoclassical. It is non-Sraffian in that it does deploy a form of supply and demand analysis, and it does incorporate subjective elements. It is non-Neoclassical in that it does not rest on the axioms of rational choice when it comes to modelling human behaviour, although rationality in the form of prudence is a cardinal Smithian virtue.

This is an intellectually stimulating book. It does for the Sraffian school what Samuel Hollander's work does for the mainstream. It requires us to rethink some of the most fundamental issues in economics, issues which all too frequently are glossed over. It is a major study of Smith's political economy. While I have focused my attention on some points of economic theory, the book is a comprehensive overview of all of the central themes in that political economy. This is probably the most ambitious and thorough reading of Smith from the Sraffian perspective, and as such it deserves to be carefully and widely read. I recommend it for Smith scholars and historians of economics generally, particularly those in parts of the world where Sraffian economics is virtually unknown. It is in many ways a plausible, although I think ultimately flawed, approach to Smith.

Notes

1 By 'extreme' I do not mean 'outrageous' or 'outlandish'. I simply mean to indicate that Hollander is one of the staunchest defenders of the 'single paradigm' view of the history of economics and a strong opponent of Sraffa's interpretation of Ricardo. Elsewhere I have written a very positive assessment of Hollander's work, which I will not revisit here (Young 2001).

2 Joan Robinson asserts that, 'it [*Production of Commodities*] is the Marscian [*sic*] c+v+s with particular emphasis on c', and that Sraffa was a 'devoted Marxist' (Robinson 1978). The latter comment is a marginal note she wrote in copy of my doctoral dissertation.

3 As is well known, English Classical economists used Malthusian population dynamics to set the subsistence wage, while Marx developed the theory of the reserve army of the unemployed. As is less well known, Malthus and Ricardo were well aware that the population dynamics assumed that the preventive checks to population growth were absent or weak, leaving the positive checks of disease, war, and famine, to do the job of maintaining population equilibrium. In a population where preventive checks prevail, the subsistence/luxury distinction breaks down, and the surplus concept becomes problematic. This was a result that the Classical economists were well aware of, and even hoped would happen.

4 Not only does subjectivity enter into the picture, but also Smithian agents are not the rational maximizers of Neoclassical theory. Natural confidence in one's own ability leads to an over-supply of entrants into certain professions (WN I.x.b.23).

5 On this point I think Aspromourgos too quickly dismisses 'toil and trouble' or the 'pains' of labour as 'empirically empty psychologizing' (96) on the grounds that they do not represent, 'a homogeneous substance which could provide a unit or standard for measurement' (298, n55; I might also note that my work [Young 1997] is cited here, and I would refer the reader to the arguments I have made there about the subjectivity of Smith's conception of cost). Isn't 'substance' in this context a throwback to Aristotelian and Scholastic metaphysics?

Bibliography

Boss, Helen (1990) *Theories of Surplus and Transfer*, Boston: Unwin Hyman

Hollander, S. (1979) *The Economics of David Ricardo*, Toronto: University of Toronto Press.

——(1987) *Classical Economics*, Oxford: Basil Blackwell.

Meek, R. L. (1961) 'Mr. Sraffa's rehabilitation of classical economics', *Scottish Journal of Political Economy*, 8(2): 119–36.
——(1977) *Smith, Marx, and After*, London: Chapman and Hall.
Robinson, J. (1978) Letter to the author, dated 11 October.
Skinner, A. S. (1974) 'Introduction', in A. S. Skinner (ed.) A. Smith, *The Wealth of Nations Books I–III*, Harmondsworth: Penguin Books.
Smith, A. (1976) *An Inquiry into the Nature and Causes of the Wealth of Nations*, (eds) R. H. Campbell and A. S. Skinner, Oxford: Oxford University Press; Glasgow edition. Reprinted, Liberty Press (1981).
——(1978) *Lectures on Jurisprudence*, (eds) R. L. Meek, D. D. Raphael and P. G. Stein, Oxford: Oxford University Press; Glasgow edition. Reprinted, Liberty Press (1982).
Sraffa, Piero (1960) *Production of Commodities by Means of Commodities; A Prelude to a Critique of Economic Theory*, Cambridge: Cambridge University Press.
Young, J. T. (1997) *Economics as a Moral Science: The Political Economy of Adam Smith*, Cheltenham: Edward Elgar.
——(2001) 'From Adam Smith to John Stuart Mill: Samuel Hollander and the classical economists', in S. G. Medema and W. J. Samuels (eds) *Historians of Economics and Economic Thought: The Construction of Disciplinary Memory*, London and New York: Routledge, pp. 129–65.

AUTHOR'S RESPONSE

Tony Aspromourgos's response to review by Jeffrey T. Young

I am most grateful to Jeffrey Young for providing such a lengthy review of my book, and for his commendation of much of it. I am surprised, however, by how much he wishes to talk about matters other than Smith – in particular, the interpretation of classical economics (supposedly) associated with Sraffa. Young devotes a far greater proportion of his review to these matters than does my book. I cite, quote or discuss Sraffa on fifteen of the 354 pages of the text proper, and some of these are about post-Smithian developments rather than the interpretation of Smith. I do not have the space to respond to all Young's comments on these wider matters. But since his commentary on Sraffa-related issues informs his views on some parts of my interpretation of Smith, I offer some response on these as well.[1] Furthermore, as a matter of preference, I would rather focus on 'Smith *before* Sraffa' (paraphrasing the title of Ian Steedman's well-known book).

I may also add here, without further comment, that a large part of my book (approximately 35 per cent) is devoted to the 'prehistory' of Smith's concepts in earlier literature, back to the earliest times, a fact which could easily be lost on readers of the review. Similarly, my chapters 2 and 5 – addressing respectively Smith's conception of the character of political economy as a science, and his understanding of the purpose and content of policy, and its relation to theory – are hardly touched upon by Young, who focuses on chapters 3 and 4 (the 'economic theory' parts, one might say). My Epilogue also addresses Smith's enduring relevance.

Sraffa, Smith and classical economics

Young's characterization of Sraffa's theory, and Sraffa's (to a considerable extent, only implied) conception of classical economics, is I think in some respects insufficiently nuanced. I nowhere suggest that 'demand' has no role to play in Smith's price theory, and I think it is also not true that '[d]emand plays no role' (Young) in Sraffa's price theory, or in that of other classical economists more widely.[2] In Sraffa's 1960 book one element of the data of price determination is the gross outputs of the economic system. Since he is evidently theorizing a decentralized capitalist economy, it may be taken for granted that the gross outputs are those that satisfy the system's aggregate demands for commodities. Hence, so long as technical input–output ratios or coefficients depend upon the scale of outputs, which in general will be true, prices depend indirectly on demand. This is obvious also in Ricardo, for example, via the dependence of the price-determining production method for agricultural output (or 'corn') upon the extent of cultivation, in turn a function of the demand for agricultural outputs. It is likewise evident in Smith, since his natural prices are defined by reference to output levels which satisfy 'effectual demand'. And it is very explicit in Smith that changes in the scale of outputs (a function of demand or 'extent of the market') in general lead to technical change via changing division of labour, as well as there being a role for natural scarcities to alter production methods as some categories of outputs expand (81–82, 91–93, 136–39).[3]

Young also suggests that in Sraffa's theoretical construction, and in at least some of the classical economists, absence of a role for demand means that there is also 'no room for ... rational choice'; 'the axioms of rational choice ... play no role'. Further on, he also agrees with me, that in a certain sense, the latter-day marginalist ('neoclassical') 'theory of rational behaviour cannot be ascribed to Smith' (Young). To state my view more precisely, Smith's approach does not partake of the peculiar form of methodological individualism associated with modern general equilibrium theory (including autonomous preferences), and with marginalism generally – or any other form of methodological individualism.

But let us not push this too far. The tendency towards a uniform net rate of return on capital – in Smith, the classical economists generally, and Sraffa – entails a form of economic rationality on the part of the decision-makers allocating capital: pursuit of the highest available returns. I explain that this is a weaker or more elementary form of rationality than that of marginalism (258–59, 261, 267); but it *is* a form of rationality. The tendency also for rates of remuneration more generally, and commodity prices, to tend towards uniformity (again, in Smith, the classical economists generally, and Sraffa) entails that this kind of rationality is also more widely operative than merely in the behaviour of the 'capitalists'.

This elementary economic rationality holds even for classical writers who subscribe in some sense or other to the labour theory of value, notwithstanding Young's suggestion that if 'labour time … determine[s] the exchange ratios between goods … there is no room for demand and rational choice'. Acceptance of the labour theory does not render such elementary rationality superfluous. Ricardo and Marx endorse the labour theory under conditions in which prices are proportional to capital advanced (due to that elementary rationality) – *and* capital advanced is proportional to labour time required to produce commodities. The labour theory is also consistent with demand influencing value, so long as scale influences input–output ratios and hence, labour time required to produce commodities.

In any case, the subject of the labour theory of value is an unhelpful and irrelevant digression, especially in relation to Smith. As a matter of logic, the labour theory is not necessary to surplus approaches to the theory of income distribution. One need only mention (before Smith) Quesnay and Turgot. Neither had anything resembling a labour theory of value, while clearly theorizing income distribution in terms of necessary input or cost, versus a freely disposable surplus output or net revenue.[4] Smith likewise has no recourse to a labour theory of value in relation to commodity prices in commercial society (and I nowhere suggested any different). To echo a point I made in my opening paragraph, let us focus on Smith *before* Ricardo and Marx. Smith at least had the benefit of reading Quesnay and Turgot.

Smith's economic theory

The two key issues Young raises, more directly relating to my interpretation of Smith, in the latter part of the review, are the productive/unproductive labour distinction and associated concept of surplus; and the role of supply and demand in relation to price theory. In both cases, Young's own earlier interpretation of Smith's treatment of wage differentials is brought into play.

Actually, with regard to the former, Young concludes that he has 'no problem with [my] … reconstruction' of the productive/unproductive distinction. His argument seems to be with the surplus approach itself, rather than with the proposition that Smith operated within that framework (at least in Book II of the *Wealth of Nations*). Space does not allow a full response to this more general issue. Young's somewhat convoluted arguments concerning whether or not luxuries and services are outputs, and whether voluntary exchange is compatible with the notion of a social surplus, seem to me merely semantic and therefore to miss the mark. The distinction between labour that produces capital (which for Smith includes the wages of productive labour and acquired labour skills), and labour that produces surplus consumption, is the coherent form of Smith's distinction (170). This is also the view of Eltis (1984: 77–78) – not a 'Sraffian', though a scholar with a deep sympathy for classical economics. It is a distinction still meaningful today.

Young's further suggestion, that the surplus approach requires a notion of subsistence labour consumption, is more pertinent. But it is not at all necessary that this subsistence be 'a fixed constant' (Young). As I often have to tell students, in relation to the notion of exogenous variables, the only thing truly constant is God; everything else changes, usually for the worse. Nor does preserving the notion of the social surplus require denying that, today, services enter into subsistence consumption, nor denying that anything else does. And it is not the case that if 'some service production is productive' (*sic*; not quite the same thing as being part of necessary consumption), then 'all service production is … productive' (Young). Two simple points may be made in the face of all this. The proposition that most wage-rates in mixed economies today are well above subsistence level *presupposes* that 'subsistence' remains an empirically meaningful concept. Second, labour as much needs to be reproduced or 'replaced', by way of consumption that sustains its capacity to undertake labour activities, as depreciating capital goods (in the modern sense) need to be replaced – as true in 2011 as it was in 1776.

What is really at stake here, with regard to 'surplus' approaches to income distribution? In relation to the sense in which Smith's theory of distribution is in this tradition, Young is silent on my interpretation of Smith on income taxation (197–201), which provides vital evidence. The key question with regard to remunerations is whether they are a necessary payment in order for the associated contribution to production to be enabled or to be forthcoming.

Putting aside land-rents and surplus wages and taking the case of profits in particular, Smith decomposes profit rates into premia for 'risk and trouble' versus the pure rate of return on capital as such. He then makes clear that the pure profits are not a necessary payment, in the sense of being required in order for the capital to be forthcoming, and are therefore a taxable surplus – even though he adds some further practical considerations for why such taxation might be difficult or undesirable. In other words, the pure rate of profit is not a necessary remuneration. By contrast, the general rate of interest in later marginalist theory is conceived of as the necessary cost (at least at the margin) to ensure that saving (or the supply of capital) is forthcoming in sufficient quantity to balance investment (or the demand for capital), in an equilibrium entailing full employment of resources. One significant implication of this is that what 'is appropriable by taxation is also privately appropriable, via shifts in the bargaining power which governs the distribution of private income, as Smith makes clear himself' (202).

This illustration from Smith's treatment of profits may usefully be contrasted with Young's suggestion that a 'surplus' exists in modern economics, in the form of the net product of national income accounting. But a 'net product' may not be a surplus in the classical sense. The key issue is whether this net product is available for free disposal. Smith's pure profits can be redistributed to tax revenues (or to higher real wages if the balance of bargaining power around the labour contract shifts) because they are not a necessary cost of production. But in modern marginalist theory, the net product in the national accounting sense is *not* conceived of as available for free disposal in the same sense, because under competitive conditions, there are 'necessary' rates of return to *all* factors of production, including both labour and capital (at least at the margin), such as to bring forth the requisite quantities of factors to ensure the equilibrium of the economic system. Competition fully determines functional income distribution, with no scope for wider social forces to play any role.

It may be added, with regard to the question discussed above, as to whether subsistence labour consumption is relevant to modern economies, that even if human beings could subsist on fresh air, and only, say, capital and intermediate inputs used up had to be netted out of the gross product to arrive at the net product or value-added, the notion of a contestable freely disposable surplus would remain, in a classical framework.

I made the point earlier, that 'demand' certainly plays a role in Smithian and wider classical price theory. Demand 'functions' or demand 'curves' (Young: 'graphs'), on the other hand, are not at all to be found in Smith (77–90). Young suggests that I imply a 'subtle' point of distinction here. That is partly right. I have responded on this issue elsewhere (Aspromourgos 2008; in relation to a version of part of Chapter 3 of my book) and so can avoid using up space on it here, except to make this point. Demand *functions* bring out most clearly the strong assumptions required to sustain the marginalist notion of how demand enters into the determination of equilibrium prices. But do demand *curves* require less strong assumptions; or is it just that by drawing a mere 'cartoon' diagram of the function (a diagram which might be mistaken for mere 'common sense'), the question of what is required to make this notion coherent can be avoided? It is true, as Young says (and I say: 86–87), that responsiveness of aggregate market demand to market prices is required for Smith's price theory; more precisely, it is required to ensure that disequilibrium market prices are bounded from above and below. But this proposition does not require well-defined demand functions or curves.

In short, to say that demand enters into the determination of natural or equilibrium prices does not mean that demand functions or curves (and most particularly, autonomous individual preferences) are sensible constructs as parameters for the theory of equilibrium prices – and Smith has no such functions. Such lack of recourse to demand functions is only reinforced if conventional supply functions (rising 'supply-prices') are also absent. It is the *combination* of demand functions with such conventional supply functions which gives the seductive but spurious symmetry of the supply-and-demand approach to equilibrium price theory. At one point Young asserts that for Smith 'natural price does not vary with output' (wrong, except, perhaps, for disequilibrium variations of outputs: 91–93), so that 'the supply curve is flat': hence, the 'independence of price from demand' (wrong) is due to conditions that latter-day marginalism 'treats as a special case'. In fact, the marginalist normal case of rising supply-price is due to the (spurious) marginal productivity theory of distribution, which is not to be found in Smith (93–94). If that theory is rejected in favour of a surplus approach, conventional supply functions are deprived of their theoretical foundation.

With regard to Young's perception of Smith's theory of competitive wage differentials, on the one hand, Young thinks that because there is in Smith's text 'a whole structure of relative wages, which depends on differential investments in human capital, differential risks ... , social status ... and so on', that this somehow undermines the idea of a social surplus in Smith's economics. He does not explain and I do not see how. My account of Smith's theory of wages suggests that even the lowest paid labourers can be earning above-subsistence wages in commercial society (98–99, 199–201). If *they* can share in the social surplus, there is no problem in other categories of occupations taking even larger shares. In some cases these higher wages are due to sociological factors; but in others, they are a return on capital invested in skill acquisition, or a premium for risk-bearing. The latter are more akin to necessary costs of production.

On the other hand, Young thinks that Smith's treatment of wage differentials demonstrates a role for 'supply and demand' and 'subjective elements' in wage determination, and hence by implication, in production costs and natural commodity prices. This, he supposes, 'undermines the idea that technical requirements will alone be sufficient data to determine relative prices' – and by implication, undermines my interpretation of Smith's natural prices. But it is, I think, analytically clear that: (a) the natural prices depend upon production methods *plus* natural rates of remuneration to land, labour and capital; (b) with heterogeneous labour, there will be multiple natural wage rates; and (c) natural prices remain determinate since the wage differentials are independent of natural prices. This is my view of the issue.[5] Which of these three propositions would Young care to claim is not shared by Smith?

Even if this resolution of the role of wage differentials in relation to Smithian natural prices is accepted, it might still be asked: what, nevertheless, determines those differentials which are given for the purposes of determining natural prices? Are there 'subjective' determinants? It doesn't much matter, to me or for the role of surplus. Whatever psychological phenomena might be in play here they do not seem 'subjective' in the sense of being grounded in individually idiosyncratic and autonomous preferences, in the manner of latter-day marginalist theory, and I am glad to see that in his penultimate paragraph, Young seems to agree.

Conclusion

While it might be too much to expect that this response will put an end to the disagreements between Professor Young and myself, I may hope that my comments narrow the gap between us – and perhaps also, that the reader might even prefer my side on those issues where we continue to disagree on the meaning of Smith's text. But in any case, on these important matters let us continue such civil conversation as this.[6]

Notes

1 My silence concerning other of Young's Sraffa-related comments should not be read as acquiescence in them.
2 I indicate 'Young' in parentheses when quoting his review.
3 Throughout, I cite my book by way of just page numbers in parentheses.
4 Young quotes me as saying net revenue is 'the important scientific development for economic theory in the eighteenth century' (156). The context indicates that I intended merely that it is the most important development *of a revenue concept*, at the societal level.
5 I nowhere suggested that 'technical requirements' alone determine Smith's natural prices.
6 Young does allow himself a mild touch of rudeness though, when he comments on my dismissal of Smith's appeal to 'toil and trouble', as not representing 'a homogeneous substance which could provide a unit or standard for measurement' (298): 'Isn't "substance" in this context a throwback to Aristotelian and Scholastic metaphysics?' (Young). On the one hand measurement *does* require homogeneity. On the other, my sarcasm here was evidently too subtle: I was precisely meaning to lampoon the idea that there could be a substance such as 'disutility' (or its opposite for that matter).

Bibliography

Aspromourgos, T. (2008) 'Demand and Smith's price theory: a rejoinder', *History of Economic Ideas*, 16: 125–29.

Eltis, W. A. (1984) *The Classical Theory of Economic Growth*, London: Macmillan.

Magali Bessone and Michaël Biziou (eds), *Adam Smith philosophe. De la morale à l'économie ou philosophie du libéralisme*

Rennes: Presses Universitaires de Rennes, 2009, 220 pp.

ISBN Paperback 978-2-7535-0785-2

Reviewed by Sergio Cremaschi

This is a collection of seven essays by French Adam Smith scholars with three papers by Anglo-American scholars. At least two among the latter, originally invited lectures at an Adam Smith workshop in Paris, are strictly related to each other, since they deal with the relationship of state and civil society. Donald Winch in 'Civil Society and the State in Adam Smith' adds some useful comments to what he has been writing on Smithian politics since the 1970s. He shows how the dichotomy state–civil society is absent from Smith and how the ideas of the homo oeconomicus and the autonomy of the economy are still to come. Winch then examines Smith's peculiar idea of politics as a special kind of prudence, the virtue of a legislator who has to be able to cope with the ebbs and flows of society while keeping in view the common good with a kind of reasonableness that is almost the opposite of the attitude of the man of system. Knud Haakonssen's 'Adam Smith and Civil Society' sets out to prove how Smith's discussion of morality, justice, and government does not 'forerun' eighteenth-century discussion of the opposition between the state and civil society, but also that his own occasional use of the term civil society shares very little with the meaning current in his century and that even his discussion of government has little to do with any notion of the state qua juridical subject. I would say that neither Winch nor Haakonnsen would understand their own contributions in terms of a discussion of Adam Smith's 'liberalism', one key-word casting in the book's title and discussed at length in Biziou's paper. The third invited lecture is 'Justice and Market according to Adam Smith' by Charles Griswold, who summarizes what he had said on justice in his book.

Coming to the French papers, Magali Bessone discusses Smith's theory of penal justice, arguing that it is partly 'utilitarian' and partly anti-utilitarian, punishment being partly justified by the moral sentiment of resentment. Michaël Biziou discusses Smith's views on the relationship between merchants and master-manufacturers and the working poor. Arguing quite appropriately that Smith's argument in favor of the system of natural liberty was far from an argument from efficiency, being rather a moral argument for institutional

The Adam Smith Review, 6: 359–366 © The International Adam Smith Society
ISSN 1743-5285, ISBN 0–415–66722–7

arrangements which would foster the re-establishment of a fairer balance of power in favor of the less privileged class, and besides that, if applying the same approach to contemporary society Smith would probably argue for more active intervention by the state aimed at protecting the poor. This is fair enough, and indeed it has been illustrated by Winch and more recently by Fleischacker (2004) and others, but it seems to the present reviewer that this is not just a proof that Smithian 'economic liberalism' was a normative doctrine to be contrasted with positive doctrines such as Chicago-School kinds of 'liberalism' fancy they are, but rather demonstrates that Smith's political views were not primarily liberal ones. What Winch's and Haakonssen's papers show is that Smith's agenda was a different one, and that it could be better described, in the reviewer's words, in terms of 'disenchanted Republicanism' (Cremaschi 1989).

Another group of papers discusses Smith's moral theory. François Calori treats Smith's relationship to Hutcheson; Claude Gautier compares Hume and Smith on sympathy; Vanessa Nurock also discusses the notion of sympathy and Eléanor Le Jallé compares Hume and Smith on the admiration for the rich and powerful as well as on the opposite sentiment of envy.

A reviewer is expected to discuss and criticize at least something in a book and so, in order to be fair to everybody, let me proceed randomly, discussing at length the paper which happens to come first in the table of contents. Philippe Hamou, 'History of Science Naturalized: Adam Smith from the History of Astronomy to Moral Sentiments' (pp. 19–36) is an examination of the *History of Astronomy* which concludes that Adam Smith's view of natural science makes it consist in the reduction of particular phenomena to general principles and that he works out his own moral theory on the basis of this very model of a scientific theory. He also claims that such a view of science is reached by Smith through an historical approach that resembles Kuhn's, and an attempt at naturalizing science that foreruns Quine's, and yet this attempt co-exists with that 'meta-sceptical dimension' which, according to Hamou, has been appropriately highlighted by Griswold (p. 36).

The first comment is that Hamou for some reason seems to have chosen to ignore all the secondary sources on Smith's epistemology apart from Raphael (1977). That is Moscovici (1956); Becker (1961); Thompson (1965); Megill (1975); Wightman (1975); Skinner (1979); Cremaschi (1981, 1984, 1989, 2000); Freudenthal (1982); Hetherington (1983); Fiori (2001); Montes (2004); and Schliesser (2005).

The second point is that one claim in the paper, namely that Smith wanted to naturalize epistemology along the lines later designed by Quine (p. 30), is indeed original but it is mistaken. One could object to this claim on three grounds. First, Bittermann (1940) claimed that Smith could be read as a logical-empiricist, Campbell (1971) assumed that his methodology was Popperian, Lindgren (1973) that Smith was a 'forerunner' of Thomas Kuhn and Peter Winch, and Brown (1988) discovered striking similarities between Smithian and Lakatosian methodologies. Such a story should have made

Hamou wary that his own could turn out to be one more anachronistic reading into Smith of the latest epistemological fashion. Second, an attempt at reducing natural science to a production of the imagination sounds prima facie like a strong anti-realist program with a rather heavy commitment to epistemological subjectivism. Quine's program instead was that of dropping the Cartesian subject–object opposition (allegedly still haunting both analytic philosophy of science and such Continental schools as phenomenology) in order to study the production of science as one more natural phenomenon among others. Thus, the reader is likely to find in the *History of Astronomy* more a piece of Rortian post-modernism than any manifesto for a naturalization program. Third, according to a not too uncommon diagnosis concerning fin-de-siècle philosophy, Quine's was one among several attempts at getting rid of the last vestiges of Cartesianism still left after two centuries critique starting with Condillac, d'Alembert, Hume, and the Scottish philosophy as a whole (Cremaschi 2000), and reaching Peirce, Dewey, and the post-empiricist philosophy of science. Smith's character in the plot may have been that of a scout trying, and failing to find, a way out of the Cartesian subject's conundrums. The reviewer's own wild conjecture is that the main reason for having his own manuscripts burnt was that he was aware of such a failure, and believed that in such papers the reader would have found 'more refinement than solidity'.

A third point is that Hamou's main conclusion, namely that both in his philosophy of the natural sciences and in his moral epistemology Smith ends up with a stalemate, is correct but not original. Hamou writes that in both epistemology and ethics

> the issue of relativism comes to the fore, and in both cases I would say that Smith leaves us without an answer to the question asked, by suggesting more than once that on principle he does not endorse the relativist's claims, that he even rejects them, but without offering us the means for understanding how we could escape relativist claims. This holds true for the sciences […] And it is apparently the same in the domain of morality.
>
> (p. 35)

This brings us back to the 'more refinement than solidity' clause, which Hamou would have better quoted, and which had been quoted by Moscovici who, while pronouncing Hamou's own conclusion, had remarked that there is

> a twofold aspect of the Newtonian theory, namely that of a system of nature that the mind may view as its own creation, and that of a tool useful to everyday life, trade, navigation, and yet this twofold aspect is not yet a splitting into two. And while the instrumental dimension of other systems has gotten lost to the point that we tend to think that it never existed, Newton's is still too much present, it is actually the present

> time. We cannot be sure that Adam Smith did clearly bring to the fore such a conundrum, but for sure he did sense it.
>
> (Moscovici 1956: 10)

Moscovici added that 'we meet in his historical considerations the idea, that one is tempted to label Pascalian, that the system may be wholesale true if it is not true at retail price' (Moscovici 1956: 18–19). The impasse diagnosed by Moscovici is the point which the present writer took as his own starting-point, thanks to the not-too-extraordinary skill of reading French, which has apparently disappeared among Anglo-American scholars, while trying to add something, for example the conclusion that Smith

> while leaving The History of Astronomy unfinished, apparently felt [...] that it was impossible to account for the historical phenomenon 'science' as precomprehended by our culture, so far as the Cartesian presuppositions are accepted. The separation of the order of ideas from the order of things and the atomistic nature of phenomena (which makes the individual phenomenon unintelligible) are presuppositions that make it impossible to acknowledge any kind of rationality in the history of science, or to formulate any idea of the truth of scientific theories that makes sense.
>
> (Cremaschi 1989: 103–4)

It may be appropriate to add that in recent discussion the issue has been not so much whether Adam Smith's account presents us with conundrums, but instead where their roots lie. Schliesser (2005) suggested that Smithian epistemology is a kind of modest realism, and the present writer's suggestion is that it is radical anti-realism combined with an attempt at immunizing skeptical implications by quasi-transcendental constraints provided by technology in natural science and by social interaction in morality (Cremaschi 1989, 2009).

The book ends with a list of books on Adam Smith including 150 titles. Since it is neither a bibliography of the works cited nor a select bibliography organized by themes, the purpose it may serve is not clear. Besides, were such lists useful, its compilation is seriously defective. It includes books published after 1900 in English, French, German, Italian, and no reason is spelled out for excluding Spanish. Besides it omits as many books as it includes. It is as well to assume that the selection was not carried out on the basis of quality, since even such an – to say the least – 'oddment' as Lux (1990) has been included.

By way of conclusion, one could say that most papers by French contributors suffer from a tendency to overlook specific secondary literature on the various subtopics dealt with in each paper. One could add that all contributors overlooked the opportunity to read generally neglected French literature on Smith, such as the abovementioned Moscovici (1956) or Mathiot (1990), a book whose balanced suggestions on Smith and Kant nobody seems to know, and which is instead cited in this book only once by Gautier, just in order to declare that something Mathiot says 'doesn't make any difference' (p. 86).

Bibliography

Bittermann, H. J. (1940) 'Adam Smith's Empiricism and the Law of Nature', *Journal of Political Economy* 48: 487–520 and 703–34.

Becker, J. F. (1961) 'Adam Smith's Theory of Social Science', *Southern Economic Journal* 28: 13–21.

Brown, M. (1988) *Adam Smith's Economics: Its Place in the Development of Economic Thought*, London: Croom Helm.

Campbell, T. D. (1971) *Adam Smith's Science of Morals*, London: Allen and Unwin.

Cremaschi, S. (1981) 'Adam Smith, Newtonianism and Political Economy', Manuscript. *Revista de Filosofia* 5: 117–34.

——(1984) *Il sistema della ricchezza. Economia politica e problema del metodo in Adam Smith*, Milan: Angeli.

——(1989) 'Adam Smith: Sceptical Newtonianism, Disenchanted Republicanism, and the Birth of Social Science', in M. Dascal and O. Gruengard (eds) *Knowledge and Politics. Case Studies on the History of the Relationship of Epistemology and Political Philosophy*, Boulder, CO: Westview Press, pp. 883–110.

——(2000) 'Les Lumières Écossaises et le roman philosophique de Descartes', in Y. Senderowicz and Y. Wahl (eds) *Descartes: Reception and Disenchantment*, Tel Aviv: University Publishing Projects, pp. 65–88.

——(2009) 'Newtonian Physics, Experimental Moral Philosophy, and the Shaping of Political Economy', in R. Arena, Sh. Dow and M. Klaes (eds) *Open Economics*, London: Routledge, 2009, pp. 73–94.

Fiori, S. (2001) *Ordine, mano invisibile, mercato: una rilettura di Adam Smith*, Turin: UTET.

Fleischacker, S. (2004) *On Adam Smith's Wealth of Nations: A Philosophical Companion*, Princeton, NJ: Princeton University Press.

Freudenthal, G. (1982) [1986] *Atom and Individual in the Age of Newton: On the Genesis of the Mechanistic World View*, Dordrecht: Reidel (first published in German).

Hetherington, N. S. (1983) 'Isaac Newton's Influence on Adam Smith's Natural Laws in Economics', *Journal of the History of Ideas* 44(3): 497–505.

Lindgren, J. R. (1973) *The Social Philosophy of Adam Smith*, The Hague: Nijhoff.

Lux, K. (1990) *Adam Smith's Mistake: How a Moral Philosopher invented Economics and ended Morality*, Boston: Shambala.

Mathiot, J. (1990) 'Adam Smith: Philosophie et économie: de la sympathie à l'échange', Paris: PUF.

Megill, A. D. (1975) 'Theory and Experience in Smith', *Journal of the History of Ideas* 36: 79–94.

Montes, L. (2004) *Adam Smith in Context*, Basingstoke: Palgrave Macmillan.

Moscovici, S. (1956) 'À propos de quelques travaux d'Adam Smith sur l'histoire et la philosophie des sciences', *Revue d'histoire des sciences et de leurs applications* 9: 1–22.

Raphael, D. D. (1977) 'The "True Old Humean Philosophy" and Its Influence on Adam Smith', in G. P. Morice (ed.) *David Hume: Bicentenary Papers*, Edinburgh: Edinburgh University Press, pp. 23–38.

Schliesser, E. (2005) 'Wonder in the Face of Scientific Revolutions: Adam Smith on Newton's "Proof" of Copernicanism', *British Journal for the History of Philosophy* 13: 697–732.

Skinner, A. S. (1979) [1996] *A System of Social Science: Papers Relating to Adam Smith*, Oxford: Clarendon Press.

Thompson, H. F. (1965) 'Adam Smith's Philosophy of Science', *Quarterly Journal of Economics* 79: 212–33.

Wightman, W. P. (1975) 'Adam Smith and the History of Ideas', in A. S. Skinner and T. Wilson (eds) *Essays on Adam Smith*, Oxford: Clarendon Press, pp. 44–67.

AUTHOR'S RESPONSE

Magali Bessone and Michaël Biziou's response to review by Sergio Cremaschi

We are very thankful to Professor Cremaschi for his reading of the volume we have edited and are happy to have the opportunity to respond to his review.

After having summarized Donald Winch's and Knud Haakonssen's papers, Professor Cremaschi starts his critical remarks by suggesting that the label 'liberalism', which appears in the subtitle of the volume, could be a misleading way to characterize the interpretations given of Smith by these two contributors. He could also have added that most of the papers in this volume do not even directly discuss Smith's liberalism. Indeed, the word 'liberalism' has been inserted in the subtitle to refer to the common interpretation of Smith pointing to the way he is so often read (or maybe misread). But the full title of the book is *Adam Smith as a Philosopher, from Morals to Economics: Philosophy of Liberalism*. As is explained in the introductory essay, such a title means that in order to understand the liberalism which is (appropriately or not) so frequently attributed to Smith, we need first and foremost to read him as a philosopher. To read Smith as a philosopher supposes two things. First, all his different works have to be seen as strongly connected, since Smith himself describes philosophy as the construction of a system. Second, Smith's thought has to be interpreted in the light of other philosophers, considered as his historical sources, or his contemporary allies and adversaries. All the essays in this collection consider Smith as a philosopher in this double manner. They do not necessarily discuss Smith's liberalism, but they all study the philosophy which it is necessary to know in order to discuss this (alleged) liberalism.

More precisely, these essays are dedicated to the exploration of the core of Smith's philosophical system: the connection between his science of morals, his theory of jurisprudence and politics, and his political economy. This exploration, which has more coherence than Professor Cremaschi's review suggests, runs as follows: a first essay explains the methodological ties between Smith's theory of science and his theory of moral sentiments within the general framework of a science of human nature; then four essays investigate various aspects of the theory of moral sentiments, focusing on the central concept of sympathy; four further essays apply the theory of moral sentiments to juridical and political issues, focusing this time on the concept of justice and on that of civil society; and the concluding essay deals with economic themes and discusses explicitly the category of 'liberalism'. In other words, the architecture of this volume is built on the three successive presuppositions: that the theory of moral sentiments is part of a whole science of human nature which determines its methodology; that jurisprudence, politics and political economy are based on the theory of moral sentiments and that it is necessary to understand the connections between all these different parts of the system in order to decide whether or not the category of 'liberalism' can possibly be relevant to interpreting Smith's thought.

Indeed, in the last essay of the volume, entitled 'Economic Liberalism, Poverty and Social Inequalities according to Smith', Michaël Biziou does argue that this category of 'liberalism' is relevant, provided that it be understood mainly as a normative doctrine. Smithian liberalism is grounded on moral values, and it would be a mistake to interpret it as an amoral or apolitical discourse interested only in market efficiency. This Professor Cremaschi is ready to concede. However, he adds that it might well be a proof of 'the fact that Smith's political views were not primarily liberal ones', but should rather be described as 'disenchanted Republicanism'. One might respond that the problem, in fact, may not be to decide if Smith is a liberal or a republican, nor even 'primarily' one or the other. These two are not mutually exclusive notions, though their relationship is certainly very tense, and Smith can very well be both republican and liberal at the expense of some theoretical intricacy. The problem rather seems to be to what extent reading Smith can help us to make sense of the categories of liberalism and republicanism, and reciprocally to what extent these categories can help us to make sense of Smith. In his essay Biziou chooses to address the problem of Smith and liberalism because it is the most visible popular characterization of Smith to regard him as being a liberal. But of course this does not amount to a claim that Smith is nothing else than a liberal, nor that liberalism can be nothing else than Smithian.

After his discussion of liberalism, Professor Cremaschi chooses 'at random', as he says, to give a somewhat detailed account of Philippe Hamou's paper on 'History of Science Naturalized. Adam Smith from the History of Astronomy to Moral Sentiments'. This is a very good choice indeed, inasmuch as Smith's epistemology and methodology are topics Professor Cremaschi has already written much about. This gives him the opportunity for a set of very interesting and knowledgeable remarks, to which a few lines can be added by way of reply. Hamou's contribution is the work of a historian of science whose perspective is developed around a more general question about how the progress or dynamics of science has been conceived at different times in history. His intention is to sustain three main points. First, Smith's position appears to be singular in his own time, compared to the way other thinkers of the Enlightenment, such as Condorcet or d'Alembert, viewed the progress of science. Second, this singularity results from Smith's application of a principle he found in Hume: the principle that all productions of the human mind, including scientific productions such as astronomical theories, should be referred to the science of human nature, that is to the laws of imagination. Third, this Humean origin of Smith's theory is the reason why it can be labelled 'naturalism', and also explains its sceptical dimension. Contrary to Professor Cremaschi's reading, Hamou does not assert that Smith anticipates Quine's or Kuhn's theses on epistemology, as can be clearly seen from pages 30 and 31 of the paper. These two authors are referred to as a matter of comparison, in order to allow the reader to understand what is meant here by Smith's – paradoxical – 'naturalism'.

Professor Cremaschi's long discussion of this paper is extremely stimulating. The one drawback to this choice – for any choice has to have some drawback – is that it leaves aside all the moral, political and economic themes which are dealt with by the other papers in the volume (no less than the nine tenths of it). We dare to hope that this will not alter too much the perception of the book that the reader may get from its review.

Bibliography

Bessone, M. and Biziou, M. (2009) 'Adam Smith philosophe. De la morale à l'économie ou philosophie du libéralisme', Rennes: Presses Universitaires de Rennes.

Gavin Kennedy, *Adam Smith: A Moral Philosopher and his Political Economy*

London: Palgrave Macmillan, Great Thinkers in Economics Series, 2008, 272 pp.

ISBN 10: 1-4039-9948-1; ISBN 13: 978-1-4039-9948-1

Reviewed by Michael J. Clark

In his overview, Kennedy provides insight into modern interpretations of Adam Smith. With encyclopedic ability Kennedy highlights the most pertinent debates, and does not shy away from expounding his own conclusions. He starts with a brief background of Smith's life before turning to *The Theory of Moral Sentiments*. Kennedy then gives a chapter to main points in Smith, from the division of labor and the invisible hand, to his take on mercantilist policies and the labor theory of value.

Kennedy's work is a solid contribution to the Great Thinkers in Economics series for which it is written. Each chapter in Kennedy's book can stand alone as a reference on a Smithian topic, but the book also works as a whole. It develops two major themes. The first theme, salient in the first half of the book, is Smith's emphasis on process and on emergent phenomenon. The second theme, developed in the latter stages of the book, is the nuance of Smith's political views, notably that Smith was not an ardent supporter of laissez-faire.

The first two chapters of the book foreshadow the two themes which are to follow. In the first chapter, the brief biography highlights Smith's behind-the-scenes political connections. Kennedy starts with Smith's father's connections and then shows how they may have influenced Smith's own political ties. Throughout the book Kennedy harkens back to the importance of these ties. Kennedy even suggests the possibility of Smith using political influence to block his friend David Hume from an academic appointment. Kennedy is trying to present a picture of Adam Smith without accepting any reputational distortions that may have developed over the past 200 years. The real human being, Adam Smith, is set forth by Kennedy as the central figure running through the book.

After the biography of Adam Smith, Kennedy explores how Smith's works fit together. The theme of the first half of the book really starts to develop in the second chapter. Kennedy shows how many of Smith's works tie together when one sees Smith's appreciation for emergent phenomena burgeoning into complex ends. Kennedy argues that the many interpretations of Smith are a result of his complex approach tied in with his pragmatic desire to deal with

The Adam Smith Review, 6: 367–374 © The International Adam Smith Society
ISSN 1743-5285, ISBN 0–415–66722–7

the reality outside his window. As a result Smith's ideas take on many intricacies and nuances that can be misinterpreted using modern assumptions. The complexity of reality was not lost on Smith. The social evolution from rude states of society to the age of commerce, development of language, wealth creation, and even his moral philosophy, involved an evolutionary process. Kennedy points out that an evolutionary approach runs through numerous aspects of Smith's thinking. In Smith's thinking human experience inherently involves unplanned and unconscious exchange, the interactive effects of which are central to understanding social life.

In emphasizing emergent phenomenon, Kennedy is on familiar and solid ground, and in the following chapters he continues to stress and explore this notion. Kennedy provides important insight that is often mentioned but not really examined. When possible, the reality-driven Smith avoids over-simplification and sees time and human interaction as vital aspects to understanding political economy, morality, and society in general. Kennedy drives this point home in the first half of the book and thus provides an integrated interpretation of the body of Smith's work. Meanwhile, Kennedy is providing a caution or criticism against modern interpretations that assume away the processes Smith so clearly thought central to his thinking.

In the third chapter Kennedy provides an overview of *The Theory of Moral Sentiments* and discusses the minimal conditions Smith believed were necessary for society's continuance. While most of the book focuses on *The Wealth of Nations*, Kennedy's overview of TMS is instructive. The chapter further deepens the two major themes of Kennedy's work.

First, Kennedy emphasizes the process involved with the impartial spectator and the development of a moral society. 'Smith asserts that we approve or disapprove of our conduct according to how we imagine others see, or are likely to see, our behavior … Society mirrors our person' (p. 48). We make observations in many situations including when others react to our intrusions upon them. We observe and learn and our sentiments develop. Kennedy highlights in Smith the emergent nature of moral sensibility, which, he believes, helps us understand *The Theory of Moral Sentiments* and Smith's other work as well.

Second, Kennedy shows how Smith made sure to show the imperfection of the process. Kennedy deprecates any interpretations holding that Smith pushed a simplistic 'greed is good' message for humanity. For Smith there is no neat system of human behavior from which we could derive an outlook. Society is instead a developing, experienced process from which we learn to co-exist and even thrive. By showing the complexity of our outward nature and avoiding the self-love model, Kennedy points towards the second theme of his work where he discredits the simplistic self-interest interpretation of Smith.

The major theme of the first half of the book culminates in chapter 4. Kennedy covers Smith's four ages of society, and keeps us aware that Smith sees social change as evolution rather than revolution. Society passed through four distinct ages – of hunters, shepherds, agriculture, and commerce – an evolution centering on forms of property. Kennedy makes sure to note Smith's theory is not naively progressive, highlighting how in many cases society did not evolve towards commerce. The evolutionary story of society's ages is put forth as anything but certain about the future.

Kennedy also highlights the evolution of justice in chapter 4, capping off the main thrust of his evolutionary interpretation of Smith. The evolution of justice occurred in conjunction with the ages of society. Also, the enforcement of justice became more important and thus more complex. Kennedy explains that social evolution is a discovery process that is undirected and does not follow some rational construction of progress. He contends that Smith put forth similar views about social evolution. Kennedy explains that Smith's views on the matter go under-appreciated, including his historical analysis of the British evolution towards constitutional monarchy in the fifteenth century.

Kennedy's fifth chapter includes Smith's interpretation of the history of British governance. Kennedy covers Smith's narrative of how the feudal lords slowly lost their power and how the politics and incentives of the day changed. He reiterates Smith's emphasis that social evolution can stall at any one of the four ages of society and also points out that they could bypass an age all together.

Next comes Kennedy's analysis of Smith's economic theories found in the *Wealth of Nations*. He starts with what he calls Smith's central theme for the creation of wealth – the division of labor. Kennedy shows that the origin of the division of labor is also tied into another of Smith's theoretical constructs – the propensity to truck, barter, and exchange. The critical point is still that the cooperation is not directed or organized and that the division of labor spreads via this propensity. Kennedy's analysis of the division of labor is nothing new, but is a nice exploration of the topic. We are now near the center of Kennedy's book, and he is highlighting what is most central to Smith – exchange. Kennedy states, 'exchange is the most important concept in the *Wealth of Nations*' (p. 108). It lies at the heart of the social evolutionary process, the division of labor, and the creation of wealth.

Kennedy also explores how exchange impacts bargaining and argues that Smith's treatment of bargaining went under-appreciated for far too long. Smith felt awe in pondering that so many peaceful transactions take place between strangers. His marvel came as a result of the immense challenge that bargaining would seem to represent. Smith was not naïve and he knew that exchange and bargaining was often far from polite and full of niceties. But Smith also had an understanding of the man within the breast of each individual and how judging oneself the impartial spectator helped facilitate bargaining. Kennedy shows the many sides of Smith's theories that allowed for bargaining, and thus much exchange, to take place. In order to get at the core of Smith's entire economic philosophy, Kennedy implores us to look at the exchange process and the dividing of labor.

In chapter 7 Kennedy takes a bold stance on the interpretation of Smith's labor theory of value. He suggests that Smith was only very weakly, if at all, committed to a labor theory of value. Smith has long been associated with the errors of the labor theory of value view, but Kennedy suggests a different interpretation. Kennedy argues that Smith's rhetoric shows signs of only mild support for the labor theory of value and that Smith may have applied it only in certain situations. In more rudimentary societies the labor theory of value might meaningfully apply, but in a more advanced society exchange would take place and the labor theory of value would be far less applicable. Kennedy suggests that the misunderstanding of Smith is the result of those who came after Smith who tried to measure value. As Kennedy points out, measuring value is not a theory, and Smith was putting forward a theory of value. It may even be that scholars got confused about Smith's statements as they tried to take them further than they were ever meant to be taken. Kennedy's conclusion on Smith's labor theory of value is that there was no credible role for it outside of the early ages of a rude society. He points out that Smith 'asserted explicitly that labor was not the sole source of value in a commercial exchange society' (p. 129) by stating that profit from a borrower's use is divided between the profit for his risks and the profit from the lender who affords the opportunity. Kennedy's remarks are somewhat controversial and bold, but he provides solid argumentation and an appropriate overview of Smith's labor theory of value to support his claims.

In chapter 8 Kennedy begins to hint at his less than laissez-faire interpretation of Smith. Kennedy highlights Smith's philosophical construct of perfect liberty. While Kennedy acknowledges that Smith favored perfect liberty pure and simple, he spends most of the chapter setting up and refuting the laissez-faire caricature of Smith. Kennedy shows how Smith put forth many ideas showing the commonplace divergence from perfect liberty and notes that Smith accepted these divergences within wide margins. While Kennedy highlights the pecuniary gains found in different jobs that cause differences in wages and imperfect markets, he nonetheless shows that Smith's main thrust was against the imperfections caused by European governments. Kennedy gives his readers the liberty-focused Smith, but he nonetheless begins to make arguments about Smith's understanding that perfect liberty was not always benign.

In chapters 9, 10, and 11 Kennedy reviews what modern economists would call Smith's growth theory. Here Kennedy starts to put forth a less traditional interpretation of Smith. Kennedy argues that Smith was more government-friendly than most give him credit for. But I feel that Kennedy is knocking down a straw man by frequently placing his argument against a purely laissez-faire interpretation of Smith. In reality it is very hard to find a Smith scholar who believes Smith put forth a simple system of 100 per cent perfect liberty. Kennedy's chapters on growth theory do provide a nice overview of a number of differences between Smith's nuanced approach to growth and the modern approach.

It is important to Kennedy to point out that Smith has a different kind of growth theory. Smith talks about the phenomenon of growth in real-world settings. Perfect liberty is only a theoretical tool in the background, whereas speaking about wealth creation to those who could influence the policies impacting growth was Smith's true agenda. Smith focused on the core elements of growth within a context of mercantilist policies, in ways understandable and relevant to the policymakers and practitioners of the day. For Smith, growth was about looking out his window at the real world. Smith wanted to explore ways that could help the people around him to accrue capital and eventually to garner a surplus so that the division of labor could be expanded and deepened.

Kennedy argues that Smith was mainly concerned with getting rid of the mercantilist policies that he so opposed. However, Smith's desire to get rid of these policies does not mean that he was opposed to government action in all cases. Kennedy argues that Smith made this quite clear by showing the misbehavior of men in free economic systems. Kennedy notes that there are over fifty counter-examples to the benign system of natural liberty in Books I and II of the *Wealth of Nations*, and he ends chapter 9 with a list of measures that Smith showed could hurt growth.

Kennedy points out the very harmful mercantile policies that Smith argued against – he lists them in chapter 11 (p. 189). But he makes sure to remind us of Smith's departures from pure laissez-faire, such as his support of the Navigation Acts and his views on banking regulations. While Kennedy does acknowledge that Smith's main concern was to get rid of mercantilist policies, he also makes sure to put this in the context of his argument against seeing Smith as a strong and simple proponent of free markets. Kennedy finds it important to emphasize that Smith 'considered exceptions to natural liberty on their merits and not on whether they offended purist doctrine' (p. 188). Kennedy's aim is to persuade his readers to look a bit more deeply at exactly what it is that Smith is arguing for.

In all, Kennedy presents Smith as attacking very harshly the tremendously hurtful mercantile policies of his day while making sure to note that certain free activities add to wealth creation while others certainly do not. He wanted to influence those making the policies around him and did not care nearly as much about the purely theoretical. He had little to no interest in a perfect model of liberty or a more modern mathematical theory of growth. Smith didn't want to get rid of bad polices in order to make society perfectly free or to meet some theoretical standard: he wanted it to get rid of people's deprivation.

In chapter 12 Kennedy shows the many interpretations of Smith's invisible hand metaphor. He goes through the uses of the invisible hand to clarify the context and meaning. Similar to his previous chapters, Kennedy shows that Smith feels the wrong rules can cause outcomes of spontaneous orders to turn out poorly. If spontaneous orders can turn out poorly, the invisible hand is really a neutral aspect of Smith's theory. Smith's use of the metaphor doesn't seem all that pertinent to Kennedy. The main thrust of his argument lies elsewhere. Kennedy argues that once one looks at the uses of the invisible hand metaphor, one can conclude that Smith wouldn't have placed the emphasis on the invisible hand metaphor that many do today. While Kennedy reviews the interpretations that see the metaphor as something of great significance to Smith, he finds little evidence for such claims. For any reader interested in the debate over the invisible hand, Kennedy provides a thorough overview and a solid criticism of common interpretations. Overall, Kennedy's interpretation is that the invisible hand is more of an isolated metaphor than the centerpiece of Smith's laissez-faire approach.

In his final chapters Kennedy explores Adam Smith's lasting legacy. Kennedy covers two areas: The extent of Smith's laissez-faire and his views on the redistribution of income. The selection of these two areas fit well with the way Kennedy builds up the book towards a less-than-laissez-faire interpretation of Smith. Most of chapter 13, entitled 'Peace, Easy Taxes, and Justice', centers on Smith's non-laissez-faire stance, arguing that Smith is much more open to the redistribution than commonly assumed.

Overall, Kennedy's work is full of great commentary and useful overviews of the most important Smithian concepts. Kennedy's fine book is put in simple language and with great flow. The first half of the book centers around one important way in which Smith's corpus fits together around his evolutionary views of society. The second half of the book builds on the first half and shows that Smith's spontaneous order view of the economy lead to his disdain for harmful government interventions. He stresses that Smith shows that the emergent phenomenon in an economy may not always be positive. Kennedy sees the pragmatist in Smith and emphasizes Smith's evolutionary take on society and economies while providing a more interventionist interpretation of Smith than is common. Even if one doesn't find Kennedy's interpretation of Smith highly convincing, his work is a valuable guide for anyone interested in digging deeper into the thoughts of Adam Smith.

AUTHOR'S RESPONSE

Gavin Kennedy's response to review by Michael J. Clark

I am grateful to Michael J. Clark for his fair and thorough review of my account of Adam Smith's moral philosophy and political economy, which necessarily takes in his historical perspectives in his *Lectures on Jurisprudence* (1762–63), and his *History of Astronomy* (c.1744–50), plus his *Lectures on Rhetoric and Belles Lettres* (1762–63), including his *First Formation of Languages* (1761).

Today's secondary literature on Adam Smith tops many thousands, and shows no signs of drying up. Reading Adam Smith's works, I am struck by the fact that many shibboleths associated with his name are of questionable provenance. Smith's lifetime's work throws up many points of difference with the modern consensus. Michael Clark notes some of the areas where I disagree with mainstream historians of Smith's thinking, for example those 'modern interpretations that assume away the process so clearly central to [Smith's] thinking'; 'the simplistic self-interest interpretation of Smith'; 'the under appreciated … historical analysis of the British evolution towards constitutional monarchy'; 'the interpretation of Smith's labor theory of value'; the 'laissez-faire interpretation of Smith'; the fact that he 'was more government-friendly than most give him credit for'; the evident 'misbehavior of men in free economic systems'; contrasting with those who see 'Smith as a strong and simple proponent of free markets'; and those who deny that Smith 'wouldn't have placed the emphasis on the invisible hand metaphor as many do today'.

Of course, many of these ideas have precedents in the work of earlier scholars. Jacob Viner (1966) on Smith's alleged laissez-faire credentials springs to mind, as does much of the work on 'spontaneous order', emergent order', and 'evolutionary processes', which find resonance in some of Smith's ideas. Terry Peach has criticised, with his usual patience, my take on Smith's labour theory of value in private communications, and it is from such exchanges that productive debate shapes the discipline's common knowledge. In this respect, I commend the recent work of younger scholars (Leonidas Montes, Craig Smith, Maria Paganelli, Ryan Hanley, etc.) without necessarily agreeing with all of their interpretations.

James Otteson's *Adam Smith's Market Place of Life* (2002), which has not yet received the attention it deserves, is a remarkable example of the power of original thinking about what Smith was trying to put together. He identifies a four-step process, throughout Smith's works on Moral Sentiments, Wealth of Nations, and First Formation of Languages (in LRBL), which I found works when applied to the *History of Astronomy* and *Lectures on Jurisprudence,* (Kennedy 2008: 40–43). New ways of looking at Smith's oeuvre contrast with the erroneous schema offered in too many modern commentaries, of which the so-called 'Adam Smith problem' is pre-eminent and, surprisingly, still current.

Of course, the main problem with studies of Adam Smith is the wholly ubiquitous, modern assertion of the invented 'doctrine' of Adam Smith's invisible hand. The mainstream view that Smith taught that the pursuit of 'selfish' outcomes by each individual, 'as if led by an invisible hand', resulted in the 'best good of all' is a wild generalisation, not supported by Smith's texts (Samuelson 1948, 1st edition, 36; cf. Samuelson and Nordhaus in their 19th edition, 2010: 29).

The nine paragraphs in pages 452–56 of *Wealth Of Nations*, containing the invisible hand metaphor, show that Smith discussed merchant traders deciding between investing their capital in foreign trade versus investing it locally, the latter perceived by some merchants, but not all, to be less risky than the former. It was not the general case at all, as asserted by Samuelson. Those (risk-averse) merchants who chose to invest locally, by the arithmetic of the 'whole is the sum of its parts', added to the national output of the 'necessaries, conveniences, and amusements of life', which to Smith was consistent with the 'public good'. The rest of Book IV shows the likelihood that the same domestic contributors to the 'public good' were the main constituency from which the mercantile pressures for tariff protections, prohibitions and hostility to trading partners contributed to the pubic 'bad'.

Smith also lectured on rhetoric (1748–63), in which he described metaphors as giving 'due strength of expression to the object to be described and at the same time [doing] this in a more striking and interesting manner' (LRBL, 29). What then was the 'object to be described' by this particular metaphor? For Smith, the 'object' was the necessary consequence of the individual, risk-averse, merchant's 'own security' which led to the individual contributing to total output. Yet, modern economists, since the 1950s, have made the invisible hand metaphor its own object!

For that, and other reasons, I have tackled other errors of attribution to Adam Smith of ideas he never held, or where he might be said to hold weak versions of them; it is necessary to be mindful of their context before generalising too much, e.g. chartered merchant companies.

Bibliography

Otteson, J. R. (2002) *Adam Smith's Market Place of Life*, Cambridge: Cambridge University Press.

Samuelson, P. A. (1948) *Economics*, 1st edn, New York: McGraw-Hill.

Samuelson, P. A. and Nordhaus, W. D. (2010) *Economics*, 19th edn, New York: McGraw-Hill International.

Smith, A. (1976a) *The Theory of Moral Sentiments*, (eds) D. D. Raphael and A. L. Macfie, Oxford: Oxford University Press; Glasgow edition.

——(1976b) *An Inquiry into the Nature and Causes of the Wealth of Nations*, (eds) R. H. Campbell and A. S. Skinner, Oxford: Oxford University Press; Glasgow edition.

——(1978) *Lectures on Jurisprudence*, (eds) R. L. Meek, D. D. Raphael and P. G. Stein, Oxford: Oxford University Press; Glasgow edition.

——(1980) *Essays on Philosophical Subjects*, (ed.) W. P. D. Wightman, Oxford: Oxford University Press; Glasgow edition.

——(1983) *Lectures on Rhetoric and Belles Lettres*, (ed.) J. C. Bryce, Oxford: Oxford University Press; Glasgow edition.

Viner, J. (1966) [1928] 'Adam Smith and Laissez-Faire', *Adam Smith 1776–1926: Lectures to Commemorate the Sesquicentennial of the Publication of Wealth of Nations*, Fairfield, NJ: Augustus M. Kelly.

Deepak Lal, *Reviving the Invisible Hand: The Case for Classical Liberalism in the Twenty-first Century*

Princeton, NJ: Princeton University Press, 2006, 336 pp.

ISBN 10: 0691-12591-0; ISBN 13: 978-0691-12591-6

Reviewed by Paul Gunn

As we enter the second decade of the twenty-first century, the future is by no means assured for international liberalism. The looming spectre of climate change and the legacy of the recent recession have rendered liberal economic policies particularly unpalatable for democratic polities, whilst the continued rise of the East and South will only increase the political odds stacked against Western globalists. In what is consequently a timely defence of globalisation and free trade, Lal forcefully rejects these 'dirigiste' pressures in order to remind us all of the extensive benefits of economic liberalism. Economic freedoms not only brought the West vast wealth and comfort, but – where they have been allowed to operate – they have also helped to spread those goods eastwards. Capitalism's laissez-faire respect for others, moreover, underpins the world's greatest hope for peace and order, and its tendency for innovation provides the best defence against all possible environmental threats to our well-being. To succumb to the new dirigisme, Lal convincingly argues, would therefore be to renounce these benefits, to stem the global spread of wealth, and to capitulate to the destabilising forces of moral imperialism.

Since the economic arguments Lal mobilises are well-versed (as the title suggests, his basic arguments for free trade and the division of labour refer back to Scottish Enlightenment thought), the great potential of this book is humanistic. For, the most desirable effects of Lal's questioning of the dubious and, in many cases, simply bogus claims against globalisation would surely be to the good of the world's poorest, the very people deep Greens and anti-capitalists ostensibly want to help. Indeed, Lal is at his best when, taking their perspective, he shows just how the impoverished would be the most harmed by the foreclosure of global enterprise. Yet the force of this demonstration is undermined by his imprecise identification of many of his opponents – at times he seems to be arguing against a vague idea rather than a set of clearly defined actors and viewpoints – and his attributing to those opponents unworthy motives. However counter-productive their attempts, for instance, it is unwarranted to label those who feel genuine distress at the poverty, morbidity and working conditions in developing countries, or those who believe that multinational companies can contribute to social goals, as interfering and supercilious. More to the point, Lal's argument is based upon a seemingly wholehearted rejection of international politics. As such, it risks alienating the very political moderates Lal would need to persuade if his attempt to resuscitate liberalism is to succeed.

Nowhere is this clearer than in Lal's historical account of liberalism. It is significant that this history is intended to highlight the contingencies upon which our economic prosperity depends. In particular, Lal traces the liberal fortunes of the West to the two 'papal revolutions' initiated by popes Gregory I and VII in the sixth and eleventh centuries. The first restructured the 'cosmological' views embodied by Christianity by emancipating the individual from traditionally strong family ties and legal customs. While it was intended to decrease the number of male heirs in order to increase the amount of wealth bequeathed to the Church, this revolution had the unintended effect of weakening the culture of shame which had inhibited the pursuit of self-interest amongst the masses. The productive forces of this self-interest were subsequently unleashed when Gregory VII, seeking to protect the Church's wealth, sought to elevate the power of God above the predatory Byzantine political elites. With the subsequent rise of the Church-state, an administrative and legal framework emerged within which bartering became the main source of income. The West's 'material' beliefs – regarding how to make a living – were thus aligned with its individualism, setting the scene for what would later become a Promethean surge in economic growth.

It is in his discussion of this growth that we find the most extensive references to the classical political economists. Lal draws variously and insightfully upon Smith, Hume and Ricardo to show that the West's steadily intensifying growth was incomparable with the experiences of Eastern nations. For, while the expansion of Eastern agricultural economies was subject to diminishing returns to land use, and fuelled only by meagre increases in the labour supply, Europe benefitted extensively from the proceeds of the bartering, trading and innovation undertaken by its increasingly free peoples. Indeed, it was these Smithian proclivities which led the European economies in time to industrialise and harness the immense power of fossil fuels. This led to significant reductions in the costs of transport, communication and supply, and it therefore converted many previously non-traded goods with their attendant local monopolies into competitive, tradable goods. As the classical account goes, Western nations were thus able to discover and capitalise their comparative advantages through ever-increasing levels of international trade, whilst the East languished.

Remarkably, given the title of Lal's book, this classical analysis plays a limited role in his argument. Just as important as our natural tendency to create wealth for Lal is the role that the British empire played in securing international trade routes in the nineteenth century. Thus, he spends much of the early part of his book developing his argument – which builds upon his previous volume, *In Praise of Empires* – that the health of the global economy depends upon the actions of the de facto imperial power. It was ultimately the Victorian 'liberal international economic order' which facilitated the global expansion of wealth, and it is ultimately up to the United States, the world's only superpower, to continue this expansion and secure its future. To be sure, Lal shows that the success of the Victorians relied upon their assuming a stoic commitment to fairness not dissimilar to that set out by Smith's *Theory of Moral Sentiments*. But the geopolitical nature of this argument leads Lal to explicate a sharp divergence with classical theory. The hope that the success of free trade and laissez-faire policies will alone 'lead to a spontaneous global order', Lal (p. 21) argues, 'is likely to be belied in the real and dangerous world of power politics'.

This position sets the scene for much of the rest of the book. Lal deploys various analytical political economic arguments to support two basic suggestions for American policy-makers. The first is that it should wind-down the IMF and the WTO. Both of these multinational and multilateral institutions have outlived their useful lives and, in their rent-seeking search for a new role, threaten to undermine global liberalism. Lal's defence of this claim is both strong and edifying. He demonstrates, for instance, that the numerous roles that these two institutions were set up to perform are actually unnecessary on the classical liberal argument. The adjustment assistance supplied by the WTO, for instance, is completely unnecessary and actually counter-productive, given that it introduces harmful and opaque distributional judgements into the otherwise automatic adjustments prompted by demand and supply schedules. Similarly, the IMF's original role of supervising exchange rates after the failure of the Bretton Woods system is equally pointless. The movement towards freely adjusting exchange rates represents perhaps the biggest advance for the global economy under American supervision, as it allows for a much more efficient allocation of international capital than could ever be shepherded by either the IMF or the WTO.

Lal uses an impressive breadth of knowledge and experience to show that the presence and activities of the IMF and WTO have had far-reaching effects for the world's poor. For they have fed a subversive narrative that the only form of successful international action is multilateral. Thus, there is a widespread belief that it is not for nations to consider the effects of their own policies on developing markets, because they have a far more important role in supporting the multilateral assistance provided by the WTO and international aid agencies. Similarly, it is not for governments to consider restrictions on trade from only their own perspective, because, under the auspices of the IMF (and ultimately the US), trade is instead an issue for multi- and increasingly bilateral negotiation. Lal is persuasive here, and recent negotiations concerning climate change and banking regulation bear his point out. Yet, as Lal shows, all countries, especially the poorest, have much to gain from supporting the free and unfettered movement of goods and capital. Of course, this does require bearing the pain of the economic cycle. Even taking recessions into account, however, Lal's data show that those citizens of developing countries lucky enough to experience free trade have benefitted substantially from it.

While this passive defence of the benefits of liberalism is convincing, Lal's second line of argument, which takes the fight to his moral opponents, is less so. He believes that the prominence of multilateralism has allowed anti-capitalists and moralists to exert illiberal and undemocratic pressure upon the international political process. With the aim of encouraging 'sustainable development', protecting the environment and giving capitalism a 'human face', these groups threaten to disrupt the flow of wealth from the West to the East and present a convenient excuse for protectionism. Lal's disdain for these groups is palpable. He accuses Greens of being misanthropic and parochial, and he provocatively applauds those nations which refuse to enter negotiations about climate change. The EU is similarly derided as a coalition of cynical governments united by a rent-seeking executive. Perhaps Lal's most egregious claim, however, is his comparison of communitarianism with Mao's Cultural Revolution. This broad-brush claim disregards the nuanced forms of communitarianism offered by liberals such as Michael Walzer and Will Kymlicka, and ignores completely the possible economic benefits of communitarianism set out by Elinor Ostrom.

Moreover, Lal's trouble is that, by verging into moral condemnation, his strong critique of these movements requires that he set out his own account of ethics. That is, his claims surpass the mere classical liberal defence of individual liberty, embodied by Smith's limited role for moral judgement, beyond anything other than interpersonal exchanges, in order to claim that moral intervention is itself wrong. Thus, he briefly rejects the claims to rights he sees as underpinning paternalism in order to affirm a 'Common Law' conception of freedom as access to the full range of feasible actions, subject to the harm principle. Since this is true for everyone, he suggests, there can be no foundation for the on-going interference in the global economy. Lal leaves this under-theorised – perhaps understandably, given the economic focus of the book – but this leaves him open to the objection that the political process is necessary to decide what the feasible range of actions actually is for international economic actors, which externalities constitute harm, and whether or not they should be compensated for. As an economist, Lal is well-placed to highlight how inefficient this politicking is. He offers little, however, to justify its general rejection.

This is a shame, because *Reviving the Invisible Hand* offers much that is relevant to debates about trade. As I mentioned at the outset, if the invisible hand is to be revived to help those who have yet to reap the rewards of its beneficent direction, classical liberals need to persuade the political moderates who broadly support curbs on free trade. Many of these would no doubt be persuaded by Lal's passionate defence of the improvements the developing world has already seen. But others – especially those who, however erroneously, believe the moral arguments Lal attacks – will likely be angered by

Lal's seeming contempt for politics, and his effective advocacy of American imperialism. This imperialism ignores the contribution of all those non-American voters, who could collectively achieve far more for international liberalism than America alone could just by voting for laissez-faire policies. And it is based upon a pessimistic view of human nature which is antithetical to the classical liberal tradition. Even within the US, it is unlikely to convince sceptics who require a more positive case for the invisible hand. The positive message for the world's poor in Lal's account could not be stronger, but it is unnecessarily undermined by his derisive attack on paternalism.

Stephen J. McKenna, *Adam Smith: The Rhetoric of Propriety*

Rhetoric in the Modern Era Series
State University of New York Press, 2006, 184 pp.

ISBN Hardback: 0-7914-9581-0; Paperback: 0-7914-6582-9

Reviewed by Catherine Labio

It is fair to say that Smith's views on rhetoric have not yet received the sustained critical attention they deserve.[1] *In Adam Smith: The Rhetoric of Propriety*, Stephen J. McKenna proposes to fill this gap. His stated goal is twofold: demonstrate that Smith's rhetoric is central to our understanding of his entire body of work and establish that for Smith rhetoric and propriety are inextricably linked.

In the opening paragraphs of the first chapter, 'Smith and the Problem of Propriety', McKenna argues that '[i]n LRBL, Smith makes rhetoric the genus to which all communication is species' while Smithian propriety 'mediates virtually all forms of social interaction' (p. 1). McKenna does not define either communication or social interaction. Nor does he tell us how they relate logically or hierarchically to one another. He then goes on to note that 'Smith's approach to the study of human society was fundamentally rhetorical in conception' (pp. 1–2). This claim suggests a primacy of the rhetorical over the social that is never fully explained. Nor is, problematically, the exact nature of what McKenna sees as the fundamental relationship between rhetoric and propriety. The bulk of the first chapter, aimed primarily at the non-specialist, does not focus on this issue, however, but consists of succinct introductory remarks on the Scottish Enlightenment and a summary of Smith's life. Smith scholars will not learn a great deal from these, but may appreciate the author's decision to begin his discussion of WN by quoting early readers' admiring comments on its innovative style. Only then does McKenna make the case for the economic impact of WN with the words: 'and indeed, the effects of WN were not merely literary … ' (p. 21).

In the second chapter, 'Smith and Propriety in the Classical Tradition', McKenna surveys Greek and Roman views on propriety in speech and action in order to demonstrate that Smith's debts to the classical rhetorical tradition are greater than has usually been acknowledged. The author covers a lot of ground in a few short pages and the chapter occasionally loses its focus. Nevertheless, McKenna makes a convincing case for the ancient connection between propriety and sense-perception, particularly with respect to sight, as well as between the attendant notions of social judgment and aesthetic

The Adam Smith Review, 6: 380–385 © The International Adam Smith Society
ISSN 1743-5285, ISBN 0–415–66722–7

pleasure. In a thought-provoking demonstration, McKenna argues that *to prepon*, one of the Greek terms for appropriateness, can be traced back to the Homeric verb *prepein* – 'to appear before the eyes', or 'to be seen conspicuously' (p. 26). Proceeding chronologically, McKenna later submits that scholars have tended to underestimate the importance of Aristotle's *Rhetoric* and *Poetics* in relation to Smith's rhetoric. He emphasizes in particular the thinkers' shared belief that propriety allows for ethical action and involves a similarity of emotional response between speaker and audience.

The third chapter, 'Rhetorical Propriety in Eighteenth-Century Theories of Discourse', focuses on the fate of rhetoric in the Enlightenment. Displaced by the *res* of Baconian and Lockean thought, *verba*, exiled from the philosophy of science, found refuge in the emerging discourse of aesthetics. The latter was marked above all by an interiorization of codes belonging to the social sphere and the primacy of the imagination, defined as a faculty grounded in sight. As a result, aesthetics replaced rhetoric as a vector of socio-ethical behavior and came to play an important role in Smith's conceptualization of the impartial spectator.

The first three chapters are interspersed with references to Smith. By contrast, the fourth and longest chapter, 'Propriety in Smith's Rhetoric Lectures', consists of a close reading of LRBL. First, however, McKenna makes clear that he rejects the work of literary scholars Court, Crawford, and Miller who, he believes, have mistakenly identified Smithian rhetoric as the means to teach politesse to the sons of a new Scottish elite and have misinterpreted LRBL as a 'manifesto' (p. 77) in support of bourgeois capitalism. McKenna suggests instead that the form and content of LRBL clearly manifest Smith's concern with propriety in the aesthetic as well as ethical meanings of the word.

McKenna's analysis of LRBL rests on the core belief that an essential continuity exists between the *Lectures* and TMS. I am not convinced, however, that LRBL cannot be studied independently from TMS. Indeed, McKenna's insistence on the centrality of propriety to LRBL blinds him to some of the ways in which Smith's lectures are representative of other trends in eighteenth-century intellectual history. Smith's inclusion of a speculative history of the origins of progress and language in the third lecture, for instance, is hardly 'unexpected' (p. 82), let alone 'simply entertaining' (p. 83), in the age of conjectural histories. Also, knowing Rousseau's views on sympathy makes it difficult to agree with one of McKenna's key claims, namely that 'Smith's idea that the intention to communicate a given passion or affection originates in sympathy is an entirely new contribution to the theory of rhetorical propriety' (p. 88). This being said, McKenna's analysis of LRBL contains some valuable insights, particularly in the section on rhetorical propriety and sight (pp. 98–104), in which the author contends that indirect descriptions play a key role in Smith's rhetoric of propriety because they create 'something like a stereoscopic effect which strengthens the audience's sense of the object' (p. 100).

In the fifth chapter, 'Propriety in *The Theory of Moral Sentiments*', McKenna attempts to underscore that 'Smith's rhetorical practice … constitutes his ethical metatheory' (p. 111). The demonstration is not convincing, in large measure because the structure of the chapter is somewhat haphazard. Moreover, McKenna's claim hinges in part on the notion that sympathy is both natural and learned (through the practice of rhetoric), a claim that may or may not be true, but seems driven largely by a desire to rout aesthetics out of ethics. The main contribution of this chapter is that it ties together Smith's rhetoric with his views on justice and utility and paves the way for concluding remarks on the contemporary implications of Smith's 'rhetoric of propriety'.

McKenna's work is commendably ambitious. He wants to offer a new reading of LRBL, demonstrate the centrality of Smith's views on rhetoric and propriety to his entire corpus, make a case for their originality, and study their application to contemporary ethical situations. This is too big a series of propositions for such a slender volume, however, especially when half of it consists of historical surveys one would expect to find in a doctoral dissertation. Moreover, as noted above, McKenna's demonstrations are not uniformly persuasive, even in the case of such essential questions as the exact nature of the relationship between rhetoric and propriety. In this context, one cannot help but wonder at the omission of any examination of the etymological connection between propriety and property in a work devoted to arguing that Smith's views on rhetoric and propriety inform his entire corpus, up to and including WN.[2] These problems are compounded by the fact that McKenna is trying to address two very different audiences: readers interested in rhetoric and Adam Smith scholars. The work cannot satisfy these two sets of readers, both of whom are likely to find some passages too allusive and others too detailed. This is a significant drawback for a book on rhetoric, as is the fact that many errors remain that should have been caught at the copy-editing stage. In conclusion, though individual passages are undeniably perceptive – I think, in particular, of the thread that traces the connection between sight and rhetoric/propriety – the work as a whole is uneven and its central tenets need further clarification.

Notes

1 See Labio (2006: 153–55) for a review of the secondary literature on Smith and rhetoric.

2 Etymology of 'Propriety':

> Anglo-Norman proprietie, Anglo-Norman and Middle French proprieté, propriété (French propriété) ownership, proprietorship (a1176 in Old French), personal property (1212), particular or individual character of a person or thing (c1265), landed property, lands (a1377) and its etymon classical Latin propriett-, propriets ownership, special property or character, proper or specific meaning of a word, fitness, appropriateness, rightness, property (2nd cent. A.D.), in post-classical Latin also special character of a language, idiom (4th cent.), landed estate (7th cent.), possession of worldly goods, in violation of a vow of poverty (frequently 1234–1443 in British sources), correctness (c1363 in a British source).
> (OED online. Accessed 23 March 2010)

Bibliography

Court, F. E. (1992) *Institutionalizing English Literature: The Culture and Politics of Literary Study, 1750 – 1900*, Stanford, CA: Stanford University Press.

Crawford, R. (ed.) (1998) *The Scottish Invention of English Literature*, Cambridge: Cambridge University Press.

——(1992) *Devolving English Literature*, Oxford: Oxford University Press. Reprinted by Edinburgh University Press (2000).

Labio, C. (2006) 'The Solution Is in the Text: A Survey of the Recent Literary Turn in Adam Smith Studies', *The Adam Smith Review*, 2: 149–76.

Miller, T. P. (1997) *The Formation of College English: Rhetoric and Belles Lettres in the British Cultural Provinces*. Pittsburgh, PA: University of Pittsburgh Press.

AUTHOR'S RESPONSE

Stephen J. McKenna's response to review by Catherine Labio

One never gets the last word on Adam Smith, but it's helpful that *The Adam Smith Review* affords authors an opportunity to respond to reviews. While my book is no doubt far from perfect, in suggesting that it tries to 'fill the gap' on all there is to be said on Smith and rhetoric, Professor Labio criticizes it for failing to succeed in ways never intended by me or the editors of the SUNY series, 'Rhetoric in the Modern Era', for which it was written. Had she adverted to the flyleaf description of the series, which clearly lays out that the books in it are aimed at non-specialists and are intended to be 'first books on their subject, not the last', or had she attended to the final line of the book, which acknowledges that a great deal more work needs to be done on Smith's theory and practice of rhetoric (the entire sixth chapter and postscript apparently escape her notice), she may have better appreciated what she was reading.

Such inattention characterizes much of Labio's review. While some points are well taken –I wish I had been clearer on what is meant by 'communication' and 'social interaction' –and while I am pleased by her positive assessment of my analysis of the relations between sight and rhetorical propriety in Smith and the rhetorical tradition, a contribution heretofore undervalued in other reviews, her verdict merely that 'some passages are undeniably perceptive' seems to be the product of some spotty reading. Instead of addressing the argumentative trajectory of the book, Labio prefers to take passages out of context and unfairly deride them. To take one example (there are others), what is 'unexpected' about Smith's turn in the third lecture of LRBL to a treatment of 'the origin and progress of language' is not that he would be interested in such a thing, as Labio would have me naively portraying it. On the contrary, I explicitly contextualize Smith's effort in relation to Condillac, Rousseau and Gabriel Girard (Smith's immediate spur to the conjectural history of language). What is unexpected is simply its inclusion in a practice-directed rhetorical theory, as well as the particular juncture at which it appears in the lecture sequence. That it might additionally have been entertaining to the young men and women in Smith's audience is hardly beside the point.

Unfortunately, such miscomprehension by Labio extends to the larger scope of the book as well. As to her complaint that I am not clear about the relationship between rhetoric and propriety, I would direct readers to pp. 109–10 (to cite just one articulation): 'By showing how propriety communicates sentiments – emotions that issue as judgments about subject matter – Smith assigns propriety both heuristic and probative roles in addition to its usual stylistic one of abetting clarity.' This is because '[S]ympathy is achieved only if sentiments are accompanied by a sufficient etiological account of their unfolding in response to a set of original circumstances'. Labio protests that she is not convinced 'that LRBL cannot be studied independently from TMS'. That's good, because I never take any such position. Would that her conviction had come, however, from attending to my argument, affirmed in chapters 1, 4, 5, *et passim*, that it is TMS that should not be read independently from the rhetorical theory underpinning it as its otherwise missing epistemological or metaphysical infrastructure: 'Smith's notion of rhetorical propriety functions architectonically within his moral philosophy' (p. 24); 'Smith implied and applied his own stated conception of rhetorical propriety in his account of the development of conscience in moral agents' (p. 112). And so on. I spend several pages in chapter 3 (pp. 76–79) explaining how my reading of LRBL *counters* those approaches that put TMS as philosophically antecedent. This is a central tenet of the book, one repeatedly put forward. It is hard to see how any reader, specialist or non-specialist, would miss it. Other reviewers, from specialized journals such as *Rhetoric Society Quarterly*, to a more general interest outlet like the *Times Literary Supplement*, have not.

Perhaps Labio would favor a more reductively Marxian interpretation of Smith's rhetorical theory. She contends that my reading of LRBL 'rejects' the work of Court, Crawford and Miller, who, in different ways, do give priority to TMS in service to at least quasi-Marxian interpretations of Smith's belletrism. It's true that I think their interpretations err in varying degrees, but I do not in any way 'reject' the idea that belletristic rhetoric had a significant ideological role to play. On the contrary, I accord Miller's argument its place (p. 152) and positively praise Court's work (p. 153). But again, that is in a section of the book nowhere referenced in her review.

Labio seems most troubled by what she sees as my 'desire to rout aesthetics out of ethics'. But how could a book that reads Smith's theory of appropriate rhetorical style as essential to moral thinking do that? Moreover one that accords heuristic power to style? The answer is that it couldn't, and doesn't. Smith does aestheticize ethics in large measure, but in a manner far more sophisticated than that of, say, Shaftesbury or Hutcheson, thanks mainly to the coherence of his theory of appropriate style and its imbrication into his observations on the genesis of moral sentiments.

One thing Labio gets right, and demonstrates, is that it is difficult to please all the different potential audiences for a book on as interdisciplinary a thinker as Smith. I can only hope that readers of *The Adam Smith Review* might advert to the several other consistently positive reviews the book has received in a range of other publications before they take Professor Labio's more negative judgments to heart. Or better yet, they might simply read the book.